Management
Structures, Functions, and Practices

ARTHUR ELKINS

University of Massachusetts

ADDISON-WESLEY PUBLISHING COMPANY

Reading, Massachusetts · Menlo Park, California
London · Amsterdam
Don Mills, Ontario · Sydney

Sponsoring Editor: Janis Jackson
Production Editor: Evelyn Wilde
Designer: Marshall Henrichs
Illustrator: F. W. Taylor
Cover Design: Ann Scrimgeour

Library of Congress Cataloging in Publication Data

Elkins, Arthur.
    Management: structures, functions, and practices.

    Includes bibliographies and index.
    1. Management. I. Title.
HD31.E55   658.4   79-5371
ISBN 0-201-01517-X

ISBN 0-201-01517-X
BCDEFGHIJ-DO-89876543210

PREFACE

The purpose of this book is to train students to be effective, efficient real-world managers. I view the essential task of the introductory management course as teaching people to manage—allowing them to sample management as a discipline and showing them how to behave or function in a managerially professional manner.

Therefore, this book is not bound to any one particular approach—classical, behavioral, or quantitative; nor does it attempt to set forth that delineation of approaches. Rather, the point of view adopted here is that anything useful for teaching managers to manage effectively and efficiently should be integrated into the text. Although the book's format is almost functional—e.g., basic functions of design, implementation, and control—it is not tied to the rest of the traditional functional format. For example, the areas of organizing and motivating—building an organizational structure and constructing motivation systems—are treated here much like planning, as design activities. Findings from the field of organizational behavior are injected into sections where they can be of help to the aspiring or functioning manager. Quantitative tools are closely wedded to decision-making and planning situations, not tacked on at the end of the book. In sum, this book is eclectic and as "real-world" as possible.

The book has five parts. The two chapters in Part I delineate a manager's role in terms of functions and skills and show the integration of managerial and technical roles. Part II (Chapters 3 and 4) explores the world of organizations and their managers—how organizations get started, how they grow, and how managers adapt to their demands, and vice-versa. Part III (Chapters 5–11) focuses on managerial design processes: setting objectives, making decisions, planning, making policies, determining organizational design, and building motivational systems. Part IV (Chapters 12–16) places the manager in the role of implementer, putting into effect the plans and systems that he or she (or other managers) previously designed. Here the manager procures resources, is a trainer, communicates, and provides leadership. Finally, managerial control activities are the focus of Part V (Chapters 17–20). We include consideration of the effect of control on human beings and some processes for overcoming the dysfunctional effects of control processes. Chapter 20, on the organizational audit, provides not only an introduction to a valuable managerial process, but also a comprehensive review and over-view of management in organizational settings.

All of the material in this book has been class-tested and refined in light of classroom use and reviewers' comments. Most of the case contexts are real, the majority gained from my own experiences as a manager, teacher, trainer, and consultant. Some cases are from the literature of business and organizations. But most organizations' and people's names have been disguised, and generally product line, location, and industry have been changed.

LEARNING AIDS

This text incorporates several learning aids for the student and teaching aids for the instructor:

1 *"Chapter Highlights":* Each chapter opens with a brief description of the chapter's main contents. This helps to establish for the student the overall framework of the chapter as he or she begins reading.

2 *"Learning Objectives":* The learning objectives listed at the beginning of each chapter are designed to alert students to the specific knowledge and skills to be acquired in the chapter.

3 *Opening case:* Most chapters begin with a case study, which sets the stage for that particular chapter. "Solutions" to the case problems are woven throughout the chapter discussion, thereby providing the student with direct and immediate application of concepts and theory.

4 *"Summary and Conclusion":* This section of each chapter synthesizes the key points presented in the chapter, thereby serving as a study aid for the student.

5 *"Discussion Questions":* Each chapter concludes with several discussion questions to aid the student in reviewing his or her mastery of the material of the chapter. Many of the questions are set in an action, or experiential, mode.

6 *Closing cases:* The end-of-chapter cases provide the instructor and student with the opportunity to analyze the problems illustrated in light of the principles, functions, and practices of management explored in the chapter. To facilitate this process, case questions direct attention to the major concerns.

7 *"Selected Readings":* Extensive suggested reading lists are included at the end of each chapter. Students who wish to read further in the particular area covered will find suggested books and articles from both the popular and scholarly press included in the references.

 • **8** *Glossary:* Students can use the glossary included at the end of the book to check their knowledge of key terms (from both the learning objectives and the discussion questions).

 9 *"Comprehensive Cases":* The five articles in the Appendix serve to integrate the entire book. The cases illustrate the actual problems faced by a cross-section of well-known firms: a public utility (American Telephone and Telegraph), a large multiproduct manufacturer (General Motors), a retail food chain (A&P), a retail chain that went bankrupt (W. T. Grant), and a large government contractor (Electric Boat). These cases can be used to apply much of what has been learned throughout the course.

10 *Appendixes:* For more in-depth treatment of managerial tools for decision making and planning, two chapter appendixes cover linear programming and PERT.

11 *Supplements:* A comprehensive *Instructor's Resource Manual* includes teaching suggestions, additional lecture resources, answers to discussion questions, and analyses of all cases appearing in the text. The extensive *Test Bank* provides a wealth of class-tested, objective test questions as well as numerous essay-type questions.

ACKNOWLEDGMENTS

Writing and developing a project such as this depends on contributions from many people and groups. I want to thank all of them for their assistance, and I hope that I haven't inadvertently left anyone out in this listing.

Extra special appreciation goes to my good friend and colleague George S. Odiorne. Very early, Professor Odiorne expressed interest in what was a germ of an idea, encouraged me in the formulation, and gave me numerous suggestions for the book's development. For over three years, he has used the manuscript in his introductory management course, at the University of Massachusetts, providing me with the valuable evaluation that obviously helped build a better book.

Also during those years a number of Teaching Associates at the University of Massachusetts have worked with Professor Odiorne and me on the course, and they too gave me vital input and advice. Most are now earning recognition on their own as faculty members at other universities: James Lang (University of Kentucky), Aileen Cavanagh (Boston University), John Preble (SUNY—Albany), Arie Reichel (New York University), Ed McDonough (Northeastern University), Dick Pyle (University of Massachusetts—Boston), David Flynn, Hugh O'Neill, Mark Lipton, John Oni, Ken Schoen, and David Sear.

Colleagues at other institutions provided critical reviews during several stages of the book's development, helping me to improve my presentation of several topical areas and in some cases for calling my attention to some important material to be included in the text: David Gray (University of Texas at Arlington), Gus Bloomquist (Del Mar College), David Blevins (University of Mississippi), John Martin (Mount San Antonio College), William Dickson (Green River Community College), Ralph Todd (American River College), Gene Lebrenz (College of DuPage), George F. Croffort (Fullerton Junior College), Edward J. Morrison (University of Colorado), Bernard C. Reimann (Cleveland State University), John W. Newstrom (Arizona State University), Raymond T. Ruff, Jr. (Monroe Community College), H. Nicholas Windeshausen (California State University—Sacramento), and Bertrand B. Heckel (Sinclair Community College).

Richard Leifer and D. Anthony Butterfield, my colleagues at the University of Massachusetts, read some portions of the manuscript and gave me comments, suggestions, and encouragement. Dennis W. Callaghan of the University of Rhode Island, my coauthor on *A Managerial Odyssey* (Addison-Wesley), read several early drafts of chapters of this book and also kindly consented to my using some *Odyssey* material in this book. Michael J. Merenda (now at the University of New Hampshire) did some of the work on discussion questions and assisted me with the research for the text. C. N. Hetzner III, my diligent, "take-charge" Research Associate, made substantial contributions, working on questions, the index, the instructors' manual, the glossary, and footnotes. Tom Sanderson, formerly an undergraduate assistant at the University of Massachusetts, helped with questions, proofreading copy, and numerous trips to the library.

To about five thousand students who have used this book in various forms, my thanks for your patience. To those who took the time to give me their impressions of the book, my thanks for your help and your interest. To one student in particular, Ken Berman, I owe a debt for helping me to clarify some of the quantitative presentations. To all who have suffered through multilithed versions of the book—with their inevitable missing pages and blurred print—my apologies and thanks.

Judy Rose did her usual efficient typing of several of the chapters, but more importantly, carried out many of the administrative chores for the Department of Management while I closeted myself for writing. For her efficiency I am fortunate; for her patience, grateful.

The people at Addison-Wesley have been wonderful to work with. Keith Nave, a former senior editor, initiated the project with me and prodded me for several years. Janis Jackson, Keith's successor, has also been very supportive and extraordinarily creative in her approach to the market. Shirley Rieger, assistant to Keith and Janis, was always there and cheerful when I needed information or help. Carl Hesler is just the friendliest and most supportive vice-president one would ever want to meet. Evelyn Wilde did a superb job in copy editing and shepherding the manuscript through the various stages of production.

Finally, to my family—Barbara, my wife (a budding manager in her own right), and my sons, Mike and Steve, my apologies for all those late nights in the office, all those lost weekends, and all those missed Red Sox games. We'll make up for them now, I hope.

Amherst, Massachusetts   A.E.
September 1979

CONTENTS

PART III
MANAGERIAL DESIGN PROCESSES

PART V
MANAGERIAL CONTROL/ADAPTATION/AUDIT

APPENDIX
ILLUSTRATIVE COMPREHENSIVE CASES

PART I
Introduction

The two chapters of Part I are introductory in nature. In Chapter 1 we define Management as a professional organizational activity, describe what a manager does on the job, and then categorize management into three major functions: design, implementation, and control/audit/adaptation. In Chapter 2 we introduce some of the specific skills managers need and should find useful, and we also differentiate between a manager's technical and managerial roles and activities.

Chapter 1
WHAT IS MANAGEMENT?

CHAPTER HIGHLIGHTS

In this chapter we introduce the topic of management and its functions. We illustrate the complexity of a manager's job, the different categories of managerial tasks, and the intensity of a manager's commitment. In addition, the chapter covers standards by which managers are judged and the similarities of managerial activities in both profit and not-for-profit organizations.

LEARNING OBJECTIVES

1 To see and to understand the busy role managers fill.

2 To observe management as an organizational process.

3 To realize that management is primarily a mental activity.

4 To understand the categories of managerial activity: design, implementation, and control/audit/adaptation.

5 To define and to apply the concepts of effectiveness and efficiency.

6 To know the similarities and differences of managerial tasks in profit and not-for-profit organizations.

INTRODUCTION

As you start this book, you may be sitting comfortably in a chair; possibly you are muttering to yourself, "Okay, here goes *another* semester." Well, let us leave your anticipation (or, more likely, your apprehension) aside for the moment and concentrate not on you or on this introductory management course or even on this book, but rather on the chair that you're sitting on.

Did you ever stop to wonder how that chair got there in the first place? Most of us take for granted the commonplace activities or properties in our lives, but those commonplace things usually exist only because some rather complex systems or long chains of interrelationships occurred. For example, someone had to design the chair, perhaps even using a computer to model the chair. The designer took into account the weights of bodies sitting down in the chair; considered proper posture and the esthetic and utilitarian qualities of furniture; and then related design, weight, posture, utility, esthetics, and other factors to the myriad of materials available, such as plastic, rubber, steel, wood, fabric, straw, paints, varnishes, etc.

3

Then one or more people built the chair. Perhaps one craftsperson built the entire chair with painstaking care and time-consuming precision. More likely, your chair progressed along an assembly line, being screwed, stapled, stuffed, pinched, nailed, and sprayed by literally dozens of people. Next, someone packed the chair for shipment, carefully placing protective sheathing around the scratch-prone areas and then putting the chair into the carton in such a way as to minimize its being jostled during shipment. After that, the chair was probably delivered to a distributor, trucked to your dormitory room, carried in, unpacked, and placed precisely where it rests now.

In the process of manufacturing and getting the chair to you, screws, nails, staples, and stuffing miraculously appeared on the assembly line when needed; boxes were available in the packaging department; gasoline was in the tanks of the delivery trucks; everyone involved received his or her weekly paycheck; suppliers sent bills; buyers paid bills; factories were swept out; burned-out light bulbs were replaced; machines were oiled and tightened; and the "muzak" kept blaring out the latest in conservative, soothing music. The end result of all of these activities is that you have your chair.

But who put all of those activities together? Who made sure that the assembly line was configured to make chairs, not typewriters or bookcases; that a procedure ensured that the chair went to *your* room rather than to one in Moscow, Lisbon, Abu Dhabi, or Bangkok; that a standard ensured that 1½″ nails rather than six-foot threaded bolts ended up at the assembler's workbench; and that the person who designed the chair really knew something about chairs?

We know that many different individuals performed many different physical tasks just to get you a chair. But in addition, there were other people involved in making sure that those individuals building your chair (and the equipment and supplies that they used) all linked, or meshed, together. Who, for example, considered that chairs might be profitable to manufacture and then set the designer to the task of creating a chair? Who planned the assembly areas where the craftspeople built the chair? Who established and mapped the distribution network by which the chairs moved from factory gate to warehouse to distributor to the room you occupy? Who scheduled the date and time at which the chair was delivered to your room? Who? *Managers.*

MANAGERS: EXAMPLES OF THEIR WORK

Managers perform all sorts of mental tasks, as well as some physical ones, in making sure that even a very commonplace thing like a chair actually gets produced and delivered. What are some of the things a manager might have done in relation to your chair?

1 First, a manager would have had to decide that the chair business was profitable. This activity would have entailed a manager's studying the chair market, including the need for chairs, the profit potential from catering to chair buyers, as well as the availability of resources capable of producing chairs in order to realize that profit.

2 Next, designers would have had to be hired. Here a manager would have established the qualifications necessary for chair designers, written job descriptions and specifications, advertised, interviewed, matched qualifications against necessary specifications, and then hired the best-qualified persons relative to the job specifications.

3 Assembly lines for producing the chairs would have had to be designed. Here managers had to consider the production process, break it down into component subprocesses, and arrange those component subprocesses in such a way as to minimize the amounts of time, material, and motion lost. In essence, a manager's objective here might be to maximize the number of chairs produced and to minimize the expense of producing them. (This may well be a production engineering job as well as a management job—more on that in later chapters.)

4 Sales networks had to be designed. After deciding what agencies other than the manufacturing company, if any, were to participate in getting the chairs to the consumer, managers had to map out a system of ensuring that these buyers were aware of the product and had an opportunity to order it. Usually, this means that salespeople have to be assigned to call on the buyers. Do managers just turn salespeople loose to call on buyers? No, territories must be planned on the basis of such factors as time for travel, time for visits, sales volume per customer, equalization of sales earnings, etc.

5 Procedures for ordering materials, paying salaries, paying outstanding invoices, etc., had to be designed.

6 Managers had to ensure that supervised personnel were working to capacity and that they were producing products of the correct specifications and quality. The determination of those specifications and quality standards is, in itself, another management problem and task.

7 Deliveries of chairs (and maybe tables and beds as well) had to be scheduled.

As one can see, in the chair business there are many different managerial duties to perform, just as there are many different kinds of physical tasks to be done. Clearly, we have covered only a few of the managerial tasks. Also obvious is the fact that some managerial tasks involve a broad scope, tying together plans and pieces of the whole company. Others involve more minute parts of the operation—scheduling five trucks, for example.

Most management work is mental, but sometimes the people doing these mental tasks may also do some of the physical ones. Our scheduler of trucks, for example, may pitch in and help load some of them too (union rules permitting, that is). Or, a sales vice-president may get out on the road to sell when there is need for an extra sales effort.

Managerial work is, however, mostly mental. Managers most often work at desks; attend meetings; read pages of reports; originate all sorts of letters, memoranda, and sketches; manipulate numbers; and make decisions.

That may sound easy enough—far better than physical drudgery—and even like a lot of fun. Managing, however, is not easy, is often not fun, and can be more exhausting than even the most difficult, most tiring operative task. Managing can be difficult, challenging, time-consuming, emotionally exhausting, and rigorous work. But it also can be financially as well as intrinsically rewarding—if you become good at it.

An example of a manager's day

Let us for a moment trace a day in the life of Chuck Martinelli, the 29-year-old sales manager for the Greco-Roman Chair Company. Perhaps viewing Chuck's day will give us greater insight into what managing really is.

7:00 A.M.: Chuck leaves home, having risen at 6:00, showered, dressed, and eaten breakfast.

7:30 A.M.: Arrives at plant, parks car in assigned space.

7:30–8:30 A.M.: Checks calendar for meetings and appointments; prepares folders, data, and materials necessary for meetings.

8:30–9:00 A.M.: Reviews computer printout of yesterday's sales reports, inventories, and sales expenses.

9:00–10:00 A.M.: Meets with product planner and production manager to review plans for introducing Model 64 Hercules chair. Also takes first look at preliminary designs for the Cyclops footstool.

10:00–10:30 A.M.: Has coffee over morning mail.

10:30–11:30 A.M.: Meets with market research director to review results of style survey. Reviews plans for a redirection of survey technique.

11:30–12:00 noon: Has conference call with marketing vice-president and account executive of Achilles and Paris Advertising Agency to settle final specifications of advertising campaign on Model 48 Samson chair. Call results from questions raised at conference in Chicago last week on the efficacy of using religious symbolism in the advertising matter. Orders are given to go full speed on the advertising campaign.

12:00–1:00 P.M.: Has working lunch with president to formulate preliminary sales objectives for the next fiscal year.

1:00–2:30 P.M.: Places calls to all regional sales managers to begin formulation of regional sales quotas for next fiscal year.

2:30–3:00 P.M.: Reviews Midlands district sales performance, which is coming in at thirty-two percent under projections for the current fiscal year, although other districts are up five to eighteen percent. Martinelli notes need to formulate a plan for redirecting effort.

3:00–4:00 P.M.: Attends meeting of Executive Committee for Coordination for review of general corporate finances, profit objectives for the next fiscal year, integration of objectives of key functional departments, and preliminary budget requests.

4:00–5:00 P.M.: Dictates letters and memoranda; reads *Wall Street Journal* and daily *Furniture Market Report*. Makes a note to call his broker about new issue of Soybean Associates warrants.

5:00–6:30 P.M.: Attends emergency meeting to discuss the impact of competitor's Model 4 Eros chair, a clear substitute for the Hercules model under development. Meeting orders design review of Hercules and reassessment of product planning, sales, and production planning. Marketing vice-president suspects a "leak" of information on the design for Hercules, and the president orders corporate security to investigate the possible leak.

6:30–7:00 P.M.: Drives home, stopping at a store for some cigars.

7:00–8:00 P.M.: Has supper (watching Walter Cronkite) and has conversations with wife and children (two sons, ages nine and eleven).

8:00–10:00 P.M.: Works on budget and objectives for sales unit for next fiscal year. Reviews performance of Midlands district and plans personnel changes; dictates memorandum to president informing him of decision to replace regional manager and two low-performance sales representatives.

10:00–11:15 P.M.: Watches *Streets of San Francisco* and the news.

11:20 P.M.: Goes to bed.

Our friend Chuck has just put in a 14½ hour day on his job, with minimal time out for meals and his family. Not all of his days will be that long, but he can count on some even longer ones occasionally. Indeed, sometimes he will be traveling away from home for extended periods of time.

Before we begin analyzing what Chuck's work consists of, let us have a brief look at some of the personal sacrifices he is making and some of the pitfalls that might confront him. First, while on the job, Chuck is almost totally absorbed with the business at hand. Although there will be moments of levity, relaxation, and even loafing or casual conversation, Martinelli is a busy person; he is responsible for quite a bit of the organization's activities and works hard at his job.

Second, Chuck's home life mixes with his work life. Like a student, he has homework. Most executives couldn't accomplish their jobs unless they worked at home, and Chuck is no exception.

Third, Chuck must keep his social and political antennae up and tuned in. Although he coordinates well with other vice-presidents, district managers, and fellow executives, he is always aware of his own need to move up in the organization. In fact, Chuck is balancing the welfare of Chuck Martinelli with that of not only the Greco-Roman Chair Company, but also the other executives in the organization. In other words, Chuck the manager is also a politician, watching his words, associations, and opportunities.

Fourth, Martinelli works much of the time meeting and consulting with other managers. Although decision making by individuals still occurs in organizations, most decisions are made either in groups or as a result of a manager's seeking out information or views from other managers or sources. Technology, size of organizations, and the specialization of functions and tasks make these consultative arrangements very necessary in modern organizations.

Last, Chuck's job is almost totally mental. We would hope that he gets some physical exercise, but while on the job, it's his brain power that is at work, not his muscle power. His job taxes his ability to analyze, see through complex situations, apply analytical tools to problem solving, make decisions, and provide for the implementation of these decisions.

CATEGORIES OF MANAGERIAL ACTIVITY

Let us now try to analyze Chuck's work. In broad terms, we can say that his work falls into three categories. First, he is a designer (very much like the designer of the chair), but as a manager, he designs interrelationships among systems and resources. Much of a manager's day is spent setting objectives and designing plans, programs, systems, and procedures. Second, Chuck sets into motion activities to implement the plans he has designed (or has worked to design as part of a team); he purchases supplies, hires people, orders services, etc. Finally, Chuck is a controller, auditor, and adapter. When things do not go according to plan, he seeks to learn why the deviation exists, determines whether the objectives were attainable, and then either changes the plan or orders appropriate changes in resources or personnel so that objectives are reached and plans fulfilled. In other words, we can divide his activities into three general functional categories: *design, implementation,*

DESIGN

IMPLEMENTATION

CONTROL/AUDIT/ ADAPTATION

FIG. 1.1
Categories of managerial activity.

and *control/audit/adaptation* (see Fig. 1.1). Some of the specific activities that we saw in Chuck's day on the job may thus be assigned to the general functional categories as follows:

1 *Design* activities:
   a) Determining the tasks involved in introducing the Model 64 Hercules chair;
   b) Developing specifications for the advertising campaign for the Model 48 Samson chair;
   c) Formulating sales objectives and quotas.
   d) Undertaking budgeting and financial planning for the next fiscal year.

2 *Implementation* activities:
   a) Ordering new sales kits;
   b) Authorizing the go-ahead for the advertising campaign for the Model 48 Samson chair;

3 *Control/audit/adaptation* activities:
   a) Reviewing styling survey and ordering change in survey technique;
   b) Taking all of the actions relating to the Midlands division, including the release of the sales manager and the two sales representatives.

The concepts of design, implementation, and control/audit/adaptation are convenient ways to categorize managerial activity. But two very crucial points need to be made. First, managerial activity in the real world is not a series of discrete steps that can be neatly categorized; rather, it is a continuous cycle for each action or program undertaken. Second, the real-world manager rarely has the luxury of being able to pigeonhole or line up problems, handling one problem at a time from initial ideas to adaptation and auditing. We have seen that Chuck was confronted with a multitude of issues, each in various stages of the cycle; on some he was at the designer stage, on others an implementer, and on yet others a controller/auditor/adapter.

And always there will be emergencies—the fires to put out. In the Greco-Roman's manager's case, the possible security leak was a problem demanding immediate attention and investigation. Little time was available for quiet contemplation or design activities, since the future of the company depended on preventing competitors access to designs and plants. Perhaps sometime in the near future, the company will have to assign someone to restudy all security procedures, but at the present time there is only one problem—to catch a thief.

THE STANDARDS BY WHICH MANAGERS ARE JUDGED

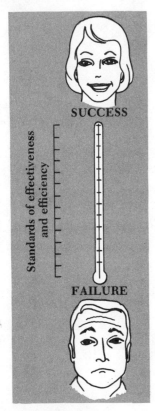

FIG. 1.2
Judging managers.

Obviously, some managers succeed—receive promotions, make fabulous salaries, and reap all the benefits of success. But other managers fail. Putting aside managers who are related to the boss, attain success by unethical means, or practice in an industry protected by monopoly market situations, why is it that some managers are promoted, some fail, and some get fired?

Ideally, managers are judged on the basis of how well and how much they produce. Although the standards by which managers are evaluated generally are not exact, two criteria usually stand out either explicitly or implicitly: *effectiveness* and *efficiency*.

Effectiveness can be simply defined as the achievement of objectives. Your objective may be to climb Mount Everest. If you reach the summit, you have accomplished your objective and can be judged effective. A sales manager's objective may be to sell one million units during the current fiscal year. If a million units are sold, the sales manager was effective.

But although objectives might always be achieved with unlimited resources, most organizations are not so blessed. More important, however, such wasteful effectiveness is rarely desirable. Aside from some military-type objectives—e.g., the enemy must be stopped at all costs—most objectives in organizations must be achieved under resource constraints. Therefore, managers under a proper evaluation scheme are also judged by efficiency criteria, that is, whether they accomplished the goals (effectiveness), but used the planned amount or a minimum amount of resources in achieving effectiveness (see Fig. 1.2).

For a business organization, efficiency is generally measured by profit, but other standards often are employed for evaluation at various levels of the organization: economical use of space, motion, hours, personnel, fuel, etc. So a sales manager may be judged not only on the basis of units sold by the division, but also whether those sales were accomplished with a minimum of salesperson effort, expense, or time—in a word, whether the division minimized expenses for the time period involved while accomplishing objectives.

PROFIT AND NONPROFIT ORGANIZATIONS

Not all managers operate in a business situation; many—and their numbers are increasing—operate in nonbusiness organizations such as hospitals, social agencies, government offices, schools, libraries, and transportation systems. Some of these institutions are classified as nonprofit (or more recently as "not-for-profit"). To a layperson, managing a nonprofit enterprise differs from administering a profit-oriented business, with managers in nonprofit organizations operating by standards different from those in profit-making situations.

But to a manager, this different treatment of profit and nonprofit organizations is a false one. Managers in nonprofit organizations are subject to the criteria of effectiveness and efficiency, just as their counterparts in profit-making organizations are. Once the primary objective of the organization has been set (e.g., to provide patient care, education, fire protection) and the resources budgeted to accomplish the mission, managers in nonprofit organizations are expected to reach that objective using the budgeted resources or less. These managers still must plan to maximize their services for a given allotment of resources.

For example, the school you are attending has multiple objectives, one of which is teaching students. Given the standards of a good educational environment, e.g., determining optimal class size, teaching loads, length of class periods, classroom utilization, etc., the dean of your school is allocated a certain budget. The dean and the faculty are expected to teach so many students so many subjects (ideally, to a certain standard of knowledge) within the constraints of the school's allocated budget. Thus the accomplishment of the mission is related to effectiveness; the accomplishment of the mission within the budget constraints is related to efficiency. In general terms, that means that your dean must ensure that the school will teach the maximum number of students the maximum amount of material within the constraints of the budget. The mission would not be considered accomplished if the maximum number of students learned the maximum amount of material at a cost double the amount budgeted.

Sometimes the organization must make trade-offs among the objectives; in this case the definition of effectiveness will cnange. Suppose that increasing the number of students decreases the level of learning for each student. Is effectiveness now to be judged on the number of students taught? On the level of learning accomplished? Sometimes these trade-offs in objectives are painful to comtemplate. Suppose that a hospital can purchase either a cobalt unit to be used six times a year or a cardiac unit to be used fifteen times a year. How is the effectiveness of the hospital administrator to be determined? Are six cancer patients less important than fifteen heart-attack victims?

Once institutional standards have been set, administrators will be judged on how well they achieved them, given the allocated resources. If the university's objective is to teach the maximum number of students, but it teaches only seventy-eight percent of the maximum possible (and refuses admission to others) and uses up the allocated resources, its administrator might well be judged as inefficient. The same would be true for the administrator of a hospital that treats only seventy-five percent of the patients it could (and turns others away), given the resources available.

We shall have more to say about objectives and these standards of evaluation later in the book. But from the outset you should be aware that managers of nonprofit enterprises don't generally have an easier mission or a different life than their profit-oriented counterparts.

DO YOU WANT TO BE A MANAGER?

You've now had a taste of what managers do, what their days are like, what personal and managerial problems they face, and how they might be evaluated. There is a lot more to learn—indeed, a lot more than can be presented in this book or even in a whole library of books.

But if you had any notions before you came into this course that managerial work is easy, forget them. The Marine Corps used to play the popular song "I Never Promised You a Rose Garden" to recruits undergoing basic training. Organizations don't promise aspiring managers rose gardens either. But the intrinsic satisfactions of management are so great—the creativity, the satisfaction of accomplishment—that we think they're worth the costs.

PLAN OF THE BOOK

Although the managerial job is by nature a continuous one, with no clear-cut divisions and sharp boundaries, it is useful to teach managing in bits and pieces first and then tie the whole package back up. This formula of analysis followed by synthesis is the one we are adopting in this book, primarily because we feel that it is the best one.

This book has five basic parts. Part I has two chapters—this introductory one and Chapter 2, where we explore the relationship of management to a functional or occupational specialty. Most managers are managers of skills and equipment that work on a product or service. Sales managers manage sales representatives, deans manage classrooms and faculty members, controllers manage ledgers and accountants, office managers manage typewriters and secretaries. We cover these relationships in Chapter 2.

Part II consists of two chapters on the organizations in which managers work. Most modern management takes place in organizations, some of them very large. In Chapter 3 we will explore the growth of organizations—from small to large and complex ones. Chapter 4 focuses on the individual and the organization. Much has been written, particularly in the popular press, of the alleged suppression of one's individuality by organization life and demands. "The man in the gray flannel suit" or the "organization man" syndrome has many sides, and we will explore the possible role conflicts involved in organization life.

Part III, "Managerial Design Processes," consists of seven chapters on management design problems and tools: setting objectives, decision making, planning, setting policies and procedures, structuring organizations, and designing motivational processes. The chapters in Part IV, "Managerial Implementation," relate the "planning" to the "doing," i.e., putting into action that which is planned (hiring people, assembling resources, training, communicating, and leading people).

In Part V, "Managerial Control/Audit/Adaptation," the topics range from changing directions (goals) to keeping goals constant and adjusting the resources to achieve them. Managers sometimes have to fire people and close up shop; at times, they will realize that the environment changes and that even the best-laid plans go astray.

We close the book with several articles describing how some organizations meet many of the problems and apply many of the management concepts, processes, and skills covered in this book. Those readings will help to integrate many of the things that were by necessity covered in separate chapters.

Chapter format

Most chapters open with a short case vignette which sets the tone for the basic lessons of the chapter. The text material includes concepts, tools, and practices. As you read the text, try to relate the material to the opening case. Try to grasp relationships; see whether your original thoughts on handling the issue presented in the case will stand up in terms of your new knowledge of human behavior and actual managerial behavior and practice. The case at the end of the chapter gives you an opportunity to apply your new-found knowledge and thoughts. Each chapter also has a series of discussion questions and a bibliography of selected readings. Use the reading lists to explore for new ideas and expand your horizons.

Cases

A few words need to be said about cases in the management-training format. First, unlike in legal training, we are not using cases to teach you how to handle a particular situation. Chances are that during your own managerial career, you will never meet the exact situation portrayed in any case presented in the classroom or this book. Second, management is an inexact profession; managers can and do take different courses of action given exactly the same sets of circumstances. In other words, cases are not designed to train you in the handling of specific problems, and there may be no stock solutions. Solutions can and do differ among managers, professors, and students.

But what good are cases, then? Cases are vehicles for training you to think as managers—to use your knowledge and analytical powers in a way of thinking as close to a manager's as possible. We can't put you into a real-life business or organization to train you, so the next best thing is to bring some business-type problems to you. As long as you remember the two cardinal rules, you should find the case method of learning interesting.

How can you handle cases? Sometimes you can role-play them. Suppose that an employee just walked into work late for the fourth time this month. How would you handle that situation? You could take time out to map out your tactics and present an oral or written report. But real-world managers may not have all that time for such a problem. So we might confront you with your problem employee and let you act the scenario out right on the spot. This puts some pressure on you, but think of what managers go through every day with similar problems.

For other cases, the staff study, analysis, and written report are most useful, and you should get into the habit of presenting your papers to both your classmates and your professor as if your job depended on how well you do. Some day it might.

DISCUSSION QUESTIONS

1 In describing a manager's activities, we frequently categorize them in terms of designing, implementing, and controlling/auditing/adapting. What does each of these concepts mean? Give specific examples of each of these concepts—use Chuck Martinelli as an example if you like.

2 Based on your observation and personal experiences, how would you define the term "management"?

3 It has been said by some that successful management is more "luck" than skill. Do you agree? Why or why not?

4 "Managerial activity in the real world is not a series of discrete steps that can be neatly categorized; the real-world manager rarely has the luxury of being able to pigeonhole problems, handling one problem at a time from initial ideas to adaptation and auditing." What is meant by this statement?

5 By what professional criteria can managerial performance usually be judged?

6 Most laypeople consider management in a "not-for-profit" business to be different from management in a "profit"-oriented business. What arguments would you make to dispel this misconception?

7 Define the following terms from the point of view of managers:

a) effectiveness   b) efficiency

c) auditor   d) implementor

e) designer   f) profit

g) management   h) not-for-profit organization

i) trade-off   j) business

SELECTED READINGS

Albanese, R., *Management: Toward Accountability for Performance* (Homewood, Ill.: Richard D. Irwin, 1975).

Albers, H. H., *Principles of Management: A Modern Approach,* 4th ed. (New York: Wiley, 1974).

Bakewell, K. G. B., ed., *Management Principles and Practices: A Guide to Information Sources* (Detroit: Gale Research Co., 1977).

Begosh, Donald G., "So You Want to Be a Supervisor," *Supervisory Management* **23,** 2 (February 1978): 2–10.

Cappeto, Michael A., "Liberal Arts versus Business Administration," *Journal of College Placement* **38,** 1 (Fall 1977): 37–39.

Carroll, Stephen J., Frank T. Paine, and John B. Miner, *Management Process: Cases and Readings,* 2d ed. (New York: Macmillan, 1977).

Cowan, John, *The Self-Reliant Manager* (New York: AMACOM, 1977).

Dale, E., *Management: Theory and Practice,* 2d ed. (New York: McGraw-Hill, 1969).

Donnelly, J. H., J. L. Gibson, and J. M. Ivancevich, *Fundamentals of Management: Functions, Behavior, Models,* rev. ed. (Dallas: Business Publications, 1975).

Drucker, P. F., *Management: Tasks, Responsibilities, Practices* (New York: Harper & Row, 1974).

———, *The Practice of Management* (New York: Harper & Row, 1954).

Galbraith, J. K., *The New Industrial State* (Boston: Houghton Mifflin, 1967).

Killen, Kenneth H., *Management: A Middle-Management Approach* (Boston: Houghton Mifflin, 1977).

Koontz, H., *Appraising Managers as Managers* (New York: McGraw-Hill, 1971).

Koontz, H., and C. O'Donnell, *Management: A Book of Readings* (New York: McGraw-Hill, 1968).

———, *Principles of Management,* 5th ed. (New York: McGraw-Hill, 1972).

Luthans, Fred, David Lyman, and Diane L. Lockwood, "An Individual Management Development Approach," *Human Resources Management* **17,** 3 (Fall 1978): 1–5.

Mace, Myles L., "What Today's Directors Worry About," *Harvard Business Review* **56,** 4 (July/August 1978): 30ff.

Massie, J. L., and J. Douglas, *Managing: A Contemporary Introduction,* 2d ed. (Englewood Cliffs, N.J.: Prentice-Hall, 1977).

Odiorne, G. S., *Management and the Activity Trap* (New York: Harper & Row, 1974).

Schulz, R., and C. Johnson, *Management of Hospitals* (New York: McGraw-Hill, 1976).

Shrode, W. A., and D. Voich, Jr., *Organizations and Management: Basic Concepts* (Homewood, Ill.: Richard D. Irwin, 1974).

Smith, Bryan F., "TI Board: Pioneering Reform" *Directors and Boards* **2,** 3 (Fall 1977): 4–23.

Williams, Mareille Gray, *The New Executive Manager* (Radnor, Pa.: Chilton, 1977).

Wren, D. A., *The Evolution of Management Thought* (New York: Ronald Press, 1972).

Chapter 2
ADMINISTRATIVE AND FUNCTIONAL INTEGRATION

CHAPTER HIGHLIGHTS

This chapter introduces the role of the manager in terms of the skills he or she needs to develop to perform the managerial job effectively and efficiently. We set these skills into three major categories: knowledge of subordinate functions, interactive skills, and administrative skills. As you read this chapter, you should gain a greater appreciation of the differences between managerial and nonmanagerial work.

LEARNING OBJECTIVES

1 To learn and to be able to define the major categories of necessary management skills: knowledge of subordinate technical and administrative roles, interactive skills, and administrative skills.

2 To appreciate the position of the supervisor as the "person in the middle."

3 To develop an awareness of the administrative skills that managers must develop, e.g., information processing, decision making, leading.

4 To appreciate the limits to the transferability of managers between organizations of differing technical functions.

CASE: AUDREY HOLLIS

■ Audrey Hollis's association with Milopac Industries began twelve years ago, when she was hired after graduation from high school to work as a clerk typist to process purchase orders. During this time, the company has grown from a $200,000 annual business to one of $6 million, and Audrey has moved up from clerk typist to switchboard operator to calculator operator. When the firm rented its first computer, the company paid for Audrey to go to school to learn the basics of computer operation and programming. After about three years on the computer, she became the personal secretary to the vice-president for manufacturing, the job she now holds. In looking back over the past twelve years, Audrey thinks that she has held every clerical and office position in the company.

A technically oriented company, Milopac sells precision instruments to shipbuilding companies. It prides itself on being administratively lean, preferring to concentrate its resources on technical and scientific functions. Consequently, the firm allots only four personal secretaries—one for the president and one each for the three vice-presidents. All the rest of the clerical work and the bookkeeping, billing, and purchasing are routed to the "office" where twenty-four clerks perform specialized functions, but these people could be moved to other tasks if the work flow demanded. This arrangement means that the office manager has to know the capabilities of all of the clerical staff plus the potential of the clerical equipment and the computer.

Audrey was called into the president's office at 11:00 A.M. one Monday. James Truman, who founded Milopac on a shoestring about fourteen years ago, was known as a blunt person who wasted little time with pleasantries. He came right to the point with Audrey. "Ms. Hollis, we just canned Simpson, the office manager, and we want you to take over the job. You know every clerk in the place and are familiar with every machine in that office. What this will mean to you is that you'll have to schedule work as well as supervise. Of course, you'll be expected to fill in with some typing also, just like you are doing now, but the job will be primarily managerial. And, by the way, it will mean a $54 weekly raise. Do you think you can handle it?"

Audrey was a bit shaken by the offer—or was it an offer? Truman didn't offer her the job; he just about ordered her to take it. Quickly, she realized that she had many friends in the typing pool, but also that a number of younger, more independent people were coming into the office. She had no doubts about her knowledge of the tasks involved. She just wondered if she was capable of managing and supervising as well. ■

INTRODUCTION

Audrey Hollis's apprehensions in approaching a managerial position are quite understandable and indeed expected. Making managers out of functional specialists is a good deal more difficult than simply saying (as James Truman essentially did), "Now you're a manager." Managers need to master and to apply several kinds of skills in order to succeed. In most cases would-be managers will have to "learn" these skills; in all cases it will take time to master them.

In this chapter we will explore some of the skills needed by the manager in the performance of administrative duties. We will emphasize not only the differences between operative—or technical—and managerial work, but also the integration of the administrative and technical functions in order to achieve objectives.

Managerial skills can be divided into three major categories: (1) *knowledge of subordinate functions—technical and administrative;* (2) *interactive skills;* and (3) *administrative skills.* These categories, of course, are not mu-

- ■ Knowledge and appreciation of subordinate functions and roles—technical and administrative
- ■ Interactive skills
- ■ Administrative skills

Three categories of managerial skills

tually exclusive; indeed, we shall cover most of them in the latter category. Many of the skills will be further elaborated on in later chapters.

KNOWLEDGE OF SUBORDINATE FUNCTIONS—TECHNICAL AND ADMINISTRATIVE

It is often said that a good manager will not ask someone else to do something that he or she cannot do. Although this statement makes an excellent popular recommendation, *being able to perform all operative and technical tasks is not a prerequisite to good management.* Few major corporate presidents are familiar enough with all of the technical specialties under their general command to be able to perform them. Yet corporate presidents generally have enough familiarity with the *uses* of technical skills and the *power* of technical capabilities to be able to fully integrate them into the corporate scheme. For example, few top managers know how to program or operate a computer, yet they ought to know what the computer is capable of doing and most important, what the computer can contribute in terms of aiding them in decision making.

Some managers, such as Audrey Hollis, will derive some functional expertise and knowledge from experiences gained in performing some of the tasks. She has, for example, filled in at most of the jobs in her unit. But it is not totally necessary—as Mr. Truman suggested it was—that she be experienced in all of the tasks. What is important, in order for her to function as the office manager, is that she be familiar with the uses and power of the technical processes within her jurisdiction, not so that she could do them herself if necessary, but so that she can schedule, shift resources, and achieve maximum productivity from her subordinates.

Audrey manages operatives or technicians, but some managers manage other managers. These higher-level managers must not only be familiar with the technical departments their subordinates manage, but also appreciate the administrative problems subordinate managers face. A key problem in many organizations is that often executives do not consider or understand their subordinate managers' administrative problems or processes, despite the fact that they should know better. Indeed, when subordinate managers are rewarded on a production basis, sometimes the manager who achieves a high productive record, but ruins his or her unit's cohesiveness in the process is rewarded and promoted, but a successor then reaps the results of the predecessor's performance in terms of lower production, weak unit cohesion, and interpersonal problems. In many of these situations the superiors often cannot understand why the new managers have problems that the previous ones didn't have, but which in reality were always lurking below the surface.

INTERACTIVE SKILLS

The second prerequisite for the manager is the development of interactive skills. Audrey Hollis, for example, will have to know what makes people "tick," how she can get them to produce (and not, as is often assumed, through exploitation), and how she can get them to coordinate with one another to generate a satisfactorily productive work force. Mastery of interactive skills does not necessarily correlate with technical expertise, although subordinates will expect their superiors to be familiar with the technical processes.

Interactive skills are among the most difficult for a new manager to apply, since typically she or he moved up from a technical operative position to a job of "bossing" former peers. Thus Audrey Hollis will no longer be just a friend to her workmates, but their manager as well. It is precisely this duality that creates what one article termed the "man-in-the-middle" role conflict.* The manager, particularly the first-line supervisor, is caught between the expectations of the organization for production and those of subordinates for protection and advocacy of their needs to higher management (see Fig. 2.1). Note also that the situation may be complicated if a collective-bargaining agreement is present. The supervisor is the first line of management to administer the contract. And quite possibly the new supervisor's departure from the bargaining unit meant a change in his or her benefits and seniority accumulation. The contract probably also has some provision relating to a manager's return to the bargaining unit.

Some organizations recognize the "person in the middle" problem when they promote from operative nonmanagerial positions or when they promote a manager to a higher-level position. Instead of promoting from within a unit and creating a serious adjustment problem for the new manager, the organization may transfer the manager out of his or her present branch or plant to become the head of another unit physically removed from the old one. In that way the newly promoted manager will not be subject to the

---

* The article that popularized the term is Fritz Roethlisberger's "Foreman: Man in the Middle," *Harvard Business Review* 23 (Spring 1945): 285–294.

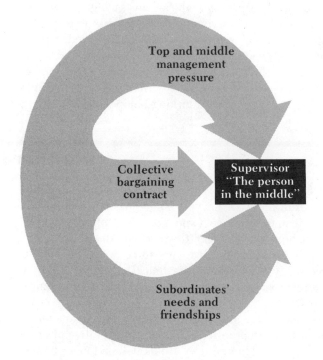

FIG. 2.1
The supervisor's position.

Top and middle
management
pressure

Collective
bargaining
contract

Supervisor
"The person
in the middle"

Subordinates'
needs and
friendships

demands of old friendships. Of course, this does not guarantee that the manager will not be caught in the middle of demands coming from subordinates and those emanating from topside. But at least one strong contributing factor to role conflict may have been diminished.

ADMINISTRATIVE SKILLS

Perhaps the most important area of new skills to be mastered is administrative. Audrey Hollis's work will now be geared to planning, forecasting, scheduling, controlling output, allocating work, and evaluating performance. More specifically, she will find herself using some of the following skills, ones that most likely will be new to her:

1 Information processing
2 Decision making
3 Scheduling
4 Evaluating, rewarding, and promoting
5 Supplying and training human and other resources

FIG. 2.2
Administrative skills for the managerial role.

6 Leading and advocating
7 Arbitrating and conciliating
8 Counseling
9 Coordinating

Most of the remainder of this chapter elaborates on these administrative skills and points out the problems and pitfalls for managers as they apply them. See Fig. 2.2.

As information processors, managers have to translate and transfer information both into and out of their units. Thus Audrey Hollis will have to translate the orders from the various departments her unit serves with respect to necessary output—specifically, by relaying information to her subordinates. In addition, she will become the interpreter and describer of all sorts of non-task information to her subordinates, such as changes in fringe benefits, new salary scales, office-hour changes, vacation schedules, or changes in managerial staffing or organization structure. Also, she will become the reservoir for all sorts of information that supervisors are expected to have—occupational safety and health regulations, affirmative action and equal opportunity

Information processing

standards, repair services available, emergency police, fire, and ambulance service, first aid, and so on. But information processing is not a one-way street. The manager's job will also include communicating upward about the status of the unit, including needs to be filled, additional positions desired, personnel performance, the status of equipment, and the inevitable gripes of subordinates.

Since accuracy in communication is a key to good management and since rumors get started and spread very easily in any organization, much of a manager's communication and information processing will need to be written. Indeed, a good deal of manager's time is spent dictating and writing the memoranda, letters, notes, and reports that form the basis for organizational maintenance.

Decision making   Anyone who shuns making decisions is certainly not well suited for a managerial role, since decision making is the basis of management. Managers make dozens of decisions every day and must develop decision-making skills and learn what considerations are important factors in their decision making.

Fortunately for Audrey Hollis, her organizational universe is much smaller than that of, say, the corporate president, so she won't have to juggle so many considerations in making her decisions. Nonetheless, whereas operative employees or workers may be able to live happily while someone else makes the decisions affecting their welfare (even though they will often gripe about these decisions), the manager has no such luxury. President Harry Truman used to have on his desk a sign reading, "The Buck Stops Here." In Truman's case the slogan meant that excuses could go no further; he was the top link in the chain of command, and he could not say, "It's not my job" or "It's the fault of upstairs" or "The decision must be made higher up." Although lower-level managers are not the ultimate sources of authority and responsibility within an organization and many areas are out of bounds to them, they nevertheless are the focal points for many decisions affecting their particular limited universes—their departments or units.

Decision making is not easy, particularly when it involves the well-being of others and the expenditure of resources. For example, during periods of economic slack or recession, many managers must make the difficult decisions about whom to lay off and whom to retain within the organization. Only a few managers may enjoy making that type of decision, but it must be made. Oftentimes, the right move can be determined by a mechanical formula, but applying the formula and making the move is a most difficult, and at times an emotionally draining, experience. It is these difficult decision situations that clearly distinguish the role of the manager from that of the operative employee.

Managers have to develop skills in scheduling, particularly as they relate to subordinates' work loads, but just as importantly as they relate to the manager's own daily routine. Often a manager's primary problem is the inability to develop disciplined scheduling of his or her own activities, and hence the "never enough time" syndrome sets in.

Much of the work in Audrey Hollis's office will be routine, and a standard schedule might be relatively easy to apply. But then, of course, there will always be crash projects, those that must be completed immediately (the "I need it yesterday" syndrome). And then there are the specialized chores that pop into the office periodically. Reports, surveys, technical papers, specification sheets, and even an occasional manuscript must be absorbed into the technical system without disrupting the normal patterns of billing correspondence, advertising, inventory reports, filing, etc.

Audrey's scheduling task is not made easier by the fact that her unit services every other organizational unit in the company. Each of these other units undoubtedly thinks that its work should be accorded top priority and so often sets unrealistic deadlines and is oblivious of the work and needs of the other units calling on the services of the office staff. Therefore, scheduling is a skill that entails not only parceling out work among the various clerks in the office, but also keeping the other organizational units satisfied that their needs are being met in a timely, equitable fashion.

This type of scheduling problem is not confined to a position such as Audrey Hollis holds. Consider the position of Chuck Martinelli (Chapter 1); as a sales manager given a finite level of production capacity, he must schedule deliveries of chairs among customers who probably think that they must be served above all the other customers of the Greco-Roman Chair Company. Sometimes managers may have to resort to favoritism to keep larger customers satisfied; sometimes new accounts must be moved to the front of the line. In essence, scheduling is a skill that might not always be purely technical; it can be political as well.

In her new position, one of Audrey's primary tasks will be to develop her skills in evaluating and rewarding her subordinates. Very early, she will have to develop standards against which to measure her subordinates, and she must then be prepared to administer those standards fairly and firmly. Hence she must develop the dispassionate, almost mechanical process by which subordinates are measured, but then temper that process with some degree of understanding and acceptance of human frailties.

Along with the evaluation process, Audrey Hollis will gain some power to reward and promote—and punish. Not everyone will receive pay raises or promotions, and it takes skill to differentiate among subordinates and determine those who will be rewarded and those who will not be—and at the same time keep those who do not receive rewards. More important, the manager

Scheduling

Evaluating, promoting, and rewarding

must develop skills to turn those nonrewarded employees around so that they *do* become more productive and eligible for the rewards the manager has available.

Occasionally, a manager has to discipline, downgrade, or sever an employee from the organization. These activities take not only the skills of ensuring that the action is justified and is backed by integrity—and of meeting the employee and informing him or her of the decision—but also those associated with preventing the situation from getting out of control and disrupting the rest of the organization. Often employees will rally about a fellow worker being disciplined. All sorts of rumors will fly about the unit, and the manager has the unenviable task of keeping the unit intact while terminating the ineffective or disruptive employee.

Resource provision and training
Any manager will have to master skills involved in resource provision and training. In relation to resource support, the manager will have to learn to understand the desires of employees for certain support systems, ranging from ample supplies to specialized equipment for task performance. For example, as we shall see in the next chapter, a hospital administrator must somehow deal with doctors who might desire all sorts of esoteric medical equipment, and decisions must be made as to the necessity of that equipment, given limited financial resources. In Audrey Hollis's case, questions might relate to who gets the new typewriter, who sits at the front desk, who receives authorization to operate the copying machine and other expensive equipment, or who is allowed access to the supply cabinet.

These problems are not as easily solved as one might imagine at first glance, since they entail all sorts of human reactions. For example, one state agency thought that clerks could be differentiated in the office by giving each category of clerk (determined by civil service pay grade) a different color desk and chair; all of the clerks would seem identical in the bullpen-type office except for the color of their furniture. Needless to say, the attempted move for identification caused a minor revolt in the office, as employees balked at the color scheme. It seemed that although the utility and the quality of the equipment were equal among employees, the color differential emphasized status differentials which the clerks involved were doing everything to hide. The desks were rapidly repainted.

So simply supplying resources is not as easy a task as one might envision. A director of research and development in any major corporation must make decisions on projects to be parceled out, technical equipment, allocation of laboratory assistance, distribution of travel money, assignment of computer time, secretarial service, etc. In a department wrought with status problems —and research and development departments often are—any minor differences in allotments could cause havoc, despite the fact that some members of the department may have little need for additional resources.

Providing resources includes the provision of skills to subordinates—in a word, training. All employees require some training, whether it means a simple indoctrination and introductory ceremony or on-the-job training in the use of specialized or complex equipment. Often older employees must be retrained to operate new equipment or be brought up to date on new systems or new company policies and procedures.

Many times organizations will arrange to have outside agencies conduct the training, but just as frequently the chores of training and indoctrinating will fall on the immediate supervisor. Audrey Hollis, then, will have to develop some skills in training—perhaps herself learning how other people learn—so as to maximize the amount of training effectiveness and to minimize the expense and time needed to train.

Sometimes training involves pairing the new employee with one experienced with the methods and processes that the new employee will have to learn. Although some employees may take pride in being selected to "break in" the new employee, others may resent having to take time out and explain the "obvious."

Whether she likes it or not, Audrey Hollis in her new position has become the leader and advocate of her work group. In this context she represents her group to higher-level management, carrying members' complaints to higher-level authority and assuring her group that she is able to get its equitable share of organizational resources. In a very real sense, Audrey is being evaluated not only by her superiors for performance, but also by subordinates for her delivery of their need satisfaction. Thus if her subordinates feel overworked and if their work overload can be demonstrated as fact, it will fall on Audrey to carry that message to higher management and obtain authorization for additional positions. If a general layoff occurs, Audrey's subordinates will expect her to represent the unit's personnel. Here is where the "person in the middle" syndrome comes into play the hardest. Whereas top management expects managers to perform according to organizational objectives, constraints, and expectations, those managers' subordinates look on them as their protectors and advocates.

Leading and advocating

And so the manager must also develop leadership skills in order to temper the demands of the organization with those of subordinates. This will entail knowing when to act independently and when to seek consultation with subordinates.

Many studies indicate that leadership effectiveness is a function of the problem environment in which the leader exists (along with the followers), and the environment may be diverse. That is, at different times, given the same leader and group, the problems may necessitate varying leadership styles. Thus the leadership style a manager may adopt may vary from tough, unilateral "ordering around" to a conciliatory, consultative, group-oriented one, depending on the attributes and information available to the leader, the problem at hand, and the willingness or need of the subordinates to participate. Being able to vary leadership styles, however, is a difficult, if not impossible, task to master. Audrey Hollis will have to learn and carefully determine when to apply various leadership styles in handling her unit's problems.

Arbitrating and conciliating

No unit made up of diverse individuals will ever exist without an occasional conflict developing among its members. Whether the conflict results from a simple "got up on the wrong side of the bed" situation or is a long-simmering one resulting from status differentials or personality differences, the manager in charge is faced with the problem of arbitrating and conciliating among the conflicting parties. Sometimes the problem is easily resolved, perhaps with a simple conference over coffee or by a move of one of the parties. Other times, however, the manager will be required to find the root causes of the conflict and to attempt to get two parties to understand each other's views. This may take several sessions, and the manager must become skilled at conducting "rap" sessions. In still other situations, the manager may find the situation so disruptive that the best alternative would be to remove both parties to the conflict from the scene. (We shall have a great deal more to say about conflict resolution and the role of the manager in later chapters.)

Counseling

Many work-related problems are caused by personal problems, and managers may find themselves acting as counselors to their subordinates. Oftentimes this is dangerous territory for the manager to tread in; he or she may find that the best alternative is to seek professional assistance from either top management or other trained professionals within the organization.

But at other times the counseling takes on a distinctly work-related character, and the manager cannot abdicate taking a role. Absenteeism, poor work habits, office romances, medical problems, marriage problems, alcoholism, and similar personal difficulties may have to be dealt with at the level at which they are having the adverse effect. Indeed, many commentators have labeled alcoholism as a number-one problem facing modern organizations and industry and are encouraging managers to become familiar with counseling and assisting employees seeking help in overcoming the problem. Similar concerns have been expressed about drugs.

But counseling also has its brighter sides—for example, coaching employees on the routes of promotion and advancement within the organization. Managers are often faced with employees who say, "I'd like to go that route, but I don't know if I can make it or whether I'll be happy there" or "I like it so much here, I don't know if I can duplicate it on that other job." Many employees, therefore, are feeling the same syndrome of insecurity that Audrey Hollis felt when told about her new position as office manager. And it is the manager's job to be able to allay those feelings and to encourage talented employees to accept more challenging assignments.

The counseling role for managers is a cross between confession hearer and ardent advocate. Most managers quickly develop a feel for how deeply they should become involved in problems of their subordinates as well as learn quite early the limits of their expertise in the areas of counseling. Caution is the best advice for any manager here. Too much amateur psychology often takes place in organizations, and the manager ought to quickly arrive at a realization of the limits of his or her competence.

Finally, managers are coordinators, not only of all the technical operative tasks under their jurisdiction, but of all their own personal skills as well. Of course, the manager applies skills concurrently. No neat lines exist for identifying managerial activity as technical, interactive, or administrative. We can sift through the elements in pieces, but the experienced manager knows that the job is a conglomeration of skills and functions.

Coordinating

Figure 2.3 sums up our approach to this chapter. It is often said that management is getting the work done through others. As Fig. 2.3 shows, the manager applies knowledge of technical roles, interactive skills, and administrative skills to activate the operative employees' technical and operative skills and to create task action leading to objective achievement under, of course, the criteria of effectiveness and efficiency.

FIG. 2.3
The application of managing skills.

SKILL TRANSFER

Many writers on management have written about the universality of management skills. That is, managerial skills are necessarily the same in all types of organizations and in all types of functions. But often, laypeople will carry this universality to the point of saying that a good manager can move from one position to another or from one organization to another and that so long as he or she has mastered managerial skills, he or she will be successful.

Although one may view the administrative skills as necessary in all managerial positions, the necessity of technical skill and, particularly, knowledge is also always present. Apart from figureheads who are placed into organizations for prestige purposes but who actually manage very little, few managers will agree that they can function effectively and efficiently without some understanding of the technical functions of their organizations and units.

Thus many managers will spend a good deal of time learning *about* the technical processes either before or while on the job. Rarely will they find themselves functioning well without that knowledge. Thus the universality of managerial skills should be taken to merely connote their necessity in all managerial positions; other knowledge—of a technical nature—is also necessary, however.

SUMMARY AND CONCLUSION

In this chapter we explored some of the skills needed by the manager in performing administrative duties. Those skills can be divided into three major but not mutually exclusive categories: knowledge of subordinate functions, interactive skills, and administrative skills. Under the third category, we included such specific skills as information processing, decision making, scheduling, evaluating, rewarding, and promoting, training and supplying human and other resources, leading and advocating, arbitrating and conciliating, counseling, and coordinating. We then considered the transfer of skills from position to position or from organization to organization, concluding that effective management still requires some appreciation, if not intimate knowledge, of the technical processes of the unit or the organization.

DISCUSSION QUESTIONS

1 What skills would you say are necessary to be an effective and efficient manager?

2 Managerial skills can be broken down into three categories: knowledge of subordinate functions (technical and administrative), interactive skills, and administrative skills. Briefly define each of these managerial skill areas.

3 A prerequisite of being a good manager, some laypeople have argued, is possessing the ability to perform all operative tasks under a manager's control. Do you agree with this statement? Why or why not?

4 What is the "person-in-the-middle" problem relative to a manager's interactive skills?

5 What are some of the problems and pitfalls for managers relative to applying the following administrative skills: information processing; decision making; scheduling; evaluating, promoting, and rewarding; resource provision and training; leading and advocating; arbitrating and conciliating; counseling; and coordinating? Pick any four administrative skills and elaborate on some of the inherent problems associated with each.

6 Do managers of not-for-profit organizations apply the same, similar, or different skills as managers of profit-oriented organizations?

7 What do we mean by the phrase "universality of management"? Do you agree with this concept? Why or why not?

8 Define the following terms:
   a) managerial skills   b) interactive skill
   c) administrative skill   d) manager in the middle problem
   e) universality of management   f) management
   g) skill transfer

9 List, define, and illustrate five administrative skills.

CASE: DICK HERNANDEZ

■ Dick Hernandez graduated from the University of Santa Clara in 1976, having already accepted a position with Sunshine Oil Company, a national, vertically and horizontally integrated energy refiner and marketer. Dick knew what to expect: several months working at one of the company's stations, a year or two on the road visiting gasoline stations and garages selling the company's products, and then maybe a promotion to territorial sales manager. That was the standard company training and upgrading sequence.

Dick spent the summer and autumn of 1976 working at a busy company station in Phoenix, Arizona. This was one of the company's larger stations, with eight rows of pumps and twelve service bays, plus a vending machine and self-service convenience-item store. While in Phoenix, Dick pumped gasoline, changed oil, greased cars, changed tires, learned to do minor repairs and maintenance work such as tuneups and brake overhauls, and performed general maintenance and housekeeping around the station. He worked all the shifts: 8:00 A.M. to 4:00 P.M., 4:00 P.M. to 12:00 midnight, and even put some time in on the 12:00 midnight to 8:00 A.M. graveyard shift. Dick knew that the company training program began with a stint in the service station, yet he still disliked the work. Surely it bore little relationship to management, his major in college. He counted the days until January 15, 1977, when he would go onto the road as a company service representative.

The time came for Dick to graduate out of the station. His station manager gave him an extremely high evaluation for his work, and Dick admitted that he had learned a great deal about the operation of a gasoline station. He hadn't got much managerial experience, but he had learned about the company's products and services.

He then spent a year on the road, his territory covering western Missouri and eastern Kansas, basically around Kansas City. Dick called on company-owned stations, independent operators handling the Sunshine line, and some retail stores carrying accessories and products such as motor oil. His job was to take orders; push tires, batteries, and accessories (called TBA in the trade) onto independent dealers; introduce new products to dealers; decorate stations with special promotional material; and file reports to his territorial manager on station condition, personnel appearance, and customer satisfaction.

The next year, Hernandez was transferred to a territory in northern Florida, where he performed essentially the same duties as he had in Kansas City. During the next two years he filed reams of reports, opened several new stations and accounts, but most of all did a great deal of traveling. And that was starting to get on his nerves.

On February 12, 1979, Hernandez finally was promoted to territorial sales manager. Only occasionally now would he visit stations and dealers. His basic job was to manage the routes of nine sales representatives (the same position he had previously held) who operated out of the company's Southeast regional office in Atlanta. He was one of six territorial sales managers in the Atlanta office. Specifically, the sales managers were to schedule their sales representatives; study sales and recommend territorial quotas; plan the introduction of new products; plan and execute the opening of new dealerships; coordinate with shipping, advertising, real estate, and the various other departments concerned with the company's services in the territory; evaluate sales representatives; and hire sales personnel (sometimes from the very company training program from which Hernandez came—college graduates now doing their time in company stations).

Before he was actually placed in his job, however, Hernandez was sent to New York for a two-week training program for new territorial managers. At 8:00 A.M. on February 19, the trainer walked into the classroom on the 58th floor of company headquarters and said, "Good morning, ladies and gentlemen. You are now managers, and the purpose of this two-week program is to get you thinking like managers." ■

Case questions

1. Why does Sunshine Oil Company require its future sales managers to work in service stations? On the road?

2. What new skills do you think will be stressed in the training program that Dick Hernandez is attending?

3. Evaluate some of the changes in outlook that Hernandez will have to make in becoming a manager.

SELECTED READINGS

Barnard, C. I., *The Functions of the Executive* (Cambridge, Mass.: Harvard University Press, 1938).

Baughman, J. P., *The History of American Management: Selections from the Business History Review* (Englewood Cliffs, N.J.: Prentice-Hall, 1968).

Bramlette, Carl A., Donald O. Jewell, and Michael H. Mescon, "Designing for Organizational Effectiveness: How It Works," *Atlanta Economic Review* **27,** 6 (November/December 1977): 10–15.

Champion, D. P., "Developing the Knowledge and Skills of Federal Executives," *The Bureaucrat* **4** (April 1975): 66–82.

Cleveland, H., *The Future Executive: A Guide for Tomorrow's Managers* (New York: Harper & Row, 1972).

Driscoll, James W., Daniel J. Caroll, Jr., and Timothy A. Strecher, "The First-Level Supervisor: Still One 'Man in the Middle,'" *Sloan Management Review* **19,** 2 (Winter 1978): 25–37.

Glover, J. D., R. M. Hower, and R. Tagiuri, *The Administrator,* 5th ed. (Homewood, Ill.: Richard D. Irwin, 1973).

Greenwood, W. T. (ed.), *Management and Organizational Behavior Theories: An Inter-disciplinary Approach* (Cincinnati: South-Western, 1965).

Guyllenhammar, Pehr G., *People At Work* (Reading, Mass.: Addison-Wesley, 1977).

"How Successful Executives Handle People: 12 Studies on Communications and Management Skills," *Harvard Business Review* (special edition, 1970).

Katz, R. L., "Skills of an Effective Administrator," *Harvard Business Review* **52** (September/October 1974): 90–102.

Keeley, Michael, "A Social-Justice Approach to Organizational Evaluation," *Administrative Science Quarterly* **23,** 2 (June 1978): 272–292.

Levinson, Harry, "The Abrasive Personality," *Harvard Business Review* **56,** 3 (May/June 1978): 86–94.

Liles, P. R., "Who Are the Entrepreneurs?" *MSU Business Topics* **22** (Winter 1974): 5–14.

Maccoby, M., *The Gamesman: The New Corporate Leaders* (New York: Simon and Schuster, 1976).

McGregor, D., *The Professional Manager* (New York: McGraw-Hill, 1967).

Mintzberg, H. D., "A New Look at the Chief Executive's Job," *Organizational Dynamics* 1 (Winter 1973): 2–30.

———, *The Nature of Managerial Work* (New York: Harper & Row, 1973).

Mowday, Richard T., "The Exercise of Upward Influence in Organizations," *Administrative Science Quarterly* **23,** 1 (March 1978): 137–156.

Peter, L., and R. Hull, *The Peter Principle* (New York: Morrow, 1969).

Sloan, A. P., Jr., *My Years with General Motors* (Garden City, N.Y.: Doubleday, 1964).

Stewart, Nathaniel, *The Effective Woman Manager: Seven Vital Skills for Upward Mobility* (New York: Wiley, 1978).

Townsend, R. *Up the Organization* (New York: Knopf, 1970).

Wallach, Arthur E., "The Man in the Middle," *Personnel Journal* **56,** 12 (December 1977): 622–624.

PART II

Organizations and Their Managers

In Chapters 3 and 4 we explore the organizational setting for managerial activity and the individual manager in relation to the organization, respectively. Chapter 3 focuses on the structure of organizations; Chapter 4, on the vital question of changing individual values relative to organizational demands.

Chapter 3
THE ORGANIZATIONAL SETTING

CHAPTER HIGHLIGHTS

Contemporary managers manage organizations. In this chapter we introduce the various principles and concepts of organization design. We will see how an organization grows both vertically and horizontally, differentiates its basic (primary) functions from secondary ones, and develops specialized units. We introduce the concept of authority and relate it to the various types of organizational components. We also will cover the placement of decision responsibility within organizations.

LEARNING OBJECTIVES

1 To appreciate the problems brought about by organizational growth.

2 To learn the distinction between primary and secondary organizational functions.

3 To learn the meaning of vertical specialization and delegation.

4 To learn the meaning of horizontal specialization.

5 To recognize the bases on which to divide an organization horizontally.

6 To start appreciating the problems in multiunit operations.

7 To differentiate between line and staff.

8 To learn the relationship of various types of staff units to line units.

9 To understand the bases for line staff conflict.

10 To be aware of the line staff relationships in a multiunit organization.

11 To learn the meaning and various bases of the term authority.

12 To understand the concepts of span of control and levels of command and the problems between the two.

13 To know what a decision center is and what decentralization and centralization mean in an organizational context.

INTRODUCTION

All contemporary managers function within purposeful organizations. Organizations come in all shapes and sizes, ranging from extremely small (one or two individuals) entrepreneurial ones through large, complex, multinational conglomerates employing hundreds of thousands of people and spanning continents and oceans. Larger organizations are characterized by high degrees of specialization as tasks are broken down into smaller and more specific entities. Smaller organizations have less specialization; larger and varied tasks are usually assigned to singular positions.

Our objective in this chapter is to explore the world of formal organizations and to understand the relationships and problems that go into constructing them and making them run. We can do this by tracing the growth of an organization to demonstrate how complexity evolves and to illustrate some of the devices used to handle larger masses of tasks and the increase in the number of tasks inherent in any growing organization. With a few exceptions that we shall point out, organizations in the context of this chapter should be thought of as groupings of functions rather than of people. That is, every organization has certain functions to perform in order to accomplish its objectives, and the relationships among these functions are more important to us now than the interpersonal relationships among people filling the various positions. Later on we shall tackle "people" problems, but for the purposes of studying organization design, it is the *task* that we are concerned with, not the person who fills the position related to the task.

In a small, one-person organization, all functions are performed by that one person. But as the organization grows, each function becomes so time-consuming that more than one position is required to handle it. So each function must be broken down into subfunctions. This is the process that John Smith, a budding young entrepreneur, who decided to open a hardware and paint store, went through. Initially, John will have, at a minimum, the following functions to perform: selling and merchandising, buying, accounting, maintenance, hiring, and public relations.

The organization chart for his business—John's Hardware Store—would not be very elaborate at this stage, consisting of one box denoting one position. But within that box would be all of the functions that John would have to perform in order to make the business succeed (see Fig. 3.1).

John may not realize it yet, but he has the embryo of a rather complex organization within that little business he has opened. Although none of those functions included in his one position is as yet time-consuming enough to take up more than a portion of his time, if his business is successful, sooner or later he will have to decide to either break some of them out into separate positions or limit his business's growth.

John Smith
President,
Chief Buyer,
Salesperson,
Merchandise Manager,
Bookkeeper,
Head of Maintenance,
Personnel Manager

FIG. 3.1
John's Hardware Store—
organization chart.

PRIMARY AND SECONDARY FUNCTIONS

At this point, we can start to recognize one of the first fundamentals of formal organizations—the distinction between primary and secondary functions. In formal terms, some of those functions that John is performing are called primary ones. *Primary functions* are those that contribute *directly* to the achievement of organizational objectives. Secondary functions, by contrast, are those that facilitate the achievement of the primary functions and hence contribute only indirectly to the achievement of the firm's primary objectives.*

Let us suppose, for a moment, that the organizational objective of John's Hardware Store is to procure and distribute utility in the form of hardware, paint, wallpaper, plumbing supplies, etc. The degree to which the organization meets this objective can be measured by the criterion of efficiency; efficiency in this case could be defined as *profits* (the maximization of which may be John's personal objective).

In theory, the functions that contribute directly to the achievement of the objective of utility procurement and transfer are those that work directly on the passage of the product or service of the organization from vendors to consumers. For example, the two functions in John's Hardware Store that fulfill this definition are buying and selling. Therefore, buying and selling are the organization's primary functions. The other functions—bookkeeping, maintenance, personnel, and public relations—do not work directly on the product or service, but do facilitate the achievement of the primary functions; therefore, they may be considered secondary functions.

"Secondary" in no way suggests "lesser" or "inferior." Even though most secondary functions start out as segments of a primary component's job, they are no less important to the organization's well-being. Secondary functions *are* important, and if poorly performed can certainly have a damaging effect on the organization's performance.

VERTICAL SPECIALIZATION AND THE LINE ORGANIZATION

Now let us suppose that John Smith's business has prospered to the point that he finds it necessary to hire a salesperson. John intends to remain the buyer, bookkeeper, maintenance director, personnel manager, and public relations expert of the organization, but he will now have someone to share the sales work with him. John must now assume, however, the responsibility

* *See* Ralph C. Davis, *The Fundamentals of Top Management* (New York: Harper and Brothers, 1951), p. 205.

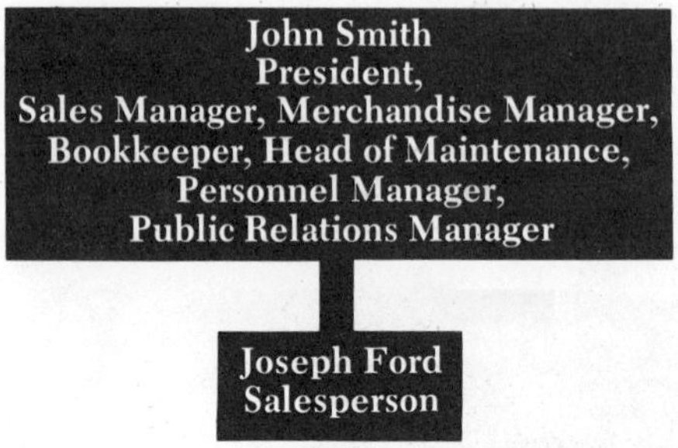

**John Smith
President,
Sales Manager, Merchandise Manager,
Bookkeeper, Head of Maintenance,
Personnel Manager,
Public Relations Manager**

**Joseph Ford
Salesperson**

FIG. 3.2
John's Hardware Store—organization chart showing
beginning of vertical specialization.

for supervising the new salesperson. By hiring this new salesperson, John is
taking the first step toward making his organization more complex (see
Fig. 3.2).

The hiring of Joseph Ford, John's first organizational subordinate, represents the first step toward *vertical specialization* within the organization. The
subordinate's role is much more narrowly defined than John's own. This is
precisely the feature of hierarchical organization. Positions at the top have
broader, more encompassing functions and roles than do those at the lower
levels of the organization; the latter have more specialized functions and
narrowly defined roles. In our case, Mr. Ford's work-related universe is confined to sales; he would rarely venture out of that function.

Just as important as the creation of vertical specialization, however, is
the fact that John, in hiring a salesperson as his first subordinate, has started
building what is called a *line* organization. The line organization is that part
of the organization or the chain of command that works principally on the
functions that contribute directly to the achievement of the organization's
objectives—in short, the primary functions. Line personnel may still perform
secondary functions (for example, our salesperson may sweep the floor, thus
performing some maintenance functions, and John is still the bookkeeper
and personnel manager), but their principal functions and roles would be
related to the buying and selling of hardware. Hence they would be considered as part of the "line."

HORIZONTAL SPECIALIZATION

John's business continues to grow, and he is once again forced to add a salesperson. The addition of a second salesperson makes John's organization more
complex (see Fig. 3.3).

In order to maintain some order in his store and to develop specialized
expertise, John makes one of his two employees the paint and wallpaper
salesperson; the second, the hardware salesperson. In so doing, John Smith

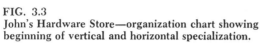

FIG. 3.3
John's Hardware Store—organization chart showing
beginning of vertical and horizontal specialization.

has started his organization along the path of *horizontal specialization.* That
is, his subordinates have differing tasks, even though they are on the same
organizational level (both are immediate subordinates to John Smith). The
horizontal specialization of John's salespeople is on the basis of differing
products; one person is in charge of paint, and the other is in charge of
hardware.

As we move through the growth of John's Hardware Store, we will find
other possible bases for horizontal specialization: *location* (e.g., North Division, South Division, East Division), *function* (e.g., sales, production,
finance), *customer* (e.g., wholesale or retail or main store and bargain basement), *time* (e.g., day shift, night shift), or *process* (e.g., painting, machining,
sanding).* In an organizational hierarchy, every level is divided horizontally,
and typically all subordinates reporting to a single superior are classified
according to a single horizontal-specialization scheme. (Exceptions do take
place, however.)

Let us continue to see what happens as John's single-store organization
grows. Before long, it might look something like that shown in Fig. 3.4.

Now what has John done? Instead of having a two-level organization,
he now has a four-level organization, creating greater *vertical* specialization.
Certain functions that had been held exclusively by John have now been
delegated, and management positions have been created at lower levels.
Note, however, that as one moves down the organization, the scope of the
manager's and employees' functions become narrower and narrower. For
example, whereas Joseph Ford has a universe consisting of the entire hardware department, one of the buyers subordinate to him may be concerned
only with hand tools.

Note also the horizontal specialization in the larger organization. On the
second level, the organization is divided by products; on the third level, by
function. On the fourth level, although this is not specified on the organiza-

* William Newman, *Administrative Action,* 2d ed. (Englewood Cliffs, N.J.: Prentice-
Hall, 1963).

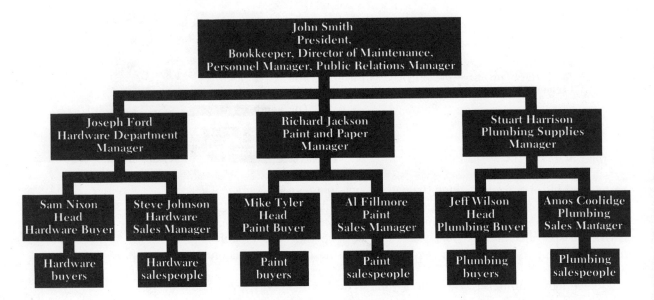

FIG. 3.4
John's Hardware Store—organization chart showing greater vertical and horizontal complexity.

tion chart, we might assume a division based on differing products, at least among the buyers. For example, one of the buyers may deal with hand tools.

MULTIUNIT ORGANIZATION

What might happen to John's organization if he opened a second store and then a third and fourth? He might simply duplicate the organization of the first store. But that type of structure would not be very efficient. After all, why let each store have its own set of buyers for commonly carried items? It would be much less costly to have a central buying unit for all stores. Indeed, this is one principle exercised in chain-store organizations. In effect, then, proper organization design is essential to fully meeting the criteria of economy and efficiency.

John's multiunit operation, now called John's Hardware Stores, might adopt the organization structure depicted in Fig. 3.5. The opening of new stores has led to a reshuffling of the organization. The basis of vertical specialization now differs from that of the old, one-store organization, and the task universe of nearly everyone in the organization has become smaller. Department managers are no longer responsible for buying, and buying has been elevated within the organization. The organization now has five levels instead of the four it had previously.

Note also that the *horizontal specialization* within John's multiunit organization now includes *location* as well as *function* and *product*. The second level is organized by function; the third, by product in the buying unit and by location in the store operations unit. The fourth level is organized by products within the stores and probably by products (or vendors) in the buying unit. Salespeople in the stores (the fifth level) are not organized according to any basis within their particular departments.

John Smith's function is now chiefly one of coordination; he must concern himself with managing the managers (coordination), the continued existence of the total organization as a system, and the growth or expansion of the organization. For example, John may now be considering taking over some of the wholesaling functions or even some of the manufacturing of products the chain now buys. He would not, however, be overly concerned about a given item's specific shelf location in a particular store, although one of the merchandise managers or buyers might be so concerned.

FIG. 3.5
John's Hardware Stores—multiunit organization chart.

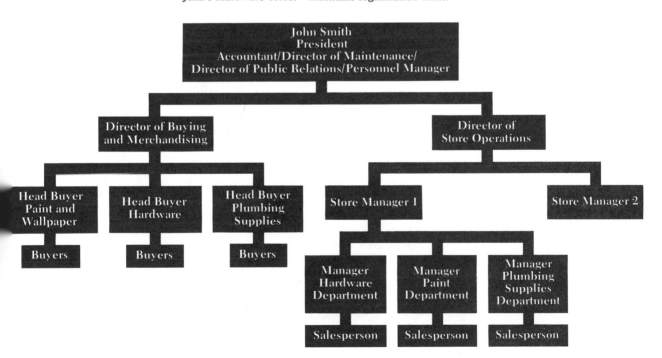

STAFF UNITS

But this pattern of vertical and horizontal specialization has left John with the functions of accounting, maintenance, personnel, and public relations—in short, the secondary functions. Is he still performing them, or does each person in the organization perform part of them in addition to performing his or her primary functions? Although the consideration of these functions in a real-life situation would have occurred long before now, it is now time for us to consider consolidating those secondary functions into specialized positions. We call this specialization and consolidation of secondary functions the creation of *staff positions*.

Staff positions evolve in unique ways within different organizations, but basically they are created to aid, assist, service, and abet the primary functional units. Staff positions result because the primary work of the operating manager grows so large that the primary organizational component allots less and less time to the secondary functions assigned to it. When this phenomenon starts occurring throughout the organization, it becomes useful to create positions to handle all of those segments of noncompleted or non-attended secondary functions. Another reason to create staff units to handle the secondary functions is to ensure that those functions are handled consistently throughout the organization. As an organization grows larger, this latter reason becomes increasingly important.

In the beginning of staff-unit evolution, there usually is not enough work involved in a single specialized secondary function (e.g., public relations) to warrant creation of a single specialized unit to handle that function alone. But the organization may have enough bits and pieces of several secondary functions (e.g., personnel, maintenance, accounting, public relations) to create a *general* secondary unit. So the initial evolution of staff would usually be a general staff person, quite possibly with the title "Assistant to." That "assistant" would be assigned the chores of handling all of the secondary functions, as if that person were acting for the boss he or she is assisting.

As time moves along and the duties grow, some of the assignments given to the general staff person may become large enough in volume to be split off on their own. When this occurs, the organization generates *specialized staff units*—personnel departments, public relations departments, maintenance departments, etc.

Relationship of staff to line units

Staff units have several types of relationships with the primary line units. These relationships are governed by the types of work allocated to staff units and the types of authority the staff units are either granted or bring to bear themselves.

Service units   Service units are formed principally to perform some secondary physical operative function: mail room, tool room, parts manager, files room, testing section, etc. The advantages of having such service units are obvious: They form central repositories for tools and records and contribute to better control over materials, records, costs, etc. Although service units occasionally exercise some control over operative (line) units, the typical service unit has extremely limited authority in relation to the rest of the organization. About the only control the mail room may exert over the rest of the organization is in scheduling mail pickup and delivery times; it may keep track of a particular department's mail budget and warn the department when it is approaching budgetary limits, but the mail room may also have no authority to stop handling the mail from that department should its budget be exceeded.

The limitations described and prescribed are not meant to belittle the importance of such service units. Indeed, any line manager knows better than to cross the head of the mail room, particularly if that unit does the sorting, stapling, folding, and stamping of an important survey the manager of the line unit wants distributed.

Staff units   Staff units in their purest form are planning units; that is, they conduct studies and present recommendations for line management's approval. For example, a staff unit may be asked to analyze a market, prepare a survey, tally the survey, present a recommendation for entering or not entering the market, and then—if the recommendation is to go into the market—prepare a plan for implementing the market penetration. These plans will then be presented to top management (or to the unit of the organization to which the staff unit is attached). Line management may or may not approve the plan, but if it does, the plan is assigned for implementation to the primary, or line, unit involved. The staff unit may then move on to further studies assigned to it (or it may undertake studies on its own initiative, if that mode of staff operation is consistent with company policy), or the unit may be dissolved and its members reassigned to other units.

Staff/service units   By far the most common type of secondary unit is the combination staff and service unit. In addition to planning, this type of unit is assigned a portion of the nitty-gritty implementation of that planning. Much of the authority for final decision making, however, will probably continue to reside with the line unit.

A good example of a staff/service unit is the personnel department in many organizations. Suppose, for instance, that a firm's personnel department is ordered to prepare a plan for a selection procedure for operative personnel in the production department. The personnel unit might develop a procedure such as the following (along with the requisite standards of applicant passage that go with the various steps of the procedure):

1 Initial interview

2 Aptitude tests

3 Reference check

4 Physical examination

5 Credit check

6 Secondary interview

7 Decision

Job applicants would have to progress step by step, being favorably selected in one step before proceeding to the next. Progressively fewer applicants would remain in contention in the later steps.

Of course, each of these steps could be carried out by the production superintendent for whom the new person is being hired. But for the same reason that the line officer was relieved of personnel planning—i.e., little time available and/or a lack of consistency throughout the organization—the line officer too would have little time or inclination to implement this procedure. So the staff unit is usually assigned the task of implementing some steps of the procedure as well.

With this selection procedure, the personnel department might be given the authority to screen out candidates who obviously do not meet job specifications, fail tests, have poor references, fail the physical, or create a poor impression. But the final choice, among the few candidates who make it through the screenings conducted by the personnel group, will be made by the office to which the new applicant will be assigned—in this case, the production department. The choice will be made by the production manager, section manager, or a supervisor, but the personnel department will have performed a service activity by relieving the line department of the secondary functions involved in evaluating applicants.

In some cases, however, the personnel department may even make the final choice, e.g., for a routine or standard job. If the unit involved simply "puts in an order" for a new person, the personnel department will make the final selection and simply send the hired individual to the unit. In essence, the chore of making these choices is taken from the shoulders of other executives whose primary function gives them little time to make the choice well.

Functional units   We noted earlier that a staff unit typically has its plans or projects approved by line or top management before those plans are either assigned to the line for implementation or absorbed in some sort of joint line/staff or line/staff/service arrangement. But suppose that top management says: "Look, we know so little about personnel that we're wasting our time having to approve all of these policies and plans. Why don't you (the personnel department) just devise the policy and the procedure and send them down the organization for implementation? You're acting under our authority in only the area where your expertise applies." Here the personnel department assumes *functional authority;* it has been granted the authority to issue policies and to disseminate decisions throughout the organization in its own name, but only *in its area of expertise.*

Oftentimes functional authority for staff units is not explicitly assigned. Rather, it often evolves through usurpation by the staff unit or as a tacit resignation by the line in the area covered by the staff departments.

Control units Some stafflike units are specifically designated control units and have the authority to make or order specific corrective changes in line operations. Although the original chartering standards and guidelines of operation for these units are typically approved by top management, the fact is that these types of units have a great deal of power to act on their own accord. Examples of control units are quality control, fiscal or cost control, and production control.

So far our discussion of organizational structure has focused on the tasks and functions involved in an organization. We should now briefly cover the area of staff/line conflict. Staff/line relationships are quite easy to write and speak about in the abstract, but in real life these relationships are not always cordial and are sometimes subject to serious conflict. Some of this conflict results simply from an insufficient understanding of the role and function of staff personnel. Line officers often distrust staff officers and sometimes cannot understand what staff officers do or why staff officers make certain decisions. **Line/staff conflict**

More often, however, the conflict results from "human" interaction problems in the organization. Staff officers, for example, are generally younger, better educated, and more analytical than line officers, who typically have come up through the ranks and tend to be pragmatic. Thus age, dress, education, social status, and mode of operation might create barriers to understanding and cooperation between line and staff personnel.

Staff officers are typically *physically* located near the centers of line power. Whether at the corporate central headquarters or in the plant manager's office, the staff personnel exude an aura of importance because they are from "topside." In reality, staff persons may receive lower pay, be ignored at central headquarters, and hold little, if any, of the power they are thought to have. Yet the perceptions of both line and staff personnel prolong the potential for conflict in many situations.

Staff officers are *organizationally* attached to the line officers to whom they report and from whom they receive their authority to act. In most cases

- ■ Insufficient understanding of staff role
- ■ Age differences
- ■ Educational differences
- ■ Differences in dress
- ■ Social-status differences
- ■ Physical location in building
- ■ Organizational location of line and staff units
- ■ Mode of operation and style
- ■ Organizational advance rate
- ■ Differing organizational universes

Sources of line/staff conflict

this puts a staff person high on the organization chart. In reality, however, the staff person often advances in pay and rank more slowly than his or her line counterpart, but the staff person's location on the organization chart leads to a "topside" reputation.

Finally, line and staff people exist in different organizational universes. The staff person often views the entire organization as his or her universe, even though he or she operates within a very limited function. The line person's universe is the limited area over which she or he has control. These differing perceptions can cause problems because of the importance each of the managers attaches to his or her own function. The line person may have little patience with the staff person's needs; similarly, the staff person may have little respect for the fast pace and demands of the line person's position.

Staff in a multiunit operation

Let us now return to our original example of a multiunit organization, John's Hardware Stores. John now heads an organization of 130 stores, each with 60 employees, and the organization has split off staff units throughout the various divisions. In addition, since the organization is now so large, additional units (such as warehousing) have evolved. Organizationally, John's Hardware Stores might look like the chart in Fig. 3.6 (note, however, that the chart depicts only a small portion of the entire organization).

Now the organization has staff units at several levels, each with the same or similar titles. What relationships exist between these similarly named staff units, and what functions does each unit perform? Now that you know the terminology, we can explain these relationships quite simply.

Central-level staff groups establish or devise (for top-management approval) policy for the entire organization when consistency is necessary throughout the organization. The central staff units also perform those ser-

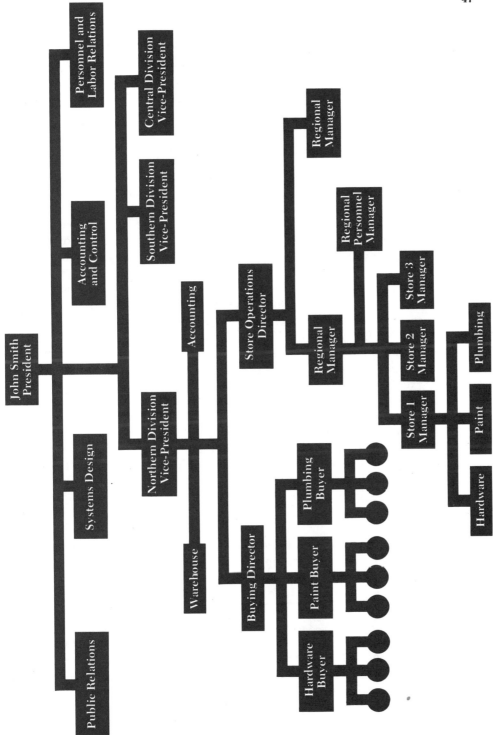

FIG. 3.6
John's Hardware Stores—organization chart showing staff units.

vice functions necessary for the top levels of the organization, such as hiring for other units, initiating search processes for the hiring of key executives, maintaining personnel files, handling payroll records, conducting corporate-wide public relations campaigns, etc.

Lower-level staff units apply the centrally devised policy at the lower levels (usually in a service capacity to the lower-level line units), make or recommend local policy when necessary, and perform services for the local-level line and other staff units, such as maintenance of local files, etc. All local-level staff actions (like their line counterparts) must be consistent with, and subordinate to, those policy and planning parameters made at higher levels of the organization. For example, if the higher-level personnel policy states that each employee in the organization shall receive two weeks of vacation per year, lower-level units cannot devise a policy of granting three weeks.

To whom is the lower-level staff person responsible—the line manager or the higher-level staff person? In theory, the local staff person is responsible to the local line manager, just as the central-level staff operative is responsible to the central-level line executive. All authority flows, supposedly, down through the line, so that in theory again, central-staff directives are coming down from line superiors to line subordinates and then assigned to local staff units.

In fact, however, the flow of information and command from central to local staff units is more direct. Oftentimes this is the result of either conscious organization design or tacit abdication by line management. Indeed, the lines of promotion for staff people often are from local to central staff rather than from local staff to local line and then up. This makes the natural relationship of local staff to central staff much closer than it appears to be on paper.

Recognition of staff units   It is often said that organization charts tell very little, that the guts of an organization are the job descriptions and policy statements usually contained in the accompanying manuals and in actual behavior. Later in this chapter, when we try to locate decision centers within the organization, we shall see that this statement is accurate. Here, however, we are concerned with trying to locate and identify staff units. Staff units may not be identifiable by their titles. Often a unit with a primarylike title of Production Planning or Marketing Planning, with vice-presidents in charge, is in reality a staff unit which is assisting the primary line units in planning, data gathering, or other services. In essence, one cannot always determine the true nature of a particular unit by glancing at its title on the organization chart. Rather, one must examine the actual functions and roles assumed by the unit, and this takes more than cursory examination.

AUTHORITY

Although we briefly touched on authority in relationship to staff and line units, it is now time to study the concept more closely, recognizing that the term "authority" can be used in many different contexts. The concept of authority, of great importance in the functioning of any organization, is often seriously misunderstood.

A subordinate who has been given the authority to utilize resources— say, to sign purchase orders up to the amount of $500—has the power, or the right, to make the commitment of resources, without having to gain a superior's concurrence. But what makes this subordinate accept the limits on his or her spending over $500? Why does the subordinate respect the superior's "authority" to withhold permission to make expenditures of more than $500?

Many commentators regard authority as the "right to command," and subordinates are expected to respond accordingly because their superiors hold that mystical "right." This treatment is very similar to the "divine right of kings" concept, except that the right in a profit-making operation, also often treated as sacrosanct, is derived from the ownership of property (or, in a socialist enterprise, from the legitimacy of the state).

It might be more useful, however, to define authority in terms of the *relationship* between two parties, not just the "rights" of one.* Thus the relationship equation would include the elements of influence and power.

When one party in a relationship accepts the authority of the other party, the former is giving up making a judgment on a particular issue to accept the judgment of someone else. Why might that happen? What are the bases of this acceptance? First, the subordinate might not care; if the issue is routine, he or she has filtered it out of consciousness, or it might be too trivial in his or her scheme of values to be concerned about.

Second, the subordinate may respect the other party's knowledge, expertise, or competence in the area under consideration so much as to be willing to forego personal judgment in favor of the other person's. This is a typical process in organizations, and the authority being respected by the subordinate is often ascribed to "influence" on the part of the superior. Influence is often the key to line people's accepting the recommendations or judgments of staff people. "Why should I question a computer expert? I've never had a computer course in my life."

---

* The background for this treatment of authority comes from several important contributions to management literature: Chester I. Barnard, *The Functions of the Executive* (Cambridge: Harvard University Press, 1938), Chapter 12; Herbert A. Simon, *Administrative Behavior*, 2d ed. (New York: Macmillan, 1957), Chapter 6; James G. March and Herbert A. Simon, *Organizations* (New York: Wiley, 1957) Chapter 4.

Third, and this is the closest concept we may find to the "rights" approach described earlier, the subordinate may recognize the superior's position as legitimate. But in recognizing the basing of authority on perceived legitimacy, we must also acknowledge that this linkage is only a cultural phenomenon, and cultural phenomena are subject to change. Indeed, the challenges to "established authority" taking place on campuses and within government and business organizations might dash anyone's thoughts that the recognition of legitimacy by subordinates is a permanently grounded phenomenon.

Fourth, authority may be accepted because the superior has the resources available to apply sanctions—to grant rewards or to punish. A person who holds such resources over another person is said to have "power." In other words, the superior holds resources that directly affect the subordinate. In order to obtain those resources, e.g., rewards or to avoid punishment, the subordinate must perform according to the superior's expectations and values. This does not necessarily mean that the superior flaunts the power. Rarely is the subordinate reminded daily that "you can be replaced." But the simple fact that there is an unequal distribution of resources (the skills of the subordinate are resources also) requires that we recognize the power relationship.*

If we recognize the concept of authority as a relationship rather than a right, and most modern managers are coming to that view, we need to determine why some subordinates are willing to be "manipulated" more than others are. A useful explanation is that each person in an organization has a unique "zone of acceptance." † Thus each subordinate will be willing to accept the authority of his or her superior if the superior's actions, commands, judgments, and values fall into the subordinate's zone of acceptance. Using our discussion of the past few paragraphs on the bases of authority, we can now construct some conceptual models for determining the relative width of a particular subordinate's zone of acceptance.

A zone of acceptance may be wide (reflecting a subordinate's willingness to accept authority under a vast array of conditions) simply because the subordinate is conditioned to think that the zone should be wide. This may reflect the subordinate's cultural heritage. But, of course, a culturally based concept may also be quite transitory.

A zone of acceptance can be made wider through the use of the reward system within the organization; thus a superior may try to induce a subordinate to accept authority in return for rewards. This is not simply an "any person can be bought" approach; other work-related organizational attributes

---

* For an excellent discussion of power as a relationship, *see* Richard Emerson, "Power-Dependence Relation," *American Sociological Review* **27** (February 1962): 31–41.
† Simon, *op. cit.*; Barnard, *op. cit.*, p. 167 ff.

may motivate people to perform, and indeed modern management stresses the intrinsic value of work. But nonetheless, one should not downgrade the power inherent in a large organization possessing great resources.

Conversely, a zone of acceptance can be narrowed by the subordinate's gathering resources. These resources may be in the form of expertise, independent wealth, or indispensability (learning corporate secrets or being the only person in the organization to have knowledge of a particular process or function). In essence, the subordinate gains power relative to the superior and hence is less likely to be overcontrolled or restricted.* Many scientists, for example, do not hold high positions within organizations, but their expertise gives them substantial autonomy or freedom from authority.

In short, authority, particularly in a voluntary organization, is a more fluid concept than it is popularly characterized to be. Authority flows not only from superior to subordinate, but also in the other direction. The amount and type of authority are not constant, but instead depend on the participants' ages, economic conditions, personal values, personal alternatives, and a whole host of other variables. This means that managers working in an organizational setting must be more aware of the factors affecting the acceptance of authority among subordinates. The manager who utters, "I order you to do this because I have the authority," may be uttering nonsense in most organizational situations.

Aware of the bases and ranges of authority, we can now proceed to classify "types" of authority bases existing in an organization relative to the types of units—line or staff. Line units are often classified as "command" units. Managers who operate in line units would probably be expected to use all of the available bases underlying their authority. But in most productive organizations, one might find line managers relying principally on power trade-offs. Subordinate managers may tend to attempt to equalize the power of their superiors by gaining expertise, alternative offers of employment, or by harboring a particularly small portion of the organization's intelligence.

Authority related to line and staff units

Operatives in line units attempt to equalize power and hence reduce the authority of managers by collective action—union contracts—and by the ability to "sabotage" the productive processes of the organization. It is within the line units that legitimacy-based authority is most emphasized conceptually; in fact, however, the manager is dealing with zones of acceptance and the bases underlying those zones.

Staff units, by contrast, tend to gain authority through the use of expertise or influence or even the indifference of line units. For example, a manufacturing firm's production department may be indifferent as to who provides the light bulbs as long as they are available when needed. So whether the

---

* Emerson, *op. cit.*

bulbs are purchased from the Jones Bulb Company or the Smith Bulb Company is a decision of no concern to the production department (although of significant concern to the purchasing department). On the other hand, a job description devised by the personnel department for an expert machine operator may be of prime importance to the production department, and the personnel department will have to use its influence and expertise to gain the acceptance of the production executives. The personnel department, however, will have little "power" to force the production department to accept its work.

In summary, we find that authority bases are related to organizational unit type (line or staff) in many ways. The manager soon learns to know the limits of his or her authority, whether in terms of power, expertise, or influence. Yet it is useful for the manager to be aware that authority as a "right" is not universally accepted and that he or she must be constantly aware of the need to employ differing bases in order to achieve organizational objectives.

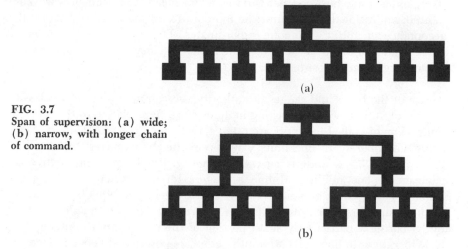

(a)

FIG. 3.7
Span of supervision: (a) wide;
(b) narrow, with longer chain
of command.

(b)

**Span of control and
levels of command**

Another issue must be covered before we conclude this section on organization—the concern with the number of units (or subordinates) that a superior can effectively supervise. Many studies have been conducted and rules of thumb put forth concerning the number of subordinates that a manager can effectively supervise, but there is really no exact science to determine the appropriate number.* The "correct" span of supervision depends on a

* See V. A. Graicunas, "Relationships in Organizations," in Luther Gulick and L. Urwick (eds.), *Papers on the Science of Administration* (New York: Institute of Public Administration, 1937), pp. 183–187. This classic article developed a formula to determine the geometric growth in relationships relative to the arithmetic growth in subordinates.

number of variables: the repetitiveness of the work, the necessity for inter-relationships among subordinates, the degree of subordinate autonomy possible (or, conversely, the intensiveness of supervision necessary), the amount of discretion allotted to subordinates, the physical proximity of subordinates, and the quality of personnel in subordinate positions.

The converse of a wide span of control is a longer chain of supervisory levels. This means that solving one problem often creates another, for a long chain of levels means possible malfunctions in information flow and possible alienation of managers who are placed at increasingly longer administrative distances from higher levels (see Fig. 3.7).

At the very least, additional levels add to the complexity of information channels and the need for more precise communication. For the longer the communication chain, the more likely that the message will become distorted. On the other hand, a wider span offers the possibilities for inadequate supervision and ineffective and inefficient performance.

DECISION CENTERS

Organizations are sometimes referred to as collections of decision-making centers. The location of these decision centers will determine whether an organization is administratively decentralized or centralized. But just like the difficulty of trying to identify staff units from an organization chart, so too one would have difficulty in trying to pinpoint where decisions are made by consulting the chart. The title "manager" may be meaningless if the "manager" has little authority to make decisions or operates in a mode that has been mapped out by higher levels within the organization.

To the layperson, physical dispersion of facilities might mean that decision making is also decentralized, or occurs at a number of lower levels. But that is often not the case. All the buying and merchandising decisions for John's Hardware Stores may be made centrally; the store and department managers may have only very narrow limits of discretion in implementing the decisions made at the central office. Indeed, in one chain of leased departments in discount department stores, the department manager is little more than a stock clerk. All of the merchandise is prepriced at the central warehouse, ordered by centrally located buyers, and the chain makes its account settlement with the principal owners of the stores at central levels. In many of the large, national fast-food restaurant chains, local employees have very little discretion; all of the systems and procedures are carefully mapped out and programmed at the central level; the local manager has relatively little discretion and few areas for substantive decision making.

Several factors affect whether decisions are to be made at higher or lower levels of the organization. One such factor is the degree of consistency

- How far apart are the organizational units located?
- How necessary is consistency in behavior?
- What is the competence of employees at local levels?
- How important is it to have knowledge of local conditions?
- What is the effect of technology in communications and decision making?

Factors in decision-center placement

necessary in the local units or throughout the organization. McDonald's, for example, very centralized, prides itself on total consistency; a unit in California is almost a twin to one in Massachusetts.

Other factors conditioning the location of decision making are competence of local employees, the importance of local conditions, and technology. Sometimes a manager may be granted some degree of decision-making autonomy, whereas a counterpart on the same level in another unit may not be given similar organizational autonomy. For example, one manager in a discount department store reported many calls for a locally produced product not available on a national basis. This manager was given very restricted "authority" to order a limited amount of the product from local sources and to reorder as necessary. The reverse has occurred too. A major automobile company had trouble with one of its divisions; the profitability of the division was destroyed, and its management did not seem capable of pulling it out of the tailspin. Whereas the other divisions of the company were left to operate in the old, decentralized manner, the troubled division's decisions were centralized into top management's jurisdiction.

Technology is a primary contributing factor in the current trend toward centralization. In the 1930s and 1940s decentralization was the cornerstone of organization design, as the so-called General Motors model, developed by Alfred Sloan, was duplicated by many large firms and organizations. The principal distinguishing feature of the General Motors model was the delegation of decision making to lower levels and then holding the executives in charge responsible for their decisions on a profit basis. Thus division managers at GM were under no compulsion to use General Motors parts in their cars if they could find better and cheaper substitutes outside the organization. Managers of key units were encouraged to push decision making down even further.

But the advent of the electronic computer and new information-transmission devices has made possible the centralization of even minute decisions. For example, one large chemical company used to have its sales representatives allocate orders to the various plants producing the firm's products; that is, upon receiving an order for sulfuric acid, a salesperson had the authority to send the order to a plant making sulfuric acid. Generally, salespeople were instructed to use the plant nearest to the customer. Although this resulted in fairly routine decision making for the salespeople and gave them the prestige of having a certain amount of decision-making authority, the practice also resulted in imbalances among the firm's plants; some had extensive backlogs, whereas others had excess capacity.

With the installation of a computer and a leased telephone line, however, the firm was able to have accurate daily data on production capacities channeled to the home office. Now the sales representatives no longer make decisions on order allocation; all orders are transmitted to the home office, and the computer aids in the decisions on allocations.

Many retail chains are now able to link the cash registers of the various physically dispersed outlets into a central office computer, giving the central office buyer almost daily reports on sales by item. Accounting for stock shrinkage (pilferage, damaged goods, etc.) with standard formulas and using the daily inventory reports, the buyer can relieve the manager of some of the latter's decision making. The store manager does not have to physically count the inventory or make any judgments as to what products are moving swiftly or slowly. Except when the system breaks down or the formulas don't hold up (unfortunately, these are the situations we most often hear about), the central office buyer is able to keep the inventory under control very swiftly and quite accurately. The system allows the buyer to either rush-order goods or shift inventory from another location, steps the manager might not be aware of or incapable of taking.

In short, the pattern of decision making that exists within an organization is dependent on many factors and may change if changes occur in conditions of the environment, skill levels, and/or effectiveness.

NONBUSINESS ORGANIZATIONS

Although we have used examples from business firms for most of this chapter, most of the organization-design problems and principles apply equally well to all other types of organizations. All organizations have primary and secondary functions; all have staff and service units; all should be concerned with spans of supervision and levels of command; and all make decisions on the placement of decision-making centers within the organization.

For example, a university has a primary function—education. The line in your university runs from the president through the academic vice-president, the deans, the department heads, and on to the faculty. Units such as the library, dormitory administration, dining commons, admissions office, building and grounds, student affairs, personnel, and the like exist to facilitate the performance of the primary function, education, and hence are staff or service units. Faculty decisions on hiring, promotion, and tenure may be made at the department level (decentralized) or at the president's level. Class size, course and curriculum changes, scheduling, enrollment standards, the balance of research and teaching—all are decisions that could either be decentralized to the faculty or made at central levels.

Similarly, a hospital has a primary function—the care and cure of patients. Hence those units directly providing medical service are the line; units such as housekeeping, pathology, pharmacy, fund raising, accounting, and building and grounds are secondary functions existing in order to service the primary function. Decisions on operative care, therapy, drug administration, types of service to be offered or not offered (abortions and vasectomies are two current controversial examples) could be either left to the medical staff or centralized to the governing medical board. Again, factors such as the maintenance of consistency throughout the organization would determine the degree of decentralization.

Nonprofit organizations do have one unique problem, however. Unlike business firms, nonprofit organizations typically are based on the professionalism of one key group, e.g., educators or doctors. Professionals generally judge issues on the basis of considered professional standards, and these standards may conflict with norms of efficiency and effectiveness. Indeed, one of the conflicts now current in hospital administration is the trade-off between the medical staff's wishes for complete facilities, with all the associated esoteric equipment, and those of the hospital's administrative board, which must operate the hospital under the constraints of limited resources. Choices at the highest levels of the institution may then be painful, since opposition to life-saving equipment and techniques is never very popular.

SUMMARY AND CONCLUSION

In this chapter we discussed the formal organization, the structure in which managers operate. We used as our partial tool for exploring organizations the growth of one hypothetical organization, illustrating the evolution of complexity and change.

Organizations are initially built around functions, not people. We then differentiated between primary and secondary functions and the types of units that relate to those functions. We covered vertical (or administrative) specialization and the line organization, horizontal (or work) specialization, and multiunit organizations. We described the function of staff units and how they relate to line units and discussed line/staff conflict, staff in a multiunit operation, and the recognition of staff units.

In exploring the concept of authority and its various bases, we concluded that authority functions on the basis of acceptance, not right. Authority relates to line and staff units in a variety of ways, affected by a number of variables.

Finally, we covered the concepts of span of control, levels of command, and the locus of decision making (administrative centralization or decentralization). We concluded by relating the entire subject of organizational processes to nonbusiness organizations.

Knowledge of organization design is important to aspiring managers, since that is the world in which they will function and operate. Growth of an enterprise, as we have seen, means change in the design of the organization. Some technical expertise in organization principles is necessary to accomplish such growth and organizational change both effectively and efficiently.

As we mentioned earlier, most managers work in large organizations and may think that they are nothing more than little cogs in rather large wheels. The question always arises as to whether such managers are losing their individuality and sacrificing their values by being part of large organizations. Probably every manager has engaged in introspection on the question of maintaining individuality in the face of bigness. This question of personal gains and losses for managers in large organizations is the topic of Chapter 4.

DISCUSSION QUESTIONS

1 Large organizations are usually characterized by high degrees of specialization; smaller organizations, by less specialization. What do we mean by this? Why is this so?

2 What do we mean by an organization's primary and secondary functions? Give an example of a primary function in a manufacturing firm, hospital, law firm, CPA firm, university, personnel office, professional football team. Give an example of a secondary function in each of these organizations.

3 Distinguish between vertical and horizontal specialization in the formal organization of a company.

4 What are some of the bases for horizontal specialization in the formal organization?

5 What is meant by the classic "line/staff" conflict found in large organizations?

6 In describing a staff unit's relationship with the primary line unit, we describe staff units as: service units, staff units, staff/service units, and

functional units. On what basis are these distinctions made, and what is meant by each of these different categories of staff units? Give a specific example of each type of secondary function listed above.

7 Define the following terms:

a) entrepreneurship   b) multinational corporation

c) international corporation   d) conglomerate

e) formal organization   f) line function (primary)

g) secondary function (staff)   h) vertical specialization

i) horizontal specialization   j) delegation

k) service unit   l) staff unit

m) functional unit   n) authority

o) zone of acceptance   p) "command" unit

q) span of control   r) decision center

s) centralized organization   t) decentralized organization

CASE: CARLTON INDUSTRIES

■ "Only five years ago, we were a quiet, moderately successful little electronics switch company," mused President and Chairman of the Board Cecil Whiting. "Now we're an uncontrollable little conglomerate, and we've got to get all of these divisions and departments straightened out and into some order."

Carlton Industries' recent (five-year) history has been nothing short of amazing. It was acquisition after acquisition. The first was a plastics company, acquired because it was a supplier of plastic parts to Carlton, and Cecil Whiting and the owner of the plastics company were old college friends. That merger seemed a natural. But then came the minicomputer company, the small hardware manufacturer, the business-forms paper company, the toy company, the chain of retail electronics stores, the telephone-equipment company, the stereo-equipment company, and then (incredibly, thought some observers) a specialty-clothing (cold-weather gear) maker and a book publisher.

Even though all of the acquisitions were one-plant operations located primarily in the Northeast, Carlton Industries was having difficulty controlling and operating such a diversified group of businesses. Even though the corporate accountant concluded that all of the divisions were profitable, he also said that profits could be larger if the company just got its house in order.

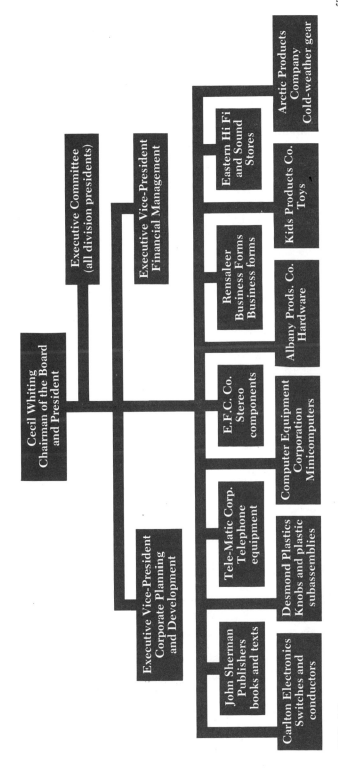

FIG. 3.8
Carlton Industries—organization chart.

The mode of organization during the acquisition wave was simple; just attach the new organization to the present company, leaving the old management in charge, but control from the top level via financial controls, capital budgets, and long-range plans. A minimum of staff services was offered by central headquarters, on the assumption that the businesses were so different that companywide controls over most of the business functions were impossible.

Organization of Carlton Industries

The organization of Carlton Industries is shown in Fig. 3.8. Operationally, the entire company was decentralized, at least down to the chief executive officer (CEO) of each of the divisions. What follows is a brief description of each of the divisions, along with its organization structure.

Carlton Electronics The original corporate base, this division produces switches, conductors, printed circuits, and miniature and microcomponents for computer manufacturers, television and consumer-products companies, and other electronic companies, including military-hardware producers. Its primary group is research and development, which works to develop new switches and equipment as the orders are brought from the field by the sales staff. The small sales group works closely with customers and relays information back to R&D for special problems. R&D develops prototypes which are then put into production. All administrative services are consolidated under one director, but the division is technically oriented, and most of its organizational resources are devoted to technical and production departments. The division employs 270 people. See Fig. 3.9.

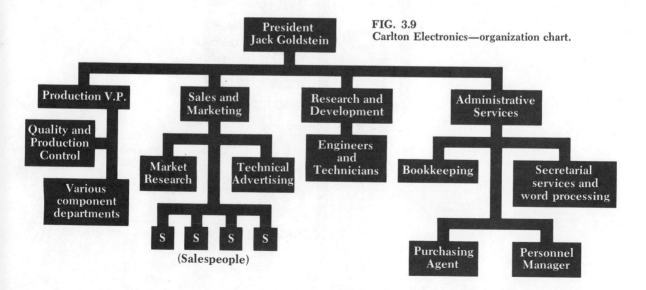

FIG. 3.9
Carlton Electronics—organization chart.

Desmond Plastics This is a smaller division, employing thirty-four people. Six salespeople visit industrial accounts, and the company is able to fabricate knobs, specialized cabinets, and plastic parts to order for the customers it serves. The company is organized by function and coordinated by Tom Desmond, the president, who also does most of the planning for the firm. See Fig. 3.10.

FIG. 3.10
Desmond Plastics—organization chart.

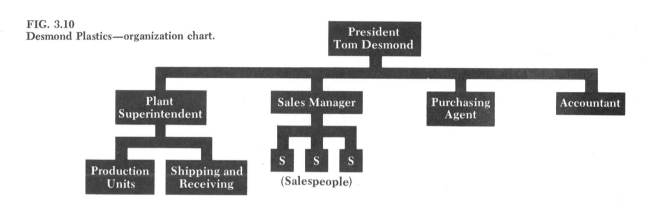

Computer Equipment Corporation As another of Carlton's divisions, CEC employs 182 people and manufactures a line of minicomputers marketed in both kit and completed form. All CEC sales are made by mail order, and advertising is done in electronics and hobby magazines. The minicomputer market is an expanding, increasingly competitive one, with nationwide chains of hobby shops moving into the "home computer" business. As a result, CEC is concerned with product refinement and testing of all products. In addition, the technical-development group is charged with developing easily read and understood manuals. See Fig. 3.11.

FIG. 3.11
Computer Equipment Corporation—
organization chart.

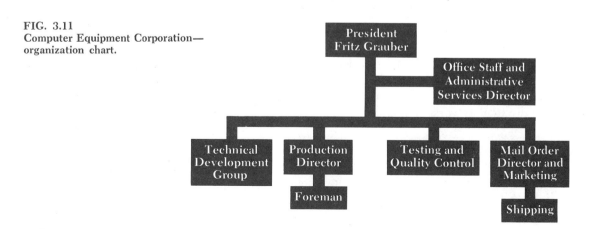

EFC Corporation Named after its president, Edward F. Colski, EFC markets a line of stereo receivers and speaker systems. This business is highly competitive, with most manufacturers switching to purchasing and marketing Japanese-made components. But Colski remains convinced that EFC can compete by offering quality products and cutting costs to the bone. He sold out to Carlton Industries in order to tap its capital and gain an entrée to its chain of stereo stores, and to profit by some of the electronic technical expertise available in the organization. But he still wanted to maintain some independence in product development and marketing. So far, he has received little technical help, but was able to convince top management to finance development of a new turntable line. EFC employs 197 people. Its sales are handled through manufacturers' representatives, who sell EFC components as well as other lines. At one time, EFC employed more than 250 people, but cut back when the division eliminated its lower-priced lines when cheaper components started pouring in from overseas. See Fig. 3.12.

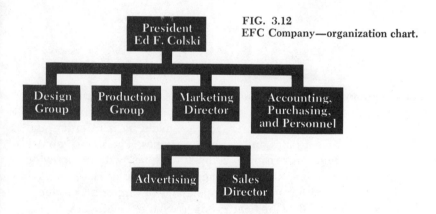

FIG. 3.12
EFC Company—organization chart.

Albany Products A small division employing thirty-four people, Albany manufactures hardware items, principally hinges, door lock sets, hasps, metal knobs, and latches. Originally a specialty machine and die shop, Albany became a production firm when the shoe industry, for which it was making dies, started disappearing from the Northeast. Albany has no sales force but sells through several jobbers, with whom it has good relations, and one large discount chain, for which it manufactures under a private label. Most of the employees are production workers operating semiautomatic machinery. See Fig. 3.13.

Rensaleer Business Forms Employing 178 people, RBF manufactures and imprints sales forms, letterheads, carbonless multicopy sets, and other types

FIG. 3.13
Albany Products—organization chart.

of business paper goods. Starting as a small print shop in 1952, RBF was able to standardize its product line and to offer imprinting services for shelf items as well as specialty items such as purchase orders for public agencies. Most of the employment is in production, with eight salespeople on the road visiting industrial accounts. Most of the purchasing is for paper and ink and is the full-time job of one manager. See Fig. 3.14.

FIG. 3.14
Rensaleer Business Forms—organization chart.

Kids Products Corporation One of the largest of Carlton Industries subsidiaries, Kids Products employs 490 production people and is the only division to have anywhere near national distribution of its products. It manufactures toys, games, some low-priced sports equipment, and some school products. The company is organized functionally within the plant, and the sales division is organized along a geographical basis. The key unit to the company's success is its market research and product development unit. Toys are often related to popular TV characters or movies (although the company does have a number of old standbys), and a mistake on one product can break a good year on a great many of the others. Cancellation of a TV show or the downfall of a current hero can have a devastating effect on the whole year's effort. Consequently, it is up to the market research and product development group to be keenly aware of the directions markets are taking. Yet MR and PD is a small, closely knit unit. The majority of KPC's employees are in production, although the sales force and marketing people number about eighty. See Fig. 3.15.

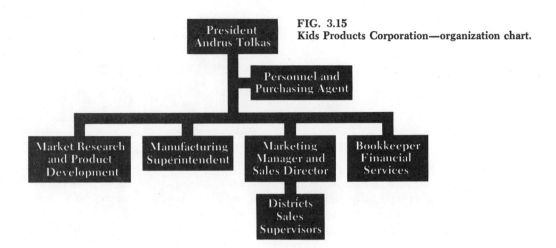

FIG. 3.15
Kids Products Corporation—organization chart.

Eastern Hi-Fi and Stereo Stores Started by four college students in Cambridge and Amherst, Massachusetts, Eastern Hi-Fi stores now number twenty-six and are located in most of the major cities and college towns in the New England states and New York, New Jersey, and Pennsylvania. Selling a number of lines of stereo equipment, hobby supplies, and records, Eastern operates out of a central warehouse in Acton, Massachusetts. The division is organized as a typical retail chain, with the buyers in charge of purchasing and promotion development and the stores under the direction of a stores operation unit. Eastern is a very seasonal business, with perhaps 50 percent of its volume taking place during the last quarter of the year. See Fig. 3.16.

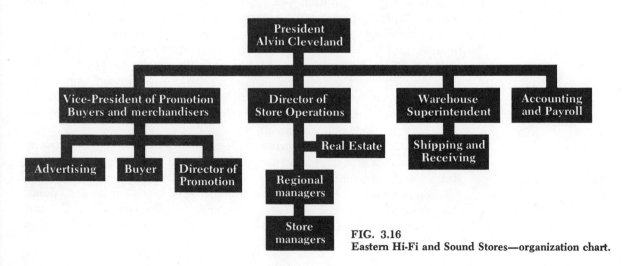

FIG. 3.16
Eastern Hi-Fi and Sound Stores—organization chart.

Arctic Products Inc. "Why we bought this one, I'll never know," thought Whiting. A small clothing factory in New Hampshire, Arctic manufactures down-filled ski jackets and down-filled vests, selling to about three or four major outlets in New England and the Northwest. Most of the forty-six employees work on production; the company has two commission salespeople (who handle other lines as well), and the president maintains personal contact with the largest account. There is plenty of work around the production employees. The division's biggest problem is obtaining a consistent and good supply of down feathers; this takes most of the president's time. See Fig. 3.17.

FIG. 3.17
Arctic Products Inc.—
organization chart.

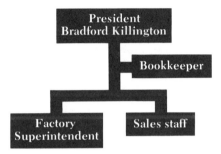

Tele-Matic Corporation This company is into a new, growing business—private PBX telephone systems. With various court decisions and Federal Communications Commission rulings challenging the Bell System's requirements that only Bell-provided equipment be hooked to Bell System lines, a number of specialized companies are springing up offering equipment equal to or exceeding the quality of Bell products. These companies allow customers to purchase equipment rather than rent from Bell.

Basically, the equipment is a main switch allowing the customer a large number of services that conventional telephone equipment generally does not offer. Often the switch is a programmable computer, so that services to individual lines can be added or subtracted easily and daily reports can be printed out for control purposes. The systems are sold by independent dealers who couple the main switch with hand sets and installation equipment made by other manufacturers.

Tele-Matic makes a computer-controlled switch at the rate of two to three units per month. The company provides the technical help to its dealers and always has its people on site for any new installation. Since new developments are constantly coming on the scene, the research and development component of the firm is important. Since the product is so technical and specialized, the production work is custom and carried out by very skilled workers. See Fig. 3.18.

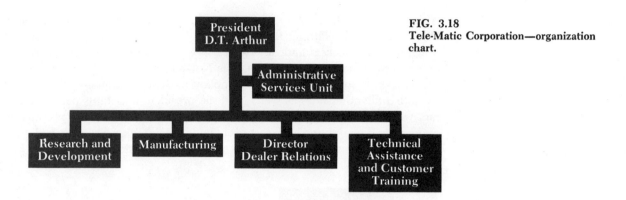

FIG. 3.18
Tele-Matic Corporation—organization chart.

John Sherman Publishers A small publishing house, John Sherman was purchased by Carlton from a larger publisher which established JS as a semi-independent venture. Sherman publishes a few trade books, but centers primarily on professional books which can be marketed to schools and professionals alike (particularly in business and management). Like most publishers, JS does no printing or setup, but does do copy editing, art work, and production scheduling in-house. The editors function as product managers, selecting books to be published and turning them over to production when they are ready for copy editing. Upon publication of the books, the sales force takes over, seeking guidance from the various editors. Among the 175 John Sherman employees are officers, editors, copy personnel, proof readers, and secretaries. See Fig. 3.19.

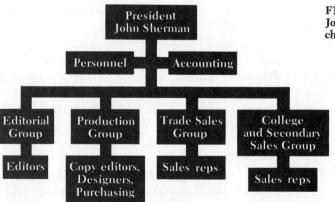

FIG. 3.19
John Sherman Publishers—organization chart.

A need for reorganization

Each of the acquired companies retained essentially its premerger organization and its own functions, shown in Figs. 3.9–3.19. Whiting knew that he had a hodgepodge on his hands. Each of the divisions was operating completely independently, with no standardization within the company. Several functions were duplicated, decisions were inconsistent throughout the divisions, quality of personnel varied, and possible economies from combined activities were being missed. "This is getting too big to leave this way," he thought. "Perhaps some divisions should go, some combined, and some reorganized. We've got to get a better handle on this miniglom." ■

Case questions

1. Why is Carlton Industries' present organization not conducive to efficient operation? Discuss.
2. On what basis of horizontal specialization might the second level of the line organization be divided?
3. Draw the organization chart for a reorganized Carlton Industries. Justify your new structures.

SELECTED READINGS

Allen, L. A., "Identifying Line and Staff," in J. A. Litterer, *Organizations: Structure and Behavior* (New York: Wiley, 1963), pp. 94–104.

Anthony, Robert N., and R. Herzlinger, *Management Control in Nonprofit Organizations* (Homewood, Ill.: Richard D. Irwin, 1975).

Applebaum, Steven H., "The Middle Manager: An Examination of Aspirations and Pessimism," *Business and Society* 18, 1 (Fall 1977): 5–12.

Badowy, M. K., "How Women Managers View Their Role in the Organization," *Personnel Administrator* 23, 2 (February 1978): 60–68.

Carroll, Stephen J., and Henry L. Tosi, *Organizational Behavior* (Chicago: St. Clair Press, 1977).

Cullet, Ray C., and Herbert G. Hicks, "Power and the Functioning of Organizations," *Baylor Business Studies,* Issue No. 115 (February/April 1978): 35–45.

Cyert, R. M., *The Management of Nonprofit Organizations* (Lexington Mass.: D. C. Heath, 1975).

D'Aprix, Roger M., *The Believable Corporation* (New York: AMACOM, 1978).

Dale, E., *Planning and Developing the Company Organization Structure* (New York: American Management Association, 1952).

——, *The Great Organizers* (New York: McGraw-Hill, 1960).

Davis, R. C., *Fundamentals of Top Management* (New York: Harper & Row, 1951).

Filley, A. C., and R. J. House, *Managerial Process and Organizational Behavior* (Glenview, Ill.: Scott, Foresman, 1969).

Frank, H. E., *Organization Structuring* (New York: McGraw-Hill, 1971).

Gantt, H. L., *Organizing for Work* (New York: Harcourt Brace Jovanovich, 1919).

Graicunas, V. A., "Relationship in Organizations," in L. Gulick and L. Urwick (eds.), *Papers on the Science of Administration* (New York: Institute of Public Administration, Columbia University, 1937).

Gruber, W. H., and J. S. Niles, *The New Management: Line Executives and Staff Professional in the Future Firm* (New York: McGraw-Hill, 1976).

Katz, Daniel, and Robert L. Kahn, *The Social Psychology of Organizations* (New York: Wiley, 1978).

Litterer, J. A., *Organizations: Structure and Behavior* (New York: Wiley, 1963).

——, *The Analysis of Organizations* (New York: Wiley, 1973).

Lorsch, J. W., and P. R. Lawrence (eds.), *Studies in Organization Design* (Homewood, Ill.: Richard D. Irwin, 1970).

Lutz, C. F., and A. P. Ingraham, "Design and Management of Positions," *Personnel Journal* **51** (April 1972): 234–240.

March, J. G., and H. A. Simon, *Organizations* (New York: Wiley, 1958).

Mooney, J. D., *The Principles of Organization* (New York: Harper and Brothers, 1947).

Rice, George H., Jr., "Structural Limits on Organizations," *Human Resources Management* **16**, 4 (Winter 1977): 9–13.

Scott, W. G., "Organizational Theory: An Overview and an Appraisal," *Journal of the Academy of Management* **4** (April 1961): 7–26.

Sutherland, John W., *Administrative Decision Making: Extending the Bounds of Rationality* (New York: Van Nostrand Reinhold, 1977).

Taylor, R. W., *The Principles of Scientific Management* (New York: Harper & Row, 1911).

Urwick, L. F., *Notes on the Theory of Organization* (New York: American Management Association, 1953).

————, "The Manager's Span of Control," *Harvard Business Review* **35** (May/June 1956): 39–47.

Vesey, Joseph T., "Vertical Integration: Its Effect on Business Performance," *Managerial Planning* **26**, 6 (May/June 1978): 11–15.

Weber, M. "Bureaucracy," in J. A. Litterer, *Organizations: Structure and Behavior* (New York: Wiley, 1963), pp. 94–104.

Whelton, David A., "Coping with Incompatible Expectations: An Integrated View of Role Conflict," *Administrative Science Quarterly* **23**, 2 (June 1978): 254–271.

Chapter 4
ORGANIZATIONS AND INDIVIDUAL VALUES

CHAPTER HIGHLIGHTS

In this chapter we seek to explore a very important problem of organization design—the role of the individual, particularly the manager, relative to the demands of the organization. You will be exposed to some data and discussion of job satisfaction and personal values, some questions about the data, and then some strategies—organization development and others—for building concurrent job satisfaction and organizational goal achievement.

LEARNING OBJECTIVES

1 To appreciate the changes in managerial values and outlooks that have occurred in recent years.

2 To learn some of the organizational mechanisms for responding to managerial values, needs, and outlooks.

3 To see the benefits of decentralization in building committed managers.

4 To learn the rudiments of Management by Objectives.

5 To understand the uses and limitations of sensitivity training.

6 To learn the uses of team-building techniques in management.

CASE: SUE HARRISON

■ Sue Harrison began her career at the Spofford-Hendricks Advertising Agency immediately after graduating from Midwestern American University, where she majored in English. Sue started as a copy writer in the agency's creative shop and worked on automobile, travel, and detergent advertising. Two years later, she was transferred into account training and eventually worked her way up to become account executive for Super-Smile, a leading toothpaste, manufactured and marketed by Mason-Holden Chemical Corporation.

While in college, Sue had been deeply involved in many of the various political protest movements sweeping the nation's campuses, particularly during the Vietnam War. She had been a leader of the disruption of Dow Chemical's recruiting program at Midwestern American, protested against the university's holding of Gulf Oil stock in its endowment portfolio, and joined with a group of about forty students and professors to protest the award of a contract for a new computer to Honeywell. Generally, Sue had had an antibusiness attitude, and more than a few people were surprised when she accepted the Spofford-Hendricks position offer.

During her two years as a copy writer, Sue was pleasantly surprised; she thought that she was really accomplishing something. Her ideas were accepted, her creativity praised, and she was genuinely and warmly welcomed as a member of the creative team. She also was learning more about business, started valuing the need for advertising, and began to appreciate the role of business. Spofford-Hendricks sent her to school at night to earn an MBA. Gradually, her lifestyle became more conservative.

As an account executive, Sue faced some new challenges, and she was on her own to solve them. Within the agency for the Super-Smile account, her job involved coordinating and planning among media-selection specialists, copy writers, and market researchers. She also had to sell the plans and coordinate the agency efforts with Mason-Holden, the product's manufacturer.

Although she knew that the products she was working on cost very little to manufacture and that its ingredients were not overly complex or differentiated from competing products on the market, Sue nonetheless reveled in the challenge of keeping Super-Smile on the top of the industry's sales charts. In essence, Sue found that she liked the challenge of managing, enjoyed being in charge of "her own shop," and believed that she was growing intellectually. ■

CASE: MONTE KLINGER

■ Monte Klinger went through the University of Wilmington as an almost straight-A student. The classes at Wilmington were practically no challenge to him, and he mechanically ground out his good grades. He spent a good deal of his time at the movies, playing touch football, and reading novels. Monte was not involved in any political protest; as a matter of fact, he was highly critical of his fellow students who did take part. And while others were busily studying for their marketing and management final examinations, Monte played tennis. Even so, he still received the highest grades in the class.

Monte was a recruiter's dream come true. Tall, good looking, athletic, involved in extracurricular activities, and a good student, he fit to a tee most of the prerequisites for hiring. He received excellent recommendations from his professors, who recognized his achievements in their classes. It was no surprise that he received six job offers when his classmates were struggling to land a single one.

Monte accepted a position with Mason-Holden Chemical Corporation as a marketing trainee. Mason-Holden was a large conglomerate firm with many product lines, some of which competed with one another. Marketing trainees were expected eventually to move into product-management positions, taking charge of a particular product and shepherding it through manufacturing, sales, promotion, etc. After moving about from several detergents to salad oil to soap to peanut butter and then to bleach, Monte was assigned to be assistant product manager for Super-Smile toothpaste, a leading brand in the nation.

All during his two-year training period, Monte was doing what he considered useless make-work jobs—checking salespeople's reports, meeting with grocery and department store buyers and executives, accounting for various "cents-off" promotion campaigns, and the like. He never got into the design phases of either product development or a marketing plan. He considered the work about as challenging as his college work had been, but at Mason-Holden he was totally constrained by rules, policies, procedures, and standard methods. Monte gradually learned that Mason-Holden was very centralized in terms of decision making. One day, he even fantasized that the organization was governed by an invisible wizard; he never saw the policy makers and imagined that none really existed. The rules just came down from some invisible source, and everyone in the organization dutifully followed them.

However, when he was offered the position as assistant product manager with the Super-Smile division, Monte thought that maybe at long last he would be able to make some decisions. He arrived at the Springfield office at 8:00 A.M. on his first day to meet the product manager, his new boss. He was pleasantly, but formally, greeted and shown around the plant, facilities of which were shared with three other Mason-Holden brands.

Monte's first shock came when he learned that the product cost only a few cents to manufacture (and sold for nine times that) and was practically identical to any competitor's brand. The big difference, he was told, is that "our marketing program is so much more effective. We're doing a great job keeping the buyers thinking Super-Smile is better, and we're going to continue doing it."

Monte was assigned to coordinate the company's relations with its advertising agency, Spofford-Hendricks. The agency planned the programs, arranged the marketing appeals, planned and produced the commercials, and arranged for the placement of advertising. Mason-Holden determined the advertising budget and accepted and approved the plans of the agency before they were implemented. The company did have certain guidelines for its advertising. Earlier research had indicated that the primary buyers of toothpaste, and indeed most soap products, are housewives and that the best way to reach them is with standard "Gee, I didn't know that" commercial styles. Anything smacking of an intellectual, creative approach was considered ineffective. In addition, no advertising programs could be approved except by the product manager, and even he had to receive budget approval from the corporate headquarters.

Monte traveled to Chicago for his first meeting with the account staff at Spofford-Hendricks. He met the new young account executive, Sue Harrison, and listened to the presentation of the agency's plan for the advertising campaign for the first six months of next year. He was impressed. The campaign was creative and imaginative. And the agency had new research data to show that a creative approach, appealing to the intellect, had an excellent chance of being successful. Monte offered some suggestions, which surprisingly (and to his satisfaction) the agency people liked and incorporated. But both parties knew that final acceptance had to come later from Monte's boss.

Monte returned to Springfield and reported to his boss. He was excited because he had participated in the design of what seemed to be a promising new type of advertising campaign. When he related the details to his boss, he saw a frown spread across his boss's face. Finally, the product manager said, "Monte, your job, first of all, is simply to report back to me, not as an advocate, but as a liaison person. Second, you know the company's policy regarding the type of campaign we will buy; this new approach is out. I'm sorry, but you'll have to tell those Spofford-Hendricks hot shots to get back down to earth."

That night, Monte complained to his wife about the experience. "I don't know who is running that company, but I'm nothing but a darn messenger boy. Wow, were all those profs back at Wilmington, who sold me on business and that creativity garbage, out of it. They should see what their prize student is doing now."

Two weeks later, Monte saw his boss and announced that he was quitting. "What do you have, another job with more money?" his boss asked.

"No," Monte replied, "I'm going back to school to learn woodworking." ■

INTRODUCTION

These two vignettes about young middle managers introduce a subject area that has been the grist for both nonfiction and fiction writers. Undoubtedly, you are familiar with such terms as "organization man" and "the man in the gray flannel suit," both derived from books of those titles. Other creative outlets have also liberally covered the area—notably, motion pictures and television. But the key theme of many of these books, screenplays, novels, and dramas is that the organization, particularly the business firm, is a people crusher, that somehow the organization demands and obtains obedience to its objectives and values and that the individual who is inherently creative, ambitious, and human bucks into the demands of the organization and is psychologically destroyed. In the context of a novel of these types, Monte would continue to fantasize, but would never know who the invisible wizard was; he would know only that the wizard was keeping him frustrated and crushing him mentally.

The tragedy of a great deal of the fictional writing and some of the non-fiction as well is that it sets a generally inaccurate stereotype of managers, businesspeople, and organizations. Obviously, organizations, by necessity, demand some sacrifice from their members. But not all managers are ulcer-ridden, hypertensive, frustrated automatons who have little creativity left, little leeway for individuality, and are inwardly suffering. Many a manager is healthy, well motivated, and satisfied with his or her creative role.

Some emerging data, on the other hand, do show increasing dissatisfaction with managerial work, particularly among young managers—middle managers—and with the roles they are playing in organizations. In this chapter we will briefly explore this new evidence, the pressures that managers do in fact feel in terms of conformity and organizational loyalty, and particularly the problems of middle managers. But we also include some organizational and managerial mechanisms for enhancing individual creativity and growth—mechanisms being employed by many business firms and other organizations.

SOME RECENT FINDINGS ON MANAGERS' OUTLOOKS TOWARD WORK

In 1970 the Department of Health, Education, and Welfare commissioned a study on the problems and role of work among Americans. The results of the study were described in a book entitled *Work in America*.* The study and the book focused on the work-related processes of this nation's work force and the problems that work poses for the physical and mental health of individuals and the well-being of society. Not too surprisingly, significant discontent with work was detected among skilled and unskilled operative employees—these results paralleled those of earlier studies—but surprisingly, discontent among managerial employees was noted as well.

The types of data in the *Work in America* study have been the subject of some criticism.† The methodology used in gathering the data and in reaching the conclusions has also been criticized. For example, one question

---

* *Work in America: Report of a Special Task Force to the Secretary of Health, Education and Welfare* (Cambridge, Mass.: MIT Press, 1972).
† For a comprehensive critique, *see* Harold Wool, "What's Wrong with Work in America?—a Review Essay," *Monthly Labor Review* **LCVI**, 3 (March 1973): 38–44.

in the surveys was: "What type of work would you try to get into if you could start all over"?* Forty-three percent of the responding white-collar workers answered "same." Only twenty-four percent of blue-collar workers answered "same." These data, particularly those for blue-collar workers, correlate positively with some of the earlier studies, particularly in the automobile industry, where assembly-line workers often stated determination to have their children follow a different occupational path.

Such a question as previously cited, however, has been criticized as measuring not necessarily dissatisfaction with present conditions at all, but merely a propensity for change. In essence, people may be perfectly (or nearly perfectly) satisfied with present conditions, but obviously ready to consider a change if something better comes along.

Nevertheless, the *Work in America* survey and other studies have reported that one of three middle managers is now willing to join a union,† and a similar study by the American Management Association found that fifty percent of the middle managers surveyed favored a change in the law (National Labor Relations Act) to allow collective bargaining between middle and top managements.‡ These are significant findings when compared with the ideological commitment to management prerogatives and the anti-union stance that managers are presumed to maintain.

Generally, middle managers have several substantive complaints. One is their lack of influence on the organization's goals, policies, and mode of operation. In another study, some managers were cited as concerned with the lack of their organizations' commitments to socially responsible corporate activities.§

Managers were outspoken about the need to compete to gain attention and resources and complained about the tension, frustration, and infighting that this intraorganizational competition led to. Some middle-management executives reported feeling like parts of a machine, to be replaced when a technologically superior part became available. Indeed, in a rapidly advancing technological age, many executives feel obsolescent.

In a *DUN's Review* article, many middle-management executives complained that their firms exhibited little reverse loyalty during a recession period.‖ Executives were expected to show complete loyalty and to work hard for the corporation, they protested, but when the slightest shrinkage in

---

* *Work in America, op. cit.,* p. 15.
† *Ibid.,* p. 40.
‡ American Management Association, *Manager Unions* (New York: American Management Association, 1972), cited in *Work in America, op. cit.,* and also in George J. Berkwitt, "Management, Sitting on a Time Bomb?" *DUN's Review* (July 1972).
§ Berkwitt, *op. cit.*
‖ *Ibid.*

bottom-line profits appeared, the corporation showed no hesitancy to "take a meat cleaver" to its staff.

The notion that the needs and outlooks of individuals today are identical to those of people twenty years ago perhaps should be discarded. Many observers think that today's young managers are being drawn from a population much more questioning, cynical, and demanding than that of their predecessors.

The new managers: are they different?

For example, today's young managers view authority much differently than did managers of bygone years, including many who are now in the top echelons of organizations. Heady from victories in college protests over the Vietnam War, Watergate, and such mundane education-related phenomena as grades, residence-hall requirements, and control over social lives, today's young managers are less likely to automatically accept authority than their predecessors were.

Moreover, routine, repetitive, nonchallenging work will have a greater negative impact on the new middle manager than on the older one working toward the gold watch. In essence, today's younger managers have higher expectations, less tolerance for nonrewarding jobs, more alternatives, including nonbusiness and societal-furnished perquisites, and less loyalty to "good ole Magnet Products Company."

But will time dull both the cynicism and enthusiasm of the younger manager? It may be that the longer a person remains in the organization, the more likely that he or she will become acculturated to the rhythms and demands of the organization. In other words, the longer-term employee has learned either that organizational life can be very satisfying or that it just doesn't pay to rock the boat, e.g., "What's the use, I might just as well sit back, take it easy, and live with it." Either one learns that life in a large organization can be satisfying, or one's definitions of satisfaction (or aspiration levels) come down several notches.

The *Work in America* study contained a table of data that might prove interesting in this regard. Respondents were asked: "How often do you feel that you leave work with a good feeling that you've done something particularly well?"* The results are shown in Table 4.1.

Many would probably interpret these data to mean that the young are intrinsically less satisfied with work. An equally plausible interpretation, however, is that older people might have been acculturated to accept the values of the organization, might have acquired different or changed notions of satisfaction as they aged, or might have given up. Indeed, it would be interesting to repeat this survey when the under–twenty-nine groups reach fifty-five to sixty-five years of age.

* *Work in America, op. cit.,* p. 45.

Age group	Percentage answering "very often"
Under 20	23
21–29	25
30–44	38
45–64	43
65 and over	54

Source: *Work in America*, p. 45.

TABLE 4.1
Data on positive feelings
toward work

Effects of economic conditions

"There's nothing like a good recession to make an employee thankful to have a job." That statement is often heard during economic downturns, oftentimes in gleeful, if not spiteful, tones over the number of previously outspoken middle managers scurrying for jobs. According to the prevailing ethic, whereas middle managers can pick good times to complain, cop out, or threaten to unionize, when the chips are down—and the economy with them—many top executives will opine that they "can buy any kind of skill they need." Then, they say, they hear little about the needs of managers for intrinsic organizational or work satisfaction.

Obviously, there is some truth to the notion that economic conditions have an effect on managerial outlooks and the relationship of extrinsic and intrinsic job satisfactions. But limited evidence continues to show that some middle managers are continuing to leave industry for different living modes—recession or no recession. They can do so, in part, because they are protected economically in much better fashion than their predecessors were. Welfare, food stamp, and similar programs provide a cushion of support that, although not luxurious, was not available to preceding generations of managers. Thus whereas years ago an older manager might have accepted corporate life and swallowed personal values because of economic uncertainty, today's younger manager might not be so easily persuaded.

ORGANIZATIONAL RESPONSES

Some companies and top executives respond to any challenge to corporate norms viscerally, labeling the departed or the complainers as misfits, cop-outs, failures, or the like. Indeed, in a *DUN's Review* article one corporate president remarked, "The creative, innovative managers generally have not gone anywhere. The competitive misfits who can't stand the pressure of bottomline performance have."* In essence, according to this assessment, the fault definitely does not lie with the system, but with the few managers who cannot handle the inherent demands of corporate life.

* Robert Levy, "Top Management—and Turned-Off Executives," *DUN's Review* (August 1972).

To other top executives, however, industry and organizations are much less cognizant of the needs and potential of younger middle managers than they should be. These executives note the need not only for middle managers to participate and make decisions, but also for top management "to listen to and to communicate with middle managers."

Some companies underutilize middle managers, know it, and are prepared to face any problems and turnover resulting from this attitude. After all, the nation's business schools seem to be turning out an endless supply of new potential managers. Other companies, however, do attempt to maximize the challenges available for younger managers by delegating meaningful tasks to them and by sharing decision-making power. Several of these approaches come under a widely encompassing label of organization development. Some of these approaches are structural changes, a redesigning of organization structure, whereas others entail behavioral and value changes.

Some techniques to increase managerial commitment

- Decentralization
- Management by Objectives
- Sensitivity training
- Team building

Decentralization

In Chapter 3 we discussed the concept of decentralization and the placement of decision centers within the organization. Decentralization is one of the key methods of building management commitment and a sense of value in the minds of middle managers.

In some companies wide spans of control and minimum levels of supervision can be engineered. Middle managers (and lower-level managers as well) can be then given wide latitude and be responsible not only for making things happen, but for design stages and command capacities as well.

Companies that are decentralized through restructuring can thus compel younger managers into design and decision situations by forcibly expanding the lower-level manager's universe of decision and reducing the superior's capacity to interfere because he or she has so many subordinates to deal with.

In other organizations, however, wide spans and minimum levels are not possible, because of the character of the tasks involved and other factors. In those organizations decentralization requires a conscious managerial effort to push decision making down to lower-level managers and a design not of structure, but of procedures.

Whenever decentralization is the expressed norm, however, the intent may be undermined by overzealous (and probably overworked) and untrusting superiors. That is, executives who do find time to continually interfere with subordinates' activities, call for reams of activity and results reports, or consistently "suggest" ways of doing things are defeating the purpose of any prescriptions of decentralized structure or practice.

Despite the problems, however, it is in the decentralized companies and organizations that we should expect much less dissatisfaction over the manager's role.

Management by Objectives

Another method—one related closely to decentralization—of overcoming some executive dissatisfaction is through the use of the managerial technique known as Management by Objectives.* Briefly, Management by Objectives, or MBO, rests on the processes of agreement, consultation, compromise, support, and contract that go on between a superior and a subordinate. Under MBO, a manager and his or her superior will meet in predetermined cycles to map out a set of objectives for the subordinate to attempt to attain during the next evaluation period (say, one year). These objectives are usually classified as routine, problem solving, and innovative. Routine objectives are related to the maintenance of the unit involved and include basic production, sales, cost-control goals, etc. Problem-solving goals relate to managerial problems that are affecting the unit. For example, problems of motivating workers, accelerating work flows, and reducing wasted time would fall under this category. Innovative goals relate to new programs and expansion activities for the unit.

This process of objective setting may take several meetings between superior and subordinate, during which the objectives should become increasingly clarified and should gain more precision. Ideally, these goals should be quantifiable; for example, the subordinate may set as an objective to train a specific number of employees, to manufacture so many widgets, etc., within the prescribed time period.

At the conclusion of the objective-setting sessions, both superior and subordinate must agree on the usefulness and necessity of the objectives, the standards of acceptable achievement, and the projects that go with them. Generally, the subordinate proposes the objectives and attempts to "sell" them to the superior during the negotiating process.

Obviously, the objectives must be attainable and not "pie-in-the-sky wish lists." The superior must agree to provide the necessary resources to accomplish the objectives. If a superior is unable to supply or commit the resources, either the subordinate's objectives must be modified or, when the day of reckoning comes, the subordinate should not be held responsible for the nonattainment of objectives. Indeed, this step is a major problem source in MBO; managers on both sides of the process must be very careful to spell

* The definitive book on MBO is George S. Odiorne, *Management by Objectives* (New York: Pitman, 1965).

out the necessary resources and be able to supply them in order for MBO to remain a viable management tool.

Finally, at the beginning of the evaluation period, the superior and subordinate should agree on the rewards to be granted when the subordinate achieves the objectives, and then the two parties should sign a written statement detailing objectives, resources, rewards, etc. Subordinates should be given maximum latitude in achieving the agreed-on objectives.

Periodically during the evaluation period, superior and subordinate should meet to review the progress being made toward attainment of objectives. Many companies require that these meetings be held at least quarterly. The review should also be in quantitative terms and should account for any changes in environment, e.g., scarcity of resources, disasters, etc. Perhaps corrections will be made in the objectives, the plan for reaching those objectives, the amount of resources needed, or the standards by which the subordinate will be evaluated.

At the conclusion of the period, superior and subordinate will again meet to evaluate progress, determine if the objectives were met according to the standards agreed on, and, if the objectives were not achieved, try to determine why they were not. Of course, if any rewards are to be granted, this is the appropriate time for them to be given. Another caveat for the superior in MBO, of course, is to be sure to have the authority to grant rewards before making commitments to subordinates. Nothing can dull the motivating force behind MBO faster than the relevation that promises made at the beginning of the process cannot be fulfilled at the end. Of course, the conclusion of one evaluation period should be coupled with the start of another, with both parties applying lessons learned to the expectations established for the next period.

Management by Objectives may be a tool to alleviate many managerial-satisfaction problems. What might have happened to Monte Klinger, for example, if he had operated under MBO? Perhaps his motivation would have been restored. Perhaps, for the first time in his life, standards might have been set high enough for him to find some challenge in his work.

MBO assigns definite organizational tasks along with the authority to use organizational resources to achieve those tasks. A clearly defined MBO program leaves no question on the authority granted to subordinate managers or on what is expected from them.

MBO ties rewards into accomplishment, offers the challenge to a manager of fitting in his or her own ideas and prescriptions to the achievement of corporate goals, eliminates much of the wheel spinning that goes on in organizations (one writer termed this the "activity trap"), and minimizes the organization's concern with petty rule making for rule-making's sake.[*]

[*] George S. Odiorne, *Management and the Activity Trap* (New York: Harper & Row, 1974).

In essence, MBO introduces flexibility into dealing with employees, but also includes the stability of expectations for individuals once the process has been set in motion.

Are there any problems with MBO? Yes, and some of these have already been alluded to. Basically, the problems involve not the concept of MBO, but the ways in which MBO is applied. All too often, managers do not spend the time refining objectives into precise statements, but allow vague and unclear standards to creep into the process. Further, introducing MBO into an existing work force might be problem-laden. Older managers, who for years might have been evaluated on loose, qualitative standards, become fearful when the newer, more precise MBO standards are introduced. But careful, competent management should be able to overcome these problems and realize the positive effects of MBO.

Sensitivity training

One process, once widely heralded but now used by only a few companies, is sensitivity training. Within a small group (the T-group, or training group), participants gradually come to expose all of their inner feelings about the organization and their co-workers. The aim of the process is to get an equal and open environment—often antiauthority and nonhierarchical—in which people are free to relate to one another in very personal ways.

Often, however, the relationship of the session to the organization, its problems, goals, and processes is illusive, and the technique, although building a feeling of equality and participation, may be nonpurposeful or indeed disruptive to the organization. Consequently, its popularity has declined in favor of other methods of organization development.*

Team building

Another change process is variously called team building or organization development (although the latter term, as we have seen, has been applied to the general category of change techniques, including MBO and T-groups). Under team-building strategies, sections of an organization are designated into groups, and these groups are geared to organizational problems in ways that call for teamwork and cooperation, as opposed to the intraorganizational competition that may characterize some managerial relations.

Generally, this means changing an organization's values—encouraging more cooperation—rather than its structure (wider spans of control, for example), although structural changes and redesign of organizations can be the end result of the organization-development process, once sharing of power and decision making has become an accepted organizational value.

Often team building makes use of an outside trainer, although one is not necessary. The first stage is generally data collection to diagnose the problems. Later stages include dissecting the existing values of an organization, building new cooperative values, and then making the new values a part of

* William J. Kearney, "Sensitivity Training: An Established Management Development Tool?" *Academy of Management Journal* 17, 4 (December 1974): 755–760.

the managerial style. This process is sometimes described as the unfreezing, intervention, movement to change, and refreezing elements of organizational change.*

In any event, the result is supposed to be a better-functioning team. Unlike pure sensitivity training, however, team building is geared to organizational problems. On the other hand, the process does reduce status differentials, and although there may be significant attitude changes, it is not totally clear that the technique leads to improvement in organizational goal achievement.†

In the cases presented at the beginning of the chapter, we see some rudiments of the team approach. Sue Harrison was welcomed as part of the team, and this obviously pleased her. But she was also given more and more responsibility, so components of decentralization and even MBO could have been part of her organization's managerial philosophy.

SUMMARY AND CONCLUSION

Back to Sue Harrison and Monte Klinger

In the two vignettes at the beginning of the chapter, we observed some rather surprising results. Sue Harrison, the college activist, has been turned around and obviously is challenged and motivated by her job—in business, an institution she had little use for while in college. It might be interesting to speculate on the reasons for the change. Perhaps Spofford-Hendricks gave her encouragement, authority, and a free rein over her account—authority as well as responsibility—or perhaps advertising agencies deserve their reputation as the most free-wheeling of all business organizations. Perhaps Spofford-Hendricks practiced MBO or team building, and Sue Harrison in turn managed her account team using those techniques. The agency is obviously quite decentralized, and its mode of operation seemed to work wonders with Sue Harrison.

What happened to Monte Klinger, who was a business student, well above average in intelligence, undermotivated all through college, and able to choose among several jobs? Did he make a poor choice to start with? How did his company fail him? The easiest of all answers, of course, is to say that Monte's company was so overcentralized that younger middle-management executives were smothered. Or perhaps Mason-Holden did not keep track of and monitor its young talent. Monte wasn't seriously challenged, received very little guidance, and seemed to be treated as a spare part rather than as a valuable member of the product-management team.

* Kenneth D. Benne, "Changes in Institutions and the Role of the Change Agent," in Paul R. Lawrence and John A. Seiler, *Organization Behavior and Administration* (Homewood, Ill.: Richard D. Irwin, 1965), pp. 953–955.
† John B. Miner, *The Management Process*, 2d ed. (New York: Macmillan, 1978), pp. 347–349.

Conclusion Both Sue Harrison and Monte Klinger were affected by the norms of their respective organizations. This chapter focused on this issue of organization/individual relationship—the possible conflict in values that may occur between an organization and its members. However, it would be an error to overgeneralize about organizations and their effects on managers' satisfaction; indeed, some organizations are pleasant places in which to work, are intrinsically motivating, and provide satisfactory employment experiences.

But there is also little use in trying to rationalize our way out of the problem of middle-management dissatisfaction. It does exist, and although not all employees may be mentally disturbed as a result of organizationally generated frustration, there is some evidence of significant middle-management dissatisfaction. Businesspeople may say that the problem doesn't exist, that managerial dropouts are misfits anyway, and that business organizations continue to be challenging. But the data starting to flow and the reported changes in young people tend to indicate that some managerial practices do not quite mesh with the values, needs, and aspirations of young people or middle managers and that although this value conflict doesn't cause violent behavior, it does lead to dissatisfaction. Obviously, economic conditions will have an effect on younger managers' choices and may downgrade their aspirations, although with cushioning social alternatives, today's middle managers may be much less tied to an organization than their predecessors were.

However, several managerial techniques are available to combat the problem of increasing managerial satisfaction. These approaches take several forms: the expansion of decentralization schemes to ensure a balance between authority and responsibility, the institution of Management by Objectives, and a variety of organization development and team-building techniques.

DISCUSSION QUESTIONS

1 The *Work in America Study* cited survey results showing that one of every three middle managers was ready to join a union. Discuss some of the reasons why middle managers are now willing to join labor organizations.

2 As a potential owner or employer, what might you do to stop the flight of managers toward union membership?

3 Comment on the assertion that today's new manager is different from a manager of, say, twenty years ago.

4 It has been said that the work ethic is dead in this country. Is it? Was it ever alive?

5 One of the newer managerial techniques to overcome the malaise of executive dissatisfaction is MBO. Specifically, what is MBO? What processes is it based on?

6 MBO depends on a sound understanding of its advantages and disadvantages. What are some of the advantages and disadvantages of MBO? In particular, what have been some of the problems in applying MBO?

7 In addition to MBO, what are some of the other management techniques that might be used to increase managerial satisfaction?

8 Some senior chief executive officers have claimed that the departed or malcontent managers are "misfits, corporate copouts, failures, or the like, who cannot withstand the pressure of bottomline performance when the economy gets tight." Do you agree with the accusations? Why or why not? What counterarguments might you offer in defense of the departed or malcontent manager?

9 How might wide spans of control and minimum levels of supervision help middle managers from falling into the ranks of the discontented?

10 Define the following terms:
a) span of control   b) MBO
c) work ethic   d) new manager
e) sensitivity training f) team building

CASE: DON LaPOINTE

■ "I put in a nine-to-five day, and that's it. At 5:00 P.M. I'm my own boss." Don LaPointe held firmly to that philosophy. His wife always answered the telephone after he came home from the office, and she would not refer any calls from colleagues, clients, or suppliers to Don, telling them to "call him at the office in the morning, because he is busy for the evening." Don would not work late at the office voluntarily; it was a rare and sometimes unpleasant occasion when his boss persuaded Don to work after hours to finish a project.

Don was an assistant purchasing agent for Pylon Metal Products Corporation, which manufactured office furniture, household items such as breadboxes, step-on garbage cans, etc., and cabinets for refrigerators, washers, dryers, and other major appliances. The last group of products was made under subcontract to various private-label appliance manufacturers.

Basically, Don's job was to work with both the product-design group and the design-engineering group. The former worked on products that the company intended to market itself; the latter was charged with designing and engineering the components made under subcontracts with other manufacturers.

His work with the product design group consisted of pricing material needs, seeking alternate materials, suggesting suppliers, and contracting to assure the company of a ready and steady supply of any necessary materials. His predecessor had been fired for contracting for seat cushions with a fabricator who was too small to handle the rush order resulting from an unanticipated contract for 10,000 sets of office furnishings for a federal office complex. Only some quick footwork by the purchasing agent who found two additional suppliers with sufficiently available capacity saved Pylon from defaulting on the contract.

On subcontracts, LaPointe's role was to work with the engineers preparing the prototype and the bid, if the contract was a competitive one. Sometimes a saving of a penny or two on one component was enough to get the bid price into the winning range.

Both of these tasks kept Don busy for the better part of his work day. While at the office, Don was totally cooperative; he consulted with his colleagues, was service-oriented in the true tradition of a staff person, and put in a solid day's work. He offered to solve problems and was freely and cheerfully available to anyone who called. In essence, he was good, productive, and a storehouse of knowledge.

But once 5:00 P.M. came around, he gave of his time grudgingly, no matter how important the project was thought to be by his fellow managers. "Nothing," he would comment, "is so important that it can't wait until morning."

One day his boss called him in, assured him that his work was good, but asked him point blank why he was so insistent on keeping such regular hours. "It's my own life-management scheme," he answered. "If I don't manage my time and provide for my personal life, I'll slowly but surely become a prisoner of my work."

"But what about the importance of the company and its goals? Aren't you a professional?" asked his boss.

"I watched my dad give thirty-five years of devoted service to a corporation. His family always came second, and sometimes we kids didn't see him for days, as he came home late at night. I made up my mind that I would never become a slave to my job. There are too many other important things in life. I'm sorry, but that's the way I've got to operate." ■

Case questions

1. Discuss Don LaPointe's values relative to those of higher management and relate this comparison to LaPointe's role in the organization. Why are there differences in outlook?

2. Do you think that Don's job offers enough challenge? Why or why not?

3. What practices can Pylon's top management and Don's superiors engage in to increase his commitment? Why might they work?

SELECTED READINGS

Abboud, Michael, and Homer L. Richardson, "What Do Supervisors Want From Their Jobs?" *Personnel Journal* **57,** 6 (June 1978): 308ff.

Ackerman, R. W., "How Companies Respond to Social Demands," *Harvard Business Review* **51** (July/August 1973): 88–98.

Agee, William M., "The Moral and Ethical Climate in Today's Business World," *MSU Business Topics* **26,** 1 (Winter 1978): 16–19.

Baumback, C. M., and K. Lawyer, *How to Organize and Operate a Small Business*, 5th ed. (Englewood Cliffs, N.J.: Prentice-Hall, 1973).

Carr, A. Z., "Can an Executive Afford a Conscience?" *Harvard Business Review* **48** (July/August 1970): 58–64.

Carroll, A. B., "Managerial Ethics: A Post-Watergate View," *Business Horizons* **18** (April 1975): 75–80.

Cherrington, David, "The Values of Younger Workers," *Business Horizons* **20,** 6 (December 1977): 18–30.

Connor, P. E., and B. W. Becker, "Values and the Organization," *Business Horizons* **18** (August 1975): 85–88.

Coxon, Anthony P. M., and Charles L. Jones, *The Images of Organizational Prestige: A Study in Social Cognition* (New York: St. Martin's Press, 1978).

Dyer, W. G., *Team Building: Issues and Alternatives* (Reading, Mass.: Addison-Wesley, 1977).

Elkins, A., and D. W. Callaghan, *A Managerial Odyssey: Problems in Business and Its Environment* (Reading, Mass.: Addison-Wesley, 1975). Note particularly Part II, Section A, "New Lifestyles and Corporate Response."

Grupp, F. W., Jr., and A. R. Richards, "Job Satisfaction Among State Executives in the United States," *Public Personnel Management* **4** (March/April 1975): 104–109.

Heisler, W. J., and J. W. Houch, eds., *A Matter of Dignity: Inquiries into the Humanization of Work* (Notre Dame, Ind.: University of Notre Dame Press, 1977).

Jun, J. S., *MBO in Government: Theory and Practice* (Beverly Hills, Calif.: Sage Publications, 1976).

Krantz, David L., *Radical Career Change: Life Beyond Work* (New York: Free Press, 1978).

Levinson, H., "Management By Whose Objectives?" *Harvard Business Review* **48** (July/August 1970): 125–134.

Long, J. D., "The Protestant Ethic Re-examined: What Kind of Value System Is Implied?" *Business Horizons* **15** (February 1972): 75–82.

Luthans, F., and R. Kreitner, *Organizational Behavior Modification* (Glenview, Ill.: Scott, Foresman, 1975).

McConkey, D. D., *MBO for Nonprofit Organizations* (New York: AMACOM, 1975).

Mayer, Richard J., "The Secret Life of MBO," *Human Resources Management* **17,** 3 (Fall 1978): 6–11.

Melcher, A. J., *Structure and Process of Organizations: A Systems Approach* (Englewood Cliffs, N.J.: Prentice-Hall, 1976).

Myers, M. S., and S. S. Myers, "Toward Understanding the Changing Work Ethic," *California Management Review* **16** (Spring 1974): 7–19.

Newstrom, J. W., and W. A. Ruch, "The Ethics of Management and the Management of Ethics," *MSU Business Topics* **23** (Winter 1975): 29–37.

Odiorne, George S., *Management by Objectives* (New York: Pitman, 1965).

———, *Management Decisions by Objectives* (Englewood Cliffs, N.J.: Prentice-Hall, 1969).

———, "Politics of Implementing MBO," *Business Horizons* **3** (June 1974): 13–21.

———, "A Management Style for the Eighties," *University of Michigan Business Review* **30,** 3 (March 1978): 7–11.

———, "How to Succeed in MBO Goal Setting," *Personnel Journal* **57,** 8 (August 1978): 427–429.

Sargeant, Howard, *Fishbowl Management: A Participative Approach to Systematic Management* (New York: Wiley, 1978).

Terkel, S., *Working* (New York: Pantheon, 1974).

Toffler, A., *Future Shock* (New York: Random House, 1970).

Waters, James A., "Catch 20.5: Corporate Morality as an Organizational Phenomenon," *Organizational Dynamics* **6,** 4 (Spring 1978): 2–19.

Work in America: Report of a Special Task Force to the Secretary of Health Education and Welfare (Cambridge, Mass.: MIT Press, 1972).

Managerial Design Processes

The first major category of managerial functions mentioned in Chapter 1 was that of *design*. Design, as you recall, is the manager's activity of mentally interrelating problems, resources, needs, outputs, etc., into goals, plans, organizations, and systems.

Part III consists of seven chapters reflecting the manager's performance of design activity. These activities are varied: setting objectives and goals, making decisions, using quantitative tools for decision making, planning, setting policies and procedures, designing organizations, and designing motivating systems and practices.

Often the malfunctioning of a project can be traced to insufficient or otherwise inadequate design. Thus the manager's design activities can probably be judged the most important, since everything else she or he does depends on the effective setting of goals, standards, plans, and policies as well as on the design of an efficient organization structure.

Chapter 5
SETTING GOALS AND OBJECTIVES

CHAPTER HIGHLIGHTS

In all organizations the managing, operations, activities, and processes are directed toward the achievement of some objective or set of objectives. In this chapter we shall explore the basic nature of objectives. Organizational objectives range from very broad to very specific, reflecting or corresponding to the organizational hierarchy; hence the term "hierarchy of objectives."

Our discussion of hierarchy will be followed by a discussion of the goals of business and some of the many models of the firm and its objectives. Then we shall cover the setting of goals, including forecasting, accounting for organizational strengths and weaknesses, recognizing the importance of timing, considering standards of efficiency and effectiveness, and setting subunit goals. Finally, we shall consider some of the problems of conflicting goals (suboptimization), goal displacement, and other human problems in setting and pursuing goals.

LEARNING OBJECTIVES

1 To understand and to be able to apply the concept of the hierarchy of objectives.

2 To learn the various concepts of top-level business goals.

3 To understand the notions of profit, service, social responsibility, and sales maximization as top-level corporate goals.

4 To learn the role of forecasting in setting goals.

5 To understand the goal-setting process, the choosing of goals, and standards of efficiency and effectiveness.

6 To appreciate that managers set goals to both capitalize on organizational strengths and avoid organizational weaknesses.

7 To appreciate the importance of time in goal setting and pursuit.

8 To learn how goal pursuit is constrained by government regulation and resource availability.

9 To learn to define and recognize the concepts of suboptimization and goal displacement.

CASE: TERRY PETERS

■ Terry Peters formerly worked in the assembly department of the Small Appliance Division of Switch-On Products Corporation. He had been employed there for seven years, moving up from general help to skilled assembler. During his time at Switch-On, Terry had learned a great deal about appliances, and this experience, plus his tinkering at his home basement workbench, triggered the idea that he might open a small appliance-repair business. He had always wanted to be his own boss.

Terry borrowed $3000 on his life insurance policy and scraped up another $2000 from friends and relatives. He rented a small, inexpensive shop in an out-of-the-way section of town, moved his tools into the shop, bought some additional tools, installed a sign and fixtures, and acquired an old cash register. In addition, he purchased from Switch-On $1800 worth of appliance repacks. (Repacks are items that were returned under warranty to the manufacturer. The original customer was given a new appliance and the returned one was later repaired and resold at a price considerably below normal wholesale. Often, these appliances are marked as repaired or repacked, but just as often they are not. For the small stores, they are a blessing, since they allow the dealer to compete on price with the big chain buyers and still make a decent profit.) "Now, I'm in business for myself," gloated Terry.

Terry's business progressed slowly for several months. He was confident that a small appliance-repair business was really needed in his city, and he thought that his basic labor charge of $5.00 an hour was very reasonable. With parts, the average appliance repair took an hour of time and cost about $7.50. After seven months, Terry had exhausted all of his working capital (in most cases, withdrawing it as salary) and was grossing only $350 a week on the average—about $200 from the repair service and the rest from miscellaneous sales of appliances, small electrical gadgets, and keys made on a second-hand key-making machine he had purchased at auction. But he was barely paying the rent and utilities, let alone turning a true profit.

During the eighth month, Terry grew even more frustrated. He tried newspaper advertisements; they resulted in one sale. He distributed handout flyers, yet there was no increase in business. He even offered a discount on repairs to people bringing in coupons attached to the flyers.

One day, Terry said to his wife, "Maybe this town doesn't need a small appliance-repair service." Two weeks later, Terry closed his shop and reapplied for his job at Switch-On. ■

INTRODUCTION

Terry's dilemma illustrates the need for well-thought-out and realistic goals, or objectives, in any business venture. In its own small way, Terry's story points out a problem that many businesspeople have—an inability to establish a scheme of objectives based on realistic consumer need and demand and factual expectations rather than on wishes. It is not enough that the actions taken to attempt goal achievement (plans) be logical and well planned; the goal itself must be, first, attainable and, second, explicit. Terry's goals were always implicit—to make some money by providing a small appliance-repair service. But did he ever go beyond his personal desires, skills, and interests and think about the usefulness and demand for his proposed business? In essence, were his goals attainable?

In this chapter we shall explore goals and objectives, focusing on the things that managers must consider and do when they establish goals for their organizations. (For our purposes, we use the terms "goals" and "objectives" interchangeably.)

All activity, including organized activity, is geared toward the accomplishment of some end or a series of ends. For organizations, the process of attempting to achieve an overall objective or objectives means that subunits within the organization aim toward their own particular subgoals. Indeed, in its ideal sense (according to what some have called the "rational model" of organization), the organization can be defined as an integrated set of units pursuing interrelated and coordinated goals and subgoals; the achievement of one lower-level goal furthers the achievement of a second, higher-level goal, and so on to the total-organization-level goals. In essence, then, managers at all levels of the organization are involved in selecting and formulating goals and planning activities to reach those goals.

THE HIERARCHY OF OBJECTIVES

Managerial goals form a hierarchy that corresponds to that of the formal organization. For example, let us suppose that your college or university has only one overall objective—to provide a high-quality education to the maximum number of qualified students, given the level of allocated resources. This goal statement is very general and says little in terms of specific output. But higher-level goals *are* expressed in broad, general terms. Indeed, the higher up one moves in the organization, the broader, more encompassing, and general the goals seem to be.

Let us look further at the university. Suppose for the moment that it has three schools, or colleges—the second level within the line organization—the schools of arts and sciences, business administration, and engineering. What might the goals of each of these schools be? Probably each school's goal would be a restatement of the overall goal, but reflecting the unique nature of each school or college. Thus, for example, the engineering school would have as its objective the provision of high-quality engineering education to the maximum number of students; the business school would aim toward quality education in business administration to the maximum number of students. Note that these objectives are still quite general, but they are somewhat more specific than the overall university goal in that they start zeroing in on particular disciplines. They are, however, all consistent with the overall university goal. Note also that at the school level we need no longer concern ourselves necessarily with stating "qualified" in the goal, since the admissions function is at the university level, and the schools can assume that the students will be qualified generally throughout the university. (For the time being, we will not be troubled with defining "high quality" in relation to education.)

Farther down the hierarchy are the various departments, and their goals are more specific than those at the school and university levels. The department of management, for example, would have as its goal the provision of

1. First-level administrative unit—total university: goal, quality education for maximum number of qualified students, given allocated resources.

2. Second-level administrative subunit—business school: goal, quality education in business for maximum number of students, given allocated resources.

3. Third-level admininstrative subunit—department of management: goal, quality education in management for maximum number of students, given allocated resources.

4. Fourth level administrative subunit—professor of organizational behavior: goal, quality education in organizational behavior for maximum number of students, given allocated resources.

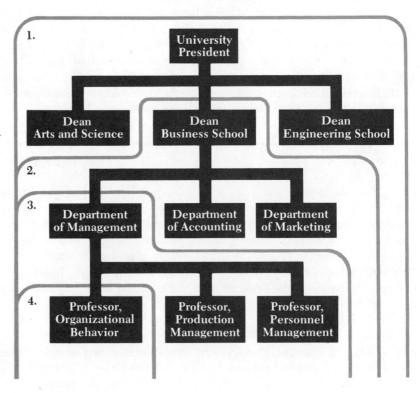

FIG. 5.1
Administrative units and the hierarchy of objectives.

high-quality education in management (within business administration); lower yet in organization, a professor of organizational behavior might have as an objective the teaching of a high-quality course in organizational behavior.

Note that the goals at the level of the professor are much more specific, centering on one course. Across the breadth of the university, many courses are being taught by many different professors, each of whom has a specific goal. But each of these specific courses is consistent with the objectives of the schools in which it is taught, and each of the schools follows objectives that are consistent with that of the total university. No professor in the school of business, for example, will be teaching biochemistry, and no one in arts and sciences is likely to be teaching accounting. Finally, within the overall objectives of the university fit the various staff objectives relating to such things as ensuring that the buildings are kept clean, providing adequate secretarial assistance to faculty, ensuring a steady supply of examination books, keeping the lights burning, etc.

In essence, what we have been describing here in general and simplified terms is sometimes called the hierarchy of goals and objectives. Within an organization, *each subunit or administrative unit has goals which are consistent with and subordinate to the goals of the next higher administrative unit, which in turn has goals consistent with and subordinate to those of the next higher unit, and so forth up the organization.* (An administrative unit is a vertical part of the organization which peaks at a single office, or box, on the organization chart.) Objectives at the highest level of the organization are the most general; those at the lowest level, the most specific. In our simple example, quality education moved steadily down the line until it became quality instruction in an organizational-behavior course. Figure 5.1 illustrates both the administrative-unit concept and the hierarchy of goals and objectives.

TOP-LEVEL GOALS—BUSINESS

A good deal of management and business literature focuses on the topic of top-level business goals, and much controversy centers on the choice of goals—profit, provision of a product, maximum sales, social responsibility, and the like. Here we shall discuss the various approaches to top-level business goals.* A warning is in order, however. Much of the literature on corporate goals is normative; that is, writers generally *prescribe* goals based on some preconceived value system. It is important to recognize this underlying

---

* Much of the following discussion on top-level business goals is adapted from Arthur Elkins and Dennis W. Callaghan, *A Managerial Odyssey: Problems in Business and its Environment,* 2d ed. (Reading, Mass.: Addison-Wesley, 1978), pp. 7–15, 41–47.

problem of values when discussions of goals occur. On the other hand, we will also cite some studies of a descriptive nature—theories or observations of actual or operational goal systems. We will, in our approach, be careful to differentiate between the prescription and description of goals and then set up a system of trying to sort out the competing prescriptions.

Traditional economic notions

The notion that profit is the primary goal of business firms derives from both the economists' descriptive model of the firm and the normative political and economic doctrine of a free-enterprise society and economy. However, the economists' descriptive model of the firm uses profit maximization only as a simple assumption device to allow the generation of reasonably good predictions of resource allocation and income distribution. The assumption itself is not meant to be an accurate description of real-world managerial or business behavior or motivation, but simply a "good enough" concept to get economists where they want to go. Indeed, for prescriptive management the assumption and its associated constructs are of limited use.

Normatively, however, the classical economist believes that the business person *should* pursue maximum profits primarily, and it is from these capitalist dogmas that profit-motivated or -directed management gets its impetus. Business decisions under this doctrine are expected to have extremely simple parameters; the businessperson simply arranges the lowest cost resources in the most efficient configuration, sells to customers willing to pay the highest price, and derives maximum profit (see Fig. 5.2).

FIG. 5.2
The profit-maximization concept.

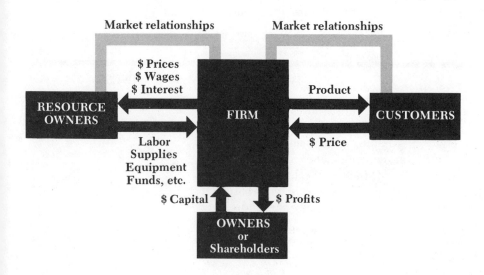

But empirically, the notion of a maximum profit-motivated or -directed business is tenuous. Today's business, particularly when operating under conditions of monopoly or oligopoly, is often under no compulsion to maximize profits; as a matter of fact, a monopolist or oligopolist may be under compulsion from several quarters to limit profits. More important for our perspective, however, are the studies that have found some firms to be satisfied with "adequate profits" or those studies that indicate that most managers do not know how to maximize or indeed cannot determine whether or when they have in fact maximized profits.

The economic concept of profit maximization in the descriptive economic model is tied to the equally important conceptual assumption of rationality—the ability of the decision maker to survey all opportunities and to select the one most appropriate path to maximum profit. The normative, or prescriptive, economic doctrine, to a great extent, also includes that concept. But the real-life businessperson is not that rational; indeed, most studies have shown managers to be bounded in rationality, so that they accept "good enough" rather than maximizing outcomes.* In essence, although profit maximization is an attractive concept (and indeed may still be the goal of many businesspeople), any illusions about either the generality of acceptability or ease of achievement should be well tempered.

Chapter 3 introduced the notion that the primary functions of a firm relate to its primary objective—providing and distributing utility. This making and selling of some product or service has been called the "service objective," and many management writers have often gone to great lengths to displace the profit objective with the service objective in management theory. In their view the business organization is granted a right to exist by society, and its objective should be to produce a product for the use of the society. Accordingly, an individual investor's objective is to maximize return. The profit gained by investors, however, is only a collateral side effect of achieving the service objective.† (See Fig. 5.3.)

Service-objective model

Obviously, these are two alternative ways of approaching ultimate business objectives. Whereas the economist's view is based on individual rights and motivations, the management theorist's view is based on a societal grant of the right to function as a business. Perhaps we can simplify these frames of reference by looking at the problem using the terms "objective," "function," and "result." Thus according to the economist's view, profit maximization is the objective that will be fulfilled by efficiently performing the firm's

* Herbert A. Simon, *Administrative Behavior,* 2d ed. (New York: Macmillan, 1957), pp. xxiv, 40–41.
† Ralph C. Davis, *The Fundamentals of Top Management* (New York: Harper and Bros., 1951), Chapter 4.

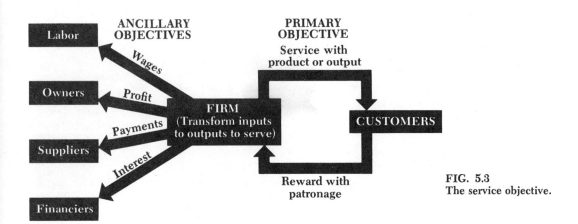

FIG. 5.3
The service objective.

function—production and distribution (although not always maximizing production). According to the management theorist's view, by contrast, profit is the corollary result of achieving the primary objective—production and service. Really, it makes little difference which of these ways of saying the same thing you adopt. Obviously, your own values will influence which of these two objectives you view as primary.

Sales-maximization model   But profit and service orientations are not the only prescriptions or descriptions of management or business goals. Some managers supposedly aim for highest sales or highest market share. According to the proponents of this theory, managerial prestige rides more heavily on those two indicators than on anything else.* And as you should recall from economics, maximizing or attempting to maximize sales and market shares may not be the same in terms of either result or behavior as maximizing profits, because the firm moves into a scope of operations resulting in diminishing returns to scale.

Social-responsibility model   Some of today's writers on management are prescribing an entirely new set of corporate objectives—social responsibility.† These writers view the business organization as not only an economic unit, but a social one as well.

* William J. Baumol, *Business Behavior, Value and Growth,* rev. ed. (New York: Harcourt, Brace & World, 1967), Chapter 6.
† *See* Committee for Economic Development, *Social Responsibilities of Business Corporations* (New York: CED, 1971); *also see* Keith Davis, "Social Responsibility Is Inevitable," in Elkins and Callaghan, *op. cit.,* pp. 20–28.

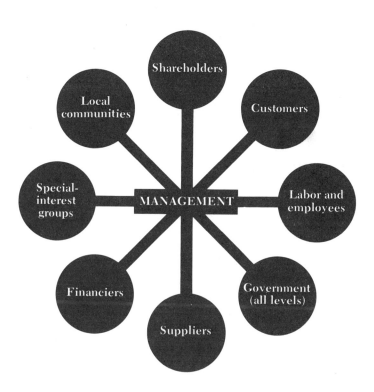

FIG. 5.4
The concept of social responsibility. (Arthur Elkins and Dennis V. Callaghan, *A Managerial Odyssey: Problems in Business and Its Environment*, 2d ed., Reading, Mass.: Addison-Wesley, 1978, p. 11.)

According to the social-responsibility doctrine, firms are surrounded or made up of various constituent or interest groups, each having some legitimate call on the firm's resources, rewards, energies, or efforts (see Fig. 5.4). Profit-seeking shareholders are only one of these interest groups and hold no special place in this prescription, sharing importance with labor, government at all levels, customers, neighbors, suppliers, minority groups, and so on. Management, as the hub of the activity, is entrusted with equitably distributing its effort and its corporate rewards or resources among each of these groups. Thus, according to social-responsibility advocates, companies may be expected to provide not only serviceable products and collateral profits, but also fair wages, employment opportunities, support for community functions, special charitable contributions and support, etc. The rationale behind the social-responsibility thesis is that society is changing rapidly and is making new and different demands on the corporations it created. These demands are or must be reflected in new corporate goals and objectives.

The social-responsibility thesis is not without its critics.* Such criticism usually centers on the social-performance capacity of business managers, the

* The most notable critic is Nobel Laureate economist Milton Friedman. *See* Milton Friedman, "The Social Responsibility of Business Is to Increase its Profits," in Elkins and Callaghan, *op. cit.*, pp. 28–34. *See also* Paul T. Heyne, *Private Keepers of the Public Interest* (New York: McGraw-Hill, 1968).

power entrusted to self-elected managers, the misallocation of economic resources, and the propriety of decision making on the basis of nonuniversally
accepted values. Indeed, some critics have commented that social responsibility is nothing but profit making in disguise or a recognition of newly imposed cost constraints on regular corporate behavior—in essence, public
relations.

Managerial self-interest   Other groups of management writers, using descriptive models and studies,
contend that corporate goals are shaped not by investors, owners, society, or
by societal expectations—e.g., profit, service, or social responsibility—(even
if they look that way or even if managers say they are), but by the needs
and desires of the controlling managers.* That is, rather than the corporation
being operated for the ends of the owners or society and managers occupy-
ing a trustee role, these writers contend, the managers are operating firms in
their own self-interest. Long ago, and indeed in much of economic doctrine
and theory even today, managers and owners were considered synonymous—
the goals of the owner were considered the goals of the firm and consequently the goals of management (see Fig. 5.2). But by the 1930s, the recognition of separation of ownership and management had become almost
universal.† This recognition, plus the fact that few corporate managements
can be challenged by shareholders for control of corporate decision making,
can lead one to the conclusion that managers have a great deal of power
over the ultimate goals and objectives of most American corporations. Those
goals and objectives may well be framed according to the well-being of
management and not according to prescriptions of managerial or corporate
duties. Thus high salaries, maximum sales, social responsibility, large size,
and the like may really be more closely aligned with managers' personal
needs and desires than with any expressed societal or investor criteria.

This brief discussion of corporate goals is neither a complete catalog nor
a treatise on identifying what goals are the correct ones or in whose interests
business firms and organizations really operate. Rather, it simply points out
the wide diversity of descriptions and prescriptions of primary corporate
goals. You should also be aware that explicitly stated corporate goals may in
fact be a mask for other, implicit goals. For example, objectives relating to
high sales may be the manifestation of a need to enhance managerial prestige as much as or more than a reflection of actual corporate goals.

* *See*, for example, R. Joseph Monsen and Anthony Downs, "A Theory of Large Man-
agerial Firms," *Journal of Political Economy* **LXXII** (June 1965): 221–236. *See also*
R. J. Monsen, B. O. Saxberg, and R. A. Sutermeister, "The Modern Manager: What
Makes Him RUN?" in Elkins and Callaghan, *op. cit.*, pp. 48–61.
† Adolph A. Berle and Gardiner C. Means, *The Modern Corporation and Private Prop-
erty* (New York: Macmillan, 1932).

SOME PROCESSES AND CONSIDERATIONS IN GOAL SETTING

Whatever the real primary goals or however one views an organization, somewhere within the organization the functions are expressed in goal forms. For example, the General Motors Corporation, somewhere in its hierarchy of goals, may state as an objective the production of three million Chevrolet automobiles. Having considered the concept of hierarchy of goals in simplified terms, we now move on to more complexity and cover goal-setting processes and the factors to consider in setting goals.

Note that these processes will vary in importance given the organizational level with which one is concerned; that is, some considerations are more important at top levels than at lower levels. Note also that both the considerations and the practices apply to all types of organizations—profit or not-for-profit, service or manufacturing, etc.

A key factor in setting goals is selecting ones that are attainable, and this often means that elements outside the organization must be willing and capable of absorbing the organization's output. No university would set as its divisional objective the training of 600,000 students in sword making if it wasn't relatively clear that there were 600,000 young men and women interested in sword making. Obviously, we don't always know off-hand whether a "market" exists for our product or service, so as we set goals and objectives, we must estimate our market potential. This requires forecasting.

Forecasting

Of course, managers and firms also must be aware of resource availability, changes in legal requirements and government and other constraints and costs. Although here we focus our discussion on forecasting in the output market, managers also use forecasts in the many other goal- and subgoal-related settings.

In "seat of the pants" estimates, one method of forecasting, little research goes into the goal-oriented decisions. Often, a manager will proceed convinced that the market is "out there somewhere." Although one often hears stories about the genius who was able to make decisions based on intimate and uncanny market sense and knowledge, there are many more stories of failure—sometimes underestimating, but more often overestimating a market's potential. Terry Peters, the small businessperson cited at the beginning of this chapter, was convinced that there were thousands of people in the city needing appliance repair. Only after a short time in business did he realize that most consumers apparently felt that his products and services were not worthy of any special patronage. Terry's perceptions of the market were apparently totally wrong, and hence his business objectives were doomed to failure. (In fact, later research established that many of Terry's potential clients would rather throw away an appliance costing up to $20 and purchase a new one rather than spend $7.50 and up repairing the old one.)

When perceptions can't be trusted and security of knowledge is necessary, so is some type of formal forecasting. Formal forecasting has many variants, and obviously some firms can afford and indeed need more sophisticated methods. For some other firms, however, the loss associated with error in objective setting may be less than the cost of overusing sophisticated forecasting methods.

Forecasting methods may range from using the wealth of information available in the public library (census data, Chamber of Commerce data, state income data, advertising agency studies, etc.) to commissioning full-blown, sophisticated, and rather expensive market-research studies. Successful large firms rarely set market objectives without some fairly substantial data backing them up. We don't necessarily have to accept the entire thesis in John Kenneth Galbraith's *New Industrial State* to agree with him that big-business organizations are finely tuned to the pulse rates of the markets in which they operate.*

Forecasting methods can be simple or complex. Often the least expensive and easiest method is simply extrapolating future trends from historical data. So, if sales rose an average of five percent per year over the past eight years, a prediction of a five percent increase may be a natural and appropriate forecast. More sohisticated forecasting would attempt to set up a model of the market (or work force) and try to determine what would happen to that market if certain actions were taken by the company (e.g., advertising, price changes) or if certain things happened over which the company had no control (e.g., increase in price of a complementary product, as has occurred with gasoline for automobiles). Many companies are now simulating their environments on a computer and by setting in alternative constraints or occurrences, the computer will generate predicted outcomes. Caution should be followed, however, that the output from a computer simulation is only as good as the data that flow into it. Computer specialists use the phrase GIGO —garbage in, garbage out—to describe the efficacy of computer-assisted simulation based on poor input data.

Utilizing organizational strengths   An organization may have unique strengths that enable it to reach goals that other companies or organizations cannot. For example, a company with an unusual and strong research-and-development component should realize that strength and develop a set of goals to capitalize on it, e.g., new-formula

---

* The Galbraith thesis is that the modern corporation, because of the imperatives of large-scale production, heavy capital commitments, and sophisticated technology, must plan far into the future. In order to ensure success for the plans, consumers must be managed so that their behavior will correspond to the needs of the corporation. Furthermore, the state must be an active participant, moderating economic fluctuations and providing certainty in the economic environment. *See* John Kenneth Galbraith, *The New Industrial State* (Boston: Houghton-Mifflin, 1967).

products every year. Similarly, a strong design capability in the automobile industry can allow a company to develop a set of goals emphasizing change and modern styling, whereas a competitor without such an effective department might consider only a line stressing stability of design.

Just as we can point to the necessity to capitalize on strengths in the setting of goals and objectives, so too we can stress the need to recognize and consider organizational weaknesses. Indeed, many an organization has failed to achieve its goals because its internal resources would not allow goal achievement—something that should have been recognized in the first place. Thus a company that has no sales force in seventeen states would be hard pressed to meet a goal of national distribution of its product, despite the fact that its advertising department is second to none. Indeed, the company would be wasting its advertising effort if it could not supply the product to customers in those states. Similarly, an automobile company that purchases its transmission units from another firm but still has the industry's best stylists must temper its optimism on objectives with the realization that its transmission dependency may be a liability in the achievement of goals. In essence, then, the setting of goals involves considering not only market acceptance and capitalizing on strengths, but also recognizing organizational weaknesses.

Recognizing organizational weaknesses

In many cases, those weaknesses can be rectified, but often they cannot be, at least in short term. Moreover, strengths often do not compensate for weaknesses. No automobile can be sold without a transmission, no matter how hard the stylists try.

Assuming that a company's primary goal is profit-oriented and that its function is, for example, associated with producing washing machines, what is the next step? As in the university described earlier, each division and department in the company will develop sets of standards and output goals which when fitted together will, ideally, make the operational and primary goals come to fruition. For example, if we are concerned with washing machines, our next step is to determine how many we are to produce and market. And then each component in the organization sets its goals according to that number. Sales quotas are set in sales divisions, production expectations of the various components—right down to the last bolt—are set up in the production units. If 600,000 washing machines take 1.6 million $1'' \times \frac{1}{8}''$ bolts, that input requirement becomes the output objective of the bolt machinists in the machine shops or a purchasing department objective if the company buys its small parts externally.

Setting subunit goals

Earlier, we spoke about the standards necessary to measure when and if objectives were achieved. But how are those standards established? How, for example, does the university know when it is providing a "quality" education?

Standards of efficiency and effectiveness

Generally, goals can be set with some quantitative statement: so many units sold, so many units machined, so many students taught, etc. Often, a goal may have several standards to meet: for example, ninety percent of 4000 students will achieve a score of eighty-five percent or more on a standard examination or 12,000 washing machines will be produced per month with only a .25 percent rejection rate.

Qualitative goals, such as quality education, high profits, high sales, etc., should be tied to some quantitative standard so that one can measure at the appropriate time whether, in fact, those goals were attained. If they weren't attained, managers can then determine why they weren't and can determine whether or not the goals should be changed. For example, if a baseball team sets as its goal winning the league pennant, it should set as its standard winning about 100 of its 162 games; if the team wins only 65 games (and, of course, comes nowhere close to the pennant), it has a standard against which to evaluate its relative performance. Was the goal reasonable? Should the team have originally settled for second or third place? Or, could changes be made in the team to allow it to win 100 games, e.g., better pitching, a new shortstop, etc. And, of course, all sorts of lower-level standards will aid the team's managers in evaluating the team's performance—earned-run averages, batting averages, fielding percentages, won-lost records, numbers of home runs, runs batted in, etc.

Later in this book, we shall discuss the manager as an evaluator, auditor, and adapter. There we shall see the importance of quantifying standards to match goals and discuss the steps an organization may take in either changing goals and standards or revamping the organization and its processes.

Timing of goals and objectives

So far, we have said nothing about the timing involved in the establishment and achievement of goals, but it should be obvious that timing is important, particularly for the subgoals of the various departments and divisions of an organization. Some goals are timeless and are maintained by the organization over the long haul, perhaps in perpetuity. For example, the profit-maximization goal may be a constant one in the organization, as may be the goal of organizational survival. At your university, the provision of a quality education may be a constant goal over the life of the institution.

But other goals may be related to some general time period and be classified by the organization as a long-term, short-term, or intermediate-term goal. Other goals may have specific time benchmarks, e.g., one month, two months, three years. For instance, in setting goals the washing machine maker must consider *when* the washers will be produced and sold—on January 15 or July 20 or on December 23. Obviously, they will be produced all during the year. Thus 600,000 units will be manfactured in batches or in a timed sequence, not all at the end of the year. This means that the bolt makers making $1'' \times \frac{1}{8}''$ bolts must also produce required batches of bolts early or throughout the year, not suddenly deliver 1.6 million bolts on December 30 and declare that their objectives were achieved. In essence, appropriate objective setting requires proper consideration of the *timing* of required performance.

This factor—timing—suggests that we can establish another hierarchy of goals—that of time. The *continual,* or *perpetual,* goal of an organization will remain quite stable; indeed, only a change of organization or ownership might alter it. These goals may be expressed in terms of profit, survival, service, quality education, social responsibility, or any other general category. Such goals are not only relatively stable, but also extremely resistant to change.

Long-term objectives could be more specifically oriented to product lines or operational functions. These goals, often called strategic goals, are stable and long-lasting, but are subject to change. For example, one might find a firm shifting from one major product line to another (necessarily altering long-term objectives). This would likely occur without alteration of higher-order perpetual goals (e.g., the maintenance of the survival of the firm).

Intermediate goals in this time-based hierarchy would likely include the year's projection for production and sales. These goals are generally changeable, depending on changing environmental conditions. Finally, *short-term* goals are the most easily changed or altered. For example, the firm might plan to produce 60,000 units for the month of February, but this figure could be raised or lowered as constraints or opportunities arose.

Figure 5.5 shows the time-based hierarchical composite of objectives or goals. Note that although the time hierarchy pervades the entire organiza-

FIG. 5.5
Time-based hierarchical
composite of objectives or
goals.

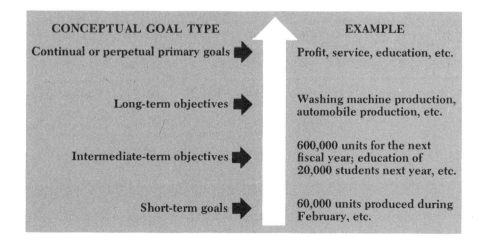

CONCEPTUAL GOAL TYPE	EXAMPLE
Continual or perpetual primary goals ➡	Profit, service, education, etc.
Long-term objectives ➡	Washing machine production, automobile production, etc.
Intermediate-term objectives ➡	600,000 units for the next fiscal year; education of 20,000 students next year, etc.
Short-term goals ➡	60,000 units produced during February, etc.

tion, a similar time hierarchy is in force within each unit, although each might have a horizon extending only to long-term objectives. For example, the bolt makers have an objective to produce so many bolts during the entire year—1.6 million—but they also have a short-range goal of 300,000 bolts for the month of February. Or, the painting department may have an average employment objective of 440 workers for the year, but know that in March 490 workers will be needed to handle an overload.

External constraints on goals

Simply because an organization says that it wants to reach a goal doesn't necessarily mean that it can freely engage in any behavior to reach that goal. There are constraints on the easy achievement of goals. One of the most important constraints on goal attainment is societal regulation, normally expressed through government control. Suppose, for example, that a firm has a finite capacity to produce three million automobiles annually. Suppose further that the government, in response to, say, the energy crisis, orders a cutback in production-oriented power use. A goal of three million automobiles may not be feasible under such a regulation, no matter how hard the firm tries or how much it may desire to reach the goal. Or, suppose that the company's goal is maximum market share in an industry dominated by four firms. Together, the firm and a competitor could capture seventy-five percent of the market by merging. But such an action would undoubtedly invoke the antitrust laws. Is the goal attainable? Possibly, but not by merger.

In short, one important constraint to goal achievement is government regulation and legislation. Another is resource availability—materials, money, labor, energy, and the many other inputs into production and distribution systems. No rational manager will set a goal of producing six million washing machines if steel is available to manufacture only 2.4 million units or labor is available to produce only three million.

OTHER PROBLEMS AND FACTORS IN GOAL ATTAINMENT

Subgoal conflict— suboptimization

In theory, the organization is supposed to be a finely tooled instrument, with goals meshing to accomplish the overall organizational objective. Indeed, as we mentioned earlier, this is the orientation presented in the so-called rational model of organization and in much of the theory of bureaucracy. Realistically, however, since organizations are collections of people and their efforts, often the parts of the organization do not mesh so smoothly as designers would like. Max Weber, the creator of the term "bureaucracy," theorized that in the ideal organization, individuals leave their own feelings, needs, and values outside of the organization and adopt the organizational ethic.* Hence we could expect (hopefully) the automatic integration of

* See Hans H. Gerth and C. Wright Mills (trans.), *From Max Weber: Essays in Sociology* (New York: Oxford University Press, 1946).

organization goals and personal goals. We know, however, that this ideal case rarely occurs and that indeed, the real goals of subunits (and the entire organization, possibly) may differ from formally stated goals because of individual and group values, needs, and personal objectives.

Possible problems resulting from the relationship of individual needs to organizational goals can be shown by a simple example. Salespeople are often paid by commission and obviously would want to sell as many of their high-commission items as possible. Following that behavior, their real (rather than stated) sales objectives and subsequent actions may be totally out of synchronization with those of the production department, which may want to maintain as smooth a flow as possible on the production line.

Often conflicts of this type may force a reassessment of the total organization goal(s) because they make the organizational goal nonachievable, and there is no way of controlling or reconciling the aberrant behavior.

This process of goal conflict and subsequent reassessment is called "suboptimization." Most commentators say that all organizations will probably have to suboptimize in order to achieve any goals at all. For example, assume that the salespeople referred to above sell washing machines; in order to achieve a yearly sales goal of 600,000 washing machines and keep the production line smooth, each might take home a weekly paycheck of only $75.00, since they are forced to substitute lower-commission washing machines sales for their higher-commission items.

In order to keep them on the job (obviously few salespeople would stay on the job at that salary), the firm may have to either alter its ideal objective of 600,000 washers or tolerate less profit (as a result of realigning salespeople's commission rates) or scramble its production priorities so as to achieve a different product mix and satisfy the salespeople's need for higher salaries.

Suboptimization is another constraint on *ideal* goal achievement, and it is one that an organization may have to "learn," as often goals and objectives are set with little knowledge of the reactions of people inhabiting the organization. Indeed, most often managers set goals with little concern with the "human element."

Goal displacement

Another problem described extensively in the literature of bureaucracy specialists is the phenomenon of goal displacement. Often, according to these writers, people working in organizations "learn" to look on the methods and procedures of achieving goals as more important than the goals themselves; gradually the strict adherence to and preservation of the methods become the real goals.[*] If the organization tries to change goals and the attendant procedures, there is resistance, as the people involved rationalize the need for the long-ingrained procedures.

[*] This process was first pointed out in Robert K. Merton, "Bureaucratic Structure and Personality," *Social Forces* **22** (1940): 560–568.

Examples of goal displacement are quite common. Managers may be more concerned with the neatness with which forms are filled in than with the information on the forms. Other managers may demand that the simplest requests be put into writing before they will act on them, simply because "everything should be in writing." In one case, a unit strongly resisted a change in name and broadening of functions simply because it possessed an ample supply of stationery imprinted with the old name!

Goal displacement is a serious problem for management and organizations. Sometimes the organization's reputation will seriously suffer from goal displacement, as it is often the basis for what we commonly refer to as "red tape."

Other human problems　Goal displacement and suboptimization are only two of the elements that can cause organizations to fail in meeting its goals. Organizations in the abstract are marvelously efficient mechanisms, much the same as the all-powerful entrepreneur of economic theory. But in the real world, organizations tend to be less efficient, less automatic, and less rational than any imagined ideal.

In the eyes of employees, however, there may be nothing wrong with the organization's being "less efficient," "less automatic," and "less rational." Given these employee values, the organization may have to lower its aspirations, since the constraints imposed by this human element mean that the most efficient the organization can actually be is much less than the ideal. In essence, the "ideal" concept of organizational optimum is tempered, and a new "number" emerges.

At the very least, organizations and managers must make some new assumptions about goal acceptance. Not all managerially formulated goals are going to be accepted automatically by subordinates; if they are not accepted, but management insists on imposing them, they are likely to be sabotaged.

Thus another constraint to goal achievement often is the population of the organization itself. Managers have two tasks here. The first is to "sell" the goals to subordinates, carefully explaining them and offering training and acceptance in reaching them. In this case, it becomes imperative that all parties be operating "on the same wavelength."

But suppose that goals are seemingly accepted, but later are rejected. Here managers may have to reexplain and recycle. If, however, this human relations effort doesn't work and reaching the established goal is necessary to the organization, changes in personnel and organization may be called for. This is the process of control/audit/adaptation. Later we shall have more to say about the control and change process, but suffice it to say now that keeping the organization attuned to its goals—if those goals are considered optimum—or knowing when to change the goals are key problems for management.

In Chapter 4 we introduced Management by Objectives, a management method to motivate personnel by setting mutually agreed on goals and objectives for each subordinate, allowing subordinates maximum latitude in achieving goals, and then regularly reviewing and evaluating each subordinate's performance in relation to those objectives. Goals and objectives set in the MBO process are not distinct from or unrelated to goals as we have been discussing them—in the context of organizational vitality. MBO goals, ideally, must also be consistent with and subordinate to organizational primary and functional goals. Indeed, the whole process of MBO means that an organization gives greater amounts of attention to its goal-setting process and becomes more precise in the setting and relating of goals and standards. MBO may be one of the better methods for a manager to induce acceptance to goals and to avoid some of the pitfalls of goal displacement and rejection.

Motivating with goals

SUMMARY AND CONCLUSION

In this chapter we explored the concept of goals and objectives and some of the processes and problems in selecting and formulating goals. Most organizations have a hierarchy of goals or objectives reflecting the arrangement of administrative units. We then explored the controversial topic of top-level goals for business, considering whether it is even pragmatically possible to maximize any of the ends prescribed for business—profit, service, or social responsibility.

Following that we covered some of the processes and factors involved in setting goals: forecasting, the recognition of organizational strengths and weaknesses, the setting of subunit goals, standards of efficiency and effectiveness, timing in goal setting, and external constraints to goal achievement. Finally, we dealt with some human problems in goals, goal setting, and goal attainment—subgoal conflict (or suboptimization) and goal displacement—as well as some of the ways of coping with these human problems.

All organizational effort is predicated on reaching some goal(s) or objective(s), and the managerial role is made easier if clear and attainable goals and objectives are established.

DISCUSSION QUESTIONS

1 What is meant by the hierarchy of goals and objectives? Give a specific example of the hierarchy, say, in an educational institution, manufacturing firm, insurance company, and retail store.

2 The social-responsibility doctrine prescribes a varied goal approach. Describe the social-responsibility view of the firm from a normative perspective, and a positive perspective.

3 There are obvious constraints to goal achievement. What are some of these constraints?

4 Organizations possess various strengths and weaknesses associated with their goal setting. Generally, what are some of these strengths? Weaknesses?

5 How does one use forecasting methods in the setting of organizational goals? What type of forecasting methods are available for managerial use?

6 What effect does timing have on the setting and attainment of goals? How might a hierarchy of goals be established in terms of time?

7 Distinguish among continual, long-term, intermediate, and short-term goals.

8 Define the following terms.

a) goal
b) objective
c) hierarchy of goals
d) social responsibility
e) normative model
f) positive model
g) managerial theory of the firm
h) continual, or perpetual, goals
i) long-term objectives
j) intermediate objectives
k) goal displacement
l) suboptimization

CASE: BROCKPORT WHOLESALERS, INC.

■ "Are you kidding," retorted Lee Chang, newly hired management consultant to Brockport Wholesalers, "are you seriously telling me that you don't have a single written objective in this whole place?"

"We never thought we needed any," replied Mike Boardman, the firm's president. "Hey, look, we're making enough money here; we work hard, but we're satisfied. I just called you in to find out how to get the salespeople to hit some of those smaller stores that cluster around some of the bigger ones they call on. They don't think it's worth their time. What's that got to do with objectives?"

"Quite a bit. Look, I really think you've got a deeper problem here. Nobody seems to know where they are headed here. Let me think for a while about how to put some perspective on this firm."

Brockport Wholesalers, a full-line food and grocery wholesaler, serves independent supermarkets in northwestern Pennsylvania and the Cleveland, Akron, and related areas of Ohio. Brockport grew from a small fruit and vegetable wholesaler which collected produce from local farms and delivered it to local "mom and pop" stores, to a company now doing $188 million sales a year in groceries, fruits and vegetables, boxed meats (portions of meat that come from the packing houses either already cut or ready for cutting), health and beauty aids, tobacco products, and other related lines.

But the firm just seemed to grow "by the seat of the pants." Boardman, like his father before him, made decisions daily on just about everything from building warehouse space to whether to discipline a stock clerk. Fifteen-hour days, and nights spent sleeping on the office couch, were not uncommon for Mike—as well as the other managers. The firm just struck out in all directions at once, and no one seemed to know where they were going.

This was the situation that confronted Lee Chang when he spent the first morning talking over what started out as a salesperson-motivation problem. He thought for a while and then called Boardman on the phone. "Mike, do you suppose we can spend some time trying to develop a coherent set of objectives for your firm? I really think your salesperson problem stems from the fact that the salespeople have no objectives other than personal ones involved."

"Sure, come on by and we'll write up a set," responded Mike.

"Hey, wait, it's not as easy as that. We've got a lot of research to do, and then I want your people to know how objectives throughout the firm fit together."

Mike then answered, "You know, at first I thought you were just trying to pad your fee, but you sound real convincing. Let's talk some more about it. What kinds of things should we start thinking about? What kinds of questions do we start answering? What do my managers need to know?" ■

Case questions

1. As Lee Chang, what kinds of questions would you recommend that Boardman ask himself?

2. How would you make the point to managers that they must start thinking about goals and objectives?

3. Why does the salesperson problem stem from a lack of corporate goals and objectives?

SELECTED READINGS

Aguilar, F. J., *Scanning the Business Environment: Studies of the Modern Corporation* (New York: Graduate School of Business, Columbia University/Macmillan, 1967).

Ansoff, H. I., *Corporate Strategy* (New York: McGraw-Hill, 1965).

Aran, J. D., *Dilemmas of Administrative Behavior* (Englewood Cliffs, N.J.: Prentice-Hall, 1976).

Armstrong, J. S., *Long-Range Forecasting: From Crystal Ball to Computer* (New York: Wiley, 1978).

Bassie, V. Lewis, *Economic Forecasting* (New York: McGraw-Hill, 1958).

Bliss, Edwin, *Getting Things Done: The ABC's of Time Management* (New York: Scribner's, 1976).

Bridges, F. J., K. W. Olm, and J. A. Barnhill, *Management Decisions and Organizational Policy: Text, Cases and Readings*, 2d ed. (Boston: Allyn and Bacon, 1977).

Butler, W. F., and R. A. Kavesh, *How Business Economists Forecast* (Englewood Cliffs, N.J.: Prentice-Hall, 1966).

Cyert, R. M., and J. G. March, *A Behavioral Theory of the Firm* (Englewood Cliffs, N.J.: Prentice-Hall, 1963).

Eilon, S., "Goals and Constraints in Decision Making," *Operational Research Quarterly* 23 (March 1972): 3–15.

Fish, D. C., "Decentralized Staff Planning Leads to Better Management," *Association Management* 29, 10 (October 1977): 94–97.

Fusfield, A. R., and R. N. Foster, "The Delphi Technique: Survey and Comment," *Business Horizons* 14 (June 1971): 63–74.

Galbraith, J. K., *The New Industrial State* (Boston: Houghton Mifflin, 1967).

Gilmore, F., *Formulation and Advocacy of Business Policy* (Ithaca, N.Y.: Cornell University Press, 1970).

Heilbroner, R. L., *Beyond Boom and Crash* (New York: Norton, 1978).

Katz, R., *Management of the Total Enterprise* (Englewood Cliffs, N.J.: Prentice-Hall, 1969).

Khachaturov, T. S., ed., *Methods of Long-Term Planning and Forecasting* (New York: Halsted Press, 1976).

King, D. C., "Long-Range Thinking," *Personnel Journal* 57, 9 (September 1978): 504–509.

Lipinski, A. J., "Communicating the Future," *Futures, The Journal of Forecasting and Planning* 10, 2 (April 1978): 119–127.

McCaskey, M., "A Contingency Approach to Planning: Planning with Goals and Planning without Goals," *Academy of Management Journal* 17 (June 1974): 281–291.

March, J. G., and H. A. Simon, *Organizations* (New York: Wiley, 1958).

Morell, R. W., *Management: Ends and Means* (San Francisco: Chandler, 1969).

Moore, B., and J. Talbott, "An Application of Cost-Volume Profit Analysis, *Cost and Management* 52, 2 (March/April 1978): 31–38.

Paine, F. T., and W. Naumes, *Organizational Strategy and Policy: Text, Cases, and Incidents* (Philadelphia: Saunders, 1975).

Paul, R. N., N. B. Donavan, and J. W. Taylor, "The Reality Gap in Strategic Planning," *Harvard Business Review* 56, 3 (May/June 1978): 124–130.

Stevenson, H. H., "Defining Corporate Strengths and Weaknesses," *Sloan Management Review* 17 (Spring 1976): 51–68.

Tersine, R. J., and W. E. Riggs, "The Delphi Technique: A Long Range Planning Tool," *Business Horizons* 19 (April 1976): 51–56.

"Theory Deserts the Forecasters," *Business Week* (June 29, 1974): 50–54, 59.

Thomas, J. S., "Demand Analysis: A Powerful Productivity Improvement Technique," *Public Productivity Review* 3, 1 (Spring 1978): 32–43.

Williamson, O. E., *The Economics of Discretionary Behavior: Managerial Objectives in a Theory of the Firm* (Englewood Cliffs, N.J.: Prentice-Hall, 1964).

Chapter 6
MAKING DECISIONS

CHAPTER HIGHLIGHTS

Decision making is the pervasive activity of management. This chapter focuses on the decision-making process and its various stages. You will also be exposed to the relevance of timing to decision making. Finally, we shall cover group decision making and the advantages and disadvantages of the various types of group decision making.

LEARNING OBJECTIVES

1 To define decision making.

2 To differentiate between decision making and planning.

3 To learn how decision making is constrained by goals and policies.

4 To learn and to be able to apply the steps of the decision-making process.

5 To appreciate the need to find problems in the forms of challenges, risks, and opportunities.

6 To learn the limits of information search and information sources.

7 To consider the constant possibility of backstepping to a redefinition of the problem.

8 To appreciate the need for decision rules and to understand their use.

9 To learn how one's personal values can affect organizational decision making.

10 To learn three timing considerations in decision making.

11 To understand the values and disadvantages of the various group processes for decision making.

CASE: McDONALD'S*

■ McDonald's, the nationwide chain of hamburger restaurants, has a policy of flying the American flag in front of each of its outlets. This policy was personally promulgated by Chairman of the Board Ray Kroc.

* The substance of this incident was reported in J. Anthony Lukas, "As American as a McDonald's Hamburger on the Fourth of July," *New York Times Magazine,* July 4, 1971, p. 26.

On Monday, May 4, 1970, four students at Kent State University were killed by National Guardsmen. The Guard was ordered to Kent State after students, like those all around the country, struck and rioted in protest to the Vietnam War and the invasion of Cambodia. At Kent State, the students had burned the ROTC building a few nights earlier.

The Kent State killings created shock and confusion among the nation's students. At the Carbondale campus of Southern Illinois University, students asked that all flags be lowered to half-mast in memory of the Kent State students. When they confronted the manager of the local McDonald's, he complied and lowered the flag.

A neighbor who witnessed the confrontation reported it to the McDonald's chairman, who in turn called the manager and ordered that the flag be hoisted to full mast. The manager complied with the chairman's directive.

A few hours later, the students returned, disturbed that the manager hadn't kept his word. They threatened in no uncertain terms to burn down the restaurant.

Perplexed, the manager called McDonald's headquarters for guidance. The manager's call was put through to the president of the corporation. ■

INTRODUCTION

Both the local manager and the president of the corporation in this vignette are faced with resolving a very sticky situation. In a word, they must make decisions—not just any decisions, but decisions that will have reasonable expectations of success when they are implemented.

Decision making is the overriding activity in managerial design functions. Indeed, managers at all levels face situations requiring decisions—decisions on goals to be pursued, decisions on hiring, decisions on purchasing, and decisions about firing. Chuck Martinelli, for example, made decisions on budgets, on replacing the Midwest sales manager, and on advertising appeals. Audrey Hollis was apprehensive about the decision situations into which she would be placed as a manager. John Smith obviously made decisions about the growth of his small hardware store; there were many decisions to be made as his initial store grew into a large national chain.

The decision-making process permeates goal setting, planning, policy making, and indeed adapting and change as well. Most managerial activity in one way or another includes decision making. In this chapter we shall explore the decision-making process—the mental activity a manager engages in when making decisions—the importance of timing in decision making, the role of groups and interaction in managerial decision making, and the necessity for consistency of decisions with organizational rules and policies.

SOME DEFINITIONS AND DIFFERENTIATIONS

In our discussions about managers so far, you may have noted that there are two levels of decisions. Goal selection, the topic of Chapter 5, is a decision process. Managers view environments, scan potential and possible market opportunities, research organizational strengths and weaknesses, and then select the objectives for their organization or unit. This goal-selecting process is one kind of decision process, or level of decision making. In addition, however, there are the decision processes followed in designing activity to reach those goals—for example, who is to be hired, who is to be entrusted with funds, how the product is to be delivered, at what speeds the lathe in the milling department should be operated, and how often payrolls should be processed.

Decision making in the context of this chapter refers to decisions of the latter dimension. *Decision making here is often defined as that mental activity that takes place in moving an organization from the existing state of affairs to an anticipated desired state* (see Fig. 6.1). The goals and objectives established are the desired state, and the current conditions or place of the organization are the existing state. Once the goals have been determined, the executive or manager must decide how to reach those goals; that is, he or she must engage in decision making.

FIG. 6.1
The concept of decision making.

Later in this book we will differentiate more fully between decision making and planning, another managerial activity. For now, however, decision making and planning can be treated as synonymous *only* when the goal to be reached is one in isolation. But generally, the goal to be reached is only one segment of the path to a broader goal or is a short-range goal on the road to a longer-range one. Planning, then, usually encompasses a *series* of decision processes in a sequential or multiple-goal structure. Planning is, in effect, a series or set of linked and interrelated decisions.

In the action-oriented decision making to be covered in this chapter, goals become a constraint to the actions managers may contemplate as well as a state to be achieved. The goals that are set for a unit or for the higher-level units establish a limit or frame of reference beyond which the manager may not operate while making decisions.

Thus, for example, if the goals of the total organization include one of selling life insurance, investment procedures and decisions are constrained

Decision making and goals

by the fact that life insurance sales efforts—even apart from the rules of the regulatory agencies—are conditioned by the need to emphasize safety in investment and prompt payoff upon death to potential buyers. Thus the firm will be required to maintain sufficient liquidity and abundant security to ensure that policyholders will be paid in the event of death. Decision makers, then, cannot invest the funds of the organization totally in, for example, a very risky wildcat mining adventure paying no dividends. The portfolio must include reasonable security to assure present and potential policy-holders.

Similarly, decisions must be consistent with company policy (policy setting is itself a decision-making process which we shall cover later). Policies are guides to action which reflect the goals of the organization. Policies have also been described as constraints on the latitude of managerial activity. For example, if the goal of the organization is low-overhead sales, a policy may be to sell for cash only. This policy constrains alternative actions in any plan to expand sales or offer customer services. Thus a sales manager who is planning a new sales campaign will always (unless one can induce a policy change) have to gear the campaign to cash-only sales. The sales manager cannot consider offering budget terms, use of credit cards, or down-payment plans as possible sales inducements.

In other words, *decision content* and substance are constrained by other, earlier decisions, e.g., those on goals and policy. Goals and policy also limit *decision opportunities or situations* from arising. The very same policy cited above of "cash only," for example, limits the need for decision situations to develop. No clerk will ever have to decide if a customer is credit worthy, *if* the clerk is not empowered to make that decision in the first place because of the cash-only policy.

Decision centers   In an earlier chapter we discussed centralization and decentralization, or the placement within the organization of decision-making authority. We noted that organizational policy will place the location of decision centers within the organization and that different organizations can have different arrangements. In some organizations all lower-level managers will be given little decision making opportunity. Thus a local manager of a fast-food restaurant may have very few areas in which to make decisions, most decisions being made higher up in the chain.

Other situations may find managers at lower levels making a wider variety of decisions. The manager of a store with its merchandise differentiated from others in a chain of stores may have much more discretion in terms of merchandising, inventory management, and employee training, for example. Finally, there are situations in which the manager of one organizational unit may have greater design opportunities—decision-making authority—than another, even though the second manager may be on the same level as the first. This latter arrangement often occurs when the operating results of one of the units is markedly different from those of the others; the decision-making authority for the less productive unit is then moved upward in the organization, but the authority for the other units remains intact.

THE DECISION-MAKING PROCESS

Whether we are going to a movie, purchasing an automobile, deciding on a home, hiring an employee, or making an investment, we utilize mental choice processes. If we stopped to analyze those mental processes, we would find that they are remarkably similar for all situations. That is, we do fairly standard things when we make choices, no matter how complex or how simple those choices may be.

In this section we will detail the mental decision process that is probably used for most managerial decision situations and indeed for most of our own personal decisions. The seven parts of this process are as follows:

1 Problem search and formulation
2 Information gathering and evaluation
3 Formulation of alternative courses of action
4 Application of decision rules and decision tools
5 Choice of desired alternative
6 Choice of implementation scheme
7 Provision of check and audit procedures

In the context of this chapter, problem search is considered to be the explicit definition of the existing state of affairs—where we are now and/or what is now wrong in the organization. Oftentimes the problems will present themselves rather vividly. The security problem at the Greco-Roman Chair Company (Chapter 1) is one such example. The possible theft of plans had to be checked out and if verified, had to be stopped. In this case, there were no ifs, ands, or buts about the problem or its sources.

Problem search and formulation

In other instances, however, problems (or the real definition of the existing state of affairs) are more illusive or more difficult to recognize and define. Suppose, for example, that a company is experiencing decreasing sales in one of its product lines. Decreasing sales may not be the problem at all, but simply a symptom of the real problem. Investigation may reveal that sales are slumping because no product was available—even though customers were calling for it. In that case, the company may really have a production problem (scheduling does not result in sufficient manufacture of the product in question), an inventory problem, or a transportation problem, not a sales problem.

This type of problem location is similar to medical analysis. If a patient has a temperature of 102 degrees, that temperature is not the basic problem; rather, the problem is the ailment causing the fever. Even though a competent physician will prescribe methods to bring the fever down, he or she will still recognize that the disease must first be diagnosed.

In both cases, then, the problem is not what is staring the decision maker in the face. The real problem lies much deeper, and the decision maker must then search and be careful to precisely define the real problem.

This problem-formulation step is not simple, and an error in defining the problem can have disastrous consequences. The strategies selected will be useless if they are geared to the wrongly selected problem. Suppose that a company has a high absenteeism rate and that the problem is diagnosed as poor motivating or insufficient supervision. As a result, the manager in charge is replaced. But the real problem might be that all of the employees in the unit are short termers and do not look forward to any career with the company. Hence they simply are using up all of their allotted sick days plus a few additional days. The newly assigned manager probably would do little better than the replaced one. Possible ramifications resulting from a decision based on the original problem diagnosis may be a drop in a managerial morale—a particularly crucial factor with supervisory and middle management—and a possible breaking up of as productive a supervisory subordinate relationship as one could expect under the circumstances.

Another consideration of problem formulation is problem finding. Much of the management literature stresses problem solving and decision making. Very little encourages managers to seek out and find problems to solve. But it seems to us that one of the primary tasks of a manager—particularly one who wants to advance—is to "create" problems by finding risks, challenges, and opportunities. One of the easiest traps a manager can fall into is to ignore problems, not seek them out, or try to pretend that they don't exist. *Challenges and opportunities should be classified as problems.* And solving problems results in payoffs.

The manager who sits back and thinks that he or she is in good shape because no "problems" are apparent may not be running a smooth ship at all, but may simply be either neglecting the recognition of problems that do exist or not seeking them out. In essence, that "manager" may not be managing, but simply maintaining a custodial role.

Information gathering and evaluation   Once a problem has been formulated in precise terms, all information pertaining to the problem or to its possible solution must be gathered. At times, the gathering of information will lead to a reformulation of the problem, as the new information may indicate that initial perceptions or diagnoses of the problem were in error. For example, suppose that the initial diagnosis in our low-sales example cited earlier was that the inventory-control process was at fault. But further information gathering reveals that salespeople are not submitting their orders immediately upon signing them, but are holding them to submit them in batches in order to even their commission payments. The real problem, then, may be the sales representatives' commission schedules or indeed even the sales-reporting procedures rather than the inventory-control process.

In a department store operation, a central buyer was once confronted with a zero-inventory count every month from one particular store on one particular item. The store had no special characteristics to justify such a sales record, but the buyer, assuming that the problem really was that he was sending insufficient amounts of the product to the store, progressively doubled and tripled the amounts sent to the particular store. Finally, after a few months of this astronomical sales-growth pattern, the buyer, anxious to determine how this particular store was selling so many units, called the manager. He was informed that the warehouse was full of the item and then asked, "Why the hell are you sending me so many?" The problem quickly shifted from meeting an abnormal demand to determining how the organizational procedures had allowed so many units to be tied up in one store. In this case investigation revealed that the stock clerk checking inventory never bothered to count the units in the warehouse. He was, incidentally, fired.

A major consideration in information gathering is determining when enough information has been gathered. This entails consideration of both cost and relative importance. In selecting a janitor, for example, the amount of information to be collected on any particular candidate would probably be minimal, except, of course, if the custody of valuable property were at stake. In selecting a corporate-level vice-president of finance, however, the reputation, efficiency, and operation of the firm are at stake, and the information-gathering process will probably be very extensive and quite costly. Oftentimes a manager will spend more time gathering information than the decision is worth in terms of payoff. In any case of information gathering, clear demarcations as to the types and amounts of information to be gathered should be delineated.

Most of the rational models of organizations (and those in economics as well) make the assumption that managers will seek *all* information available and will then develop *all* possible alternative courses of action.* Real-life managers, however, know the impossibility and implausibility of these pre-

---

* This is the assumption of rationality we alluded to in Chapter 5. Most management theorists no longer use the notion of total rationality.

scriptions. Most *satisfice,* in both information gathering and making alternative choices; that is, they choose "good enough" solutions or seek "just enough" information.*

Sources of information   Managers making decisions will search all kinds of sources for information. They will find much of the needed data in their own units, but they might commission staff studies, do research themselves, or seek information from other line managers. For example, suppose that a plant manager is trying to schedule vacations for the work crews. The problem will be to determine if and when the company can tolerate either no production or a slower-than-normal production rate from the unit. The plant manager's information must include input from sales departments at the very least and perhaps from the purchasing department as well.

Or, suppose that a department chairperson at your university is scheduling classes for the following semester and has a problem deciding how many sections to schedule of a particular course necessary for graduating seniors who are, however, majoring in another department. The chairperson, as part of the information-gathering process, would try to contact the chairperson of the second department to get information on the number of graduating seniors who would need the course. This would be one information input to the decision process; faculty availability and capability would be two other types of information.

The manager, however, will have to learn what sources of information can be trusted as reliable purveyors of information. Material gained from other units, for example, may be biased in favor of those units. Few managers will voluntarily offer information that casts a bad light on their units. At other times information may be gained from sources who are either extreme optimists or extreme pessimists. Some individuals tend to look only to the bright side of things; others are always seeing dark clouds on the horizon.

Managers must also avoid the "halo" effect when evaluating information received. For example, a manager who in the past received accurate forecasts from the market research unit may be likely to trust without question the forecasts of that unit at any time, even to the point of questioning his or her own decision-making process first if the whole program fails because of poor information.

Later in this book we shall cover the entire area of communication. Even though we shall explore that subject under the section generally covering implementation of decisions, the communications problems cited here and there are equally applicable to the information-seeking manager in a decision-making situation.

---

* Herbert A. Simon, *Administrative Behavior,* 2d ed. (New York: Macmillan, 1957), pp. xxiv, 40–41.

"There is more than one way to skin a cat" is a familiar adage about decision making. But for a manager, although there may be many possible ways of solving a problem, many of those ways may be fraught with dangers, and only one might have the fewest number of adverse effects. The manager who is making decisions will usually try to trace out a scenario that might result from each possible alternative, measuring the possible ramifications and the possible pitfalls and impacts of each of the available alternatives.

Development of alternatives

For example, let us return to the beleaguered restaurant manager cited in the vignette at the beginning of this chapter. What alternatives would this manager have had in his confrontation with the students? The manager might have done one of the following:

1 Call the police and request protection for the establishment and its clientele

2 Lower the flag to half mast in deference to the students' demands

3 Reason with the students, hoping to convince them of the rationale for the corporate policy and the possible predicament in which he, the manager, was finding himself placed

4 Reason with the chairman of the board, hoping to convince him of the dangers in the student confrontation and the possibility of physical damage to the establishment

5 Refuse, without any consultation with corporate headquarters, to lower the flag and call the students' bluff

The first alternative would obviously be loaded with problems. Police were not well regarded at that time, violence could have erupted, the future sales of the establishment definitely would have been affected, the police could not patrol the restaurant forever, and so on.

If the manager concurred with the students' demands and lowered the flag to half mast, he might have momentarily placated the students, but he would have incurred the wrath of the board chairman for violating company policy and perhaps even been fired. More than likely, the manager would have been ordered to rehoist the flag, at which time the confrontation would have intensified once again. And even if nothing happened this time, his future relationships with both the students (to whom he has now caved in) and the board chairman (whose policy he has violated) would be unpredictable.

If the manager refused to lower the flag, he would have maintained the integrity of the company's policy, but perhaps at the expense of one of its restaurants.

If he tried to reason with the students, several possible results or ramifications might have occurred. He might have convinced them to leave (probably unlikely), might have further enflamed them, or might have delayed them until he could receive further direction from corporate headquarters.

If he attempted to reason with the board chairman, he might have won him over to a compromise (probably unlikely), talked himself into being fired, or further solidified the corporation's opposition to the students' demands.

Thus for each of the projected alternatives, the manager must trace out a "if I follow this alternative, what will follow, and then what would be the consequence" type of scenario. The *manager's* objective is to solve the problem with the minimum cost and the maximum benefit to the organization (we shall leave the manager's own values to a later section). In this particular case, that meant protecting the restaurant and moving the protesting students off the premises with minimum damage to property and reputation.

In most cases the manager who traces out the ramifications and possible outcomes of each alternative will reach one that will accomplish the objective with the minimum of cost and effort. In other cases, however, the exercise of tracing alternatives might recycle the manager back to a reformulation of the problem or a reexamination of the existing state.

For example, in the case cited in the vignette, the president of the corporation realized that the source of the real problem was not the students or the intransigence of the chairman or even the moral issue of the Vietnam War. *Rather, it was the existence of the flagpole itself.* The corporate president solved the problem by eliminating its source. He simply ordered a truck to "accidentally" knock the pole over, thus eliminating the source and the problem.

But it takes some skill to recycle back to the problem definition. Many managers, in a case such as McDonald's, probably would have formulated the various alternatives based on the original problem (student demands), and probably few would have come up with a satisfactory set of alternatives. The McDonald's president backtracked, reformulated the problem, and solved it by eliminating the problem source.

Here again, we must reiterate the importance of problem formulation. A "correct" formulation in this case might have saved one harried manager much grief.

Constraints on the formulation of alternatives In most managerial situations there are always alternatives which, although plausible, are not possible. We have already seen how goals and policy constrain decisions, but there are other constraints as well. In essence, the manager is "prevented" from considering every possible alternative.

Law, customs, mores, norms, values, public policy, and similar factors are the constraints operative here. For example, a very feasible way of eliminating a competitive threat would be to commission an arsonist to burn the competitor's plant. This is a plausible alternative, but not a possible one for a professional manager of a legitimate organization. Similarly, public managers are constrained by budgets and conflict-of-interest laws. A commissioner may find that his or her brother is indeed the most qualified to fill the second highest-paying job at the commission, but the law, if not public opinion, will constrain the commissioner from making that appointment.

Organizations are said to "learn" standard routines for handling decisions, and even if they do not learn, they have available to them formulas for determining optimum choices.* Often a problem will recur, and the organization will "remember" that some time in the past, the problem was "satisfactorily" resolved. If conditions are similar, it may be more economical for the manager simply to reach back into the organizational memory, apply the previous solution, and move on to new issues. It might not matter that the organization is not maximizing or that the solution is possibly not optimum. The solution works, it is quickly decided on, and it is "good enough." Some authors say that organizations seek to avoid uncertainty by applying such standard decision rules to problems. At least the managers know how the situation turned out in the past, and the only risk they would be running is that it turn out differently this time. But this risk might be less than trying a new, untried action. Of course, as the organization resorts to memory over and over on the same problem, the solution might eventually become policy or standard operating procedure—that is, an automatic rule to be applied in all cases.

Application of decision rules

Often, formulas are available to assist the manager in making decisions. Although a flip of the coin is not always recommended, it is used at times. But here we are concerned mostly with quantitative techniques available to assist the manager in both formulating and evaluating alternatives. Although the necessary level of sophistication for quantitative tools can be quite high, many involve rather simple formulations. In Chapter 7 we shall cover some quantitative decision techniques. Here we will only say that many times these formulas become decision-making rules for the organization to follow.

Some of the quantitative techniques described in the next chapter will almost automatically "select" the correct alternative. But for other decisions the selection process is not so automatic. As mentioned earlier, the alternative selected should solve the problem with the fewest dysfunctional ramifications (or the minimum costs and maximum benefits). With problems to which quantitative formulas cannot be applied, this is quite difficult. Many a manager has used up reams of paper trying to select a correct course of

Selection of alternatives

* Richard M. Cyert and James G. March, *A Behavioral Theory of the Firm* (Englewood Cliffs, N.J.: Prentice-Hall, 1963).

action and justify it. But if one keeps in mind the criteria of efficiency and effectiveness, the process eases—somewhat.

Here we should mention that despite admonition to the contrary, *personal values* might have some strong impact on the decision, particularly on those issues on which value judgments are necessary or when formulas will not yield definitive solutions. Thus religion, nationality, moral and ethical imperatives, propensity for risk taking, concepts of loyalty, personal needs as opposed to organizational demands, and other such factors may all temper the outcome of the decision process.*

There is nothing inherently unnatural or evil about this intrusion of personal values; indeed, it probably would be unnatural if personal values did not intrude. Although the rational model of organization predicts and prescribes that values be left outside the framework of organizational decision making, many an organization is guided not by officially promulgated organization values, but by the personal whims, values, and desires of its important decision makers.

However, the manager must be alert to his or her own values' intruding into the decision process so greatly as to cause harm to the organization or to allow the organization to miss good opportunities for growth and progress. Even more important, the manager should be alert to subordinates' making decisions overladen with personal values.

Provision for implementation

Even though an alternative has been selected as optimum, the process is still incomplete. Someone must be assigned the responsibility for implementing it, perhaps some resources must be secured, and perhaps some change in organization must be made. One might look on this activity in itself as a decision situation (or a subset of a decision situation), and indeed it is. Perhaps it is not on a level with the major decisions of which it is a part, but the activity entails decisions nevertheless.

Provision for audit and control

As mentioned earlier, generally a decision puts into effect some activity geared to moving from an existing state to a desired state. Obviously, some standards must be established to ensure that the contemplated activity does indeed reach the desired state, and some checkpoints must be established to monitor the activity. The manager who is making a decision will therefore decide when and how (and possibly who) to check the decision. Again, the degree of importance attached to this step relates directly to the degree of importance of the decision. One would not care too much for the expenditure of thirty cents for a pad of writing paper, but might be very much concerned

* See R. J. Monsen, B. O. Saxberg, and R. A. Sutermeister, *"The Modern Manager:* What Makes Him RUN?" in Arthur Elkins and Dennis W. Callaghan, *A Managerial Odyssey: Problems in Business and Its Environment* (Reading, Mass.: Addison-Wesley, 1978), pp. 48–62.

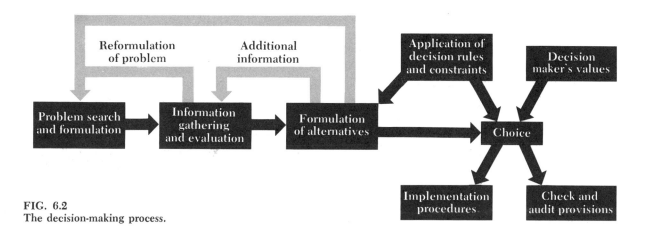

FIG. 6.2
The decision-making process.

with the contemplated outcome of the expenditure of $30,000 for sales-promotion brochures.

Most decisions follow some pattern using the steps traced here. For some decisions—going to the movies or buying the pad of paper, for example—some steps of the process may be engaged in only fleetingly. For other decision situations, each step may be a ponderous and laborious undertaking.

Summary of the decision-making process

In summary, then, the decision process is rather elaborate, with each step being the possible prelude to feedback or recycling to a redefinition of some previous step or steps. Figure 6.2 illustrates this process of feedback, along with the entire decision-making process as outlined in this chapter.

TIMING IN DECISION MAKING

Earlier, we wrote about several kinds of decisions. Let us now establish a dichotomy of decisions in terms of two examples. On one end of the continuum is the decision to go to a movie; on the other end, the decision to locate a new plant. Are there differences between these two types of decisions? Obviously, there are. You might be tempted to pronounce the movie example as frivolous. But close examination of both decision situations would reveal that the same process is engaged in for the solution of both problems; only the plant-location decision, being more important and costly, will absorb much more time and mental energy than the movie decision. *Hence the time allocated to the various steps of the decision process will be directly related to the importance (and cost) of the issue under consideration.*

Timing is important in decision making in two other ways also. First, the time in which the entire *decision process* must be completed is often critical.

Often a manager is faced with the dictum: "Let me know your decision on that tomorrow." The reason behind that dictum is that deals may be lost if the manager cannot come up with a decision quickly enough. The purchase of a building may be the result of competing bids due on the same day. If an executive doesn't enter the company's bid on time, the company loses the building. An auction forces quick decision timing. One must bid quickly or lose the item. Of course, the decision maker then has to be sure that an error forced by demanded timing will not be overly costly.

Second, the time when the *decision implementation* must be completed is crucial also, particularly if the phase under consideration is but one in a series or part of a plan. Thus in purchasing paint, for example, the manager must decide not only that 1500 gallons of Jones Paint will be purchased to paint the company's product, but also when that paint is to arrive at the plant. If the paint arrives a year later than the product is produced, it does the company little good to have decided that Jones Paint was the best for its use in the first place.

GROUP PROCESSES IN DECISION MAKING

Decisions are often made by groups, or part of the decision process is carried out through the use of groups. Group decision making generally utilizes the same process as that of individual decision making, but the group adds the dimension of bringing together additional sources of information and various insights into problem definition.

But groups are composed of diverse individuals with diverse values, propensities to risk and uncertainty, and outlooks on optimism. Groups often tend to reach decisions by consensus, compromise, or even majority vote. The resulting decisions of these finalizing mechanisms for decision making depend not only on the agreement of the participants on ends to be pursued or means to reach those ends, but also on the sum of the differences in values and perspectives among group members. Thus although the advantage of groups is the bringing to bear of multiple points of view and all possible sources of information, there is also the inherent possible disadvantages that a really optimum decision from the point of view of the organization—in terms of risk, quality, timeliness—will be watered down in the group's approach to decision making.

Since much contemporary decision making requires the input of information from multiple sources (due to organizational complexity, technology, and information specialization), some managements substitute the group process for the individual process *simply and only to expedite the information-gathering step of decision making*. The selection of alternatives may still reside with one manager or executive, but the group will be available to process information. Other managements use the group to not only process information, but also stimulate thinking on new, alternative solutions. Often called collective genius, but also going under other names (Synectics, for-example), the process is designed to stimulate original and sometimes bizarre alternatives and to allow one participant to hitchhike on another's ideas.*

Group processes, however, also run the risk of having the group dominated by either higher-level executives—if the formal authority structure permeates the group—or by the more talkative and forceful members of the group. Either way, the purposes for which the group was brought together—free flow of ideas and stimulating thought—may be defeated if the group members are inhibited from making their contributions, not to mention the time of expensive executives that may be lost.

Delphi techniques

To overcome the problems involved in face-to-face meetings, yet still obtain the value of group input, a technique developed by the RAND corporation is quite useful. This technique is called Delphi.† Under Delphi, executives do not meet as a group; rather, questionnaires soliciting opinions on issues are submitted to them. After they respond, a coordinator prepares a composite of the group members' views, and the participants are asked to resubmit opinions. Eventually, after several rounds of reevaluation, a consensus of opinion *may* develop. This consensus will, of course, not suffer from the inadequacies of face-to-face pressures, since without group meetings, no participant knows either the position or title of anyone else associated with particular viewpoints.

The Delphi technique, however, suffers from being extremely time-consuming, and thus it is most useful when time for decision making is not a crucial factor. These situations are usually confined to those such as long-range forecasting and futuristic prediction.

Group decision making is more expensive in terms of the time tied up, and as pointed out, there is no guarantee that "better" decisions will be made. Therefore, executives contemplating using groups should consider whether the added input of many minds will be worth the cost and whether the resultant decision output will be enhanced.

On the other hand, groups are often employed when the consideration is *acceptance* of the decision even more than the development of the decisions. When people have had a hand in the development of the decision, they may be more likely to accept it and to enthusiastically implement it than if the

* William J. J. Gordon, *Synectics: The Development of Creative Capacity* (New York: Harper & Row, 1961).
† A. R. Fusfeld and R. N. Foster, "The Delphi Technique: Survey and Comment," *Business Horizons* **14** (June 1971): 63–74.

decision is imposed on them from a single executive. Thus the group process may have benefits beyond information provision and the development of alternatives. This is particularly likely when the decision involves professionals whose status is an important factor in decision implementation.

SUMMARY AND CONCLUSION

Our primary coverage in this chapter was of the decision-making process. That process includes the following steps: problem search and formulation, information gathering and evaluation, formulation of alternative courses of action, application of decision rules and decision tools, choice of desired alternative, choice of implementation scheme, and provision of check and audit procedures. We also explored timing in relation to decisions and group processes in decision making.

Many commentators have pronounced decision making as the most important managerial activity; indeed, some have said that managing *is* decision making. Although we shall not go that far, we do view systematic decision making as an important process for prospective and practicing managers to learn and master.

There are many tools which managers may use when making decisions. In Chapter 7 we sample some of the quantitative tools for decision making.

DISCUSSION QUESTIONS

1 List the steps involved in the mental decision process used for most managerial and personal decisions.

2 Describe the "problem search and formulation" step in the decision process. Describe the rest of the steps in the management-decision process.

3 What are some of the constraints on the formulation of alternatives?

4 Some factors that constrain the alternative-formulation step in the decision-making process are: laws, customs, mores, norms, values, and public policy. How does each of these constraints affect the formulation of alternatives?

5 What differentiates the steps and processes associated with a decision to attend a movie from those associated with a decision to build a power plant? What role does time play in the decision process?

6 How does group decision making differ from individual decision making? What are some of the benefits of participative decision making? Disadvantages?

7 Describe the Delphi technique as used in decision making.

8 Define the following terms:

a) decision making   b) policy

c) decision centers   d) decision process

e) problem   f) decision rules

g) Delphi technique

CASE: FILTCO, BELGIUM*

■ In July 1972 John Hartley, President of Filtco Corporation, headquartered in New York City, was contemplating whether to allow the Managing Director of Filtco, Belgium, to assume control of the sales and marketing functions of the Belgian operation.

Background of William Patterson

In 1961 William Patterson, Export Manager of Filtco Corporation, had developed a $2,000,000 export business. Export sales included various types of precisely engineered filter products used in industrial plants and in products they produced. Ninety percent of Filtco export sales were made to companies in Germany, France, Switzerland, Italy, the Netherlands, Belgium, and the Scandinavian countries. Primary growth had been in the European Common Market countries. Overseas sales of Filtco products were handled by Patterson, a salesperson in Brussels, and agents in Italy, Germany, Sweden, and Switzerland. Since the number of customers was relatively small, this sales staff could manage the job satisfactorily. Shipments of products were made from three American manufacturing plants.

Patterson had started his career with Filtco in 1945, after serving five years in the United States Army. He had gone to college for two years prior to entering the service, but he decided not to continue his formal education after leaving the Army. He joined Filtco as a sales trainee and rapidly gained a reputation as an outstanding salesperson. When Filtco decided to enter the export market in 1955, Patterson was chosen because of his superior sales skill, his thorough study of sales prospects, and his sensitivity to customer needs and personalities. In addition, he was a bachelor. Since his export sales job required considerable travel (often fifty percent of his time outside the United States), this was a critical factor in the decision to select him. (Patterson could not speak or write any foreign language.)

---

* Case prepared by Thomas M. McAuley. From Arthur Elkins and Dennis W. Callaghan, *A Managerial Odyssey: Problems in Business and Its Environment* (Reading, Mass.: Addison-Wesley, 1975), pp. 393–399. All rights reserved.

Planning the future

In 1961 Patterson, Hartley, and Robert Bailey (Manufacturing Vice-President) met to review the objectives of the corporation, with special emphasis on what the strategy should be concerning its export business. In this review consideration was given to long-range domestic plans, opportunities in the United States and abroad, threats to the domestic and foreign business, and a long, hard look at the future. The products made by Filtco were growing in domestic sales at the rate of twelve percent annually, and export sales growth exceeded twenty percent. Hartley and Bailey knew that additional plant and equipment would be required to achieve long-range sales forecasts. Patterson believed strongly that a European manufacturing operation would be necessary to accommodate the future health of Filtco's export market, which he had so carefully developed.

Filtco Corporation had accumulated an excellent patent estate on its processes and products, and patents had been either issued or applied for in all the countries to which the company exported products. In spite of this, Hartley was reluctant to establish a foreign operation that in any way would jeopardize the know-how which had been achieved. In two instances foreign-born technical employees had left the company and had allegedly divulged certain critical technical information regarding its manufacturing operations. This had caused embarrassing problems, though it had not hurt Filtco's business. Patterson agreed that this could be a problem, but he strongly believed that either a foreign manufacturing facility must be built or the export business would decline rapidly and eventually cease.

Patterson pointed out several compelling factors favoring a foreign operation:

1 Boat shipments to Europe took up to three months in some cases. Furthermore, the incidence of dock strikes had caused late deliveries at an increasing rate.
2 Problems in quality or the use of Filtco products on its customers' machines were becoming more difficult to solve. Salespeople and agents were not equipped to handle technical problems adequately.
3 Freight costs and tariffs were becoming prohibitively high when consideration was given to competitive products available in foreign countries. Though American manufacturing costs were relatively low, freight and tariff costs amounted to over twenty percent of sales.
4 Because of the potential and real growth in the market for Filtco's products, several European companies were starting to make competitive products. At this time, they were not of good quality, but Patterson did not underrate the ability of these companies to develop improved products.

5 Raw materials represented over fifty percent of the cost of Filtco products, and these materials were available in Europe at costs lower than those in the United States.

6 The concept of the "Ugly American" was strong in Europe. Although Filtco had excellent relations with its customers, Patterson had been told several times by many of them that they would prefer their own domestic sources rather than American products. He further related that even with customers who appeared to understand English well, there was language confusion and often distrust.

This "side of the coin" was strong, but Hartley saw difficulties. There would be high investment to get an operation going, high training costs, language barriers, and lack of familiarity with the culture and laws of a foreign country. There would be difficulty in selecting a good manager. There were nascent, competitive technologies which might make Filtco's equipment obsolete. The narrow product base and the possibility that major customers would integrate backwards and make their own product bothered Hartley. He was also cognizant of the possibility of shrinking American demand, which might idle some of the company's domestic capacity. He wanted to make sure that all avenues were considered before a decision was reached.

Bailey's concern

Robert Bailey was a long-time Filtco employee, having spent more than twenty years working his way up in the manufacturing organization to his present job as Vice-President and Manager of Manufacturing. He recognized the problems he would face in starting a manufacturing operation in Europe. He had an adequate engineering staff, and machine builders had service personnel they could send to overseas locations to assist Filtco's people. Bailey was concerned about the language barrier and the difference in culture of any continental European country compared to the United States. He knew that he would be the one responsible for getting the operation started, and he was very uncertain as to how quickly foreigners could assimilate the complexity of company operations. He also felt that the three American plants were all that he could comfortably control.

The decision

Hartley reviewed the pros and cons and concluded that a site search should be undertaken. It was decided that a plant should be located as geographically central as possible to potential markets, that it would start as a small operation in a rented building, and that preferably it should be located in a small community. A further requirement was that a nearby site should be available on which to locate another company-owned plant should growth occur as anticipated. Hartley also concluded that the operation should be managed by a national and that no Americans should be in plant management after the initial engineering and installation work. The national manager would report to Bailey. Patterson would maintain supervision over sales and marketing.

Filtco, Belgium

A site was eventually selected in the quiet little town of Brusk, Belgium. The 40,000-square-foot building on the site would be adequate as a starting point. Hartley, Patterson, and Bailey had made several trips to Belgium. They talked at length with local government officials, bankers, and national officials, exploring the source of employees, local and national laws and practices, and the attitude of the Belgians regarding a foreign-based manufacturer entering their country. Hartley knew that Filtco could succeed in Brusk only if it contributed as much to the community as (or more than) the community contributed to the company. The decision to locate in Brusk was made quickly, however; there was a genuine feeling of mutual trust.

Jon Voder

Bailey's knowledge of Belgium and its languages was nil, and now he faced the responsibility of finding a manager for Filtco, Belgium. After many interviews (during which he happily discovered that many Belgians spoke English well), he selected a twenty-six-year-old engineering graduate, Jon Voder, who had some experience in a field related to Filtco products. Bailey immediately recognized that Voder was bright. His relative youth and limited industrial experience bothered Bailey somewhat, and Voder's stiff and formal demeanor disturbed him. Voder had excellent references, however, among which was high acclaim by the local mayor (who had considerable power and prestige in this little town). Bailey considered Voder the best prospect of any of those he interviewed.

Voder immediately got to work, and he assisted in negotiating a renewable three-year lease on the property which had been selected. He spent two months in the United States, familiarizing himself with Filtco equipment, processes, products, cost systems, work assignments, financial reports, quality control, etc. He became acquainted with company personnel, with whom he and his staff would later have contacts. He became "the manager" immediately; it was his operation in Belgium even before anything was physically in existence. Bailey was often upset by Voder's self-confidence, his almost arrogant manner at times, and his reluctance to be informal. In a shirt-sleeve conference, Voder always wore a jacket. Bailey cringed at this.

Operations

Engineers were sent from the United States, and servicemen from American machinery builders assisted in the installation of equipment. Voder hired a few supervisors and workers who became familiar with operations through vestibule training and on-the-job experience in helping the machine erectors. Luckily, most of the people Voder hired could understand some English, certainly enough to grasp what was going on. The Americans did not understand the Belgian languages, and because of their limited time there, they made no attempt to learn. This disturbed Voder, but the other personnel did not appear to mind. Machinery and equipment were in place and ready to go less than a year after the decision was made to establish a plant in Belgium. The job had gone smoothly, although Bailey and Patterson continued to have difficulty in understanding Voder. Patterson commented to Bailey many times that he was glad that Voder was Bailey's responsibility and not his.

Startup problems were normal, no greater than those experienced in the United States. Voder established reliable sources of raw materials, selected excellent associates and workers, and dedicated himself to make Filtco, Belgium, an asset to the community. For all his rigidity, he was a good manager. He knew the Belgian people and what was acceptable and unacceptable in the community. Though he was highly ambitious, he knew that he must establish this little plant and make it successful. It was evident early that he wanted to manage the plant with as little interference as possible, and very often he eloquently expressed this point of view to Bailey and Patterson.

In 1963 it was decided to build a larger plant in Belgium. Voder's staff developed the plans and hired the contractors. A review of the plans by Hartley and Bailey revealed that Voder had planned a huge office for himself and a large hall "for me to give talks to employees." Voder defended his desire for these forcefully, much to the chagrin of Hartley and Bailey. He finally agreed to a sliding partition in the middle of his office to make half of it available as a conference room. "You Americans just do not understand us," was Voder's lament. Aside from the two "luxuries," the plans were accepted and a beautiful plant was built. Filtco, Belgium, continued to grow, and Voder continually pressured Hartley and Bailey for additional plant and equipment. Over the next several years production expanded tenfold.

Growth

Contributing significantly to the growth of the Filtco, Belgium, operation were the efforts of Patterson. He had built a sales force of ten people on the Continent, with his Brussels salesperson now being sales manager. He hired two Belgians as product managers, reporting directly to him. Though these two people were housed in the Filtco, Belgium, office building, Voder made sure that they were given the smallest offices and that they were not involved with his operations or invited to attend any of his meetings. Both of the product managers, as well as the sales manager, told Patterson that they would resign if they had to report to Voder. Patterson tried to get these people together, but Voder remained aloof. At the same time, however, Patterson recognized that Voder's people had done an outstanding job in assisting customers. Despite more competitive conditions in Europe and the necessity to lower prices, profitability of Filtco, Belgium, was excellent, having a higher rate than the American operation.

The manufacturing operation of Filtco, Belgium, was fully mature by 1972, and Bailey felt strongly that he no longer could add anything to the activity. He suggested to Hartley that Voder was capable and that it was no longer necessary for Bailey to be involved. Hartley agreed and made plans to have Voder report directly to him in the future.

When Hartley announced this to Voder in a late-morning meeting, Voder was dismayed, not because he was no longer reporting to Bailey, but because he had anticipated that Hartley was also going to give him responsibility for sales and marketing. "It is five minutes to twelve," said Voder toward the scheduled close of the meeting.

Hartley was very upset by the apparent arrogance of Voder's remark. Voder had the nerve to tell him that the time had arrived for him to come to the decision to consolidate the sales and marketing functions with manufacturing! Hartley was not aware that such a comment was considered perfectly acceptable in Belgium as a means of ensuring that a decision is made prior to the scheduled termination of a meeting. He simply interpreted it as another evidence of Voder's rigidity.

Patterson was a sensitive man. He was still relatively young, only fifty-two. His entire career was in selling, and he had done an outstanding job. Where was his future? He felt very strongly that Filtco, Belgium, was his creation. He prided himself on the organization he had built in Europe. His subordinates were intensely loyal to him. Relationships with customers had never been better. His Brussels sales manager was extremely competent, and his marketing manager (previously one of the product managers) was doing a splendid job. Both of these people spoke French, German, and Dutch fluently and knew the cultures of every country in which Filtco, Belgium, sold products.

Hartley was also proud of Filtco, Belgium. He was thankful for his decision to initiate this operation. He was elated over the respect that the company had in the Brusk community and indeed in the country of Belgium. He had often smarted under Voder's demands, but could not deny that Voder had done a very fine job. Perhaps he did not really understand the Europeans. ■

Case questions

1. Referring to the decision model in the text, state the problem in the Filtco case.

2. Develop a set of alternative solutions to present to Mr. Hartley, and evaluate the costs and ramifications of each. Which would you choose?

3. Are there any special circumstances—e.g., Voder, Europe, international business practices—that might temper your selection of an alternative? Explain.

SELECTED READINGS

Alexis, M., and C. S. Wilson, *Organizational Decision Making* (Englewood Cliffs, N.J.: Prentice-Hall, 1967).

Bross, I. D. J., *Design for Decision* (New York: Macmillan, 1953).

Buffa, E. S., *Modern Production Management* (New York: Wiley, 1965).

———, "Aggregate Planning for Production," *Business Horizons* **10** (Fall 1967): 87–97.

Buzzell, R., B. Gale, and R. Sultan, "Market Share—A Key to Profitability," *Harvard Business Review* **53** (January/February 1975): 97–106.

Carnarius, S., *Management Problems and Solutions* (Reading, Mass.: Addison-Wesley, 1976).

Churchman, C. W., *Prediction and Optimal Decisions* (Englewood Cliffs, N.J.: Prentice-Hall, 1961).

Dent, J. K., "Organizational Correlates of the Goals of Business Management," *Personnel Psychology* **12** (August 1959): 365–393.

Dror, Y., "Policy Sciences: Some Global Perspectives," *Policy Sciences* **5** (March 1974): 83–87.

Ford, C. N., "Time to Redesign the Decision-Making Process," *Management Review* **67**, 7 (July 1978): 50–53.

Gorman, R. H., and H. K. Baker, "Brainstorming Your Way to Problem-Solving Ideas," *Personnel Journal* **57**, 8 (August 1978): 438ff.

Goshen, C. E., *The Management of Decisions and the Decisions of Management* (New York: Vantage Press, 1975).

Groser, C. W., and R. T. Peterson, *Business Forecasting* (Boston: Houghton Mifflin, 1976).

Hughes, C. L., *Goal Setting: Key to Individual and Organizational Effectiveness* (New York: American Management Association, 1965).

Kassouf, S., *Normative Decision Making* (Englewood Cliffs: Prentice-Hall, 1970).

Koontz, Harold, "Making Strategic Planning Work," *Business Horizons* **19** (April 1976): 37–47.

Kristy, J. E. "Managing Risk and Uncertainty," *Management Review* **67**, 9 (September 1978): 15–22.

Kurfman, D. G., ed., *Developing Decision-Making Skills* (Arlington, Va.: National Council for the Social Studies, 1977).

McClean, E. R., and J. V. Soden, *Strategic Planning for MIS* (New York: Wiley, 1977).

Malley, D., "Lawrence Klein and His Forecasting Machine," *Fortune* (March 1975): 152–157.

Miller, E. C., *Objectives and Standards of Performance in Marketing Management*, AMA Research Study 85 (New York: American Management Association, 1967).

Mintzberg, H., D. Raisinghani, and A. Theorel, "The Structure of 'Unstructured' Decision Processes," *Administrative Science Quarterly* **21** (June 1976): 246–275.

Mueller, R. K., *New Directions for Directors* (Lexington, Mass.: D. C. Heath, 1978).

Oxenfeldt, A. R., "Effective Decision Making for the Business Executive," *Management Review* **67**, 2 (February 1978): 25ff.

Prince, T. R., *Information Systems for Management Planning and Control* (Homewood, Ill.: Richard D. Irwin, 1966).

Ramsgand, W. C., *Making Systems Work: The Psychology of Business Systems* (New York: Wiley, 1977).

Sherwood, J. J., and F. M. Hoylman, "Individual versus Group Approaches to Decision Making," *Supervisory Management* **23**, 4 (April 1978): 2–9.

Simon, H. A., *The New Science of Management Decisions,* 3rd ed. (Englewood Cliffs, N.J.: Prentice-Hall, 1977).

———, *Models of Man* (New York: Wiley, 1957).

Smith, Thomas B., "The Policy Implementation Process," *Policy Sciences* (Spring 1970): 83–87.

Vancil, R. F., and P. Lorange, "Strategic Planning in Diversified Companies," *Harvard Business Review* **53** (January/February 1975): 81–90.

Vickers, G., "Values, Norms and Policies," *Policy Sciences* **4** (March 1973): 103–111.

Von Bergen, C., Jr., and R. J. Kirk, "Groupthink: When Too Many Heads Spoil the Decision," *Management Review* **67**, 3 (March 1978): 44–49.

Vroom, V. H., "A New Look at Managerial Decision Making," *Organizational Dynamics* (Spring 1973): 66–88.

Chapter 7
QUANTITATIVE TOOLS FOR DECISION MAKING

CHAPTER HIGHLIGHTS

This chapter introduces some of the quantitative aids and tools available to the decision maker. We classify these decision-making tools under the condition categories of certainty, risk, and uncertainty. You will be exposed to break-even analysis, inventory-control models, linear programming, and decision matrices, among other techniques.

LEARNING OBJECTIVES

1 To learn the distinctions among certainty, risk, and uncertainty.

2 To master the concept of break-even analysis.

3 To learn the basics of inventory control.

4 To learn the basics of graphic linear programming, the technique for allocating limited resources over multiple uses.

5 To learn techniques of decision making under risky conditions.

6 To learn techniques of decision making under uncertain conditions.

7 To understand the following: principle of insufficient reason, maximin, maximax, weighted optimism, and minimax regret.

8 To be able to define and know how to use subjective probability.

9 To learn the algebraic solution to linear programming.

CASE: SALLY TURNER

■ Sally Turner is the market forecaster for a company manufacturing aluminum snow shovels, among other products. Once a year, Turner is assigned a project involving a prediction of the number of snow shovels that the company might sell during the coming winter season. This information is then transferred to the various sales, production, and purchasing units so that planning for the year's output of shovels can begin. The importance of her prediction is evident to all of the company's officers; based on her analysis, the company could hit the season correctly, be vastly overstocked, or underproduce.

Sally knows a great deal about the company's prospects. She knows the number of households in the market area, has hard information on the sales of various dealers, and also knows that snow shovels have an average life of four years of steady, hard use. But she also knows that snow shovel sales have a strong relationship to the severity of the weather. A winter with over eighty inches of accumulated snowfall could easily translate into sales of over 3.5 million units, whereas one with twenty to forty inches of snow would likely result in sales of only 1.5 million shovels. Snowfalls in the range of fifty to seventy inches would probably result in sales of 2.5 million shovels. The key to the recommendations, then, and to the subsequent production decisions is the weather. And on that, Sally has no hard data on what to expect—only her best guesses. ■

INTRODUCTION

Sally Turner is a decision maker of sorts upon whose shoulders rests a great responsibility in terms of a profitable operation for her company. The entire success or failure of the year's production of snow shovels and the entire planning effort of the company are predicated on her projection. Some would say that Turner's recommendation is but a guess, because her opinion of the severity of the next winter would be but a guess. But as we shall discover, some tools are available that might assist her to "guess" with a higher degree of reliability than she might attain through mere guessing.

In this chapter we cover some decision tools—quantitative techniques—that assist the manager in decision making. These tools are not guaranteed to be foolproof; nor are they substitutes for poor performance in the gathering of data. Inaccurate data and faulty collection will inevitably result in poor decisions (unless one is lucky and the conditions change favorably). No powerful or esoteric techniques will overcome the effects of GIGO.

We group these decision techniques in three general categories of decision conditions—certainty, risk, and uncertainty. Under conditions of certainty, the various possible values of all of the variables and outcomes or of the variables interacting are known, and each is attainable or controllable; the decision maker simply has to arrange operations in their most efficient configuration according to the objectives sought. Under conditions of risk, the decision maker may be aware of the values of all of the variables and/or possible outcomes. However, the likelihood of an event's occurring may be neither under the control of the decision maker nor certain to occur. But the decision maker has available the *objective* probabilities of each value or outcome's occurring and can make decisions based on probable occurrence. For example, if we flip a penny, we don't know whether a head or a tail will fall, but we do know that there is a probability of .50 that a head will fall. With uncertain decisions, the decision maker also knows the possible outcomes, but can assign neither definite certainty nor objective probabilities to their occurring. In decision situations under risk and uncertainty, the decision techniques are often quite similar, but the objectivity or subjectivity of the data may result in different decisions.

DECISION MAKING UNDER CERTAINTY

Decision making under conditions of certainty—with all variables known and all values of those variables known, certain, and controllable—is a luxury. Few managerial decision situations ever present themselves as completely certain. Indeed, since much of business decision making depends on the fickle variable of consumer demand, only in those situations in which demand is totally certain (such as when the customers are under contract or as in a regulated industry) will decisions under certainty ever present themselves as totally pure ones. But in other cases the situation facing the manager does approach the conditions assumed by many of the rational models in economic and organization theories. That is, the decision maker knows all of the data (in terms of values) that enter into a situation, the entire range of outcomes, and is capable of manipulating the variables and the projected outcomes to reach an optimum decision. Only uncontrollable or rare circumstances (acts of God, strikes, fires, etc.) will cause the decision maker to miss the mark.

The decision situations that we will cover under this category of certainty are break-even analysis, inventory control formulas, and linear programming. Although each of these tools can have high degrees of complexity and sophistication, we shall present only some simple models and then note the potential for introducing complexity.

The question a decision maker often wants answered is: "How many units must the firm produce in order to cover all costs completely?" The real question is, of course: "When do we start turning a profit?" The tool that many managers use to determine these levels is called break-even analysis. Break-even analysis is a decision tool under certainty, because all of the variables and outcomes (and their values) that enter into the process are either certain or under the control of the manager.

In order to calculate a break-even point, the manager must have available several pieces of information. Generally, these are readily available or obtainable. The first piece of information is the level of fixed costs—those

Break-even analysis

costs that the firm incurs regardless of the level of output. Such costs include real estate taxes, insurance, some salaries, and some maintenance. In essence, these are the costs that the firm will have to bear even if it produced nothing at all. Conversely, however, these costs would not increase in total over those incurred at the zero-production level even if the firm produced at the output possible at maximum capacity. The total remains constant.

The manager must then know the variable costs per unit of output. Variable costs (VC) include the labor put directly into the product, materials and supplies consumed in making the product, utilities necessary, etc. In essence, variable costs are directly related to the production level of the firm and are incurred only if the firm produces. Total variable costs (TVC), then, are a function of production and can be expressed as

$$TVC = x(VC),$$

where x is the number of units produced.

Total costs (TC) for the firm are the sum of the fixed and the variable costs. For any level of production, the firm's total costs can be expressed as

$$TC = FC + x(VC),$$

where FC is fixed costs.

Finally, the manager must calculate the revenue the firm will gain from selling its product. This will, of course, vary with the level of output. The total revenue (TR) of the firm can thus be expressed as

$$TR = x(p),$$

where p is the price of the finished product.

The break-even point, then, is the level at which the total revenue of the firm is equal to the total costs that the firm incurs:

$$TR = TC$$

or

$$x(p) = FC + x(VC).$$

To determine the break-even point in units, we must solve for x:

$$x(p) - x(VC) = FC$$
$$x(p - VC) = FC$$
$$x = \frac{FC}{p - VC}.$$

To illustrate, assume that a firm has fixed costs of $20,000 and variable costs of $10 per unit of output. At a price of $30, what level of sales would constitute the break-even point? Applying the formula, we would obtain the solution as follows:

$$\frac{\$20,000}{\$30 - \$10} = 1000 \text{ units.}$$

Break-even analysis is often graphed. Figure 7.1 shows the previous problem in graphic form. The fixed-cost function is a horizontal straight line, indicating that it is a constant over all levels of production. The total-cost line increases with the level of production. Note that the total-cost line starts at the fixed-cost line, since it includes both fixed and variable costs (a total–*variable*-cost line would start at the zero origin point and parallel the total-cost line, but it is unnecessary to include it). The total-revenue line starts at zero, since the firm would receive no revenue if it did not sell any units of its product.

The break-even point is where the total-cost line intersects the total-revenue line. At any point prior to that intersection, the firm incurs a loss, but it generates a profit at any point beyond the intersection.

Break-even analysis essentially calculates the contribution toward the coverage of fixed costs achieved by each additional unit produced and sold. When fixed costs are totally covered, along with variable costs, the firm is at the break-even point. Note, however, that the loss is less in total as the firm approaches the break-even point. A question often asked by managers is whether it is more beneficial to produce at a loss or to close the plant. In this case, one can see the value of maintaining production in the short run. If the firm produces nothing, it will still pay the $20,000 in fixed costs. On the other hand, if the firm produces and sells 800 units, its total revenue

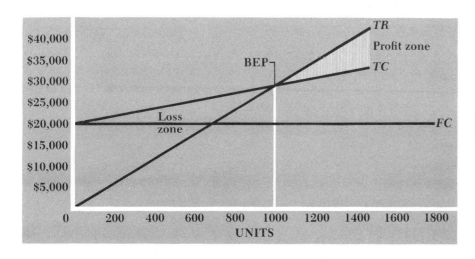

FIG. 7.1
Break-even analysis.

would be $24,000 against a total cost of $28,000 for a loss of only $4000. What has occurred is that the firm, by producing and selling 800 units, has made a $16,000 contribution toward covering the $20,000 fixed cost.

Producing "at a loss" is a viable strategy for the firm only in the short run. In the long run, all costs are variable and must be met totally in order for the firm to remain viable. So in break-even analysis, all of the relationships are viewed as static, short-run expressions. Producing in order to make a contribution toward fixed costs often is practiced in the clothing industry, however. Large buyers will often contract with a manufacturer to produce a large order for variable costs plus a small increment. The manufacturer, anxious to keep the plant operating or to dispose of an excess inventory and looking for a contribution to fixed costs, generally will be anxious to produce and sell. Hence, the "closeout" or overrun sales one often finds in retail stores.

A serious limitation of break-even analysis *as we have graphed it* (and also related to its short-run character) is the assumption that unit variable cost and price remain stable over the entire range of output. In fact, however, quantity discounts and lower prices for both inputs and outputs are quite common. So are higher prices on some inputs that will become in short supply as output expands—labor costs for skilled machinists, for example, might increase per unit as the local pool of skilled machinists is recruited and put to work. Indeed, it would probably be rare for a firm to face constant price and cost situations except over a very small range of capacity.

A variant of break-even analysis useful for profit planning—and one that overcomes the objections of linearity cited above—is the familiar set of total-cost and revenue curves of microeconomic theory. Here the objective is to determine not only break-even points, but also the point of maximum profits. The curves can be constructed to reflect the economies and diseconomies of scale the firm encounters (quantity discounts as well as extra costs caused by plant congestion, for example), as well as the more common negatively sloped demand curves.

Figure 7.2 illustrates the curves for total cost and revenue. It is, of course, at the point where the slopes of the total-revenue and total-cost curves are equal that profit is maximized. To the economist, this is the point where marginal cost is equal to marginal revenue—where the increment to total cost is equal to the increment in total revenue.

Note that short-run nonlinear total-cost and revenue curves will yield two break-even points—one at lower range of output, where the firm is just approaching the profit zone, and one where the firm is well into suffering diminishing returns. In regard to the second break-even point, the firm may produce beyond it for a short period of time and gain a contribution to fixed costs, but note that the loss will exceed fixed costs at a relatively small increment of production beyond the break-even point.

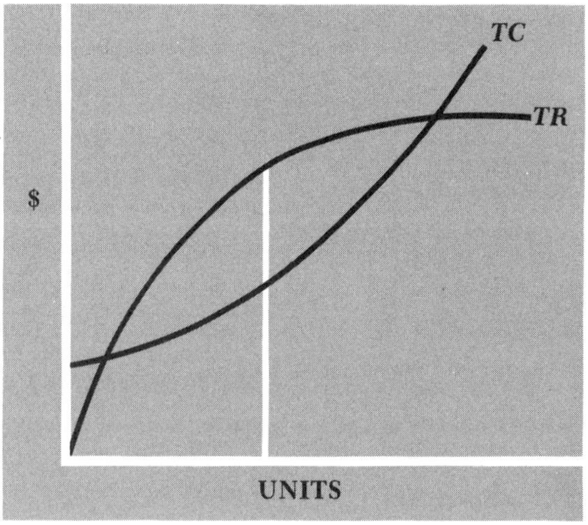

FIG. 7.2
Total-cost and total-revenue curves.

For a manager who knows the rate of usage of a component being stocked, the costs of placing orders for that component, and the costs of carrying an inventory of them, the controlling of inventory may become a relatively simple process with relatively certain results. Essentially, the decision is one that will minimize the costs associated with keeping an inventory flowing. The objective is to determine the costs that enter into an inventory situation and to minimize the combinations of costs.

Inventory control

The two key costs in the problem are *carrying costs* and *ordering costs.* Carrying costs relate to holding an inventory on hand, such as insurance, physical depreciation, spoilage, pilferage, and interest on the money invested in inventory. Obviously, the larger the amount of inventory held on hand, the higher these carrying costs will be.

Ordering costs are those clerical, freight, and other costs related to the placing and receiving of an order. As the size of the inventory carried decreases (to conserve carrying costs), the number of orders increases, and thus ordering costs (per period of time) increase. Conversely, as the inventory size increases (to reduce the number of orders and ordering costs), the total ordering costs decrease, and the carrying costs increase.

The efficient inventory-control process, then, minimizes the combination of the increasing costs (carrying) and the decreasing cost (ordering). The determination in that process will yield the optimum number of orders per period of time and the optimum size of each order. We can now develop a formula that will accomplish this in a very simple situation; we will comment on the modifiers of this simple model later.

If a manager can determine the annual usage of inventory (in dollars) and call that total Q, the average inventory can be calculated as:

$$\frac{Q}{2N},$$

where N is the number of orders placed in a year (or in the period of time under consideration). This formula is nothing more than a simple arithmetic average and accounts for the fact that inventories are high when an order first arrives and are reduced to practically nothing just before the next order is to arrive. The average, in effect, subtracts the low level from the high and divides by 2, yielding the midpoint inventory for the time in question.

If we let C denote carrying costs and F ordering costs, we can derive the formula by setting carrying costs equal to ordering costs:

$$NF = (C)\left(\frac{Q}{2N}\right).$$

Solving for N, we calculate as follows:

$$NF = \frac{CQ}{2N}$$

$$N^2F = \frac{CQ}{2}$$

$$N^2 = \frac{CQ}{2F}$$

$$N = \sqrt{\frac{CQ}{2F}}.$$

N, of course, yields the number of orders per period of time. Simply applying a formula Q/N will result in the total size of each order in dollars. Dividing that number by the cost per unit will then yield the order size in units.

As an example of the application of the formula just derived, let us assume that a firm uses $200,000 worth of an input per year. Each order costs the firm $100 for processing shipping and receiving, and the carrying costs of the inventory are estimated at ten percent of the inventory value. This can be expressed as

$$N = \sqrt{\frac{(.10)(200,000)}{2 \times 100}} = 10.$$

Thus the firm would place ten orders per year of $20,000 each. The application of this formula to the specific problem we just solved is illustrated graphically in Fig. 7.3.

Once the number of orders per period of time and the size of each of those orders have been determined, the manager who is armed with one additional piece of information—the lead time required to place an order or the time that elapses from when an order is placed to when it arrives at

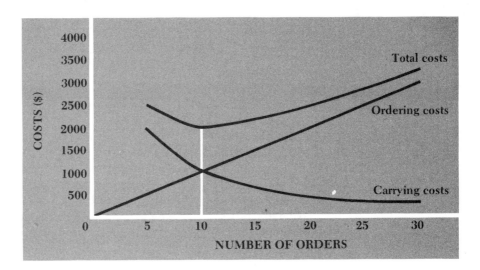

FIG. 7.3
Inventory costs.

the company's door—is then in a position to determine the ordering point in terms of inventory value. When the stock reaches that point, the order is placed, and the inventory is expected to reach the minimum level (generally not zero, since the firm would normally carry a reserve minimum inventory) just at the time that the new shipment arrives to replenish the depleted inventory. Figure 7.4 shows graphically how this ordering point is calculated. Of course, the entire success of this calculation rests on an ensured constant

FIG. 7.4
Derivation of
ordering point.

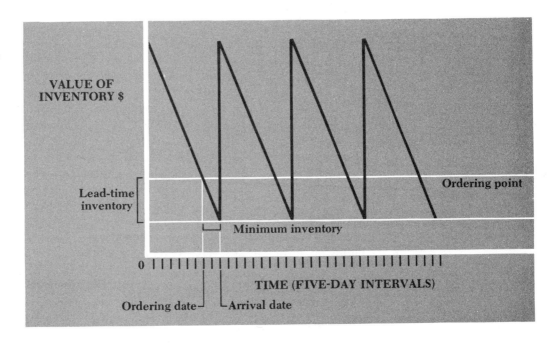

usage of the material at hand and a reasonably ensured delivery schedule, variables not always under the control of the manager using the material.

These inventory formulas are very simple ones and cannot, without some qualification, handle the complexities that might arise in inventory management. For example, sometimes batches cannot be ordered regularly; suppliers may be able to supply only at a constant flow or may be able to supply at only certain times of a year. The demand for the company's finished product might be unknown or at least may be more variable than we have assumed, and as we have mentioned, guarantees that deliveries will be made on time cannot always be taken for granted. But the basics are the same in all inventory-management problems. In every situation, the manager will face the problem of balancing inventory carrying costs and inventory ordering costs. A manager who is blessed with good information should be able to bring those costs within reasonable lines and close to a reasonable optimum balance.*

Linear programming   One of the more common management problems is the allocation of limited or finite resources among multiple uses in order to optimize or maximize output and profit. Most managers face capacity limitations in one or more resources—at least in the short run—and the multiproduct situation is probably more common than the single-product one.

The problem managers face in such situations is classified as one of certainty, since the values and limits of the variables are all known and certain to the decision maker. Only the configuration, or mix, of resources to reach optimality is unknown, and this can be determined and controlled.

Suppose, for example, that a firm produces two products—automobile bumpers and fence gratings. Each product yields a profit, but the bumpers yield less of a profit: $5 for each grating and $4 for each bumper. Each of the products requires the input of three materials, which we shall call input X, input Y, and input Z. Our problem, then, would be to determine the mix of bumpers and gratings that will maximize the joint profit. Linear programming is one method to assist the manager in making this decision.

To repeat, our manager knows all of the information except the outcome, and if conditions do not vary, the manager can be certain that the outcome projected will be achieved. One limitation in this problem is that all of the relationships are assumed to be linear; that is, the proportions of substitution of inputs among outputs are assumed to be constant throughout the entire range of outputs. This simplifying assumption may not always be valid in real-world situations, however.

* Most standard production-management texts carry expanded treatments of the inventory problem. For example, *see* Leonard J. Garret and Milton Silver, *Production Management Analysis*, 2d ed. (New York: Harcourt Brace Jovanovich, 1973), Chapter 15.

TABLE 7.1 Information matrix	Product	Amount of input X	Amount of input Y	Amount of input Z	Profit per unit
	Bumper	20 lb	10 lb	25 lb	$4
	Grating	20 lb	20 lb	10 lb	$5
	Capacity	1000 lb	800 lb	950 lb	

Aware of the limitations, however, we can condense the information for the bumper-grating problem as shown in Table 7.1. The first point to recognize is that the number of bumpers and the number of gratings produced must be zero or more. The firm cannot produce less than zero of each of the products, and this becomes, obviously, a constraint on the range of possible solutions. Thus the output of bumpers ≥ 0, and the output of gratings ≥ 0.

Next, we must establish our objective, which is, of course, to maximize the profit attainable from the mixture of bumpers and gratings. The profit function can thus be expressed as:

$$\text{Profit} = \$4B + \$5G,$$

where B denotes bumpers and G denotes gratings.

Then a manager must recognize that the limited resources set constraints on their use. Relationships must be established for each of the inputs to the products being produced. In this problem these relationships are:

$$20B + 20G \leq 1000 \text{ for input X,}$$
$$10B + 20G \leq 800 \;\; \text{for input Y,}$$
$$25B + 10G \leq 950 \;\; \text{for input Z.}$$

These inequalities recognize that 1000 pounds of input X must be distributed between the bumpers and gratings, with 20 pounds necessary for each bumper and 20 pounds for each grating. Similarly, 800 pounds of input Y must be distributed between the two products (only 10 pounds will be to each bumper and 20 pounds to each grating, however), and 950 pounds of input Z will be distributed between the two products. The inequalities also recognize that the use of the input between the two outputs cannot exceed the availability of the input. That is, for example, the production of bumpers and gratings can use only 1000 pounds *or less* of input X. These inequalities can be graphed as shown in Fig. 7.5.

Each of the lines on the graph represents one of the functions explained above. The vertical axis of the diagram represents production of gratings; the horizontal axis, production of bumpers. If the firm made only bumpers, it could produce a maximum of 50, given the available amount of input X (1000/20). Similarly, if the firm made only gratings, 50 would be the most produced with the available supply of input X (1000/20). So the line of

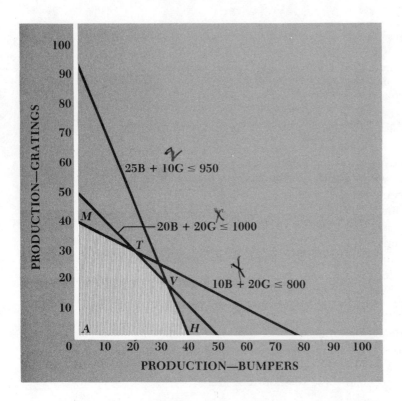

FIG. 7.5
Linear programming: Pro-
duction input/output com-
binations.

possible combinations of bumpers and gratings capable of being produced
with the given amount of input X is that which connects 50 bumpers on the
horizontal axis to 50 gratings on the vertical axis. Similar lines must be constructed for the other two inputs—Y and Z.

If the firm made only bumpers, it could produce a maximum of 80 with
the amount of input Y available (800/10). With the 800 pounds of Y, the
firm could also produce 40 gratings (800/20); hence the line of possible
combinations for input Y runs from 40 bumpers to 80 gratings. For input Z,
if the firm made no gratings, it could manufacture 38 bumpers (950/25).
Similarly, if it made no bumpers, it could produce 95 gratings (950/10).
Therefore, the line of possible combinations for input Z runs from a point of
38 bumpers to that of 95 gratings.

Now, a look at the diagram will indicate that there are only certain production combinations of the two products that will satisfy *all* of the constraints posed by the limited combined resources. That is, when we consider
the resources available together, there are only certain combinations of
bumpers and gratings that can be produced, given the available quantities
of inputs X, Y, and Z. These combinations are those enclosed in the space

bounded by the letters *AMTVH*. Once the firm moves out of the *feasibility space,* it cannot produce, since not enough of one or possibly two of the inputs would be available. For example, the firm cannot produce 50 gratings under any circumstances, since it has only enough of input Y to make only 40 of that product. Similarly, the firm could not produce a combination of 35 bumpers and 15 gratings, since not enough of input X would be available.

Now, let us bring back the profit function:

$$P = 4B + 5G,$$

and let us assume any level of profit, e.g., $100. A profit of $100 would result from producing 25 bumpers *or* 20 gratings:

$$100 = 4(25) + 5(0)$$

or

$$100 = 4(0) + 5(20) \text{ (with rounding)}.$$

If we assume a profit of $160, this can be generated by producing 40 bumpers or 32 gratings. A profit of $180 can be generated by either 45 bumpers or 36 gratings.

The profit function allows us to construct a series of *iso profit* lines on our graph. The one for a $100 profit would connect the point of 25 bumpers with that of 20 gratings. The iso profit line for $160 would connect the points for 40 bumpers on the horizontal axis with that of 32 gratings on the vertical axis (and so on for various assumed profit levels).

The maximum attainable profit for the firm (remember, that is the objective) *will always be at one of the corners of the feasibility space (AMTVH).* More specifically, it will be at the point where the iso profit line which is furthest from the origin is *tangent to a corner of the feasibility space.* One can, therefore, determine the point of maximum profit graphically. But one can also determine this point more quickly and with less trouble by applying some simple algebra.

Remember that the maximum profit will occur at one of the corners of the feasibility space: points *A, M, T, V,* or *H.* Profits at points *A, M,* and *H* are the most easily determined, and we shall consider those first.

1 At point *A,* no bumpers and no gratings are produced; hence the profit is 0.

2 At point *H,* only bumpers are being produced; hence the profit is $96:

$$\$152 = \$4(38) + \$5(0).$$

3 At point *M,* no bumpers are produced, but 40 gratings are manufactured; hence the profit is $200:

$$\$200 = \$4(0) + \$5(40).$$

Points *V* and *T* are only a bit more complicated to solve.

4 Point V involves the simultaneous solution of the two intersecting equations (see Fig. 7.5):

$$25B + 10G \leq 950$$
$$20B + 20G \leq 1000.$$

To solve these equations, multiply the first by 2 and subtract the second equation from the first:

$$50B + 20G \leq 1900$$
$$\underline{20B + 20G \leq 1000}$$
$$30B \qquad 900 \quad B = 30.$$

Substituting 30 in the basic inequalities yields:

$$20(30) + 20(G) \leq 1000$$
$$600 + 20(G) \leq 1000$$
$$20(G) \leq 400$$
$$G \leq 20.$$

Substituting the values for B and G in the profit equation gives us:

$$\$4(30) + \$5(20) = \text{Profit}$$
$$120 + 100 = \$220.$$

5 Point V involves solving simultaneously the intersecting equations:

$$20B + 20G \leq 1000$$
$$10B + 20G \leq 800.$$

Subtracting the second equation from the first yields:

$$10B \leq 200$$
$$B \leq 20.$$

Substituting the value for B back into the equation yields:

$$20(20) + 20(30) \leq 1000,$$

and substituting the values of B and G in the profit function yields:

$$\$4(20) + \$5(30) = \$230.$$

Now the profit has been identified at the five corner points of the feasibility space:

at point A, $P = \$0$
at point H, $P = \$152$
at point M, $P = \$200$
at point V, $P = \$220$
at point T, $P = \$230$.

The maximum profit occurs at point T, where the firm will produce 20 bumpers and 30 gratings. Any other combination of bumpers and gratings, given the available resources, will yield a lesser profit and will not fulfill the objective function.

Other linear programming methods are available, but our objective in this chapter is simply to demonstrate the possible uses of the tool. (We will cover an algebraic solution to the same problem in the appendix to this chapter.) A variant of linear programming, called the transportation method, is useful for solving problems involving multiple shipping points and multiple destinations.

But the lesson to be learned here is the use of linear programming and its limitations. The tool is designed to assist the decision maker in maximizing the profit resulting from the output of multiple products given finite levels of multiple inputs. With the aid of a computer, much more complicated types of problems involving more inputs and products than we illustrated here can be tackled. The limitations of the tool, however, are inherent in its name; all relationships are assumed to be linear. Substitutions of inputs among outputs are assumed to be attainable on a proportional basis over the entire range of output. These assumptions are not always applicable to real-world problems, necessitating the use of nonlinear methods.

DECISION MAKING UNDER RISK

Unlike a decision maker facing certain and controllable conditions, a decision maker facing a risky situation is not able to pinpoint precisely or control all conditions. The decision maker in risky situations faces an environment in which the event, outcome, or the values of at least one of the parameters are not known with precision. For example, in our opening vignette Sally Turner knew precisely all of the information she needed except whether the winter would be a long, arduous one or whether the area would have little snow. In risky situations, however, the occurrence of the event can be estimated using probabilities.

Probabilities allow decision makers to make judgments using data generated over a large series of events. Suppose that Turner had data from 150 past winters which showed that snowfalls of over 80 inches occurred 10 percent of the time, snowfalls of 50 to 70 inches occurred 50 percent of the time, and snowfalls of 20 to 50 inches occurred 40 percent of the time. Since she had a large number of winters from which the data were available (large numbers are the basis for the use of probabilities), she would then be able to assign probabilities to the various events—in this case, the possible snowfalls in a winter. The types of winters possible in this sort of problem are called *states of the world,* or *states of nature,* and the data from the past winters would give her the probability of each of the state's occurring:

20″–50″ snowfall	50″–70″ snowfall	80″ snowfall
.40	.50	.10

If Turner knows the costs and prices of the snowshovels (including the fixed costs, carrying costs, etc.) that her company produces and the various projected output levels, she can establish a *payoff matrix* (Table 7.2) combining the various production strategies with the various possible states of nature.

Production strategies	States of nature and probabilities of occurrence		
	20″–50″ .40	50″–70″ .50	>80″ .10
3.5 million units	$100,000	$ 500,000	$350,000
2.5 million units	$300,000	$1,250,000	$125,000
1.5 million units	$600,000	$ 500,000	$ 60,000

TABLE 7.3 [handwritten]
Payoff matrix— conditional payoffs *TOTAL EXP. VALUE* [handwritten]
950,000 [handwritten]
1,675,000 [handwritten]
1,160,000 [handwritten]

The data in Table 7.2 indicate the possible profit resulting from any of the strategies combining with any of the possible states of nature. For example, if the firm produces 3.5 million shovels and there is a moderate winter, the profit will be $1 million. If, however, the firm produces 1.5 million shovels and there is a severe winter, the profit will be only $600,000. The profit values in each of the cells of the matrix are called *conditional payoffs*.

But Sally Turner in this problem now knows the probabilities of each of the state's occurring. Applying the probability to the conditional values of each of the cells (multiplying) would yield the *expected value* of each cell (or each combination of strategy and state of the world) (Table 7.3).

Production strategies	States of nature		
	20″–50″	50″–70″	>80″
Produce 3.5 million units	$ 250,000	$1,000,000	$3,500,000
Produce 2.5 million units	$ 750,000	$2,500,000	$1,250,000
Produce 1.5 million units	$1,500,000	$1,000,000	$ 600,000

7.2 [handwritten]
TABLE 7.3
Expected values *TOTAL EXP VALU* [handwritten]

The decision maker facing these risks is interested in maximizing profits for the firm. The technique in this type of decision situation would be to select the strategy that would result in the highest total expected value (profit). *Summing the expected values across for each strategy would yield the following total expected values:*

> strategy 1,   950,000
>
> strategy 2, 1,675,000
>
> strategy 3, 1,160,000.

In this case, Sally Turner would recommend a production strategy of 2.5 million shovels, since the expected value of the profit would be the highest at $1,675,000. Given the severity of past winters, her decision, using that strategy, would entail the least risk and would have the highest probability of maximizing payoff for the the firm.

Using a payoff matrix of the type described above is but one example of decision making under risk (i.e., using probabilities). Another decision situation involving risk is that of quality control. In a quality-control situation, the decision maker is armed with a record of past performance in terms of defective and passable products and is able to gear sampling of the firm's output for quality checking based on the probability of a certain number of defectives in a batch. We shall not cover quality control here, but the key is that the decision maker knows all of the precise values of the problem except that being predicted. And for that he or she knows the probability of occurrence. This allows the decision maker to predict with reasonable certainty that the decision will be the most accurate—and most profitable—one.

DECISION MAKING UNDER UNCERTAINTY

As mentioned earlier, under uncertainty the decision maker not only is unable to control the outcome, but also has no objective probabilities of occurrence on which to base the decision that must be made. That is, the knowledge of the future is blank in terms of precise or probable predictions. Under this condition the decision maker ostensibly has no criteria for choosing one course of action or strategy over another. Indeed, a bystander might just say to a decision maker, "Close your eyes and choose" or "Throw a dart and select the outcome indicated by where it lands."

But many scholars have worked on this problem of decision making under uncertainty, and some criteria and methods have been developed to assist the decision maker. As we shall learn, however, much of the choice depends on the decision maker's aversion to failure and risk—in a word, on the decision maker's propensity for taking chances. We shall cover five of those methods and criteria in this section: the principle of insufficient reason, maximax, maximin, weighted optimism, and minimax regret. In addition, we shall briefly comment on the applicability of *subjective probabilities*.

For all of the problems in this section, we shall assume a similar conditional payoff matrix to that faced by Sally Turner in our risk problem. (See Table 7.2.)

Principle of insufficient reason* Decision makers under this criterion feel that they have no reason to assume that one state of nature will occur over any other. Therefore, they assume that each state of nature has an *equal* probability of occurring. Applying an equal probability of each state of nature to our conditional payoff matrix would yield the expected values for each cell as shown in Table 7.4. Under the conditions and criteria shown in the table, the obvious strategy would be to produce 3.5 million shovels, since the expected payoff would be $1,582,000, and this sum is larger than any of the other summed expected values.

Production strategies	States of nature and probabilities 20″–50″ .33	50″–70″ .33	>80″ .33	Total expected value
3.5 million	$ 83,000	$333,000	$1,116,000	$1,582,000
2.5 million	$250,000	$833,000	$ 413,000	$1,496,000
1.5 million	$500,000	$333,000	$ 200,000	$1,033,000

TABLE 7.4
Principle of insufficient reason

The obvious problem with the principle of insufficient reason is that the likelihood of equal probabilities' residing with all outcomes is most times extremely small. Also, the possibility of adding ridiculous states of nature to which "equal" probabilities will be assigned is always present. In this problem, for example, suppose that the decision maker added the absurd option that the temperature would average 110° above zero throughout the winter. Under the principle of insufficient reason, such a projected state of nature would draw an equal probability as the other states of nature. But even simple knowledge of weather conditions would preclude this from being a very rational possibility. We use this ludicrous example only to point out the possible deficiency of this criteria, however.

The maximin criterion Under this criterion, the decision maker assumes that the worst possible state of nature will *always* occur and acts to maximize the outcome under

* Often referred to as the LaPlace criterion.

this pessimistic assumption. In the problem of this chapter, the worst condition to be expected is a snowfall of 20 to 50 inches (remember, the product is snow shovels). The payoffs for each of the strategies with that state of nature would be:

Strategy	Conditional value
Produce 3.5 million shovels	$250,000 profit
Produce 2.5 million shovels	$750,000 profit
Produce 1.5 million shovels	$600,000 profit

The decision maker here would select a production level of 2.5 million shovels, because if the expected worst state of nature did occur, the firm would end up making $750,000—the best it could do under the projected worst possible state of nature.

The maximin criterion is one based on pessimism, and the decision maker is seeking to make the best of the worst situation. That type of decision maker, of course, has an opposite—the extreme optimist.

The maximax criterion

The decision maker could be an optimist and see silver linings in every dark cloud. Under this condition, the decision maker might "go for broke" and always select the maximizing solution. In the case of our snow-shovel problem, the decision maker would recommend production of 3.5 million shovels, since there is the possibility that the firm would profit by $3.5 million if the winter was severe; that profit is greater than any other combination of winters and possible production outputs.

Weighted optimism

Under this criterion, often called the Hurwicz criterion, the decision maker, rather than being a total pessimist or a total optimist, would assign probabilities to his or her optimism and pessimism. The best possible outcome of each strategy would then be factored by the optimistic probability. Similarly, the worst outcomes for each strategy would be factored by the pessimistic probability. The expected value of the pessimism is then subtracted from the expected value of the optimism for each strategy. The decision is based on the highest product of the subtractions.

For example, in the problem involving Sally Turner, suppose that she assigned a probability of .7 to the best always happening and a .3 probability to the worst occurring. The expected values that would result from her outlooks are shown in Table 7.5. Using the criterion of weighted optimism, Sally, as a decision maker, would choose to produce 3.5 million shovels, since the expected value would be $2.375 million and would be higher than the expected values of the other two production strategies.

Minimax regret

Using this criterion, our decision maker asks, "If I select a strategy and a state of nature different from the one which would maximize under that

TABLE 7.5
Weighted
optimism

Strategy	Profit from best occurrence	Profit from worst occurrence	Conditional values × weights
Produce 3.5 million	$3.5 million	$250,000	$2,450,000 — $75,000 = $2,375,000
Produce 2.5 million	$2.5 million	$750,000	$1,750,000 — $225,000 = $1,525,000
Produce 1.5 million	$1.5 million	$600,000	$1,050,000 — $180,000 = $870,000

strategy occurs, what would be my regret?" and then seeks to minimize that regret.* For example, if Sally Turner selected strategy 1 (production of 3.5 million shovels) and state of nature 1 (20″ to 50″ of snow) occurs, her regret would be $1,250,000, because with that state of nature, she should have selected strategy 3 (1.5 million shovels). The decision maker using the minimax regret criterion would attempt to minimize the amount of regret to be suffered in the decision situation. For Sally Turner's problem, a regret matrix could look like that shown in Table 7.6.

Production strategies	States of nature 20″–50″	50″–70″	80″+	Max regret
3.5 million	$1,250,000	$1,500,000	0	$1,500,000
2.5 million	$ 750,000	0	$2,250,000	$2,250,000
1.5 million	0	$1,500,000	$2,900,000	$2,900,000

TABLE 7.6
Regret
matrix

The maximum regret that Sally would suffer *if she selected strategy 1* (3.5 million shovels) would be $1.5 million (the difference between the possible maximum payoff of $2.5 million and the actual $1 million that would materialize *if state of nature 2 occurs*). *If she selected strategy 2*, the maximum regret would be $2.25 million (the difference between 3.5 million possible payoff and the $1.25 million that would actually materialize *if state of nature 3 occurs*. The maximum regret *for strategy 3* would be $2.9 million (the difference between $3.5 million and the actually realized $600,000 *should state of nature 3 occur*).

In this problem the decision maker seeking to minimize the maximum regret would choose strategy 1 and produce 3.5 million shovels, since the maximum regret under that strategy would be $1.5 million whereas maximum regrets of $2.25 million and $2.9 million could result under strategies 2 and 3, respectively.

* L. J. Savage, "The Theory of Statistical Decision," *Journal of the American Statistical Association* XLVI (March 1951): 55–67.

One last mechanism is the use of subjective probabilities. Suppose that Sally Turner did not have large enough numbers of observations from which to draw and assign objective probabilities to the various possible states of the world. Might she still assign probabilities? In a variation of the uncertainty problem, some observers have suggested that the decision maker can assign best guesses of probability to the various states of the world and then proceed to solve the problem as if the probabilities were objective.

Subjective probability

Oftentimes, decision makers have reservoirs of information which, although not precise, would yield remarkably accurate predictions. Applied to problems, the *subjective* probabilities may differ among decision makers, but they may yield "acceptable" decisions. As a problem, figure what Sally Turner's recommendation would be if, from her knowledge of the situation, she assigned the following subjective probabilities to the various states of the world: 20–50 inches, .25; 50–70 inches, .45; and 80+ inches, .30.

CONCLUSION

In this chapter we offered an introduction to some quantitative tools for decision making. We introduced relatively simple and unsophisticated tools; others, more complex and powerful, exist and are also used. Our objective in this chapter is simply to point out the uses of mathematical and statistical tools under conditions of certainty, risk, and uncertainty and to point out their limitations and pitfalls. Tools such as those demonstrated in this chapter are making the manager's job somewhat more complex, but they can, when used effectively, increase the accuracy and potential of the manager's decision making.

DISCUSSION QUESTIONS

1 Define the following terms:
   a) Decision making under certainty
   b) Decision making under uncertainty
   c) Decision making under risk
   d) Linear programming
   e) Break-even analysis
   f) Maximin
   g) Minimax
   h) Principle of insufficient reason

2 Decisions can be made in three types of environments or states of nature: certainty, risk, and uncertainty. Define each state of nature and give a specific example.

3 The Keep-it-Going Motor Company currently buys exhaust valves for its motors at $2.50 each. An estimate of the cost to the company to manufacture these valves reveals that the fixed costs will be $4800 per year and that the variable costs per valve will be $1.25. Each motor requires one exhaust valve, and Keep-it-Going's annual capacity is 6000 motors per year. At what unit volume does it pay the company to manufacture its own valves? Show graphically.

4 The Smith Manufacturing Company produces chairs. An analysis of the company's accounting data reveals:

a) Fixed cost, $50,000 per year

b) Variable cost, $2.00 per chair

c) Plant capacity 20,000 chairs

d) Selling price $7.00 per chair

Compute the break-even point in number of chairs. Show graphically. Find the number of chairs Smith must sell to show a profit of $30,000.

5 How many orders would a firm make given the following data?

a) Annual requirement in units, 5000   b) Cost per unit, $1,000

c) Inventory carrying charge, 10%   d) Cost per order, $25

6 Joe Smith can make hammers and screwdrivers. He makes $5 per hammer and $6 per screwdriver. Both require the same kinds of input, as shown in Table 7.7. If Joe wanted to maximize his profits, how many of each product should he produce?

Product	Units of input A	Units of input B	Units of input C	Profit	TABLE 7.7 Product inputs
Hammer	4	6	8	$5	
Screwdriver	6	3	2	$6	
Capacity limit	84	66	80		

SELECTED READINGS

Agee, M. H., R. E. Taylor, and P. E. Torgersen, *Quantitative Analysis for Business Decisions* (Englewood Cliffs, N.J.: Prentice-Hall, 1976).

Altev, S., "A Taxonomy of Decision Support Systems," *Sloan Management Review* 19, 1 (Fall 1977): 39–56.

Churchman, C. W., *Prediction and Optimal Decision* (Englewood Cliffs, N.J.: Prentice-Hall, 1961).

Coltar, M., and E. Richman, *Problems in Operations Management* (Englewood Cliffs, N.J.: Prentice-Hall, 1974).

Darden, B. R., and W. H. Lucas, *The Decision Making Game: An Integrated Operations Management Simulation* (Englewood Cliffs, N.J.: Prentice-Hall, 1969).

Doktor, R. H., and J. A. Moses, *Managerial Insights: Analysis, Decisions and Implementation* (Englewood Cliffs, N.J.: Prentice-Hall, 1973).

Duchworth, W. E., A. E. Gear, and A. G. Lockett, *A Guide to Operational Research* (New York: Wiley, 1977).

Duncan, L. R., and H. Raiffa, *Games and Decisions* (N.Y.: Wiley, 1958).

Hoyt, D. B., *Computer Handbook for Senior Management* (New York: Macmillan, 1978).

Kabak, I. W., and A. I. Schiff, "Inventory Models and Management Objectives," *Sloan Management Review* **19**, 2 (Winter 1978): 53–59.

Kazmier, L. J., *Statistical Analysis for Business and Economics* (New York: McGraw-Hill, 1967).

Keen, P. G. W., and M. S. Scott Morton, *Decision Support Systems: An Organizational Perspective* (Reading, Mass.: Addison-Wesley, 1978).

Leithold, L., *The Calculus: With Analytic Geometry*, 2d ed. (New York: Harper & Row, 1972).

Levin, R. I., and C. A. Kirkpatrick, *Quantitative Approaches to Management*, 2d ed. (New York: McGraw-Hill, 1971).

Miller, D., and P. H. Friesen, "Strategy-Making in Context—Ten Empirical Archetypes," *Journal of Management Studies* **14**, 3 (October 1977): 253–280.

Miller, D. W., and M. K. Starr, *The Structure of Human Decisions* (Englewood Cliffs, N.J.: Prentice-Hall, 1967).

Mohr, N. Carrol, and C. L. Hubbard, "How to Reduce Uncertainty in Sales Forecasting," *Management Review* **67**, 6 (June 1978): 14–22.

Plossl, G. W., and O. W. Wright, *Production and Inventory Control* (Englewood Cliffs, N.J.: Prentice-Hall, 1967).

Radford, K. J., *Managerial Decision Making* (Reston, Va.: Reston Publishing Company, 1975).

Raiffa, H., *Decision Analysis: Introductory Lectures on Choices under Uncertainty* (Reading, Mass.: Addison-Wesley, 1970).

Rector, R. L., "Value of Perfect Information," *Industrial Management* **19**, 6 (November/December 1977): 20–21.

Thompson, G. E., *Statistics for Decisions: An Elementary Introduction* (Boston: Little, Brown, 1972).

Wessel, R. H., E. R. Willett, and A. J. Simone, *Statistics as Applied to Economics and Business*, rev. ed. (New York: Holt, Rinehart and Winston, 1966).

Youse, Bevan K., and A. W. Stalnaker, *Calculus for Students of Business and Management* (Scranton, Pa.: International Book Company, 1969).

APPENDIX: ALGEBRAIC LINEAR PROGRAMMING

Another method of solving the linear programming problem is by the algebraic method. To demonstrate this method, we shall utilize the same problem detailed in the chapter section about the graphic method. To repeat the functions: The objective is to maximize

$$P = \$4(B) = \$5(G)$$

under constraints

$$20B + 20G \leq 1000$$
$$10B + 20G \leq 800$$
$$25B + 10G \leq 950.$$

To solve the problem by the algebraic method, we must convert the inequalities to equalities; for this we must add slack variables to complete the total utilization of each input:

$$20B + 20G + slack_X = 1000$$
$$10B + 20G + slack_Y = 800$$
$$25B + 10G + slack_Z = 950$$

or

$$slack_X = 1000 - 20B - 20G$$
$$slack_Y = 800 - 10B - 20G$$
$$slack_Z = 950 - 25B - 10G.$$

Four possible production solutions are available in this problem: produce nothing, produce only bumpers, produce only gratings, or produce a combination of bumpers and gratings.

1 To produce nothing obviously means a profit of $0.

2 To produce only bumpers, we must find the maximum number of bumpers the firm can produce, given the finite level of all three of the inputs.

   a) What output is possible for input X?

$$20B + 0 + slack_X = 1000$$
$$20B = 1000$$
$$B = 50.$$

   b) What output is possible for input Y?

$$10B + 0 + slack_Y = 800$$
$$10B = 800$$
$$B = 80.$$

   c) What output is possible for input Z?

$$25B + 0 + slack_Z = 950$$
$$25B = 950$$
$$B = 38.$$

The maximum amount of bumpers our firm can produce, given the constraints posed by the available resources, is 38. The key limitation is input Z. At a profit of $4 each, the total profit for making bumpers would only be $152.

3 To produce gratings only, we must find the maximum number of gratings the firm can produce, given the finite level of all three of the inputs.

a) What output is possible for input X?

$$0 + 20G + slack_X = 1000$$
$$20G = 1000$$
$$G = 50.$$

b) What output is possible for input Y?

$$0 + 20G + slack_Y = 800$$
$$20G = 800$$
$$G = 40.$$

c) What output is possible for input Z?

$$0 + 10G + slack_Z = 950$$
$$10G = 950$$
$$G = 95.$$

The maximum number of gratings our firm can produce, given the constraints posed by the available resources, is 40. The key constraint is input Y. At a profit of $5 per grating, the total profit for this firm making gratings only would be $200.

4 Finally, we need to solve the problem of producing a combination of bumpers and gratings. Our objective here is also to use all possible amounts of the available resources; in other words, the firm wants a minimum of slack left. We start with three possible slack relationships:

$$slack_X = 0, slack_Y = 0, slack_Z \text{ remains}$$
$$slack_X = 0, slack_Z = 0, slack_Y \text{ remains}$$
$$slack_Y = 0, slack_Z = 0, slack_X \text{ remains}$$

a) Solving for $slack_Z$, we establish the following three equations:

$$20B + 20G + 0 = 1000$$
$$10B + 20G + 0 = 800$$
$$25B + 10G + slack_Z = 950.$$

Solving the first two equations of the set simultaneously:

$$20B + 20G + 0 = 1000$$
$$\underline{10B + 20G + 0 = 800}$$
$$10B \qquad\qquad = 200$$
$$B = 20$$

and substituting:

$$20(20) + 20(G) = 1000$$
$$G = 30,$$

or

$$10(20) + 20(G) = 800$$
$$G = 30.$$

These values, placed into the slack equation, yield:

$$25(20) + 10(30) + slack_Z = 950$$
$$slack_Z = 150.$$

Slack is positive, so this solution is feasible. Substituting the two values for B and G in the profit, or objective function, yields a profit of $230.

$$\$4(20) + \$5(30) = \$230.00.$$

b) Solving for $slack_Y$, we establish the following three equations:

$$20B + 20G + 0 = 1000$$
$$10B + 20G + slack_Y = 800$$
$$25B + 10G + 0 = 950.$$

Solving equations 1 and 3 of the set simultaneously:

$$50B + 20G + 0 = 1900$$
$$20B + 20G + 0 = 1000$$
$$\overline{}$$
$$30B \qquad\quad = 900$$
$$B = 30$$

substituting:

$$20(30) + 20(G) + 0 = 1000$$
$$G = 20$$

or

$$25(30) + 10(G) + 0 = 950$$
$$G = 20.$$

These values, placed into the slack equation, yield:

$$10(30) + 20(20) + slack_Y = 800$$
$$slack_Y = 100.$$

Slack is positive, so this solution is feasible. Substituting the two values of B and G into the profit, or objective function, yields a profit of $220.

$$\$4(30) + \$5(20) = \$220.$$

c) Finally, solving for slack$_X$, we establish the following three equations:

$$20B + 20G + slack_X = 1000$$
$$10B + 20G + 0 = 800$$
$$25B + 10G + 0 = 950.$$

Solving the second and third equations of the set simultaneously:

$$50B + 20G = 1900$$
$$\underline{10B + 20G = 800}$$
$$40B = 1100$$
$$B = 27.5.$$

Substituting:

$$10(27.5) + 20(G) = 800$$
$$G = 26.25$$

or

$$25(27.5) + 10(G) = 950$$
$$G = 26.25.$$

These values, placed into the slack equation, yield:

$$20(27.5) + 20(26.5) + slack_X = 1000$$
$$slack_X = -80.$$

We should not be concerned that the values for B and G are frac-tional, since they can be rounded to the next lowest whole unit. But solving for slack$_X$ does yield a nonfeasible solution, since the firm cannot have negative slack in any input.

So the firm has five potential profit levels: $0, $152, $200, $230, and $220. The profit-maximizing firm would choose the profit level of $230 and would produce 20 bumpers and 30 gratings.

Chapter 8
PLANNING

CHAPTER HIGHLIGHTS

Planning is the management activity involving the arrangement of multiple linked decisions—ends and means—to accomplish one or more long-range or major objectives. In this chapter, after an initial simple single-path planning illustration, progressively more complex planning situations will be presented. In addition to analyzing many of the important considerations in planning and the concept of dynamic planning, we will cover several planning tools, including PERT (Program Evaluation Review Technique).

LEARNING OBJECTIVES

1 To learn the definition of planning.

2 To appreciate the concept of linked ends-and-means decisions.

3 To learn multipath planning.

4 To learn to integrate short-term and long-term plans.

5 To appreciate the complexity of multipath, multiunit, multitime planning.

6 To learn the practice of planning backwards.

7 To understand the effects on planning of such factors as organizational resources, public policy, organizational policy, timing, allowance for unforeseen events, the organization's capacity for controlling, and the cost of failure.

8 To be able to define and apply the concept of dynamic planning.

9 To know how to use a planning matrix.

10 To know the uses of a Gantt chart.

11 To learn the basics of PERT.

CASE: JIM SHERRY

■ The decision was made; Magnum Industries was going international. Over the past twenty years, Magnum's export sales had grown to $12.6 million—about fourteen percent of the company's total sales. Export sales were now a significant factor in the company's prosperity and growth, and forecasts indicated that the potential market in export sales was both solid and expanding. This was a far cry from that bleak November day when a bespectacled, slightly graying Danish businessperson just walked into the office and asked to see samples of the company's microstrain filters—and then placed a $20,000 order on the spot.

In those days the sales manager didn't have the slightest notions on selling to Europeans. "Wow, what a pleasant surprise that first order is," he thought. "Now, what do I do with it?" The shipping department needed a week just to figure out how to send a shipment abroad. In some cases, on follow-up orders, the products required government clearance, since the filters had potential military uses. The company didn't find that out until one order had been loaded and was on the road to the shipping port. The finance department spent hours with bankers, befuddled by the intricacies of exchange rates and letters of credit in Danish kroner, Swiss francs, German marks, and Italian lire. But the company learned and learned quickly, because the Danish order led to Italian orders, then German orders, French orders, and so on.

The export business expanded with the appointment of a Munich-based firm as Magnum's European agent. Exports became an important input into sales forecasting, production planning, and corporate strategy.

Now, however, the development of the European Common Market was making it much more difficult for Magnum to compete with European firms. American-made products, and Magnum's in particular, were at a competitive disadvantage, as preferential treatment in terms of tariffs and customs duties was given to companies located within the Common Market. Moreover, European technology was gaining rapidly.

Magnum's American capacity was geared toward accommodating the export market, but it was strained and could easily be filled through readily obtainable domestic orders, particularly if the projections of high growth in the chemical industry materialized and the emphasis on environmental controls continued. Nevertheless, Magnum executives did not relish the idea of the company's going backward or stagnating, even if such stagnation was only a short-run phenomenon. The European business was too good to lose. Therefore, the decision was made to build a branch plant somewhere in Europe.

The European facility would be the company's first venture into a multiplant operation, let alone into a multicountry one. The company had not only no policies or procedures on plant location, but also little accumulated experience. Practically all of Magnum's executives had grown up with the company; few had experience in multiunit operations, and none had experience in operating a multinational business. Only one executive spoke a foreign language—Spanish.

Top management began searching for a general manager who had experience managing a European operation. After a long search, including checking out numerous leads offered by customers and the European agent, the company selected as manager for the European plant Jim Sherry, who managed the Netherlands branch of a large American-based chemical firm. Sherry knew Magnum's products well and had spent more than eight years in Common Market countries. He was given the assignment of getting the European plant built and into operation within twenty-four months.

Jim's two-year objective, then, was to get the plant built and staffed and into operational condition. He anticipated that the first six months of his new job would be spent in planning. ■

INTRODUCTION

Planning? What do we mean by planning? What kinds of managerial activity will Jim Sherry be engaging in when he plans? In the chapter on decision making, we looked on planning as a very special kind of decision making; we called planning, in a way, a series of linked decisions. We can now define planning more precisely. Planning is a mental managerial activity involving the arrangement of multiple linked decisions on ends and on means to accomplish a long-range, or major, objective. In essence, the accomplishment of one goal is a necessary and essential occurrence preceding the effort to achieve another goal, and so on until the major objective has been accomplished. Planning is the tool to bring these decisions and the linkages together.

As such, planning can have many interesting and challenging facets. For example, as one department plans—links together means and ends—those who plan at the next higher level of the organization must integrate those lower departmental plans with similar sets of linked decisions from other subordinate departments. This is called the integration of plans.

Also, planning means the integration of short-range plans with longer-range ones. For example, your own short-range plans are probably concerned with this semester, with the various courses that you are now enrolled in. This semester's work, however, is linked to your longer-range plan for the year, then to your four-year plan for your college education, and if you really are a long-range planner, to your entire education, perhaps through graduate school, law school, a night-MBA program, and the like.

Now, to complicate the subject of planning even more, consider the plans of each department of the organization (i.e., linked ends/means decisions) integrated with other departments' plans, and then consider that integration with a time-frame continuum of short range to longer range. Looking at such a mind-boggling exercise should indicate that planning is not a subject to be trifled with. Such a consideration should also indicate how we can distinguish the successful managers from the mediocre ones.

In this chapter we will explore some of the ideas and concepts touched on in the paragraphs above, starting with very simple planning situations and then moving to relatively more complex ones and finally to even more complex multidepartmental, multi–time-frame planning efforts. Then we shall see what kind of planning situation faces Jim Sherry. After those explorations into the complex world of organizational planning, we shall reiterate some of the constraints on planning, cover the dynamics of planning (the updating and refining of plans), and then describe some planning tools.

PLANNING SITUATIONS

A simple plan would entail moving beyond a single decision to a string of decisions, each a part of a sequence of events to be implemented. For example, assume that Steve Student has an especially called 8:00 A.M. class at which a distinguished visitor will analyze the students' solutions to an assigned problem. Normally, we might think that this single class is not worth the time that it takes to plan for it. For the moment, however, we are simply trying to illustrate the conceptual bases for planning. Assume also that the longest-term objective Steve has is to arrive safely at that special class. What sequence of subobjectives might precede the achievement of the long-term objective? Simplifying a bit, we might consider the following sequence of projected subgoals for Steve.

Simple unipath planning

1 Get out of bed by 6:45 A.M.
2 Ensure good appearance
3 Get dressed
4 Eat
5 Arrive at class (also long-range goal)

Steve has just completed the first step in planning for reaching that class (and the longer-term objective). He has assembled a group of subobjectives that must be accomplished before the major goal can be attained.

Next, he would want to place time benchmarks on the accomplishment of the group of subobjectives. After all, it would be silly if one had a long-range goal of reaching class by 8:00 A.M., but spent fifty-eight minutes in the shower and only seventeen minutes remained in which to accomplish the other subgoals leading to the major goal. Figure 8.1 shows the time benchmarks along with the various subgoals.

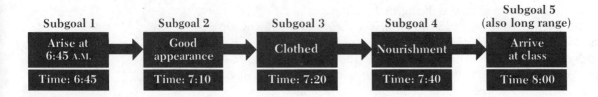

FIG. 8.1
Subgoals and time benchmarks—single-path plan.

But our student doesn't just set goals and hope that they materialize. As we learned in the chapter on decision making, he must select the *means* of going from the existing state to the desired state. How is Steve to arise at 6:45 A.M.? A list of some possible alternative methods might include:

1 Have roommate awaken him
2 Use an alarm clock
3 Have girl friend call at 6:45
4 Make arrangements with telephone operator to call at 6:45

For grooming, the next step, Steve has not only multiple chores, but also multiple choices of how to accomplish each of the chores, e.g., wash, shower, or take a bath. Shaving might entail use of an electric shaver, blade, or straight edge—or, indeed, going without a shave. Brushing the teeth means a choice of paste or power, and combing the hair entails a choice of brush or comb, aerosol spray, or rub-in oil, etc.

In dressing, Steve will have to select color combinations (what else goes with blue jeans?), be geared to the appropriate temperature, be dressed for comfort, etc. For breakfast, there are all sorts of choices of juices, eggs (scrambled, lightly over, poached), toast, coffee, milk, tea. And to achieve the final objective, he can ride, walk, bicycle, take the bus, or jog. Each of these choices involves a decision on reaching the desired state, which is a subgoal on the road to the main, desired goal.

No matter how trivial you view this example (and it is trivial, we admit), our student still has established goals, subgoals, and benchmarks in terms of timing and has made decisions on reaching those goals. The student has *planned*—has linked ends and means in a sequential arrangement to reach the longer-range goal.

Even within this simple example, however, the extent of planning could have been carried to finer and finer gradations. For example, Steve could have broken the planning for dressing down into further subgoals of trousers, shirts, socks, shoes, and indeed could have planned so minutely as to program whether to put his right or left leg into the trousers first. Indeed, *in many planning situations it may be necessary to move down several steps in developing subgoals and means to achieve those goals, spelling out in minute detail the methods and procedures for meeting each objective.* In other situations it might simply be appropriate to spell out the subgoals and allow the implementer to develop further refinements of subgoals and methods for reaching them. Obviously, cost and time available for planning have important roles to play in the amount of effort put into planning, as will the difficulty of the assignment, the capacity of the subordinate, the importance of the decision, the value of accuracy, and the degree of tolerable flexibility.

So far we have discussed a single-path planning process, which generally involves one person or unit and one sequence. Suppose, however, that in order for an event to occur, several diverse chains of events must take place simultaneously and involve several different people or divisions. The process is the same—decisions on linked goals and means—just more complicated.

Multipath planning

For example, in order for the eight o'clock class to function, not only the student, but also the professor must arrive there. In addition, both must be prepared: the student with homework and the professor with a lecture or daily class exercise. Figure 8.2 shows what these paths might look like.

Now, if we were managing this student and the professor, we would, in order to have them both in class at 8:00 A.M., sketch out a plan—linked ends and decisions—as shown in Fig. 8.2. That plan, however, is a very

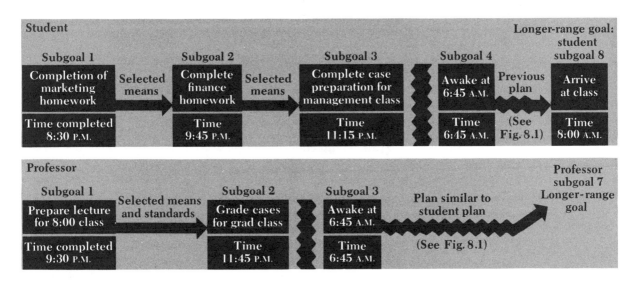

FIG. 8.2
Multipath planning.

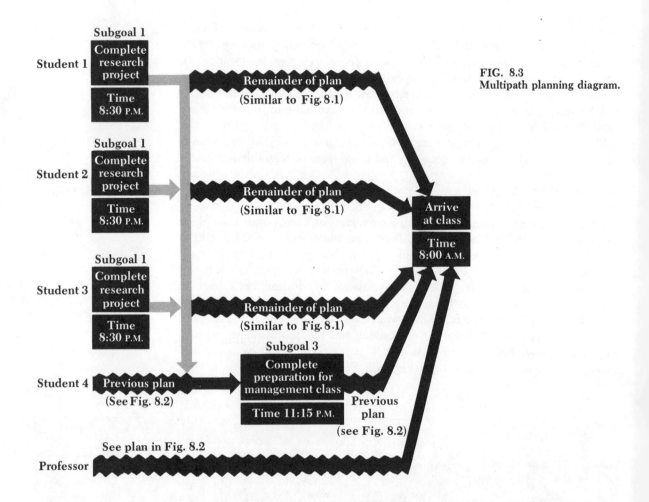

FIG. 8.3
Multipath planning diagram.

simple multipath one, since the only place where the plan of one person is dependent on the completion of the plan of another is at 8:00 A.M., when they both must meet in room 201 of Joseph Bumpkin Hall.

Let us now complicate the process a bit. Suppose that at the previous class, the professor had assigned a group project to four students; three of them were to prepare research studies on a particular problem, and the fourth was to bring the work of the other three together, synthesize it, and derive conclusions and recommendations. Now we have three students working and a fourth who cannot start to work on the project until the other three complete their reports. This situation, which is very common in business and other organizational situations, might look like the planning diagram shown in Fig. 8.3.

The plan has become a bit more complicated, because several units of our organization are dependent for fulfillment of their own goal on other units' successful completion of subgoals at a point other than at the final subgoal (e.g., 8:00 A.M. in class). If we were planning this arrangement, we would have made determinations of subgoals plus decisions on means links at every stage of the process, down to the gradations necessary or relevant.

Of course, we know that some decisions probably could be made more quickly than others; their importance might be so minute to the accomplishment of the major goal and the cost of the wrong choice in terms of goal achievement so insignificant that the decision maker—or now, the planner—would spend little precious time on elaborating alternatives, gathering information, etc.

In real life the 8:00 A.M. management class in room 201 at Joseph Bumpkin Hall during this particular semester is only one part of a longer-term plan for our student, whose long-term plan—often called a strategy—would probably be related to an employment goal. Suppose that Steve would like to be a production manager following graduation. He has eight semesters in which to prepare for this career, and his planning would entail arranging an educational program for the eight semesters in order to reach that ultimate objective of preparation for a career as a production manager. Obviously, he would be constrained by required courses, availability of courses, sequencing of electives, etc., but could nonetheless lay out a long-range four-year plan such as the one shown in Fig. 8.4.

Integrating short- and long-term planning

In essence, the student's short-term plan for one semester (and the incidental shorter-term one for getting to the 8:00 class) are integral parts of the longer-term strategy of preparing for a career in production management. If we could, with the aid of a computer, program every second as this student progressed through the four years at Moccasin University, we would have the complete integration of short- and long-range plans. Obviously, such minute programming in this case is not necessary, but the conceptual problem of tying short-range plans to the longer-range strategy would be illustrated by such a program, and that conceptual framework is appropriate for many organizational planning situations.

Short- and long-term planning for multiunit organizations   Conceive now of the problem of an organization engaging in unit planning for the short term, having that unit plan integrated into a multiunit plan for the short term— indeed, having those plans mesh so that the completion of one unit's task triggers another's activity—and then having all of the short-term plans becoming building blocks for the longer-term strategy. Such a long-term strategy might look like that shown in Fig. 8.5.

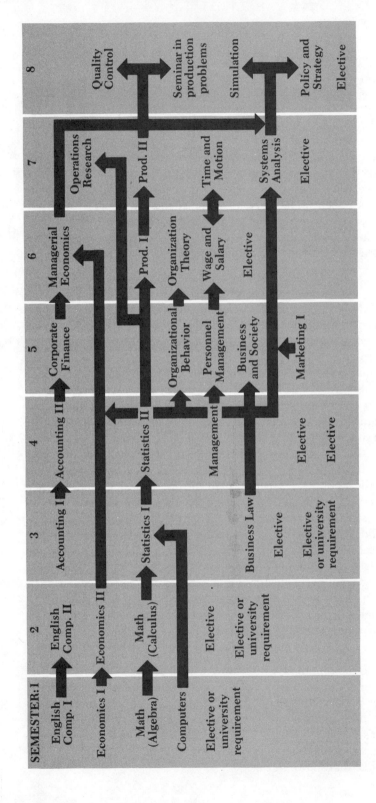

FIG. 8.4
Eight-semester plan for student desiring production-management training.

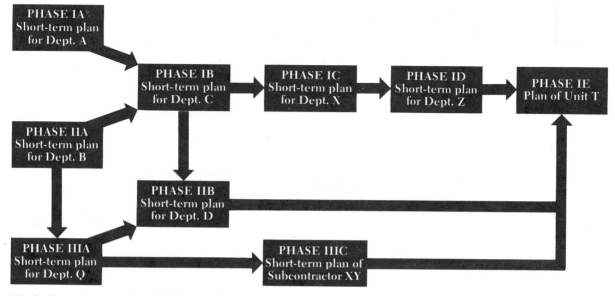

*Each phase is an amalgam of decision linkages of subunits and personnel.

FIG. 8.5
Short-term plans integrated into long-term strategy.

Each phase, in fact, may be an amalgam of hundreds of short-term multiunit ends-and-means decision linkages. Indeed, the firm may have a planning process so complex that a computer is necessary for keeping track of all the linkages among departments, subunits, and the various time frames involved. Consider, for example, the management-planning problem involved in the Apollo spacecraft project. This particular objective—articulated by President Kennedy as landing a man on the moon by 1970—took almost ten years from the date the final objective was stated to the day astronaut Neil Armstrong stepped onto the moon's surface. During that time, some 30,000 companies were involved in the contracting and subcontracting for the project, and numerous test phases had to be completed before the final run could be made. Simply keeping a planning diagram involving the 30,000 linked *final* objectives of the subcontractors is a horrendous enough planning problem, but then adding in each company's plans (subobjectives plus means decisions) would yield one monumental plan. Conceptually, you should be able to envision what such a plan would entail; operationally, you would need a very large computer to assist you.

Let us summarize our discussion to this point. First, we defined planning as a set of linked ends and means decisions. Then we added a time dimension for a single unit, made that problem more complex by adding a second unit, added further complexity by making one unit's task completion dependent on another's completing its tasks, and finally considered all of the unit parts of a multiunit longer-range, multitime configuration.

Planning situations: a review

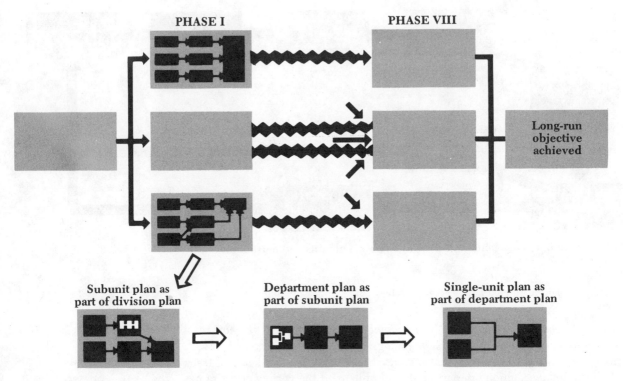

PHASE I

PHASE VIII

Long-run
objective
achieved

Subunit plan as
part of division plan

Department plan as
part of subunit plan

Single-unit plan as
part of department plan

FIG. 8.6
Conceptual diagram of a major multiunit, multitime plan.

Figure 8.6 illustrates these breakdowns of means/ends chains in conceptual fashion. The total plan is one breakdown, each box is broken down into further subplans, each part of the subplan is further divided, and so on until we come to the point where planning is no longer feasible, useful, or economical.

ADDITIONAL PLANNING BASICS

Planning backwards   Planning is often best accomplished by working *backwards* from the final objective to the initial starting point. This process entails determining what must be achieved before that final objective is attained by detailing in reverse the preceding subobjectives that must be met. Thus our student would begin planning by considering that the class began at 8:00. He would then work backwards to plan the time needed for transportation, nourishment, clothing, awakening, etc. In order to determine when to get out of bed, he would subtract from the 8:00 final benchmark the amount of time needed to complete the series of immediately preceding subobjectives.

Similarly, a training director for a major corporation planning a seminar on, say, affirmative action for the corporation's personnel officers might start by considering the date and content of the program. Once these items had been determined, the director could plan backwards to consider location; contracting with speakers; recruiting participants; arranging transportation, lodging, and meals; assembling and producing course materials; procuring audio and visual equipment, etc. On a first pass at the plan, the training director could determine if all the necessary prerequisites could be completed in order to have the program occur on the scheduled date.

Seasoned planners will often plan a complex process both forward and backwards to determine not only the sequence of activities, but also the attainability within necessary time constraints of the entire operation. Suppose, for example, that Chuck Martinelli heard that in thirty weeks one of his competitors would be placing on the market a new rocking chair that was likely to be successful. Planning forward to meet that challenge might not get the Greco-Roman Company very far, because the process then might entail a sixty-two-week implementation period. By imposing the thirty-week constraint on the completion of the project, however, and then working backwards, planners would be forced to eliminate all waste, cut corners, pour extra resources into bottlenecks, speed up processes, select only subcontractors who could deliver on time, and schedule overtime and the other necessary activities to meet the deadline.

One problem in planning is that we cannot always pinpoint the substance of every decision in an extended long-range planning process. For example, in planning a long-range sales effort, we cannot, at the time the major plan is laid out, detail who will be the sales representative hired on December 24 of the fourth year of the plan, but we know that if all goes well, we will need an additional salesperson on that date. Part of the planning process, then, is determining not only the substantive results expected and the means by which to reach those results, but also the injection of procedures to ensure that those events happening in the future for which substantive results cannot be foreseen at the present planning period will be controllable, well planned, and within acceptable limits. Thus although we may not know who that salesperson will be, we can plan now how one is hired and what the requirements might be in terms of output and expectations.

Planning for planning and decision making

In essence, part of the planning process is to plan for future managerial activity—future decision making and planning. Rarely will a long-range plan be so complete that the manager's design job is complete before he or she begins implementation of the plan. Often, it may not even be necessary at the time of planning to collect information and make a subsequent decision. The data may not be available or may not be reliable enough for a future decision. So the manager might plan now that a subplan or a decision will be made sometime later in the context of the total strategy. Thus a manager also plans for planning, and a long-range plan might be some combination of plans for implementation and plans for future planning activities.

Back to Jim Sherry   To illustrate some of these planning concepts, let us return to the vignette at the beginning of the chapter. Jim Sherry has a great deal of work to do in planning the construction and startup of Magnum's first overseas plant. Obviously, one of his first tasks is to plan for determining the location of the plant, the capacity of the plant, and the financing of the venture. Probably he would set these as his first subobjectives of his general plan, and as he starts he would consider the decisions and implementation processes relevant to those subobjectives. In this case, then, part of the plan is to determine when decisions would have to be made in the future—i.e., a plan for planning. For example, right now Jim does not know who his personnel manager will be, but he would consider early in the planning process how he would go about hiring a personnel manager, when that person would be hired, and what that person would do once hired.

Indeed, at the present time he does not even know where the plant will be located or what its capacity will be; he simply knows that he must build a plant in twenty-four months and that if he wants to complete that assignment, he must choose a location within two months. So his first planning step is to map out his objectives and subobjectives to get the plant in operation within twenty-four months—each of these with a rough timetable for completion (see Fig. 8.7).

The next step is to develop decision processes by which those objectives would be achieved. In essence, Sherry is planning his managerial, or mental, or planning, activities for the next two months. *How* is he to decide where that plant will be located and how much it will produce?

Thus Jim Sherry's initial run at a long-range plan is a combination of both substantive results and future planning situations. With the substantive planning segments, he will make decisions on what should occur at a future date. For the planning or decision-making segments, he will plan what kinds of information inputs and decision processes are necessary for the decision at that point—and possible immediate implementation.

If Jim Sherry were an oracle with perfect future vision and had all information perfectly and readily available at his fingertips, all substantive decisions on ends and means could be mapped out immediately; for example, he would plan to hire not just a salesperson on June 18 two years hence, but to hire John Smith as a salesperson on June 18. Since, however, no managers are endowed with such clairvoyance, most, including Jim Sherry, would probably settle for a subobjective of having a sales representative on June 18 and would develop a procedure for making the decision on who the salesperson employed at that time might be in terms of qualifications.

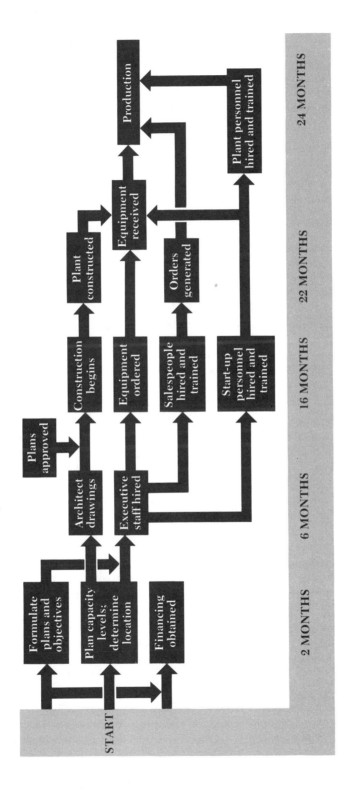

FIG. 8.7
Initial detailing of objectives and rough time frames for Magnum Industries' overseas venture.

The first step in Sherry's plan is to set down the benchmarks. Next, he will select substantive alternatives for all of the areas possible, then proceed to the first step of the long-range plan—itself a subplan—of selecting the location and capacity of the plan—with his decision model planned.

Some additional considerations in planning

Until now we have been concerned primarily with a process approach to planning. However, in doing his or her planning, the manager must consider several types of organizational as well as environmental constraints on the viability and fruition of plans. Among these constraints and factors are:

1 Availability of organizational resources
2 Public policy
3 Organizational policy
4 Timing
5 Allowance for unforeseen events
6 Ability of the organization to monitor, audit, and adapt
7 Cost of failure

In terms of available organizational resources, managers will obviously be constrained by the resources available or attainable. A public hospital, for example, can plan to add all sorts of new and esoteric programs, but if resources are not already available or if they are not forthcoming from the legislature or beneficent donors, the plan to phase in the new programs may be a useless exercise. Indeed, under such conditions one might justifiably question the amount of resources devoted to a planning exercise when everyone knows that the organization is sailing against the wind; an alert organization, however, will attempt to forecast changing environmental conditions and plan accordingly.

Plans must, of course, be consistent with public policy. For example, a firm cannot plan to sell military supplies to South Africa, because such an action is prohibited by the United States embargo of military sales to that nation. Nor can a new drug be marketed without extensive testing, since public policy demands such testing before a drug can be offered for sale to the public.

Organizational policy is generally thought of as a constraint to planning. That is, one plans within the guidelines set by policy. For example, sales organizations may be constrained in their marketing plans by an objective of low-cost operation, and hence no-credit sales and cash-only policies may govern the behavior of those organizations.

Most organizations subscribe to the approach whereby policy constrains planning, and generally this posture is supportable, since, as we shall see, policy governs repetitive-type activities. Furthermore, a policy often is borne out over time and experience to be the least costly guideline for the organization's action in the affected area.

However, planning, particularly long-range planning, may also become the audit or adaptive trigger for policy change. Few organizations would regard policy as sacrosanct; when changes in environment or business conditions demand a change in policy, policy is usually changed. Indeed, modern firms schedule periodic reviews to determine the possible need for such change. However, firms may also use their planning activities to reevaluate their need for continuation of policies (or indeed objectives) that may constrain some imaginative plans and attainable goals for the firm or organization.

Timing is important, since the planning must be completed and the implementation of the plan must be completable before any deadlines or the impact of the action has been lost. Few plans have no time constraints, particularly if competition is involved. If a plan cannot be completed or brought to fruition in the allotted time frame, it probably is back to the drawing board, or it may mean the scrapping of the project.

Insofar as possible, the planner should allow sufficient flexibility in planning so that unforeseen events such as inflation, recession, strikes, fires, deaths of key executives, etc., will not be totally catastrophic to the plan's implementation. For example, the marketing plan for a new product must include enough latitude for contending with price increases in resources, changing market size, renegotiations of labor contracts, changes in style, etc. Often this flexibility is related to the planner's leaving decisions to be made later on, in the implementation phase. That is, if a decision cannot be made now, it would be made later, when better information is available. But at the same time, the nonfinalizing of this one particular decision would not be crucial enough to destroy the effectiveness of the total planning process.

The planner must also consider the ability of the organization to monitor the plan's progress, to react swiftly to changes in the environment, and to adapt the plan to unforeseen problems and unanticipated events. Thus, for example, a plan that calls for sophisticated measurement of results in a firm that is not equipped to provide such measurements may not be an appropriate plan for that firm. In essence, the plan must consider the ability of the firm to not only carry out the plan, but also administer it and provide the proper information and control mechanisms.

Finally, the organization must consider whether it can sustain the cost of failure. In some cases, the cost of failure may be the viability of the enterprise. For example, many firms in the aerospace industry have seen their hopes rise and fall on one aircraft. Success in meeting the deadlines for the projected costs and market acceptance will mean huge profits and organizational growth. Failure may mean bankruptcy, merger with another firm, or perhaps even a petition to government for bailing-out assistance.

Dynamic planning   Planning is never finalized. Throughout this discussion, we have alluded to the need for the organization to consider changes in environment, organizational needs, etc., *within* the context of the plan while making the initial run at the plan. But organizations must be prepared for wholesale revisions of the plan, continual updating, massive changes in environmental conditions, and changes in organizational needs and objectives. For example, a university athletic department put forward a plan entailing a six-year effort to bring increased numbers of women's sports on line. The plan was well thought out; the planners confirmed their plans and assumptions with everyone involved, and the projections were based on the best information available. Suddenly, two things occurred which sent the planners back to the drawing boards. First, Title IX of the Educational Amendments Act mandated a three-year period for the equalization of opportunity among the sexes in college and university athletics. Second, resources became increasingly scarce, as state budgets were slashed and student numbers leveled off. So rather than being able to count on a reasonable increase in resources over six years and a longer period of time to institute necessary changes, the planners are now faced with short-run shifting of resources and a problem of compressing a six-year plan into the mandated three-year one, while keeping present programs on a viable level.

This does not mean that all prior planning effort is wasted. Indeed, everyone concerned with the previous problem was committed to a continuous reevaluation of projections in line with changing conditions. The original plan still constitutes a very adequate base from which to start a new effort at replanning. But the point is that planners must maintain a dynamic context. No planner should ever consider that a plan constitutes a finality that cannot be altered under any conditions. Nor should a planner take such a proprietory interest in a plan that all parts become irrevocably cast in concrete. The key is for managers to maintain a dynamic posture on planning —continually planning and monitoring their efforts.

PLANNING TOOLS

Several tools for planning and scheduling are available for a manager to use. Although few of these tools would help the manager in selecting particular alternatives (unlike decision-making aids) or in determining *how* to carry out a plan (means), they generally are helpful in putting subgoals and priorities in order and assigning responsibilities. The three we will cover here are a simple planning chart or matrix, scheduling charts (Gantt charts), and PERT (Program Evaluation Review Technique).

Planning matrix   This tool or any similar variant simply allows the manager to keep order in the planning process by providing benchmarks in terms of times, responsi-

	Step or process	Who is to perform?	When— (time deadline)	Where— (location)	Special resource needs
1.					
2.					
3.					
4.					
etc.					

FIG. 8.8
A planning matrix.

bilities, and interrelationships and to control while the plan is being implemented. A planning matrix is illustrated in Fig. 8.8.

The manager simply sets in the process or step to be completed and assigns the responsibility, time deadlines, place, and special needs. Note that the tool does not assist the manager in making the *correct* decision on means; the manager will have to employ decision processes for each step or process, but once these have been determined, they can be easily sequenced through the planning-matrix technique.

Scheduling charts

Scheduling is a type of planning that entails assigning a certain project through various functions or processes within certain time constraints. A scheduling chart is useful not only in planning the assignment problem, but also in auditing and adapting the process should it go astray.

The originator of scheduling charts was Henry Gantt, one of the early pioneers in management; hence the tool is often called a Gantt chart, although hundreds of variants are offered by management consultants and supply houses. Gantt charts are most often used in scheduling an order through certain production processes, but they can also be used in scheduling a project through departments or units (see Fig. 8.9).

Figure 8.9, a scheduling chart, plots time against machines. Note that three projects are progressing through the system: jobs 1, 2, and 3. Job 1 starts on machine 1, job 2 starts on machine 3, and job 3 starts on machine 2. Job 1 moves to machine 2 while job 2 moves to machine 1, and so on. The objective in this exercise may be to minimize machine down-time or the time that the

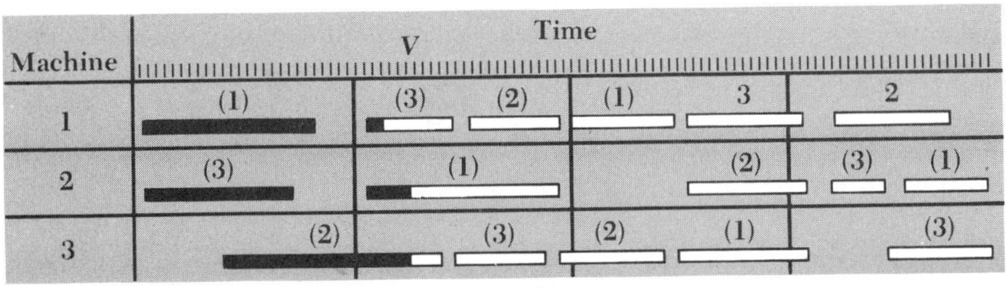

FIG. 8.9
A Gantt chart.

V = reporting date

projects are worked on. The dotted lines show actual progress and give the decision maker or scheduler control over the process, allowing the manager to set corrective action into motion if necessary. Note in this case that job 3 is slightly behind schedule; it should be about half way through its time on machine 1 on the checked date. In fact, it is only one-quarter through.

PERT (Program Evaluation Review Technique) A method of scheduling or planning very similar in concept to a Gantt chart is PERT, a method developed for use when large numbers of interrelated processes must be brought together into an integrated plan. For example, as mentioned previously, in the Apollo space program literally thousands of contractors and subcontractors were engaged in the manufacture of the various components and assemblies for the program, which itself involved several missions, long periods of training, plus the side projects of selection, housing, travel, etc. PERT, with the aid of a powerful computer, was employed to sequence those many hundreds of thousands of activities and control the process throughout its operation.

Although we shall cover the particulars of PERT in the appendix to this chapter, we shall discuss the rudiments of the tool here.* The first thing a planner engages in with PERT is to construct a network of events (objectives) and activities that must occur for completion of the project. In the project shown in Fig. 8.10, fifteen things must occur in order for the project to be completed. The "things" are called *events* and are designated by circles. The actions connecting the events are called *activities* and are designated by arrows. Note that the network includes several steps in which multiple paths of activities and events are going on simultaneously and that completion of all paths is a necessary condition for the connecting or terminal event to be completed. This occurs before events 9, 12, and 15.

Each *activity* is assigned three possible times for completion—an optimistic time (everything goes superbly and the organization is extremely lucky), a most likely time (everything goes well, according to plan, and all contingencies were accounted for), and a pessimistic time (the project will hit some unforeseen snags). Using these three times, the planner can determine an *expected time for each activity*, using the formula

$$t_e = \frac{t_o + 4(t_{ml}) + t_p}{6},$$

where t_o is the optimistic time, t_{ml} is the most likely time, and t_p is the pessimistic time.

Summing the expected times for each activity over the range of activities on each of the paths of the network yields the total expected time (T_E) for

---

* *See* R. W. Miller, "How to Plan and Control with PERT," *Harvard Business Review* 40, 2 (April 1962): 93–104. Expanded treatment and more complex models can be found in J. D. Wiest and F. K. Levy, *A Management Guide to PERT/CPM: with GERT-PDM, DCPM and Other Networks,* 2d ed. (Englewood Cliffs, N.J.: Prentice-Hall, 1977).

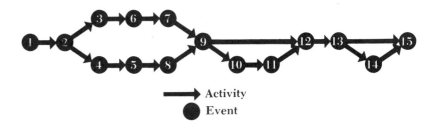

FIG. 8.10
A PERT network of events
and activities.

→ Activity
● Event

each path. The longest path in terms of time (e.g., the highest expected time total) is called the *critical path*. For example, suppose path 1-2-4-5-6-9-12-13-15 had the longest expected time relative to the other necessary paths. That path would be the critical path.

The next step is to determine the latest allowable date for the project and then for each of the events. The latest time for the entire project to be completed (T_L) is specified by the planner. The latest time for each event is obtained by subtracting backwards from the final event—subtracting in steps the expected time from the latest time. For example, suppose that the latest possible date for event 15 and hence for the project to be completed is assigned as September 30. If the expected time for the activity connecting events 14 and 15 was twelve days, the latest date for event 14 would become September 18.

For each event, subtracting the accumulated expected time (t_e summed from the beginning of the project) from the latest time (t_e subtracted from the proposed end of the project) will yield the *slack time* available for each event. Slack time on the critical path will always be equal to the term

$$T_L - T_E \quad (\text{or} \quad T_L - \Sigma t_e).$$

Slack time will give the planner some idea of how much time can be lost or wasted or will indicate possible transferring of resources to other uses—perhaps on the critical path. From a calculation of slack time, PERT allows the decision maker to calculate a probability that the project will be finished on time—using probability tables.

Again, PERT does not allow the decision maker to determine how an activity will be undertaken. It simply arranges given decisions or activities into a logical sequence, offers the planner some criteria on shifting resources and minimizing costs, and simplifies controls.

All of these planning tools—matrices, charts, PERT, and the many others that have been adapted and developed—are no panacea for thoughtful, logical analysis of means and ends. The dilemmas of the planner are not resolved by use of any tool. The planner must still determine the efficacy of the objective and the least costly or best way to achieve that objective and will still temper those decisions with his or her own values and those of the organization. The value of these tools lies in their time saving, their ability to predict the possible malfunctioning of a plan due to time problems, and their usefulness in assisting the manager in controlling the process once it commences.

SUMMARY

By now, you should realize that planning—even when it involves a single unit in a relatively short-range objective situation—is no easy matter. When the complexities of longer-range, multiunit strategic planning are added, the value and necessity for managerial contributions become obvious. Earlier, we said that managing is not an easy task; now we can add that planning is the most complex of managerial assignments. The aspiring manager would do well to heed the advice of not taking planning too lightly.

Managers often are accused of enlarging the administrative structure; building large, self-serving organizations; padding their payrolls for their own prestige; and the like. Such allegations are often expressed most vehemently during budget-setting times. We, of course, do not condone unnecessarily complex and overloaded organizations and do not recommend any more of a management structure than is absolutely necessary to accomplish the mission of the organization. One should, however, recognize the complexities of goal-setting, decision-making, or planning activities; the number of steps involved and the levels of sophistication necessary; the sources of information which need to be consulted; and the number of offices that must be tied into the process, etc., before automatically questioning the need for managers and their functions. Planning is a difficult but very necessary managerial task.

DISCUSSION QUESTIONS

1 Briefly summarize the planning process.

2 Differentiate between a unipath planning process and a multipath planning process.

3 What do we mean when we say that each phase of a planning process may be an amalgam of hundreds of short-term (multiunit) ends-and-means decision linkages?

4 What do we mean by planning backwards? Why is planning often best accomplished by that method?

5 What do we mean by the term "dynamic planning"?

6 What tools are available to assist the manager in planning? Explain at least two tools for planning and scheduling.

7 Several types of organizational and environmental factors constrain the viability of a proposed plan. Define and explain some of these factors.

8 What are some of the key differences between short-term and long-term planning?

9 Define the following terms:

a) planning   b) single-path planning
c) long-term planning   d) short-term planning
e) Gantt chart   f) PERT
g) planning matrix   h) slack time
i) critical path

10 Devise a PERT diagram for preparing a steak dinner with all the trimmings.

CASE: POSITION PUBLICATIONS: THE GENESIS OF *VOYAGER MAGAZINE*

■ "Hey, look, Sylvia, with all those Super Saver fares, Liberty fares, package tours, and what have you, more and more people are traveling. Do you realize that a person can fly from New York to California for under $300 round trip?"

Sylvia Agrow knew that her coeditor Sam Carranza was a true travel buff and had been pushing to get Position Publications into a travel magazine for the last six years. But with *Holiday*, the various guides, the *New York Times* travel section, and all the services of the oil companies, the American Automobile Association, and travel agents, she was never very enthusiastic about it and always found some reason to get him to back off. This time, however, she thought that he might have something. Travel was now within the means of most everyone.

The airlines, after an initial period of protest and grumbling, were finding that they liked the progressively deregulated structure that the Civil Aeronautics Board was moving them into. Passenger traffic had increased by seven percent since the beginning of the year, and practically all of that represented new business—people who might not have flown without the reduced rates. Regular passengers, who wanted to travel on their own schedules, would like to save the money if they could, but wouldn't alter their schedules to do so. The business traveler—considered the mainstay of the airlines' clientele—still paid full fare, although there were increased complaints about crowded planes, allegedly surly cabin crews, and the same service that the full-fare passengers received being granted to the cut-rate passengers.

The additional passengers, however, most of them traveling on a special-deal fare, represented "gravy" for the airlines, since they filled previously empty seats for the cost to the airline of essentially a meal (although additional costs in handling the increased reservation load were starting to mount). So the airlines started advertising and pushing the cut-rate fares and welcomed the new traveler. And air travel was booming for the non-business traveler.

On top of that, Laker Airlines, a private British international airline, had introduced a one-fare, no-reservations, no-frills, regularly scheduled New York–London service, introducing more Americans to Europe, although the decreasing value of the dollar made Europe and Japan less attractive to the American traveler.

"Okay," agreed Sylvia, "We probably can sell the idea upstairs, but after the way we bombed on the consumer magazine, we had better have a detailed plan to justify each step of the process."

The consumer magazine was a poor copy of the one put out by Consumers' Union, but Position Publications had changed the format somewhat. Their product tests, moreover, were commissioned to several outside agencies, and the consistency of their reliability was rather poor. Feature articles on retail chains, federal regulations, mail-order deals, vacation homes, etc., often become unresearched diatribes, and the publishers suffered through three negotiated settlements of libel suits before quietly folding the magazine.

"That's a low blow, Sylvia. I still think it was a good idea; we just didn't tie up all the loose ends."

"Oh come on, Sam, you know you were just winging that one. You went to that symposium on consumerism in Washington and came back all fired up. You didn't even consider that consumerism might be just another fad."

"That's your opinion. But I do agree that we've really got to plan this new one out. Let's be sure we can justify another travel magazine in terms of numbers first—you know, air travelers, ground travelers, the competition, income of potential subscribers, and all the other demographics of the traveling public. Maybe I can get the Spofford-Hendricks Ad Agency to come up with some of their data. They handle the Intercoastal Airways account, and I think that they've got one of the major oil companies as well. If I can't get any information from them, maybe we can get some of our own staffers to build up the numbers base.

"I'll do a pro-forma profit-and-loss statement on the thing, costing it out and comparing the costs to subscriptions and advertising revenues. I'm almost sure we can project the twelve percent net we know they'll demand upstairs."

"Okay, assuming it's a go proposition—the market is there, the demographics all check out, and the net looks reasonable—then we've got about a two-year time between the approval decision and the first edition. And you've got to plan the editorial—writers, travelers, photographers—production, marketing, space sales—the whole ball of wax."

"Why don't we lay out a preliminary plan and schedule to take upstairs with the numbers?" ■

Case questions

1. What kind of planning are Sam Carranza and Sylvia Agrow becoming involved in? Unipath? Multipath?

2. Assume that the proposed magazine's profit potential is acceptable to top management; outline a path(s) of ends or completion dates for the production of *Voyager* magazine.

3. What might you do differently from what Sylvia Agrow is now doing?

SELECTED READINGS

Ackoff, R. L., *A Concept of Corporate Planning* (New York: Wiley-Interscience, 1970).

Ansoff, H. I., R. Hays, and R. Declerck, *From Strategic Planning to Strategic Management* (New York: Wiley, 1976).

Elmaghnaby, Salah E., *Activity Networks: Project Planning and Control by Network Models* (New York: Wiley, 1977).

Enrick, N. L., *Management Planning* (New York: McGraw-Hill, 1967).

Ewing, D., "Corporate Planning at the Crossroads," *Harvard Business Review* 45 (July/August 1967): 77–86.

————, ed., *Long Range Planning for Management*, new ed. (New York: Harper & Row, 1972).

Gantt, H. L., *Organizing for Work* (New York: Harcourt Brace Jovanovich, 1919).

Glaser, E. M., "Outline for Long Range Corporate Planning," *S.A.M. Advance Management Journal* 36 (January 1971): 51–57.

Grinyer, P., and J. Wooller, "Corporate Models for Corporate Planning," *Long Range Planning* 8 (February 1975): 14–25.

Hall, W. K., "SBU's Hot New Topic in the Management of Diversification," *University of Michigan Business Review* 30, 2 (March 1978): 12–18.

————, "Corporate Strategic Planning—Some Perspectives for the Future," *Michigan Business Review* 24 (January 1972): 16–21.

Hilton, Peter, *Planning Corporate Growth and Diversification* (New York: McGraw-Hill, 1970).

Holloway, C., "Planning at Gulf—A Case Study," *Long Range Planning* 8 (April 1975): 27–45.

Hughes, R. E., "Planning: The Essence of Control," *Managerial Planning* 26, 6 (May/June 1978): 1–3, 10.

Katz, A., "Planning in the IBM Corporation," *Long-Range Planning* 11, 3 (June 1978): 2–7.

King, D. C., and W. G. Beevor, "Long-Range Thinking," *Personnel Journal* 57, 9 (September 1978): 504–509.

King, W. R., and D. I. Cleveland, "A New Method for Strategic Systems Planning," *Business Horizons* 18 (August 1975): 55–64.

Levin, R. I., and C. A. Kirkpatrick, *Planning and Control with PERT/CPM*. (New York: McGraw-Hill, 1966).

Litschert, R., "The Structure of Long Range Planning Groups," *Academy of Management Journal* 14 (March 1971): 33–43.

Mize, J. H., C. R. White, and G. H. Brooks, *Operations Planning and Control* (Englewood Cliffs, N.J.: Prentice-Hall, 1971).

Mockler, R. J., *Management Control Process* (Englewood Cliffs, N.J.: Prentice-Hall, 1972).

Preble, J., "Corporate Use of Environmental Scanning," *University of Michigan Business Review* 30, 5 (September 1978): 12–17.

Redmond, W. H., "Values in Forecasting and Planning," *Long-Range Planning* **11**, 3 (June 1978): 22–25.

Schoeffler, S., R. D. Buzzell, and D. F. Heany, "Impact of Strategic Planning on Profit Performance," *Harvard Business Review* **52** (March/April 1974): 137–145.

Sokolik, S. L., "A Strategy for Planning," *MSU Business Topics* **26**, 2 (Spring 1978): 57–64.

Spainhower, J. I., "Managerial Planning in State Government," *Managerial Planning* **26**, 5 (March/April 1978): 36–37, 40.

Steiner, G. A., *Top Management Planning* (New York: Macmillan, 1969).

Terry, P., "Organizational Implications for Long Range Planning," *Long Range Planning* **8** (February 1975): 26–30.

Vancil, R. F., "Strategic Formulation in Complex Organizations, *Sloan Management Review* **17** (Winter 1976): 1–18.

Warren, K. E., *Long Range Planning: The Executive Viewpoint* (Englewood Cliffs, N.J.: Prentice-Hall, 1966).

Wheelwright, S. C., "Strategic Planning in the Small Business," *Business Horizons* **14** (August 1971): 51–58.

Wiest, J. D., and F. K. Levy, *A Management Guide to PERT/CPM: with GERT-PDM, DCPM and Other Networks*, 2d ed. (Englewood Cliffs, N.J.: Prentice-Hall, 1977).

APPENDIX: PERT

Assume that a network has been constructed of activities and events as shown in Fig. 8.11. Event 1 is the beginning of the project, which will be completed at event 15. The next step is to assign optimistic, most likely, and pessimistic times to each activity, as shown in Table 8.1. Next, the planner will calculate an expected time for each activity, using the formula

$$t_e = \frac{t_o + 4(t_{ml}) + t_p}{6}$$

and a standard deviation for each activity, using the formula

$$\sigma = \frac{t_p - t_o}{6}.$$

Note that t_e is a measure of the mean time. Given a normal distribution, fifty percent of the possible times will fall on each side of t_e. For example, for activity 1–2, then,

$$t_e = \frac{1 + 4(2) + 3}{6} = 2.00$$

$$\sigma = \frac{3 - 1}{6} = .33$$

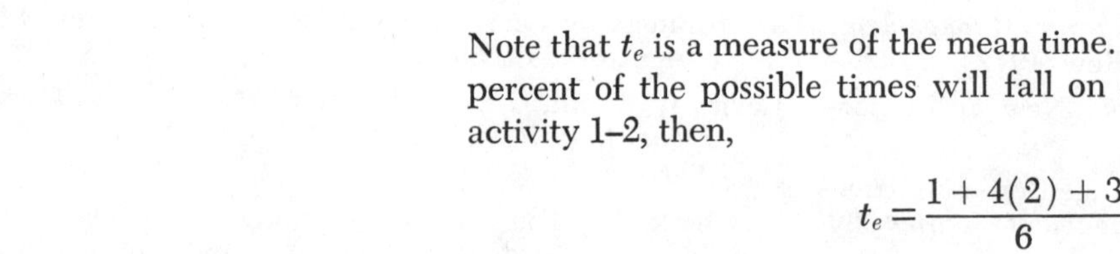

FIGURE 8.11

TABLE 8.1 Activity completion times	Activity	t_o	t_{ml}	t_p	t_e	σ
	1–2	1	2	3	2.00	.33
	2–3	2	5	8	5.00	1.00
	3–4	2	4	6	4.00	.67
	3–6	1	2	3	2.00	.33
	4–5	2	4	6	4.00	.67
	5–8	2	4	6	4.00	.67
	6–7	1	2	3	2.00	.33
	7–9	2	5	8	5.00	1.00
	8–9	6	6	6	6.00	0
	9–10	2	5	8	5.00	1.00
	10–11	6	10	14	10.00	1.33
	11–12	2	4	6	4.00	.67
	11–13	2	4	6	4.00	.67
	12–15	6	8	10	8.00	.67
	13–14	1	2	3	2.00	.33
	14–15	1	2	3	2.00	.33

and for activity 2–3,

$$t_e = \frac{2 + 20 + 8}{6} = 5.00$$

$$\sigma = \frac{8 - 2}{6} = 1.00.$$

We have inserted all of the remaining calculated t_e in Table 8.1, along with the standard deviations for each.

Next, T_E must be calculated. T_E is the sum of the t_e numbers for each of the paths. There are four possible paths to follow in attempting to sum the t_e values and obtain T_E.

	T_E (or Σt_e)
1-2-3-6-7-9-10-11-12-15	43
1-2-3-6-7-9-10-11-13-14-15	39
1-2-3-4-5-8-9-10-11-12-15	52
1-2-3-4-5-8-9-10-11-13-14-15	48

The longest path is 1-2-3-4-5-8-9-10-11-12-15, with an expected total time (T_E) of 52 units. This longest path is called the *critical path*.

Next, the planner must calculate T_L, defined as the latest possible time of completion. T_L is specified by the decision maker; assume in this problem that T_L is specified at 58 units. The t_l for each activity is obtained by starting backwards from event 15 (specified as 58) and subtracting t_e from t_l. Thus t_l for event 14 would be $58 - 2$, or 56; for event 13, $56 - 2$, or 54.

Event	t_l	—	t_e	=	Slack	TABLE 8.2
1	6		0	=	6	
2	8		2	=	6	
3	13		7	=	6	
4	17		11	=	6	
5	21		15	=	6	
6	23		9	=	14	
7	25		11	=	14	
8	25		19	=	6	
9	31		25	=	6	
10	36		30	=	6	
11	46		40	=	6	
12	50		44	=	6	
13	54		44	=	10	
14	56		46	=	10	
15	58		52	=	6	

Table 8.2 calculates the cumulative t_l and t_e for all activities and events. Note that in calculating cumulative t_e for an event that is preceded by two or more events, we use the larger sum. The t_l for an event succeeded by two or more events is the smaller of the numbers calculated.

Slack time is the difference at each event between the latest possible time an event may be completed and the expected time for that event. Note that the slack along the critical path will always equal $T_L - T_E$, or $58 - 52 = 6$.

Finally, the planner can determine the probability that the project will be completed on time. For this σT_E must be determined first:

$$\sigma T_E = \sqrt{\Sigma(\sigma)^2},$$

Using the standard deviation of the activities on the critical path (from Table 8.1):

σ		σ^2
.33		0.109
1.00		1.000
.67		0.449
.67		0.449
.67	and squaring each	0.449
.00		0.000
1.00		1.000
1.33		1.769
.67		0.449
.67		0.449
		6.123

$$\sigma T_E = \sqrt{6.123} = 2.48.$$

To determine the probability, we must determine the difference between T_L and T_E expressed in standard deviations. This is the familiar Z statistic:

$$Z = \frac{T_L - T_E}{\sigma T_E} = \frac{58 - 52}{2.48} = \frac{6}{2.48} = 2.42.$$

The Z statistic gives us the difference between the T_L and T_E expressed in standard deviations. Using the normal curve, the probability of the project's being completed on time can be calculated. (See Fig. 8.12.)

By consulting a table of areas under a normal curve, the planner will find that the 2.42 standard deviations from the mean encompasses .4922 percent of the curve from the mean. Since 50 percent of the curve already lies to the left of the mean, the probability of this project's being completed on time is .50 + .4922, or approximately 99.2 percent.

One should thus note that the greater the slack time, the higher the probability that the project will be completed on time. If slack time equaled zero, the probability would be .50, since T_L and T_E would be equal. If the project had negative slack, T_L would lie to the left of T_E, and the project would have a probability of completion of .50 minus the difference between T_L and T_E expressed in standard deviations and then converted to probability from the table of areas under the normal curve.

FIGURE 8.12

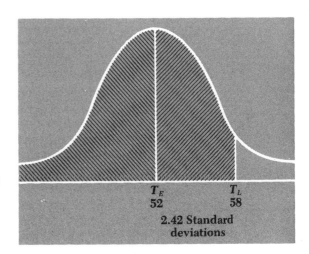

T_E
52

T_L
58

2.42 Standard
deviations

Chapter 9
DESIGNING POLICIES AND PROCEDURES

CHAPTER HIGHLIGHTS

In this chapter we cover the concepts of policy and procedure, often referred to as standing plans, since they are put into effect to allow managers to quickly handle repetitive events. We will relate policy to organizational level and to planning as well as to the shaping force of environment. We will then cover the policy-formulation process and the responsibility of various organizational components in policy making.

LEARNING OBJECTIVES

1 To be able to define "policy" and "procedure."

2 To learn the functions of policy and the reasons for using it.

3 To know why policies and procedures are often referred to as standing plans.

4 To learn why we need policy, who is constrained by policy, and why consistency is necessary.

5 To learn where in the organization policy may be promulgated and how that relates to decentralization and centralization.

6 To understand the relationship of policy to planning.

7 To understand the need for continual reexamination of policies and procedures.

8 To understand the effect of law and public regulation on organizational policy.

9 To learn how societal changes can impact on policy.

10 To understand the process of policy formulation and implementation and the usual organizational units (line and staff) that carry out each step.

11 To learn what a policy audit entails.

CASE: SEABOARD MANUFACTURING COMPANY: THE PERSONNEL DEPARTMENT

■ In November 1956 President Oswald P. Clarke of Seaboard Manufacturing Company hired the organization's first personnel officer, Sigmund Heller. Seaboard had grown from a small tool and die shop specializing in shoe dies into a company of 280 employees. Company growth had resulted from basically one product: barbecue grills. The simple, easily manufactured pan-shaped grills became very popular with suburban Americans in the early 1950s, and by 1956 practically every family owning its own home had one on the back porch or in the yard.

Clarke knew, however, that a company could not continue to subsist on one primary product, particularly a seasonal one, and one that he considered a fad at that. So he already had a new-products committee working on developing inexpensive, but useful steel-fabricated products.

Like many fast-growing companies continually planning for future growth, many of the secondary functions of the firm were just not given the attention they needed. Inventory control was a disaster. No standards were in force in the purchasing area. Bids were not taken for the widely used items such as sheet steel; suppliers were just old friends of Clarke's. For the accounting function, an outside certified public accountant came in once a week to make sense out of desk drawers full of invoices from suppliers and bills to customers.

But the biggest shock came with an attempt by a militant union to organize the company's production workers. The attempt failed by just seven votes and only after Clarke had delivered a fatherly speech to the production unit, stressing the benefits to be derived from the company's planned growth.

Clarke, in bringing in Heller, gave him virtual carte blanche in the personnel area. Clarke said that his company needed personnel policies so that everyone—from the president to the workers—knew where they and the company stood in terms of recruitment, selection, placement, and maintenance of the work force. Aside from wage rates, which were standard throughout the company (and basically were copied from the contract of the local plant of a large electrical equipment manufacturer), foremen and supervisors handled all of the personnel work, from hiring to firing. Practices varied from department to department, and it was not uncommon for an applicant rejected by one supervisor to be hired by another one in another part of the plant. No salespeople were hired at Seaboard, since personal connections of the owners with the operators of four large discount department-store chains resulted in sufficient orders to keep the plant operating at full capacity.

Heller's first task was to cement down the relationship of his position to the rest of the units within the company. Initially, foremen were requested to channel all of their needs for personnel to his office. Although Heller realized that this was only a start, at least the step prompted the foremen to think in terms of a personnel office and allowed him to keep track of requests for personnel, with an eventual aim toward standardizing personnel-requisition procedures.

Heller then spent the better part of the next two years developing personnel policies and procedures for recommendation to the top management of Seaboard. Policies and procedures were developed and adopted in the following standard areas related to personnel management:

1 Job descriptions and labor specifications

2 Recruitment

3 Employee selection

4 Job evaluation and wage determination

5 Merit rating and employee evaluation

6 Fringes and benefits

7 Safety

8 Employee communications

With very few exceptions, all of Heller's recommendations were accepted by Seaboard's top management, and the company's first manual of personnel policy was published for distribution in early 1958.

Selection—or hiring—was one particular area on which Heller spent a great deal of time standardizing while formulating policy. Based on the job descriptions he had developed in consultation with the foremen and supervisors, Heller established some standard policies and procedures that covered the entire production force within the plant. For example:

> All hiring for the plant is to be carried out by the central personnel office, except for skilled machine operators (job categories 21, 22, and 23). Applicants for those jobs will be screened by central personnel office according to standard instruments, and the two most qualified applicants will be sent to the relevant department supervisor for final selection.

> Only high school graduates between the ages of eighteen and thirty will be employed in entry-level positions.

> All applicants for positions at Seaboard Manufacturing Company will be required to attain satisfactory scores on selected aptitude and ability tests.

The tests selected by Heller for administering to applicants were some general intelligence and various specialized ability-measurement tests.

Heller felt, and top management concurred, that these policies and standards were necessary in order to contribute to a high-quality, stable work force. This type of work force, he was convinced, would in turn contribute to the overall company objective of profitable operation from maximum production of high-quality products.

The standard policies and procedures developed by Heller in 1958 remained relatively unchanged until the mid-1960s. Although Heller was aware that policies and standards are subject to occasional incidents of a particular policy's not being the best rule for a particular case, in general he felt that the efficiency of having standardized guides to action and rules of behavior more than compensated for the occasional loss incurred in the exceptional case.

And so, Sigmund Heller's department and its relationships with the operating departments settled down to a general routine. The company continued to grow, and new products were introduced.

Occasionally, a new policy area was developed. For example, when the company outgrew the sales relationships of the owners and employed salespeople to expand the market area, a new set of policies, procedures, and standards relating to the compensation of salesmen was developed. But generally, Heller's job settled down to processing applications, hiring, maintaining payroll and fringe-benefit records, etc.

In the mid-1960s Seaboard's personnel policies and procedures were challenged not by any new move or plan of the company, but by changes in legislation and court decisions striking down some time-honored personnel policies and procedures present in most companies, including Seaboard. First, the Civil Rights Act of 1964 specifically outlawed in companies of more than fifteen employees discrimination on the basis of race, religion, national origin, and sex in any personnel-related matter such as hiring, wages, job assignment, promotion, personal facilities, etc. This law seemed innocuous enough to Heller. Both Heller and Seaboard's top management had always prided themselves on being color blind in hiring and other personnel matters and felt that all of their standards and policies were as objective as humanly possible.

But then in rapid succession came an act prohibiting discrimination based on age (for applicants or employees between forty-five and sixty-four years of age) and a court case that struck down tests and education requirements unless such requirements and instruments could be related specifically to the jobs involved. These were followed by other cases and administrative rulings that struck down time-honored applicant-evaluation instruments such as credit checks and arrest-record checks; for female workers, pregnancy status and the number of children under care could not be considered as employment standards, unless the employer could show definite job relatedness of the information.*

Although Seaboard had not been sued and had no explicit notification that its policies were in violation of the law, Clarke called in Heller and asked what effect the new legal requirements were having on company personnel policies and procedures. Heller replied that to his knowledge, "Seaboard is clean." No one had challenged the policies, and in any event the tests were not being relied on, and he felt that he could justify the age stan-

* These rulings and cases are discussed more fully in Chapter 12.

dard for entry-level jobs. Clarke was unconvinced. He felt that the company was not only courting danger, but also in technical violation of the law. He ordered Heller to immediately audit *all* personnel policies, standards, and procedures not only in light of changing laws and social demands, but also in line with the company's latest product planning, including the possibility that Seaboard would be bidding for government contracts. ■

POLICIES AND PROCEDURES

Definitions   So far, throughout this book, we have used the terms *policy* and *procedure* without ever fully defining the terms or relating how policy ever becomes embedded within the organization in the first place. It is now time to explore those issues more carefully and more fully, since policies and procedures are important elements in organizational operation, and managers are the people who design the policies and procedures.

Although most organizations are continually engaging in planning and strategy building related to short-term, intermediate-term, and long-term objectives, the organization also has an underlying code of rules and regulations which reflect the firm's character or its ultimate and continuous objectives. These rules and regulations, which are ongoing and reflect the continuous or philosophic goal of the organization, are policies and procedures.

Policies are *general guides to action* that are standard within and throughout the organization. For example, suppose that a business firm has a goal of maximum profits (or profitable operation). A general guide to all activity and planning related to that goal might be a policy such as the following: "All projects planned in this company must show a potential return on investment of twenty percent in order to be considered for future continuation." This rule, or policy, *effectively limits all of the planners or decision makers* in the firm from considering projects in their planning that promise a return of less than twenty percent. Furthermore, the policy encourages the decision makers to search out and consider and promote opportunities capable of gaining returns of greater than twenty percent.

Standard procedures are the sequences that decision makers and planners follow in implementing policy. For example, how is the project planner to know that a particular project would yield eighteen percent, twenty-two percent, or twenty-eight percent? What costs are to be included? How is investment to be measured? What overhead charges are to be allocated to the particular project under consideration? How many years is the project to be allowed a low return before the high rate of return is expected to materialize? All of these questions would be covered by a step-by-step process for planners to follow for determining the rate of return for each project. Such a step-by-step process is called a procedure.

Or, suppose that Sigmund Heller is able to maintain his policy of employing only applicants between the ages of eighteen and thirty for entry-level positions. How is the evaluator of applicants to determine if that policy is being met for each particular applicant? The evaluator should also be provided with a procedure to follow to verify the applicant's record. This procedure could include requiring the applicant to submit a transcript of high school grades, a birth certificate, a high school diploma, or some other certification of graduation. The procedure might also include a call to the high school, checking out previous employers, etc.

In short, policies are standard general guides to action, and procedures are the sequential instruments for carrying out policies. Some authors have referred to policies and procedures as *standing plans,* and indeed that is precisely what they are.* Policies and procedures are the stable building blocks on which the organization functions on a day-to-day basis, and they form the stable base while the organization cuts new ground with planning and strategy building.

As we shall see later, however, a policy is never so constraining that it is never challenged nor so sacrosanct that it is never changed. Sometimes a new plan may signal a need to reexamine established policy. And organizations ought to establish organizational mechanisms that encourage the periodic reexamination of standards, policies, rules, or procedures that allow a reassessment of such standing rules if a plan can better achieve objectives with a revised policy or procedure.

Rationale for policy

The chief advantages of policies and procedures are the consistency and standardization that they inject into an organization's operations. Action is guided on a consistent basis throughout the organization, and an individual or other organization, in dealing within any part of the organization where a particular policy applies, can expect the organization to act in a certain predictable manner because the policy is in existence. On the other hand, consistency of action as a result of policy is also a function of the extent of centralization or decentralization within the organization (centralized organizations feature greater consistency). Thus the advantages of consistency may be limited only to the administrative unit in which that policy is operational.

Policies and procedures also constrain and program the behavior of an organization's executive and operative personnel. If a particular policy, for example, calls for three competitive bids on purchases of over $1000, an executive knows that he or she cannot award a $7000 contract to a friend or relative unless that individual also happens to be the low bidder (and even then, the firm may have a policy against nepotism, which would preclude the relative's being considered at all). What policy is accomplishing in these cases is a limitation on the freedom or discretion of organizational personnel

* *See* William Newman, *Administrative Action* (Englewood Cliffs, N.J.: Prentice-Hall, 1951).

to act, presumably because such a limit would better serve organizational purposes than allowing executives total or the maximum amount of leeway in decision making.

Although consistency and programmed behavior are usually cited as advantages of policies and procedures, critics have pointed to those outcomes as inherent limitations of policy as well. Some have argued that the consistent level of decisions demanded by policy often restricts the choice of the best alternative for a situation, thereby causing the firm or the organization to reach less than an optimum solution. Often critics claim that firms and managers are then forced to satisfice—to pick solutions that are good enough or, in this case, that fall within the guidelines of policy.

But defenders of the concept of policy retort that the costs involved in continually assessing the same problems and making the same decision over and over—or perhaps having a different decision being made for the same problem situation—are not compensated for by the infinitesimal advantages accruing to a possibly more optimum outcome. Moreover, the inconsistency in decisions on repetitive problems or situations may well lay the basis for future organizational conflict. Under a policy, at least, every member of the organization is presumed to know what to expect and so be subject to the same treatment.

Critics also assert that *excessive* policy binds the organization up in red tape, causes its members to lose sight of the organizational goals and objectives, and engenders as much ill will as is relieved by the consistent treatment afforded by the presence of policy. In essence, compliance with the policy itself becomes more important than the end the policy was originally intended or designed to pursue.* These conditions are more likely functions of the organization and managers' forgetting to monitor the administration of the organization or of executives' setting substantively bad policy in the first place; they are not necessarily indictments of the concept of policy per se. Like laws that outlive their usefulness, organizations may find policy piled upon policy, with little attempt to prune, codify, or relate one to another. That results from just poor management, not from an inherent disadvantage of policy, however.

Organizational levels and policy   Policies are instituted and applied at all levels of the organization, and a key to understanding where a particular policy is to be instituted rests with the determination of the need for consistency below various organizational levels (or within what administrative units, to use the terminology adopted in Chapter 3). For example, if a corporate goal is maximum profit, as in one of our previous examples in this chapter, the policy of twenty percent return on investment would obviously be instituted at the top levels of the organiza-

---

* This is the goal-displacement argument discussed in Chapter 5.

tion and would apply to and permeate all of the divisions. Similarly, if dress standards are deemed important to the profitable operations of the organization, policies on appropriate dress might also be set at the top or central level and then be applicable throughout the organization.

But suppose that a consistent or standardized dress policy is not considered that important to total company operations. If consistency in dress is not an important input into company profit, such a policy might not be instituted at the central level, but the organization might allow different standards at the lower levels. Under such conditions one division might impose dress codes for reasons *relating to that division's objectives.* Another division might not do so. Both divisional policies could be consistent with the overall corporate objective or philosophy, simply because central management rested silent on the issue. If, however, central management imposed a policy that no dress codes could be set anywhere within the organization, the second division's policy would not be consistent with the organizational goal or philosophy and probably would be overruled.

Placement of policy determination and formulation functions within an organization obviously relates to the degree of decentralization or centralization practiced by the organization. If, like many of the fast-food chains, total consistency in all aspects of the organization's operations is so important to the overall corporate objectives, minute procedures and policy would be set at the central levels and followed or implemented throughout the total organization. (An example is the standard policy throughout at least one major chain relating to the length of time food can remain under the warming lights before being disposed of.) On the other hand, decentralized conglomerates composed of divisions selling different products and aiming at different markets usually have only limited numbers of general organizational policies set at the central level (usually covering finance, return on investment, capital budgeting, accounting, and auditing procedures, etc.). Much of the policy making remains in the various divisions. The divisions, in turn, might further push policy formulation to lower levels, depending on the philosophy of organization practiced within each.

Recall from Chapter 3, however, that the extent of centralization and decentralization need not be consistent throughout a large organization. Some divisions will be operated from "topside," whereas others may be operated with decisions made at the lowest possible levels. Often these decisions will be the result of performance over time; a particularly bad long period for a division may result in all decisions and all policy setting being transferred to top-level, central management.

Policies and planning

Policies and procedures are generally viewed as constraints to the decision-making and planning processes. That is, planners usually accept as givens, or constants, the established policies and procedures of the organization, and they are supposed to plan around the established policies. For example, suppose that a state university has a policy of open admissions. Under such a policy, any student who is graduated from an accredited high school within that state must be accepted to the state university. This type of policy effectively constrains any of the individual schools and colleges within the university from planning a program limiting their offerings to applicants who graduated in the highest ten percent of their high school graduating classes or who scored in the 90th or higher percentiles on scholastic aptitude tests.

Other examples have already been cited throughout the book. A cash-only policy would restrict the planning of a sales-promotion campaign to those alternatives involving only cash sales. A policy of conservatism in design practiced by an automobile manufacturer would restrict a designer from indulging fantasies of racing stripes, high-horsepower engines, vinyl roofs, and red-striped tires. In essence, the policies and procedures governing the organization or the unit within the organization often act as the frame of reference, or the basic starting point, for the planner. Figure 9.1 reflects this relationship of policy to planning.

On the other hand, experienced managers would never fail to reexamine the need for any policy should a particular plan show promise of fulfilling objectives, but require a modification in a long-standing policy or procedure. Often it is this planning function which spurs the organization to reexamine its standing rules and underlying procedures. For example, suppose that a medical clinic has a policy requiring a certified medical doctor to be present in *all* situations of patient care, including taking of tests. The rationale for

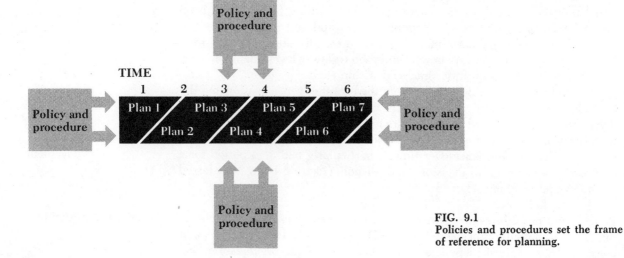

FIG. 9.1
Policies and procedures set the frame of reference for planning.

this policy is relatively easy to understand; doctors are trained, and the protection of the patient's health (presumably the objective of the clinic) led to the early adoption of the policy. Suppose, however, that a plan was suggested for handling a larger number of patients—reflecting the growth or expected growth of the community in which the clinic was located—and that the planner included larger roles for nurses, nurse practitioners, and paraprofessionals. For example, blood-pressure tests, electrocardiograms, blood tests, X-rays, and out-patient treatment of fractures, cuts, etc., might have been included as operations to be handled by the nurses, technicians, and paraprofessionals. Under some circumstances, such a plan would be rejected outright or not even considered, since its implementation would violate an established policy. But as medical facilities are faced with increasingly large case loads—and, incidentally, the need to handle those larger case loads more economically—and as social standards change, they are reexamining the need to use the highly qualified physicians in many of the roles relating to patient treatment and care. Thus, the plan might be the impetus to a reexamination of the patient-care policy within the clinic.

Suppose that a discount department store maintained a policy of plain pipe racks, old factory locations within inner cities, and no frills in order to project an image of economy and reach a clientele that might be attracted to low-priced merchandise. That firm would probably reexamine those policies as a result of a plan calling for the tapping of suburban market segments. Indeed, this was the process followed by many of the discount department chains which started business in old mills (even using the title Mill Store) and slowly gravitated to newer stores in less congested locations.

In essence, we are saying that although policies and procedures normally play a constraining role for the planning process, the planning process can also force a reexamination of policy. Planning processes often lead to a reexamination of policy and procedure, perhaps triggering a change in certain policies or indeed a full-scale reevaluation of whether a particular policy is necessary at all.

The key word is flexibility, and rarely does an organization regard established policies as untouchable, unless the organization falls into the malaise of trained incapacity—policies and the adherence to them become ends in themselves.

Policy and environment

Much of an organization's policies and procedures result from an interface or impact with various environmental groups and conditions. Thus a business firm's marketing policy in terms of pricing, returns, product selection, etc., relates and is conditioned by its market, type of customer, location, and the like. Similarly, a firm's policy on charitable contributions generally results from the social forces within the community where the firm has its home office.

One of the stronger environmental influences on an organization's policy is government at all levels. Labor laws, antitrust laws, antidiscrimination laws, and the like have all forced organizations to set new policies or alter established ones. But government does not have to pass laws to influence an organization's policy making. Often policies are formulated and implemented to prevent regulation or to forestall it at the very least.

An example of governmental influence on organizational policy occurred in the case at the beginning of this chapter. Sigmund Heller's initial activity involved defining a set of policies on hiring and job classification. Many of those policies were based on what might be called the standard temperament of personnel work in the 1950s. Tests and psychological evaluations were deemed important, and a certain aura of certainty, if not mystique, surrounded their use. All sizes and types of firms adopted the use of tests because "it was the thing to do." Prevailing attitudes about the capacities of women, minorities, and older workers found managements classifying certain jobs "for men only" or "for women only" or prescribing age limits for certain jobs. Although very few companies would admit that they discriminated overtly on the basis of race, religion, or national origin, many did set overly high and often irrelevant standards on jobs—standards that few members of certain ethnic groups, because of educational deficiencies, could pass.

The Civil Rights Act of 1964 was only the first of many legislative and judicial actions which broke down the old policies based on the prevailing mores of the time in which they had been instituted and which had never reevaluated or altered. *Griggs* v. *Duke Power* was a landmark case that should have caused the reexamination of all job descriptions that contained test and education requirements for the applicant. A company was found unable to prove the job-relatedness of certain of the tests administered and of the education required. Even though all applicants were treated equally, the net result of using the education and test requirements as conditions of employment was to screen out minorities who, in greater proportions than whites, tended not to have many years of education. Hence if the tests and requirements were not *explicitly job-related*, but were simply general screening devices, they were found to be effectively discriminatory. Similar types of discrimination in effect were established by the courts and subsequently by interpretation of the law by the Equal Employment Opportunity Commission, e.g., those relating to arrest records, pregnancy, credit ratings, and number of children cared for by a working woman. (These will be discussed more fully in Chapter 12.)

Now you should be able to understand how and why Heller's policies at Seaboard must be altered—because the law requires them to be changed. Even though the company has no cases pending against it, its policies are illegal. The president, Clarke, also ordered Heller to prepare the company for possible bidding on government contracts. Government agencies administering contracts impose affirmative-action requirements on the contractor. Such a regulation (established under Executive Order 11246 and revised to include women under Executive Order 11375) requires any contractor with fifty or more employees and contracts in excess of $50,000 to set goals for minority and female employment and to develop policies and procedures for affirmatively reaching those goals. Heller, in essence, like all his fellow personnel officers in firms contracting with the government, is now required to develop policies for actively seeking out minorities and women for employment in all job categories within the firm. Affirmative action sets no firm quotas for the firm—only goals—and if the firm cannot reach those goals, the burden of proof is on the firm to show that its management, through formulation and implementation of policies and procedures, tried to attain the goals.

Personnel management must now become more professional in terms of hiring and selection. No longer is the management of a company free to set policy based only on internal company considerations or on the past practice of personnel managers. The environment has forced new considerations onto the policy process as well as the substance of the policy output.

Sometimes changes in the environment are not as powerful as government or law, yet just as demanding and persuasive for change. For example, when fast-food restaurants were just starting to catch the public's imagination, many were garish, plastic kinds of establishments often littered with the paper remains of thousands of meals dispensed to automobile-borne eaters. Putting aside, for the moment, the communities that zoned such restaurants out of their jurisdictions, most of the companies have responded to increased public environmental awareness and the need for visual attractiveness. The chains have developed whole new sets of policies relating to the design of buildings, periodic cleanups, and proper disposals of used papergoods. A number of these chains have installed eating areas inside the buildings and responding to conservationist concerns, have switched from paper to other types of serving materials.

In summary, the environment has an enormous impact on organizational policy making, ranging from governmental regulations which force the generation of certain policies and obsoletes others to consumer and public pressure which forces the adoption of new and revised policies.

THE PROCESS OF POLICY FORMULATION AND IMPLEMENTATION

The policy-formulation process is very closely related to the decision process delineated in Chapter 6. *Policy formulation is a decision-making exercise.* Expanding on that base, however, we will in this section discuss the location

- Define problem
- Research and gather information
- Analyze alternatives
- Make selection
- Recommend policy
- Choose policy choice or get approval at top level
- Explain policy rationale
- Implement policy and establish controls

The policy-making process

within the line and staff organization of the various elements of such a decision-making process, along with the special considerations such organizational unit types must take into account.

Problem definition

The formulation of a policy results from an activity or problem facing the organization repeatedly over a period of time. For example, if customers are consistently asking if a store will accept one or more of the major bank credit cards, the store may need to consider developing a policy relating to the acceptance of the cards. Or, if an organization finds increasingly large numbers of its employees taking off on the days before and after holidays, forfeiting pay for those work days or applying sick days to them, while collecting holiday pay for the legitimate day off, it might be time for the firm to develop a standard policy for that problem rather than have each case investigated and dealt with separately.

In general, then, the need for a standard policy (and procedure) arises from a definite need resulting from a problem's presenting itself to the organization repeatedly. It is usually a function of the line organization to *define these needs and to frame the problem,* since the line is the part of the organization that has as its primary function interaction with the environment. If the problem is so clear and the answer so obvious, the proper policy may well be adopted in the part of the organization concerned—at the top levels for a corporatewide policy or at the divisional or departmental levels for policy embracing less than the entire organization. Generally, however, the solution to the problem is not so clear-cut, and the development of the policy will require analysis and investigation. This task is usually delegated to a staff unit or to a committee that will function in a staff capacity.

Research, information gathering, alternative analysis, and policy recommendation

The important elements of the decision-making process on a policy issue requiring analysis, namely, information gathering and evaluation of alternatives, are usually assigned to a staff unit. Such a unit may be specialized, if the organization is so divided and the problem is related to the function of the staff unit, or general, if the organization is not so functionally specialized and/or the problem cannot be neatly pigeonholed into a particular unit. If the policy bridges a number of areas or if staff units are not available, a committee or task force may be established to deal with the issue in a staff role.

Staff personnel do the work in policy derivation and might, if requested, present only one proposed policy to the line. Alternatively, the staff unit could be asked to present a number of alternatives to the line organizational unit concerned, and the choice would be made by the line unit from among the alternatives. Of course, if the staff unit has functional authority, either explicitly or implicitly, the final decision on the selected alternative policy would be made by the staff unit.

In most cases the choice of the policy is reserved to the line function or unit involved. The line unit may accept or reject the alternative proposed by the staff unit. Staff studies and recommendations may then be implemented, totally rejected and forgotten about, sent back to the staff unit for further modification, or returned to staff for further study and analysis.

Policy choice or approval of policy

Although the line organization might hold the final responsibility for implementing the proposed policy or at the very least be affected by its implementation, often staff units are given the responsibility of explaining the need for the policy throughout the organization. In any case, *effective policy statements generally carry an explanation of the need for such a policy.*

Explanation of policy

Although many policies are accepted within the organization with little need for elaboration on the necessity for them, others are not so readily understood. Sound managerial practice emphasizes that individuals need to know the rationale for a policy that will affect them. Often a written attached explanation will be sufficient. Although present members of the organization may find little necessity in such a written explanation, it is necessary also to cover and inform future members of the organization, who might be unaware of the reasons for the policy adoption.

But in complex policy issues, the selected policy must often be "sold" to the members of the organization—managerial and operative. In this case, managerial teams, often including members of the researching staff unit, are sent down into the line as representatives of top management to explain the need for such a policy. The danger here relates to the possible mistrust surrounding the central staff function (see Chapter 3), but generally the members of the researching staff unit are the best equipped to handle the explanation, since the personnel involved are intimately familiar with the problem and its analysis.

This part of the process may be either a line or a line/staff function. In terms of putting policy into effect, the key rests with the understanding by all concerned of the requirements of the policy and its rationale. Often staff units

Implementation of policy

have the responsibility for effecting policy, and line units must conform (note that line units may have approved the policy). For example, suppose that an organization sets as a policy the requirement to hire all new secretaries on a first-come basis of minimally qualified individuals. The rationale for this policy is to broaden the employment opportunities for members of the local community, who might be frozen out of the positions if the best-qualified person were always employed. A particular department within the organization will then know that it is requisitioning a typist and will have little choice over the typist's skills, even though it may grumble over them. So long as the individual meets the minimum required standards, that individual is employed by the staff personnel department.

Or, a company may have a policy that all expenditures must first be submitted to the accounting department for approval and then made by purchase order sent from the accounting department. Presumably this policy is in force to encumber funds so that a particular line unit will not go over budget. Staff implements and line complies, but at some point the line organization approved the policy.

Policies such as these work well if the line units involved have had either reasonable explanations of the policy or some input into the policy-making process. Often large organizations will neglect one or both of these prerequisites, and chaos in terms of organizational functioning—particularly that involving line/staff—results.

Often the policy is for line units alone to implement. Customer-selection policies, credit granting, executive hiring, services to be offered, etc., are line functions, and the line units will often bear the sole responsibility for implementing the policy. If the policy is imposed from above in the organization, the importance of a reasonable explanation of the need behind the policy becomes paramount. With good preparation and proper consultation, however, there is little reason for a policy not to succeed. Indeed, it is often *improper preparation and consultation* in the policy-setting process that lead to confrontation and conflict in policy implementation. The confrontation and conflict are not necessarily the result of the policy concept itself.

POLICING POLICY

Enforcement of policy is the responsibility of the chain of command within the organization. Enforcement usually occurs through periodic checks of operations, standard reports, and in management meetings and conferences at which probes are directed to subordinate officers.

If the organization is serious about a policy, however, its managers must telegraph that they demand complete compliance with policy. Otherwise, the entire system can break down and become a farce. General Electric Company, for example, always maintained a policy of complete compliance with the antitrust laws, and managers were forbidden by the policy to discuss pricing, contracts, or market shares with competitors' managers. But for many years, up to 1959, executives at many levels disregarded the policy, and subordinates were brought along into a major price-fixing conspiracy.* After the company and its managers (and several other companies) were apprehended, prosecuted, and convicted (resulting not only in firings, but also lawsuits and embarrassment for the company), a new procedure to reinforce the policy was established; each manager is now required to file with the company's legal office a signed statement that the company policy on antitrust has been reviewed, is understood, and is being complied with.

Commitments to corporate policy in the area of affirmative action are also being filled only in the breach at many companies, according to some critics. According to these observers, while the company president may be off on the speaking circuit bragging about the company's commitment to affirmative action and its progressive policy, subordinate managers may be "inventing" all sorts of mechanisms to circumvent the policy. Serious companies, however, will have built-in mechanisms to ensure compliance with the policy.

THE POLICY AUDIT

Although policies provide stability in an organization, this stability should never be an excuse for creeping lethargy's preventing the organization from keeping up to date. Some students of organizations have suggested that policies turn the organization into a closed system, one that assumes stability in an environment and certainty outside the bounds of the organization. But environments rarely stay stable and certain, and neither do organizations.

Effective managers will be aware of environmental and organizational instability and periodically review policies and procedures to determine if they are still applicable, efficient, and effective. Many organizations routinely schedule such reviews, dropping outmoded policies and procedures, modifying others, and adding others for newly found problem areas. Indeed, one of the most stable policies in some organizations is that calling for periodic review of policies and procedures.

But policy change is often a difficult topic for managers to handle. Armies are often accused of being prepared to fight the last war, and this occurs because reviews covering changes in doctrine, technology, enemy

---

* For a history of this antitrust case, *see* Clarence C. Walton and Frederick W. Cleveland, Jr., *Corporations on Trial: The Electric Cases* (Belmont, Cal.: Wadsworth, 1964).

strengths and dispositions, and tactics are not undertaken periodically. So too, such a malaise can affect an organization and its policies. Too often, managers and subordinates develop trained incapacity; that is, policies and/ or procedures may become so ingrained that the end, or objective, is lost sight of, and maintenance of the policy becomes the end in itself. Professional managers resist such a natural temptation if their organizations are to be kept effective and efficient. In sum, the policy audit should be a regular feature of the organization's routine and an important feature in the organization's ongoing campaign to keep current.

DISCUSSION QUESTIONS

1 Define the following terms:
   a) policy   b) procedure
   c) strategy   d) standing plans
   e) policy audit   f) policy formulation and implementation process

2 Distinguish between "policy" and standard procedures—standing plans.

3 As a general manager, why is it to your advantage to establish detailed policies and procedures? What are some of the disadvantages to strict adherence to detailed policies and procedures?

4 How would you as a proponent of detailed policies and procedures counter a critic's claim that *excessive* "policy binds the organization up in red tape, causes its members to lose sight of the organizational goals and objectives, and engenders as much ill will as is relieved by the consistent treatment afforded by the presence of policy."

5 At what level of the organization, generally, would you expect a policy of twenty percent return on investment to be instituted? Why?

6 Why are policies and procedures generally viewed as constraints to the decision-making and planning processes?

7 How can the planning process force a reexamination of policy?

8 What impact might environmental change have on the policy-formulation process?

9 Match the following policy-formulation steps with the appropriate organizational function:

(1) problem definition

(2) research, information gathering, alternative analysis, policy recommendation

(3) policy choice or approval

(4) explanation of policy

(5) implementation of policy

(a) line

(b) line and staff

(c) line or line/staff

(d) functional

(e) service

(f) staff

Briefly describe why you matched each policy-formulation step with a particular organization function.

10 Describe the policy-formulation and implementation process.

11 Describe in detail how you might police a policy, that is, perform a policy audit.

12 How might the degree of decentralization or centralization practiced by an organization affect the placement of policy-determination and formulation functions within an organization?

13 How might a landmark case such as *Griggs* v. *Duke Power* affect the existing personnel policies of an organization?

CASE: SOCIETY LIFE INSURANCE CO. (C)*

■ "It's hitting the fan all over town," remarked Mr. Berrigan to his colleague, Mr. House, while reading the morning papers over breakfast in the company cafeteria. "Even the Boston papers are on us for trying to run the town or for being unfair. There's even a note of conflict of interest."

What Berrigan was referring to was a decision by the Salem (Massachusetts)–based Society Life Insurance Company's management to donate $125,000 to the fund drive of Essex Hospital Center and conduct an in-house solicitation of employees (which resulted in an additional $26,000 going to Essex). Three matters seemed to be causing the most concern, according to the newspaper accounts. First, another hospital, Clinic Hospital, was conducting its fund-raising campaign at the same time. Clinic was not only smaller than Essex, but also less well financed, incapable of offering as wide a range of services, and was continually being badgered by Essex directors to merge. Clinic's rates, however, were much lower than those of Essex.

Second, Society's president, Frank Seward, was chairman of the Essex Hospital fund drive and was instrumental in directing the company toward the Essex donation and the in-house solicitation on behalf of Essex.

* For more details of this case, *see* "Society Life Insurance Company (A) and (B)" in Arthur Elkins and Dennis W. Callaghan, *A Managerial Odyssey: Problems in Business and Its Environment*, 2d ed. (Reading, Mass.: Addison-Wesley, 1978), pp. 554–560. Although (A) and (B) are based on a real-life situation, this case (C) is fictional.

Third, Society allowed Clinic to solicit company employees at office exits and entrances later on in the week after the proceeds of the company-conducted in-house solicitation and the company contribution were announced. One local doctor was quoted as saying something to the effect of "leaving the crumbs for the beggars."

When Berrigan and House arrived upstairs at the office, the whole place was abuzz. The public relations officer was meeting with members of the press, who wanted to know whether the company would entertain solicitations from other community organizations, what the bases were for the company meeting a request for assistance, whether Seward's chairmanship of the Essex drive had anything to do with Clinic's being shut out, whether it was now the official company position that Essex should be the dominant hospital in that area and that Clinic should disappear, merge with Essex, or become a low-service medical out-patient treatment center. The public relations director answered most of the questions with a "No comment" or "We'll have something for you later." He seemed particularly stung, however, when one of the reporters read a statement from Clinic's board chairman accusing the company of discrimination among community services, and a disservice to the lower-income residents of the area. He further alleged that Seward was trying nothing less than to force an elimination of competition in the dispensing of medical services.

Some of the company's employees were now openly critical of the method used to solicit them. At that time management meetings were held, and payroll deductions were announced as the preferred method of contribution. All employees received a pledge card with their paychecks. Many employees believed that the personnel department would now have a record of who gives and who doesn't to "Seward's pet project." The use of this information in personnel evaluations, promotions, and pay raises was suspected by many.

Berrigan and House, on getting to their respective offices, found notes on their desks calling a 9:30 A.M. meeting of the company's top management. The word around the office was that the meeting had been called by Chairman of the Board of Directors Elton Braff, not by Mr. Seward.

When the meeting opened, it was indeed Braff who was chairing it. Seward, however, was present and was sitting next to Braff.

"Ladies and gentlemen," Braff opened, "we do have a minor crisis here, and we will solve it. Within a few days, much of it will blow over. This hospital contribution, however, is only the sign of a deeper problem in the company.

"Society Life has encouraged community involvement on the part of its management and employees, and we are proud of the many contributions made by members of the Society organization. Frank Seward was right in tune with our philosophy when he accepted the prestigious chairmanship of the Essex fund drive. And we have always given some of our funds away to worthy causes—usually to the United Fund, although the board of directors, at Frank's urging, concurred with this contribution to Essex.

"These days, however, corporations are being called on to contribute to more and more causes—some worthy and some not so worthy. Society Life is no exception. I still have no quarrel with our donation of funds to that particular hospital, but the fact that our president was chairing the fund drive and that we have no standards on the size of contributions or policies on to whom we give and do not give seems to be the basis of the current problem. And the lack of policy in this area is bound to cause us community-relations problems in the future.

"We also need some policies relating to the solicitation of our employees. We can all agree that this is an easy way for them to give to worthy causes, but maybe its not the right way. I understand there's quite a bit of resentment in the ranks."

The chairman then appointed Mr. Berrigan and Mr. House to design a set of policies and procedures relating to the company's donative activity and report back to the board of directors. "If we can come up with some set of guidelines, we can stay out of any messes like this one again. We're not alone here, by the way. All of the major companies in our industry are going through similar policy evaluations.

"I also want to repeat that this particular decision was ratified by the board of directors, so we'll all take responsibility for it. I retain the fullest confidence in Frank Seward and urge him and all of you not to cut back on community involvement.

"Finally, I should like all of you to say nothing to the press or anyone else about this issue. We'll talk to the press out of public relations. The company will weather this storm, and we'll all be better off for it, particularly if it results in a stable and useful set of policies and procedures. Meanwhile, let's keep our problems in-house. Thank you for coming this morning." ■

Case questions

1. If you were Berrigan (or House), what kinds of policies and areas of concern would you cover in relation to company donations of funds?

2. What policies would you recommend relative to the solicitation of employees?

3. You have determined a set of policies on recipient organizations and their eligibility; outline the procedures and the organizational relationships that you would recommend to implement those policies.

SELECTED READINGS

Ackerman, R. W., *The Social Challenge to Business* (Cambridge, Mass.: Harvard University Press, 1975).

Andrews, K. R., *The Concept of Corporate Strategy* (Homewood, Ill.: Richard D. Irwin, 1971).

Ansoff, H. I., ed., *Business Strategy* (Baltimore: Penguin, 1970).

Bonoma, T. V., and D. P. Slevin, "Management and the Type II Errors," *Business Horizons* 21, 4 (August 1978): 61–67.

Bowman, E. H., "Epistemology, Corporate Strategy and Academe," *Sloan Management Review* 15 (Winter 1974): 35–49.

Bridges, F. J., K. W. Olm, and J. A. Barnhill, *Management Decisions and Organizational Policy: Text, Cases and Readings,* 2d ed. (Boston: Allyn and Bacon, 1977).

Broom, H. N., *Business Policy and Strategic Action: Text, Cases, and Management Game* (Englewood Cliffs, N.J.: Prentice-Hall, 1969).

Carroll, A. B., ed., *Managing Corporate Social Responsibility* (Boston: Little, Brown, 1977).

Chandler, A. D., Jr., *Strategy and Structure: Chapters in the History of American Industrial Enterprise* (Cambridge, Mass.: MIT Press, 1962).

Christensen, C. R., K. R. Andrews, and J. L. Bower, *Business Policy: Text and Cases,* 3rd ed. (Homewood, Ill.: Richard D. Irwin, 1973).

Cohen, K. L., and R. M. Cyert, "Strategy Formulation and Implementation and Monitoring," *Journal of Business* 46 (July 1973): 349–367.

Ein-Dor, P., and E. Seqev, "Information-System Responsibility," *MSU Business Topics* 25, 4 (Autumn 1977): 33–40.

Elkins, A., and D. W. Callaghan, *A Managerial Odyssey: Problems in Business and Its Environment,* 2d ed. (Reading, Mass.: Addison-Wesley, 1978).

Gilmore, F. F., "Formulating Strategy in Smaller Companies," *Harvard Business Review* 49 (May/June 1971): 71–81.

Greenwood, W. T., *Issues in Business and Society,* 3rd ed. (Boston: Houghton Mifflin, 1977).

Hamermesh, R. G., M. J. Anderson, and J. E. Harris, "Strategies for Low Market Share Businesses," *Harvard Business Review* 56, 3 (May/June 1978): 95–102.

———, *Harvard Business Review on Management* (New York: Harper & Row, 1975).

Hodgetts, R. M., and M. S. Wortman, Jr., *Administrative Policy: Text and Cases in the Policy Sciences* (New York: Wiley, 1975).

Lasswell, H. D., *A Pre-View of the Policy Sciences* (New York: American Elsevier, 1971).

Lucas, H. C., "The Evolution of an Information System: From Key Man to Every Person," *Sloan Management Review* 19, 2 (Winter 1978): 39–52.

Mitroff, I. I., and R. H. Kilmann, "Teaching Managers to Do Policy Analysis—The Case of Corporate Bribery," *California Management Review* 20, 1 (Fall 1977): 47–54.

Paine, F. T., and W. Naumes, *Organizational Strategy and Policy: Text, Cases and Incidents* (Philadelphia: Saunders, 1975).

Patel, P., and M. Younger, "A Frame of Reference for Strategy Development," *Long-Range Planning* 11, 2 (April 1978): 6–12.

Pickle, H. B., and R. L. Abrahamson, *Small Business Management* (New York: Wiley, 1976).

Robinson, S. J. Q., R. E. Hichens, and B. P. Wade, "The Directional Policy Matrix—Tool for Strategic Planning," *Long-Range Planning* 11, 3 (June 1978): 8–15.

Smith, T. B., "The Policy Implementation Process," *Policy Sciences* 4 (June 1973): 197–209.

Staw, B. M., and J. Ross, "Commitment to a Policy Decision: A Multi-Theoretical Perspective," *Administrative Science Quarterly* 23, 1 (March 1978): 40–64.

Thompson, J. D., *Organizations in Action* (New York: McGraw-Hill, 1967).

Van Maanen, J., "People Processing: Strategies of Organizational Socialization," *Organization Dynamics* 7, 1 (Summer 1978): 18–36.

Wrapp, H. E., "Good Managers Don't Make Policy Decisions," *Harvard Business Review* 45 (September/October 1967): 91–99.

Chapter 10
DESIGNING ORGANIZATIONS TO CARRY OUT PLANS

CHAPTER HIGHLIGHTS

In this chapter we shall relate the design of organization structure to plans and strategies of the institution or firm. We will discuss situations in which the organization is stable and the plan is adapted to an existing organization, those in which the organization is a variable subject to change to match a proposed strategy, and finally situations in which the redesign of an organization is itself a strategy. Finally, we cover the matrix, or product manager, type of organization and its design to cover certain kinds of product-line or programmatic strategies.

LEARNING OBJECTIVES

1 To appreciate organization design as an integral part of the total design process.

2 To recognize situations in which organization is a variable: organizational growth, added products or services, functional breakaway, or technological change.

3 To learn under what conditions the organization structure stays stable relative to the plan: inability to conceive of the organization as a variable, vested interests, resistance to change, recognition of the organization as a stabilizing force.

4 To learn to consider organization structural change as a strategic move in itself.

5 To understand the concept of the matrix organization.

CASE: STATE UNIVERSITY AT PIERPONT ATHLETIC DEPARTMENT

■ Prior to 1974, the athletic department at the State University at Pierpont was basically an all-male operation in terms of programming, personnel, and mission. Although women's teams were fielded by the university in six intercollegiate sports, those teams were organized under the jurisdiction of the department of physical education for women rather than the athletic department. All of the functions of eligibility determination, staffing, and scheduling, as well as game operations for the women's sports, were the responsi-

211

bility of the department head's office in women's physical education, although the budgets for the individual sports were allocated from the athletic department's general budget. In September 1974 the whole intercollegiate sports program for women was placed within the department of athletics, and all functions relating to the women's program were assumed by that department.

Personnel within the athletic department are basically of four types: administrators and staff; full-time coaches, who are members of the athletic department, but do not hold faculty status; personnel partially "borrowed" from other departments to coach a sport while holding full-time faculty status within the other departments; and graduate students hired to coach a sport or a junior varsity team.

With the reassignment of jurisdiction of women's athletics to the athletic department, all of the women's sports were transferred to their new department, but the coaches remain under their former statuses. In the short run, then, all of the women's sports are to be coached by personnel from other departments (chiefly women's physical education) and graduate students. In the long run, however, the objective is to integrate the entire athletic department into one functioning unit, with as many of the coaches as possible holding full-time status within the department.

Anticipating the need for such integration and also the pending issuance of the guidelines under which Title IX of the Educational Amendments Act of 1972 would be administered, Alex Blanchard, director of athletics at Pierpont, set about developing a long-range plan for the department. The objectives of the planning exercise were to expand the offerings in women's athletics and to integrate the entire expanded program of women's athletics and the presently functioning men's program.

Title IX of the Educational Amendments Act called for all schools and colleges receiving federal funds to develop plans to ensure that equal opportunity was offered to both sexes in all activities. In athletics this amounted to equal access to sports activities and opportunities. Although precise guidelines for Title IX had not yet been issued by the Department of Health, Education, and Welfare (and approved by Congress), the enactment of the law meant expanded numbers of sports open to women in most of the colleges and universities affected.

Prior to 1974, the athletic department's staff consisted of the director, an associate director, a director of sports promotion and publicity, and a business manager, along with the various coaches, assistant coaches, and support personnel, such as trainers and maintenance personnel. The department was allocated a position to be filled with an assistant director in 1975. The associate director generally handles scheduling, eligibility requirements, athletic scholarships, etc. The director of sports promotion supervises tickets, advertising, programs, and radio and television broadcasting arrangements. The business manager keeps the departmental financial records and monitors the purchasing and payment rolls of the department. Although their positions are very much distinct and the role of each of the administrators is fairly clear-cut, often one administrator would help another, and they all consult on any major problem arising in the department. Blanchard stresses the management-team approach to administration, having reinforced that approach by not developing a formal organization chart for the department prior to 1974.

Coaches generally have little to do with the administration of the department. Their tasks center on the training and maintenance of the various teams; often they rebel at what they consider minor administrative tasks such as budgeting, expense control, and developing administrative procedures.

In developing the long-range plans for the department, Blanchard had one additional constraint with which to deal—money. The state's budget was being severely slashed, and this meant that the university would be receiving little in the way of additional funds over the next several years. In addition, student-fee funds were leveling off simply because the enrollment at the university was stabilizing. Approximately one-half of the department's operating budget was supported by state funds and one-half by a student athletic fee. Even though this student fee had not increased in more than fifteen years, rising enrollment generally guaranteed an increase in the total available funds. But with the leveling off of student enrollment and the stabilizing or even decrease in state support funds—plus the almost double-digit inflation of the 1974–1975 period—the department was left with little if any slack with which to build the necessary women's program equivalent in scope, size, and quality to the men's programs. And the administration was committed to maintaining the quality of the men's programs.

Given these objectives and constraints, Blanchard's long-range plan centered on the development of programs that would use resources economically. Initially, a search was made for common denominators between women's sports and the existing men's sports, and the department decided that such common denominators would be used as the benchmarks for the early addition of new sports. For example, economies of joint scheduling, joint promotion, sharing transportation, sharing equipment, or perhaps having existing coaches assume expanded duties with the women's sports function were to be considered. Given these common-denominator considerations, several models of program operation were developed—a program being defined as an identifiable sports activity, such as volleyball or track and field.

In some sports, for example—although few at the beginning—joint teams could be developed; in others, separate teams for men and women might exist, with the occasional transfer of athletes from one team to another. With a third model, several levels of mixed teams—such as varsity, junior varsity, and freshmen—might be the norm. Finally, in some sports separate teams based on sex might be the norm. There would always be some single-sex sports, such as football for men and field hockey for women.

Given the possible models, the dimensions of the plan over the five-year period included integrating the already existing comparable teams in some sports to achieve greater economies in personnel and equipment, adding and integrating women's sports for which a comparable men's sport already existed, and adding and integrating men's sports for which a comparable women's sport already existed. Time schedules for each addition were established along with estimates of resource needs to accomplish the addition.

Now Blanchard was faced with the question of economically and effectively organizing the department. If he continued the present administrative pattern, he and the associate director (who headed what might be called the department's staff services) would face as many as thirty-six separate coaching positions—that is, if each team, men's and women's, had its own coach—each with its own unique problems. Was there a way of facilitating the plan and reducing the span of supervision as well as pushing the operational decision making down into the line organization? ■

INTRODUCTION

Planning can assume several relationships to the structure of the organization. First, the organization structure can be a variable in the planner's deliberations, allowing him or her to mold the strategy and the optimum structure around which to carry it out. That is, everything becomes a variable, and the planner is given carte blanche in assuming that the existing structure can be altered. In implementing the plan—or getting it accepted —the planner may have problems, but in the planning exercise the existing organization is not considered sacrosanct or impervious to alteration.

Second, plans can be developed with the existing organization treated as an unalterable given. Thus the organization structure becomes a constraint to the planner's freedom of action. For example, in many universities new programs are often planned with an eye to using the established departments *as they are structured rather than creating a new structure*. If any new coordinating office is created, it is often established with the control being left to the existing departments (although the control might eventually pass to the new central office despite the admonitions and promises to the contrary). In business firms a new product or service is often planned for marketing through the existing sales organization rather than the planner's creating a new type of structure or adding a new sales department for that product. In these cases the organization is thought to be inflexible, and the planner is expected to maintain flexibility by adapting the plan to existing organizational style and structure.

Finally, in some cases the structural change *is* the basic strategy. That is, the key to the plan is a change in the organization, since that may be determined to be the only appropriate response to an opportunity or threat to the organization.

We shall be considering all of these cases in more detail in this chapter, and we shall explore some of the reasons why each of the cases would be in force. In all cases, however, the structure of the organization really is a design problem related to the strategy and planning exercises. Even if the planner does nothing about the structure or is constrained from doing anything about it, it is still—explicitly or implicitly—a consideration in the total design. Simply being constrained by something means that the planner has to consider it in his or her deliberations.

Organization design relative to strategy building and planning is so important that many organizations maintain specialized staff units to monitor organization and administrative structure and to propose changes when the existing organization is not responsive to environmental change, when objectives must be altered or units integrated to reflect strategy, or when the organization just goes stale. These planning units engage in continual planning and information gathering. Of course, they generally are attached to the central-level or corporate headquarters, and their plans for organizational change must be approved by top management. Such units may be under an officer such as a vice-president for planning and development, and their functions will be closely related to total organizational strategy development.

ADAPTING THE ORGANIZATION TO THE STRATEGY OR PLAN

Changing the structure of the total organization or altering the structure of units of the organization can result from any number of factors in a plan. The following situations might make such an inclusion of change appropriate:

1 Planning for organizational growth
2 Planning for additional services or products
3 Planned functional breakaway
4 Planning for technological change

Even if the managers do not consider adding new products or opening new locations or any other such growth factors, sheer growth in the present market or clientele may force them to plan an entirely new organization structure. In John's Hardware Store, for example, the addition of persons at the initial location resulted from additional customers' partaking of the original

Planning for organizational growth

FIG. 10.1
Present organization.

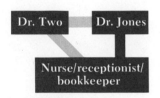

FIG. 10.2
Phase I of organizational growth.

services and products that John initially offered. As another example, consider a medical practice in an area that suddenly undergoes a population increase—a new military or space installation in the locality, the building of a large plant in the town, or an oil strike within the vicinity. No change in special services is contemplated by the doctor, who plans to continue a general practice. But adding more general practitioners and nurses to the practice must be planned for. New patients will be calling for service—that is easily predictable. Of course, the doctor can always opt to turn any new patients away and remain small, but in this case he has chosen to expand. The doctor's fairly simple present organization is pictured in Fig. 10.1.

Suppose that the doctor hires a planner, who forecasts an increase in patients from the present 250 families to 1700 families over the next five years. Dr. Jones cannot handle all 1700 families alone. Without the planning, he might decide to share an office or might encourage other general practitioners to move into the area as independents. But suppose further that the planner encourages him to establish a medical partnership and to plan to add new general practitioners to his partnership as the growth in population continues. The plan then would include not only a move to larger offices and the purchase of additional equipment and facilities, but also a change in the duties assigned to the peripheral staff. For example, instead of jamming more work onto the bookkeeper, who now also functions as a nurse and receptionist, the bookkeeping and receptionist functions will eventually have to be separated. As a first phase, however, Dr. Jones adds only Dr. Two, and the organization appears as in Fig. 10.2. Drs. Jones and Two share the nurse, who continues to function as a receptionist and a bookkeeper for the entire practice.

In the planned phase II of the growth, which would probably happen very quickly after Dr. Two's arrival, a second nurse would probably be employed; that nurse would be assigned to Dr. Two. Dr. Jones's nurse would continue to perform the functions of receptionist and bookkeeper for the entire organization. Figure 10.3 illustrates the phase II organization structure as planned.

In the final phase of the plan's implementation, however, drastic changes in the organization structure are anticipated. These changes would have been planned for—timed to coincide with the growth in the partnership's clientele

FIG. 10.3
Organizational structure in phase II of growth.

and the practice. First, Dr. Three has been added to the staff of doctors by the planner. And each doctor is to have his or her own nurse. Dr. Jones, the managing partner, will remain as the supervisor of the secondary functions, but it is anticipated that he simply will not have the time to handle that supervision and that his nurse no longer will be able to do double duty as the receptionist and bookkeeper. Therefore, a director of administration is planned for, under whose direction the bookkeeping, clerical, and receptionist functions will reside.

Under the organizational structure developed for this phase of the practice's growth, more doctors and nurses can be added very easily, since the secondary functions are now sufficiently planned so as to be able to handle growth. Figure 10.4 shows the planned phase III organization structure.

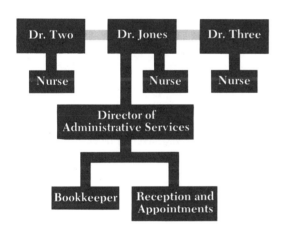

FIG. 10.4
Organizational structure in phase III of growth.

In this general-growth situation, the organization was planned for change simply because the plan included market growth in terms of patients. The plan in this situation detailed the organizational charts to reflect the new growth. Indeed, in such a situation one of the planner's prime considerations would probably be structural change of the organization.

Planning for additional services or products

The previous case demonstrated a situation in which an organization must plan its structural change simply because it is anticipated that the organization will be doing more of what it always did. But suppose that Dr. Jones is not so conservative and thinks that his small general practice might eventually offer not only greater numbers of general practitioners, but some specialized services as well. For example, the community would probably need some X-ray, laboratory, physiotherapy, and other peripheral services, as well as medical specialists. The question for the planner becomes one of determining when each of these additional services is to be added and how the organization will change to reflect the additions. The first question is answered by determining when it will pay off to cease referring patients to outside specialists and service organizations and to expand one's own resources to secure additional equipment and a facility to provide such services. The second question relates to correlating the organization structure to such additional offerings.

Under conditions where both the expansion of already offered services and products and the addition of new services or products occur, the planner could also adapt the organizational structure in phases. Such a phasing is illustrated in Fig. 10.5.

In this case as the new services (products) were considered (along with the growth of the previously offered services), the planner would have to not only anticipate phases when each of the services would be added to the or-

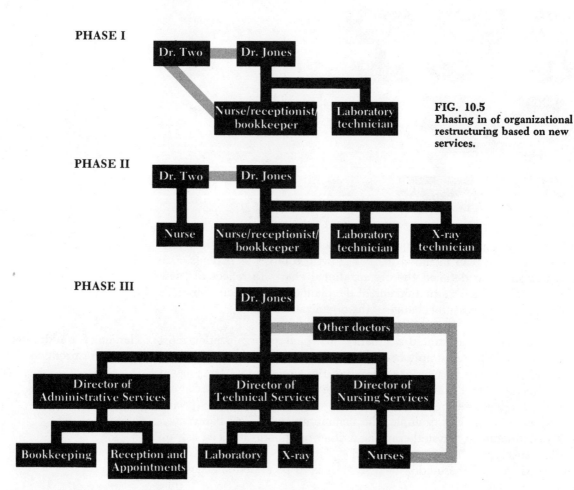

FIG. 10.5
Phasing in of organizational restructuring based on new services.

ganization, but also consider when the organization was ready to consolidate the added services into groups. Phases I, II, and III comprise the gradual addition of the technical services and their consolidation into groupings. The phases also encompass the consolidation of existing administrative and nursing services as they too expand, reflecting the growth of the entire organization.

In Chapter 3 we discussed both horizontal and vertical specialization (or functionalization) as well as the breakout of the secondary functions into general and specialized staff units. Such change in an organization can occur in either of two ways. First, it might result from a topsylike arrangement and be instituted as or after the need arises. In that case units would be added (or others subdivided) simply because the organization seemed to need such structural change or the problems became so intense that "things just aren't being taken care of any more." Or, the organizational growth can be planned for. Questions can be posed early, such as: "When in the progress of the firm should the personnel functions be consolidated into a staff unit?" or "At what point in the organization's future should sales territories be allocated?" For example, in Seaboard Products Corporation, we saw Clarke and his fellow top managers doing all of the sales work through personal connections. Did salespeople and a sales department mysteriously appear, or was such a change planned for and developed in sequence with the planning for product market expansion? Was Sigmund Heller hired because Clarke felt that it was time for a personnel manager, or did the organization plan to relieve the line officers of their personnel duties at a specified time? In planning for the European plant (see Chapter 8), Jim Sherry should include the time, within the twenty-four months during which the plant was to be established, when the organization would require the addition of a personnel function, a research function, or an advertising staff, etc. When was an accounting staff to be added, and when were the functional line units to be established?

Functional breakaway

In setting goals, making decisions, solving problems, or planning, much of the work, as we have noted often, involves the gathering of information. Often this means forecasting or gathering data on the future of various trends. One of the more difficult aspects of the future to anticipate is the rate of technological change as it will affect the structure of the organization. For example, when will data processing and communications equipment become so inexpensive or so efficient and effective that the organization can begin installing such equipment and changing the relationships among local and central organizational units in terms of authority and decision making? When will it be possible for the organization to rely on real-time central decision making?

Technology

Because of the difficulty in forecasting changes in technology, the technologically induced organizational changes are often not planned for until after the technology has become available. Although one might reasonably ask if the organization is then using only the historical past to plan for the future, the difficulty in accurately forecasting the future in this particular area may make such an arrangement more practical than trying to "crystal ball" developments yet to appear on the suppliers' drawing boards. Few companies, for example, in the late 1950s could predict the power and efficiency of the third-generation computers to be available within ten years and then, moreover, accurately map out the changes in the organization that such computers would create.

Some technology is easier to forecast, however. Supersonic air transportation will undoubtedly be a reality, for example, and the effects that a two-hour trip from Europe to the United States will have on the ability of the head office to supervise subsidiary offices across the ocean are relatively easy to predict. Similarly, the changes in structure that will result from such a foreseeable technological breakthrough can be planned with reasonable certainty that the event will occur.

ADAPTING THE PLAN TO THE ORGANIZATION

The previous examples have all considered the organizational structure to be flexible and adaptable to planners and decision makers in their alternative-selection process. But the reverse too can be true; the organization can be a fixed constraint. Plans are often constructed with the organizational structure as a given for at least the short range, but often in the long run as well.

This fixed situation is very obvious in public organizations; their structures are often static, having been mandated by a legislative or executive body, or their numbers of internal positions are limited by annual legislative appropriations. Similarly, in organizations where trustees or directors establish a structure and generally a long period passes between reorganizations or changes, plans may also be adapted to the established structure.

But just as often, organization structure assumes an unchangeable character because of the following internal considerations, many related to the mental sets in which the planner or other organizational members find themselves:

1 Planners suffer from tunnel vision and are unable to mentally conceive of organizational structure as a variable in the plan

2 The organization assumes a sacred position for managers and planners with vested interests

3 Personnel are resistant to change, and planners know it

4 The organization is recognized as a stabilizing force

Often a planner or a decision maker is unable to conceive of the organization as a variable to be altered for the plans being developed. For example, in some organizations committees are "a way of life" and are established rather routinely when various problems arise. When planning task forces consider new programs or revisions to existing ones, a role for some of the established committees is almost automatically figured into the plan. It sometimes never occurs to the planners that the existing structure might not be appropriate to the plan or may even be dysfunctional to the operation of the plan. The committees are there, they are to participate, and hence are included in the plan. In essence, a certain structure may be resistant to change simply because *planners are conditioned to think of the organization in terms of the existing structure* and thus consider it a fixed factor in planning.

Planners' tunnel vision

A related reason why organizational structure is resistant to planned change is that the managers who may be doing the planning often have a vested interest in the existing structure. As we shall show in the next chapter, individuals are motivated by all sorts of needs, not the least of which may be esteem or personal growth. This need may manifest itself in the managers' desire to seek and hold prestigious and larger organizational units under their supervision.

Managers' vested interest in existing structure

Once those units have been established and the managerial relationships developed, however, it is only the rare manager who will surrender them voluntarily while still capable of effectively controlling the unit. Indeed, many managers who worked hard to move into a position of organizational unit control will fight just as hard to retain such control. One can hardly expect such managers to plan their own units' shrinkage or decrease in prestige.

Of course, for some managers the future of an organizational unit may also mean their future in the organization as well. Few managers will plan themselves out of a job; few others will passively allow another planner to reduce their chances of continued employment either (although in a recession, even active resistance may be futile). Other managers, who may be planning, could be reluctant to plan colleagues out of jobs also, for fear that similar fates may befall them in the future.

In short, the continued viability of an organizational unit will temper a plan despite the fact that the plan may be a better one if the organizational changes are made.

Not only managers are resistant to losing status and positions; so too are operative and clerical personnel, and planners—either consciously or tacitly —take such resistance into account when devising plans. Even the slightest hint that something is afoot will often alarm personnel. Questions of physical movement, new supervision, new organizational and personal relationships, revised seniority and status positions, retraining, and the threat of displace-

Personnel resistant to change

ment (particularly on the part of the older worker) become key factors in reducing the ability of a planner to consider organizational realignment in planning decisions. Although there are mechanisms for overcoming some of this resistance to change, many times the easy path to follow involves minimizing the change.

In the data-processing department of a large insurance company, the manager always kept the unit's organization chart prominently displayed on a blackboard in his office. Subordinates and co-workers could always easily see the chart as they passed his office. One day, however, the chart was gone. Although the manager was simply using the blackboard for another purpose, the chart's absence sent tremors through the department. Only when the chart was restored unaltered were the departmental personnel reassured that a major reorganization was not in the offing.

Another example is quite common. Most of the major office-equipment manufacturers offer systems—called word processing—so that the bulk of clerical work can be centralized and the number of clerical personnel reduced and transferred into a central typing pool, with only occasional bits of typing left to the one or few remaining departmental or unit secretaries. One of the key problems in installing such a system, obviously, is the resistance to the organizational change demanded by such a system despite the technical efficiency that the system offers.

Organization structure as a stabilizing force

Like policies and procedures, defined structure is often a key stabilizing force in an organization, and hence planners try to maintain this stability. Many planners, then, do not always assume that the organization is a variable. Generally, they consider that *only a complete strategy change* can be the basis for altering the structure of the organization, not necessarily because of the resistance by managers, planners, or operatives, but because they are aware that it is not a healthy process to continuously tear and retear the underpinnings of the total organization or any organizational unit.

ORGANIZATIONAL CHANGE AS A STRATEGY

Often the organization structure will be altered not because such an alteration is a *part* of a planned change in corporate strategy, but because the organization can find no better or usable alternative strategy or response to an environmental change or threat than to alter the very structure of the organization. As we have been suggesting throughout this book, planning or designing *includes* the planning or designing of organization structure. Responding to an opportunity or challenge by including *only* a restructuring of the organization is quite appropriate as a design or planning activity.

Often restructuring the organization is the *easiest* step that a planner can contemplate or consider, but it is not the easiest to implement. All of the problems related to organizational change are obviously present. So, in response to an environmental opportunity, threat or challenge, other, less drastic mechanisms might be considered initially.

An example will illustrate the use of structural change as a strategy. A common practice among conglomerates or firms built from mergers is to simply tack a new acquisition on as a separate division, integrating it into the total organization through central policy on finance, officer selection, and accounting routines, but otherwise leaving the operations of the division to be decided on at the lower levels. Thus the divisions continue to look like and act as the former independent companies they were before the mergers. The typical structure of such an arrangement is illustrated in Fig. 10.6.

As more companies are acquired, each could simply be tacked on as another division, retaining separate identities and distinct physical facilities. This structure is a very common one for conglomerates to maintain. In terms of the markets each of the divisions (or former independent companies) serves, it is often more advantageous to have the division continue to stress its reliable brand name rather than the conglomerate's name. On the other hand, for some purposes, particularly with financiers or suppliers, the image of strength conveyed by the conglomerate name has its value too.

This type of organization is also relatively easy to administer, particularly if the units are noncompeting and relatively independent of one another. Goals and standards can be set for each division; no excuses of one product or group of products getting in the way of another are possible; and sales forces, production lines, markets, and sources of supplies are sufficiently separated to ease administrative and coordinative problems. Indeed, the continual adding of divisions is a useful strategy under these conditions.

Suppose now, however, that the conglomerate aims to increase profits by ten percent, but without adding new firms to its collection (perhaps because of antitrust enforcement) or marketing new products or services. Rather, the firm could—or must—achieve its goal by cutting costs; eliminating duplicated departments, units, or efforts; combining similar functions; pruning unnecessary organizational units; and consolidating offices. Such a move often occurs after a conglomerate has reached a certain stage of growth. Indeed, some conglomerates have had subsidiary units competing with one another for government contracts, salespeople from two or more subsidiaries calling on clients and customers, and uncoordinated research and development efforts resulting in two units' working on similar problems.

Thus an organization undergoing such a cost-cutting scheme might perhaps accomplish savings by restructuring its entire organization to consolidate divisions. (This was essentially the problem facing Carlton Industries in Chapter 3.) In the process the company might centralize more of its decision

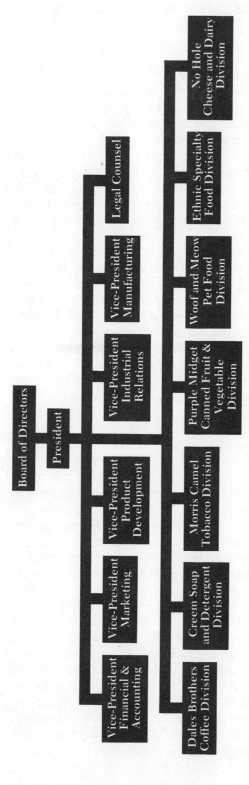

224

FIG. 10.6
Organization chart of XYZ Conglomerate.

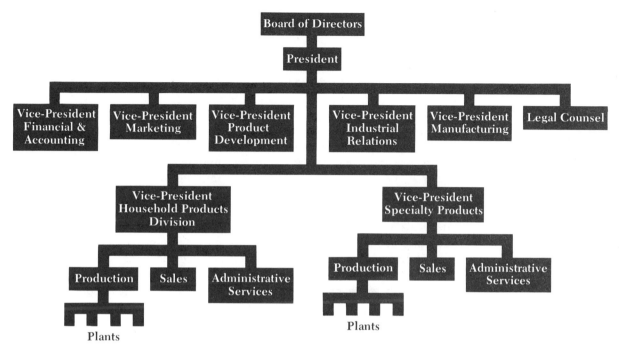

FIG. 10.7
Revised organization chart of XYZ Conglomerate.

making and insert control devices to ensure increased coordination. Essentially, however, units having needs for similar resources or serving similar or identical clientele would be brought together to cut costs. After such a restructuring, the company organization shown in Fig. 10.6 might look as depicted in Fig. 10.7. No longer is each of the original divisions readily identifiable (although the product brand names probably would be retained), and production facilities and sales forces would be merged.

This strategy of structural change may not guarantee that costs will be reduced. Indeed, the shock waves sent through the organization, particularly if divisions are sold off, closed up, or moved, may mitigate against any significant savings. But the integration and control of the organization may result even though the company is giving up the specialization gained through the old organization structure.

However, we must repeat our earlier warning. Structural change is often a last-resort activity, since the many problems it generates may overwhelmingly outweigh the ease with which it can be proposed. In essence, the implementation may be much more difficult than the proposing.

MATRIX ORGANIZATIONS

Another way certain complex multiproduct organizations can be designed (or redesigned) is to move to a special type of structure called the matrix organization, or the product manager—type organization.* The matrix organization is used widely for defense-related, highly technical products. This type of structure is most often found in multiple-product firms, where even though each product can be thought of as distinct and different from the others, many of them employ common production and sales resources. For example, most soap manufacturers have multiple brands, but the difference among those brands may be minimal, requiring no unique functional processes. That is, the various brands may have only different formulations of chemicals or ingredients and have different appeals. Consequently, although each product is planned for and marketed separately—and accounted for separately—all or most of the products *can* use the same research, production, and sales facilities of the organization.

Basically, then, the matrix type of organization entails coordination of the relationship of many and varied products or programs overlaid on a group of multipurpose functional resources. Thus in a multiple-product firm, each of the products, under the direction of a product manager, is woven through the functions (production, sales, operations, etc.), each under the direction of a functional manager (hence the term "matrix"). See Fig. 10.8.

Book publishing can be used as an illustrative and explanative case of matrix organization. The acquisitions editor is a product manager, and each acquisitions editor has a speciality, e.g., business, mathematics, English, his-

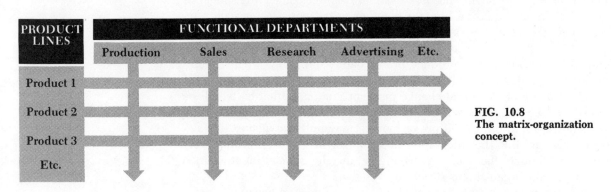

FIG. 10.8
The matrix-organization concept.

* *See* Jay Galbraith, "Matrix Organization Designs," *Business Horizons* 14 (February 1971): 29–40; and Stanley Davis and Paul R. Lawrence, *Matrix* (Reading, Mass.: Addison-Wesley, 1977).

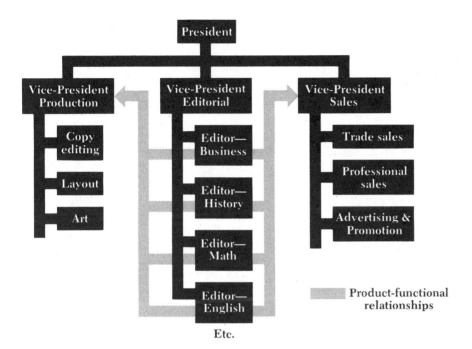

FIG. 10.9
The matrix-organization concept as applied to a publishing company.

tory, economics, etc. But there is only one production department (copy editing, layout, etc.), one advertising department, one sales department, etc. Each of the acquisitions editors must negotiate and coordinate his or her books through (for example) the production system, and it is the production manager's task to coordinate and schedule through that department the output of several editors' projects. Figure 10.9 illustrates a very simplified product-manager concept for a publishing company.

Authority and responsibility patterns must be carefully delineated for the matrix system to work. Cooperation and consultation are necessary, and potential conflict is a real possibility. Although each of the product managers usually thinks that his or her product is the most important and thus should have priority, the functional manager must schedule and balance his or her resources among the various programs (or products) having need of those resources. Thus the product manager often has authority over the design and planning of the product, but then must negotiate (often purchase through internal pricing mechanisms) the manufacturing time and resources from the manufacturing department. Similarly, the product manager must negotiate sales efforts from the sales department. The product manager must negotiate with his or her functional counterparts just as if he or she were buying their services on the open market. The functional managers have control over balancing and allocating the resources, whereas the program or product managers have control over the program or product design, content, and marketing efforts.

This brief explanation of the matrix system only introduces the problems and complexity of the concept. A matrix organization is complicated and depends on cooperation, clear delineation of roles and responsibilities, and a healthy appreciation of the organizational needs and pressures of the various parties involved.

DESIGNING STRUCTURE: THE ATHLETIC DEPARTMENT

Let us now return to the case with which we opened this chapter. One of the first things one must consider about the athletic department at Pierpont State University is that no prescribed organization structure was in force even though functions were assigned to particular individuals. Indeed, aside from the fact that all of the coaches ran their own teams and reported to an athletic director and that some secondary functions were carried out by assistants, little in the way of a formalized structure existed. But even if a structure had existed before 1974, it might have been of little future use. Essentially, the department was being required to absorb and expand a whole new program, bring it up to the standards of the existing men's program, and complete the task without the promise of additional resources.

In the actual planning process, Blanchard considered the possibilities of utilizing existing resources in terms of coaching types, joint scheduling, multiple uses of existing equipment, etc. It was decided that insofar as possible, one constraint to adding any new sports was that a comparable women's or men's sport had to already be in existence. Thus sports for the two sexes would eventually be paired, and the economies in support services and instruction would then be realized to a maximum.

Another decision relating to organization was that the various sports could be best developed and decisions on which of the various team and participation models was used should be made at the coaching level, not necessarily at the level of the director of athletics. Thus each program, encompassing a men's and a women's comparable sport, would receive a budget, and the coaches within that program would, as a group, determine how their particular sport would be organized. For administrative purposes, each grouping of sports or program would have a program head, who might be one of the coaches. That program head would report to the director, and the coaches, assistant coaches, and the program head would comprise a decision unit for that particular sport. This arrangement would not only decentralize decision making, but also reduce the number of line managers (coaches) reporting to the director from approximately thirty to a maximum of fifteen, when all the new sports for both sexes were phased in over the five-year period.

Secondary functions, such as scheduling, bookkeeping, game operations, sports promotion, and publicity were reorganized under the associate director, who was also named director of administration. The devised organization is shown in Fig. 10.10.

One coach and the newly hired assistant director served in joint positions because of particular problems facing the department. Since women's athletics is so new and the integration problem so crucial, the assistant director, whose normal duties entailed assisting on eligibility, scheduling, and other administrative service tasks such as departmental research, also served as special adviser to the athletic director on women's athletics. One of the program directors also served as a special adviser to the director in the area of curriculum development. Since many of the individuals in the department also taught courses for other departments, developed special courses that were offered as services to other departments, or were asked to appear as guest lecturers throughout the university, it was felt that this coordinative advisory position was needed. In addition, special programs, such as football, baseball, swimming, and basketball clinics, were offered for high school coaches and players. All of these required development and coordination, and the special adviser served in this coordinative role on behalf of the head of the department.

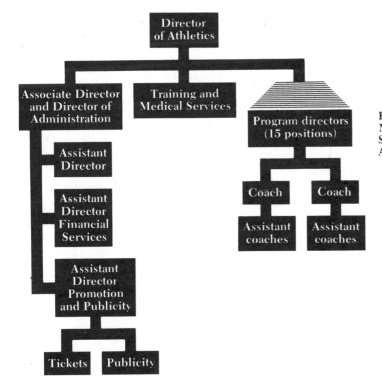

FIG. 10.10
New organization chart for State University at Pierpont Athletic Department.

With this organization structure, Blanchard felt that he could phase in women's sports, utilizing more effectively the exisiting personnel and forcing decisions on team composition (e.g., two teams, one combined team, passage of athletes from team to team, or a set of varsity, junior varsity and freshman teams, etc.) down to the level of the coaches and program heads. *The responsibility for developing the sports and the composition of the teams would be placed at the program level,* and appropriate resources would be allocated to the program groups to allow them to carry out their respective mandates.

Thus the entire organization structure was revamped to face the new challenges of the environment as well as the stringency of resources allocated to the departments. The restructuring was, indeed, part and parcel of the broader strategy of phasing in new women's and men's sports over a period of five years, and the new structure would give Blanchard the flexibility of adding a program director and placing various new coaches when they were added to the department according to the time schedule of phasing in a particular sport.

SUMMARY

In this chapter our primary aim has been to relate the design of organization to planning or strategy development. We covered the alteration of structure as part of a plan or strategy; the holding of structure as a constant, with strategies and planning designed around a given structure; and the changing of structure as a strategy, particularly in response to crises that cannot be met by alternative strategies or tactics. We then briefly covered the matrix-organization concept. Analysis of the chapter case showed an organization in which redesign was an integral part of a new strategy or plan being developed in response to several simultaneously changing environmental conditions—increasing athletic awareness among women, the pending issuance of new legislative guidelines, and the freezing of resources growth.

DISCUSSION QUESTIONS

1 Define the following terms:
   a) functional breakaway   b) technology
   c) defensive strategy   d) structure
   e) decentralized organization   f) matrix organization

2 How might planning for organizational growth change or alter the structure of the total organization or units of the organization?

3 How might the following situations affect the structure of the organization or its units?

a) planning for organizational growth

b) planning for additional services or products

c) planned functional breakaway

d) planning for technological change

4 What is functional breakaway? When or why does it occur within an organization?

5 Although it sometimes seems obvious that organizational change or adapting is the appropriate action to take as a result of a plan, the organization structure assumes an unchangeable character. What are some of the legal and behavioral causes of fixed or unchangeable organizational structures?

6 It is sometimes held that planners suffer from "tunnel vision." What is meant by this description of planners?

7 How do organizational change and corporate strategy affect each other?

8 Can the organization's structure affect how a company will be viewed by the antitrust authorities?

9 It has been claimed that a divisionalized structure neatly strung out means extremely easy decisions for a court or administrative agency seeking divestiture or breaking up of the company. Why does a divisionalized organization structure *invite* divestiture?

10 What problems could result from structural change within an organization?

11 As a general manager of a plastics company, how might the EPA decisions on environmental pollution affect your organization's structure?

12 Describe a matrix-organization structure. How do product and functional managers relate to each other under such an arrangement?

CASE: THE *PEOPLE'S NEWS*

■ "A few of us just pumped out the *Revolutionary Free Press* during the late 1960s." So began Timmy Ryan as he recounted the history of the *People's News*. Ryan was the publisher and one of the founders of the newspaper. What started out as an "alternative newspaper" in Princeton, New Jersey, during the turbulent late 1960s was now a chain of five large weekly papers throughout New Jersey, Pennsylvania, and Delaware. Each of the papers now competes quite respectably with the established press and draws advertisements from not only the shops catering to the counterculture, but also chains, high-class specialty shops, local department stores, and the like. What follows is the rest of the "oral history" as recounted by Ryan.

"In the beginning, the few of us did all the writing, sold a few advertisements to sympathetic friends, ran our first twenty or so issues off on an old mimeograph, and hawked the thing on street corners. It was to be only a temporary thing, but quite frankly, putting out an alternative newspaper really got into our blood.

"We give the paper free to our readers now, and you know, the marketing advantage of that came through by sheer serendipity. We were so anti-capitalist back then, we felt that our readers shouldn't have to pay to read our exposés. We thought that we would just soak the advertisers and give the paper away free. Funny, but that turned out to be a great circulation gimmick. We don't have to go to the expense of filling subscriptions, keeping lists up to date, or dropping the paper off at every local newsstand. We just drop off big bundles at high-traffic places and let anyone pick the paper up. It's cheaper for us, people think that they're getting a bargain, and the advertisers love those huge circulation figures.

"We've cleaned up our act a little since those early shrieking days. Oh, we still print a few four-letter words, and I guess you can say that we're still to the left politically. But our material is much better researched, and we're willing to give kudos to people who, years ago, we wouldn't have given an inch of space to.

"I guess our biggest problem was growth. For the first two years, it was uncontrolled and completely unorganized. It was chaos; we didn't plan at all. Pamela Cohen, Mark Reeson, or I did everything—many times forgetting to tell one another what we did. We sold advertising, delivered papers with our own cars, wrote copy, and swept out the offices. We paid ourselves only a few dollars a day—just enough to pay the rent and buy some food. Our stringers and reporters got no pay. They just did their work for the love of it.

"Then the thing started getting the best of us. We were literally pooped. We found that despite our disposition toward running things loosely and our professed distaste for bureaucracy, there was a genuine need for organization and administration. Actually, you might say that that realization was our first turn into the straight mode. From there on in, we became recognized as a really serious newspaper.

"Our first stage in reorganizing came when we started separating editorial from business functions. We were grossing about $40,000 to $50,000 a month, and the accounting for monies, keeping track of advertising lineage, paying bills, going out to bid, and the other business activities were becoming as important to this paper as the editorial and news side. We split off a business department and under it put advertising, circulation, accounting, and purchasing. Next came the separation of production—layout, photography, art, etc.—from editorial. We don't do our own composition or printing; those we contract out. Those reorganization steps left us with three major departments—editorial, production, and business. We also incorporated and retained a legal counsel. This paper was becoming very successful.

"In the mid 1970s we started thinking of hitting some other communities. Our original venture centered on Princeton, New Jersey, and we went looking for other college communities to test our ideas. We planned out the Wilmington paper. Pamela moved there and essentially created a duplicate organization to the one we have here. We organized a subsidiary corporation, with the Princeton corporation as the sole shareholder. That went well.

"We then repeated the process by adding papers in Philadelphia, Camden, and Dover. But we organized them a little differently. We tied the Camden operation closely to our home shop; we did the production and handled the business affairs. But we opened a local office, added some advertising salespeople, and hired some extra reporters especially for that area. All of the people in that local office reported to their respective departments in the Princeton office. Dover is tied to Pamela's organization in Wilmington just as Camden is tied to us. Philly is a separate organization modeled after the Princeton and Wilmington groups.

"I guess we're now in need of some control and consolidation. Mark Reeson left the paper years ago, and both Pamela and I are running large organizations. We've known each other a long time and so are completely honest with and confident of each other. But we don't have that same sense of personal confidence with the Philly operation, even though we've known Tom Craft, the editor, for three years. Each of the organizations is semi-independent enough so it controls its own costs and revenues. At the end of the year a CPA firm audits the books of each, and then the subsidiary corporations declare dividends payable to the parent.

"But we have no idea whether costs are being held in line at all. Also, we probably could be picking up some advertising for all five papers, but we do that only occasionally now—when one of us gets the time to call the others. And we're really not that far apart physically.

"I guess what I'm saying is that we now have to reorganize. I think we planned our growth up to now really well. We knew what our strategies had to be for the markets we went out for. I think that allowing each of the major papers a maximum of freedom was also correct. Now, however, we need to standardize and be prepared for further expansion—including buying established papers or even other media. And I think that we must emphasize cost cutting and control. Newspapers are a tricky business. We have a nice niche to fit into, but that could blow away at any time. Now we've got to get our act together in terms of control and organization." ■

Case questions

1. What types of organizational problems now face this chain of newspapers?

2. Evaluate Ryan's statement: "I think that allowing each of the major papers a maximum of freedom was . . . correct." Do you agree? If you were in Ryan's place (or Pamela Cohen's), what would you have done differently?

3. As a consultant to the *Peoples' News,* what type of organization structure would you recommend for the chain of papers? Diagram it.

SELECTED READINGS

Albrecht, K., *Successful Management by Objectives* (Englewood Cliffs, N.J.: Prentice-Hall, 1978).

Barnes, L. B., and S. A. Hershon, "Transferring Power in the Family Business," *Harvard Business Review* **54** (July/August 1976): 105–114.

Bennis, W. G., K. D. Benne, and R. Chin, eds., *The Planning of Change* (New York: Holt, Rinehart and Winston, 1961).

Cason, R. L., "The Right Size: An Organizational Dilemma," *Management Review* **67,** 4 (April 1978): 24ff.

Cleland, D., and W. King, "Organizing for Long Range Planning," *Business Horizons* **17** (August 1974): 25–32.

Cyert, R. M., *The Management of Non-Profit Organizations* (Lexington, Mass.: D. C. Heath, 1975).

Davis, S., and P. R. Lawrence, *Matrix* (Reading, Mass.: Addison-Wesley, 1977).

———, "Problems of Matrix Organizations," *Harvard Business Review* **56,** 3 (May/June 1978): 131–142.

Famularo, J. J., *Organization Planning Manual* (New York: American Management Association, 1971).

French, W., and C. Bell, *Organization Development: Behavioral Science Intervention for Organization Improvement* (Englewood Cliffs, N.J.: Prentice-Hall, 1970).

Galbraith, J., *Organization Design* (Reading, Mass.: Addison-Wesley, 1977).

———, *Designing Complex Organizations* (Reading, Mass.: Addison-Wesley, 1973).

Gilbert, T. F., *Human Competence—Engineering Worthy Performance* (New York: McGraw-Hill, 1978).

Guest, R. H., P. Hersey, and K. H. Blanchard, *Organizational Change Through Effective Leadership* (Englewood Cliffs, N.J.: Prentice-Hall, 1977).

Hayes, R. H., and R. W. Schmenner, "How Should You Organize Manufacturing?" *Harvard Business Review* **56,** 1 (January/February 1978): 105–118.

Huffmire, D. W., "Strategies of the United States Airlines," *Long Range Planning Journal* **8** (April 1975): 72–79.

Huse, E. F., *Organization Development and Change* (St. Paul, Minn.: West, 1975).

Lorange, P., and R. F. Vancil, *Strategic Planning Systems* (Englewood Cliffs, N.J.: Prentice-Hall, 1977).

Lorsch, J. W., "Organization Design: A Situational Perspective," *Organizational Dynamics* **6,** 2 (Autumn 1977): 2–14.

McCaskey, M., "An Introduction to Organizational Design," *California Management Review* **17** (Winter 1974): 13–20.

McNeil, K., "Understanding Organizational Power: Building on the Weberian Legacy," *Administrative Science Quarterly* **23,** 1 (March 1978): 65–90.

Margulies, N., and J. Wallace, *Organizational Change* (Glenview, Ill.: Scott, Foresman, 1973).

Newman, W. H., "Strategy and Management Structure," *Proceedings: Academy of Management 31st Annual Meeting,* Boston, Mass., 1972.

Rue, L. W., "The How and Who of Long Range Planning," *Business Horizons* **16** (December 1973): 23–30.

Steiner, G. A., *Top Management Planning* (New York: Macmillan, 1969).

Youker, R., "Organization Alternatives for Project Managers," *Management Review* **66,** 11 (November 1977): 46–53.

Chapter 11
DESIGNING MOTIVATING SYSTEMS AND PRACTICES

CHAPTER HIGHLIGHTS

In this chapter we are concerned with the design of systems and practices that will contribute to optimum relationships of individuals and groups to organizational goals and purposes. We first cover several theories of individuals and motivation, then explore the effects of group processes on individuals within organizations, and, finally, introduce some of the ways that managers may capitalize on behavioral knowledge to build effective and efficient organizations and management practices. In conclusion, we emphasize the need for a manager to use all of the background information available, but to retain the flexibility necessary for meeting differing situations. In essence, there is no singular approach to management.

LEARNING OBJECTIVES

1 To appreciate the many theories of individual motivation.

2 To learn the traditional management theories of motivation.

3 To understand some contemporary models of motivation.

4 To learn Argyris's approach, Maslow's hierarchy of needs, Alderfer's ERG model, Herzberg's two-factor theory, McClelland's achievement-need theory, and expectancy theory.

5 To learn the behavior-modification approaches.

6 To understand some critiques of behaviorally based theories.

7 To understand the role of group processes in motivation.

8 To be able to differentiate between Theory X and Theory Y.

9 To understand the concept of job enlargement.

10 To understand the concept of job enrichment.

CASE: MOVING THE BETA ASSEMBLY DEPARTMENT

■ The Halston Company's plant at Peoria, Illinois, is the key component in the manufacture of electronic subassemblies. After being manufactured, the subassemblies are sent to the company's other plants for synthesis into the finished products. The Peoria plant became a division of Halston when the parent company, a large manufacturer of private-label electronic equipment, undertook a concerted effort to acquire all of its key suppliers. This consolidation effort materialized after the company had experienced difficulties acquiring tuners for one of its crucial products and had endangered its relationship with its major customer, a large retail chain. With increasing competition from Japan, Taiwan, and Korea, Halston occupies a tenuous place in a cost-conscious and extremely competitive industry. To some extent Halston relied on its fast and accurate delivery times to compensate for its somewhat higher prices.

The Peoria plant manufactured nine subassemblies, each of which was sufficiently unique so that a separate assembly line or production room was in operation for each. The Beta assembly, a component for the company's 19-inch color portable television set, was produced by seventy assemblers, packers, and support personnel in a large room sixty feet by eighty feet. The room was divided so that the product moved through eight distinct operations before it was packed. Seven employees worked on each of the operations and four worked in packaging. Two employees were in charge of the stock room, and eight were "runners" who carried the subassemblies from one workplace to another and kept the various workplaces supplied with parts that were added to the total subassembly. Figure 11.1 shows the department's production layout.

Each production employee worked on only one of the processes involved in the subassembly. After finishing the task on a piece of work, the production employee placed the product in a basket at his or her right side and took a new piece from a similar basket at his or her left side. The runners had the

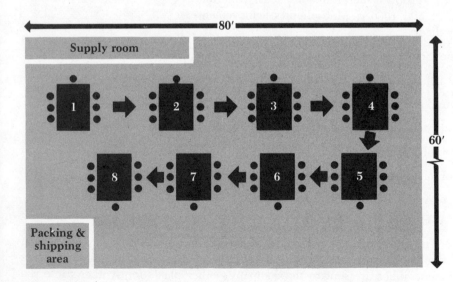

FIG. 11.1
Beta assembly department
production layout.

responsibility of moving the finished work of one worktable to the next work-table, where the next process would be applied to the product. Thus the runner became the supplier to the next assembly table. The runners also had the responsibility of keeping their assigned areas supplied with the parts and components which were to be added to the subassemblies at their stations. These parts were drawn from the supply room as needed.

Most of the work at the various stations involved relatively simple tasks such as soldering, bolting together parts, adding "plug-in" parts, etc. Qualifying for the work required little training, and most of the skills could be taught in one day or less. The chief problem was that of teaching new workers to solder and to avoid "cold joints."

Most of the employees adjusted well to the system. Although each employee at a work station did exactly the same work as the others at that station, enough repartee and camaraderie developed to relieve any boredom that might be expected from working on a simple repetitive operation. Workers practically always met the production standards demanded of them.

For one month, however, industrial engineers from the central engineering staff had been studying all of the operations at the Peoria plant with an eye toward increasing production. Rumors were rife throughout the plant that the "slide-rule boys" were going to turn the place upside down. No official communication of the staff's purposes was delivered to the production employees.

The plant closed for its annual three-week vacation in July. When the workers returned, they found that the "slide-rule boys" had indeed been working. The group working on the Beta assembly were sent to a new home, and the production workers were routed to a long room forty feet by eighty feet on the second floor. Four of the runners were told to report to the personnel office, where they were informed that they were no longer needed at the plant.

The new plant layout for the Beta assembly section was composed of four long tables, with eight workers seated on each side. Each side of each table was a complete assembly unit, with a part starting with the first person and being completed by the last person. The four remaining runners kept the tables supplied with the parts and then took the finished assemblies to the packing area. Figure 11.2 illustrates the new arrangement for Beta.

Very few of the workers were ecstatic about the new layout. A few went home on the first day, but returned later in the day. Most loafed for about two hours before starting work. All grumbled about the "brainchild" of the slide-rule boys. "They didn't tell us a damned thing about this change" was the least vulgar of the many remarks made about the new system. The supervisors on the assembly line tried hard to explain the promised efficiency of the new setup, but the workers were not easily convinced.

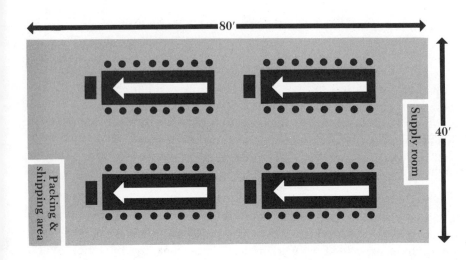

FIG. 11.2
Beta assembly department
revised production layout.

For the first four months, production levels never came close to the previous ones under the old system, although the central staff engineers were convinced that output would be one and one-half times the level under the old system and with less direct labor cost. ∎

INTRODUCTION

In designing or altering organizations to carry out plans, managers are also attempting to direct the behavior of individuals and groups into prescribed channels or patterns. Organizational designers also have the functions of limiting personal frames of reference and of relating one unit or task to another. In the Beta assembly case—which ostensibly may be viewed as a production problem, but in reality is one of organization—the relationships were altered from one homogeneous work unit relating to another homogeneous unit and so on to a department composed of units, each with a number of heterogeneous tasks.

Whether this new arrangement will be as successful as the former will depend on not only the technical arrangement of one task or group of tasks to another task or group of tasks, but also the mental sets of the individuals and groups employed in the processes.

Traditional, or classical, management thought, beginning with the early pioneers of management, prescribed that organizations be designed around tasks, not people. The bases for this prescription were some rather simple notions that tasks could always be efficiently related to one another in one best way and that people were motivated by very simple kinds of things and thus could be manipulated very easily to plug into the one efficiently designed productive system. Current management thought, however, is not so sanguine. First, it is argued that technical efficiency can be reached through many avenues. More important, however, is the new knowledge on human beings operating as individuals or in a group. The human being is seen as one who is much more complex in needs, wants, and feelings and who cannot be simply packed into a technically efficient structure.

In this chapter we shall explore the organizational systems-design process as it must consider the entire conceptual framework of human behavior. After discussing the various theories of human needs and motivation and then group processes, we will explore how the manager may capitalize on this knowledge to build possibly more efficient and effective organizational relationships and systems.

THEORIES OF INDIVIDUAL MOTIVATION

Individuals relate to an organization in terms of an exchange. Individuals have needs and organizations have objectives. In fulfilling one's own particular needs, the individual is motivated to perform some act and to achieve some result desired by the organization. When the act is performed satisfactorily, the organization rewards, and hence the individual satisfies his or her own particular need. Such an arrangement is pictured in Fig. 11.3; individual need leads to some activity, which in turn leads to the achievement

FIG. 11.3
Individual motivation in an organizational context.

of the organizational objective. This achievement leads to a personal reward that satisfies the need. What are those needs composed of? What makes the individual want to continue to perform organizationally prescribed tasks? Are there any limits that might diminish the amount of effort an individual will exert for the organization?

Traditional management thought

Until well into the 1930s, the dominant assumption underlying most of management thought and practically all of management activity was that people work primarily for money and that the more they are paid, the more they will work and—even more important—the more malleable they will be to supervisory direction. The earliest pioneers—the first to view management as a discipline to be studied and learned (circa 1890)—stressed money motivation in the practical business and production procedures. Thus, piece-rate systems, work analysis, time-and-motion study, and reward systems relating increased pay to increased production were part and parcel of a creed that came to be known as *scientific management*. The father of this scientific-management movement was Frederick W. Taylor.*

Even when one moved from the production floor or the operations tasks into the administration of the total organization or to the design of the total organization, the overriding assumption about individual motivation was still very implicit, if not explicit. Formal organization theory and bureaucratic theory stressed the need to organize around the job, not the individual.† All individuals were assumed to have similar simple needs; hence differences in human behavior were rarely factored into the design process. The box on the organization chart (related to other boxes) and the job description, along with the concept of hierarchical control and the notion that those at the top of the pyramid always knew better than those at the bottom of the pyramid, were based on the assumptions that one could place an individual in one of those boxes, pay that individual sufficient wages, and expect him or her to perform according to the specifications of the box and the job description.

The type of managerial style (practiced in relating to employees and subordinates) resulting from this chain of assumption to structure was, of course, autocratic. Management had the right to set standards as it knew best; the employees were there for money and were expected to conform to organizational demands. If the employee could not or would not perform, then, of course, another money-motivated individual could always be found.

* See Frederick W. Taylor, *Principles of Scientific Management* (New York: Harper and Brothers, 1911), and *Shop Management* (New York: Harper and Brothers, 1919). Other key participants in the scientific-management movement were Henry Gantt, Frank and Lillian Gilbreth, and Harrington Emerson.
† Probably the first of the management books to focus on total organizational management was Henri Fayol, *General and Industrial Administration,* trans. C. Storrs (London: Sir Isaac Pitman & Sons, Ltd., 1949).

Parenthetically, although one might think that employee unions would force management to rethink its underlying assumptions, until well into the 1970s, unions stressed wages, job security, pensions, seniority, supplemental unemployment benefits, and other job extrinsics—things that employees personally carry away from the workplace. Some observers have noted that such union behavior and demands simply reinforced the traditional management assumption that employees are motivated by extrinsics, particularly money.

Newer theories of individual motivation are now making their impact on management and are affecting the underlying assumptions of organization design and the styles of managerial behavior practiced with employees and subordinates. Generally these theories all have one common denominator; they look at the human being as a complex bundle of needs, abilities, motivations, and attitudes. As such, these models relate the individual to the formal organization in such a way that the organization comes out being designed as a more flexible mechanism, and managerial styles are more contingent on a task/people combination than on the task alone. In Chapter 3 the area of organization was essentially covered in a traditional manner, although we did inject a number of "human" factors in topics such as decentralization, centralization, and span of control. Here, however, we will make further modifications as a result of learning more about individual and group behavior.

Contemporary models and impact

Argyris's personality and organization model   In examining the relationship of individuals and organizations, Chris Argyris concludes that the highly structured organization is a gigantic personality crusher.* Argyris suggests that psychologically healthy individuals *must* grow personally and develop mature personalities, whereas organizations are built on the assumption of very low levels of personal maturation. Hence, according to Argyris, organizations have been built to demand control, compliance, and conformance to tightly prescribed standards.

In the Argyris model, when the healthy, psychologically maturing individual, who needs autonomy and responsibility, bumps into the organization, which is demanding conformance and compliance, the organization generally stands firm, and the healthy, maturing individual becomes increasingly frustrated and therefore turns to defense mechanisms, generally regressing to childlike behavior and becoming submissive and dependent on superiors (parent substitutes) for direction. The behavior exhibited under regression, of course, "proves" to the management of the organization or the organization-design experts that their assumptions about individuals were right in the first place. The result is that management imposes more controls. Hence the crushing of motivation starts all over again in ever more constraining cycles.

* Chris Argyris, *Personality and Organization* (New York: Harper & Row, 1957).

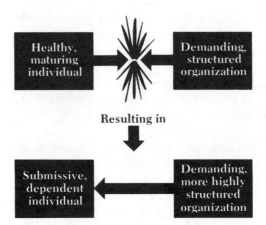

Resulting in

FIG. 11.4
Argyris model of individual/organization interaction.

In short, Argyris is attempting to tell us that formal organizations are designed for very low-level individuals and that there are just not enough of those to go around, so the organization "creates them." Figure 11.4 pictures the Argyris argument.

Maslow's hierarchy   One of the most important and widely cited theories of motivation in the management literature is Abraham Maslow's concept of the hierarchy of needs.* Maslow pictures the individual as having five levels of needs (see Fig. 11.5). The most basic needs are the physiological ones—food, water, sex, etc. These are the most important needs, and the individual will seek to satisfy this important group first. The second-level needs Maslow terms the safety needs, which generally refer to physical safety, but can be

FIG. 11.5
Maslow's concept of hierarchy of needs.

* Abraham H. Maslow, *Motivation and Personality,* 2d ed. (New York: Harper & Row, 1970).

extended to include economic safety as well. Third, the individual has needs for love and belongingness—social needs. These needs refer to the individual's need to belong, to be accepted as part of a group, and be loved, not in a physical sense, but in a human, emotional sense. The fourth level includes the self-esteem needs—ego gratification, status, etc. Finally, the individual has needs for self-actualization, or self-fulfillment, articulated by the desire to create.

According to Maslow's model, individuals first seek to satisfy the lowest level of needs—physiological. When those have been sufficiently satisfied, the individual moves to seek satisfaction of the next higher-level needs. Generally, then, when one level of needs has been satisfied, the individual will then seek to satisfy a next higher-level need.

Relative to motivation, needs are the basis for motivating activity, as we saw in the simple model presented in Fig. 11.3. Maslow states, however, that a satisfied need is no longer a motivating need. Hence a continuous infusion of money by the organization to the individual would have little or no incremental effect on motivation, according to Maslow, since the organization would have already effectively satisfied the individual's physiological, probably the safety, and perhaps part of the belongingness needs through the money mechanism. Reliance on offering satisfaction of the higher-level needs as inducements to motivating is thus a necessary fact of organization life. This prescription, of course, is in direct contradiction to the implicit assumptions of the older, formal management theories, i.e., that money is a consistent motivator.

One can ask, of course, what affects the nature of satisfaction. Why might some individuals satisfy their hunger need with a hamburg, whereas others need steak in order to satisfy themselves? Maslow recognized that needs satisfaction depends a great deal on the particular culture to which the person belongs. Thus certain needs will be easier to satisfy in a cultural situation in which people are satisfied with minimal provisions than in a more developed culture in which need satisfaction requires greater infusion of provisions.

Maslow did caution, however, that very few individuals ever reach the highest-level needs of ego and self-realization. Many individuals are still motivated by lower-level needs and may continue to be motivated by greater infusions of money, just as the traditionalists had contended.

One last caution must also be made. No empirical verification of the Maslow model has yet been offered, even though the model is cited extensively throughout the literature.

Alderfer's ERG model   A need-based theory of motivation similar to Maslow's is Alderfer's ERG approach.[*] Alderfer postulates that individuals have

[*] *See* Clayton P. Alderfer, *Existence, Relatedness and Growth: Human Needs in Organizational Settings* (New York: Free Press, 1972).

three basic need sets: existence, relatedness, and growth (ERG). Existence needs are analogous to Maslow's physiological and safety needs—food, water, security, etc. Relatedness needs are those connected with the maintenance of interpersonal relationships with friends, family, co-workers, etc. Growth needs in the Alderfer model are similar to Maslow's two upper levels —personal development and creativity.

The fundamental difference between Alderfer and Maslow, however, is that Alderfer maintains that for an individual who is frustrated in attempts to satisfy higher-level needs, lower-level needs will increase in importance, and the individual will pursue them with more intensity. For managers, then, Alderfer's approach, unlike that of Maslow, would seem to recognize the ability to motivate with larger doses of existence and relatedness need satisfaction.

Herzberg's two-factor theory   Another theory that gained popularity among management analysts and practitioners alike is Frederick Herzberg's two-factor theory of motivation.* Herzberg's thesis is based on the notion that individuals have essentially two needs: (1) the need to grow psychologically and to achieve, and (2) the need to avoid pain from the environment. The growth need is the motivating one, and the pain-avoidance need, although not motivating, will result in increased unhappiness if satisfaction is decreased.

Psychological growth and achievement needs are stimulated by organizational mechanisms that induce psychological growth and occur in the content of the job. Hence, according to Herzberg, *the growth, or motivating, factors are intrinsic to the job*. These factors are:

1 Perceived opportunity for advancement
2 Recognition for achievement
3 Interesting or important work
4 Responsibility
5 Growth or advancement

Those factors stimulating *pain avoidance* (Herzberg calls those the hygiene factors) are in the job environment and hence they are *extrinsic to the job*. These factors are:

1 Company policy and administration
2 Supervision
3 Interpersonal relationships
4 Working conditions
5 Salary, status, and security

* Frederick Herzberg, *Work and the Nature of Man* (New York: World, 1966).

The hygiene factors, according to Herzberg, increase unhappiness if they are negatively applied, but neither the negative nor increasingly positive application of hygiene factors will increase the motivation of individuals. Only the positive application or presence of the growth or motivating factors will increase motivation on the part of individuals.

Herzberg's work has come in for its share of criticism. One of the most crucial concerns is his extrapolation of the conclusions from the research methodology employed. Herzberg's conclusions were based on oral reports by respondents. Critics, however, argue that people will always take credit for things that go well, but will tend to blame failure on their environment. Hence the factors that do show motivation will inevitably be instrinsic, whereas those that show unhappiness will usually be the extrinsic ones.

One might note the similarities in the Maslow and the Herzberg presentations. Theorists following Maslow often contend that many of the lower-level needs are met by money and that much of the need for belongingness and love is satisfied in the workplace or out of it. Herzberg's thesis includes most of these needs in the hygiene category, reserving for the motivating factors those areas that seem to correspond most closely to Maslow's higher-level need classifications.

McClelland's three-need theory   David C. McClelland's extensive and long research program has generated a theory centering on three needs—achievement, affiliation, and power—and relating the strength and/or dominance of each need in individuals to occupations or professions held.* His theory is particularly relevant for the selection and motivation of managers.

Individuals with a high need for achievement thrive on jobs and projects that tax their own skills and abilities. These people also set realistic goals and objectives for themselves, disdaining unrealistic or unattainable goals. Such individuals tend to be loners in the pursuit of goals—individualistic—and will seek primarily task-oriented assistance. Finally, individuals with high achievement needs want to be apprised as to how well they are doing; they want feedback on results.

Individuals with high affiliation needs value interpersonal relationships and exhibit sensitivity toward other people's feelings. By contrast, individuals with strong power needs seek to dominate or gain power, influence, or control over people.

McClelland's research has found that managers and entrepreneurs generally score high in the need for achievement. This indicates that the motivating forces for managers should lie in the challenge and potential of the job. There is, of course, the necessity for a manager to possess some degree of all three needs—that is, some need for affiliation and some for power to go

* David C. McClelland, *The Achieving Society* (Princeton, N.J.: Van Nostrand, 1961); also David C. McClelland and David G. Winter, *Motivating Economic Achievement* (New York: Free Press, 1969).

along with the strong need for achievement. But the dominant need, according to the research, is the one for achievement.

Expectancy theory   An approach that seeks to link the needs of the individual to the process of converting those needs into choices of behavior is expectancy theory, which is based on the notion of rational choice.* That is, individuals will perform if they can *expect* to receive a reward or group of rewards *and* if that reward or the sum of the grouping of rewards *seems important* to them (see Fig. 11.6).

According to this theory, individuals attempt to determine the probability of gaining personal goals if they achieve a particular organizationally demanded goal. This determination is a measure of expectancy of outcome. These personal outcomes are rewards that the organization can provide, e.g., pay raises, promotions, time off, and other perquisites. They can also be, however, intrinsics such as relationships with workmates, more interesting work, and the like. The values of expectancy that the individual attaches to each of the rewards result from such things as past experience, others' opinions, one's opinion of oneself, etc.

In addition, there is a measure called valence, which is a measure of the importance of each of those outcomes or rewards to the individual. The val-

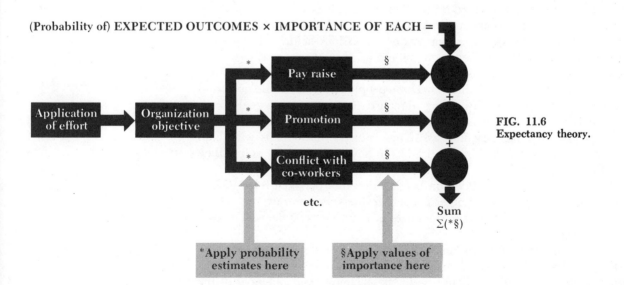

(Probability of) EXPECTED OUTCOMES × IMPORTANCE OF EACH =

Application of effort → Organization objective

Pay raise §
Promotion §
Conflict with co-workers §

etc.

*Apply probability estimates here

§Apply values of importance here

Sum
$\Sigma(*§)$

FIG. 11.6
Expectancy theory.

* Victor Vroom, *Work and Motivation* (New York: Wiley, 1964). *See also* Larry Cummings and Donald P. Schwab, *Performance in Organizations* (Glenview, Ill.: Scott, Foresman, 1973); Lyman W. Porter and Edward E. Lawler, III, *Managerial Attitudes and Performance* (Homewood, Ill.: Irwin/Dorsey, 1968).

ues of these measures are a result of the attractiveness of the reward and the opinion of oneself and those opinions of others about the reward in question.

According to the expectancy theory, employees are able to make rational calculations summing the products of each probability (expectancy) factored by its respective desirability. In order to dramatically improve motivation, then, managers should improve the expectancy and attractiveness of those items which tend to drive the motivation way down—those that contribute to a lowered motivation index or sum.

For example, if an employee already has a high expectation of a pay raise, a slight increase in expectations of a pay raise (e.g., the organization "telegraphs" that it is going to increase pay more) may induce less of a motivational change than working to alter a factor that has a high expectancy multiplied by a very low personal value. For example, if high production is expected to also result in higher conflict with fellow employees and the worker has a high *negative* value of this conflict, managers might be better off working to effect a significant decrease in the conflict-generating conditions than in promising modest pay increases.

The major problem with expectancy theory is its assumption of rationality. Individuals are not always as calculating as the theory assumes they are. Indeed, as we have seen, managers may seek "good enough" solutions to their problems by satisficing. There should be no reason to assume that employees reacting to organizational reward systems should be any more rational.

Finally, in order for expectancy theory to work for the individual manager, she or he must have control over the availability of rewards, and the organization must communicate clearly the reward system to employees.

Behavior-modification approaches

A somewhat different, and perhaps frightening, approach to controlling—indeed manipulating—human behavior in organizational settings, draws heavily from the work of B. F. Skinner and the behavioral school of psychology.* Proponents of this approach rely not on notions of internal phenomena determining behavior, but rather on the observation of overt behavior. Thus the behaviorists in psychology argue that when a person is given a certain reward after specified behaviors and then the promise of the same reward's being repeated again induces the correct behavior, the person has been *conditioned* to behave in the "correct" way. Such outcome is without reference to such internal factors as needs, emotions, anxieties, etc.

The Skinnerian followers emphasize primarily positive reinforcements to condition toward, or shape, desired behavior. That is, they emphasize rewards, not punishments. They conclude that over time positive reinforce-

* B. F. Skinner, *Beyond Freedom and Dignity* (New York: Knopf, 1971). *See also* Craig Schneier, "Behavior Modification in Management: A Review and Critique," *Academy of Management Journal* **17** (September 1974): 528–548.

ments will generally induce the desired behavior and that undesirable behavior will gradually disappear because it is not reinforced.

Behavior-modification approaches are interesting in that they stress that an individual can be manipulated and that managers and organizations can be the manipulators. Unlike in some of the other theories we have covered, the individual looms rather helpless under behavior modification. There is, on top of the question of whether the basic conclusions hold up, the whole area of the ethics involved in managers and organizations' using that manipulative power.

Theories of motivation: summary

In summarizing all of the foregoing theories of motivation, we can say that they do exhibit certain consistencies. They all deal with the individual as a very complex mechanism. But one must note that the models also stress different things—different needs, different levels of importance attached to the environment, differing actions by managers, etc. They all, perhaps with the exception of behavior modification, credit individuals with a great deal more complexity and inner motivation than did the traditional, money-centered concepts.

There is some concern lest the contemporary models raise managers' interest levels and get them involved in all sorts of behavioral jargon, which they then find unusable or incapable of paying off in the hard, cold figures of productivity or profit. For example, soon after some of the behavioral models began appearing in the managerial literature, one critic, George Strauss, responded to the Argyris- and Maslow-type approaches.* In effect, Strauss scolded his fellow university professors for ascribing their own self-actualizing needs and behavior to everyone else, when there was a very strong possibility that production employees and other organizational members did not care for such need satisfactions. Even if they did care, the costs of participation, intrinsic job satisfactions, and mechanisms for satisfying higher levels of needs might be too great. Other critics, noting that many behaviorally centered processes were introduced into very small firms and seemed to work primarily in very special types of operations, also ran up the caution flag. The critics argue, in essence, that people might have to bear the burden of work and some of the unpleasantness that goes with it, since the costs of change would be too great—and they might not care about the burden either.

The behavioral theorists too issue cautions to overzealous managers. Maslow, for example, wrote: "Clearly, different principles of management would apply to these different managerial levels. We don't have any great

* George Strauss, "The Personality-versus-Organization Theory," in Leonard Sayles, *Individualism and Big Business* (New York: McGraw-Hill, 1963), pp. 67–80.

need to work out management principles for the lower levels in the motivational hierarchy."*

Frederick Herzberg, in discussing steps to job enrichment, wrote as step one: "Select those jobs in which (a) the investment in Industrial Engineering does not make changes too costly, (b) attitudes are poor, (c) hygiene is becoming very costly, and (d) motivation will make a difference in performance."† Clearly, this statement implies that some jobs do not or cannot fit a prescription of increased intrinsic satisfaction. It seems a bit more efficient and realistic to recognize the inapplicability of the theories to certain situations than to advertise them as panaceas for all of an organization's ills.

What we are saying here is that a great deal of motivation theory *may* be applicable to management personnel, highly skilled production personnel, and people with variable and interesting work tasks. It may not be universally applicable to low-skilled people working in relatively unchallenging jobs.

GROUP PROCESSES AND INDIVIDUAL BEHAVIOR

The small informal group has a most definite effect on employee behavior, from fully supporting the employee to informally, but harshly, disciplining him or her for breaking group norms. If Maslow-type theorizing is correct, people are often motivated to come to work to find sociability and work grouping. But the group also is very definitely a controlling unit through the various "natural" processes that arise in it.

Group characteristics

Informal groups within the organization do participate in motivating, acculturating, and indeed in controlling individuals (see Fig. 11.7). Groups develop goals of their own; sometimes these goals are consistent with those of the organization; sometimes they are not. But group members do share some purposes—perhaps only one or two—and although they may look trivial to the outside observer, they are nonetheless shared and important to the members. For example, one of the widely shared goals among many production employees is protection of the weaker or less capable members of the group. Thus the group will establish production norms—or "bogies"—that limit the output of the more able members. This goal becomes very observable when management is using piece-rate systems, and the employees fear that high

---

* Maslow, *op. cit.*
† Frederick Herzberg, "One More Time: How Do You Motivate Employees?" *Harvard Business Review* **46** (January/February 1968): 58.

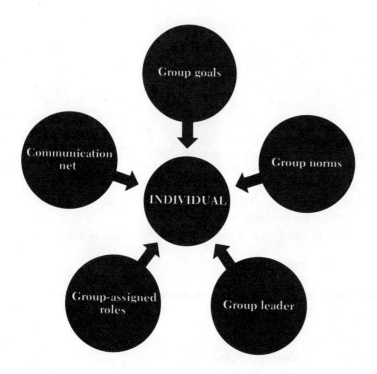

FIG. 11.7
Group processes affecting individuals' behavior.

production on the part of the more capable workers will cause management to raise the quotas beyond the reach of the least capable worker.

The norms established in pursuit of goals, then, guide group members behavior. Such norms condition the behavior of the group members toward one another. Some norms, however, like the production quota, are geared toward the formal organization. These norms are enforced by the group, but generally accepted by members.

The groups also develop some semblance of a structure and a communication-flow network. Certain individuals informally assume or are assigned certain tasks within the structure, such as "breaking the rookie in." People in the group develop member-to-member affinity, and the group develops some degree of group identity.

Finally, the group develops a leadership function. The leaders hold their position through acceptance by the group rather than through appointment by management. Hence informal leaders can change rapidly if they lose acceptance by members, although experience has shown that there is surprisingly high longevity among informal leaders.

An interesting perspective on the important role of groups as motivators is detailed in a 1970 set of articles in the *New York Review of Books* by Elinor Langer, describing her experiences as a service representative with the Commercial Department of the New York Telephone Company.* Ms. Langer went into the telephone company to find out why lower-middle-class women worked, why they adhered to and supported a rigorous, demanding, and (according to Ms. Langer) demeaning management system, and what they hoped to and actually did get out of their jobs. She came away with some interesting findings, although her research approach was admittedly one of radical journalism. The key motivating force for the women seemed to be the social groups that evolved. The women were coming to work to be with friends and to socialize, and this resulted in adherence and sometimes even loyalty to a rigid management system. Fortunately for the company, production was a by-product of the socializing process, and perhaps the telephone company could not have found a more effective way of getting the work done than by relying on the development of those social groupings, although observation and control were extremely strict on the job.

Indeed, one of the first breakaways from the traditional management approach of the turn of the century resulted from the recognition, albeit accidental, of the sociability need. In 1924, at the Hawthorne plant of Western Electric Company, Elton Mayo and a group of his associates from the Harvard Business School selected and segregated groups of employees to study the effects of variations in working conditions (light, heat, humidity, etc.) on productivity.† These types of experiments were quite standard in the scientific-management literature, and the hypothesis was that the improvements in working conditions or the work environment would have a positive effect on productivity.

In the Hawthorne study, lighting intensity was increased for the test group, but not for the control group. Surprisingly, productivity increased in both groups. Lights were decreased for both groups, with the expectations that production would decrease in both. It did not! Indeed, productivity continued to increase in both groups.

The well-told, but then unexpected, conclusions of those experiments were that *social* rather than physical working conditions played the key role in raising production. The people involved knew that they were being tested, took pride in the fact that they had been selected, thought that the company

Groups in work situations

---

* Elinor Langer, *New York Review of Books:* "Inside the New York Telephone Company" **14**, 5 (March 12, 1970): 16–24; and "The Women of the Telephone Company" **14**, 6 (March 26, 1970): 14–22.
† *See* Fritz J. Roethlisberger and W. J. Dickson, *Management and the Worker* (Boston: Harvard University Press, 1939). *See also* Elton Mayo, *The Social Problems of an Industrial Civilization* (Cambridge, Mass.: Harvard University Press, 1945).

really cared for them, enjoyed the social contacts of the work group, reveled in the freedom from supervision which the experiment offered them, and hence, as a group, produced more.

Management, then, is coming to realize that socialization and cohesive work groups may have a highly positive effect on production. This realization runs counter to the often-heard fear of management that work groups, spawning, as we noted, natural leaders and their own internal communications systems, are always counterproductive to the organization's objectives.

Sometimes, however, the activity relating to satisfying social needs may not be functional to the organizational output objectives, and if the organization or management cannot institute any other behavioral mechanisms to stimulate productivity, it may have to resort to old-fashioned rules or environmental engineering. For example, in a fast-food restaurant the various bins for the hamburgs and other meat products were placed in behind the counter work area, directly in front of the cooking area, exposed to the lines of customers. The french fry supply was over to one side of the work area, out of the sight of the manager, who usually worked in the back on the meat-preparation area. The french fry area thus became a natural area of socializing for the counter help. Although the conversations were usually brief, they were enough to irritate a customer who had been standing in line for five minutes and who expected instant service. The problem became so severe that the french fry dispensers were relocated to the center of the service area, within sight of the managers. In this case the elimination of an area that enhanced sociability did not affect the work relations in the shop, but did increase production—if only by a few minutes time here and there. But one must remember that time is one of the most valuable factors in a fast-food operation.

MOTIVATIONAL THEORY, ORGANIZATIONAL SYSTEM DESIGN, AND MANAGEMENT PRACTICES

One widely quoted writer, Douglas McGregor, used the various models about individuals to develop his classification of managers into Theory X or Theory Y types.* According to McGregor, a Theory X manager makes certain assumptions about people and work, as follows:

1 Work is inherently distasteful and should be avoided

2 Since people don't really want to work, they must be directed, coerced, and controlled in work situations

3 Individuals work only to make money and be secure

* Douglas McGregor, *The Human Side of Enterprise* (New York: McGraw-Hill, 1960).

A Theory Y manager, on the other hand, assumes that:

1 Work is a natural activity for individuals

2 Individuals will commit themselves to work objectives

3 The degree of commitment is a function of the rewards

4 The average person seeks responsibility and does not shun it

5 Such capacity for psychological growth is widely rather than narrowly distributed within the population

Obviously, the superior subordinate posture adopted by a Theory X manager will differ from that adopted by a Theory Y manager. A Theory X manager tends to be autocratic and production- or output-centered, whereas a Theory Y manager tends to be more people-centered, being democratic and supportive of the growth needs of subordinates.

For most practicing managers, however, the choice of a managing philosophy is not an "either/or" one for total application, and the current literature reflects this need for flexibility. Our objective in this section, then, is to relate the various background theories of individual (and group) motivation into practical work and organizational design situations. Through examples, we shall illustrate that some situations call for the manager to apply a strictly technical solution using a high degree of structure based on the simplistic assumptions similar to the traditional approach (or the first-level needs of the behavioral approach), whereas other situations might require the manager to adapt designs because of the necessity to compensate for the complexity and needs of the individuals and the groups he or she is dealing with.

Money-oriented systems

In many cases money is the only motivator that will work, and managerial activity undertaken to introduce complex behavioral systems based on higher-level needs may be a waste of time and effort in terms of incremental return in productivity and profitability. An interesting example involves a chain of ice cream parlors. The jobs in general are not overly challenging, certainly not very interesting, do not require very much skill and training, and generally are not widely regarded as offering promising and lifelong careers. Indeed, most of the positions were filled by part-time workers who wanted to earn some pocket money for a short-term purchase (such as an automobile for a teenager) or who were working at the job to supplement the family's income.

The company suffered high rates of turnover, tardiness, and absenteeism. As hard as it tried, management could not redesign the jobs or the supervision to give the workers greater intrinsic satisfaction. Management tried meetings, allocating individual work stations, meetings with top management, colorful uniforms, allowing employees to design new ice cream "creations," etc. Nothing seems to work; absenteeism remained high, and tardiness remained a major problem. Finally, in desperation, management raised the pay by thirty-five cents an hour; this gave the company the highest-paid ice cream shoppe workers in the area. Presto! Absenteeism fell, tardiness dropped off, and the turnover decreased dramatically.

One could, of course, argue that working in the highest-paying shop was a status-inflating activity, and thus the need that had to be fulfilled was status, not money. This argument was discounted, though, by management and employees alike. The employees simply had not been getting enough money, and the decision on whether or not to come to work was a simple one of matching the added income with the "pain" of a boring job for several hours. When the "pain" won out, the employee simply took the day off.

One may, of course, find the effect of this pay raise leveling off over time or quite quickly, however, since more pay increases will not be forthcoming. Many companies seek to overcome this leveling effect by using piece-rate plans or other methods of relating pay to productivity. Piece-rate systems were a primary result in traditional management thought and analysis, and many modern-day, behaviorally oriented management analysts and practitioners look on them with disdain. But they are another tool in the kit of the manager, and when the situation is right in terms of the types of jobs and employees one is dealing with, they should not be disregarded simply on dogmatic grounds.

By endorsing piece-rate plans and money as a motivator in certain situations, we are, of course, not proclaiming the contemporary theorists wrong. In fact, they are probably very much correct. Here we are dealing with jobs needing no high degrees of skill, and people are at those jobs to earn money. That is their primary need. Such things as status, prestige, participation, and all the other items on the motivation menu may be irrelevant in the managerial situations involved in these cases.

Job enlargement One of the mechanisms strongly suggested by the new theories on motivation and highly recommended by management theorists is job enlargement. Job enlargement, applicable in many instances, simply means adding additional operative tasks to a worker's responsibility. To use the language of Chapter 3, it means expanding the worker's job horizontally.

To illustrate job enlargement, let us consider the assembly line. The assembly line typically is based on the classical, or traditional, prescription that a process should be broken down into minute tasks and that an individual should be trained to do the simple, repetitive, minute task over and over again. In essence, the organization is designed down to the simplest functions, and the individuals hired to fill the "boxes" are not expected to be very sophisticated. All of the minute tasks are then engineered to mesh together to "create" the whole product at the end. In an assembly-line situation, job enlargement would entail giving the individual workers a number of tasks to complete, thus allowing them to vary their work and input. For example, instead of continuously operating a machine that simultaneously tightens the five or six lug nuts on the two left wheels of an automobile, a worker might also be given the responsibility for installing the radio and the steering wheel.

Job enlargement is often not associated with adding jobs or tasks to an individual's role on a preexisting assembly line, but rather is more likely to lead to a redesigning of the entire line and work-station routine. In *Man on the Assembly Line*, a popular training film, one of the workers, complaining about the monotony of doing the same simple task over and over again on the assembly line, asks: "Why can't we build a whole car?" He sounds silly in the film, but in Sweden, Volvo and Saab are doing something very similar, having a group of workers make complete subassemblies, such as engines or transmissions. The workers thus achieve "closure"—they can "see" the final product on which they are working. Worker groups are free to develop their own standards of pace and to allocate and reallocate the tasks among themselves. Similar experiences of junking the assembly line and enlarging jobs have taken place in the United States, although the results are mixed in terms of both worker motivation and organizational output.

The Volvo and Saab plant experiences, however, may be affected by the unique Swedish culture and environment, and hence the results may not be replicable in the United States. Indeed, a group of American automakers spent some time at the Saab plant, and the consensus of opinion was that they did not care for the plant.* However, observers noted that the American workers went to Sweden without their families, and the cultural and language differences may have been crucial factors in their opinions. Also, the scale of the Swedish operations is much smaller than that in most American auto plants.

Job enrichment

The objective of job enlargement is to increase motivation by broadening the operative tasks of workers; in job enrichment, by contrast, decision-making or managerial tasks are added to the workers' jobs. Thus operative employees can plan their own work paces, production standards, and work allocations (note that the Volvo plant experience is a combination of both job enlargement and job enrichment); or, salespeople can be given the authority to plan their own territorial coverage, to route their own orders to the company's various plants, to authorize credits, etc.

Job enrichment seeks to respond to the higher-level, creative needs of individuals. As such, its use falls right into the prescription of McGregor's

* "Doubting Sweden's Way: American Workers View Team-Assembly Methods at Saab Engine Plant," *Time*, March 10, 1975. *See also* Pehr G. Gyllenhammar, "How Volvo Adapts Work to People," *Harvard Business Review* (July/August, 1977); and *People at Work* (Reading, Mass.: Addison-Wesley, 1977).

Theory Y. On the other hand, not all work groups or individuals are ready for job enrichment. For example, suppose that a job-enrichment design calls for significantly less interaction among employees in exchange for their greater involvement in individual decision making. This may cause a dysfunctional result, with workers resenting not being able to socialize with old friends and co-workers. In essence, although job enrichment might be highly successful among some groups of workers and in certain situations, it could be a complete disaster when applied to other groups and individuals and in other situations. In addition, some job-enrichment experiments have been criticized for taking credit for increased motivation, when in fact some additional, more traditional incentives, including money, were also added at the same time.*

Management by Objectives and other organization-development techniques

In Chapter 4 we described at some length the practices of Management by Objectives and other organization-development and team-building techniques. In that context, we were mostly concerned with overcoming what many observers perceive as a malaise coming over organizations and managers because of changing values. All of that material is relevant here too; all of those techniques are also motivational tools for the manager to use. We should note that MBO and OD (organization development) techniques are often thought of as being applicable to situations of managers' managing other managers. The relevance of those techniques to the management of operative and technical employees, however, should not be overlooked.

We should also note that MBO is particularly attuned to McClelland's achievement-need theory. Managers with strong achievement needs want the feedback on results and like to pursue realistic, achievable goals. They also want independence of action. Achievable goals, feedback of results, and independence of action, as we saw in Chapter 4, are precisely the ingredients of the MBO concept.

Management practices and the Beta assembly department

Now let us apply some material in this chapter to the Beta assembly department. Why did the redesign fail to excite the employees? Indeed, why did it aggravate and upset them?

First, the fact that the central-office staff personnel were around for several weeks before the vacation obviously had an effect. No one communicated to the workers on the purpose of the central staff's being in the plant, and this obviously affected the workers' security perceptions.

Second, the change was precipitously dropped onto the workers after their vacation. This no doubt had an effect on their security, and the employees, seeing that four of their co-workers (the runners) were summarily

* E. Lauck Parke and Curt Tausky, "The Mythology of Job Enrichment: Self Actualization Revisited," *Personnel* **52,** 5 (September/October 1975): 12–21.

dismissed, might have interpreted that action as a threat to not only employee security, but also their earning power.

Probably the most important factors, however, were the changes in group structure that the new design imposed on the work force. Instead of the homogeneous groupings that the workers were used to, the new design called for four heterogeneous groupings. Old friendships that might have been developed under the old arrangement were broken up. Old social groups were eliminated. Even though each of the new heterogeneous groups completed an entire subassembly (job enlargement), that factor might not have compensated for the breakup of friendships.

How might have Halston handled this situation differently? One approach, of course, would have been to consider whether the change was really necessary. If that question could not be answered satisfactorily, perhaps another, more effective mode of motivating for increased production could have been found—group piece rates, for example. What about involving the workers in the new design process? When asked whether the workers were involved in the decision process, the real-life company answered, "No, we never thought of that." If the move was necessary, a job-enrichment solution in terms of having the employees designing and planning the system —and using the central-staff personnel as resources for advice and counsel— might have been a great deal more productive and less disruptive than the actual solution imposed.

SUMMARY AND CONCLUSION

Our approach here has been to review some behavioral theories available to the manager and then to explore the possible applications of them in terms of designing production systems or organizations. We note immediately that there is no correct answer. Each design situation facing the manager and the possible solution is a combination of the following factors:

1 The task to be performed

2 The skills of the employees

3 Technology available

4 Need levels of the various employees involved

5 Culture of the society

6 Projected incremental gains in productivity

7 Costs

As we have seen, some situations call for high structure in the system and low discretion for the employee. In other situations, low organizational structure is present, and high discretion is allowed. Of course, in between these two extremes are the various gradations. To our list, we might add all of those factors covered in Chapter 4. For example, the level of the general economy obviously has an effect on the employees' willingness to accept structure and imposed controls.

It is appropriate here to repeat a statement from Chapter 1. That is, management is an inexact profession. No one manager or management analyst has all of the answers, and the actual solution to a managerial problem may differ among practitioners and analysts. Two groups of management experts recently disagreed on the structure of a major university's decision network. Both groups had high credibility. Both had cogent and legitimate arguments, and both had adequate management theory to back them up. Their conclusions, though, were diametrically different.

Managers are, however, increasingly being armed with new knowledge that allows them to factor into the decision process (in this case, the system or organization-design process) many additional variables. So today's managers need not run into the pitfalls of their predecessors in terms of extracting the most out of employees, since today's managers have a good deal more basic knowledge of what makes the employees "tick."

DISCUSSION QUESTIONS

1 Traditional, or classical, management thought prescribed that organizations be designed around tasks, not people. What was the basis for this prescription?

2 Modern management thought takes issue with the classicist prescription of structuring organizations around tasks. How do modern management theorists view the approach to organization design?

3 How can exchange theory be used to explain individual motivation in an organizational context?

4 What is the philosophy, or creed, behind scientific management?

5 Compare traditional management thought to contemporary, or modern, management thought relative to organization design and theories of individual motivation.

6 Briefly review the theories of the following theorists relative to the relationship of individuals and organizations.

   a) Chris Argyris   b) Abraham Maslow
   c) Clayton Alderfer   d) David McClelland
   e) Frederick Herzberg   f) Douglas McGregor

7 What types of jobs might status, prestige, and participation lose out to increased hourly pay or piece-rate compensation system in motivating individuals? Why is this so?

8 How might you counter the claim that socialization and cohesive work groups in the organization are counterproductive to the organization's objectives? Cite any studies verifying your claims.

9 Distinguish between job enrichment and job enlargement. How might these mechanisms influence individual motivation?

10 Define the following terms:

a) classical school of management   b) achievement need

c) modern school   d) scientific management

e) need hierarchy   f) motivation hygiene theory

g) McGregor's Theory X, Theory Y   h) Hawthorne effect

i) job enlargement   j) job enrichment

11 No management theory is a panacea to organizational effectiveness. Each organization-design situation facing the manager and its possible solution are a result of a combination of a number of factors. What factors might affect how a manager designs the organization and motivates its employees?

CASE: KINGSFORD MOTOR SALES, INC.*

■ Kingsford Motor Sales, Inc., is a dealer for three lines of new cars—two domestic and one foreign—located in Kingsford, New Hampshire, a community about twelve miles north of the Massachusetts border. Kingsford Motors is one of New England's highest-volume auto dealerships outside of the Boston area. Aggressive price cutting and a reputation for good service have attracted customers from an area radiating up to about seventy-five miles from the company's facility. On an average day, Kingsford sales personnel would move six to eight new cars and perhaps another six used vehicles. Sometimes sales reached twenty new cars a day. During the 1974 energy crisis, KMS was fortunate. Although more than 120 large cars were on hand, and these did not move well despite price cutting to below cost, KMS also had more than 200 compact and foreign cars to sell; salesmen had little difficulty moving the smaller cars for full sticker prices.

* Adapted from Arthur Elkins and Dennis W. Callaghan, *A Managerial Odyssey: Problems in Business and Its Environment*, 2d ed. (Reading, Mass.: Addison-Wesley, 1978), pp. 107–111.

Kingsford, the community

Kingsford is a community of some 68,000 people. It is primarily an industrial city, but its periphery and the surrounding towns are agricultural. Kingsford is an old community, founded in 1670 and incorporated as a city in 1864. The city's industrial plants are old and relatively inefficient and have suffered the vicissitudes of business cycles, changing markets, import competition, and physical depreciation. Recently, two new plants were built on the outskirts of the city, the first new construction since the Second World War. The city's population is a mix typical of many New England industrial centers: old-line families descended from early settlers and factory owners, descendants from the immigrations of the late 1800s, and the "new" immigrants—unskilled blacks and Puerto Ricans—who have moved into some of the older homes in the city's core. Currently the community is experiencing the serious emigration of its younger citizens.

Kingsford's youth have not been isolated from the events and trends generally affecting youth throughout the country. Long hair and sloppy clothing are the vogue, along with the speech patterns common to the young. Some drugs have been reported in the high school. Students at the high school have won concessions such as the elimination of lunchroom attendance, restroom passes, and compulsory study hall, and the student newspaper was recently the object of a state legislative investigation because of an article studded with four-letter words. The city's newspaper periodically runs editorials denouncing the new lifestyles and the general "lack of discipline" among Kingsford young people.

Kingsford Motor Sales, the organization and history

KMS was founded in 1929 by John Tilden to sell and service one prestige line of cars. Until 1950 John Tilden kept the agency relatively small, selling about one car a week and knowing all of his customers. Service was a byword with the agency, and the company was known as a place where "you paid the price but were assured of being well taken care of." John Tilden was a conservative man, and his dealership reflected that philosophy. Convertibles and station wagons were not stocked; of the ten or so cars kept on hand, all were sedans, and rarely was there a two-toned car on the lot. Tilden prided himself on the highest ethical conduct. In 1946 one local resident offered Tilden $400 extra to put his name higher on the waiting list for the first postwar automobiles. Tilden not only turned down the sum, but refused to sell the man a car at all.

After John Tilden died in 1952, his two sons, Jim and Steve, took over the business. In 1954 the Tilden brothers purchased fourteen acres of land on the outskirts of town and built a new showroom and service center. They dropped the prestige car agency and took on one of the low-priced three. In 1959 they accepted the agency for a medium-priced, high-fashion line, and in 1965 added a foreign-car line as well. Soon after the new agency opened, the Tildens started advertising in the Boston papers and on TV stations around New Hampshire, Massachusetts, and Maine. Price cutting became standard (advertising stressed the low overhead of the New Hampshire location), and the agency used appeals with the newest style of vehicles and flashy accessories. In essence, the younger Tildens aimed at a mass-selling dealership and keyed in on what they were convinced buyers were looking for—lowest price combined with high-style, high-performance automobiles. KMS salesmen felt no reluctance in pushing accessories, particularly those of a style appealing to the younger auto buyer. One of the city's sage older citizens, when passing the Tilden operation, was heard to comment, "If old John could see what those two kids did to his business, he'd turn over in his grave."

New-car preparation

After selling a car, the salesman would fill out the sales papers, arrange for financing, and prepare a work order to service the car for delivery. KMS guaranteed twenty-four-hour delivery of a new vehicle picked off the lot; and if the customer insisted, the car could be ready by the close of business on the day it was purchased.

Since cars were sold so rapidly, a special service area and crew were employed, separate from the repair-service unit. The new-car preparation team consisted of two mechanics, an undercoating specialist, a body man, and a wash man. One of the mechanics, Sam Forbes, acted as foreman of the crew, but generally the salesman went directly to whoever was working on "his car" to rush the work along. KMS had a twelve-step standard new-car preparation procedure (called the "dirty dozen" by salesmen). These steps were:

1 Check lubrication and oil levels (sometimes cars were found to come from the plant unlubricated or with less oil than specified)
2 Winterize to 40 degrees below zero
3 Check timing and ignition; adjust if necessary
4 Align and balance wheels; check tire pressure
5 Check and adjust brakes
6 Check and adjust transmission
7 Undercoat (if ordered by customer)
8 Install radio and other dealer-installed accessories
9 Check and adjust door, hood, and trunk alignments
10 Touch up scratches

11 Test-ride

12 Wash, clean, and vacuum

The wash rack

Of all the jobs, the wash rack required the least skill, but was the dirtiest. After a car had gone through all of the mechanical and body checks, it was delivered to the rack, where it was washed and vacuumed, the stickers peeled off the windows, and the floor mats installed. This was the last station of the dirty dozen, and the one where salesmen waited impatiently to get the car for delivery. Sometimes a salesman directed his customer to the wash area to wait for the car. The wash-rack attendant was thus under pressure to get the car out. And if any scratch or imperfection, such as leaks, showed up, he was usually the first to hear about it in no kindly manner. Even though the wash-rack attendant had no role to play in the car's manufacture or preparation, he bore the brunt of a buyer's dissatisfaction. He was often asked: "Can I trust that salesman?" or "Did he give me the best deal?" or "Is this car really gone over like they say it is?" Occasionally he was asked, "How do you disconnect the air pollution device on this car?"

Tim Wallace

Tim Wallace was the fourth wash-rack attendant KMS had employed in the last two years. He was twenty years old, having quit Kingsford High School at age sixteen to work in a paper plant. He lasted at the paper plant three months, walking off the job and complaining that the chemical smells made him nauseous. Tim then pumped gas on the 11:00 P.M. to 6:00 A.M. shift at the independent gas dealership on Main Street for about four months (one night, he just didn't show up). The next morning, he enlisted in the Army. After basic training, Tim was sent to infantry school and then to Vietnam for a year; he was wounded slightly and spent the final year of his service at Fort Dix, New Jersey, in a training company. Tim reached the rank of corporal before his discharge.

The Army and his war experience added little to Tim's skills for civilian life, but they did have an effect on his lifestyle. He grew a beard, wore long hair with a headband, and moved in with a radical commune in Desmond, Massachusetts. Tim experimented briefly with drugs, but stopped abruptly; he left the commune when that style of life started becoming unpopular and returned with his girl friend, Lucille, to Kingsford, where they took up residence in an old farmhouse north of town. Tim had a motorcycle for transport. Some of the older residents had unkind things to say about Tim and Lucille, but generally they were not harassed.

When he applied for the wash rack job at KMS, Steve Tilden at first was reluctant to even interview him. Tilden was hoping to get someone who was "straight," who could be relied on, and who would work hard, be punctual, and appreciate the fact that he had a job to do. After all, even though the wash rack required little skill, it was still an important phase in new-car delivery, particularly for a high-volume dealer such as KMS. But when no one else applied for the job, Tilden hired Wallace.

Tim Wallace on the job

For about four months, Wallace performed well; he showed up on time, and his production rate and the quality of his work were quite satisfactory. One day, a customer complained about paper shavings in the back seat; the salesman brushed them out and said nothing, thinking the event a minor annoyance. But salesmen started receiving complaints about unwashed windows, cleaning compound left unwiped, water on the floors, etc. Steve Tilden talked to Wallace, who shrugged and said, "I'm doing my best. What do you have to do to please all those rich fat cats?"

Tilden also noted that Wallace started arriving five to ten minutes later and leaving five to ten minutes earlier each day. One day Tim called in sick (on sick days, a grease-and-oil man from the regular maintenance shop was called into service on the new-car wash rack). When asked the next day what was wrong, Tim just said, "Nothing much; just a twenty-four-hour bug." Tilden could see no aftereffects of illness.

About a month later, Wallace called in sick again. At about 2:00 P.M. Sam Forbes, the foreman, called Wallace's house to find out how long he was going to be out. No one answered the phone. The next morning Wallace replied to Tilden's questioning by saying that he was over at the drug store buying some aspirin. He seemed upset at having his whereabouts checked on.

Wallace called in sick again a week later. About 10:00 A.M., Forbes called Wallace's home and got no answer. At about the same time, a salesman told Tilden that he thought he saw Wallace and "some hippy girl" motorcycling down the interstate highway toward Boston.

Forbes burst into Tilden's office. "That damn Wallace is out again, and I can't reach him. God, I know that they've got the same problems in the maintenance shop with the guys on the grease and wash racks, but the wash rack on our end is too important. We've got to get those cars to customers. What the hell is this younger generation coming to?" ■

Case questions

1. Why is Tim Wallace losing interest in his job?
2. What can the Tildens or Forbes do to Wallace to motivate him to perform better? What would you recommend to the Tildens?
3. As a consultant to the Tildens, what might you recommend relative to the job processes? Would you recommend any changes in their new-car preparation procedures? Why?

SELECTED READINGS

Argyris, C., *Personality and Organization* (New York: Harper & Row, 1957).

Anthony, W., *Participative Management* (Reading, Mass.: Addison-Wesley, 1978).

Bartlett, A. C., and T. A. Kayser, *Changing Organizational Behavior* (Englewood Cliffs, N.J.: Prentice-Hall, 1974).

Berg, I., M. Freedman, and M. Freeman, *Managers and Work Reform: A Limited Engagement* (New York: Free Press, 1978).

Champagne, P. J., and C. Tausky, "When Job Enrichment Doesn't Pay," *Personnel* 55, 1 (January/February 1978): 21–29.

Connellan, T. K., *How to Improve Human Performance: Behaviorism in Business and Industry* (New York: Harper & Row, 1978).

Cooper, C. L., *Developing Social Skills in Managers* (New York: Halsted Press, 1976).

Ends, E. J., and C. W. Page, *Organizational Team Building* (Cambridge, Mass.: Winthrop, 1977).

Fisher, J. E., "The Authoritarian as Anti-Manager," *Public Personnel Management* 7, 6 (January/February 1978): 33–42.

Friedlander, F., "Motivations to Work and Organizational Performance," *Journal of Applied Psychology* 50 (1966): 143–152.

Gellerman, S. W., *Managers and Subordinates* (New York: Dryden Press, 1976).

Hampton, D. R., C. E. Summer, and R. A. Webber, *Organizational Behavior and the Practice of Management*, rev. ed. (Glenview, Ill.: Scott, Foresman, 1973).

Hersey, P., and K. H. Blanchard, *Management of Organizational Behavior*, 2d ed. (Englewood Cliffs, N.J.: Prentice-Hall, 1972).

Herzberg, F., *Work and the Nature of Man* (New York: World, 1966).

Huse, E. F., J. C. Bowditch, and D. Fisher, *Readings on Behavior in Organizations* (Reading, Mass.: Addison-Wesley, 1975).

King, B., S. Streufert, and F. Fiedler, eds., *Managerial Control and Organizational Democracy* (New York: Wiley, 1978).

Klein, L., *New Forms of Work Organizations* (New York: Cambridge University Press, 1976).

Korman, A., *Organizational Behavior* (Englewood Cliffs, N.J.: Prentice-Hall, 1977).

Lazer, R., "Behavior Modification as a Managerial Technique," *Conference Board Review* 12 (January 1975): 22–25.

Likert, R., *The Human Organization* (New York: McGraw-Hill, 1967).

Luthans, F., and R. Kreitner, *Organizational Behavior Modification* (Glenview, Ill.: Scott, Foresman, 1975).

Maslow, A. H., *Motivation and Personality*, 2d ed. (New York: Harper & Row, 1970).

McGregor, D. M., *The Human Side of Enterprise* (New York: McGraw-Hill, 1960).

Merton, R. K., "Bureaucratic Structure and Personality," in W. L. Warner and N. H. Martin, *Industrial Man* (New York: Harper & Row, 1958), p. 70.

Salancik, G. R., and J. Pfeffer, "A Social Information Processing Approach to Job Attitudes and Task Design," *Administrative Science Quarterly* 23, 2 (June 1978): 224–253.

Sayles, L. R., and G. Strauss, *Human Behavior in Organizations* (Englewood Cliffs, N.J.: Prentice-Hall, 1966).

Viola, R. H., *Organizations in a Changing Society: Administration and Human Values* (Philadelphia: Saunders, 1977).

PART IV

Managerial Implementation

In the five chapters of Part IV we cover the second major category of managerial functions—implementation, or the putting into effect of the plans and strategies developed in the design stage or function. Thus we will discuss as implementation activities the activating processes of staffing, training and development, acquiring capital resources, communication, and leadership. In all possible instances the linkage of design and implementation is made quite clear; that is, the effective and efficient implementation of activities depends heavily on the drawing up of effective and efficient designs.

Chapter 12
STAFFING: SECURING HUMAN RESOURCES

CHAPTER HIGHLIGHTS

In this chapter we will discuss the first of the implementation functions, staffing. We cover the background planning that is necessary for the staffing to proceed smoothly. Then we will present some of the problems in staffing, including the delineation of labor markets and the new legal considerations that managers must take into account. We will review regulations and cases under both the Civil Rights Act of 1964 and affirmative action. Finally, we will consider internal sources of personnel and promotion and upgrading of employees.

LEARNING OBJECTIVES

1 To learn the basic elements of human resource planning.

2 To learn the essentials of forecasting human resource needs.

3 To understand the roles of manning tables, turnover rates, and position descriptions.

4 To appreciate the importance of forecasting labor availability.

5 To understand the importance of personnel-selection policies and procedures.

6 To be aware of the basics of and need for labor-market analysis.

7 To understand how the Civil Rights Act of 1964, the Age Discrimination Act, and the Equal Pay Act affect hiring practices.

8 To learn the case law as it affects testing; hiring women, minorities, and single female parents; use of arrest records and credit checks; recognition of religious practices; and hiring males for previously female jobs.

9 To learn the reasons for and the procedures to be followed under affirmative action.

10 To understand the value of promotion and upgrading as sources of personnel.

CASE: TONY ZANOTTI

■ The forthcoming store opening in Indianapolis was to be Cardinal Stores' first outside of the northeastern United States. Cardinal is a chain of discount department stores (or mass merchandisers, as they are called in the trade) that was founded in the Worcester, Massachusetts, area during the mid-1950s. Expansion was rapid in the early 1960s, with twelve stores opened in Massachusetts and nine more throughout New England. In the late 1960s the firm also moved into New York, New Jersey, and Pennsylvania, opening thirty-two more stores. The strategic long-range plan calls for movement into the midwestern states, with Indianapolis as the first location targeted there. Manager of the new Indianapolis store is to be twenty-six-year-old Tony Zanotti.

Cardinal Stores has a set procedure for building and opening a new store. The Real Estate and Store Construction staff unit is in charge of locating the necessary property, negotiating its purchase, and erecting the physical structure. All of the company's stores are built to a standard specification, depending on the class of store being constructed. Cardinal has three basic classes of stores: class A, full-line stores, including major appliances and automobile service centers; class B, all lines except the major appliances and auto service centers; class C, stores that carry a basic line of soft and hard goods, but with a minimum of big-ticket items. Most of Cardinal's new stores are of class A and are located in larger cities; the Indianapolis store is in this category.

Once the construction of a store shell has been completed, the structure is turned over to the store manager, who hires the necessary help, receives the merchandise, and sets up the store for the opening. The central merchandising staff plans the opening event, and the manager is given detailed procedures and numbers on opening specials and advertising.

The personnel department at the Worcester headquarters had developed some chainwide standards and policies on hiring. Job descriptions were prepared for assistant managers, department managers, stock clerks, cashiers, security guards, and snack bar attendants, and standard numbers of nonmanagerial personnel were adopted. Personnel numbers are related to the sales volume of the various departments. So the manager has to do little about anticipating or determining a store's personnel needs, except to keep a watchful eye on departmental sales volumes. The managers did have the latitude of not following the prescribed personnel-to-sales-volume ratios on the smaller side, provided they were sure that the work could be accomplished with fewer personnel. Although maintaining well-stocked shelves is an important merchandising concern for discount department stores, the various companies in the field are also extremely cost-conscious, and personnel cost savings are encouraged throughout most of the larger chains.

Zanotti arrived with his family in Indianapolis about three months before the scheduled store opening. After a week of settling in with his family and tending to personal business, Tony took practical control of the almost completed but empty store. Cardinal's market research staff had done extensive marketing studies on the Indianapolis area, but the company had conducted very little research on the availability of personnel to fit the needs of the store. Since many of the jobs did not require skill and since most of the merchandising decisions were made at the central level, central headquarters assumed that there would be little problem filling all of the personnel needs. Past experience seemed to bear out that assumption, although the chain's stores did suffer from a high turnover rate of both managerial and operative personnel.

This is Zanotti's first storewide managerial post. He started with Cardinal as a trainee, moved through various department-manager posts, spent about a year in central merchandising and buying offices, and then took an assistant store manager's job in Manchester, New Hampshire. He was selected for the Indianapolis store post over twelve others. The company felt that it had a real winner in Zanotti, who showed more promise than most of the other trainees and was excellent in merchandising and inventory control.

One deficiency in all of Zanotti's training and experience, however, was in personnel management. He had never before hired people and had no idea of how he could go about procuring personnel resources. Since the merchandise would begin arriving very shortly, however, he knew that he had to get moving. Also, he did not want to ask for central-office assistance during his first week on the job.

Tony placed a single advertisement in the *Indianapolis Star,* soliciting applicants for the positions of assistant manager, department managers, and stock clerks. On the first day following the advertisement, Zanotti received 472 responses by telephone and in person. "What a mess this is," he said to his wife. "We've got 472 responses, and everybody and his uncle wants to be a department manager, but most aren't even qualified to be a stock clerk. There's just got to be a better way of doing this." ■

INTRODUCTION

Tony Zanotti has just learned that he must put some effort into planning his activities. But for our purposes, the primary lesson to be learned is that energizing the organization by hiring people to carry out the plans of the firm is a special managerial process requiring some degree of sophistication and attention. All managers hire and allocate the human resources who will staff the organization which will carry out the plans to achieve the objectives. We call this activity an implementation activity, and it is the first one we shall cover in Part IV. However, as we pointed out in Chapter 1, there is no neat breakdown between planning or design activities and implementation activities. Thus the manager who acts or implements already has a frame of reference(s) within which implementation activities take place. We turn first, then, to the particular practices of human resource planning.

HUMAN RESOURCE PLANNING

Human resource planning is a crucial subdivision of general organizational planning. As one plans programs or activities and determines which elements of both will occur at some future date, one must also plan for the provision and obtaining of resources—the people—to carry out those plans. Such human resource planning involves at least three major steps:

1 Forecasting human resource needs
2 Forecasting personnel availability
3 Developing policies, procedures, instruments, and standards for recruitment and selection

We might note here that only the first of these three categories was attempted in the Cardinal organization described in the opening vignette. Although job descriptions were available, only the internal forecasting—relating personnel needs to sales volume—was prescribed by the central personnel staff. The relationship of the store to the external labor market was left to the manager in charge.

Forecasting human resource needs Need forecasting is essentially an internal organization consideration, although naturally the needs for personnel are ultimately related to the forecasted and planned growth of the demand for the organization's services. In the Cardinal organization, need was related to sales volume by formula. Need forecasting involves, however, not only consideration of the future growth of the organization, but also a forecast of retirements, resignations, terminations, and an analysis of turnover rates in order to maintain the existing personnel component. In general, the managerial task in staffing is in trying to predict personnel needs well in advance of their actual arising, so that recruiting efforts will be successful.

Many organizations, particularly smaller ones, use only a crash-program approach to staffing; that is, the search for a replacement or a new employee begins only when the need is at hand. An adequately planned personnel program, however, usually is much more efficient and less panic-ridden and makes available adequate time to find the right person for each job or position. In cases of replacement, the transition from the incumbent to the new person can be made smoothly. Of course, we must caution again about the possibility of overplanning. For unskilled positions (perhaps like the stock clerk positions at Cardinal), extensive planning is neither necessary nor prudent. Such positions are relatively easy to fill, and the organization would waste valuable planning time being concerned with a position-by-position planning exercise on them.

For managerial or executive positions, the most useful tools in need forecasting are organization charts and manning tables. These tools are appropriately filled in with the various incumbents' names, ages, and other pertinent data such as retirement dates, promotion dates, etc. Each of the boxes on the organization chart has a corresponding job description detailing the duties of the position as well as the qualifications necessary for successful fulfillment of the job demands.* Figures 12.1 and 12.2 illustrate an organization chart detailed as a manning table and a job description of one of the positions shown. A manager who must obtain personnel can easily spot, by periodically reviewing the manning table, the times when search-and-hire

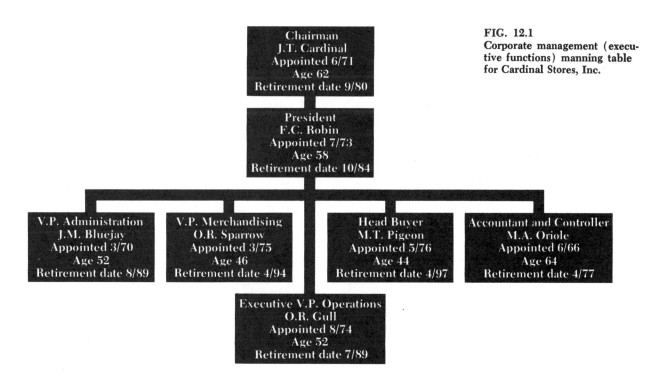

FIG. 12.1
Corporate management (executive functions) manning table for Cardinal Stores, Inc.

* See Max S. Wortman, Jr., and Joann Sperling, *Defining the Manager's Job,* 2d. ed. (New York: AMACOM, 1975), particularly Chapter 3.

CARDINAL STORES, INC.
VICE-PRESIDENT FOR MERCHANDISING

FIG. 12.2
A position description

1. Basic function

Controls the merchandising and promotion of all merchandise throughout the stores of the organization. General responsibility for advertising, promotion, point of purchase, and topical promotions. Coordinate with buyers and store operations.

2. Reporting relationships

   a) Reports to: President
   b) Reported to by:
      (1) Director of Advertising
      (2) Director of In-House Promotion
      (3) Director of Topical Promotions
   c) Staff relationship: Executive Vice-President of Operations and All Store Managers
   d) Total Personnel in unit: 26

3. Principal responsibilities

   a) Developing plans and yearly budgets for chainwide promotion projects
   b) Developing within budgets special promotion activities for areas within the company coverage
   c) Planning new-store openings and promotions
   d) Planning and coordinating the developing and producing of all advertising
   e) Coordinating with buying staff for promotional opportunities
   f) Contacting all outside agencies involved in advertising delivery
   g) Coordinating cooperative advertising with participating manufacturers
   h) Developing and presenting capital budgets for promotion needs
   i) Delegating responsibilities within unit

4. Incumbent specifications

   a) College degree in marketing or business administration
   b) At least five years' experience in merchandising management or advertising agency with managerial and supervisory responsibilities
   c) Familiarity with technical processes of promotion and advertising
   d) Ability to function effectively in a coordinative role and interact with offices of equal organizational stature

5. Present incumbent

   a) O.R. Sparrow
   b) Salary $125,000
   c) Background:
      BBA University of Massachusetts, 1953
      Advertising Manager 1970–1975
      With Silver Star Stores 1964–1970
      With ARC Advertising 1953–1964

activities must be undertaken in order to replace a retiring or terminated individual.

If the organization is expanding or growing, the complete chart or projected chart becomes the basis for a schedule of expansion. Related to the overall growth plan of the organization, the "blank" boxes would have a date of need specified, and the manager, also armed with a preplanned job description, would then be able to schedule in the times for initiating the search for new personnel.

In the case of nonmanagerial or operative personnel (often called nonexempt, since they are covered by wage and hour legislation), turnover rates are excellent scheduling aids, particularly where multiple similar positions are involved. The turnover rate is defined as the percentage of resignations, terminations, and retirements relative to the particular workforce over a specified period of time. Thus if the organization had a necessary workforce of 250 employees and during the year 50 left the organization, the annual turnover rate for the organization would be twenty percent. One could, of course, calculate the turnover rates for each job classification, and these would be more precise indicators for the manager's use than would be an overall measure.

With planned expansion of organizational services and various specialized jobs to be occupied, the problem of forecasting becomes more critical than, say, Cardinal's standard stock-clerk needs. Either each job classification must be planned separately, or equations of job classifications to particular output levels must be developed. This is necessary because a proportionate increase in organizational products or services will not typically require an equally proportionate increase in all of the jobs involved in the organization. For example, increasing the output of a ten-person machine shop by thirty percent may require three new machinists and one supply attendant, but no more janitors, painters, or packers. On the other hand, a forty-percent increase in sales or production might require the same three machinists and one supply attendant, but also an additional packer. Sophisticated planners can develop equations far in advance of actual need to guide the managers in such expansion activities.

In personnel-need forecasting, however, no planning tool is ever perfect. But the manager who does coordinate human resource forecasts with organizational planning is obviously in a better position to ensure that the organization is not left understaffed as vacancies occur in the present positions and that new positions are adequately anticipated and filled with enough lead time to allow orderly expansion.

Forecasting personnel availability

This planning activity is basically the external consideration, or the forecast of the available supply of personnel for the organization. Here the manager is concerned with questions such as: What is the depth of the various labor

- What are the depths of the various labor markets faced by the organization?
- Are plentiful pools of personnel available in areas where new units or services are contemplated?
- Can we move people if necessary?
- What is the effectiveness of the various sources of personnel?
- What is the effectiveness of the informational media in the areas where we operate?

Questions for
personnel-availability
forecasting

markets for the types of personnel needed by the organization? Is there a plentiful labor pool in areas where new services or units of the organization are planned to be? Will people be available and at the time and places that they are needed; if not, can the slots be filled by moving people from areas with surplus labor pools? Considerations such as the effectiveness of various sources and media to inform potential employees, e.g., schools and colleges, newspaper advertisements, employment agencies, state employment services, casual walk-ins, etc., relative to the organization's needs are relevant to this type of planning.

Forecasting personnel availability is the type of employee-related planning that the central personnel staff of Cardinal stores and Tony Zanotti failed to do prior to actually starting the hiring process. As a result of a shotgun approach, Zanotti was faced with an absurd hiring situation.

Also, Tony made no effort to sequence his hiring, so that his managers would be on line initially to direct his operative personnel. A well-planned personnel effort would have included not only an awareness of the depth of various types of labor available, but also a schedule to have the managerial personnel on line first to direct the hired operatives. Thus the assistant manager should have been hired first, then the department managers, then stock clerks, and finally cashiers. Given this type of scheduling, Zanotti could also have delegated some of the lower-level hiring activities to the various lower-level managers. And his training effort—if needed—could have been adequately spaced out.

Designing and implementing personnel-selection policies and procedures

The recruitment and selection process is complex and continues after an applicant has walked through the door. For any particular job, the selection process may be thought of as a series of screens, one overlaying the other, with the mesh of each screen being progressively finer until only the most appropriate applicant passes through the final screen. The planning that precedes the implementation is crucial to successful staffing. Based on job descriptions, the manager should have a set of policies and procedures and standards available for recruiting and evaluating candidates for positions.

A typical selection process would probably involve many of the following steps (although not necessarily in this order):

1 Applicant completes application form

2 Appropriate testing

3 Initial interview

4 Check of references

5 Further interviewing

6 Medical examination

7 Further interviewing, particularly for managerial positions

8 Final selection (by immediate supervisor for operatives or by management committee for high-level managerial personnel)

Recall from Chapter 3 that much of this process is done by a personnel staff department in a service role for the operating departments, if such a service-oriented department exists. If a personnel department has not been established or, as in the case of Cardinal Stores, is physically removed from the hiring site, each hiring manager might undertake all of the necessary steps in the selection process.

Although each of the steps in an organization's recruitment and selection process should be adequately planned for, the selection process is not uniform for all organizational positions. If tests, for example, are of no value to screening for a particular job, their inclusion in the selection process is a needless expense in dollars and time. If precision is not needed in terms of filling job qualifications—as in the case of stock clerks in a discount department store operation—it would be a similar waste of resources to apply a prolonged and sophisticated screening process, when hiring the first person through the door would suffice.

PROBLEMS IN STAFFING AND IMPLEMENTING THE PERSONNEL PLAN

The process of staffing the organization is affected by the environment of the organization, and that environment rarely remains stable over long periods of time. Two aspects of the environment we will explore in this chapter are the changing nature of labor markets and the new laws affecting staffing, particularly the equal-opportunity laws and the Executive Orders on affirmative action.

Labor markets are generally unique for the various jobs within the organization. For lower-level, operative, nonmanagerial jobs, particularly those requiring a minimum of skill, the labor market for the organization may be

Labor-market analysis

very local, extending only a few miles from the organization's installation. That is, sufficient personnel capable of filling the positions within the organization are readily available. Managerial positions, on the other hand, usually draw from a geographically wider labor market, although the numbers of eligible candidates may be smaller than those available for the operative skills in the geographically narrower markets. For some of the organization's positions, the labor market may be national or even international in scope. Top executives in most organizations are drawn from a national market, as are many middle managers. Supervisory and lower-level managers (foremen, clerical supervisors, etc.) may be drawn from much more narrowly defined, geographically, labor markets. Within universities, professors are recruited nationally, whereas staff personnel, secretaries, and custodial personnel are recruited locally. As a general rule of thumb, therefore, the higher one moves in the organizational hierarchy, the greater the geographical scope of the relevant labor market.

As with any general rule, however, there are exceptions. In some cases managers may have to induce movement or expand the market if certain types of labor are not available or trainable in the traditional market. One company, located in an isolated community of 50,000 people, was forced to widen its labor-search market when its demand for skilled toolmakers outstripped the available local supply, even though in years past, the local market had always been sufficient for the firm's needs. The company advertised in newspapers up to one hundred miles from the plant. Some recruits commuted; others relocated in response to the job opportunity.

Labor-market determination looms important as the organization confronts the increasing mobility among people—making past years' determinations relatively obsolete very quickly. In addition, conformity to new government regulations, particularly affirmative-action orders, requires careful analysis of the labor market for each job category within the organization.

New legal considerations in staffing

In recent years the latitude of managers in hiring personnel has been increasingly proscribed by government legislation and court decisions. What seemed like freedom of choice making personnel selection a matter only of managerial discretion is now severely constrained. Whereas personnel decisions used to be easy, sometimes routine, and often unimportant decisions in the eyes of much of the organization, those decisions are now becoming vitally important. Indeed, it may be argued that a new professionalization of the personnel function is resulting from the new roles being forced onto personnel managers by the ever-increasing legal requirements and the growing sophistication of various activist groups.

The manager who is hiring human resources may be involved in two types of situations relative to new legal requirements. In the first, the organization is in the civilian business only and is covered by the law, primarily the Civil Rights Act of 1964. In the other situation, in which the organization is doing business with the federal government, is subcontracting on a government contract, or is the recipient of a government grant, the manager will have to comply with not only the various statutes, but government contracting regulations as well, primarily Executive Order 11246, commonly referred to as affirmative action. It should be noted that up to thirty percent of the gross national product is generated by federal spending, and therefore a *large* organization is likely to be subject to affirmative-action rules. These rules extend not only to business firms, but universities and other organizations receiving federal funds and aid for their programs as well.

Since 1964, the federal government and many of the states have enacted legislation aimed at preventing discrimination in employment.* The major federal law in this area is the Civil Rights Act of 1964 (as amended in 1968 and 1972). Title VII of the act covers employers with "fifteen or more employees for each working day in each of twenty or more calendar weeks in the current or preceding calendar year . . . ," as well as labor unions and employment agencies, and prohibits discrimination on the basis of race, color, religion, sex, or national origin in hiring, firing, compensation, and/or any other condition of employment. The law also prohibits the segregation or classification of employees in any way that adversely affects an employee's status because of race, color, religion, or national origin. Finally, the act normally bars the publication of job openings or notices specifying race, sex, color, religion, or national origin as job requirements.

There are very few exemptions to the act. Although religious institutions are exempt for the activities of the particular religion at hand, they cannot discriminate on the basis of sex, color, or national origin—only religion. In general, the law also exempts jobs for which a particular sex is a *bona fide* occupational qualification (BFOQ).

Sex discrimination is also the subject of an earlier law, the Equal Pay Act of 1963, which barred pay and fringe-benefit differentials based on sex. All major businesses and institutions are covered by this act.

Another discriminatory pattern, and one that is receiving increasing attention, is that involving age. The Age Discrimination in Employment Act of 1967 (amended in 1978) protects individuals between the ages of forty and seventy from being discriminated against because of age in employment and job conditions. The act also forbids employers to exclude newly hired individuals, ages forty to seventy, from participation in pension plans if that age group is already included among existing employees.

---

* This section is adapted from Arthur Elkins and Dennis W. Callaghan, *A Managerial Odyssey: Problems in Business and Its Environment,* 2d ed. (Reading, Mass.: Addison-Wesley, 1978), pp. 113–117, 118–120.

Enforcement of Title VII rests with the Equal Employment Opportunity Commission. The EEOC, created by the 1964 act, originally was empowered only to attempt rectification by conciliatory methods, with the complainant taking the case to court should EEOC intervention fail. The 1972 amendment, however, empowered the Commission or the United States Attorney General to file suit in federal courts.

The court may issue injunctions against unlawful discrimination. Affirmative action in terms of quotas for future employment in an organization may be a remedy *if past patterns of discrimination have been found to exist*. More often the awards concern "making the individual whole again." This means that if a person has suffered discrimination, as defined by the act, the employer may be ordered to hire or promote that person; in addition, the worker may be awarded back pay or given other benefits.

The EEOC has been winning its cases, and its ability to go to the courts has given it some clout to negotiate some substantial out-of-court settlements. American Telephone and Telegraph Company paid, in an out-of-court settlement, over $45 million in back pay to women and minority-group employees who had been discriminated against in terms of pay and job advancement. Nine major steel producers agreed to a back-pay, interest, and future-pay settlement that could run as high as $80 million the first year.

Much of the case law and guideline regulation relate to the finer points of generally routine processes of personnel selection. Open, explicit discrimination or bigotry is practiced by very few managers these days (though, unfortunately, this was not always the case), but many of the so-called standard tools of personnel selection have been held suspect or implicitly discriminatory, and it is in these areas that the EEOC and the courts have made significant impacts. Some of these areas will be covered as we explore the following situations:

1 Testing
2 Hiring women
3 Hiring minorities
4 Hiring single female parents
5 Using arrest records and credit ratings
6 Recognizing religious practices
7 Hiring males for previously female jobs

Tests   Personnel tests—aptitude, intelligence, ability, and psychological—have had ups and downs in terms of their use as aids in the employee-selection process. At times the use of tests has been extremely popular; at other times, regarded as faddishness. In recent years the controversy has been on the possible cultural biases involved in tests. That is, some have charged that most of the commonly used tests are designed for a white, middle-class world and that blacks and other minority groups are at a disadvantage if their environments do not correspond to the implicit world of the test.

The challenge to tests in general came on the issue of their job-relatedness. In a landmark case, *Griggs* v. *Duke Power Co.*, the use of certain tests (and the requirement of a high school diploma) was challenged on the grounds that they were unrelated to performance on the job. Hence, if they purported to measure intelligence or achievement or ability and if these factors *could not be related to job performance in any precise manner,* and if certain groups would normally score lower on these tests (in the *Griggs* case, specifically blacks) because of lower educational levels, then the tests were discriminatory, and their use was condemned by the act. The key burden of proof is job-relatedness—not the fact that the tests were applied equally to all applicants.*

The Civil Rights Act does not prohibit the use of tests if they are directly related to job performance. Thus a typing test for a typist would be perfectly appropriate, but an educational achievement test might not be. And, in a recent case, verbal-ability tests were ruled appropriate if discriminatory *intent* was not present in the situation.† But this case should not necessarily be thought of as overruling *Griggs*. The employer, the Washington, D.C., Police Department, had an active program of soliciting minority applicants and was hiring a large number of nonwhites. More blacks were failing the test because more were being recruited.

Hiring women Several principles (mostly myths) formerly dominated management thinking on the hiring of women. Women were thought to be early quitters in order to get married, to follow their husbands to better-paying jobs, or to bear children, and generally inclined to be absent more often than males. Further, managers were often concerned about how women would blend in with an all-male work force or with customers who were primarily male. Such considerations are now illegal.

In hiring, management can make no assumptions about the marital intentions of a female applicant, her family plans, or her ability to perform because of family situations. Nor is the compatibility of a woman with other employees to be a factor. As with religion, sex can be a factor in hiring only when such a factor is a *"bona-fide* occupational qualification," and such cases are extremely rare. Indeed, an applicant's pregnancy at the time of application is no bar to hiring, and leaves of absence for maternity must also be granted. Although in the very controversial *General Electric* v. *Gilbert Case,*

---

* Griggs v. Duke Power Co., 401 U.S. 424 (1971).
† Washington v. Davis, 426 U.S. 229 (1976).

the Supreme Court ruled that a company is not obligated to include pregnancy within the coverage of health insurance plans, legislation has been enacted since to require such inclusion.*

Hiring minorities   Similar strictures against discriminating against blacks, Hispanic-Americans, and other minorities are provided for in the law, subsequent court cases, and interpretive regulations. Compatibility with employees' or customers' wishes may not be a factor in employment; neither are language or speech patterns if they are not a factor related to success on the job at issue. But in *Espinosa* v. *Farah Manufacturing Co.* the Supreme Court ruled that the Civil Rights Act's prohibition of discrimination based on nationality does not protect noncitizens of the United States against an employment policy of hiring only citizens.†

Hiring single female parents   Organizations often take a paternalistic view toward the families of employees and have often refused an individual, particularly a woman, if the manager feels that the children of the applicant could not be cared for adequately while she worked. Obviously, such a concern was not altogether altruistic; the organization was concerned about the possible absenteeism of the mother in order to care for the children.

In one court case, however, this "concern" was ruled illegal, and the woman involved was ordered hired. The court ruled that the company could not presuppose that the existence of the children would affect the work or the reliability of the parent on the job.‡ Obviously, if the employee proved unreliable as an individual in the future, then the company could take action for cause, but again, it could not *presuppose* that child-care activities would interfere with work performance.

Using arrest records and credit ratings   Again, job-relatedness is the criterion in this area. It was a common practice to check out arrest records and credit ratings, and adverse reports in these areas were often causes for not hiring. But there are several problems in using such data. Often the data are inaccurate, particularly the credit ratings. Second, arrests are not convictions, and certain groups may be shown to have higher per capita arrest records than others simply because of residence in an area populated by minority groups who are subject to "sweep" arrests.

In one case a black applicant was denied a job because he had a large number of arrest citations on his record. The company argued that such a long arrest record indicated a degree of instability that it was unwilling to

* General Electric v. Gilbert, 13 FEP Cases 1 (1976).
† Espinosa v. Farah Manufacturing Co., 414 U.S. 86 (1973).
‡ Phillips v. Martin Marietta Corp., 400 U.S. 542 (1971).

accommodate. The court ruled, however, that blacks would tend to have a higher number of arrests than whites, since ghettos were subject to frequent sweep arrests and hence to use the arrest record—not a conviction record—against a black applicant constituted discrimination.*

Religious practices   The EEOC regulations contain stipulations requiring the employer to reasonably accommodate employees whose religious practices require a schedule differing from the normal work week. Thus Jews and Seventh Day Adventists, whose Sabbath is Saturday (beginning at sundown on Friday), or Moslems, whose Sabbath is on Friday, must be accommodated if the company *can reasonably do so.*

In many cases employers were ordered by lower and state courts to reinstate employees who had been fired because they could not work on Friday evening and Saturday. Often the employer also operated on Sunday and could have easily rescheduled the employee for Sunday work hours and an evening at another time. In *TWA* v. *Hardeson*, however, the Supreme Court held that an employer's duty to accommodate an employee's religious beliefs does not require violation of the seniority rights of other employees or require the employer to incur additional costs.†

Hiring males for previously female jobs   The opening of male-dominated jobs to females is not the only result of the changing social mores and the passage of the Civil Rights Act of 1964. Female-oriented jobs are now open to males as well, and it is against the law to deny a male a job simply because of sex. Thus such positions as airline cabin attendant, nurse, and secretary are now increasingly being opened to males.

Another stage in the government's campaign against discrimination is affirmative action. Under Executive Order 11246 (amended by E.O. 11375) issued by President Lyndon B. Johnson, all businesses and institutions holding federal contracts (or subcontracting for a federal contract) of $50,000 or more and having fifty or more employees are often required to develop numerical goals, plans, and timetables for implementation to increase the numbers of females and minority-group employees in all job categories within their firms. Compliance is guided by the Office of Federal Contract Compliance of the Department of Labor (OFCC).

Affirmative action

Affirmative action goes beyond the Civil Rights Act of 1964 in that employers are required to not only practice nondiscrimination, but also take steps to *actively search* for qualified minorities and women to fill positions and to upgrade the skills and utilization of women and minorities within the

* Gregory v. Litton Systems, Inc., 472 F 2d 631(9th Cir. 1972).
† TWA v. Hardeson, 14 FEP Cases 1697 (1977).

firm. (Department of Labor Orders were issued in 1975 requiring similar affirmative action for handicapped persons and Vietnam veterans.) In one very real sense, affirmative action is requiring the government contractor to do what sound personnel management might prescribe also, that is, to make as wide a search as possible for qualified applicants.

Affirmative action requires the government contractor to:

1 Take a racial and sexual census of employees. No employee can be forced to participate in such a census; hence, it can be gathered visually for women, blacks, and Asian Americans, and by names on the payroll records for Spanish-surnamed Americans.

2 Determine the proportion of women and minority members in the labor market from which the organization draws. (In terms of universities and many managerial positions in industry, such a market may be a national one. For operative employees, the labor market may be very local one.)

3 Determine in which of the areas (in terms of job classifications) the company is deficient in its utilization of minority-group members and women, relative to the determined proportions of those groups in the general workforce or labor market.

4 Establish goals, timetables, and plans for action for increasing the utilization of minority-group members and women in the deficient areas.

5 Apply good-faith efforts to meet the goals.

6 Periodically report on the actions taken and the progress toward meeting the established goals.

Government officials repeatedly stress that affirmative action does not require an organization to follow a quota system; nor does it require the organization to hire nonqualified personnel. The contracting organization can fail to meet its goals, so long as it shows good-faith efforts in the attempt to meet them.

But that raises several problems for the organization. First, the burden of proof in terms of "good faith" is on the contractor, and some overzealous government bureaucrats may subject an organization to a real quota system by rejecting the organization's attempts at good faith. Second, in attempting to keep the government away from the organization, a manager may simply "fill the quota" without regard to the superior qualifications of rejected candidates.

Some legal experts have charged that there is a contradiction between the Civil Rights Acts and affirmative action, in that rejected white males' civil rights may be violated if individuals with inferior qualifications are hired on the basis of race and sex. In one case, involving university admissions, a University of Washington Law School applicant sued the university for violating his civil rights when minority students with qualifications inferior to his were admitted and his application was denied. A lower court ruled for the applicant, and he was admitted to the law school and remained enrolled even though a higher court reversed the decision. The student continued the case. When the case finally reached the Supreme Court, the student was ready to graduate, so the Court ruled the issue moot.

In 1978, however, the United States Supreme Court grappled with these questions in *Regents of the University of California* v. *Allan Bakke.** Bakke, a white male, was denied admission to the medical school at the University of California at Davis. Minority students, with lower admissions scores than his, however, were admitted on a separate track. Bakke sued under the Fourteenth (equal protection) Amendment of the Constitution and Title VI of the Civil Rights Act of 1964, which prohibits discrimination in programs funded by the federal government.

California's supreme court ruled in Bakke's favor, but the university regents elected to carry the case to the Supreme Court of the United States. The Supreme Court, in a complicated 5–4 ruling, ordered Bakke admitted to medical school. The Court did agree that race could be used as one of the factors in admission, but stated that affirmative-action programs featuring specific quotas could not be used except as a remedy where there was a legal finding of past discrimination. The latter was not the case at Davis.

However, in *United Steelworkers of America and Kaiser Aluminum & Chemical Corporation* v. *Weber et al.,* the Supreme Court held as legal under the Civil Rights Act of 1964 a voluntary preferential-selection plan favoring minorities, although no legal determination of past discrimination had ever been found.† In this case a quota system for a company training program was established as an affirmative action effort by agreement between Kaiser and the Steelworkers. Brian Weber, a white male, was denied admission to the training program; certain numbers of blacks and whites were admitted to the program, and each group was selected on the basis of seniority from separate seniority lists. Weber had more seniority than some of the blacks who were admitted. Weber sued and won his case in two federal courts. The union and the company appealed, and the Supreme Court, in a 5–2 ruling, supported the negotiated plan.

Finally, in terms of problems, affirmative action has the possibility of attaching a stigma to individuals hired under the program even when the stigma is undeserved. Thus a reputation that one was hired only because of race or sex may be difficult to live with in terms of relationships with fellow employees, customers, and even one's friends.

Penalties under affirmative action are strictly related to economic loss. The only penalty is loss of contract. No civil or criminal penalties are possi-

---

* Regents of the University of California v. Allan Bakke, U.S. 76-811 (1978).
† "High Court Backs a Preference Plan for Blacks in Jobs," *New York Times,* June 28, 1979.

- ■ Tests
  - *Griggs* v. *Duke Power*
  - *Washington* v. *Davis*
- ■ Hiring minorities
  - *Espinosa* v. *Farah Manufacturing Co.*
- ■ Hiring single female parents
  - *Phillips* v. *Martin Marietta*
- ■ Use of arrest records and credit checks
  - *Gregory* v. *Litton Systems*
- ■ Religious practices
  - *TWA* v. *Hardeson*
- ■ Affirmative action
  - *Regents of the University of California* v. *Allan Bakke*
  - *United Steelworkers of America and Kaiser Aluminum & Chemical Corporation* v. *Weber et al.*

Some civil rights areas and key cases

ble (except in court-ordered cases under Title VII); but loss of contracts can be a serious penalty for a business firm, particularly if key components of the organization's resources are tied to government work. In addition, OFCC may refer cases to EEOC when discrimination is suspected, whereupon EEOC would proceed under Title VII of the Civil Rights Act.

Affirmative action is a complicated area, and its relationship to the Civil Rights Act is just now starting to be adjudicated. Ten years may be a very conservative estimate of the time necessary to reach definitive judgments.

The laws and the hiring function

Most of the new regulations and laws governing staffing are duplicated on state levels as well as in the federal context. The significance of these laws lies primarily in their impact on the staffing function. The new laws, regulations, and court interpretations of them impose several obligations on management. First, traditional sources of recruitment may no longer be adequate. Management must expand its practices to include not only offering equal opportunity in the selection process, but also ensuring that potential applicants have equal access to notices of job openings. Second, traditional selection devices such as tests, profiles, and employment reviews must be reevaluated for validity, reliability, cultural bias, and necessity. The *Griggs* test of job-relatedness is still the one for management to follow.

Companies must also reevaluate their concepts of sex requirements for jobs and discard many of the prevailing myths about the performance of women and minority-group members. All of this, of course, increases the need for competent professionalism in the personnel departments of organizations. In fact, many observers credit the new regulations with pulling the personnel department (of which staffing is a part) out of the dustbin of management. The personnel function is now an important and critical area for the well-being of the organization.

Lastly, some critics argue, companies and society should realize that having an essentially black or minority work force with a white supervisory staff might entail costs in terms of lost productivity, job disruption, poor communication, and frustration. In essence, by actively promoting minority-group members to supervisory positions and managerial ranks, companies develop productive links with operative employees that they might not be able to develop with white-only supervision.

PROMOTING AND UPGRADING AS SOURCES OF PERSONNEL

Very often, human resources are not brought in from the outside to fill a specific position, but are developed, nurtured, and promoted from within the organization. A policy of promotion from within on the managerial levels and seniority on the operative ones may restrict the manager's interaction with the labor market to entry-level positions only. That makes the manager's task in filling positions from the outside much easier, but the problems of filling from the inside are not simple either. How are new managers to be assessed, spotted early, and coached along? In essence, how is the manager to make the resource-procurement decision when the source (or market) for such procurement is restricted?

Most organizations have well-defined sets of personnel policies relating to the appraisal and rating of personnel. Some of these are quite mechanical —indeed, perfunctory—on the operative or nonmanagerial level. They may consist of simple checklists or standards lists, which the manager or supervisor fills out on each employee once or twice a year. Since the movement of operative personnel into managerial ranks is rare and the number of opportunities for an operative employee few, the ratings at that level are more useful for pay raises than for promotion.

With managerial positions, however, the evaluation process is more important for promotion and grooming purposes. Tony Zanotti was hired and periodically moved along in the organization until he landed his present post as store manager. Along the way, Cardinal Stores' management should have been periodically assessing his progress in order to determine his promotability.

A number of procedures for assessment are in use. One is Management by Objectives, which is a continuing evaluation process based on task accomplishment, not popularity or favoritism.

Other instruments include an annual self-evaluation by the employee, supervisory evaluation on an annual basis, and a combination of both. Some organizations maintain special centers to which employees are sent, put through various managerial exercises, and assessed as to their capability for further advancement in the organization. Often, new employees are programmed through a number of increasingly difficult challenges, for assessment and evaluation of their progress and achievement.

The aim in this section, however, is not to cover the mechanics of the many evaluation procedures used by organizations. We simply mean to establish the notion of using the internal organization as a source of personnel and hence emphasize the need for managers to develop an evaluative process by which promising subordinates are recognized for their potential upgrading.

SUMMARY AND CONCLUSION

In this chapter we studied some of the specifics of human resource planning —internal needs forecasting, external labor market forecasting, and design of personnel policies, standards, and procedures. In addition, we analyzed some of the newer problem areas in staffing—labor market analysis and definition and the legal aspects of hiring. The latter included equal opportunity laws and affirmative action regulations. Finally, we considered the practices of promotion and upgrading as sources of personnel.

Often the human resources readily available do not fit into the organizational plan or the position prescriptions. And in only the rarest of cases is the fit between a newly hired person or a promoted one and the organizational needs totally perfect. Under these conditions, the organization may seek to upgrade already existing personnel or hire less-qualified personnel and teach them the skills needed within the various processes. In this case, the manager's staffing function is broadened to include training and development in order to properly staff the organization to fill the needs, complete the plans, and accomplish the objectives. This element of staffing is called training and development, the focus of Chapter 13.

DISCUSSION QUESTIONS

1 Define the following terms:
   a) Manning tables   b) Civil Rights Act of 1964 as amended
   c) Affirmative action   d) Reverse discrimination
   e) *Griggs* v. *Duke Power*

2 Human resource planning and physical resource planning are in many cases very similar. How are they similar?

3 Human resource planning involves at least three major steps. What are these steps? Briefly describe these steps relative to human resource planning.

4 How can organization charts and manning tables be used in need forecasting?

5 How does forecasting human resources differ between skilled and unskilled jobs; managerial and nonmanagerial positions?

6 In forecasting personnel availability, what factors should a manager consider? What activities should be undertaken?

7 List the steps involved with the selection of prospective employees.

8 Briefly review the equal-employment legislation and its effect on securing human resources.

9 What effect have the EEOC and recent courts rulings had on each of the following personnel functions or activities:

a) testing   b) hiring women

c) hiring minorities   d) hiring single female parents

e) using current records and credit ratings   f) recognizing religious practices

g) hiring males for previously female jobs

10 What are some of the penalties for violating Title VII of the Civil Rights Act of 1964? For violating affirmative-action orders?

11 What problems does Executive Order 11246 (affirmative action) pose to managers in securing human resources?

12 What are your obligations under each of the following:

a) Affirmative action   b) Civil Rights Act of 1964

c) *Griggs* v. *Duke Power*

CASE: STAN'S MAIL-ORDER STAMP SERVICE

■ In 1976 Stan Corbin decided that the time had come to either go full-time into the stamp business or forget the whole thing. He was operating a part-time approval business out of a basement room in his home, spending most of his spare time on the business. Approvals are stamps sold through the mail, with the customer receiving them, selecting some items, and returning the rest to the dealer along with payment for those kept. It's a risky business, and hundreds of would-be stamp dealers go in and go out of business in short time.

Corbin grossed about $3000 per month on stamps, netting about $500. He had little spare time for his family, and the business was just getting too much for him to handle on a part-time basis. One weekend, he spent considerable time analyzing his alternatives and the possible way he might operate a full-time mail-order stamp business. He decided to quit his job at a major oil company and go into business for himself.

System design and job planning

Corbin thought that traditional stamp merchandising was archaic. Typically the dealers were small, one-person operations. The owner did all the functions; there was little specialization; and in general the business usually was very disorganized. He thought that most dealers rarely considered the costs of serving customers or of handling particular items. That's why so many of these businesses failed each year.

The key to success, he reasoned, was not necessarily in buying established collections and breaking them down completely; that consumed inordinate amounts of labor. Rather, the key was in getting the inventory turned over fast. Also, the costs involved in selling penny stamps were generally the same as those for selling more expensive ones. Finally, so many countries issued so many stamps that to be a new-issue dealer—stocking worldwide stamps—was virtually suicidal.

Corbin decided that in his business, he would be guided by the following principles. First, the minimum price for a stamp or set of stamps would be $2.50. Groups of singles could be combined, but nothing under a unit price of $2.50 would be sold. Second, in breaking down collections, only complete sets or better singles would be extracted. The remainder of the collection could be assembled into packets and wholesaled. Third, the business would be operated in such a way that nonstamp collectors could be trained rapidly to break down collections, price the stamps, put them into inventory, and handle customer mailings. Corbin felt that a professional philatelist (stamp expert) should be needed only for specialized collections and evaluation of very rare material.

He started to think about systems. He thought that he would spend the bulk of his time buying and appraising collections and lots. This was not an easy process, as he had to peruse auction catalogs, go to some of the larger sales, visit sellers' homes when buying private collections, and appraise material sent to him. Purchasing would consume most of his time.

He would then need someone with some philatelic knowledge to administer the office and handle the breakdown of more expensive material. In the office two separate procedures would be needed. One would be the breakdown of collections and inventory-replenishing process. People would have to be trained to take a collection, extract the complete sets or valuable singles, catalog them according to the standard American catalog, price the material (usually at fifty percent of catalog value), grade the stamps, package them in glassine envelopes, and place them in inventory.

The other system involved customer service. Corbin thought that each customer should have a card on file. When the customer was sent stamps, the amount of material sent would be noted on the card. Attached to the card would also be a listing of the material sent, i.e., country, catalog number, value, etc. When the stamps were returned, the amount of the purchases would be tallied and recorded. The returned merchandise would be checked against the inventory sheet as well. Also on the card would be noted the customer's specialties and particular wants, and an employee could then assemble another selection to send, prepare a new inventory sheet, and return the card to the file. Some cards would have a maximum value of a selection to that customer noted, and this could be periodically upgraded if necessary.

Stamps not purchased would be returned to inventory by the person handling the breakdown of lots and collections. Periodically, Corbin thought, he or his manager would scan the cards, deleting customers whose purchases consistently ran below twenty-five percent of the selection sent.

Personnel specifications

Corbin thought about the kinds of people who could best fill the proposed positions. No particular skills would be required except for the manager and bookkeepers. He was convinced that he could reasonably train people in less than a week to break down collections. Order fillers could be trained in about the same time, provided the inventory was broken into special categories by country and location (such as British Commonwealth, Western Europe, Asia, etc.). Corbin thought that any reasonably intelligent person could handle the jobs. He decided that a high school diploma would be sufficient educational background, but just to be safe, he would administer one of the intelligence tests—the Wonderlic Personnel Test—that he knew his present employer was using. Finally, since stamps had high value in small size, he knew that he must be assured of the complete honesty of his employees. He decided to check credit, arrest, and previous-employment records.

The operating stamp service

After buying some old library-card cabinets and some used office furniture and renting an office in downtown Chicago, Corbin started. He hired a friend from the Evanston Stamp Club to be his manager; at first, the manager performed many of the routine tasks of breaking down collections and sending out selections. Corbin initially did the bookkeeping as well as the buying, and his wife sometimes came in to help sending out selections. He hired his first two employees about three months later, and they took to his systems quite well.

By 1979 the business was a success. Corbin had more than 5200 active accounts and was grossing about $64,000 a month. The company had seventeen active employees besides the manager and himself. "Things are really looking good," he thought. The 1978 income statement showed a net profit of more than $56,000 and the firm now had an inventory valued at more than $500,000.

Joan Clark

After the first few months, Corbin left the hiring to his manager, Fred Towne. One day in April, Towne interviewed a young black woman, Joan Clark, for a job in the selection processing system. Ms. Clark responded to an advertisement in the *Chicago Bugle*. The company employed no blacks, but most of the employees were women. Ms. Clark wasn't a high school graduate, but seemed extremely alert and capable. Although her test scores were not high, Towne was reasonably impressed. On checking her credit and employment references, however, he learned that she had once been detained by police on alleged shoplifting charges. She was released, however, when the shoplifter was identified. Although Towne realized that the arrest was improper, he decided not to take chances and rejected Ms. Clark's application. There was just too much valuable merchandise around to take risks, he reasoned. Besides, she wasn't a high school graduate, and her test scores weren't very high. He informed Ms. Clark that she didn't meet the qualifications for the job.

About two months later, Stan Corbin returned from a buying trip in the eastern part of the country and started going through the mail stacked up on his desk. Halfway down the pile, he came upon a letter from the Chicago office of the Equal Employment Opportunity Commission. The first line after the address block read: "Re: Employment Discrimination Complaint v. Stan's Mail Order Stamp Service—Filed by Joan Clark." ■

Case questions

1. What do you think of Corbin's personnel requirements? Are they reasonable?
2. Under what legal precedents and what laws would Ms. Clark's case be filed?
3. As a personnel consultant to small businesses, what procedures and policies would you recommend that Corbin alter or install?

SELECTED READINGS

Ash, P., and L. P. Krocker, "Personnel Selection, Classification, and Placement," *Annual Review of Psychology* **26** (1975): 481–507.

Beatty, R. W., and C. E. Schneier, *Personnel Administration: An Experiential Skill Building Approach* (Reading, Mass.: Addison-Wesley, 1977).

Benson, P. G., "Personal Privacy and the Personnel Record," *Personnel Journal* **57**, 7 (July 1978): 376ff.

Berwitz, C., *The Job Analysis Approach to Affirmative Action* (New York: Wiley, 1975).

Bright, W. E., "How One Company Manages Its Human Resources," *Harvard Business Review* **54** (January/February 1976): 81–93.

Bureau of Policies and Standards, United States Civil Service Commission, *Planning Your Staffing Needs* (Washington, D.C.: Government Printing Office, 1977).

Clague, E., and L. Kramer, *Manpower Policies and Programs: A Review 1935–1975* (Kalamazoo, Michigan: Upjohn Institute for Employment Research, 1976).

Dubin, R., *Human Relations in Administration* (Englewood Cliffs, N.J.: Prentice-Hall, 1974).

Elkins, A., and D. W. Callaghan, *A Managerial Odyssey: Problems in Business and Its Environment*, 2d ed. (Reading, Mass.: Addison-Wesley, 1978). See particularly Chapter 4, "Business and Equal Opportunity."

Giblin, E. J., "The Evolution of Personnel," *Human Resource Management* **17**, 3 (Fall 1978): 25–30.

Greenwood, W. T., *Issues in Business and Society*, 3rd ed. (Boston: Houghton Mifflin, 1977).

Griffes, E. J., "Changes Created by the End of Mandatory Retirement," *Personnel Administrator* **23**, 8 (August 1978): 13–16.

Grosskophf, T. E., Jr., "Human Resource Planning Under Adversity," *Human Resource Planning* **1**, 1 (Spring 1978): 45–48.

Guion, R. M., "Recruiting, Selection, and Job Placement," in M. D. Dunnette, ed., *Handbook of Industrial and Organizational Psychology* (Chicago: Rand McNally, 1976).

Hershey, P., and K. Blanchard, *Management of Organizational Behavior: Utilizing Human Resources*, 3rd ed. (Englewood Cliffs, N.J.: Prentice-Hall, 1977).

Hill, H., *Black Labor and the American Legal System, Volume 1: Race, Work, and the Law* (Washington, D.C.: BNA Books, 1977).

————, "Black Labor, the NLRB and the Developing Law of Equal Employment Opportunity," *Labor Law Journal* **26** (April 1975): 207–223.

Inbucon Consultants, *Managing Human Resources* (New York: Wiley, 1976).

Janger, A. R., *The Personnel Function: Changing Objectives and Organization* (New York: The Conference Board, 1977).

Mills, T., "Human Resources—Why the New Concern?" *Harvard Business Review* **53** (March/April 1975): 120–134.

Miner, J. B., *The Human Constraint—The Coming Shortage of Managerial Talent* (Washington, D.C.: Bureau of National Affairs, 1974).

Novit, M. S., "The Retirement Amendments: Why the Concern?" *Business Horizons* **22**, 1 (February 1979): 22–32.

Patten, T. J., Jr., *Manpower Planning and the Development of Human Resources* (New York: Wiley, 1972).

Pettman, E., *Labor Turnover and Retention* (New York: Halsted Press, 1975).

Rabinowitz, D., "The Bias in the Government's Anti-Bias Agency," *Fortune* (December 1976): 138–142, 147, 148.

Sahlein, S., *The Affirmative Action Handbook* (New York: Executive Enterprises, 1978).

Schneider, S. A., *The Availability of Minorities and Women for Professional and Managerial Positions 1970–1985* (Philadelphia: Industrial Research Unit, The Wharton School, University of Pennsylvania, 1977).

Stanton, E. S., *Successful Personnel Recruiting and Selection* (New York: AMACOM, 1977).

Wood, M., "What Does it Take for a Woman to Make It?" *Personnel Journal* **54** (January 1975): 38–41, 66–68.

Wortman, M. S., "Manpower: The Management of Human Resources," *Academy of Management Journal* **13** (1970): 198–208.

Chapter 13
TRAINING AND DEVELOPMENT

CHAPTER HIGHLIGHTS

In this chapter we cover the managerial tasks of upgrading employee skills and enhancing long-term learning. These efforts are generally termed training and development. After discussing some of the principles of learning entailed in training and development, we shall cover the organization needed for training and types of training programs. Then we shall emphasize the need for both top-management support for the training and development effort and determining the effectiveness of training efforts.

LEARNING OBJECTIVES

1 To appreciate the need for training for new managerial employees, new operative employees, the upgrading of presently employed personnel, and the continual development of employees.

2 To be able to differentiate between training and development.

3 To understand the relationship of learning to motivation.

4 To understand various learning principles: learning and payoffs, reinforcement, use of multiple senses, logical interrelated steps in learning, use of behavioral objectives, learning by experience, relevance of span of attention, and the importance of freedom from distraction.

5 To become aware of the various organizational arrangements for training.

6 To understand the various types of training programs: off the job, on the job, use of outside agencies, and "mentoring."

7 To appreciate the need for top-management support of training efforts.

8 To understand the importance of determining the effectiveness of training.

CASE: JOAN BAKER

■ "What kind of training program does M&H have for someone like me?" asked the young man sitting opposite Joan Baker. Joan was a college recruiter for Mason-Holden and was on the company's annual visit to Western New Jersey University.

"Well," she answered, "Mason-Holden doesn't have a formal training program. The new executive starts right out on the job. We believe in getting our new people involved right off the bat."

"But does that mean that it will be up to me to learn company policy and plans as I go along?" asked the student.

"Essentially, yes," replied Joan. "Of course, the staff services and corporate planning departments are always available to assist any manager."

"What kind of assignment will I get initially?" was the next question.

"Typically, a trainee, if you could use that term, is given a project involving analysis of a new product. Some, however, are put into sales territories as area managers. In any case, responsibility is assigned very early."

"Wow, that's quite a challenge. I think I'd love to try it, but it does sound, well, very uncertain."

Mason-Holden's program, if it could be called a program, is a unique way of breaking in new managers, but the company put high hopes into the method. Basically, it involved a new hire's being given a problem or program immediately upon arrival and sinking or swimming with that problem. The process cost little to administer, except—and this was a key factor—that the cost to the company of a new executive's failing on a first assignment could be high. In essence, the company put a great deal of reliance on the excellence of its recruitment and selection process for a steady supply of top-level young executives.

After her day at interviewing, John Baker spent some time thinking about the M&H training method. Most of the questions asked of her during the day had been about the training process, and she knew that many of the students with whom she had spoken were confused, if not apprehensive, about the company's philosophy on training.

Joan drew a line across a sheet of paper and started penciling in the advantages and disadvantages of the present approach. On the side of advantages she listed:

1 Greater challenge for new managers

2 Immediate integration of the trainee into the company's programming

3 Less time lost on the part of trainer(s)

4 Fresh problem-solving skills brought to bear on problems

5 No costly administrative support staff for training

6 Excellent evaluative basis *after* completion of projects

7 High pressure a good breaking-in process for new young managers

On the side of disadvantages, she wrote:

1 High anxiety on the part of the new manager

2 Lost time while manager learns in haphazard way

3 Slow partaking of the available staff and planning assistance (trainees invent the wheel over and over again)

4 Costs of errors or poor performance by the new executive

5 Loss of some fine job candidates who might be concerned about the uncertainties of the training and advancement possibilities

6 No ongoing evaluative procedure

Joan concluded that the disadvantages of the current M&H induction process were such that serious problems were raised in the recruitment process. In addition, the possible costs to the company were greater than the savings achieved from having no formal training director and staff.

Perhaps, she thought, a more formalized training effort was needed, even though she knew that the idea might not be well received. She decided to outline a proposal for a new training program and to discuss it with her boss when she returned to company headquarters the next week. ■

INTRODUCTION

Rarely will an organization be able to find precisely the right employee, plug that employee into the vacant position, and have him or her function precisely according to the planned and expected manner. In practically all cases new personnel require some degree of training or development before they are able to work in an effective and efficient way. And the manager's staffing task is never complete unless all positions are optimally filled, a case that is difficult to contemplate in the absolute.

Since the staffing function rarely leads to perfect matches between organization needs and employee skills, even when the new employee has been hired from within the organization, training and development are necessary and become a managerial function. Training and development generally are needed in at least four situations within the organization: (1) new managerial employees; (2) new operative employees; (3) upgraded and promoted employees; and (4) the continual improvement and development of abilities and skills for all employees within the organization.

New managerial employees Although managerial positions are usually filled by either experienced and seasoned executives or individuals trained in universities, the fact that no two organizations are identical precludes an absolute perfect fit between recruit and organization. Sometimes the training is only a simple introduction to company systems, mores, norms, and policies—a breaking-in period. But at other times the training may be a detailed and specific program designed to teach procedures and job content; this latter type of training is particularly prevalent for new management trainees fresh out of school or up from the ranks.

New operative employees   Operative employees are often hired with the requisite technical skills, but with little awareness of company policies or procedures. Even if for only a short period of time, they often must be trained in the procedures of product manufacture, service delivery, or company work rules.

A newer problem facing many organizations, particularly those drawing their new operative employees from the inner cities, is the need to perform remedial basic skill training. Recruits who cannot read or write at an acceptable level, who cannot read directions or blueprints, or have no work discipline may need instructions in those skills or be trained so differently as to cast an extra training burden on the organization and its managers.

Upgrading personnel   The best source for new employees to fill new or re-opened positions is often within the organization itself. Through promotion, lateral transfer, or upgrading, present employees can be placed into the newly created or opened positions. But those already employed personnel who are placed into new positions often require retooling or retraining to perform effectively or efficiently. If the promotion is from an operative to a supervisory or management position, the need for training is even greater, as the organization must not only break the older loyalty to the work group and instill a newer and more potent loyalty to the organization, but also train the employee to think conceptually in terms of management functions such as planning and decision making (see Chapter 2).

Continual development   Generally, training does not stop with the level of personnel placement. That is, an employee's becoming safely selected and trained for a particular position does not signal that she or he is finished with training. Most organizations continue training as an ongoing experience, updating employees in new techniques, technical changes, policy and procedure changes, revisions in the law, etc. So training is not just a tool for assisting in the filling of a position, but also one of continued improvement and updating. Given the state of continually changing technology, the truly effective and efficient organizations will program ongoing training efforts.

TRAINING AND DEVELOPMENT

Although we have used the terms "training" and "development" synonymously so far, there is, in fact, a difference in the two terms. Training usually relates to either a specific skill or a specific job or task. Thus training is a   **Definitions** short-term function, such as training for machine operators, blueprint reading, policy and procedure indoctrination, and safety-measure training.

Development, on the other hand, is not necessarily related to a specific task, but to the overall long-term maturation of individuals. Thus management conferences, released time, and reimbursement for enrolling in college or technical courses are not necessarily related to the specific job at hand, but to the general growth of the individuals involved.

Learning principles and effective training   Effective training depends on whether the individuals learn and primarily whether behavior and skills change result from the training. Too often, organizations think that they have an effective training program simply because they put on good performances, present updated material, and employ the best available instructors. But managers who are in charge of training must develop mechanisms for determining if the training succeeds and others for ensuring that the program utilizes the optimum in learning principles.

Learning theory has been the subject of much experimentation by psychologists and specialists in education. Some of these principles and rules of thumb will be noted here as being especially useful for managers who will engage in training efforts at some point in their careers. (See Fig. 13.1.) Of course, again, the true test of whether learning occurs and a training program is effective is the change in behavior, the improvement in skills, or the increase in output or efficiency obtained as a result of the training effort.

Learning and motivation   Whether or not one learns depends heavily on whether one is *motivated* to learn. Motivation, as we know, is generally thought to be related to needs, with individuals with lower-level needs being motivated more by extrinsic job satisfactions (money, fringe benefits, job security) and individuals whose lower-level needs have already been satisfied being motivated by intrinsic job satisfactions (job content, creativity, and other ego satisfiers).

In terms of training, for the operative employee whose performance in training leads to holding or not holding a job, the motivation is based on fulfilling the basic needs; in short, the motivation comes from knowing that unsuccessful performance means loss of job. The young, novice managerial trainee generally operates on this same sequence of need levels. By contrast, the higher-level manager, whose services the organization competed to obtain, will be an effective trainee if the ends are intrinsically rewarding—that is, if he or she can see that the training effort is one that offers "new" learning and not just a time-spending exercise.

Learning and payoffs   In order to be motivated to learn, then, trainees must be able to relate the ends to their needs. Therefore, the objectives of the training must be: (1) articulated clearly; (2) related to the work environment; and (3) related to the placement and advancement of the trainees in the organization.

Payoff in terms of reward must follow successful completion of the training. The payoff may be award of the job, promotion, or any other type of reward, such as a pay raise or even a certificate. Earlier, when we discussed Management by Objectives, we cautioned that MBO will fail if the superior is unable to deliver after the subordinate has accomplished the objective. Similar caveats are necessary in training; once the trainee has accomplished the training, the job must be available along with the other rewards that go with it.

Reinforcement   Reinforcement, as we noted earlier, may be either positive or negative—a reward or a punishment. The hoped-for effect of reinforcement is to keep the trainee doing the correct thing and/or correcting or changing incorrect to correct performance. Thus if someone progresses in training, positive reinforcement consists of praise, promotion, movement to the next training phase, etc. Negative reinforcement consists of criticism, punishment, or repetition of previously covered material. Most experts in learning theory agree that positive reinforcement is much more powerful than negative reinforcement in terms of the training effort. Negative reinforcement may lead to a dislike of the trainer by the trainee and hence block any effective communication or training in the future. Another problem with negative reinforcement is that it might lead to behavior being undertaken by the trainee simply to avoid the negative reinforcement rather than to actually learn. Cheating is the most flagrant of these behaviors; another is attempts to ingratiate oneself (perhaps in an attempt to disguise real dislike, however) with the trainer. The hope here on the part of the trainee is that future negative reinforcement will not occur, even though no learning will occur, and the behavior change programmed in the learning plan will not occur either.

Use of multiple senses   Involvement of many or all of the senses—hearing, seeing, touching, smelling, and tasting—have been found to enhance learning. For example, rather than listening to a lecture (hearing) with perhaps some visual aids (seeing) on the baking of an apple pie, one would more readily appreciate the pie if one could smell the aroma of some of the ingredients, feel of the dough being shaped, and enjoy the pie after it was finished.

Many management-training programs are attempting to involve multiple senses by using simulations, role plays, case analyses, sensitivity-training groups, and the like. As we noted in Chapter 4, the latter type of training, intended to focus on the deep feelings of managers and their interrelationships with one another, involves periods of time devoted to bringing those feelings into the open, exposing them, and seeking to sensitize the manager to the nuances of the psychological needs of others. The success of sensitivity training in directing behavior change toward organizational objectives is, as we noted, still open to question.

One interesting training approach involving the use of multiple senses and the feeling capacity of individuals is a process called synectics.* This method, which can use fantasy and various analogies, logic, reverse logic, and play acting, has been used for creating products, solving complex technical problems, and brainstorming new concepts. For example, in one problem involving the need to invent a new method for holding constant the speed of one shaft which was driven by another, variable-speed one (usually "solved" by using gears or wheels), the participants imagined themselves inside one of the mechanisms, trying to hold constant the speed of one of the shafts in the face of the varying speeds of the other. The eventual solution (after moans and groans of the participants trying to imagine themselves inside the box accomplishing the task) was the use of an elastic liquid in the coupling mechanism.† The essence of the problem-solving process was imagination and injecting oneself into the problem as part of the problem.

Logical interrelated steps   Many learners or trainees cannot learn an entire process at once, and hence the learning process is often broken down into logical, interrelated steps. Although there are exceptions to this general rule, the ability to comprehend and digest minute instructions in individuals is quite limited. Hence subobjectives reflecting the logical parts of a process are also established. Mastery then takes place in steps related to the subobjectives. The process of breaking down a course or a textbook into chapters is one illustration of this process. The student knows the general objectives of the course, but each day and each chapter are different, building on past knowledge and progressing one step at a time to the completion of the general objective—(ideally) in a logical and systematic manner. For example, teaching a machine operator to use the machine might start with some rather simple switch-on and -off training, then onto tool changing, to the loading process, to the safety devices, and so on until it ends with the trainee's mastering the complete complex capabilities of the machine. Each step must be mastered and integrated with the previous ones before the trainee is allowed to proceed to the next step.

Behavioral objectives   One of the latest provisions in many educational and training situations is the necessity to articulate behavioral objectives for each of the training subjects. Indeed, some school systems now require that this be done in every chapter of the textbooks they adopt. In our context, before

---

* William J. J. Gordon, *Synectics* (New York: Harper & Row, 1961).
† *Ibid.,* p. 30.

trainees start a particular phase of training, they are told what they can expect to do or know after they complete that particular phase. If they cannot accomplish that part after the training session, they repeat the session until they learn the skill. Each of these behavioral objectives (or subobjectives) is integrated to form the whole training program with its overall training objective.

Learning by experience   Related to the use of objectives in training is the finding that people seem to learn more and better and faster if they learn by doing or experience than by hearing alone. Thus hands-on training is often found to be most effective, though this does not preclude earlier theoretical and conceptual training. If the objective is to simply produce someone who is technically proficient in doing a simple task (such as changing the points and sparkplugs on an automobile), simple hands-on training might be the most efficient method for the organization. On the other hand, if the objective is to produce a skilled mechanic who can diagnose problems, understand the functions of the parts being changed, and perform the changes, both theoretical and hands-on training are necessary. As another example, few riflemen in the Army understand the theory of a gas-operated semiautomatic rifle. Nor do they need to understand it. Hence all riflemen are trained only to strip, repair, and maintain their rifles, and this is sufficient for the role they must play. The armorer—or technician who must diagnose malfunctions in a rifle —however, should have training in the theory of the rifle as well as the synthesis of its actual parts.

Span of attention   Another problem that trainers should be aware of is the decreasing span of attention on the part of trainees. Spans of attention vary among individuals—they are related to motivation on the part of the trainees —but there is a limit to the amount of continuous training anyone can effectively absorb in a given period of time. Thus a training program must have included in it breaks and recesses, socializing periods, and other mechanisms to break the decline in attention span. Generally, attention is at its height early in the training period, gradually tapering off as the time goes by.

Freedom from distraction   Finally, the learning environment ought to be as free of distraction as possible. In one training situation in a large manufacturing plant, a training class was conducted in a room filled by a huge cloth-covered table. Since the class was conducted in the plant and there were rumors afloat about a possible change in the plant, the covered table (which actually did house the model of a new plant to be built adjacent to the present site) lessened the ability of the participants to concentrate on the material being presented. The trainees were more concerned about what was underneath the cloth cover. In another case the training was carried on in an

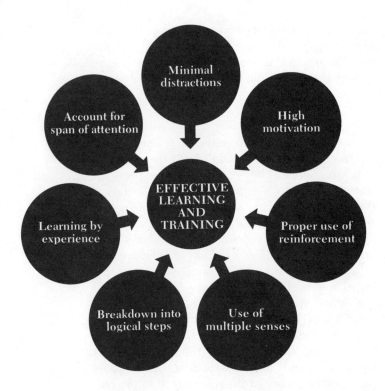

FIG. 13.1
Contributors to effective training.

insurance company's boardroom. A large divider with the company's organization chart was turned to face the wall when the training was in session. A similar disruption to that in the manufacturing plant was present in this training environment, as every one of the trainees was more interested in what was on the other side of the divider than in the material at hand.

In situations such as these, the trainer must be concerned with the physical layout and environment of the classroom or training space, including lights, heat, possible distractions, and the like. Classrooms with windows overlooking interesting activities, noise, or other types of distraction should be avoided.

Figure 13.1 illustrates in capsule form all of the contributors to effective learning and training that we have covered in this section.

ORGANIZATION FOR TRAINING

Training and development are serious organizational efforts requiring concerted planning effort. A training program also requires the development of distinct organizational relationships. Several models of staff line relationships are possible in an organization's training effort. (Refer back to Chapter 3 for a general discussion of the role of staff.)

In the simplest relationship the line individual (or other staff manager if the trainee is being groomed for a staff position) does all of the training for his or her own group. No consistency is practiced throughout the organization, and no central staff has a role in the training effort. The advantages of this mode of operation are simplicity and direct control, but the disadvantages are lack of directed expertise in training methods and inconsistency in terms of time, effectiveness, intensity, and quality of training.

Generally in organizations the training effort is planned in some central staff agency, and either general guidelines are issued for training content or, in a totally centralized situation, the specific training program is delineated at the central level. The line officer or other manager who is actually training engages in the actual on-the-spot training following either the guidelines or the specific program laid down by the central or staff-level training group.

In some organizations the actual training function is given over to the staff group as well. In another effort to relieve the line or operating manager of a secondary chore unrelated to the primary line productive function and to ensure complete consistency throughout the organization, the staff group might do the actual training and then deliver a "trained" person to the requesting line, operating, or other staff department.

Traditionally, the training director (whether a planner or a planner and trainer) has been located within the personnel department of an organization. As a component of the personnel department, the training director reported to the personnel manager, along with compensation specialists, safety directors, labor relations and contract administrators, etc. Recent evidence, however, is beginning to show that training is becoming so important to the organization that the function of training and development is being split into a separate staff operation, distinct from the personnel-management function. This phenomenon illustrates the important organizational principle that resources flow to, and organizational status is gained by, areas that assume importance to the needs or clientele of the organization. Organizations, recognizing the need for more highly trained managerial and operative personnel (perhaps in the face of finding that the public education sector is doing a relatively less sufficient job at training for a technologically complex work environment), are placing more effort and resources into their own training and development functions.

No training and development effort is going to be very good—even if designed superbly from a pedagogical point of view—if top management is not supportive of the purpose of training. Top-management support means not only providing the best available training, the finest in accommodations and facilities, and assurances that the training is relevant to the job at hand,

Top-management support for training

but also reinforcing the training when it comes time to put some of the things that were learned to work.

Sometimes a manager will send an employee off for training and then either give the employee a contradictory set of signals when he or she tries to implement the things covered in the training or not provide the resources or support to reinforce the employee's new approaches. In particular, first-line supervisors and foremen who are sent away for training often complain that management won't back them or really doesn't care what an employee learns. No conferences are held when the employee returns, and no sessions are planned to follow up on implementing the new knowledge. "Just send your vouchers to bookkeeping," was the way one company's representative described his welcome back from a training program.

The incomplete follow-up could be a major contributor to training's being ineffective. If managements are going to make the investment, monetarily, in training and development—and particularly if the programs are tailored to an organization's particular needs (often making them even more costly)—then the necessary follow-up in terms of posttraining support is essential.

TYPES OF TRAINING PROGRAMS

Training and development programs within organizations are basically of four types: off-the-job programs in separate facilities, on-the-job training, the use of outside agencies, and less formal arrangements such as "mentoring." Each of these types has its disadvantages and advantages for specific uses and for the resources available to specific organizations. Indeed, some organizations will use one basic type of program for some of its training and another type for other of its training needs. For example, on-the-job training is often given to operatives, whereas managers may be sent to specialized schools either operated by the organization or contracted for.

Separate-facility training programs

These types of programs are often used for operative trainees when the training effort would have serious disruptive effects on the ongoing job processes or when the training is so technical that it requires specialized equipment and personnel. One of the more common types is called "vestibule training"; the trainee is placed in a situation that duplicates the coming work environment with the same machines and same tasks involved, but is trained by a professional trainer. When the training is completed, the trainee is slotted into the work environment.

Another technique, used more for managerial employees, is the training center, where the trainee is actually stationed at the center for a lengthy period of time and taken through courses and experiential processes before being placed in the company hierarchy. Many companies use this system when they have unique internal processes, such as accounting or management systems, to teach those specific systems to trainees.

This type of training—commonly called OJT—has the advantage of putting the employee right onto the job in an actual hands-on experience. The employee is being trained by the actual supervisor under whom he or she will be working when the training is completed. The drawbacks to on-the-job training, however, are numerous. First, the on-line supervisors are not always the best trainers; second, they often do not have the time to do an effective job at training the new employee, considering all of the other tasks they have in completing their primary missions. But many companies use OJT simply because it is an inexpensive and easy way to accomplish training. Precision in training is often not as important as getting the job filled with an individual.

On-the-job training

For training of managers, on-the-job training is often called the "merry-go-round." Newly recruited managers are rotated throughout the organization before being placed in set departments for their first "permanent" jobs. The ideas behind this type of training are to expose the aspiring manager to as many of the company's functions as possible and to present the trainee with some understanding of the interrelatedness of the various subunits of the organization. One company does not even have the trainees hired for specific jobs; rather, each trainee completes the merry-go-round and either is bid for by various components or applies for a position in one of them. Sometimes the trainee washes out after the program in that he or she cannot find an acceptable position within the company.

In another type of managerial training program, the trainee is thrust right into the job, given a complicated task to resolve, and left alone to solve it. This is the most pressure-filled type of training, but the trainee quickly learns that she or he has responsibility and must perform. For example, in one company the trainee was brought in, given two days of company indoctrination, then assigned to the comptroller's office, where he was given the task of developing a cost-control system for a new-product line just developed. The current M&H system described in the opening vignette is similar to this type of training program.

Often it is best for the organization to use outside trainers when the organization is ill-equipped or cannot afford a first-class training effort. Thus automobile dealer franchises often use the manufacturers to train their mechanics and service personnel; managers in insurance companies are sent to associations and universities for advanced management training; other companies hire outside consultants to train sales personnel; or in not-for-profit organizations, government-funded training programs drawing trainees from a number of similar organizations are used.

Use of outside agencies

Many cities have vocational high schools and continuing-education programs which companies may use to train their technical personnel. These types of programs relieve the company or the organization of having to spend resources to develop their own programs, but they do have the disadvantages of reducing the organization's control over the trainees and of not having the programs specifically tailored to the organization's needs.

For general development purposes, organizations also rely on occasional managerial training programs put on by associations and universities. Increasingly, however, larger organizations are doing in-house development efforts for their own personnel, even though they may hire outside trainers to do the instruction.

Mentoring   One type of training procedure currently receiving some mention in the literature is called mentoring.* Often an informally established process between a seasoned executive and a new employee, the process is now tending to become more and more formal. In essence, the new employee becomes a protegé of a mentor, whose job it is to guide the employee through the problems and thickets of organizational life. Some of the recent literature on women entering the managerial ranks suggests that such a process is necessary for women to move rapidly up the organization.†

Whether formal or informal, however, the organization might consider the one-on-one mentoring process as an alternative or supplement to another type of more formal training program. The problems with such a process, of course, are that one person's training may be inconsistent with another's, and the mentor's own values and indeed organizational politics may enter into the training situation as well.

Back to Joan Baker and Mason-Holden   Now that you have been exposed to some of the learning principles and types of training programs available to organizations, you may be able to evaluate more expertly Mason-Holden's "sink or swim" type of training. It is not uncommon to find such types of programs in industry, and they do relate to many of the learning principles we have covered (although Mason-Holden's program does not seem to have a justification other than it just happened that way). Programs of that type often are related to objectives; if properly run, these programs judiciously and periodically apply reinforcement; the programs involve all of the possible senses applicable in the situation; and they offer learning by experience. On the other hand, they are not necessarily set down logically, and trainees, without guidance, can be easily distracted from the main focus of their work.

---

* See Harry Levinson, *The Exceptional Executive* (Cambridge, Mass.: Harvard University Press, 1968); and Daniel J. Levinson, *The Seasons of a Man's Life* (New York: Knopf, 1978).
† See Rosabeth Moss Kanter, *Men and Women of the Corporation* (New York: Basic Books, 1977); and Marlene A. Pinkstaff and Anna B. Wilkinson, *Women at Work: Overcoming the Obstacles* (Reading, Mass.: Addison-Wesley, 1979).

Would Mason-Holden be better off with another type of program? Mentoring perhaps? Formal classroom training? Some combination of both formal and field training? Perhaps Joan Baker's superiors, as they weigh the factors and evaluate her report, will choose to make a move into another type of training effort.

DETERMINING THE EFFECTIVENESS OF TRAINING

As we have tried to suggest throughout this chapter, the usefulness of any training and development effort depends on whether, for example, behavior changes, production increases, or new skills are demonstrated; in other words, results must be shown in daily organizational life in terms of achieving organizational objectives.[*] In essence, management must continually monitor the true effectiveness of training and development.

Management should be concerned enough to attempt to tie training and development—including the organization-development types noted in Chapter 4—directly to performance. This should be done in two specific ways. First, the training should be related directly to the process or behavior change desired. Some general management conferences and training seminars, sponsored by associations or universities, fail to impart change because they are not geared specifically to the needs, functions, or jobs of the trainees. Often, executives at conferences are heard to remark, "If I can pick up one good idea from this session, it is worth the price." One good idea may be worth the out-of-pocket cost, but that may not be what was intended by the sponsors of the training or the company that sent the executive to the program. So the first consideration is to design the training or select the program specifically to the needs of the organization. Outside programs should be selected with care so as to relate, in possibly some measurable way, to the performance goals of the organization.

Second, posttraining performance should be monitored to assess both the individual and the effectiveness of the training program. With operative or technical employees doing measurable or discrete tasks, monitoring is easier because production output can be measured rather easily, as can the reduction of rejected products in quality-control situations. Time increases on the job—reduction of absenteeism and tardiness—are also easily measurable.

With managers, however, the problem is a bit more complicated. There we are looking for results in forms of the installation of new programs, response to an organizational change, changes in behavior patterns, or the learning of new managerial skills. Installation of new programs can be measured against a projected completion date (but of course the training

[*] George S. Odiorne, *Training by Objectives* (New York: Macmillan, 1970).

for that program must then become a specific scheduled event in the plan for the program). The technical aspects of a manager's job can be easily measured; that is, the manager either does or does not know about the purchasing procedures or the product design.

The effectiveness of training instituted to bring about changes in organization or behavior or to develop new managerial skills (interactive and administrative—see Chapter 2) is probably the most difficult to measure. Here the organization may try to measure the increased use of the various topics covered in the training. That can be done roughly by the superior's evaluation, interviewing the person trained, and survey questionnaire. In connection with sensitivity training, general management development, or other general organization-development techniques, assessments by superiors of the effects of training are often relied on.

Tying training to Management by Objectives can be a useful strategy for an organization, since MBO calls for discrete measurable or describable objectives. The effectiveness of the training can then be partially assessed if the subordinate fulfills the objectives agreed on in the MBO process.

SUMMARY AND CONCLUSION

This chapter has focused on the training and development of managers and operative personnel. A major point is that managers may find the best source for positions right in their own back yards and that the best way to fill positions may be to upgrade or laterally transfer personnel already in the organization. Even when new personnel are hired, they are rarely ready to step into the position. Some training is necessary for them to function effectively and efficiently.

DISCUSSION QUESTIONS

1 Why do managers need training and development? List at least four instances when training and development are generally needed within the organization. Are training and development needed for new managerial employees?

2 Joan Baker listed the advantages and disadvantages of having no formal training program for new employees. What are some of these advantages and disadvantages? She concluded that the disadvantages outweighed the advantages; do you agree? Why or why not?

3 Compare and contrast training and development.

4 How does learning theory relate to an individual's own development?

5 Most experts in learning theory agree that positive reinforcement is much more powerful than negative reinforcement in terms of the training effort. Why do they make this conclusion? Do you agree or disagree with their conclusion? Why?

6 What are some of the management tools, aids, and techniques used in management-training programs?

7 Describe synectics. When is it particularly useful?

8 What are some of the contributors to effective training? List at least four factors contributing to effective learning and training.

9 Training and development programs within organizations are basically of three types. List and briefly describe the three basic types of training programs.

10 What criteria must be met for a training program to be considered effective?

11 Define the following terms:
   a) training
   b) development
   c) learning theory
   d) reinforcement
   e) simulation
   f) role play
   g) sensitivity training
   h) synectics
   i) on-the-job training
   j) separate-facility training programs

12 What are the implications of a decreasing span of attention for the trainer in setting up a training program?

13 When is a separate-facility training program more desirable than OJT?

14 What are the advantages and disadvantages of OJT?

15 When should a company opt for the use of outside agencies in its training program?

16 Why is there a greater need for training when an operative employee is promoted to a management position?

17 List several areas of training required for new operative employees.

18 What should characterize the objectives of a training program?

19 How does an organization evaluate a training program for nonmanagers? For managers?

CASE: OCEANSIDE STATE HOSPITAL

■ Professor Blomberg looked very satisfied as he completed the last day of a ten-session training program at the Oceanside State Hospital. "This is the best group I've had yet, and I think the material really went over," he mused. As he was passing out the certificates of completion following his lecture, one of the participants, Billy Flynn, Day Supervisor of Housekeeping, asked him, "Doc, can we get a cup of coffee after class?"

"Sure, I'll meet you down at the cafeteria," replied Blomberg. He was pleased at being asked. Blomberg liked to get as close as possible with any group that he taught or lectured.

Blomberg had been engaged by the hospital's training director to deliver a twenty-hour management-training program in ten two-hour sessions. He had planned the program around some of the newest management theory and practice. The group was exposed to motivation theory, organization structure and design, scheduling and planning, leadership, communication, Management by Objectives, and some management-union relations, since the hospital was organized by the State Employees Union.

Participants in the groups were the first-line supervisors from the various service departments. Both the day and night housekeeping supervisors attended, as did the central stores chief and supervisory personnel from the various nursing groups, maintenance, bookkeeping, and security staffs. No one from the medical staff was present; nor were there any representatives from the medical support units—radiology, pathology, pharmacy, etc.

Blomberg met Billy Flynn in the hospital cafeteria. With Flynn were Willie Washington, the night housekeeping supervisor, Joe Fontaine from the maintenance shop, and Mike Cellino, chief storekeeper.

Flynn started off: "Doc, did you notice the real lack of enthusiasm when we received those certificates? They don't mean that much to us."

"Oh, I guess I was carried away with how well I thought the course had gone, so I didn't notice anything wrong," Blomberg replied.

"Well, it's not you, professor. This was by far the best presentation of this material that we've been through."

"You mean you've had this material before?" asked Blomberg.

"Oh sure, many times," said Willie Washington. "I've got about fifteen of those pretty certificates, and I'll bet six are from courses like this one."

"Well, why didn't you say something? No wonder you guys took to the material so well."

"It's a big game," said Cellino. "They get a training budget from the state every year, and if they don't spend it, they lose it for the next year. So they try to spend every dime and send us to courses like this. And we keep piling up diplomas. But we can never use any of the stuff we learn, and that's our main complaint."

"Are you serious? Do you mean—?"

"Top management just doesn't give a damn," all four of the supervisors said practically in unison.

Flynn continued, "They send down their silly orders. If we suggest a new practice, they tell us just to do our job and to let them do the thinking. Do you know if any of them have been through these programs?"

"No, I don't," replied Blomberg.

In fact, the administration of the hospital was headed by a medical doctor, the controller had an M.B.A. degree and the director of business services had a B.S. in business. But the power of the hospital lay with the doctors and other technically trained people whose formal education in management was minimal.

Blomberg was frustrated. He thought that he had designed a good program and had been led to believe that the organization viewed it as important. On the other hand, he now recalled that the training director had introduced him on the first day but had never again come around until it was time to pass out the certificates. That's when the hospital director made his only appearance also.

On the way out of the hospital, Blomberg stopped by the training director's office to say goodbye.

"How do you think it went?" asked the training director.

"For my part, okay," replied Blomberg. "Now, what do you intend to do after this?"

"Well, the feedback we got from the course was positive. We hope the supervisors can find ways of putting the material to work. They've got some real problems in the ranks." ∎

Case questions

1. Evaluate the potential organizational effectiveness of Blomberg's training program. Explain your evaluation.

2. As Professor Blomberg, what would you say next to the training director?

3. Assuming that the training director is concerned, what should he do to increase top-management commitment to training effectiveness?

SELECTED READINGS

Albrecht, M., "Women, Resistance to Promotion and Self-Directed Growth," *Human Resource Management* 17, 1 (Spring 1978): 12–17.

Bass, B. M., and J. A. Vaughan, *Training in Industry: The Management of Learning* (Belmont, Calif.: Wadsworth, 1966). See especially Chapter 6.

Bell, C. R., "Criteria for Selecting Instructional Strategies," *Training and Development Journal* 31, 10 (October 1977): 3–7.

Berg, I., *Education and Jobs: The Great Training Robbery* (New York: Praeger, 1970).

Bigge, M. L., "Describing the Learning Process," in W. R. Nord, ed., *Concepts and Controversy in Organizational Behavior* (Pacific Palisades, Calif.: Goodyear, 1972).

Blake, R. R., and J. S. Mouton, *Corporate Excellence through Grid Organization Development* (Houston: Gulf, 1964).

Broadwell, M., *The Supervisor and On-the-Job Training* (Reading, Mass.: Addison-Wesley, 1975).

Cullen, J. G., S. A. Sawzin, G. R. Sisson, and R. A. Swanson, "Cost Effectiveness: A Model for Assessing the Training and Investment," *Training and Development Journal* 32, 1 (January 1978): 24–29.

Franklin, J. L., *Human Resource Development in the Organization* (Detroit: Gale Research Co., 1978).

Gellerman, S. W., *Managers and Subordinates* (New York: Dryden Press, 1976).

Glueck, W. F., *Personnel: A Diagnostic Approach* (Dallas: Business Publications, 1974).

Hentz, H., "How to Identify and Train Successful and Unsuccessful Foremen," *Personnel Administrator* 21 (November 1976): 16–19.

Maginn, M., "Training in Japan: What We Can Learn from Them," *Training* 15, 1 (January 1978): 59–62.

Management Development Resource Service, *The Directory of Management Education Programs* (New York: American Management Association, 1977).

Morgan, Daniel C., "Career Development Programs," *Personnel* 54, 5 (September/October 1977): 23–27.

Nunney, D. N., "Cognitive Style Mapping," *Training and Development Journal* 32, 9 (September 1978): 50–57.

Odiorne, G. S., *Training by Objectives: An Economic Approach to Management Training* (New York: Macmillan, 1970).

Paxton, D. R., "Employee Development: A Lifelong Learning Approach," *Training and Development Journal* 30 (December 1976): 24–26.

Quick, T. L., "Putting Responsibility for Training Where it Belongs," *Personnel* 52 (March/April 1975): 45–51.

Reber, R. W., and G. E. Terry, *Behavioral Insights for Supervision* (Englewood Cliffs, N.J.: Prentice-Hall, 1975).

Strauss, G., and L. Sayles, *Personnel: The Human Problems of Management*, 3rd ed. (Englewood Cliffs, N.J., Prentice-Hall, 1972).

Suessmuth, P., "Boosting Small-Group Productivity," *Training* 15, 5 (May 1978): 58–59.

Warr, P., "Redundancy, Retraining, and Reincarnation," *Personnel Management* 8 (November 1976): 23–26.

Yoder, D., and H. G. Heneman, eds., *Training and Development*, Vol. 5 (Washington, D.C.: BNA Books, 1977).

Chapter 14
FACILITIES AND CAPITAL-RESOURCE ACQUISITION

CHAPTER HIGHLIGHTS

This chapter introduces the subjects of facilities location and capital-equipment acquisition. We will review the various factors involved in site selection: managerial choice, economic factors, market considerations, and political and social climates. Then we will move into the related subject of capital-equipment decisions and cover some of the analytical methods for capital-equipment procurement. Here you will learn about discounting future earnings—or present-value analysis—as a major tool in this kind of decision making.

LEARNING OBJECTIVES

1 To become familiar with the types of decisions pertaining to facilities location.

2 To understand the relevance of the various factors in facility-location decisions: managerial convenience, economic factors, market factors, and political and social factors.

3 To become familiar with the rudiments of capital-investment decisions.

4 To be able to differentiate a capital investment from an expense.

5 To be able to differentiate between relevant factors for capital-investment decisions and financial-accounting analysis.

6 To become familiar with the concept of opportunity costs.

7 To learn the rudiments of present-value analysis and discounted cash flows.

8 To learn the other factors accounted for in a capital-budgeting decision.

CASE: MUSIC IMPORTERS, INCORPORATED

■ "We need an assembly and distribution point in the Boston-Washington-Cincinnati triangle. Somewhere in that area, we have to set up our facility so as to allow us to reach the mass of our market with the minimum operating cost." Rusty Steele was thinking aloud about the best location for his company's distribution facility.

311

Rusty Steele and two of his college friends had just established a corporation, Music Importers, Incorporated, to import prestige European-manufactured classical and dramatic phonograph records and to distribute them throughout the United States. The trio of founders had developed a unique marketing plan specifically geared to the classical-music market. Typically, the classical market was almost always treated as a stepchild in the recording industry, which stressed the popular, although volatile, rock stars. Steele and his friends, John Brass and Grant Diamond, were convinced that they could carve a profitable niche out of the total recording business by building a program catering to the prestige music stores, the discriminating music buyer, and the music and drama programs of schools and universities.

Music Importers had won the distribution rights to four prestigious Continental labels and had also picked up the franchises for three small British labels and an interesting, innovative one from Japan. The plan was to expand gradually in concentric circles from the Boston to Washington strip until the company finally blanketed the entire country.

Steele had managed to convince a venture-capital specialist of the soundness of the venture, and with the assistance and participation of banks and speculators, the specialist had raised $250,000. Each of the original founders had invested $15,000. Most of the inventory was to be financed initially by trade credit, and, if necessary, the corporation was prepared to factor accounts receivable.

But now Brass had been given the task of searching out a location for the firm's warehouse and distribution point, renting it, or getting a new facility constructed and buying the necessary equipment. Operations had to be started within a year; otherwise, the contract with the major European supplier—on whose products the whole venture hinged—would be terminated.

Brass first set himself to listing the major prerequisites of the location for the venture and the types of costs he would have to determine before he set out on the actual hunt for a location. He also started to jot down the types of questions he would have to consider when buying the equipment for the location. ■

INTRODUCTION

The three budding managers of Music Importers, Incorporated, are now facing some of the other acquisition problems that confront managers—those dealing with the acquisition of physical resources with which to operate the organization or business. In this chapter we shall cover two of these physical-acquisition problems: facilities location and capital-equipment acquisition.

Each of these areas requires high degrees of sophistication in the planning and decision processes. Although we can cover these topics only briefly, as aspiring managers you should be aware of them, along with the factors to be considered when undertaking these managerial activities.

One topic not covered in this chapter is the acquisition of materials and parts. As an example of that task, recall that at the Greco Roman Chair Co. (Chapter 1), nails, staples, material, gasoline, electric light bulbs, and all of the other things necessary to manufacture and distribute chairs were there on the assembly line, in trucks, or in the office. A great deal of specialized managerial expertise goes into effective purchasing, ranging from inventory control (see Chapter 7) to vendor selection, make-or-buy decisions, buyer-seller reciprocity, and the like. Managers who will be doing purchasing should be aware of all of the factors and processes of a technical nature that must be factored into material and parts-purchasing decisions.

FACILITIES LOCATION

Two basic kinds of facilities-location situations may face the manager who is charged with finding a suitable location for the organization's operations.* In the first situation the manager may be locating or relocating *the single facility* of the firm. In this case the objective is simply to account for all of the factors related to the organization's process and to generally minimize the total cost of the combined factors, given the present and projected scale of operation of the organization. Since environments rarely stay stable, this situation could face the manager of an existing plant or facility who is contemplating a move, as well as a manager such as John Brass who is in the process of establishing a new facility for a new venture.

Organizational facilities *do* get moved. New England, for example, suffered a loss of its textile and shoe manufacturing plants as foreign competition, population shifts, and changes in costs forced many such firms to re-evaluate the economics of maintaining their activities in the six-state region.

The multiplant manager faces a somewhat different situation, however. For that manager, the question is one of minimizing the combined costs of operating the existing plants along with the new one. The decision process in this problem involves computing the costs and efficiencies of a number of alternative locations combined with the existing locations to reach a minimum total cost. The process often uses a variant of the linear programming method (see Chapter 7), called the transportation method. The objective of

---

* For expanded treatments of plant and facilities location, see a good standard production management text, e.g., Elwood S. Buffa, *Modern Production Management,* 4th ed. (New York: Wiley, 1973), Chapter 11.

the exercise in the transportation method is to maximize service and delivery with a minimum of costs from the various combination of plants.

Managers of existing facilities who are faced with the problem of inadequate facilities often have an alternative other than moving. They can rebuild, remodel, or add on to existing plants. In this case the existing location may become one of the alternatives, and the various costs and other factors can be calculated into the decision process just as if a move were being planned. Sometimes nonquantitative factors play a dominant role in this type of decision, however, for at least the manager is sure of many of the advantages of the environment already being faced. Avoiding disruptions in routines, workforces, and relationships is not to be minimized as a factor contributing to a "no-move" decision.

Factors in facility-location decisions

The manager faced with a facilities-location decision will calculate a number of cost and environmental factors and reach a decision based on the least-cost combination of these factors. But very often other environmental—nonquantitative—factors may temper the decision. Therefore, the least-cost decision is not always the alternative selected. We should, therefore, consider in some detail all of the various factors involved in deciding on the location of an organization's facility—quantitative, cost, and nonquantitative factors (see Fig. 14.1).

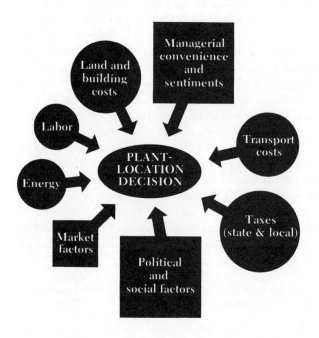

FIG. 14.1
Factors in the location decision.

We noted (in Chapter 6) the general model of managerial decision making. The facilities-location problem is a decision situation for the manager and should be thought of and solved in the context of that general managerial decision-making model. That is, problems must be defined, facts gathered, alternatives weighed, and decisions made. Sometimes new facts emerge which change the problem. The problem must then be redefined and the process started all over again.

Managerial sentimentality and convenience   At a recent conference the president of a New England manufacturing firm was arguing that his operating costs would be at least thirty percent lower if he had built his new plant in Georgia instead of New England. When asked why he had just constructed his new plant in New England rather than move, he replied, "My whole family is here, and besides, I like to ski." These factors of managerial needs, preferences, backgrounds, and family ties are often prime reasons for locating a facility in a particular place, especially for owner-managed businesses. In many cases the location is selected because the manager is from the area involved, has personal ties to a town or city, is going into business on a hunch, is unwilling to move, or does not know how to handle more sophisticated analyses of facilities location. In any event, although the optimum decision on a cost basis is not always reached, these and other personal reasons (along with other nonquantitative factors) are perfectly legitimate considerations to temper the cost analysis and locate in an area other than the lowest-cost one.

Economic factors   In the first run at analysis for a location decision, the key factors are those that have costs associated with them. It should be noted, however, that the magnitude of any one of these factors can be changed materially and quickly. As a result, many organizations contemplating facilities-location decisions are now engaging in what is termed futurist thinking in order to predict social, political, and other changes that may have an effect on future costs. For example, few firms foresaw the energy crisis and the effect it would have on changing the equations of economical plant location. Other examples are the construction of the interstate highway system, changing political philosophies regarding expensive social and public services, and the change in the laws regarding payment of unemployment benefits to strikers.

1 *Transportation costs:* Transportation availability and cost are key factors for many industries, particularly where transportation of various raw materials is significant. For example, a basic steel plant uses four primary materials—iron ore, scrap steel, coal, and limestone. Transportation costs relative to the value of each input are crucial. If coal is the relatively cheap input, but

is needed in large quantity, and if transportation costs are high, locating nearer to sources of coal might be more important than locating nearer iron ore or scrap steel supplies, whose transportation costs relative to the basic materials costs and quantity needed might be much lower. Similarly, if the cost of moving the goods to market is relatively less than the cost of assembling the necessary raw materials, a firm might want to locate nearer to the supply sources than to the markets. For a firm basically in the marketing business, such as the phonograph record importer cited at the beginning of this chapter, the calculations would have to consider the least-cost combination of transportation from port into the warehouse and then out to the company's major marketing areas.

Calculating transportation costs, however, is only part of the problem. As important is the availability and reliability of transportation in the first place. If no major highway, air, or rail transportation exists in a certain area, the rates of bringing materials in or out may be irrelevant if the reliability of service is projected to be poor and inconsistent.

2 *Land and building costs:* Availability of affordable land and reasonable building costs are two additional economic factors. Sufficient land should be available in all of the considered sites so as to allow for possible and projected expansion, and the building costs should be calculated into the equation. Sometimes the availability of land and the low cost of buildings will offset some other, higher costs such as transportation. For example, many localities, in their eagerness to attract industry, will often offer free land and low-cost buildings to organizations seeking new facilities. These places often are at out-of-the-way locations and have higher transportation costs and few amenities, but the attractive plant-siting conditions could offset the cost advantages of other alternative locations.

3 *Taxes—state and local:* Another cost factor is the state and local tax burden on the organization's profits, inventories, and buildings. Taxes among states and localities differ markedly, and some organizations are even forced to figure into their calculations the added costs they must pay for managers and executives due to the high personal burden imposed by some political jurisdictions. For example, one personnel executive estimated that the cost of a management engineer in one of the Northeastern states is anywhere from $1500 to $2000 higher than in many other areas. Contributing to this differential are the very high state and local personal and property levies prevalent in some of the Northeastern states.

4 *Energy:* Since the energy crisis descended on the United States, relative costs of energy are now more crucial to plant-location decisions, particularly for the organization that is energy-intensive. The Northeast is now at a greater relative disadvantage due to the area's need to import practically all of its current energy sources. On the other hand, although the Southwest has the advantage of being near energy sources, it is far from major markets. The Pacific Northwest has cheaper power because of the abundance of hydro-electric sources, but too is far from markets; therefore, its low energy costs can be offset by higher transportation costs. Less energy-intensive industries and organizations, of course, would not find this factor to be crucial, and the Northeast region would remain attractive—all other factors being equal.

5 *Labor:* Availability and cost of labor are very important factors to figure into the determination of plant location. The South, for example, is now less unionized than are Northern states and hence boasts lower labor costs. But the key to labor costs is not necessarily the hourly cost, but rather the per unit cost. Lower per hour labor cost may be offset by lower productivity, increased rejects, and errors. For a highly capital-intensive industry needing minimal skilled labor, the differential in productivity would not be as significant a factor as it would for an organization needing large numbers of skilled people.

Market factors   One of the key groups of factors is nearness to markets or accessibility to markets, particularly when the cost of transporting the finished product is high relative to the price of the finished goods. Sometimes this can be compensated for by other factors such as extraordinarily cheap labor or government subsidy for export, hence the location of many finished-goods industries in Far Eastern nations.

Of course, access to markets changes as other environmental factors change. Air freight, the interstate highway system, or good rail or ship transportation may eliminate the need to be in or near the major markets and thus allow the manager to reap the benefits of other, more advantageous factors. For certain types of organizations, such as services and firms with high value added from marketing efforts, nearness to markets may emerge as the crucial factor in location decisions.

Political and social factors   Increasingly, the political and social climates become factors enticing or rejecting organizational facilities. Some of the factors in these areas that organizations consider are community attitudes toward business, environmental and zoning controls, a willingness on the part of people to work, and the amenities of the various communities— housing, schools, cost of living, police and fire protection, and recreation facilities. Housing, personal taxes, quality of schools, and other amenities such as recreation, personal protection, and the cost of living are all relevant, since they affect the ability of the organization to attract and hold qualified and mobile managerial and executive personnel.

Some communities openly welcome business investment; others prefer to control closely. Statements such as "We want business, but the right kind of business" might bring a very cautious response by potential investors. Overly complicated procedures for obtaining approval of a plant or facilities plan—many communities have multiple planning boards and complex zoning requirements—sign control, and stringent environmental controls might indicate a less than enthusiastic welcome for an organization's facilities. For example, one community reportedly lost a beer-brewing plant that could have employed several hundred unemployed townspeople because the state environmental protection agency required water to be returned to the adjacent stream cleaner than it was before entering the plant and, even more crucial, cleaner than the company required for use in the beer. The company built its plant somewhere else.

Making the location decision

As mentioned earlier, the location decision fits the mode of the general decision model presented in Chapter 6. In this case the manager would want to gather all of the facts relating to the costs and other qualitative factors and to present each of the possible locations as a decision alternative. What would a total package cost in terms of transportation, costs of building, energy requirements, labor costs, and productivity, and how would these quantitative results be modified by the qualitative factors? Figure 14.2 presents a location-decision tool which brings all of the information on the various alternative locations together for comparison. The decision maker would add up all of the costs, weigh the positive and negative factors of each proposed location, and then temper each by the nonquantitative factors. This is, however, simply a decision tool; the principal thing is to bring all of the information together for easy comparison.

Locational factors for Music Importers Music Importer's location problem may be "solved" by considering the factors just covered.

1 *Managerial sentimentality and convenience:* Steele, Brass, and Diamond were all young and relatively mobile. They had moved to the college town from various locations about the country, so they probably would not be concerned about locating on a "sentimental" or convenience basis. These factors are not important here.

2 *Economic factors: Transportation* in and out would be significant factors. Essentially, a distributor or wholesaler would be breaking down and intermixing a small number of very large orders into a larger number of relatively smaller orders. The question, then, is to develop a model that will yield approximate total costs of the "in and out" combinations from the various alternative locations.

The warehouse could be in an older building, so long as clear floor space is available. *Land and building costs,* then, do not loom as a large factor if cheaper, older buildings can be secured in any of the communities projected.

Location or Site	Capital items						Operating items								Other factors							
	Land availability—yes or no	Land outlay	Building outlay	Other capital outlay	Total capital outlays		Transportation costs at capacity	Energy costs at capacity	Labor costs at capacity	Real estate taxes	State taxes	Insurance	Other operating costs	Total operating costs	Political climate Excellent/Good/Poor	Zoning Restrictive/Nonrestrictive	Personal taxes High/Medium/Low	Schools Excellent/Good/Poor	Fire protection Excellent/Good/Poor	Housing Excellent/Good/Poor	Recreation Excellent/Good/Poor	
A																						
B																						
C																						

FIG. 14.2
Location-decision analysis tool.

In one respect, being able to use an older building and not considering new construction may narrow the choice of communities to those with older buildings available. In another respect, however, the choice is widened because the lower building costs may now qualify some of the locations that might lose out because of the higher costs of other factors.

Most of the labor needed in the projected company would be unskilled, warehouse types. To the extent that this type of labor is less mobile, relative *tax rates and living costs* among communities would have minimum impact on the attractiveness of the organization to the great bulk of its employees. Taxes, both state and local, will have some impact on the organization's costs, and to this extent will be factored into the decision.

The variance of *energy costs* among locations would probably be a negligible factor for this firm. Music Importers is not an energy-intensive operation.

Although not mentioned in the case, Steele, Brass, and Diamond estimated that the firm would employ a maximum of forty people, not including salespeople and executives. These forty would be relatively unskilled, and this *labor* requirement should pose no great demands on any contemplated location.

3 *Market factors:* Markets pose the key question. Music Importers must be able to guarantee speedy delivery, and therefore the transportation cost already calculated may become a major factor here. Indeed, being closer to the major markets may, in terms of speed of delivery, necessitate taking a location other than the least-cost one, due to transportation alone.

4 *Political and social factors:* These factors are probably of little consequence to Music Importers, except if new construction is planned. This essentially is a "clean" industry, and few communities would object to its presence. On the other hand, the executives were very concerned about schools and amenities, since they were young, with growing families.

Even this small company, with its limited needs, demands, and impacts, faces a very complex locational decision, with many factors to consider and interrelate. One can easily imagine, then, the enormity of the task facing the location planner for the large firm—multiproduct, national market, energy-intensive, requiring large numbers of skilled employees, and having an environmental impact.

Multiplant location   As we noted earlier, the problem could be the location of a second facility to add to the capacity of the first and then optimally utilize both plants servicing several market locations. Part of this problem can be solved by use of the specialized linear programming technique called the transportation method, which would indicate an optimum distribution mix among the plants.* But many of the other factors—particularly the nonquantitative political and social ones—are relevant to *any* location decision, whether multiplant or not.

CAPITAL-EQUIPMENT PROCUREMENT

The manager also equips the organization with machinery, office equipment, vehicles, and the other equipment necessary to make the organization function according to plan in order to accomplish objectives. Our objective here is to delineate some decision parameters and techniques that the manager uses to make the decisions on physically equipping the organization. For ex-

* *Ibid.*

ample, the Greco-Roman Chair Company (Chapter 1) had assembly lines, machines, trucks, and all of the necessities of a functioning organization. What standards were used to determine that one particular machine is purchased or that one particular truck is acquired versus another kind of machine or another model of truck? How did the manager make those decisions?

Although our treatment of capital-equipment expenditures will be introductory only, the area is actually a complicated one, with many sophisticated alternative models; our objective is to simply introduce the problem and sample the methods. More extensive treatments are available on capital budgeting and equipment procurement.*

Also, our treatment is essentially a cost-oriented one, with analysis basically centered on savings, earnings, and return on investment. But, of course, some equipment is purchased simply because it is necessary in order for the organization to operate; for example, certain items of warehouse equipment are necessary for the record company described in the opening case. In most cases, however, cost calculations and differentials can be made. Even in the warehouse that is yet to be equipped, for example, the cost differential of a motorized conveyor system versus hand labor can be calculated and analyzed through the methods introduced in the following pages.

We are concerned here with expenditures for items: (1) that are not directly a part of the product being manufactured or service rendered; (2) that do not wear out within one year; (3) but whose cost is recoverable over a part of the period of time it is being used. For example, the purchase of a power nailer that will last many years is a capital investment, whereas the nails that are used with the product are not capital investments. Rather, the nails are a current expense. However, if by purchasing a power nailer, we are able to cut labor costs and the loss from bent nails, the resultant savings in current expense move to the profit columns of the organization. Thus in calculating the desirability of the investment, these savings in out-of-pocket costs (or current expenses) become relevant to the decision, and their magnitudes govern the desirability of the investment.

What are capital investments?

In the terminology of accounting, we are dealing here with the difference between a capitalized expenditure—which is depreciated over the life of the equipment—and a current expense—which is totally charged off in the accounting period in which it is incurred. However, some fundamental differences between financial accounting and investment-decision analysis must be noted.

Accounting concepts and investment decisions

* For example, *see* Harold Bierman and Seymour Smidt, *The Capital Budgeting Decision* (New York: Macmillan, 1966); and Jerome Osteryoung, *Capital Budgeting: Long-Term Asset Selection* (Columbus, Ohio: Grid, Inc., 1974).

The basic difference is that investment decisions are based on cash outlays and cash inflows. Depreciation and book value in the financial-accounting sense, therefore, may bear little relationship to the investment decision (except where tax savings may accrue each year). A simple if exaggerated example will explain this point. Suppose that a manager contemplated purchasing a $10,000 machine for use in a plant. For the sake of simplicity, assume that the machine is custom-built and that it is so specialized that it could be used only in this plant and therefore has no salvage value at any time. Assume that the machine has a useful life of ten years.

In such a situation, straight-line depreciation for financial-accounting purposes would yield an annual depreciation of $1000. The book value of the machine after the fifth year would be $5000. But for investment purposes, the first year's real expense is the total $10,000; it is the cash outlay that counts.

Incidentally, book value may bear no relationship to an asset's real market value. In this case, since the machine is so specialized, its market value may be zero the day after the machine is installed, despite what the books may say. Indeed, during periods of inflation, the market value may increase beyond book value on such things as buildings, general-purpose equipment, etc.

Opportunity costs

Most organizations have multiple projects in which to invest, but limited funds with which to invest; hence any capital-equipment purchase must be analyzed against others that will not be undertaken if this one is made. If an organization invests into project 1, it must forego investing in project 2. If project 2 yields a return on investment of ten percent, project 1 must yield at least as much. The possible return on project 2 thus becomes a necessary cost to project 1. Project 1 must account for not only its own out-of-pocket (interest, maintenance, electricity, etc.) costs, but also at least a ten percent return to account for the lost return on project 2. Otherwise, the organization whose goal is the maximization of return should invest in project 2.

This concept is called the principle of opportunity costs. Opportunity costs in this context are the return from the next best foregone opportunity and are as real a cost for any project as the out-of-pocket costs.

Many firms rank their investments in terms of return, thus implicitly taking into account the opportunity-cost concept. Other firms set a target rate of return, which any prospective project must meet in order to qualify for funding. These rates account for the minimum return acceptable to the organization—a variant of the opportunity-cost concept.

Analyzing a capital-investment decision

Let us now do a simple analysis of a capital-equipment decision. Again, capital budgeting, or capital-equipment investment analysis, is a complex problem area. Our analysis here serves only to introduce some of the techniques involved.

Year	Savings generated by investment	TABLE 14.1
1	$4,000	
2	3,800	
3	3,800	
4	3,450	
5	3,000	
6	2,800	
7	2,500	
8	2,400	
9	1,800	
10	1,200	
Total savings	$31,750	
Salvage	500	
Total intake	$32,250	

Suppose that an organization contemplates investing in a machine that will have a life of ten years and be worth $500 at the end of the period. The initial investment in the machine, including installation and setup, will be $15,000. Suppose that the machine will generate savings in costs (or earnings) over the presently used method of operation according to the schedule shown in Table 14.1.

The dollar return over ten years for this particular machine is $32,250, including the salvage value of $500 at the end of the tenth year. What kind of decision does the manager make? Does he or she go ahead with this investment or hold back and continue along with the existing equipment? Obviously, the investment over ten years is paid back, along with a difference of $17,250. In fact, it is paid back in four years. Is this, therefore, a "go" or a "no-go" decision?

To answer this question, the manager generally needs some more information. What is the minimum rate of return that the organization demands for its investments? What are the opportunity costs of investing in this particular piece of equipment? Suppose that the minimum rate of return (or, we might use the organization's cost of capital) is ten percent. Does this investment still qualify?

Money has time value. In other words, money has the power to earn interest. For example, if we invest $1.00 today, that dollar will be worth a dollar plus accrued interest at some future date. For example, a dollar invested at a compound rate of eight percent would be worth two dollars in nine years.

Discounting—a major tool in capital-equipment analysis—reverses the process of compounding interest. For example, if someone promised you $2.00 nine years from now and you were aware that the going interest rate

Present-value analysis

was eight percent, what would you be willing to pay *now* for that promise? The answer would be the discounted sum, or the value *today* of $2.00 earned nine years from now at the interest rate of eight percent—or $1.00.

Let us return now to our problem. Assume that the organization has set a minimum rate of ten percent as the return necessary on any capital investment. Given the yearly savings—or earnings—illustrated earlier, does this new investment now qualify for funding?

This analysis begins by taking discount factors from a table of present values and applying them to the savings being generated by the new machine. We are asking the same question that we asked earlier: Given the rate of interest, what is the worth to us today of a certain sum of dollars to be earned in so many years in the future? Table 14.2 reproduces a small portion of a present-value table.

Years from now	Rate							
	8%	10%	12%	14%	15%	16%	18%	20%
1	0.926	0.909	0.893	0.877	0.870	0.862	0.847	0.833
2	0.857	0.826	0.797	0.769	0.756	0.743	0.718	0.694
3	0.794	0.751	0.712	0.675	0.658	0.641	0.609	0.579
4	0.735	0.683	0.636	0.592	0.572	0.552	0.516	0.482
5	0.681	0.621	0.567	0.519	0.497	0.476	0.437	0.402
6	0.630	0.564	0.507	0.456	0.432	0.410	0.370	0.335
7	0.583	0.513	0.452	0.400	0.376	0.354	0.314	0.279
8	0.540	0.467	0.404	0.351	0.327	0.305	0.266	0.233
9	0.500	0.424	0.361	0.308	0.284	0.263	0.225	0.194
10	0.463	0.386	0.322	0.270	0.247	0.227	0.191	0.162
11	0.429	0.350	0.287	0.237	0.215	0.195	0.162	0.135
12	0.397	0.319	0.257	0.208	0.187	0.168	0.137	0.112
13	0.368	0.290	0.229	0.182	0.163	0.145	0.116	0.093
14	0.340	0.263	0.205	0.160	0.141	0.125	0.099	0.078
15	0.315	0.239	0.183	0.140	0.123	0.108	0.084	0.065
.								
.								
.								
20	0.215	0.149	0.104	0.073	0.061	0.051	0.037	0.026

TABLE 14.2
Discount factors for present value of future payments

Applying the ten percent rate—the necessary rate of return in our problem—to the stream of future earnings indicated in the problem above, we can calculate the present values of the projected stream of earnings. See Table 14.3. Note that the present value of the cost of the machine ($15,000) remains constant, since the discount factor for earnings in year 0 (or before they have been spent) is 1.000. The present value of the total stream of earnings over the ten-year period, including the salvage value of the equipment, is $19,250. This means that the $15,000 expenditure will be returned along

Year	Net earnings	Discount factor	Present value
0	—$15,000	1.000	—$15,000
1	4,000	0.909	3,636
2	3,800	0.826	3,139
3	3,800	0.751	2,854
4	3,450	0.683	2,356
5	3,000	0.621	1,863
6	2,800	0.564	1,579
7	2,500	0.513	1,283
8	2,400	0.467	1,121
9	1,800	0.424	763
10	1,200	0.386	463
Salvage	500	0.386	193
			+$4,250

TABLE 14.3
Present values of
projected earnings

with the ten percent interest rate *at least*. The positive figure for a total
means that the return on this investment—given this stream of earnings—is
above the necessary ten percent. The decision to buy this machine should be
positive—other things being equal—based on the present-value analysis.

Suppose that the firm wants to find the exact rate of return it will be
earning on an investment. The analysis is very similar, except that the manager searches for the rate at which the discounted inflow (earnings) will
exactly match the expenditure, or outlay. In this case the figure is a trifle
more than seventeen percent. We will show the discounting at sixteen percent and eighteen percent to show the bracketing about the final figure of
seventeen percent (see Table 14.4).

Year	Net earnings	Discount factor 16%	Present value	Discount factor 18%	Present value
0	—$15,000	1.000	—$15,000	1.000	—$15,000
1	4,000	0.862	3,448	0.847	3,388
2	3,800	0.743	2,823	0.718	2,728
3	3,800	0.641	2,436	0.609	2,314
4	3,450	0.552	1,904	0.516	1,780
5	3,000	0.476	1,428	0.437	1,311
6	2,800	0.410	1,148	0.370	1,036
7	2,500	0.354	885	0.314	785
8	2,400	0.305	732	0.266	638
9	1,800	0.263	473	0.255	405
10	1,200	0.227	272	0.191	229
Salvage	500	0.227	114	0.191	96
			+$663		—$290

TABLE 14.4
Rate of return

Year	Investment A Net earnings	Investment B Net earnings	
0	—$15,000	—$17,500	**TABLE 14.5** Stream of earnings for two investments
1	4,000	4,500	
2	3,800	4,200	
3	3,800	4,000	
4	3,450	4,000	
5	3,000	3,000	
6	2,800	3,000	
7	2,500	2,000	
8	2,400	2,000	
9	1,800	1,000	
10	1,200	1,000	
Salvage	500	750	

Since the sixteen percent factor yields a positive figure, the actual rate of return is higher. A negative figure from the eighteen percent factor means that the actual rate of return is lower. The correct percentage figure, as we noted, is about seventeen percent. For a manager who has a complete discount table, exact calculations would be a simple process.

Comparing two projects for investment

The discounting-to-present-value method of evaluating prospective investment projects can now be used to determine the actual rates of return of two or more alternative investments. In this case the cost of each investment is set against its own stream of earnings, and the appropriate interest rate is found that will exactly offset the outlay (or expenditure) with the stream of earnings. After this is done for each of the alternatives, the investment yielding the highest rate of return will be chosen.

For example, let us assume that an organization has two alternative investments: A and B. Investment A, we can assume, is the same as the one in our previous example. Investment B will cost $17,500, last ten years, and have a salvage value of $750. We set up our stream-of-earnings tables exactly as in the previous example. These figures are shown in Table 14.5.

The next step is to find the discount, or interest, rate that will make the stream of discounted earnings exactly equal to the cost of the expenditure. In this case, the values are seventeen percent (approximately) for investment A and fourteen percent for investment B. Although this process may take some time to calculate via a trial-and-error technique, the approximate outcome is shown in tabular form in Table 14.6.

The data in the table show that investment A returns about seventeen percent; investment B, close to fourteen percent. Clearly, therefore, investment A is the more profitable to consider if the case is one of choosing be-

Year	Project A Net earnings	Project A Discount factor 18%	Project A Present value	Project B Net earnings	Project B Discount factor 14%	Project B Present value
0	—$15,000	1.000	—$15,000	—$17,500	1.000	—$17,500
1	4,000	0.847	3,388	4,500	0.877	3,947
2	3,800	0.718	2,728	4,200	0.769	3,230
3	3,800	0.609	2,314	4,000	0.675	2,700
4	3,450	0.516	1,780	4,000	0.592	2,368
5	3,000	0.437	1,311	3,000	0.519	1,557
6	2,800	0.370	1,036	3,000	0.456	1,368
7	2,500	0.314	785	2,000	0.400	800
8	2,400	0.266	638	2,000	0.351	702
9	1,800	0.255	405	1,000	0.308	308
10	1,200	0.191	229	1,000	0.270	270
Salvage	500	0.191	96	750	0.270	203
			—$290			—$47

TABLE 14.6 Calculating rates of return on two investments

tween the two alternatives. If, however, the organization has a base rate of return of, say, twelve percent, then both investments, assuming that they were not alternatives for the same process, would qualify.

Many other methods of determining the desirability of an investment or of choosing between two or more alternative investments are available to the manager. These methods may be relatively simple but quick—and often accurate—payback systems based on the question: How many years will it take to recoup the initial investment? Or, they may be complex formulas accounting for inflation, tax rates, investment tax credits, different methods of financially depreciating assets (which, due to taxation, affect cash flow), and other variables. Very often, however, the simplest methods of payback determination are just as good rules of thumb for making decisions as are the more complicated systems. Here, however, we have attempted simply to outline the essential considerations in capital-equipment purchase: rates of return, the time value of money, salvage value, and opportunity costs.

Other capital-budgeting methods

SUMMARY

In this chapter we have introduced the subject of physical-resource acquisition. In particular, we have covered some of the criteria for locating facilities and plants, ranging from the attachment of the manager to a particular locale to considerations of markets, transportation, state and local taxation, building costs, land availability, political and social factors, amenities, schools, and the like. We also covered briefly the subject of capital investment and approached some of the considerations involved in equipment purchase, including the notion of the time value of money. We also explored ways of utilizing discounting methods in comparing alternatives or in determining whether a proposed investment meets a minimum return on investment.

Managers make other acquisition decisions, ranging from purchasing of everyday supplies, product components, and nonrenewable parts to negotiating for insurance, legal services, and the other intangibles that an organization needs. In all of these cases the manager is a decision maker, weighing the options, analyzing the facts, and making a decision on which way to move. Although there are specialized techniques to all of these acquisition problems, like the techniques involved in facilities location and capital acquisition, the basic decision-making model is still applicable and is one that conceptually, every management decision goes through.

DISCUSSION QUESTIONS

1 Define the following terms:

   a) single-facility firm   b) multifacility firm

   c) present value   d) discounting

   e) decision-making process   f) capital investments

   g) current expense   h) opportunity costs

2 Distinguish between the objectives and constraints facing a manager in locating or relocating a single facility of a firm and a multiplant facility.

3 List several behavioral, social, political, and economic factors that an organization should consider when locating a *new* facility, relocating an *existing* single-plant facility, and relocating a multiunit facility.

4 It is recognized that very often nonquantitative factors temper the decision to locate or relocate a new or existing facility, so that the least-cost decision is not always the alternative selected. What are some of the nonquantitative factors that could impinge on managerial decision making?

5 Describe the general managerial decision-making model.

6 What economic factors should be considered when making a decision to relocate or locate existing or new facilities?

7 How can the location-decision analysis tool as described in Fig. 14.2 facilitate the decision to relocate or locate an existing or new facility?

8 What are capital investments? Distinguish between accounting for a capital expenditure and a current expense.

9 Discuss the differences between financial accounting and investment-decision analysis.

10 Define opportunity costs. How do opportunity costs impact on the investment decision?

11 You are contemplating investing in a new automatic screw machine. It is estimated that this machine will generate savings in costs over the presently used method of operation of $3000 a year for each of the five years of its expected life. The machine will have no salvage value. The initial investment in the machine, including installation and setup, will be $10,000, and the firm's cost of capital is ten percent. Using present-value analysis, determine whether the machine should be purchased.

12 Compare the machine in problem 11 to one that also costs $10,000 but has a ten-year life and saves $1500 per year for each of the ten years. Again assume that the machine has no salvage value and a ten percent cost of capital.

13 Both projects have net earnings of $5000. Explain the difference in present value of the two investment possibilities.

CASE: THE TELEPHONE PURCHASE

■ The first thing Crosby did was to find out all he could about telephones. That was after the company executive committee had assigned him the task of investigating the company's system and reporting back with a recommendation within four months. He learned the difference between Centrex and PBX (Private Branch Exchange), the advantages of each, and the weaknesses of each. He surveyed all of the other executives in the firm to find out what kinds of features they wanted to see. Most wanted an operator intercept of calls rather than direct-in dialing to departments—that meant PBX—conference calling, call-on-hold capacity, call forwarding (enabling a person to divert his or her calls automatically to another phone in the system), dial-call pickup (allowing a phone to access another ringing phone), touch dialing, camp-on (allowing a caller to stay on the line of another busy extension, signal the busy party, and then be ringed through when the busy party hangs up), and speed calling (whereby a called number is stored in the system, and a touch of one short code number on the dial activates the whole number for the caller).

In addition, top management wanted a significant saving over the current system and data generation to allow checking against the telephone company's invoices and to accurately match toll calls to extensions. Under the system presently being used, as many as seven people shared one number, and there was no way to hold any one individual responsible for toll calls from that number.

Crosby met with the telephone company representatives. They offered a system with all of the required features, but the phone company could only rent the system. Each additional feature carried an increment in the rental fee, and that made the savings over the present system rather insignificant. In addition, the phone company was reluctant to change or upgrade the peripheral equipment such as handsets. The system did, however, offer all of the required features and did promise significant increases in productivity and convenience.

Five private companies offered to sell Crosby similar systems for one lump-sum price. Crosby's company would own the switch and all the peripheral equipment. These systems are called interconnects, since customer-owned main switches and equipment are tied into the telephone company's lines. As an example of the savings possible, the telephone company's rental charge on an extension limited service phone (e.g., five parties on one line having local-area dialing only) ran about $5 per month. The same piece of hardware could be purchased and installed for under $100.

Bids on a purchased system came in from the five companies. All of the systems were comparable—the same number of trunks, one hundred separate full-to-local-service extensions, connecting lines to a dictating unit in the secretarial pool, private lines to the company's other plant, etc. The bids ran from $65,000 to $95,000. Crosby decided that the $65,000 bid from Tele-Connect Corporation would fill the technical requirements. Now he had to sell the system to top management.

The Tele-Connect system was predicted to have at least a ten-year life span. It would probably be usable after ten years, but Crosby was predicting that more than likely, some new technology would come along in the interim. The expected availability of many first- and second-generation systems ten years hence meant a very low salvage value; Crosby estimated it at about $3000.

Also, the new system's data-generation capacity was expected to save significantly on toll calls, since they could all be pinpointed by specific extension assigned to a specific person. In addition, the switch—actually a programmable minicomputer—would allow the company to change classes of service without physically altering equipment. Maintenance service many times could be handled remotely via a terminal hookup with the servicing company's place of business. A diagnosis could be done at its location and some changes made remotely, thus saving service calls to the site.

Top management in Crosby's company dictated a fourteen percent return on all capital expenditures. Although Crosby was not able to factor in the increases in productivity and the greater convenience that the new system would offer, he did have all of the direct cost figures.

Costs with the old system on a monthly basis are detailed as follows:

1	Trunk line charges (including main phone on each trunk)	$ 687
2	Extension phone charges	639
3	Keyset charges	343
4	Toll calls (approximate per month)	1100
		2769

The proposed system would entail the following monthly costs:

1	Trunk line charges	$ 365
2	Private line to other plant	144
3	Service contract (after first year, when warranty expires)	75
4	Long-distance toll calls (approximate per month)	800
5	Operator (two-thirds time)	380
		1764

In addition, the company would receive in the first year an investment tax credit of ten percent of the purchase price, or $6500.

"Now the key question becomes," thought Crosby, "whether or not we go with the purchase." ■

Case questions

1. Was Crosby effective in developing his specifications for the new telephone system?

2. If you were Crosby, would you recommend the purchase of the system? Perform the calculation of the present value of the anticipated savings (given the 14 percent necessary rate of return).

3. Would you consider some of the nonmonetary reasons for the system of great enough importance to recommend its purchase under any reasonable rate-of-return condition?

SELECTED READINGS

Anthony, R. N., J. Dearden, and R. F. Vancil, *Management Control Systems,* rev. ed. (Homewood, Ill.: Richard D. Irwin, 1972).

Bierman, H., *Decision Making and Planning for the Corporate Treasurer* (New York: Wiley, 1977).

Brandt, A., "Evaluating Capital Expenditures Under Inflation: A Primer," *Business Horizons* 19 (December 1976): 30–39.

Brigham, E. F., "Hurdle Rates for Screening Capital

Expenditure Proposals," *Financial Management* **4** (Fall 1976): 17–26.

Butters, J. K., W. E. Fruhan, Jr., and T. R. Piper, *Case Problems in Finance*, 6th ed. (Homewood, Ill.: Richard D. Irwin, 1972).

Chen, A. H., "Recent Developments in the Cost of Debt Capital," *Journal of Finance* **33** (June 1978): 863–877.

Copeland, B. L., "Alternative Cost-of-Capital Concepts in Regulation," *Land Economies* **54** (August 1978): 348–361.

Cramer, J. J., "Nature and Importance of Discounted Present Value in Financial Accounting and Reporting," *Arthur Anderson Chronicle* **38**, 1 (1978): 46–56.

Dawkins, G. S., and R. S. Hoyle, "Accounting for Uncertainty in the Capital Budget," *Planning Review* **4** (July 1976): 16–24.

DeCoster, D. T., and E. L. Schafer, *Management Accounting: A Decision Emphasis* (New York: Wiley, 1976).

Fertig, P. E., D. F. Isturn, and H. J. Mottice, *Using Accounting Information: An Introduction*, 2d ed. (New York: Harcourt Brace Jovanovich, 1971).

Greenberg, E., W. J. Marshall, and J. B. Yawitz, "Technology of Risk and Return," *American Economic Review* **68** (June 1978): 241–251.

Horngren, C. T., *Accounting for Management Control: An Introduction*, 3rd ed. (Englewood Cliffs, N.J.: Prentice-Hall, 1974).

Hax, A. C., and K. M. Wiig, "The Use of Decision Analysis in Capital Investment Problems," *Sloan Management Review* **17** (Winter 1976): 19–48.

Hunt, P., and V. L. Andrews, *Financial Management: Cases and Readings* (Homewood, Ill.: Richard D. Irwin, 1968).

Johnson, R. W., *Financial Management*, 4th ed. (Boston: Allyn and Bacon, 1971).

Mayer, R. R., *Capital Expenditure Analysis for Managers and Engineers* (Prospect Heights, Ill.: Waveland Press, 1978).

Mintzerg, H., "Patterns in Strategy Formation," *Management Science* **24** (May 1978): 934–948.

Pekar, P. P., and D. J. Ellis, "Novel Approach for Introducing Risk Analysis," *Managerial Planning* **27** (July/August 1978): 7–12.

Pritchard, R. E., *Operational Financial Management* (Englewood Cliffs, N.J.: Prentice-Hall, 1977).

Pyle, W. W., and J. A. White, *Fundamental Accounting Principles* (Homewood, Ill.: Richard D. Irwin, 1972).

Reed, S. F., "On the Dynamics of Group Decision Making in High Places," *Directors and Boards* **2** (Winter 1978): 40–56.

Sauvain, H. C., *Investment Management*, 4th ed. (Englewood Cliffs, N.J.: Prentice-Hall, 1973).

Summers, E. L., *An Introduction to Accounting for Decision Making and Control* (Homewood, Ill.: Richard D. Irwin, 1974).

Tracy, J. A., *Fundamentals of Financial Accounting* (New York: Wiley, 1974).

VanHorne, J. C., *Financial Management and Policy*, 4th ed. (Englewood Cliffs, N.J.: Prentice-Hall, 1977).

Weidler, G., "Purchase or Lease," *Journal of Systems Management* **27** (June 1976): 28–35.

Weston, F. J., and E. F. Brigham, *Essentials of Managerial Finance*, 4th ed. (Hinsdale, Ill.: Dryden Press, 1977).

Wilkes, F. M., *Capital Budgeting Techniques* (New York: Wiley, 1977).

Chapter 15
COMMUNICATION

CHAPTER HIGHLIGHTS

In this chapter we study the topic of communication, particularly as it relates to managers and managing. We explore the communication process, the various sources of distortion in that process, and the effects of multiple trans-sending stations on communication effectiveness. We will then present some techniques of increasing effective communication and cover communication relative to organizational design considerations. Finally, we will discuss the informal communication network—the grapevine—and conclude with a consideration of increasing the formal organization's capacity for handling information.

LEARNING OBJECTIVES

1 To understand the communication process and its linkages.

2 To understand how distortions may enter the communication process through the sender, the listener, the medium, and as a result of differing perceptions.

3 To appreciate the possibility of increased distortion when sending stations are added.

4 To learn some of the steps to overcoming barriers to effective communication.

5 To be aware of the differences in efficiency and morale resulting from the wheel, chain, and free-flow communication network designs.

6 To understand the grapevine and how it may be handled by managers.

7 To understand how organizations have increased their capacity to handle both added volume and types of information.

CASE: GERALD FORD

■ Gerald Ford was the thirty-eighth President of the United States and stood for election in the campaign of 1976. During that campaign, he engaged his challenger, Governor Jimmy Carter of Georgia, in a series of three nationally televised debates. During one of the debates, the subject of the Arab boycott of American firms doing business with Israel was raised.

The boycott became an important topic during the campaign, as it was revealed that Arab nations were boycotting not only Israeli firms (which everyone conceded they had a perfect right to do), but also American firms that did business with Israel, that had Jews in managerial and directorship positions, and that did business with other American firms having business connections with Israel. Consequently, some firms were complying with the boycott by signing pledges that they would refuse to deal with other American firms.

During the course of the debate, President Ford announced, to the surprise of nearly everyone, that he was ordering the Commerce Department to release the names of firms that had cooperated with the Arab boycott. Under United States law, any firm that received a boycott request had to file a statement with the Commerce Department as to whether and how it had responded to the request. No law existed, however, that forbade a firm to comply with the boycott, although an antitrust suit had been filed against Bechtel Corporation on the grounds that its alleged agreement to exclude certain firms from subcontracting impaired competition.

President Ford's pronouncement caught everyone by surprise, including, it seems, the personnel at the Department of Commerce. Commerce officials were uncertain that they could comply with the order and the next day issued a clarifying statement that only firms filing in the future would have their names released. The rationale given against releasing the names of past filers was that the filing was based on expected confidentiality and that the new order could not violate past expectations.

Nevertheless, President Ford's use of the words "had cooperated" led supporters of stiff government action against the boycott to believe that the past participants in the boycott would be revealed also. Following the announcement, there was the usual round of complaint and clarification that accompanies vague Washington pronouncements. Commerce supporters simply wrote off the Ford pronouncement as a slip of the tenses, whereas boycott opponents looked on the Commerce Department's backtracking as a breach of promise. According to network correspondents, however, somewhere within the vast government bureaucracy, communications had indeed broken down. ■

INTRODUCTION

As we have seen throughout this book, managers deal with subordinates, outside agencies, superiors, other managers, and numerous other individuals in fulfilling their managerial roles. Managers may be called on to explain policy, give directives, place orders, evaluate others, sell a product or a service, negotiate a labor contract, draw up plans, buy a new plant site, settle a law suit, purchase raw materials, and a hundred and one other duties that must be performed. In all of those situations the manager must communicate—make his or her wishes known to other parties so that they will concur or understand completely. Thus the effective manager is also an effective communicator.

Communication is a process whereby one person transmits signals to another person; the process is effective when the second person or group comprehends exactly what the first one has transmitted and is able to act as the first person intended. Communication is complete only when the receiver receives the signal and understands it in the meaning intended by the sender. But there are many pitfalls to effective communication; there are many ways in which the message received by the second party can be changed from that intended by the first. Making communication effective, therefore, is something that every manager must be alert to.

THE COMMUNICATION PROCESS

The communication process is the mechanism by which a message gets from the sender to the receiver. The process consists of four major elements: the sender, the sensory media, the vehicle, and the receiver. The sender is the originator of the idea, the one who desires to establish a common thought pattern with the receiver. The sensory media may vary, depending on the sender and receiver location and the content of the message. Basically, the media could be sound waves (for oral communications), light waves (for visual communication), touch, and in some cases smell and taste. The most common senses used in communicating are seeing and hearing. The media vehicle could be the printed word (as in this book, memoranda, reports, telegrams, letters, etc.), oral communication (via telephone, radio, etc.), or a combination of visual and oral (motion pictures, television, etc.). The receiver is the person for whom the message is intended and whose thought patterns after the physical act of communicating should be identical with those of the sender. Figure 15.1 illustrates the communication process as we have defined it.

All sorts of breakdowns are possible in this process, and these breakdowns can disrupt and hence mitigate against the objective of effective communication being achieved. We call those breakdowns distortions, and they can originate in any part of the communication process.

Distortions

Distortions are those elements which either interrupt the communication process or effectively stifle the objective of commonality on the part of sender

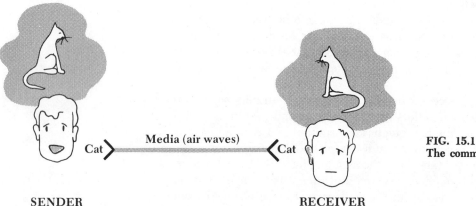

Media (air waves)

Cat

Cat

FIG. 15.1
The communication process.

SENDER

RECEIVER

and receiver. These distortions can arise with the sender, within the media or the vehicle, or on the part of the listener.

Sender distortions   Distortions on the part of the sender are often unintentional except when the sender is deliberately trying to distort the meaning of his or her communication to the listener. Let us examine some of the specifics of sender distortion.

1 *Words:* At one time, according to an old story, a professor was asked by a rather marginal student to write a letter of recommendation to a prospective employer. The professor, a kindly gentleman, did not want to say no to the student, so he agreed to write the letter. When he sat down in his study, however, he realized what a quandary he was in. If he wrote a deprecating

- Words
- Actions
- Pictures
- Numbers
- Marginal listening
- Evaluative listening
- Static
- Misprints
- Interruptions
- Perceptions

**Sources of distortion
in communication**

letter, the student would not get the job; if he wrote a praising letter, the student might get the job, fail at it, and reflect badly on his recommender and his school. So the professor (being the brilliant type) wrote the following note:

Dear Mr. Smith:

Johnny Jones has asked that I write a letter of recommendation to you in support of his application for a position with your firm.

Jones was a student in my course during the past semester, and I know his capabilities quite well. I cannot recommend Mr. Jones to you too highly. He is quite a young man.

Sincerely,

Professor Alexander Brown

Read Professor Brown's last two sentences very carefully. Does he mean to say that Johnny Jones is such a superlative student that words cannot convey his high opinion of Jones? Or do they mean that Professor Brown cannot give a very good recommendation of Jones? Professor Brown obviously had a motive for his confusing communication to Mr. Smith, and it worked. But at other times the motive may not be so conscious. Words have multiple meanings, and the sender had best be sure of what she or he is trying to say before using a word with multiple meanings. If your boss says to you, "Let's try it," are you to go full speed ahead, or are you to first test the idea out in some limited way to see if it succeeds?

Words such as *better, poorer, square, round,* and *color words* all have multiple meanings and may need further explanation if they are used. Managers who work in marketing or finance should be particularly accurate in their communications. Marketing executives must keep the firm from entanglements with government agencies, such as the Federal Trade Commission and the Federal Communications Commission, and various private consumer-protection groups on charges of false advertising or misleading promotion. Finance executives face the same situation with the Securities and Exchange Commission in the marketing of securities and the releasing of corporate financial operations data.

2 *Actions:* The physical actions of the sender often communicate as much as or more than the verbal communication. The same is true for the receiver. Nonverbal communication can alter the meaning of a message, reinforce the meaning of a message, or create a state of confusion on the part of the receiver or the sender. Activities of the receiver can confuse the sender as to the effectiveness of the communications.

Individuals often express themselves physically through hand gestures, facial expressions, and eye movements. The receiver who is given the news of a promotion verbally from a superior who frowns while delivering the glad tidings is likely to get the impression that the superior does not really endorse the promotion. Similarly, the contract agreement accompanied by a sigh of exasperation is likely to raise doubts as to the willingness of the signer to enthusiastically carry out the terms of the contract.

Just as often, the receiver gives misleading nonverbal symbols. Most instructors of classes can relate stories of lecturing to a group of actively nodding students who then turn around and perform miserably on an examination on the material of the lecture. By the same token, the listener who seems to be dozing may in fact be listening, enraptured, or may actually be dozing.

The actions of a sender may signal after or before the verbal communicating that the communicator is not serious or does not really believe in his or her communication. For example, a sender who orders employees to obey the law and then proceeds to do something illegal will obviously communicate more by his or her actions than by the words. In one of the biggest antitrust cases in history, testimony revealed that the subordinates knew that the price fixing had been going on for years—and that the bosses had been part of it—despite policy statements requiring compliance with the antitrust laws and no collusive price fixing with competitors.* Actions, in this case, spoke louder than words.

Finally, if positive action to reinforce verbal communications is truly meant as part of the communication package, those actions, to be effective in communicating, must be believable. Some of television's funniest moments occur in the advertisements in which a product is supposed to perform as expected and does (often by some miracle), or a consumer is supposed to agree that the product, in comparison to others, is the best and does agree. But the listener to the commercial always has the nagging question as to how many times the test was performed before the product or the consumer performed as expected, or how many negative endorsements were thrown out.

3 *Pictures:* A picture is not worth a thousand words if it communicates the wrong message. Usually a picture is accompanied by words, but pictures, diagrams, cartoons, and other types of visual vehicles are often confusing or misleading if they are not carefully explained. Graphs can be distorted so as to totally obscure the meaning. For example, the scale on graphs can be altered so that a ten percent increase in sales can be made to look astronomical or unusually tiny. In Figure 15.2, the two graphs show identical results, but the gradations on the axes will yield trend lines that are vastly different to

---

* This case was the Electrical Manufacturers' price conspiracy. *See* Clarence C. Walton and Frederick W. Cleveland, Jr., *Corporations on Trial: The Electric Cases* (Belmont, Calif.: Wadsworth, 1964); *see also* U.S. Congress, Senate, Committee on the Judiciary, Subcommittee on Antitrust and Monopoly, *Administrative Prices*, 87th Cong., 1st session, 1961, Parts 27 and 28.

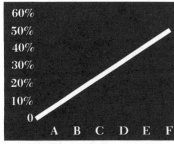

FIG. 15.2
Two graphs showing the
same results.

the perception of the viewer. Figure 15.2(a) will be perceived as the high-growth rate; Fig. 15.2(b), as the low-growth rate.

Similarly, with the illustration pictured below, if people are asked to answer which of the two lines is longer, (a) or (b), most would say (b). In fact, however, the length of the two lines is identical. The difference is an optical illusion, very easy to create with the use of pictures.

Camera angles of controversial plays in sports events often misleadingly show a possible error on the part of the game official, and television commentators take great joy in building up the viewers' suspicions by replaying the scene over and over again. Other pictures, however, taken from different angles, show the plays in different perspectives—often verifying the judgment of the officials calling the play.

In essence, the use of pictures to communicate can be deceiving—misleading (either purposely or by mistake)—and their use may lead to incomplete communication or erroneous communication. The objective of effective communication, by contrast, is to create like minds on the parts of the sender and the receiver.

4 *Numbers:* Mathematics is often called the most precise language, and supporters of increased quantification urge the greater use of the more pre-

cise symbolism of mathematics. Few people, however, understand the sophisticated techniques of quantitative analysis, so the communicator is often called on to reduce such mathematics to words. And in doing so, the communicator creates greater confusion and sometimes downright chicanery.

The mean of a distribution is often used as a quantitative indicator. For example, "On the average, people watch television twenty-two hours a week." But that average may be of a group that ranges from zero hours of watching to more than one hundred hours per week. What good is the average as an indicator for the receiver of that message? Without standard deviations or some indicator of the range of the continuum from which the average was drawn, the communication is distorted. Some wag once commented that a person could place one hand in the oven of a hot stove and the other in the freezer compartment of a refrigerator, but on the average be quite comfortable.

Yet with sophisticated receivers, the use of numbers and quantitative symbols is probably the most accurate method of communicating, since it eliminates the imprecision often associated with words and pictures.

Listening   The listener can be a source of disruption in a communications network. As we already have noted, the listener's actions can often communicate complete understanding, when in fact such understanding is yet to occur or may never occur. But listeners can affect complete communication in other ways as well.

Listening techniques can be categorized into three types: marginal, evaluative, and projective. *Marginal listening* takes place when the listener is thinking of some other subject or occasion while the sender is attempting to communicate. Perhaps marginal listening occurs because another communication is coming from another source. But often the listener is contemplating another problem, perhaps personal, when the communication is being sent. Under such conditions of marginal listening, at best only part of the message being sent is being received and hence is effective. And receiving only part of a message may be the mechanism to superdistort the original intent of the sender. In essence, receiving part of a message may be worse than receiving none of it at all.

Evaluative listening can also cause problems. Evaluative listening occurs when the receiver tries to combat the sender or argue against the sender's message. Rather than trying to understand the message, the receiver loses contact with much of the message by preparing rebuttals and counterarguments to the sender. Evaluative listening is often indicated when the listener continually interrupts the sender with "but . . . but" and similar attempts to get into the conversation.

The most effective type of listening is called *projective listening*. Under this condition, the receiver attempts to project himself or herself into the situation and state of mind of the sender, seeking to hear all of the message, understand its content, and understand the context in which the message was sent. Often called an effective listener, the projective receiver does not attempt to rebut the sender or allow his or her attention span to falter in relation to the sender and the message. Although projective listening does not automatically guarantee that communication between sender and receiver will be complete, it does eliminate one source of distortion in the communication process.

Media and vehicle noise   Mechanical breakdowns, static, misprints, erasures, and interruptions of all sorts are all sources of distortion in a communication process. One can readily imagine watching a television broadcast and losing the audio portion. Unless the listener is capable of lipreading, the essence of the message will have been lost in the breakdown. Such is the case with media or vehicle noise; these often necessitate the receiver's having to guess what was said or to ask the sender to repeat the substance of the message. Sometimes the latter is impossible. Often, in critical situations, however, such as military or police organizations, receivers are required to acknowledge receipt of the message by repeating the substance of the message just received.

Perceptual distortions   Distortions can result simply because the sender and the receiver live in different worlds or contexts and perceive issues differently. For example, for a New Englander to send the word "tree" to a South Sea Islander might be an insufficient communication, since the New Englander's perception of a tree is an oak, maple, or fir tree, whereas the South Sea Islander may perceive a tree as a palm or other tropical variety. Cultural differences, religious differences, nationality differences, and those many things which go into making up an individual's milieu will all contribute to perceptual distortion.

This problem is particularly acute in the area of international business. In the Filtco, Belgium, case (Chapter 6) a European angered his American counterparts by announcing at a meeting that it is "five minutes before twelve." The Americans took offense, but to the European the words simply meant that it was time to reach a decision. In other cases the use of American slang, for example, which may be perfectly understandable in an American context, would be completely out of place and even impolite in a foreign context.

Other instances of perceptual distortion relate to the sensitivities of the listeners. If the listeners are used to being asked to discuss a situation and cover all sides of an argument and are inclined to be sympathetic to hearing all parties, the person who comes on hard—the "heavy"—will immediately touch raw nerves because of the perception that the speaker is not in tune with the dynamics of the group being addressed. The reverse is possible also. One company had a sales force that was used to being told what to do by the owner, and the salespeople responded to his orders with considerable dispatch. When the owner died, the new manager told the salespeople to plan their own routes as well as to execute them. The receivers of that message were perplexed. Their perceptions of the manager and of his and their functions were a great deal different from those of the manager. It took two years to change those perceptions.

Communication with multiple sending stations

Messages often must pass through multiple sending stations before reaching the intended receiver. An example of such a network is pictured in Fig. 15.3; here the message comes through with the same meaning as intended by the original sender. However, distortions may often be multiplied when more transsending stations are added to the message network.

Originating
station

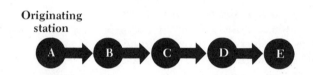

FIG. 15.3
Multiple sending stations in
a communication network.

Send 1.8 million barrels
of heavy crude
to Bayonne Refinery

Ship 1.8 million barrels
of heavy crude
to Bayonne Refinery

Inadvertent or conscious distortion along with the biases of various senders can enter into the process at any one of the stations. Such an opportunity or situation can exist in the chain of command of a formal organization (see Fig. 15.4). Suppose that the company in Fig. 15.4 is conducting market research on product X, a new product being test-marketed in a limited area. The president of the company has asked for a report of the status of the project. The people in the field may be having much difficulty with the administration of the questionnaire and will communicate these problems when asked by the project director. The manager of market research may be told that although there are problems with the questionnaire, they should be resolved by the project staff. The vice-president of marketing may then be told by the director of market research that the project is coming along, and the president, in turn, may be told that the project is going well and will be completed on schedule.

In fact, however, the project may be in deep trouble because of the faulty questionnaire, but by the time the original message gets to the top of the organization, the distortion created by the perceptions of the various senders added to the distortions in words, media, and listener has altered

FIG. 15.4
Chain of command for
survey on product X.

the entire content of the message. The communication, in essence, has been rendered completely inaccurate.

The problem in the opening vignette could possibly be the result of too many middle stations in the transmission process. The route from the President to the responsible bureau in the Commerce Department is long, and the possibility of a message's becoming distorted or indeed lost might account for some of the surprise in Commerce over the President's announcement. This assumes, of course, that the President didn't just offer a spur of the moment bit of campaign rhetoric, but had planned the announcement well in advance and had set the wheels of implementation in motion.

One instrument used by many companies in training for communication is the rumor clinic. The rumor clinic is designed to show the effects of perceptions and biases on a message as it passes through the various stations of a communications network and can also demonstrate other types of technical distortion. One group of seven or eight people is sent out of the room. The trainer calls one member into the room and shows him or her a picture; the second member is called in, and the first is asked to tell the second what was seen in the picture. A third member is called, and the second relates the story told by the first member. The fourth member is then told the story by the third, and so on until the last member has heard the story. The entire group is then shown the picture. Generally, the final story has completely altered the picture's content, reflecting the perceptions, biases, and distortions of the group members as well as their faulty memories.

One picture commonly used in a rumor clinic shows a white man brandishing a knife in a subway car while he holds up the passengers, among whom are a well-dressed black man and his wife. In several sessions with this picture, the end result has often been a reversal of black and white roles and frequently a movement from the subway car to a dining car to a fancy restaurant. Any picture with some degree of controversial subject matter will find a ready subject for the rumor clinic.

The objective of the rumor clinic is to show the increased biases and distortion in a message sent through multiple stations. And a rumor is often not far removed from the distortions in verbal messages transmitted within organizations. In essence, the verbal communications which took place as a message was passed from the marketing research project group to the president of the corporation were not that much different, conceptually, from the system engaged in between the first and eighth members of the rumor clinic.

Overcoming barriers to effective communication

In this chapter we have examined the communication process and the barriers (or distortions) mitigating against effective or complete communication. Our task now is to explore how the manager might overcome some of those distortions.

As a first step, the sender must have a clear understanding of the subject matter that he or she is attempting to communicate; then the sender must develop a clear articulation of that subject matter. This means that the sender must define terms that are likely to be missed, misconstrued, or misinterpreted. Some receivers have a tendency to ignore terms and concepts that they cannot understand, and it is the sender's obligation to reduce this possibility to a minimum. This can be done by using examples and in some cases by oversimplifying the attempted message. For example, most product advertising copy is aimed at recipients with a maximum of an eighth-grade education or equivalent. Although such copy is often belittled and ridiculed by individuals with higher intellectual and educational experiences, the advertiser knows, through literally tons of research data, that the material is at least understandable to an overwhelming number of receivers, because the eighth-grade level of education coincides closely with the world to which the message is being communicated.

- Have a clear understanding of the subject matter.
- Develop a clear articulation of the subject matter.
- Encourage questions and requests for clarification.
- Don't ridicule a confused receiver.
- Be concise; don't overload the reader or listener.
- Limit communication and information to that necessary for effective performance.

Steps to effective communication

Second, the effective communicator will encourage questions and requests for clarification in order to minimize the effects of any distraction. The receiver who is unsure of what is being communicated should be encouraged to understand before acting on the basis of the communication. All too often, a receiver will be embarrassed at not knowing the definition of a term or the meaning of a concept and hence will remain silent for fear of exposing his or her ignorance. Those receivers should be encouraged to seek clarification, with no ridicule or downgrading following their requests. This calls for some degree of sensitivity on the part of the communicator and the avoidance of such common responses as: "Oh, that's so simple" or "Come on now, you can't be serious in asking that question."

Third, as much precision as possible should be encouraged; conciseness often forces the sender to be more precise. Some organizations and managers limit any written communication to one page or less and any report to five pages or less in an attempt to encourage conciseness in form and precision in presentation. This practice forces managers to be as crisp and as definite as possible. The danger in this practice, however, is that the manager will not fully explain the intent of the message and will therefore gloss over crucial concepts and definitions. But communications often suffer from overkill, and the practice of limiting the size of the presentation has the virtue of reducing the excess verbiage.

Finally, organizations usually seek to limit the amount of information and reading to which a manager has access to only that necessary for effective and efficient performance on the job. The very essence of formal organization structure, with its various quotients of centralization and decentralization, is a breakdown of both operative and administrative tasks. Not all communications are addressed to all managers, because not all managers need to know all the information to perform their own particular tasks. Experiments have demonstrated that communication networks limiting communication flow and information availability do have an effect on productivity (and an obverse effect on morale), with different types of structures effective for different tasks.

COMMUNICATION AND ORGANIZATION DESIGN

The experimenters mentioned in the previous paragraph focused on three basic organizational designs: the wheel, the free form of organization, and the chain.* These types of organizational design are illustrated in Fig. 15.5.

* Alex Bavelas, "Communication Patterns in Task-Oriented Groups," *Journal of Acoustical Society of America* 22 (1950): 725–730; also Harold Guetzkow and Herbert A. Simon, "The Impact of Certain Communication Nets upon Organization and Performance in Task-Oriented Groups," *Management Science* 1, 3 and 4 (April/July 1955): 233–250.

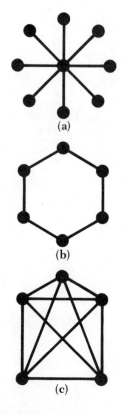

FIG. 15.5
Alternative communication network designs: (a) wheel; (b) chain; (c) free flow.

The wheel (Fig. 15.5a) is illustrative of the organizational design whereby five subordinates report to one manager; it is, in fact, the basic bureaucratic design. This type of organization was found to be the most productive for simple tasks in terms of speed and efficiency. But the morale among the participants in the wheel-type structure was lower than in the free-flow arrangement. The wheel results demonstrate that the limiting of information to each of the participants also limits their particular roles in the work process and contributes to each participant's having less time to digest and interpret extraneous information and more time to devote to the work involved.

For complex problems in which values are imporant and the need for cross-fertilization of ideas is necessary, the free-flow structure was found to be the better arrangement. The chain is frustrating and is not as effective as the wheel or the free flow in either of the work situations. The free-flow form was found to yield higher morale also.

Some critics of formal organization have asserted that the free flow of information is best for proper and effective personnel relations. But as the experiments have shown, for some tasks the information limiting formal organization is most effective despite the morale loss. Free flow is useful in think-tank types of situations. Many research and development organizations or R&D units existing in otherwise formally structured organizations are set up in the free-flow design, particularly if the units are composed of different professional skills researching a new product or new device. For example, suppose that in a company working on missile system development, management assembles a team of engineers, metallurgists, physicists, and other scientific and technical specialists to develop the particular system involved. The free flow of information among the specialists would be a necessity for the solution of the problem. Once the development process has been completed, however, the project is transferred over to the formally structured organization for production. The task team (free-flow organizational unit) may then be dissolved, with its members dispersed throughout the organization—some members into new task teams, some back into the units structured into the regular organization from which they were drawn. But for the particular problem at hand, which required the cross-fertilization of ideas and concepts, the rigidity of the formal structure was inappropriate.

THE INFORMAL COMMUNICATION NETWORK—THE GRAPEVINE

As we noted in Chapter 11, most formal organizations generate an informal structure, not necessarily sanctioned by management. This informal organization usually develops its own rules and norms and leadership patterns. But the key question for our concern here is the informal communication network that develops in most organizations.

This communication network, often called the grapevine, consists of the passage of nonofficial information through and to the members of the organization—generally by word of mouth. Often the grapevine operates with greater speed than the official channels of communication and is a particularly quick generator of leaks and rumors. Participants in the grapevine are often more likely to trust the truth of the messages they receive than those coming through formal channels. Indeed, if a message is circulated throughout the organization via the grapevine and that message is erroneous or false, the beliefs and perceptions produced by that message are extremely difficult to overcome via a corrected message.

Needless to say, the informal grapevine suffers from the same distortions —often in greater degrees—than the formal communication channels. But the participants in the grapevine make little effort to alleviate the distortive effects, and this adds to the woes of the manager trying to cope with it.

Many managers regard the informal organization and the grapevine as an evil and attempt to combat it. Management literature in the past often recommended that the informal organization be broken up through tighter supervision or transfer of the participants to other departments and areas. But the informal organization is a more natural and spontaneous phenomenon than the formal organization and does not easily disappear. Modern managers do not necessarily look on it as an evil, but rather as an interesting outgrowth of any formal organization that might be used effectively toward the formal objectives of the organization. Thus managers sometimes rely on the natural leaders of the informal organization to carry out managerial tasks (even though the formal design does not call for such a mission) and rely on the grapevine to pass along information that management wants disseminated. Since the grapevine is likely to enjoy higher believability, management's point of view may be more effectively promoted than through the formal mechanisms, be they directives or bulletins directed at employees.

Certainly there is a risk involved in using the grapevine of the informal organization. Some employees may resent being used by management, and the increased possibility of distortion might garble management messages. In the first instance, management might be faced with anything from minor resentment to a full-scale employee revolt. In the latter case, the garbled message may communicate something entirely different from what management even intended, and hence the behavior desired may be the opposite of what management intended. But a skilled manager will evaluate how and when the grapevine will be used and will avoid its use for especially sensitive information or for potentially explosive concerns. That same manager, however, will also know that the grapevine is not always totally at odds with management values or objectives and will use it and trust it when the occasion calls for such use.

INCREASING THE ORGANIZATION'S CAPACITY FOR HANDLING INFORMATION

Despite the fact that organizations limit the information available to a particular manager, that limitation is generally not to the volume of information or communications, but to the type or kind of information. As an organization grows, the volume of information which the manager normally receives or should receive for his or her particular area of concern increases very rapidly. Sometimes, however, with the advances in information-processing technology, additional kinds of information, which may increase the effectiveness and efficiency in decision making, become available, so that the *types* of information directed at the manager may be expanded also.

Fortunately, the advent of the computer and the increased availability of transmission technology have increased organizations' ability to furnish these added types of information and handle the additional volume of information as well. We mentioned in Chapter 3 that the computer has the potential of increasing centralization, since large volumes of information may now be transmitted from distant physically dispersed organizational units. For example, with cash registers tied in to a central computer and each item of merchandise assigned an inventory number, a buyer in the central office of a chain of department stores now has daily inventory and sales reports for each of the stores, broken down into totals for each product. These reports, called real-time reports, enable the buyer to make more efficient decisions more quickly. The communication is more accurate and more concise than the former hand- and person-developed inventory reports.

In some organizations, using a computer not only seems to have increased the flow of information, but also the organization appears to have discovered new types of information that the computer is capable of supplying. In essence, managers in such organizations might have to be concerned that staff units will have the computer generate so much information that, instead of increasing the organization's efficiency, channels become clogged and communication takes more time than that information is worth. The fact remains, however, that the computer and the increased ability to generate and transmit information have been boons to management attempts to increase efficiency in communications. Although organizations must always guard against overloading their managers with useless and extraneous information and communications, the computer has given them more and better basic information that is needed for decision making.

It is not our intent here to explore the world of computers and information-transmission facilities in great depth. We simply want to alert the aspiring manager to the potentials and challenges that such technology has for increasing the availability and accuracy of information needed for decision making. Computers *do* produce errors when the information fed into them is erroneous. But the speed and volume of information generated are almost always worthwhile tradeoffs.

Some human problems are associated with the computer. Individuals dealing with the computer-assisted organization often develop a dislike for the machine to which they cannot talk back. Many computer programs are too inflexible to handle the inevitable individual cases that come up. In essence, using computers makes the reverse communication for human beings very difficult. For example, I recently received in the mail my first overdue notice on a bank charge account. I ignored the first warning (computer-printed), and since a finance charge had already been assessed, I intended to withhold payment until the next due date. Five days later a second notice, threatening collection proceedings, arrived. My call to the bank with an explanation was met with assurances that the matter was taken care of. But five days later another notice arrived suspending the use of the card. My irate call to the bank produced the explanation that the "computer sends the notices out automatically" and more assurances that the account was current and that my credit ratings were not endangered.

Each of us can probably relate similar cases of Strangelovian encounters with computer-assisted organizations. When the receiver cannot communicate effectively back to the sender—i.e., the sender is an insensitive machine —problems of human relations must be attended to. The manager then must develop supersensitivity to complaints and human feedback. The costs of these, however, are often much less than the gains in speed and efficiency generated by the new information-processing equipment.

SUMMARY AND CONCLUSION

In this chapter we have covered communications as they relate to the manager and the organization. We explored the communications process, the possibility and sources of distortion, problems of organization design as they relate to communications efficiency, some managerial methods for overcoming the barriers to effective communication, the grapevine as a communications tool, and some discussion of the technology for increasing an organization's capacity for handling communications.

The manager is a communicator in most areas of administrative endeavor and hence must work hard at perfecting communications techniques and designs. Few of the other management tasks can be fulfilled effectively if they are not communicated well; hence the importance of mastering communications skills.

DISCUSSION QUESTIONS

1 Define communication and outline the communications process.

2 Explain the four major elements of the communications process.

3 Define distortion in the communications process and illustrate some types of distortion and their effects.

4 Physical actions can have the effect of distorting the intent of a verbal or visual communication. Explain how this might happen. Give illustrations.

5 Define the three types of listening—marginal, evaluative, and projective—and illustrate them with examples. How do they relate to distortion?

6 Detail the effects of a long chain of command on the communications within the organization.

7 What is a rumor clinic? How is it used as a training device? What is it supposed to illustrate?

8 As a manager, what steps would you take to overcome the barriers to effective communication? Be specific.

9 In communication experiments, what type of communication network for simple tasks results in the fastest and most efficient production? Which type results in the best morale?

10 Free-flow communication is suitable in some types of situations. What are some of those situations?

11 How does modern management react to the existence of the grapevine? Contrast that approach with older management approaches of handling the grapevine.

12 The computer and modern methods of information transmission are increasing not only the volume, but also the types of information available to the organization. What are some of the problems associated with this increased reliance on computers for information handling?

CASE: KITLON EXPORT EXPEDITERS

■ The letters arrived one or two at a time, but they kept coming in a steady stream. "Our order through your company was short by more than ten percent. We ordered 700 tons of 5-10-5 fertilizer and received less than 625 tons." Most of the letters ended politely, assuring the reader that the error was perceived as an honest one and asking for a refund, credit, or completed shipment. Some letters, however, threatened legal action.

"What happened?" thought Edward Kitlon. Kitlon, an undergraduate Spanish major at Great Eastern University, had gone on for an M.B.A. He spoke Spanish fluently and had decided to act as an export expediter and adviser for smaller businesses wishing to get into the export business with customers in Spanish-speaking countries. Kitlon would secure orders—generally through contacts with the economic attachés of the various embassies —and relay those orders to the manufacturers (who didn't and often couldn't sell overseas themselves). Kitlon would arrange all of the shipping and relay the papers back to the relevant plant. Thus the plant personnel had to be responsible only for loading the material onto the first link in the transportation chain and submitting invoices to Kitlon, who would handle payment and currency conversions. For all of these services, Kitlon received a fifteen percent commission. It seemed like a fabulous idea, but now after his first success—eighteen orders for 5-10-5 fertilizer, some 12,000 tons of it—Kitlon was justifiably concerned.

Kitlon called the plants and asked them to check the manifests. All showed that each order had received the requisite weight. Each plant also checked the records at the scales. Again, each showed that the requisite weight had been loaded aboard the railroad hopper cars.

Kitlon became so concerned that he flew to Panama City, one of the delivery points for several thousand tons. After all, these sales meant a $70,000 commission and probably the future of his business. He checked with the customer at the plant where the bulk was to be bagged for redistribution. The customer was to receive 800 tons, but claimed that only 700 tons had been delivered.

The customer showed Kitlon the scale records from the port authorities. He assured Kitlon that none of the material was stolen in transit. Kitlon produced his records from the railroad shipping agent showing shipment of 800 tons.

"I can't understand this," said Kitlon. "Are you sure your scales are accurate at 2000 pounds to the ton?"

"Pounds?" asked the customer. ■

Case questions

1. What kind of miscommunication (distortion) does Kitlon seem to have experienced?

2. How could it have been avoided? What special problems does cross-cultural communication create?

3. You are a consultant in international business; outline a set of practices, policies, and procedures for Kitlon and his employees to follow in order to avoid future communication problems.

CASE: SUSIE WATERMAN

■ After graduating from Kingsford High School in the spring of 1977, Susie Waterman took a job at the Carter Metal Stamping Company as a punch press operator. Susie was rather lucky, because there weren't many jobs around at this time in this medium-size New Hampshire city. She was one of only thirty non-college-bound seniors to be employed so far.

She reported to work on Monday, June 27, at 8:00 A.M., as instructed to by the personnel manager. She reported to Jake Deveneux, the foreman of the metal shaping area. Jake had never liked women in the shop. In fact, he had never liked breaking in new employees, preferring experienced metal workers. But the Carter Company had three major personnel commitments: one was to train some of the area's young people in order to hold them there in the city; another was to affirmative action; and a third was to cut direct labor costs by hiring less experienced employees. Deveneux's favorite hires, experienced metal workers, fitted none of these categories.

Deveneux led Susie to a punch press set up to put two holes into each end of a light brace beam for washing machine cabinets. Carter was a sub-contractor to the assembly plant of a major private-label manufacturer located near Kingsford. Deveneux showed Susie that each beam required two separate punches—one for each side—and he showed her where to get her material and where to deposit her finished products. He briefly showed her the safety devices on the machine and warned her about some of the hazards. All in all, he spent about twenty minutes with her and then left her. As he left, he mumbled something about all the rules around the shop that she would learn as she stayed on at the plant.

At 9:30 A.M., someone in spot welding and assembly yelled up that the braces weren't fitting correctly. Deveneux raced to Susie's machine, but Susie wasn't there; she had gone to the toilet. When she returned, Deveneux was fuming. "Where have you been?" he yelled.

"In the ladies room," she replied. "By the way, it's not too clean in there."

"You're supposed to ask permission," he hollered.

"Nobody told me that. Next time, I'll know," she replied.

Deveneux then asked Susie to show him how she was punching the brackets. She was punching with the wrong side up, making the holes one-eighth inch too far to the left. "That's not the way I showed you how to do it. Do you realize that you've just wrecked about $100 worth of stock? Here, let me show you again."

After Jake did about six brackets, Susie also did a few pieces, in front of Jake. Then he left, muttering about the incompetence of the younger generation.

At about 10:15, Susie noticed all the other workers leaving their stations for a coffee break, so she shut off her machine and left also. At 10:45, she was still at coffee; several of her co-workers were still there, but none were of the group that she had originally joined at 10:15. All of those workers had returned to their machines; the group she was with now had arrived at 10:30. Deveneux spotted Susie: "Waterman, what the hell are you doing here this late?"

"What do you mean? Don't I get a coffee break?"

"From 10:15 to 10:30 for your section; you don't get to share everyone else's break."

"Oh, nobody told me that. Next time, I'll know," she replied.

At 11:30, Deveneux came around to Susie's machine to check the counter. "You've done only 142 pieces in over three hours. You should be doing double that!"

"You mean I've got a quota?" replied Susie. "Nobody ever told me that."

After lunch, Susie went back to her machine. Deveneux was waiting for her again. "Where have you been? Do you realize that it is 1:45? How long do you think you have for lunch?"

"I went down to the pizza place with some old friends," replied Susie. "How long was I supposed to spend at lunch?"

"One-half hour," replied Deveneux. "We supply lockers so you can bring your lunch."

"Oh, nobody ever told me that. Next time, I'll know," replied Susie.

The next morning when Susie reported to work, Deveneux was waiting for her again. "Why didn't you clean up around your machine last night? You left little circles of metal all over the place."

"Do you mean that I've got to be a janitor too?" asked Susie.

"Hell, no, but you can't let a valuable piece of equipment get to look like a sty. It will break down fast. And what would happen if those OSHA inspectors walked in here and saw the area messed up like that? Susie, you don't seem too bright. Do you suppose you could do something right?"

Susie got her courage up. "Jake, you're not much of a foreman yourself. Why don't you and I sit down for an hour and you can tell me all those things I'm responsible for."

"What?" Jake replied. "Nobody ever told me that before." ■

Case questions

1. Evaluate Jake Deveneux as a communicator. Be specific about his strengths and weaknesses.

2. Might Jake's biases have contributed to the problem? In what ways?

3. As Jake Deveneux, how would you be sure that Susie Waterman knew all about the functions of her job and company rules? Draw up a specific list of the things you would do to ensure complete communication.

SELECTED READINGS

Bagley, C., J. Hage, and M. Miken, "Communications and Satisfaction in Origins," *Human Relations* **28** (September 1975): 611–626.

Balachandran, V., and S. D. Deshmukh, "A Stochastic Model of Persuasive Communication," *Management Science* **22** (April 1976): 829–840.

Berne, E., *Games People Play* (New York: Grove Press, 1967).

Blau, P. M., *Exchange and Power in Social Life* (New York: Wiley, 1964).

Coser, L. A., and B. Rosenberg, *Sociological Theory: A Book of Readings* (New York: Macmillan, 1969).

Hall, J. D., "Communication: Base It on Recipient Reaction," *Training* **15**, 4 (April 1978): 52ff.

Homans, G. C., "Social Behavior as Exchange," *American Journal of Sociology* **63** (May 1958): 597–600.

Hoover, J. D., "Increasing Human Potential Through Communication Effectiveness," *Supervisory Management* **22**, 10 (October 1977): 8–15.

Huseman, R. C., "Managing Change Through Communications," *Personnel Journal* **57**, 1 (January 1978): 20–25.

Keppler, R. H., "Behavior Training: Refining Communication Skills in an Industrial Setting," *Training and Development Journal* **32**, 9 (September 1978): 58–60.

Lawrence, P. R., and J. A. Seiler, *Organizational Behavior and Administration: Cases, Concepts and Research Findings* (Homewood, Ill.: Richard D. Irwin, 1965).

McDonnell, C. R., "Learning to Understand Your Trainees: Actions Speak Louder than Words," *Training* **15**, 5 (May 1978): 60–61.

Manis, M., *Cognitive Processes* (Belmont, Calif.: Brooks/Cole, 1968).

Minto, B., *"The Pyramid Principle: Logic in Writing* (London: Minto International, 1978).

Preston, R., and B. L. Hawkins, "Performance Appraisal: Evaluation and Communication," *Industrial Management* **20**, 1 (January/February 1978): 13–17.

Randolph, W. A., "Organization Technology and the Media and Purpose Dimensions of Organization Communications," *Journal of Business Research* **6**, 3 (August 1978): 237–259.

Rogers, E. M., and R. A. Rogers, *Communication in Organizations* (New York: Free Press, 1976).

Ross, J. E., *Modern Management and Information Systems* (Reston, Va.: Reston Publishing, 1976).

Russell, H. G., and K. Black, Jr., *Human Behavior in Business* (Englewood Cliffs, N.J.: Prentice-Hall, 1972).

Scheider, A., W. Donaghy, and P. Newman, *Organizational Communication* (New York: McGraw-Hill, 1975).

Sedwick, R. G., *Interaction: Interpersonal Relationships in Organizations* (Englewood Cliffs, N.J.: Prentice-Hall, 1974).

Strassmann, P. A., "Managing the Costs of Information," *Harvard Business Review* **54** (September/October 1976): 133–142.

Tsaklanganos, A. A., "Communications: A Managerial Myth," *Management Accounting* **56** (July/August 1978): 295–297.

Tushman, M. L., "Special Boundary Roles in the Innovative Process," *Administrative Science Quarterly* **22**, 4 (December 1977): 587–605.

Zajonc, R. B., *Social Psychology: An Experimental Approach* (Belmont, Calif.: Brooks/Cole, 1968).

Chapter 16
LEADERSHIP

CHAPTER HIGHLIGHTS

In this chapter we explore the concept of leadership, which we define as the process that brings about the transformation and integration of the human resources of the organization into willing, compliant and cooperative, if not enthusiastic, participants in the achievement of organizational purposes. We will present some theories and models of leadership, ranging from traditional to modern contingency and behavioral approaches. In addition, we will discuss managerial styles and organizational restructuring. Finally, we shall look at the phenomenon of informal leadership and its relationship to the informal and formal organizations.

LEARNING OBJECTIVES

1 To become familiar with the traditional theories of leadership, particularly the trait theory, the situation approach, and the emphasis on the followers, and to learn the problems associated with each of these approaches when used alone.

2 To understand the relationship of leadership and followership to need satisfaction.

3 To understand the relationship between leadership and power.

4 To understand the basics of the Fiedler contingency model of leadership.

5 To understand the basics of the Tannenbaum and Schmidt model of leadership.

6 To understand and to be able to apply Vroom and Yetton's problem-solving model of leadership styles.

7 To understand the basics of the Ohio State model and Blake and Mouton's Managerial Grid.

8 To understand the phenomenon of informal leadership and the powers and frailties of the informal-leadership position.

CASE: BILL STRATTON REPLACES SY GOLDMAN AT CHEMICAL DIVISION

■ Early in May 1977 Sy Goldman was promoted to Corporate Vice-President of Research and Development. Wednesday, May 11, was his last day at the Research Unit of Chemical Division, and the preparation for his going-away party was progressing at a feverish pitch, with beakers and test tubes being filled with all sorts of exotic concoctions.

Goldman would be moving to the Philadelphia headquarters of Consolidated Industries Corporation to head up and coordinate the research and development activities for all of the eight divisions of that multinational conglomerate. While Goldman was at Chemical Division, his operation had been judged to be particularly successful. New products and new applications of older products were continually coming out of the unit. About forty-three percent of the unit's output was put into steady and profitable production, a much higher figure than for most of the other research and development units of Consolidated.

Goldman ran a very informal shop. The chief chemists and other researchers were given almost a free hand in choosing promising areas of interest. Twice a year, Goldman would meet with each of them to map out research interests and objectives. If those interests were too out of line with the company's needs, Goldman said so, and the researchers switched gears easily. Rapport between Goldman and the group was excellent. He felt that by the very nature of the work and the fact that he was dealing with professionals who could be trusted to produce, a relaxed, nonstructured atmosphere would induce the most effective results for the unit. So far, the record of his unit had borne out that philosophy.

In mid-June 1977 Goldman was replaced by Bill Stratton, who had been "pirated" by Consolidated from Apex Chemical Corporation through a "headhunting" firm. At Apex, however, product lines were fairly well delineated, and research efforts were decided on and dictated from the top. Teams of chemists were structured into the prescribed research directions.

One of the reasons for Stratton's attraction to the Consolidated job was the free-flowing nature of the research effort there and the opportunity to branch out into new fields. He said that he didn't particularly like the idea of having research directions controlled by the sales and marketing efforts, as they did at Apex. Stratton, by the way, was a Ph.D. in Chemistry, but he also had an M.B.A. gained under Apex's arrangement with Southern State University for an evening M.B.A. program.

Right from his start at Chemical Division, Bill Stratton had some problems. First, many people resented that the company had gone outside to hire a new department head. Most people thought that Ed Riley should have moved up into Goldman's job. Riley had been with the company for twelve years, and many of his ideas eventually became "hot" products for the company. But Ed Riley had no administrative experience and had no advanced degrees. His application for the position, although he was not aware of it, was among the first to be rejected at higher levels.

Second, Stratton ordered all chemists and heads of research teams to submit weekly reports. He also started passing down to the chemists some periodically received reports and material from marketing research units within the company which detailed new-product possibilities and new product lines being offered by competitors. More than once, staff members grumbled about this new "mickey mouse" stuff.

Finally, Stratton began assigning projects according to what *he thought* was important. Indeed, in one case Steve Richards and Hal Grosser were pulled off a promising research project to work on a new application of one of the company's failing products. It didn't seem to matter to Stratton that four months of hard work on the original project went down the drain because the materials couldn't last while the chemists attended to their new assignment. Stratton just kept muttering something about "sunk costs."

All signs pointed to a decrease in productivity in the unit. Moreover, it was a wide open secret that several of the best chemists had their resumés out or were in active contact with technical search firms looking for talent for Consolidated's competitors.

Hal Grosser, who was something of the unit jester, quipped, "Well, at least Stratton can shut the lights out here when he's the last one to leave." ∎

INTRODUCTION

Perhaps the manager's primary task in implementing plans and activating programs and strategies is integrating the human resources of the organization into compliant and cooperative, if not enthusiastic, participants in the achievement of the corporate purposes. This transformation of human resources into willing participants in a cooperative venture is a complex process. Practiced by a manager or an executive, it is called leadership.

The whole area of leadership is a complex one, having drawn the attention of not only management scholars, but also psychologists, social psychologists, organization theorists, and political scientists. Studies have been ongoing for years at Ohio State University, the University of Washington, and other institutions of higher learning, as well as in business corporations and the armed forces, to try to isolate the underlying variables and determine the conditions for effective and successful leadership. What has emerged is an immense volume of literature and data and a generally accepted conclusion that effective leadership may be the result not of any *single* strength or condition, but of an amalgam of conditions particular and unique to the situation or the setting. In other words, effective managers may have to vary their approaches, or the organization may have to vary its job and task design contingent on the conditions existing in the situation at hand.

In this chapter, we shall explore the phenomenon of leadership basically in terms of the theories and models about its underlying bases. We shall review the research and literature, including some of the theories of leadership and the relation of that theoretical background to organization design and the various possible leadership styles that managers might develop. Such a discussion of styles and design, therefore, will be based on evolving research and experimentation.

TRADITIONAL THEORIES OF LEADERSHIP

Much of the early literature on leadership, and indeed much of the popular literature today, stresses the traits or characteristics of the leader as the chief determinants of effectiveness in leading. Courage, tenacity, endurance, fidelity, and forcefulness are among the terms often listed in the popular and business press as characteristics of good and effective leaders. Indeed, numerous articles contain contradicting lists between and within themselves. Other terms, considered in some of the more rigorous studies, include the ability to motivate, communication skills, delegating skills, ability to make sound decisions, decisiveness, wittiness, drive for success and advancement, social adaptation, and the like.

Some adherents to the trait theory hope that these characteristics can be developed in individuals, that they can be learned, and that aspiring managers can profit by studying existing and past outstanding leaders and then emulating their traits and characteristics. Other trait adherents believe that effective leaders are born, not made, and that no amount of training or conditioning can transform a Caspar Milquetoast into a Richard the Lion Hearted.

Many contemporary observers and theorists, however, do not believe that traits alone determine leadership effectiveness. The trait theories, these critics argue, seem to ignore too many other variables, such as the situation, the tasks involved, the relationships among diverse personalities, and other factors of a goal-directed environment. The theories also specify traits that are often held by nonleaders—followers—as well as leaders, fail to specify which traits carry the most weight, often list traits that are incompatible with one another, and make no distinction for or between the traits necessary to gain and those necessary to maintain leadership positions.

But a key problem of the trait, or characteristic, approach is that it doesn't seem to cover the many times when a seemingly ineffectual or ordinary individual rises to a leadership position for a particular instance (but then also might revert back to an ineffectual role once the crisis is past). President Harry S Truman, for example, although often pictured as a feisty, cantankerous individual, did not initially inspire many people with his capacity to lead. Yet he led his nation through some of its most traumatic episodes: the opening of the atomic era, the Korean conflict, and the firing of a national hero (General Douglas MacArthur) for insubordination. Many observers of leadership point to the literally hundreds of ordinary people who arise to lead other ordinary people to extraordinary heights—for example, the lowly ranked soldier who leads his comrades when officers have been killed or incapacitated, or the citizen who, without concern for his or her own personal safety, rescues or leads others from a burning building.

Given these limitations, other observers of leadership have looked to other bases or reasons for a leader's emerging. Some center on the situation as the most important factor inducing leadership. That is, some observers say that leadership is effective only because a situation arose which required a leader and that the individual who happened to perform the leadership role was simply in the right place at the right time.

But there are some serious weaknesses with this approach if it is unmodified by other factors. How does one explain the fact that in some situations in which leaders should emerge, none do—indeed, everyone turns "chicken"? A few years ago, a woman in New York City was attacked and murdered in full view of numbers of people. Not one of the onlookers would get involved; they would not help the woman while she was being attacked, offer her aid after she was attacked, or even call the authorities. Surely, that situation alone induced no leadership.

Nor does the situation approach—or the trait approach, for that matter —explain why followers follow a leader. Thus some theorists and students of leadership center not on the psychology (or physiology, as some theorists presumed) of the leaders or on the severity or volatility of the situation, but on the psychology of the followers.

Our conclusion in this section is that probably no one of these bases— trait, situation, or follower—by itself is the sole explanation of effective leadership. Recent work—often called the contingency approach—is determining that leadership effectiveness is the result of particular interactions of such variables as leader power, the particular task at hand, and the relationships existing among and between leaders and followers. In essence, each leadership opportunity is unique, and the challenge for managers is to be flexible enough to adapt and modify leadership styles to particular situations—or, conversely, to modify and adapt particular situations to existing and unchangeable leadership styles.

Before we turn to contingency theory and other modern approaches to leadership and the resultant styles of leadership, we should review the concept of individual needs and need satisfaction and relate that to leadership and followership. Following that, we shall relate the various concepts of power and influence to leadership.

LEADERSHIP RELATED TO NEEDS AND POWER

Leadership and need satisfaction

In Chapter 11 we discussed the relationship of needs to motivation. That discussion can also help us to understand that leading and following are often related to individuals' seeing some of their own goals being achieved by engaging in those activities. Thus followers may be motivated to follow because they have physiological needs, safety needs, or social needs which the act of followership will contribute to fulfilling. Individuals who attempt to lead or be leaders also do so partially because their needs, often higher-level ones, are fulfilled—or there is a possibility that they will be fulfilled—by that activity.

In addition to the concepts described above, the reverse may also be true. That is, individuals may be reluctant to lead and/or to follow if their needs will be better fulfilled by not participating in those activities. This may explain part of the reluctance of those New York citizens to become involved in saving a woman from assault and murder or of groups of soldiers in the Vietnam War refusing to go into combat even though ordered to do so by their commanding officers. Although we should also consider the question of power and authority in relation to this latter combat situation, we can relate compliance to followership to the promise of need satisfaction. Undoubtedly this promise was missing in the combat situation if the participants were willing to risk court martial and its penalties to avoid combat.

Leadership and power

In Chapter 3 we defined power as the reverse of dependency. That is, one person gains power by gaining resources (material goods, skills, rewards, etc.) that another individual or group does not possess but needs. We must now recognize that leadership—whether in the formal structure or in an informal group or organization—is to some extent a function of the power relationship existing among leaders and followers.

However, as we mentioned in Chapter 3, the power bases making an individual follow (or accept authority) could be of several varieties. They could be material rewards, physical coercion, respect for expertise, the recognition of legitimacy, and the fact that the followers might just like a leader and wish to associate with that person.

The classification of power or bases of authority into these types allows us also to project reasons why informal leaders sometimes achieve more followership than do formal, appointed, or elected leaders. Three of the bases of power—coercion, reward, and legitimacy—generally derive from either organizational positions or control of organizational resources. On the other hand, referent and expertise power bases—or friendship and influence —result from qualities possessed by the individual and do not necessarily bear any relationship to the position within the organization or the resources controlled within the organization.* These latter power bases are often the more potent power bases than the official bases possessed by the appointed manager. Hence the leadership of the informal organization, the controller and initiator of the grapevine, for example, is given more respect than the formally appointed task manager. (We will have more to say on informal leaders later in this chapter.)

CONTEMPORARY APPROACHES TO LEADERSHIP

A major contribution to leadership theory in recent years has been to extend the situational approach to include combinations of variables and then to study the leadership styles that are most effective under the various combinations of conditions. These theories are called contingency models; the use of a particular style of leadership is contingent, or dependent, on the mix of variables.

Fiedler's contingency theory of leadership

One of the key theories in this group was developed by Fred Fiedler.† Fiedler attempts to measure the propensity of a leader to use a particular leadership style by means of a survey instrument called the LPC questionnaire. Leaders are asked to rate their least-preferred co-worker (LPC) on scales with opposite adjectives at the ends. For example, some of the sets of terms are "unpleasant/pleasant," "distant/close," "friendly/unfriendly," etc.

Leaders who rank their least-perferred co-worker in accepting or favorable ways (high LPC scores), Fiedler terms relationship-motivated leaders; they are people-oriented and tend to be nondirective and supportive and understanding of subordinates. Conversely, leaders who rank their least-preferred co-worker in critical terms (low LPC scores) are termed, by Fiedler, as task-motivated leaders and usually stress demands, controls, etc.

Through his research into measuring and determining different leadership-style propensities via the LPC scales and then matching them to some situational variables, Fiedler was able to develop a model relating leadership style to group performance under varying combinations of situational conditions. Fiedler's model proposes that any leadership situation consists of three

---

* The sources of power identified as legitimate, expert, reward, referent, and coercive (which correspond roughly to the classifications we made in Chapter 3) are set forth in John R. P. French and Bertram Raven, "The Bases of Social Power," in Dorwin Cartwright, ed. *Studies in Social Power* (Ann Arbor: University of Michigan, Institute of Social Research, 1959), pp. 150–167.
† Fred Fiedler, *A Theory of Leadership Effectiveness* (New York: McGraw-Hill, 1967).

interacting factors: (1) the power position of the leader; (2) the task structure involved in the organizational unit; and (3) the relationships between the leader and the members of the unit.

The power position of a leader is the degree of influence inherent *in the position* that the leader holds, e.g., the leader's power to hire, fire, grant promotions, give pay raises, mete out discipline, etc. The task structure refers to the routinization of the job—the degree to which its holder follows set patterns and procedures—versus an unstructured situation—in which the subordinate has a high degree of autonomy to determine his or her task and schedules. Leader/member relationships refer to the degree of respect, confidence, loyalty, and trust the subordinates have in their leader.

According to Fiedler's research, the leadership style that will be effective will vary, depending on the interrelationship of these three factors. For example, in a situation in which the leader has a strong power position, the task is highly structured, and the leader commands respect and loyalty (called a favorable position for the leader), the leader's influence on the situation will be greater than the subordinates', and the effective leader can be a low-LPC scorer who will be able to play a stronger, more directive role. On the other hand, in a situation in which the leader has a weak power position, the job is relatively unstructured, but the leader/member relations are good (a moderately favorable position, according to Fiedler), a permissive, high-LPC, more relationship-motivated type of leadership will yield the most effective results. Low-LPC, highly directive leaders will be more effective in highly unfavorable situations consisting of poor leader/member relations, low task structure, and a weak leader position.

Figure 16.1 illustrates those relationships in the Fiedler model and further details all of the various combinations of the three factors relative to leadership effectiveness or ineffectiveness. To repeat, relationship-motivated leaders would have high LPC scores and be people-oriented. Task-motivated managers would have low LPC scores and be task- or output-oriented. The model shows the types of leadership postures that will yield the most productive results, given the various combinations of the three situational factors.

The Fiedler model can give several suggestions to designers or developers of organizations and managers. First, and this is probably the most difficult to implement, the manager can change his or her leadership style to fit the situation at hand. This is probably least possible for most managers to effect, since altering supervisory behavior styles is one of the most difficult tasks for a manager to accomplish. Second, managers can seek to avoid situations in which their particular styles will not be effective. For example, managers who are task-oriented would not be effective in situations with low degrees of task structure and weak power positions. Finally, the organization can be altered to suit the leadership styles of its managers. Jobs can be

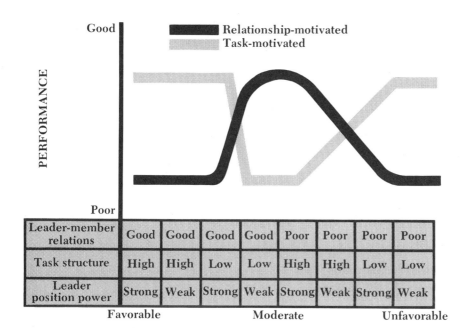

Legend
████ Relationship-motivated
░░░░ Task-motivated

Leader-member relations	Good	Good	Good	Good	Poor	Poor	Poor	Poor
Task structure	High	High	Low	Low	High	High	Low	Low
Leader position power	Strong	Weak	Strong	Weak	Strong	Weak	Strong	Weak

Favorable   Moderate   Unfavorable

FIG. 16.1
The performance of relationship- and task-motivated leaders in different situational-favorableness conditions. (Fred E. Fiedler, "The Contemporary Model—New Direction for Leadership Utilization," *Journal of Contemporary Business* (Autumn 1974): 71. Reprinted by permission of the *Journal of Contemporary Business*, University of Washington Graduate School of Business Administration.)

structured or unstructured as the case may be, and power positions can be altered to fit the styles of the executives involved in leadership positions.

It should be noted that the Fiedler contingency theory has not been without its detractors. A number of criticisms have been made of the methodology used in constructing the theory, especially the LPC questionnaire on which the theory is based.* Nevertheless, the theory has generated interest and research into leadership under differing conditions and propensities to differing leadership styles.

One of the earliest approaches to leadership that stressed variability of leadership style was contained in a classic article written in 1958 by Robert Tannenbaum and Warren H. Schmidt.† In the original version of their article, Tannenbaum and Schmidt recognized the interdependence of leader or boss authority, follower or subordinate desire for freedom of action, and the resultant leadership styles. The resulting practical and desirable leadership styles, as opposed to the possible ones, depend on three sets of factors,

Tannenbaum and Schmidt's continuum of leadership styles

* See in particular Chester A. Schriesheim and Steven Kerr, "Theories and Measures of Leadership: A Critical Appraisal of Current and Future Directions," in James G. Hunt and Lars L. Larson, eds., *Leadership: The Cutting Edge* (Carbondale: Southern Illinois University Press, 1977), pp. 9–45. Interesting rejoinders by Fiedler and a response to him by Schriesheim and Kerr appear in the same volume.
† Robert Tannenbaum and Warren H. Schmidt, "How to Choose a Leadership Pattern," *Harvard Business Review* 36, 2 (March/April 1958): 95–101.

which the authors termed "forces in the manager," "forces in the subordinate," and "forces in the situation."

Forces in the manager consist of the manager's: (1) value system, (2) confidence in subordinates; (3) own leadership inclinations; and (4) feelings of security in an uncertain situation. Forces in the subordinates include their: (1) need for independence; (2) readiness to assume responsibility for decision making; (3) tolerance for ambiguity (or strangeness); (4) interest in the problem at hand; (5) understanding and identification with the goals of the organization; (6) knowledge and experience to deal with the problem; and (7) learned expectation of sharing in the decision-making process. The third group, forces in the situation, include: (1) the type of organization; (2) group effectiveness; (3) the complexity of the problem itself; and (4) the pressure of time on the situation.

Depending on the manager's assessment of the relationships among those three sets of forces, he or she can select a leadership style that will be most effective. Tannenbaum and Schmidt, however, offer no guidelines for the managers to use in assessing those relationships.

The leadership styles are presented as a continuum with different gradations of sharing of authority and freedom among managers and subordinates.

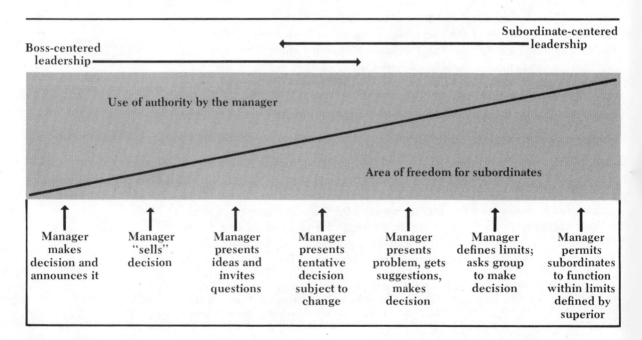

FIG. 16.2
Continuum of leadership behavior. (Robert Tannenbaum and Warren H. Schmidt, "How to Choose a Leadership Pattern," *Harvard Business Review* 36 (March/April 1958): 96. Reprinted by permission.)

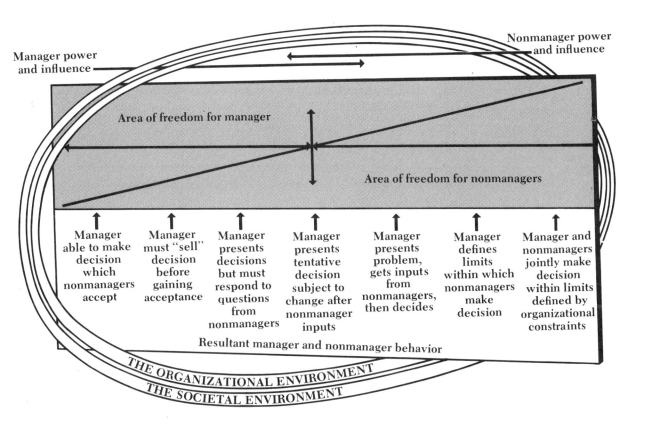

FIG. 16.3
Continuum of manager/nonmanager behavior. (Robert Tannenbaum and Warren H. Schmidt, "How to Choose a Leadership Pattern," *Harvard Business Review* 51, 3 (May/June 1973): 167. Reprinted by permission.)

The styles range from autocratic—the boss makes the decision and announces it—to subordinate-centered—the administrator permits the subordinates to function within limits defined by the superior. Figure 16.2 illustrates the original Tannenbaum and Schmidt continuum. Their revised continuum is shown in Fig. 16.3. The newer model accounts for the organizational and societal environments, but essentially the notion of a continuum drawn from the interaction of multiple variables is the same as it was in the original version.*

Victor Vroom and Philip Yetton have developed a leadership model based on problem solving, with different leadership styles geared to the particular

Vroom and Yetton— a problem-centered approach

* Robert Tannenbaum and Warren H. Schmidt, "How to Choose a Leadership Pattern," *Harvard Business Review* 51, 3 (May/June 1973): 162–180.

characteristics of different problem types.* The extent and form of subordinates' participating in the decision-making process, and hence in the sharing of the leadership, is determined by the following:

A. The importance attached to making a particular decision, e.g., whether the decision be of high quality

B. The information possessed by the leader

C. The extent to which the problem is structured

D. Importance of subordinates' acceptance of the decision

E. The probability that an autocratic decision will be accepted by subordinates

F. Subordinates' commitment to organizational objectives

G. Extent of conflict among subordinates over preferred solutions.†

Vroom and Yetton then propose a series of five leadership styles (see Table 16.1). These styles vary from autocratic—make the decision yourself (AI)—to shared decision making (GII)—a chairperson is willing to accept any group-supported solution.

TABLE 16.1
Types of management decision styles

AI You solve the problem or make the decision yourself, using information available to you at that time.

AII You obtain the necessary information from your subordinate(s), then decide on the solution to the problem yourself. You may or may not tell your subordinates what the problem is in getting the information from them. The role played by your subordinates in making the decision is clearly one of providing the necessary information to you, rather than generating or evaluating alternative solutions.

CI You share the problem with relevant subordinates individually, getting their ideas and suggestions without bringing them together as a group. Then *you* make the decision that may or may not reflect your subordinates' influence.

CII You share the problem with your subordinates as a group, collectively obtaining their ideas and suggestions. Then *you* make the decision that may or may not reflect your subordinates' influence.

GII You share a problem with your subordinates as a group. Together you generate and evaluate alternatives and attempt to reach agreement (consensus) on a solution. Your role is much like that of chairman. You do not try to influence the group to adopt "your" solution and you are willing to accept and implement any solution that has the support of the entire group.

* Victor H. Vroom and Philip W. Yetton, *Leadership and Decision-Making* (Pittsburgh: University of Pittsburgh Press, 1973).
† *Ibid.*, pp. 21–31. *Also* Victor Vroom, "A New Look at Managerial Decision-Making," *Organizational Dynamics* 1, 4 (Spring 1973): 66ff.

Problem attributes	Diagnostic questions
A. The importance of the quality of the decision.	Is there a quality requirement such that one solution is likely to be more rational than another?
B. The extent to which the leader possesses sufficient information/expertise to make a high-quality decision by himself.	Do I have sufficient information to make a high-quality decision?
C. The extent to which the problem is structured.	Is the problem structured?
D. The extent to which acceptance or commitment on the part of subordinates is critical to the effective implementation of the decision.	Is acceptance of decision by subordinates critical to effective implementation?
E. The prior probability that the leader's autocratic decision will receive acceptance by subordinates.	If you were to make the decision by yourself, is it reasonably certain that it would be accepted by your subordinates?
F. The extent to which subordinates are motivated to attain the organizational goals as represented in the objectives explicit in the statement of the problem.	Do subordinates share the organizational goals to be obtained in solving this problem?
G. The extent to which subordinates are likely to be in conflict over preferred solutions.	Is conflict among subordinates likely in preferred solutions?

TABLE 16.2
Problem attributes

Reprinted, by permission of the publisher, from "A New Look at Managerial Decision-Making," Victor H. Vroom, *Organizational Dynamics* (Spring 1973): 66–80. © 1973 by AMACOM, a division of American Management Associations. All rights reserved.

Given the possible problem *characteristics* (items A through G above), Vroom and Yetton in their model seek to generate the appropriate leadership *styles* relative to the existence or nonexistence of various combinations of the problem characteristics. Table 16.2 shows *diagnostic questions* to be asked relative to each of the problem characteristics. Figure 16.4 shows a tree diagram breaking out the resulting possible *problem types* when the diagnostic questions are asked and answered yes or no. Fourteen distinct problem types are isolated by the diagram approach.

Table 16.3 demonstrates that each path on the tree—or problem type—shown in Fig. 16.4 may result in multiple acceptable leadership methods or styles. Figure 16.4 itself, however, relates each type of problem to only one type of leadership style. Vroom and Yetton accomplish that through the application of an additional criterion, which they call "least investment in man hours." [*]

[*] Vroom and Yetton, *op. cit.*, pp. 37–38.

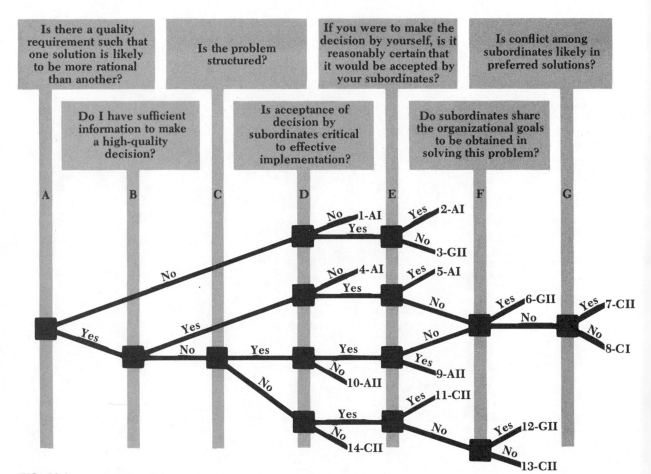

Is there a quality requirement such that one solution is likely to be more rational than another?

Is the problem structured?

If you were to make the decision by yourself, is it reasonably certain that it would be accepted by your subordinates?

Is conflict among subordinates likely in preferred solutions?

Do I have sufficient information to make a high-quality decision?

Is acceptance of decision by subordinates critical to effective implementation?

Do subordinates share the organizational goals to be obtained in solving this problem?

A   B   C   D   E   F   G

No — 1-AI
Yes
Yes — 2-AI
No
3-GII

No
No — 4-AI
Yes
Yes — 5-AI
No
Yes — 6-GII
No
Yes — 7-CII
Yes
No
8-CI

Yes
Yes
No   Yes   Yes
No
Yes — 9-AII
10-AII

No
Yes — 11-CII
Yes
No
Yes — 12-GII
No
13-CII
No
14-CII

FIG. 16.4
Decision and leadership style model. (Reprinted, by permission of the publisher, from "A New Look at Managerial Decision-Making," Victor H. Vroom, *Organizational Dynamics* (Spring 1973): 66–80. © 1973 by AMACOM, a division of American Management Associations. All rights reserved.)

Problem type	Acceptable methods
1	AI, AII, CI, CII, GII
2	AI, AII, CI, CII, GII
3	GII
4	AI, AII, CI, CII, GII°
5	AI, AII, CI, CII, GII°
6	GII
7	CII
8	CI, CII
9	AII, CI, CII, GII°
10	AII, CI, CII, GII°
11	CII, GII°
12	GII
13	CII
14	CII, GII°

TABLE 16.3
Problem types and the feasible sets of decision processes

° Within the feasible set only when the answer to question F is Yes.

Reprinted, by permission of the publisher, from "A New Look at Managerial Decision-Making," Victor H. Vroom, *Organizational Dynamics* (Spring 1973): 66–80. © 1973 by AMACOM, a division of American Management Associations. All rights reserved.

The Vroom and Yetton model, summarized in Fig. 16.5, is yet another example of an approach to leadership which emphasizes the multiple factors entering into a determination of the optimum of leadership styles.

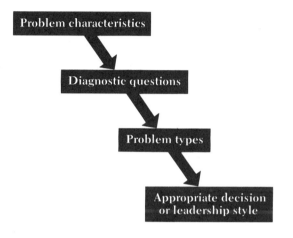

FIG. 16.5
Summary of sequences in the Vroom and Yetton decision model.

The Ohio State leadership studies

Research into leadership and leadership effectiveness has been in progress at the Ohio State University for well over three decades. One set of findings of this concentrated research effort identified two underlying dimensions of leadership behavior, which the Ohio State researchers term *initiating structure* and *consideration.* * "Initiating structure" has to do with such things as enforcing orders, maintaining standards of production and performance, and in general pursuing group or organizational production goals. "Consideration" involves treating subordinates as equal, looking after their welfare, and the supervisor's treating them with friendliness.

In the general Ohio State approach, productivity is not the only organizational output or objective. Coequal to that output are those of unit cohesiveness and drive (or pride), and the organization must seek some sort of balance, since an overstress on one objective—for example, productivity—could result in a serious decrease in the others, e.g., low cohesiveness, with further resulting excessive turnover, absenteeism, etc.

In general, then, the effective leader balances high consideration (thus meeting the organizational goal and the work group's expectation of outputs of cohesiveness and pride or drive) and high initiating structure (thus meeting the organization's concern for production). Figure 16.6 illustrates these two dimensions of effective leadership. As one moves out along *both*

---

* *See,* for example, Edwin A. Fleishman, "The Measurement of Leadership Attitudes in Industry," *Journal of Applied Psychology* **37** (June 1953): 153–158. *Also see* Edwin A. Fleishman and Edwin F. Harris, "Patterns of Leadership Behavior Related to Employee Grievances and Turnover," *Personnel Psychology* **15** (Spring 1962): 43–56. For an excellent discussion of the Ohio State developments through 1970, *see* T. O. Jacobs, *Leadership and Exchange in Formal Organizations* (Alexandria, Va.: Human Resources Research Organization, 1971), pp. 22–35.

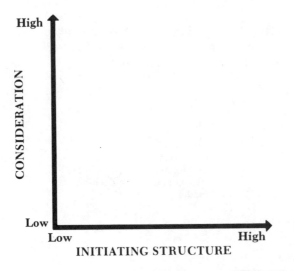

FIG. 16.6
Dimensions of leadership
behavior (Ohio State
research).

axes, one moves to a leadership style emphasizing higher structure and higher consideration—the balance process.

Further research, however, also uncovered the effects of the situation or "climate" on both leader behavior and group or organizational effectiveness and expectations. For example, if a leader's own supervisor expects him or her to show high structure to employees, that is often the kind of behavior the leader will exhibit. Other situational factors can also have an effect on the best combination for effectiveness in terms of outputs. For example, combat units, when not in combat, might expect and respond to high consideration and less initiating structure. When they move into combat, however, they often expect more structure and direction.

Any conclusion on the Ohio State University research, then, centers on the general proposition that effective leaders should optimally balance appropriate high degrees of initiating structure and consideration, but that climate or situation may have an impact on the utilized combination of the two dimensions of leadership behavior.

Blake and Mouton's Managerial Grid®

Another model, also utilizing two dimensions of leadership is the Managerial Grid approach developed by Robert R. Blake and Jane S. Mouton.* Setting the two major leadership behavior dimensions on the two axes of a matrix—concern for people on the vertical axis and concern for production on the horizontal axis (similar to the Ohio State factors of consideration and initiating structure)—Blake and Mouton established a 9-by-9 grid with eighty-one possible combinations or relationships of production and people orientations. Figure 16.7 illustrates the Grid concept, with five of the key positions illustrated.

* Robert R. Blake and Jane Srygley Mouton, *The New Managerial Grid* (Houston: Gulf, 1978).

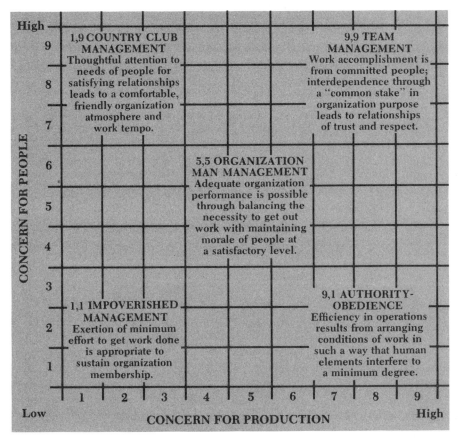

FIG. 16.7
The Managerial Grid®. (R. R. Blake and J. S. Mouton, *The New Managerial Grid* (Houston: Gulf, 1978, p. 11). Reprinted by permission.)

The 9,1 position (in the lower-right corner of the Grid) illustrates a leader who has great concern for production, but little concern for people. This is the "hardnose" who would suppress any conflict and any adversary positions. Diagonally opposite in the Grid, in the 1,9 position in the top-left corner, is the leader who puts the major emphasis on people and little on production. The manager who succeeds in achieving this position is a conflict smoother and a believer in harmonious organization. Managers in the 1,1 position are "freeloaders," contributing little to the organization or its people and who most likely should have been weeded out long ago. The center style (5,5) is termed by Blake and Mouton as the typical "organizational man"—"Don't push too hard, but don't be too easy either."

It is the 9,9 position, Blake and Mouton find in their research, that will be most effective. This type of manager has a high concern for both people and organizational objectives. The 9,9 manager stresses integrated problem solving, consultation, openness, confrontation of differences, and a cooperative effort toward the achievement of the organization's objectives.

The Blake and Mouton model, the basis for a widely used organization-development process*, seems to be at odds with some of the other approaches we have studied, particularly the contingency and decisional approaches of Fiedler, Tannenbaum and Schmidt, Vroom and Yetton, and others.

Blake and Mouton, supporting 9,9 as a one-best-way approach to leadership, argue, however, that 9,9 orientation does not rule out flexibility in application. Rather, they view the 9,9 approach not as a singular mechanistic pattern of leadership behavior, but as an *orientation* that encourages leadership "based consistently on sound principles of behavior used in creative and constructive ways that are (a) unique to particular situations, (b) unlikely to generate negative side effects, (c) optimal for problem solving and productivity, and (d) stimulating to growth and development toward maturity for those in the situation."† In essence, rather than formulating different styles, Blake and Mouton argue for adherence to an underlying set of behavioral principles as the one best way of managing, but with managers acting with versatility in the application of those principles.

FORMAL LEADERSHIP: CONCLUSION

Practicing managers are confronted with a bewildering array of contemporary theories and models to assist them in developing leadership styles or in perfecting their own approaches to leadership. Many of these models are contingency or problem-solving approaches proposing flexibility. The interested manager, however, can find much to assist him or her in all of the approaches.

But the fact remains that managers are not infallible, and it may be too much to credit them with very much ability to be flexible. Unless an organization is willing to commit itself to a maximum of organizational training and development—and the probability that such training will be successful or useful in achieving change toward flexibility on leadership styles cannot be assured—the organizational engineering approach in structuring managerial jobs may be the most effective. Under such an approach, tasks are structured and more power is added to the managerial positions if the manager's "natural" style is to be task-oriented. If the manager is by nature more consultative and democratic in style, less structure is built into his or her operation, and the power inherent in the position can be reduced. But the fact remains that it takes the truly excellent manager who can practice the often-stated prescription: "Different strokes for different folks."

* *See* Robert R. Blake and Jane Srygley Mouton, *Building a Dynamic Corporation Through Grid Organization Development* (Reading, Mass.: Addison-Wesley, 1969).
† Robert R. Blake and Jane Srygley Mouton, "Should You Teach There's Only *One* Best Way to Manage?" *Training* (April 1978).

Now we may be in a position to try to analyze some of the leadership problems at Chemical Division. What made Sy Goldman so successful and Bill Stratton so relatively unsuccessful?

Back to Chemical Division

Using Fiedler's model, we might say that Goldman, more than likely a high-LPC leader, would have succeeded. Leader/member relations were good, the task structure low, and the leader's power position not very strong. Under such a moderately favorable leadership position, a relationship-motivated leader, such as Goldman, should show success.

Stratton, on the other hand, probably was a low-LPC, task-motivated leader. When he stepped into Goldman's slot, one might have expected him to show less success than Goldman. Stratton's success would remain low if his relationships with group members deteriorated and he introduced higher task structure and strengthened his power position. Such a situation would still be a moderately favorable one, in which a low-LPC leader would show poorer performance.

Using the Vroom and Yetton approach, Chemical Division's research and development problems would have the following attributes. The division needs high quality; the manager did not have all the information; although task assignment is unstructured, problem-solving methods could be very structured (this attribute is fuzzy); acceptance of decision is relatively crucial to the department's success; it is not reasonably certain that autocratic decisions would be accepted; and subordinates seem to share in the goals of the organization.

Under these conditions, we might say that the leader faced either a problem type 6 or a problem type 12 (see Table 16.3), depending on our answer to problem attribute of structure. In both cases a decision of leadership type GII is called for, i.e., shared decision making, group evaluation of alternatives, and group decision making. Goldman came closer to meeting that type of leadership than Stratton did.

Beyond analysis via Fiedler or Vroom and Yetton, however, we might say that the abrupt change could have predictably led to problems. Goldman had developed one type of relationship (perhaps a 9,9) with his unit, and the members' routines and expectations were fairly well established. Stratton not only was an outsider, but also had been selected over the local favorite; then, despite his protestations to the contrary, he started initiating the very things at Chemical Division that he had complained about at Apex. The people at Chemical Division expected participation and the freedom to set their own goals. Stratton imposed goals and started throwing his weight about (perhaps a 9,1 on the Blake and Mouton Grid).

In sum, the Chemical case offers us some constructive lessons on leader/follower relationships. One might want to speculate on the results had it been Goldman with his leadership inclinations replacing Stratton instead of vice-versa.

INFORMAL LEADERSHIP

Much of what we have discussed so far relates leadership to the formal organizational structure and to formal managerial positions. But in addition, of course, another, very pervasive type of organization exists within every formal organization—the informal organization. The informal organization may be a loosely operating network, often called the grapevine, or it may be a series of tightly controlled, but not formal groups, related to one another through interconnecting links.

As we noted earlier, the informal organization is important for managers to know about, since its activities can be either functional—that is, contributing—to the formal organization's objectives or dysfunctional—antagonistic and destructive. In Chapter 11 we noted that informal groups have several characteristics, and it is useful to review them briefly here. Even though our primary focus is on the leadership function within the groups, those characteristics relate to the role and status of the leader. Informal groups have goals and purposes which, although not always evident to an outsider, are shared by group members. The group develops norms to guide behavior and communication networks, often called the grapevine. The group also develops some semblance of a structure, and certain tasks within the structure are assigned to or assumed by individuals. Finally, people in the group develop member-to-member affinity, and the group develops some degree of identity as a group.

The key characteristic for our purposes here, however, is that the group generates a leadership function. The key distinction between formal (or appointed leaders in formal positions) and informal leaders is that the latter hold their positions via their acceptance by the group rather than through appointment by management.* Hence informal leaders can change rapidly if the acceptance by members is no longer there, although experience has shown that there is surprising longevity among informal leaders.

Informal leaders are expected to articulate and to uphold the group norms and values and to communicate with other, outside groups. As a result, the leader of the informal group or organization may be the person who best knows the group's values and, according to observers of group processes, because of the dual role of articulation and representation, may be allowed within limits some personal deviation from those values.

The leader in the informal organization or group is also the focus of the information flow within the group and can mold group attitudes and activities; bring forth, introduce, and authorize new goals; and often educate new members. For example, after a formal training period for a new em-

* *See* Joseph A. Litterer, *The Analysis of Organizations,* 2d ed. (New York: Wiley, 1973), pp. 250–252.

ployee, the informal leader is likely to be the one who takes over to educate the new employee about the group-established rules and norms as opposed to the officially established and enforced rules and norms. If the group, for example, has agreed on a production quota for each of its members (often called a "bogie"), the leader often is called on to educate the new member on the quota—sometimes with some degree of threatened physical force. The production quota, incidentally, is generally established by the group to protect the weaker members of the group and to prevent management from raising the quota if it is seen as broken too easily. In many organizations a strong new employee can often break that quota easily and does so until the group pressure is applied.

In sum, some of the factors for effective leadership are the same for both the informal and the formal leader. But the informal leader's position may be shaky in that he or she will be eased out if group acceptance falters. The informal leader's total position is based on acceptance rather than on power. Yet since the informal leader can generally be very effective in moving the informal group in directions that either support or oppose official organizational ends, the informal leader might be a person for formal management to cultivate and rely on in greater measure.

SUMMARY AND CONCLUSION

In this chapter we studied the managerial function of leadership. We defined the function of leadership as transforming the human resources of the organization into willing participants in a cooperative process aimed at achieving organizational objectives. But the manager faces a bewildering array of information (and misinformation) about leadership. Our task was to distill some of the theories and concepts that might be useful to the practicing manager.

We first looked at the traditional approaches to leadership, which focus primarily on the personal traits and characteristics of leaders, then at the situation or the opportunity that allowed a leader to emerge, and finally on the psychology of followers. Each of these traditional approaches was found to be lacking as a complete explanation of leadership effectiveness.

We then explored and related leadership (and, incidentally, followership) to need satisfaction and power concepts. Next, we explored some of the more recent research on leadership, starting with Fiedler's approach—often called the contingency model—that relates two basic leadership styles to three interacting situational factors—the power position of the leader, the task structure, and the state of relationships between leader and members of the unit. Fiedler's model yields outcomes of projected leadership success, depending on the mix of those factors and styles. Such an approach also gives us some hints to effective organizational design.

The Tannenbaum and Schmidt approach is based on the mix of several factors—forces in the manager, forces in the subordinates, and forces in the situation. This model yields a continuum of management leadership postures with respect to relationships with subordinates' seeking decision-making opportunity.

The next model explored, the Vroom and Yetton approach, is based on the need to solve problems. Here the different leadership styles depend on various combinations of such things as distribution of information, probability of acceptance of decisions, conflict among subordinates over preferred solutions, etc. Again, several leadership styles are possible, depending on the mix of the factors.

Next, we covered the two-dimensional models—Ohio State and Blake and Mouton's Managerial Grid. Blake and Mouton related production-centered to people-centered leadership propensities and established a grid of eighty-one possible leadership styles. Concentrating on five basic positions, Blake and Mouton conclude that one of the positions—9,9—is the ideal leadership mode: the combination of maximum in people-centered and maximum production-centered orientations. The Ohio State research, however, also investigated the effect of "climate" on leadership posture and found effects from a leader's superior's expectations and other situational variables.

Finally, we explored the phenomenon of informal leadership and the leader in the informal organization and group. We determined that the leader is effective because he or she is accepted rather than appointed. But since the informal group does develop processes of its own, the leader of such a group does have functions, albeit probably less well defined than those of his or her formal counterpart.

DISCUSSION QUESTIONS

1 What is the trait theory of leadership? Give a well-reasoned critique of that approach to explaining leadership.

2 Relate leadership and followership to the concept of need satisfaction. As a manager, how would you use such a relationship?

3 Relate leadership and followership to the concept of power. As a formal manager, how would this relationship apply to you? As an informal leader, how would it apply to you?

4 Relate bases of authority or power to the types of leaders in an organization.

5 Fiedler's theory of leadership is based on three interacting factors. What are those factors, and how do they interact to provide a basis for leadership styles?

6 What are the "forces" that condition leadership styles according to Tannenbaum and Schmidt? Be specific.

7 What are some of the factors that determine leadership style in the Vroom and Yetton approach?

8 Explain Blake and Mouton's "Management Grid" approach. What five types of managers do they illustrate, and which one is defined as ideal? Why?

9 What are the characteristics of an informal organization? How does the leadership in such an organization differ from that of a formal organization?

10 What are some of the functions of an informal leader?

CASE: ANDY STENKOWSKI (A)

■ "Congratulations, honey, I'm so happy for you." That was Edith Stenkowski's elated response to the news that her husband, Andy, had just been promoted to foreman at Ajax Wholesale Foods, one of the largest food wholesalers in the Southeast.

Andy went to work at Ajax immediately following his discharge from the Army in 1955. He had been drafted right after dropping out of college, served in Korea, and married Edith immediately following his discharge. With few skills and needing money desperately, he took the first job that came along—as a sweeper at Ajax.

A wholesale food warehouse operates on two shifts, sometimes three, and, depending on the depth of product line, carries groceries, produce, meats, health and beauty aids, tobacco products, varying degrees of hard lines (housewares), and some soft goods (household accessories and sometimes standard clothing items). The operative jobs in the warehouse are few: pickers—the individuals who pull products off the shelves in response to customer orders; loaders—those who unload trailers, boxcars, and trucks and then reload delivery trucks; fork lift operators; helpers and laborers; maintenance personnel; and truck drivers.

Ajax's warehouse was unionized by the Teamsters, and over the years the union had narrowed wage differentials between the highest-paid jobs—truck drivers—and the helper/laborer category. After ten years of service, all employees were classified as truck drivers for wage purposes.

Andy Stenkowski had held just about every job in the warehouse. He took an early stint at driving, but gave it up when he found it boring. Not long after that, he qualified for driver's pay anyway under the contract. His latest job, and the one he had held the longest, was as a checker/receiver on the loading dock.

Andy is a popular person and gets along well with his work mates and his supervisors. He is a regular in the weekend poker games, bowls regularly with the company team, and he and Edith always go to company-sponsored picnics, socials, and dinner parties. At least three days a week, Andy goes with about a dozen of the men to a local bar for beers after work.

Andy was offered the job as a foreman on the day shift—Grocery Section B—when the incumbent retired. He thought about the offer for an hour when it was offered, although often in the past he had wondered how he would react to a promotion offer. He knew that he would lose some of his union benefits—e.g., his seniority would be frozen, his pension would stop growing, etc.—but on the other hand, he'd be making more money and might have a shot at moving into middle management. He called his wife, found her totally supportive, and then accepted the job. He was welcomed as part of the management team by the vice-president for operations, given a two-hour briefing about the job and his new responsibilities, was told to study the union contract, and was ordered to report ready to work in his new position on the incumbent's retirement date—two weeks hence. Meanwhile, he was asked if he would study the systems and procedures of his own foreman, so that the loss in transition time would be minimal.

Andy's appointment was announced in the company bulletin the following Friday. His co-workers *seemed* genuinely happy for him, and most offered their congratulations. A couple said, "I'm happy for you." When the day ended and it was time for the usual congregating at the local bar, however, one of the loaders yelled to Andy, "Hey, Andy, you're still going to have time to go drinking with our old friends, aren't you?"

Andy replied, "Yuh, why not?" But then at night, he thought some more about it. He mused, "Boy, with this new position, there are a lot of 'why nots.'" ■

Case questions

1. What types of new work problems, patterns, and relationships would Andy Stenkowski face as a foreman?

2. Use the general frameworks of Fiedler, Tannenbaum and Schmidt, and Vroom and Yetton to project the kinds of specific leadership situations Andy might find himself in.

3. What might you be able to project in terms of Andy's superior-subordinate relationships, his own power position, or the task structure within his unit? Might Andy be more successful by sharing decision making or being autocratic?

SELECTED READINGS

Basil, D. C., *Leadership Skills for Executive Action* (New York: American Management Association, 1971).

Bennis, W., *The Unconscious Conspiracy: Why Leaders Can't Lead* (New York: AMACOM, 1976).

Blake, R. R., and J. S. Mouton, *Making Experience Work: The Grid Approach to Critique* (New York: McGraw-Hill, 1978).

Bourque, W. L., *Leadership in Voluntary Associations* (Amherst, Mass.: University of Massachusetts Press, 1974).

Cohen, M. D., and J. G. March, *Leadership and Ambiguity: The American College President* (New York: McGraw-Hill, 1974).

Colvin, R. D., "Increasing Personal Effectiveness," *Learning and Development Journal* **32,** 1 (January 1978): 30–33.

Cowan, J., *The Self-Reliant Manager* (New York: AMACOM, 1977).

Fiedler, F. E., and M. M. Chemers, *Leadership and Effective Management* (Glenview, Ill.: Scott, Foresman, 1974).

Grayson, T. J., *Leaders and Periods of American Finance* (Freeport, New York: Books for Libraries Press, 1969).

Guest, R., P. Hersey, and K. Blanchard, *Organization Change Through Effective Leadership* (Englewood Cliffs, N.J.: Prentice-Hall, 1977).

Hennig, M., and A. Jardim, *The Managerial Woman* (Garden City, N.Y.: Anchor Press/Doubleday, 1977).

Herzberg, F., *The Managerial Choice: To Be Efficient and To Be Human* (Homewood, Ill.: Dow Jones/Irwin, 1976).

Hollander, E. P., *Leaders, Groups, and Influence* (New York: Oxford University Press, 1964).

Hunt, E. H., and K. Olmosk, "Power, Leadership, and Organizational Improvement," *Management World* **5** (November 1976): 15–16.

Hunt, J. G., and L. L. Larson, eds., *Leadership: The Cutting Edge* (Carbondale: Southern Illinois University Press, 1977).

Jacobs, O., *Leadership and Exchange in Formal Organizations* (Alexandria, Va.: Human Resources Research Organization, 1970).

Loverty, F. T., "Standards and Accountability: Managements' Missing Link," *Optimum* **9,** 2 (1978): 52–63.

Loye, D., *The Leadership Passion* (San Francisco: Jossey-Bass, 1977).

Maccoby, M., "Corporate Climber Has to Find His Heart," *Fortune* **94** (December 1976): 94–98, 101.

Peabody, R. L., *Leadership in Congress: Stability, Succession and Change* (Boston: Little, Brown, 1976).

Pollock, R., *The Leader Looks at Staff-Line Relations* (Washington, D.C.: Leadership Resources, 1961).

Richman, B. M., and R. N. Farmer, *Leadership, Goals and Power in Higher Education* (San Francisco: Jossey-Bass, 1974).

Salton, G. J., "The Focused Web—Goal-Setting in the MBO Process," *Management Review* **67,** 1 (January 1978): 46–50.

Schleh, E. C., "Handing Off to Subordinates: Delegating for Gain," *Management Review* **67,** 5 (May 1978): 43–47.

Schriesheim, C. A., J. M. Tolliver, and O. C. Behling, "Leadership Theory: Some Implications for Managers," *MSU Business Topics* **26,** 3 (Summer 1978): 34–40.

Shultz, G. P., *Leaders and Followers in an Age of Ambiguity* (New York: New York University Press, 1975).

Stogdill, R. M., and A. E. Coons, eds., *Leader Behavior: Its Description and Measurement* (Columbus: Bureau of Business Research, College of Commerce and Administration, Ohio State University, 1957).

Vroom, V. H., and P. W. Yetton, *Leadership and Decision-Making* (Pittsburgh: University of Pittsburgh Press, 1973).

Ways, M., "Hall of Fame for Business Leadership," *Fortune* **95** (January 1977): 117–123.

White, W. R., *Leadership* (Boston: Meador, 1951).

Whyte, W. F., *Leadership and Group Participation: An Analysis of the Discussion Group* (Ithaca, New York: New York State School of Industrial and Labor Relations, Cornell University, 1953).

Managerial Control/ Adaptation/Audit

The third major category of managerial functions mentioned in Chapter 1 was control/adaptation/audit. We will cover this classification in the four chapters of Part V. First, in Chapter 17 we will introduce the concept of control; the standards are assumed to be fixed, and the process or resources are assumed to need correction if necessary. Chapter 18 considers human responses to control processes. In Chapter 19, on adaptation, the goals, as well as (possibly) the resources, are considered variable. Finally, we close Part V with a chapter on the organizational audit, a device by which the managers of an organization periodically review all of the structures, processes, relationships, procedures, personnel, and even the purposes of the organization in a general effort to promote efficiency and effectiveness throughout. Chapter 20 also provides a review of the entire task of managing organizations.

Chapter 17
CONTROL

CHAPTER HIGHLIGHTS

In this chapter we introduce the manager as a controller. Applying operational control, the manager assumes that the organizational ends or standards are fixed, or unalterable; it is the operating system or parts of it that will be changed. We cover the control process and its parts and note the necessity for control. We also consider the effect of time, where controls are applied, and some of the tools for control. Finally, we explore some of the possible relationships of organizational control units to the line and functional units being monitored and controlled.

LEARNING OBJECTIVES

1 To be able to define control and to differentiate it from adaptation.

2 To understand the control process.

3 To understand the necessity for controls.

4 To learn the details of each of the steps in the control process: setting standards, measurement and comparison, evaluation, and correction.

5 To appreciate the importance of timing in control.

6 To learn the relevance and uses of precontrol, concurrent control, and postcontrol.

7 To know the different locations in the organization where controls are applied.

8 To learn some of the tools of control and their uses.

9 To appreciate the need for "independence" of control units.

CASE: GRECO-ROMAN CHAIR COMPANY (A)

■ Chuck Martinelli, the sales manager for the Greco-Roman Chair Company, was working at home this evening. Tonight he was reviewing the semiannual sales figures from the company's sales districts.

The company has five districts extending from the North Carolina main factory and home office to the Mississippi River. The area of western Pennsylvania, Ohio, Indiana, and Illinois is called the Midlands district; others are New England, Northern Atlantic, Mid-Atlantic, and Southern Midlands. The next territory G-R plans to add is the Southeast, but the implementation of that plan is still four years into the future.

The Midlands district is of particular concern at the present time. The third oldest of the districts, Midlands, until two years ago, always came in well over the sales projections planned for it. Martinelli expected a modest decrease in the *rate* of sales growth due to the saturation of the area and the increasing competition from other companies, but G-R's new products were being accepted everywhere else and should have been also in Midlands. The continued infusion of newer products should be contributing to some sustained sales growth there. The company's market research data shows no significant differences in terms of acceptability of new designs among the districts; these data were key inputs into the planning for each of the new products and the advertising campaigns associated with them.

But Midlands had slumped badly in the past two years, and this semiannual report on sales shows a continuing trend downward. In a verbal report accompanying the sales data, the Midlands regional manager cited the following as reasons for the decrease:

1 Low activity in the basic steel, auto, and heavy-equipment industries contributed to a low sales potential in furniture;

2 Increasing costs for energy in turn decreased area families' disposable income available for durable goods;

3 Dealers were carrying lower inventories;

4 Population changes within the core cities where many of the G-R dealers are located was causing potential customer shifts from middle- to lower-income families;

5 Increasing competition from other furniture companies. In some cases competitors are offering almost exact replicas of G-R's designs, but of lower quality and price.

Martinelli reviewed the regional manager's original plan and reasoning for failing to meet the expected sales projections. He was trying to determine whether the Midlands district was sufficiently different from the others, where sales continued to show their modest upswings. He carefully reread the initial planning for the district, the plan in which the current quotas were established. All of the factors cited by the regional manager in the semiannual report were accounted for in the plans, yet an increase in sales quotas had been projected and endorsed enthusiastically at that time by the regional manager.

Martinelli also reviewed some of the economic data for the area; the country's general recovery was actually increasing the economic health of the heavy industries—the base of the Midlands district—and auto sales and those in basic steel were recovering nicely.

No matter how hard he looked, Martinelli came to the same conclusion. The planning parameters were not inaccurate, and all of the contingencies cited by the regional manager were accounted for in the planning process. The problem in Midlands had to be inside the organization.

Martinelli then started to review salespeople's call records and customer account records of the Midlands district. He also contemplated reviewing the product-by-product sales in the area and comparing those figures with the data for other areas. The fault had to be somewhere within that sales unit, and he was intent on digging it out. ■

INTRODUCTION

So far in this book, we have viewed the manager first as a designer: a planner and maker of systems, goals, strategies, policies, plans, procedures, methods, objectives, and even schemes. Managers, as we have seen, are designing or planning at all levels of the organization—some are foremen or first- and second-level managers, who plan within a very limited context, narrowly constrained by the structure and authority patterns of the organization. These limit the manager's authority or sphere of influence. These lower-level managers deal with very specific plans—e.g., day-to-day time schedules or the specific assignment of persons to specific jobs. On the other hand, as we have seen, other managers plan or design at a higher level within the organization. The time span of their planning is much longer; the number of functions, units, or offices encompassed by their planning is much broader; and the authority that they have to exercise is much greater.

Then we viewed our managers as implementers of their plans—or energizers who initiate activities that put the various plans into effect. They acquire both human and physical resources; train and provide for the development of personnel; communicate the purposes, plans, and rules of the organization to subordinates; and provide the leadership and direction necessary to energize the human and material resources of the organization.

Now we come to the third major managerial role—controlling and adapting. What happens if the objective of the organization or of one of the organization's subunits is not being reached? What changes are to be made? What or who is to be altered in terms of behavior or presence? Whose behavior must be changed? What machines must be altered? Whose heads will roll? These are the types of questions to which we must now turn our attention. These are the types of issues we shall be exploring in the next three chapters of this book.

In this chapter we shall define and dissect the control portion of this major managerial process and then view how the control process is applied to various activities within the organization. We shall see why control is necessary, consider some of the tools of control, and explore some of the organizational arrangements for the control function.

Control is defined generally as the process of organizational change or correction that operates on the assumption that the goal, plan, organization, or standard against which performance or output is being compared is basically correct, infallible, or unalterable. Thus there is something incorrect with the implementation or the system being utilized, and the change required is to bring the organizational resource or its behavior in line with that contemplated by the plan or design.

The concept of control contrasts with that of adaptation, which makes no similar assumption about the sanctity of objecives, plans, standards, policies, or strategies. In essence, the fact that the environment may change or something internal to the organization may change could require the manager or the controller to redesign the plan, change the policy, alter the strategy or long-range goal, or produce an entirely new set of operating standards. We shall cover adaptation in more detail in Chapter 19.

THE NATURE OF CONTROL

Control is a general managerial process by which the output of an activity is compared and contrasted to a preestablished standard or plan. If in the evaluation and comparison to the standard, output is found not to correspond to the standard, corrective action is applied to the activity involved to bring its output in line with the standard. Figure 17.1 conceptually illustrates this process.

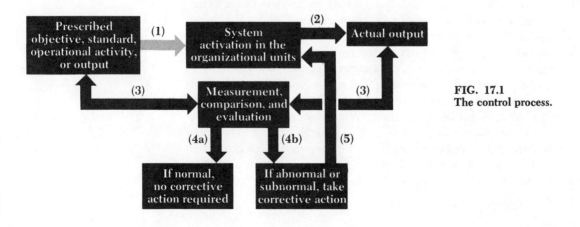

FIG. 17.1
The control process.

The standard, goal, or optimal prescription of activity is a prelude to system activation (subprocess 1), which in turn leads to actual output of some sort (subprocess 2). An evaluator (which, as we shall see, can be either human or mechanical) compares the actual output with the objective or standard (subprocess 3). If the two compare favorably and standards are being met, no corrective activity is required (subprocess 4a). If, however, the two do not compare favorably (subprocess 4b), corrective action on the system or performance is undertaken to bring the actual output into line with the prescribed standard (subprocess 5).

Conceptually, in the control process, then, the preestablished standard may be an objective, a deadline, or a desired behavior. These ends, of course, are set through the manager's *design* activities; the plans are *implemented*—resources are put to use in an attempt to reach the desired goal—and the system produces an actual output. This output is then compared to the standard—the expected output or behavior—and if the output does not deviate from the expected standard, nothing happens; production or activity just continues along. If, however, the output does deviate, intervention of some sort into the process takes place, and changes are made to bring the required output back into congruence with the expected standard.

In most cases the intervention into an organizational process is managerial. That is, some manager or supervisor says, "Stop, you're doing that wrong" or "You're not reaching objectives" or "Your division is way off target" or "The quality is deviating from standard; stop that machine and sharpen the tool."

In other situations, however, the control can be totally automatic. A standard can be set, and a machine or computer can change calibrations, flows, or output to meet the preset standards. The easiest to contemplate and most common example of this automatic type of control process is the heating thermostat in the home. The homeowner sets the thermostat according to a predetermined comfortable temperature level. The thermostat fires the boiler to heat the house; when the house is properly heated to the desired temperature (standard), the thermostat shuts down the boiler until it again compares the house temperature with the standard and finds it too cold, at which time the boiler automatically fires again.

This process is quite similar to a computer's controlling the flow of oil through a pipeline, with valves automatically closing down and opening, depending on the match between the actual flow and the preprogrammed standard. Indeed, entire oil refineries can now be computer-programmed and controlled, with flows directed toward alternative terminals and different product mixes manufactured according to predetermined and programmed standards.

Both managerial (or human) intervention and automatic control correspond conceptually to the process outlined above and pictured in Fig. 17.1.

Why are controls necessary?

The resources of an organization—human and material—are rarely directed automatically toward the achievement of the organizationally prescribed objectives or standards. Moreover, plans or standards will rarely ever be automatically fulfilled to the ultimate degree or to perfection. Human beings, for example, may have all sorts of reasons to sidetrack from the direction of achievement of the objectives. Sometimes the abilities necessary to achieve the objectives are just not present. Sometimes it is the absence of motivation. Sometimes the informal organization impedes achievement of the objective.

With physical resources, the machines may not be calibrated correctly, the cutting blades may wear out prematurely, or some other problem may arise. Whatever the case, human or mechanical, the actual behavior or output is deviating from desired behavior, and *that deviation must be corrected* if total organizational objectives are to be achieved. Hence the need for control. As a general rule, there are very few processes, either staffed by human beings or operated mechanically, that will continually strive unalterably toward the achievement of a prescribed standard. Some intervening control is necessary.

Nothing noted in the preceding paragraphs should imply anything necessarily evil, calculating, or intentionally destructive about either the controller or the object or persons being controlled. The tendency for processes or for human beings to go out of control is often unintentional, and all movements from the prescribed standard should not be generally ascribed to perverse motives.

Controllers should not function with the idea that no one can do right, nor should units or individuals being controlled feel fear of "big brother" watching over them. The rationale for control should be to aid in achieving objectives, not always in punishing or relishing the finding of errors. The well-motivated, confident manager should have little trouble operating in such a role.

STEPS IN THE CONTROL PROCESS

Let us return to Fig. 17.1 and study the control process in more detail, with some additional explanation on each step in the process. In this section we shall discuss standards, measurement and comparison, evaluation, and correction.

Standards

Standards, as the result of the planning process, are objectives, goals, quotas, expense levels, quality levels, sales targets, and the like. Or, they may be procedures that must be inflexibly followed so that some goal will be achieved. For example, most offices have some sort of dress code; the code may not be a rigid one, but it may preclude certain things such as jeans. The presumption behind many of these codes is that such a procedure will lead to higher sales or deposits or whatever it is that the organization is ultimately seeking. The dress code is a behavior standard, not an output standard. Most organizations have these behavior standards liberally sprinkled throughout.

No matter what the nature of the standard or its goal, it is set in a planning or design process and results from the mental processes that the manager went through in designing systems. In other words, the standard is a plan.

Within the context of this chapter, the key element in the control process is that the standards are relatively inflexible. They are assumed to be correct, and it is the behavior or the process that will be changed, not the standard.

Measuring the performance or the output is a crucial part of the control process. The type of measurement used is generally set in the standards-establishment phase. For example, organizations may use dollars, inches, feet, numbers, time, or any of the other enumerators available.

Measurement and comparison

It is with these standards, however, that we may run into difficulty when strictly enforcing them in day-to-day activities. Suppose, for example, that a company uses sales quotas measured in dollars as its only standard in evaluating sales territories. No consideration is given to such other types of factors as depth of market penetration, mix of products sold, and saturation of advertising. Relying only on the dollar volume may be all good and well except that salespeople may be able to reach the dollar targets very easily by overstocking customers with the popular items, with the customers not reordering during the next period. By then the original salespeople may have been promoted or moved laterally to a more promising territory, but the measure by which they were evaluated did not really measure overall contribution. Similarly, a production quota may have been reached by a hard-driving manager who leaves the unit in an organizationally chaotic condition for the successor who comes in after the manager is promoted.*

Thus managers, as controllers, must not only learn to measure the correct things, but also become conscious of modifying absolute numbers and maintaining some semblance of necessary flexibility. Managers know (or should know) what their goals and standards are, but any good controller will know that one just doesn't measure in the abstract without some reference to the possible side effects of using only absolute and singular measures.

Not all comparisons lead to corrective action. Some judgment must be used to determine if the deviation from the standard is sufficient to warrant expending the costs and energy to apply correction to bring it back into line.

Evaluation

* See Rensis Likert, "Measuring Organizational Performance," *Harvard Business Review* **36**, 2 (March/April 1958): 41–50.

For example, if an agency phone budget is exceeded by one percent, how much would be accomplished if a stringent postaudit resulted in a severe reprimand for the unit manager?

Areas in which some subjectivity in evaluation is necessary or built into the system include the statistical leeways in quality control, the optimistic/ most likely/pessimistic time estimates allowed in the PERT process, and plus or minus cost estimates. In all of these cases the evaluator knows that the planner meant to allow some limited flexibility in the evaluation of actual versus planned standards and that he or she should not expect pinpoint precision in reaching the standard.

Where the cost of correction would exceed the savings, correction should not be undertaken simply for its own sake. Only the real exception should get corrected; that instance when the cost of not correcting will be too great or an example must be established. For example, salespeople on expense accounts will be called on the carpet only for some extraordinary items that cannot possibly be justified; minor and occasional overextensions on their expense accounts generally would be ignored—unless they became habitual, of course.

Correction   After the comparison and the evaluation of whether the deviation from standard is serious enough to call for change, correction is possibly in order. Correction can take many forms. In the simplest operative cases it may mean a minor readjustment of a blade, the honing of a tool, an increase in the flow of some material or liquid, a cleaning of some sort of receptacle, and other simple types of changes. In cases involving the higher organizational components, correction may mean restricting purchase orders because costs are going out of line, restricting the replacement of personnel, reducing prices to clear glutted inventories, or ordering general changes in hiring and training practices. Or, correction may mean that the controller recognizes the inability of an individual to perform as anticipated, and the correction consists of replacing or firing the individual. This was the eventual outcome of Martinelli's analysis of the Midlands district of the Greco-Roman Chair Company.

In essence, the correction could be the refinement or replacement of a resource—either physical or human—an adjustment to a system, or the placing of a block or impediment into the process to tone it down. When we cover the human problems of control (Chapter 18), however, we will recognize that the alternatives open to the correcting agent narrow significantly. No correcting agent can charge into an organizational unit like the proverbial bull in a china shop, unmindful of the effects such behavior would have on the future organizational relationships in that unit or the responsiveness of the unit and its personnel to future managerial efforts. So correction is not an easy task; it is one requiring diplomacy, tact, and some degree of compassion.

Let us briefly retrace in terms of our control model (Fig. 17.1) what Chuck Martinelli did when he analyzed and contemplated the problem in the Midlands. First, the standards by which Midlands was being evaluated had been established during the design stage of the managerial activity. At the time it was established, all agreed that the sales quota for Midlands was both attainable and equitable. In addition to a district sales quota, each salesperson had call and sales quotas.

Actual output (the result of subprocess 2) was lower than the quota. In the comparison and measurement stages (subprocess 3), Martinelli made the comparison based on the measures prescribed in the plan. He evaluated the results by reviewing all of the environmental and other input factors that could have affected the results. For example, the area's economy was not at fault (in fact, it was on the upswing); nor were the designs insufficient. Martinelli attempted to find extenuating circumstances for the division's shortcomings and could find none. In this case corrective action (subprocess 5) was required. In essence, the performance that led to the lowered output had to be altered.

Martinelli's decision in this case was to replace the district sales manager and two low-production salespeople (see Chapter 1). He could have taken alternative corrective actions. For example, he could have assumed control of the division himself, altered sales routes, switched dealerships, altered sales allowances, put in extra salespeople, etc. He might have tried some new and different motivating strategies, perhaps even some new sales appeals. But in this case the decision was to change personnel. More than likely, this decision was not taken lightly, but Martinelli saw no other way out.

In Chapter 19, Martinelli will face a situation in which his planning or standard making could have been erroneous. In such a case the option may not be to work on the system, but rather to alter the objective or the standard. With Midlands in this case, however, that didn't seem to be a necessary step.

Back to Greco-Roman Chair Company

OTHER ELEMENTS IN THE CONTROL PROCESS: TIMING, LOCATION, AND TOOLS

Timing

Time, as we have noted, can be a standard on its own, e.g., a program must be completed by a certain date. As we discussed in Chapter 8, planning tools include Program Evaluation Review Technique (PERT), Gantt charts, scheduling charts, and other planning aids. Each of these tools not only is a planning diagram or mechanism, but also sets the framework for the control process.

With a Gantt chart (or PERT in more sophisticated processes), the intervention of a manager or human comparer is often necessary to rectify a program or a process that is off schedule. By comparing the actual process's progress with the planned progress on the scheduling mechanism, the manager is able to apply appropriate corrective devices—speedup, overtime, additional resources, or whatever is necessary—to get the program back on schedule.

Time is a key standard in that it often coexists with some other standard or standards. That is, we know that in addition to being of a certain size or weight, a certain batch of products must also be completed by a certain date. Thus the quality-control process on the size and weight measurements must also be scheduled and completed by that certain date. Conversely, it is obvious that it would be too late to schedule the control of the quality and quantity of an order that is going through the production process if one discovers that the order is behind schedule only when the customer cancels on account of late delivery.

Thus timing in the application of controls is an important consideration. Some authors have categorized control processes into three types, depending on the timing of their applications. These categories or types are precontrol, concurrent control, and postcontrol.*

Precontrols   These are applied before a process has a chance of going out of control and bringing it and the related processes to a halt. For example, many companies and organizations with large amounts of mechanically sophisticated equipment practice preventive maintenance for the machines and vehicles involved in the operative processes. Tires are changed at predetermined intervals even if the danger of a blowout or a flat is not imminent; similarly, lightbulbs, oil in machines, and other wearing components are checked and replaced. Airlines overhaul the engines on their planes after a certain number of hours of flying time. The assumption behind precontrol is that prevention is worth a lot more than cure, particularly if the cure comes after a major breakdown affecting costs, delivery, or greater damage. In the case of the airlines, the possibility of crash due to malfunction is a risk the airlines would rather avoid.

Concurrent control   This type of control is applied to a functioning process while the process is ongoing. Concurrent control corrects while the process is in motion. If automatic, like the computer-controlled oil pipeline or the thermostat on the heating system, the correction is continuous. If it involves a process of human intervention, such as statistical quality control or production control, the correction is intermittent, but scheduled in at appropriate intervals during the ongoing production or operations process. Examples of concurrent control are ongoing comparisons of expenditures versus budgeted amounts in public agencies, periodic checks on quality, midterm

* *See,* for example, James H. Donnelly, Jr., James L. Gibson, and John M. Ivancevich, *Fundamentals of Management: Functions, Behavior, Models,* 3rd ed. (Dallas: Business Publications, 1978), Chapter 6. In their book, postcontrol is termed "feedback control."

examinations in your management classes, and ongoing examinations of customers' account balances in banking institutions.

Postcontrols   Applied after a process is complete, postcontrols typically are applied to a program to determine its effectiveness and efficiency and possibly to dispense rewards and punishments to the individuals involved. For example, an audit will determine whether in a fiscal year a program has been effective and will signal the planner to determine if the program should be refunded, what alterations in the program should be made, and what personnel changes might be appropriate.

Each of these types of controls—pre-, concurrent, and post- —is appropriate in certain situations and for certain types of operations. Precontrol and concurrent control are most appropriate for operative tasks and lower-level functions and operations. Concurrent and postcontrol occur at higher organizational levels on broader and more inclusive plans and programs. Perhaps the ultimate example of postcontrol in a business organization is the closing and audit of the entire company's books made at the end of a fiscal year by outside auditors. These yield indications of whether the company management achieved its goals on return on investment, profit, sales expense controls, and other similar standards.

Controls are applied throughout an organization, but are particularly important in the line units where the primary functions are accomplished and where adequate performance is such a significant factor in the organization's overall success in accomplishing its objectives. In sales units, for example, controls are instituted on the number of calls made by salespeople, the productivity of sales unit against sales quotas established for them, the market share of a particular product, or the marginal efficiency of additional advertising expenditures. All of these controls, in addition to others, represent an attempt by the organization to maintain high and planned rates of sales, market impacts, and efficiency in marketing efforts.

Locating points for control application

Control in the production function is applied on quality, inventory, schedules, maintenance, and quantity produced. Again, these controls are applied with the objective of meeting the production needs which will allow the organization to achieve its objective of supplying sufficient products to waiting customers.

Control in the financial or cost area involves the applications of various ratios and measures applied at all levels of the organization and throughout the various units of the organization.

All of the controls described above pertain to an organization's primary functions. But secondary functions too have control procedures and standards. Personnel departments, for example, generally attempt to hold down and control personnel turnover, since high turnover results in higher costs of recruitment, selection, training, and indoctrination. Newly important safety departments are controlling all sorts of housekeeping chores and safety systems in plants and offices in order to not only comply with the ever-increasing regulation of the Occupational Safety and Health Administration of the federal government, but also reduce the accident level and the accompanying costs to the organization in terms of lost time and higher insurance rates.

At the very top level of the organization, the board of directors controls the actions of management through very broad kinds of control standards: return on investment for an entire program, marginal return on new projects, and the like. Moreover, top-level executives are held accountable to the board for the overall health of the organization. Although it may seem strange that the top-management team must bear the total responsibility for the failure or success of particular projects and must be prepared to possibly resign when such projects fail, such is the nature of high-level management jobs. Even though the failure of a project was probably the result of a myriad of factors, the chief executive officer and the top-level executives are ultimately responsible for turning approved programs into successful ones as measured by the specific criteria of efficiency and effectiveness established by the board of directors.

Some tools of control   We have already covered a great many of the tools of control, particularly when we studied planning, policy making, and the other areas of the design phase of a manager's job. Any tool that relates activity to time can also be considered a control device. Thus, as we have noted, the PERT system, Gantt charts, planning matrices, and other scheduling and planning tools are also control tools. The inventory model illustrated in Chapter 7 decision making as well as statistical quality-control methods are other instruments of control.*

Financial control tools include the use of the break-even chart, budgets (which are both planning documents and control devices), income statements, and balance sheets. In addition to the general use of those tools, a number of financial ratios are available to enable the evaluator to compare the performance of the unit or organization being controlled to standards, of either a general or a particular organizational nature. Liquidity ratios, for example, such as the current ratio (current assets/current liabilities) and the acid test ratio (cash and accounts receivable/current liabilities), are designed to measure an organization's ability to carry the current liabilities with either current assets or the current assets less inventories. These ratios are accounting standards generally accepted throughout the business litera-

* See Elwood S. Buffa, *Modern Production Management,* 3rd ed. (New York: Wiley, 1969), Chapter 20.

ture. Satisfactory ratios are 2.0 plus for the current and 1.0 plus for the acid test.

Other important ratios include inventory turnover (net sales/inventory), debt ratio (total debt/total assets), and the various profit ratios. Although it is not within the scope of this book to consider the techniques of these particular financial controls, suffice it to say that they are important measuring rods for managers to use in the controlling of the organization's performance and achievements.*

ORGANIZATION FOR CONTROL UNITS

Most designers of organizations believe that if possible, control units should be established so that they are completely independent of the line or functional units that they are to control. This placement of independent control units occurs at all levels of the organization. Thus in production units, for example, staff quality-control units are usually not placed under the authority of the manager whose unit is being controlled (see Fig. 17.2). The reason for the independence of line and control units should be easy to understand. Individuals whose units are judged primarily by output volume standards may have a tendency to disregard any consideration of quality, for example, in order to achieve greater output. With independence of the control units, such disregard is less likely.

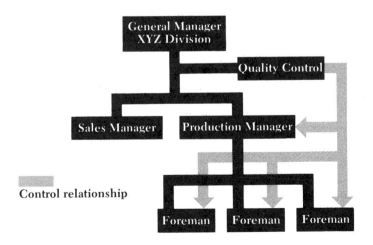

FIG. 17.2
An "independent" control unit.

Control relationship

* Any basic accounting text can give a more full treatment of these yardsticks. For example, *see* William W. Pyle and John A. White, *Fundamental Accounting Principles,* 7th ed. (Homewood, Ill.: Richard D. Irwin, 1975).

Sometimes independence is not totally possible, but other organizational arrangements can be instituted to compensate. For example, in a divisional-ized, complex organization, concurrent staff-control units would probably exist (e.g., a higher-level unit at the top of the organization having a staff-to-staff relationship with a lower-level staff unit (see Fig. 17.3). The lower-level control units take their cues from the guidelines offered at top levels, and the line managers to whom they are attached at the lower levels realize the staff-to-staff control relationship and react accordingly.

Relative independence is also in force at higher levels—sometimes pro-cedurally prescribed rather than structural. High-level control units are often financial in nature, e.g., cost or expense control or the internal audit staff, *or they deal with total organizational issues.* For example, the company controller's office or the internal audit staff or the budget officer plays the role of ensuring that *all* of the operating units are staying within budgeted accounts or that the organization is on target with respect to costs, revenues, and profit projections. They may also approve all expenditures above a certain dollar figure to ensure that they are legitimate and safeguard the organization against embezzlement and crooked dealings.

The primary point in this section, then, is that the great bulk of the controlling that goes on in organizations must—in order to retain integrity—remain independent of the activity being controlled, in terms of organiza-tional place and authority patterns.* It would be too easy for a manager whose primary interest is output to override control standards, to disregard objections, and to produce substandard goods if the quality people were

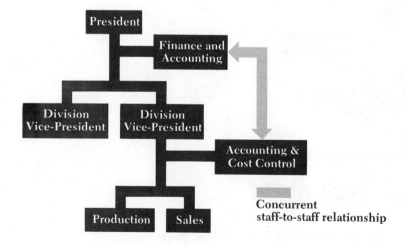

FIG. 17.3
Concurrent control units.

* William Newman, Charles Summer, and Kirby Warren, *The Process of Management,* 3rd ed. (Englewood Cliffs, N.J.: Prentice-Hall, 1972), p. 36ff.

under his or her authority. With an independent control unit, such overriding would either be impossible or create an organizational crisis.

None of this emphasis on independence of control units is meant to preclude the types of control that each and every manager practices within his or her own organizational unit. Each manager controls the behavior of subordinates in many ways that might not be related to markets, costs, or output. For example, punctuality, department safety, work pace, and correct use of equipment are obvious areas for control by the line officer at the operative level and staff officers as well. Nor is the line officer precluded from calling attention to obvious lapses in quality or output. Quality inspectors, for example, may be stationed only at certain spots on production lines and catch infractions or errors in conjunction with a great deal of other testing and observation. Often they will catch quality lapses only after they occur. Line supervisors, including foremen, are therefore obligated to correct on line any deficiencies they spot from their positions as they are occurring.

In higher managerial positions, managers are also not unconcerned about control. Simply because there are separate control units does not release the manager from being sure that his or her unit adheres to budget, for example, or achieves a prescribed level of sales calls or produces an assigned study on time.

So we see that each organization is an assemblage of control points all relating to standards, policies, procedures, and methods articulated and developed during the design phase or planning process of managerial activities. Some of these standards are so crucial that their assurances of being met cannot be left in the hands of the individual operating managers. For these standards, separate control units are established. Other standards are enforced within the operating units. The enforcement within the operating units does not necessarily mean that those standards are not important, but only that they can safely be left in the hands of the operating managers.

SUMMARY AND CONCLUSION

In this chapter we have explored the control process and each part of the process. Thus we covered standards, measurement and comparison, evaluation, and correction. We explored why control is necessary, where it is applied, what the organization for control might look like in various control situations, and some of the tools of control.

Control is applied to human beings as well as to nonhuman resources. Inevitably, applying a control process to human beings produces tensions and frustrations as well as countermeasures. Chapter 18 will explore some of the human problems of control as well as some managerial methods of overcoming those problems.

DISCUSSION QUESTIONS

1 Define control and illustrate the control process.

2 What roles do standards, objectives, or goals play in the current process?

3 What problems does the measuring function of the control process pose for the manager?

4 Differentiate among precontrol, concurrent control, and postcontrol. Give examples of each type.

5 Why is sound judgment necessary in the evaluation of performance output versus standards in the control process?

6 What kinds of actions or activities can be called for under the correction phase of the control process? Explain.

7 Why should staff control units be separated organizationally from the units they are supposed to be controlling?

8 Describe some financial control tools. What use are they to the operating manager?

CASE: THE COSTLY MAINTENANCE DEPARTMENT

■ Overland Industries is a medium-size multiproduct, single-plant firm in Milwaukee, Wisconsin. The company manufactures a number of metal specialty products. Its consumer products include metal pails and buckets, paint pots, and roller pans. Steady subcontracting has resulted in products for the automobile industry, such as air filter housings, hubcaps, wheel rings, and crankcase pans. The company employs 1180 people for its two shifts and four product departments.

The maintenance department was turning out to be the biggest headache for the company, however. That shop of forty-eight people consisted of carpenters, electricians, machine repair personnel, general maintenance laborers, plumbers, and painters. Years ago, the group had been organized by a different union from that which represented the plant's production and clerical employees. The maintenance union contract specified work crews sizes, circumstances when helpers were to be provided, extra rest and washup periods, a lunch period fifteen minutes longer than the one production employees enjoyed, and various prohibitions against one type of tradesperson's doing another type's work.

Each of the other operating and staff departments is allocated a maintenance budget, and the maintenance department charges the other departments for work done in their areas. This charge is "paid for" by an internal transfer of allocated or budgeted funds. In some cases, particularly for the outside of the building, grounds work, and the general utility and service areas, the maintenance department is allocated its own budget.

When a department wants routine work done or repairs made, the responsible manager simply calls maintenance, the work is done, and the department is "billed" according to standard rates per hour plus parts at cost. On a major renovation, maintenance sends a group of inspectors over and issues a bid price to the operating department, which then has the option of going ahead with the project or forgetting about it. The maintenance department, in turn, decides whether the work will be done by its own crew or subcontracted out.

There has always been some grumbling about the "loafers" in maintenance. Everyone in management has his or her favorite story about the "snafus" relating to maintenance. Typical of the stories related by operating managers are incidents such as three people raking out a yard of loam, four men standing and watching a backhoe dig a trench, or two electricians installing an outlet.

But it was Vice-President for Sales Bert Olson who really got hot under the collar about maintenance. Approximately one year ago, he broke into a tirade when it took two men an entire day to hang a new scheduling board and fluorescent light in his office. He fumed over the whole year that two men from maintenance spent repasting the mop boards to the walls in the tiled areas of the building. "They sure drank one load of coffee," he remarked. What contributed to his anger was that his salespeople were working overtime to secure new accounts, and he was continually being asked for reports on their outputs and activities during executive committee meetings. No such controls were ever imposed on maintenance.

The crowning touch came when Olson requested an estimate for two twelve-foot-high walls, each thirty feet long. He wanted to divide two offices into four, a project that was envisioned when the building was constructed; hence no new doors were required on the outside or corridor walls. Each of the walls was to be finished in sheetrock, packed with fiberglass insulation and sound-proofing board, have a connecting door, and be painted. Olson mentally planned to spend $1500. The estimate came in at $4480! Maintenance had figured the labor at three men for four weeks!

Olson raged over the phone to the head of maintenance. Then he called a carpenter/contractor who had worked on his house, described the project, and asked him for a ballpark figure.

"I'd say about $2000 would be a good estimate," offered the contractor.

Olson asked that the whole problem of maintenance be put on the agenda of the next meeting of the executive committee.

When the discussion came to that item, Olson reviewed all of the alleged instances of waste and inefficiency that he had encountered. He offered the opinion that maintenance was costing the company several hundred thousand dollars in lost profits and cited his own case of the proposed walls as an example. The vice-president of production joined with Olson in castigating the maintenance department's costs and time inefficiency.

The director of maintenance, who had been invited to the meeting, said that his department was tied up in all sorts of union rules that had not been negotiated by him and that the other executives who complained about maintenance did not have those rules to contend with. Also, he argued that the other executives didn't know how to estimate time and didn't know the real costs of many of the projects that he and his subordinates had estimated.

Olson and Speckle (the production vice-president) vehemently disagreed and asked the committee to authorize the company controller to do a study of the past year's maintenance cost. Olson said that going back beyond that would not be productive because of the effect of inflation on building materials and labor costs.

A month later, the auditor reported to the committee. On routine maintenance, he conceded that the company was paying about twelve percent more than if it had gone outside. On the other hand, the quick response capability of an internal department was an advantage and possibly saved more through the prevention of damage.

On the renovation projects, the auditor reviewed eighty-four projects either bid on or completed by maintenance. In six cases maintenance came in under what a contractor would have bid on the job—but only slightly under. In the remaining seventy-eight cases, maintenance was anywhere from 15 to 300 percent above possible outside bids. The auditor assembled his various outside costs by requesting bids from contractors on the original specifications and then paying them for their time preparing the bids.

All in all, according to the auditor, maintenance in its present mode cost the company $168,800 during the last fiscal year.

President Pringle looked at the report, sat back in her chair, and said, "Looks like Olson was right. Gentlemen, could we get some alternatives on the table?" ■

Case questions

1. From President Pringle's perspective, what kinds of corrective action should she apply to the control process? Or, should she delegate the problem back to maintenance?

2. If he could be convinced that something is wrong, what might the maintenance director think has broken down? Bad standard setting? Poor evaluation? No comparison or measurement? Poor correction? Make recommendations for changes.

3. In what areas would you recommend that President Pringle order that the maintenance department put control practices into effect?

SELECTED READINGS

Anthony, R. N., J. Dearden, and R. F. Vancil, *Management Control Systems: Text Cases and Readings*, rev. ed. (Homewood, Ill.: Richard D. Irwin, 1972).

Bensoussan, A., E. G. Hurst, and B. Naslund, *Management Applications of Modern Control Theory* (New York: American Elsevier, 1974).

Brodtrick, M. O., "Managerial Performance Evaluation and Accountability," *Optimum* **9**, 2 (1978): 64–67.

Bocchino, A., *Management Information Systems: Tools and Techniques* (Englewood Cliffs, N.J.: Prentice-Hall, 1972).

Bonini, C. P., R. K. Jaedicke, and H. M. Wagner, eds., *Management Controls: New Directions in Basic Research* (Papers) (New York: McGraw-Hill, 1964).

Carrol, S. J., and H. L. Tosi, Jr., *Management by Objectives: Applications and Research* (New York: Macmillan, 1973).

Chakeaborty, S. K., *Management by Objectives: An Integrated Approach* (Delhi: Macmillan Company of India, 1976).

Davis, S. M., and P. R. Lawrence, *Matrix* (Reading, Mass.: Addison-Wesley, 1977).

Hellriegel, D., and J. W. Slocum, Jr., *Management: Contingency Approaches*, 2d ed. (Reading, Mass.: Addison-Wesley, 1974). See Part II, "Managerial Process," Chapter 9, "Control Process."

Hughes, R. E., "Planning: The Essence of Control," *Managerial Planning* **26**, 6 (May/June 1978): 1–3, 10.

Iannone, A. L., *Management Program Planning and Control with PERT, MOST and LOB* (Englewood Cliffs, N.J.: Prentice-Hall, 1967).

Jones, R. L., and H. G. Trentin, *Management Controls for Professional Firms* (New York: American Management Association, 1968).

Kearing, W. J., "Improving Work Performance Through Appraisal," *Human Resource Management* **17**, 2 (Summer 1978): 15–23.

Kheva, S. S., *Management and Control in Public Enterprise* (New York: Asia Publishing House, 1964).

Kingston, P. L., "The Anatomy of a Financial Model," *Managerial Planning* **26**, 3 (November/December 1977): 1–7.

Koontz, H., and C. J. O'Donnell, *Management: A Systems and Contingency Analysis of Managerial Functions*, 6th ed. (New York: McGraw-Hill, 1976).

Larner, R. J., *Management Control and the Large Corporation* (New York: Dunellen, 1970).

Livingstone, J. L., *Management Planning and Control: Mathematical Motels* (New York: McGraw-Hill, 1970).

Lord, R. J., "Probabilistic Budgeting," *Cost and Management* **52**, 3 (May/June 1978): 14–19.

Meyer, H. H., "The Annual Performance Review Discussion: Making It Constructive," *Personnel Journal* **56**, 10 (October 1977): 508–511.

Mockler, R. J., *The Management Control Process* (New York: Appleton-Century-Crofts, 1972).

Monczka, R. M., and P. L. Carter, "Measuring Purchasing Performance," *Management Review* **67**, 6 (June 1978): 38–42.

Nicols, A., *Management and Control in the Mutual Savings and Loan Association* (Lexington, Mass.: Lexington Books, 1972).

Qureshi, M. A., and R. Babcock, "A Proposal for Integrating Budgeting and MBO," *Managerial Planning* **26**, 5 (March/April 1978): 14–16.

Radford, J. D., and D. B. Richardson, *The Management of Production*, 3rd ed. (New York: Barnes & Noble, 1972).

Strong, E. P., and R. D. Smith, *Management Control Models* (New York: Holt, Rinehart and Winston, 1968).

Tannenbaum, A. S., *Control in Organizations* (New York: McGraw-Hill, 1968).

Wiest, J. D., and F. K. Levy, *A Management Guide to PERT/CPM* (Englewood Cliffs, N.J.: Prentice-Hall, 1969).

Yoder, W. O., and C. E. Vincent, *Management and Financial Controls for Retail Hardware Store* (Bloomington: Bureau of Business Research, Graduate School of Business, Indiana University, 1961).

Chapter 18
ADJUSTING CONTROL TO HUMAN FACTORS

CHAPTER HIGHLIGHTS

In this chapter we explore the relationship and effects of human factors to control processes—and vice versa. We will look at some of the human reactions to control, particularly defense mechanisms, ineffective performance, and lowered motivation. Then we shall consider some of the organizational and managerial causes of human problems relative to the control process and finally some of the practices managers might engage in to alleviate the problems.

LEARNING OBJECTIVES

1 To realize that not all responses to control processes are negative ones.

2 To learn the general categories of negative human reactions to control: defensive behavior, ineffective performance, and lack of motivation.

3 To understand the organizational and managerial causes of negative human reactions to control.

4 To learn and to be able to apply practices to adjust control systems to the human factor: feedback of results, availability of training and information, flexibility, firmness, minimization of control points, recognition of factors beyond people's control, recognition of the need for individualism and growth, and an audit of the control package.

CASE: FIRST NATIONAL BANK OF KINGSFORD

■ Betsy Blinker was one of two class of 1977 Kingsford High School graduates hired by the First National Bank of Kingsford. The bank generally hires at least two, and often more, of the local high school's graduates for teller trainee positions. With the addition of branches in the surrounding towns and the expansion of the main branch, the bank needed to hire two or three of the graduates. The policy of going to the high school was in line with efforts by the local chamber of commerce to keep many of the younger people in town by providing jobs for them.

Betsy reported in late June to Helen LeBlanc, the head teller at the main office. Helen herself was one of the earlier hires out of Kingsford High School and in four years had advanced to her present position. Helen tried to explain all of the bank's rules to Betsy.

1 Never leave your station without permission. Usually someone can cover for you.

2 Never leave your station with the money boxes unlocked or uncovered.

3 Obtain approval from the head teller or another officer for cashing any check over $150. If none of the officers is available, call accounting to check the status of the customer's account.

4 Don't cash out-of-town checks unless the customer has an account with the bank.

5 Double-count bills paid out. That is, count the bills as you remove them from the money tray, and count them again when you pass them to the customer.

6 Count all of the cash and change being deposited, and check the amount against the deposit ticket.

7 Count the number of checks—don't worry about the amounts, as bookkeeping will check those—and check the number against that on the deposit ticket.

8 Reconcile your cash drawer twice a day—before lunch and after closing. Call the head teller on any discrepancy over $3.

Helen also briefed Betsy on the procedures in case of a robbery, fire, or injury. She stressed the bank's dress code and also cautioned her to maintain a courteous, but businesslike attitude toward customers. She mentioned the need for neatness in writing and, above all, honesty while on the job. Finally, Helen said that after a week or two, Betsy would be expected to handle twenty-five to thirty clients an hour on straight deposits and check-cashing transactions. She also said that banks try to maintain a conservative, safe image and that employees are expected to reinforce that image.

Fortunately, the bank had just instituted a new customer-control system that eliminated the line-up behind each individual teller and kept some order in front of the tellers' counters. Patrons were asked to line up between an "S"-shape system of ropes, with the first person in the line going to the first available teller. This system facilitated privacy in transactions and avoided a teller's seeing an avalanche of line-switching people in front of his or her station. For a new teller, the system made it easier to become accustomed to the routines required.

Helen stayed with Betsy for the first day at her station. She showed her how to handle some of the lesser-used procedures, such as the sale and cashing of savings bonds, the sale of travelers' checks, filing of letters of credit, etc.

During her third day on the job, Betsy was asked to join a group of fellow tellers at lunch. The group included some of the people she knew from high school—Bill Starchy, Janet Bonlison, and Carol Kelly. "How's your first week going?" asked Bill.

"Okay, I guess. Helen has been helping me, and I'm learning. I guess I'll get all the rules down before long," replied Betsy.

"Don't take all that stuff that Helen threw at you too seriously now. Once in a while, you can wear pants or even jeans, and nobody will care. And I joke a lot with customers. They're usually okay people. I don't think we have to be serious all the time," injected Janet. Then for the rest of the lunch, they talked about their teachers at Kingsford High School.

Betsy was becoming quite proficient at her job. She met the customer-service quota very easily and reconciled her accounts to the penny all but once during the first two months. And her rapport with customers and co-workers was developing very nicely. After a while, she thought that she could skip reconciling twice a day and let it go until closing time.

One day, her best friend, Ceil Braxton, came into the bank with a $250 check to cash. "Betsy, I don't have an account here, but can you cash a check for me. It's drawn on my account over at the Northborough State Bank."

"I'm not supposed to, but since it's you, well, I guess it will be okay." She counted out ten twenty-dollar bills and five tens. Ceil's check did clear—or at least Betsy didn't hear anything about it after that.

Helen caught Betsy leaving the bank after hours. Even though she saw Betsy every day, she rarely allowed herself to get personally involved with the tellers. But this time she asked Betsy how everything on the job was going. "Do you have any problems?"

"Great, just great," Betsy answered. "I like it here a lot."

Gradually, as Betsy got to know her customers better, she found herself neglecting more of the rules that Helen had taught her. For some of her regulars, she didn't count checks, often did not double-count money, and occasionally cashed checks over $150 without checking the account balance or seeking approval from the head teller.

"There's really no need for me to be so sticky with these nice people," she thought to herself. "Besides, it slows me down to do all that checking. I haven't lost anything yet, and I think I'm good enough to spot the losers and crooks." ■

INTRODUCTION

Controls and control devices can be made to perform almost perfectly—*if* the entire process being controlled is inanimate. For example, a computer-controlled production process can be programmed to compensate for tool wear, materials-flow variation, and the other variables and still keep the output flowing to the desired standard. The entire process is a closed loop, with no human interfaces involved. Assuming no breakdown in the computer, the process will just continue to operate efficiently and effectively.

However, if human beings are injected into a process and control is applied, the loop opens. Feelings, needs, anxieties, and the whole host of complicated psychological factors enter into the process. Now the corrective behavior necessary becomes more difficult to apply. Human beings don't react as machines do; they do not always automatically correct themselves or respond without any emotion to commands to change behavior. Hence the human element in the control process may cause unique problems for the manager, and this is the subject of this chapter.

SOME HUMAN REACTIONS TO CONTROL PROCESSES

Human beings react in various ways to controls. *Often the response will be positive.* That is, the person will cooperate and change his or her behavior to correspond to standards. Many times, however, the individual will react negatively toward the controls and the controller. Sometimes the type of negative reaction will depend on the power available to the controller. If the controller lacks sufficient power or influence, the controlled subordinates may react aggressively, even violently, against the controller or the system. On the other hand, if the controller possesses power, those controlled may try to find some ways to subvert the power or influence—or, alternatively, gain their own power or influence bases. In this section we shall explore some of these negative behaviors in more detail. We shall classify them into three general (and closely interrelated) categories: defensive behaviors, ineffective performance, and lower motivation (see Fig. 18.1).

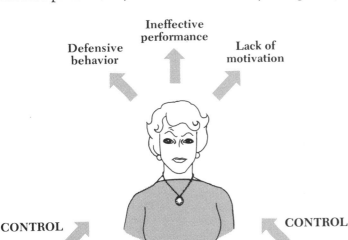

FIG. 18.1
Human reactions to control processes.

Defensive behavior   Defensive behavior, as we noted in Chapter 11, results from frustration. Frustration occurs when a person meets a system or a process that she or he cannot beat or cope with. You will recall that in the Argyris model (Chapter 11), the frustration a healthy human being meets in the controlling organization results in regression or a movement back to dependent behavior. But work situations involving the control of human beings can result in other types of defensive behavior as well. For example, the controlled individual might try to ingratiate himself or herself with the controller rather than meet the standard. This does not get the job at hand done, but it may get the controller off the back of the controlled.

Another reaction is to beat the system by trying to find ways around the standard. Betsy Blinker, for example, might be trying to beat the system, whether consciously or unconsciously, as she progressively ignores control procedures that she knows her boss doesn't check on. Thus when the control becomes so onerous, or is perceived as useless, or is so debilitating to the human being, the individual may seek to outmaneuver the controller and consciously try to beat the system and overcome the controller.

Closely allied as a reaction is the attempt to sabotage the system, slow it down, or perhaps even grind it to a complete halt. Automobile workers are famous for this type of reaction. One of the most celebrated cases involved the General Motors plant at Lordstown, Ohio.* GM engineers had designed a highly automated assembly line capable of producing more than one hundred completed Chevolet Vegas per hour. But the work pace was extraordinarily demanding and, according to the workers, punishing, a conclusion disputed by GM executives. Along with a strike, the workers did succeed in sabotaging the line through rejects and reworkings on the supposedly finished vehicles. In other cases, simple strategisms such as sand in the grease caps of machinery might be employed.

Still another type of defensive behavior manifested, when group activity or union activity is possible, is the work slowdown or the strike. Both of these actions occurred at Lordstown. Often frustration results in wildcat strikes—strikes precipitated by some real or perceived grievance but not authorized by union officers.

Ineffective achievement of goals   Another category of human reaction to control is, of course, the ineffective achievement of goals. That is, goals, despite the controller's efforts, are impossible for the controlled or the subordinates to attain. This nonachievement is often caused by the goals' being set too high in the first place, a condition that would call for a reduction of the goals or the standards involved. (Changing goals will be discussed in the next chapter.) Under adap-

* See J. O'Toole, "Lordstown: Three Years Later," *Business and Society Review* (Spring 1975): 64–71. See also Ronald K. Boyer and Richard L. Shell, "The End of the Line at Lordstown," *Business and Society Review* (Autumn 1972): 31–35.

tation, no assumption is made that the goals are impossible to change, fixed, or sacrosanct.

However, more important for our purposes here are the ineffective performances caused by the reaction to control when the standards are fixed. We have already mentioned many of the defense mechanisms caused by frustration; others are for the employee to resign or quit trying. Control can result in a conscious or unconscious inability to attain goals, despite the fact that the *person's physical and mental ability to achieve the prescribed goals are present.* That reaction is caused by the totally inflexible application of the control process. As we noted in Chapter 17, some flexibility in evaluation and measurement is needed. Inflexibility on the part of the controller, inflexibility of standards application, and inflexibility on measurement—all cause the individual to believe that the controller can never be satisfied, and hence the individual may lower output and production to an unacceptably low level—in effect, quit trying to reach standard.

A final problem that may result from overregulation is personal dissatisfaction and lower motivation. (Refer to Chapter 11, in which the theories of Argyris, Herzberg, McGregor, and other observers of modern work situations were discussed.)

Lower motivation

According to a relatively common thread running through most of the theories on motivation, if the organization and its managers operate under Theory X–type management assumptions, individuals who have high motivation are beaten down by the resultant overregulation.* Motivation is dulled and job satisfaction decreases; just being in the plant or office becomes objectionable or "a drag," and an employee becomes a clockwatcher and eagerly awaits quitting time.

ORGANIZATIONAL AND MANAGERIAL BASES OF HUMAN PROBLEMS IN CONTROLLING

A number of managerial activities—or, we might say, inactivities—contribute to human problems relative to control devices and mechanisms. In this section we shall review and investigate those kinds of ineffective activities. In the next section we shall consider some managerial actions to overcome them and to make control processes more effective.

Too often, an adverse reaction to control results from the subordinate or the controlled individual's receiving inadequate information. In essence, communication is either nonexistent or ineffective. The lack of information can relate to the standards the person being controlled is expected to fulfill or

Inadequate information or feedback

* Douglas McGregor, *The Human Side of Enterprise* (New York: McGraw-Hill, 1960).

- Inadequate information and feedback
- Measuring activity, not output
- Inflexibility in applying controls
- Inconsistency in applying controls
- Overcontrol: too many standards to fulfill
- Losing sight of the real objectives: substituting procedures for end results
- Too little confidence in people

Human problems in control:
Some managerial causes

attain, to the training that he or she was supposed to have received, or to feedback on the actual results that one did or did not achieve.

It makes little difference whether an individual does not know the standards, objectives, or results that he or she was supposed to achieve or if those expectations were not articulated to him or her with sufficient clarity and precision. In either case that individual will obviously react poorly when controlled according to standards that he or she was unaware or not informed of. This was a basic problem in one of our earlier cases. Jake Deveneux, the foreman of the shop, never did properly brief Susie Waterman on the standards that her job involved or on the rules and regulations of the organization which employed her. Consequently, she didn't realize or know that she was supposed to conform to certain standards and behave in certain ways (see Chapter 15).

Although ignorance of the law is no excuse in the courts, there is no parallel assumption for good management. Individuals who are expected to reach a certain standard or perform in a certain way have every right to know the standards expected of them.

The same is true for training information; if the performance of certain tasks requires training or information about procedures, the people being controlled should be able to expect that the necessary information will be given to them. The reaction to no training may range from a simple "How do you expect me to perform if I don't know what is expected of me" or "Nobody ever showed me how to do it" to some of the more aggressive reactions described at the beginning of the chapter.

Finally, managers frequently forget to give periodic feedback of results. Too often, frustration over control results from the supervisor's not giving the subordinate adequate feedback while the process is going on so that behavior could be altered. This allows negative factors to build up until they are no longer tolerable to the organization. Then, when the employee is finally informed, the result is usually a fantastic letdown for a person who thought all along that his or her performance was adequate at worst and superior at best.

This is an example of what George Odiorne calls the activity trap.* Sometimes managers are so intent on overmanaging that they end up emphasizing activity and not output. Then they attempt to reward or punish based on activity and not on output.

Measuring activity, not output

For example, a popular way of assessing a faculty member in a college or university is to determine if "he or she is around all the time." But a faculty member who *is* "around all the time" may be the least productive one. The faculty member who retires to a study carrel to prepare better for class may be a better teacher; one who writes more articles and hence becomes a scholar of growing reputation is also fulfilling the objectives prescribed for a professor. Keeping set office hours and seeing students, but wasting little time on faculty politics or hallway gossip is often the most productive stance for a professor. But if the personnel-evaluation process measures the faculty member on time spent in the office and visibility and not on teaching and research output, it is measuring activity—the wrong thing. Similar examples of measuring the wrong thing can be cited for industry and public service occupations as well. In our opening case, for example, many of the things that Helen LeBlanc emphasized to Betsy were activities, not output standards. Indeed, the only measurable output standards that Betsy was given were the target of reconciling within $3 and the number of people she should handle in an hour. All of the other things that Helen related were activities, but Betsy was never shown the relevance of them to output. Is it any wonder that she soon started neglecting them?

Suppose that you were ill and hence were unable to get your management assignment done, but nonetheless your professor argued, "Well, that's unfortunate, but a deadline is a deadline." How would you feel? Similar reactions arise in most organizational situations if controls are automatically applied with little thought given to the problems inherent in the system or the disabilities of the individuals being controlled. For example, control systems rarely account for physical handicaps, special circumstances that may inhibit the successful completion of a task, or incidents that require an extended deadline. Or, they may not account for the fact that completion of a particular project or attainment of a particular standard may have been missed because the person being held responsible was dependent on another person or unit that failed to complete an assignment and over which the responsible person had no control. For example, piece-rate systems, whereby individuals are paid by the number of products they produce, should not be

Inflexibility in applying controls

* George S. Odiorne, *Management and the Activity Trap* (New York: Harper & Row, 1974).

instituted unless there is complete assurance that parts are available when needed and that previous processors of the units, upon whom the people on piece rates depend for materials and a steady supply of units, do not disrupt the flow so as to cause the piece rates to be endangered.

In other words, there may be legitimate reasons for failure to meet standards, and these reasons should be taken into account. We are not saying, however, that every excuse for not meeting a standard or deadline is a legitimate one which ought to be recognized. The controller must be alert enough to differentiate between legitimate and phony excuses.

Inconsistency in applying controls

One common cause of dysfunctional human reaction to controls is a manager's applying controls and the resultant rewards and punishments inconsistently either in relation to one individual or group of individuals or between individuals. Several specific situations can be considered. First, on one day a manager is strict and precise in applying a standard, on another day is lax, and then reverts back to being strict. Or, a manager starts out being strict and precise and then levels out to an easy and lackadaisical application of standards (Helen LeBlanc seemed to behave this way). Or, finally, the manager starts out being lax and then becomes strict. Under all of these situations, the resulting possible behavior patterns by the employees who are supposedly being controlled should be fairly predictable. In the first instance, the behavior would probably be rebellious and aggressive. In the latter two cases, the employees would learn what to expect in terms of supervisory or controller behavior, and if that expectation were reinforced consistently, it would cause their patterns of behavior to be either supportive or nonsupportive of organizational objectives. If a supervisor's behavior changes from lax to strict, the employee may engage in any of the following types of behavior: produce under fear, ingratiate himself or herself with the boss, or sabotage the process. If the reverse occurs—the supervisor's behavior changes from strict to lax—employees often will slide from standards; productivity and quality will decrease. Betsy Blinker is an excellent example of this type of reaction.

Inconsistent application of controls is the reason often given for firing or replacing baseball managers. A new manager may demand strict adherence to rules and standards in terms of dress, curfew, practice sessions, signals, effort, etc. After the team wins a pennant, World Series, or just improves considerably over the previous manager's record, however, the strict *enforcement* of the standards may be relaxed, even though they are still expected. Since the team is not together during the winter season, reinforcement of the original standards is also not continually available, and the next season, under less strict application, players may learn more lax, less productive behavior patterns. That change quite often costs the manager his job.

Applying inconsistent standards among subordinates may create even more problems than applying standards inconsistently to all subordinates. If one subordinate seems to feel or perceive that he or she is being treated differently or that the standards applied to his or her work are different from those being applied to peers, a reaction of rebellion, resignation, or some other nonfunctional behavior usually will set in. If a group of individuals perceives that one of its members is being treated too harshly or even differently from others in the group, the manager might find the group solidifying, with group pressures on the superior or group slowdowns coming about.

Human problems in control systems may arise when the organization attempts to control too much. Instead, for example, of controlling an end product or end result, some firms or organizations attempt to control at every subproduct, component, or subprocess. One illustration of this is the overuse of line budget control rather than dollar total budgeting; that is, a unit is budgeted and controlled by specific predetermined expense categories rather than having a lump sum to be divided and spent according to priorities decided on within the unit.

Overcontrol—too many standards to fulfill

This is not to say that control at the subprocess level is never to be used; in many cases the control of subprocesses or subproducts is essential. Consider, for example, the Apollo space program, which succeeded in landing the first man on the moon. Relying strictly on the control of the entire system or even larger subsystems in that program might have been catastrophic. Each subcomponent and subprocess—even the very small ones—was an integral part of the entire mission, and failure of any one crucial subcomponent would have slowed down the whole mission (possibly resulting in the scrapping of the program) at a minimum, or resulted in possible disaster for the mission and its valuable equipment and crew members. In that particular case, overcontrol was necessary.

In other cases, however, too much control of the subprocesses can be inhibiting, stifle creativity, decrease motivation, and actually cause the operation of the organization to be more inefficient. Excessive paperwork in terms of reports of activity, overdetail in expense reports (some organizations, for example, require the detailed listing of every hotel telephone call made by traveling executives and salespeople) take up time and energies all out of proportion to the usefulness of the information.

The existence of too many controls may result from successive pilings on of controls and standards without ever having a management audit or some determination of whether the controls are functional or useful to achieving the overall organizational objectives. Often, added controls will be instituted during a time of fiscal emergency, lower sales, profit famines, or economic recession, but those controls are never removed when the original environmental conditions are no longer operative. Or, a scandal of some sort may impel an organization to create new control points, which will never be removed and which then may create barriers to successful achievement of objectives rather than contribute to protecting the organization and enhancing objective achievement.

Losing sight of real objectives: substituting procedures for end results

During an analysis of a business organization, one of my consultant friends told his client: "What this organization needs is a good enema." The client was taken somewhat aback until he realized that people were filling out forms, checking all sorts of records, double-checking the most minute parts of employee performance, and doing all kinds of little things. But somehow nothing was really happening in the organization. No new ideas or products were being created; employees were not motivated to take the initiative in solving problems, to plan for the future, or to deviate from an inefficient mode of operation. Everyone was literally too busy satisfying the controllers and the control systems; the whole organization had lost sight of its real objectives, and over the years, the company had built up a managerial philosophy that emphasized control. The people didn't know what was being done with the information being collected, and some didn't even know why particular standards were being enforced. But the information was being collected—indeed demanded—throughout the organization, and the standards were being enforced.

This type of "trained incapacity" we can call organizational hardening of the arteries.* The satisfaction of the procedures becomes more important than the contribution of those procedures toward the objectives of the organization. Some sociologists who have studied organizations and particularly bureaucracy see this process of substituting controls and procedures for the pursuit of objectives as being almost a natural process in organizations. Only conscious, explicit attention to preventing such a process from occurring will mitigate against its infecting any organization. The First National Bank of Kingsford, illustrated in this chapter's opening vignette, shows signs of trained incapacity, at least in terms of official outlook, although the enforcement seems so lax that the employees quickly learn that many of the standards are "paper tigers."

Too little confidence in people

Controls may be instituted because the managers have a particular philosophy that dictates the necessity for control over people—Theory X. If managers believe that individuals do not want to work, are not motivated to be creative, or do not have the abilities or knowledge to be given wide latitude in decision making or self-control, they will construct organizations and control procedures that reflect those beliefs. But as we have seen, some theorists question those assumptions, arguing that the human problems

* Robert K. Merton, "Bureaucratic Structure and Personality," *Social Forces* 18 (1940): 560–568. Reprinted in Joseph A. Litterer, *Organizations Vol. 1*, 2d ed. (New York: Wiley, 1969), pp. 240–247.

afflicting many organizations are actually the consequence of applying the Theory X assumptions about individuals and groups in the first place. In essence, applying control measures based on erroneous Theory X assumptions in effect causes the assumed behavior patterns to occur, according to the critics.

MANAGERIAL ADJUSTMENT OF CONTROL SYSTEMS TO THE HUMAN FACTOR

Many of the human problems related to control systems can probably be avoided with *sound* management practices. Managers who recognize that some situations form exceptions to ironclad rules, that there are differences in the personal problems and abilities of individuals, and that effective management usually means adapting flexibly to situations are most likely to overcome the resistance to control as a management tool. Here we shall cover a number of managerial methods and points for overcoming some of those problems. To some extent, our discussion here will parallel that in the previous section, in that we will match corrective managerial actions to the problems we note in our earlier discussion.

- Give feedback of results
- Ensure availability of training and information
- Exercise flexibility in control
- Be firm in control
- Minimize control points
- Recognize factors beyond subordinates' control
- Recognize the need for individualism and growth
- Audit the control package

Managerial practices for overcoming resistance to control

Feedback of results

Effective managers generally give quick feedback of results and evaluations. One of the better features of Management by Objectives is that *feedback is definitely scheduled as an integral part of the MBO system.* Feedback to the subordinate is a necessary and essential part of the total system. But note that MBO is based on a set of total *output* standards—ideally, quantitative—not necessarily process, behavior, or subprocess standards.

Managers having the responsibility of controlling should plan to schedule periodic feedback to subordinates; in some cases this should be written—very much like a report card on performance—but periodically managers should sit down and present results orally to subordinates and discuss overcoming inadequacies. Such a session should not be solely evaluative and corrective, but primarily supportive and future-oriented. Indeed, it is as important for the subordinate to receive positive feedback that standards and results were achieved as it is to receive criticism and negative feedback about unmet or unfulfilled standards and deadlines.

If the Theory Y assumptions are correct, feedback—particularly positive feedback—should induce people who are not performing up to standards to attempt to achieve them, e.g., to work harder or to improve skills. We might note that this was one area in which Helen LeBlanc was deficient. Her only attempt to see Betsy Blinker was on the way out of the building. She didn't schedule any feedback sessions and gave none. The lack of feedback probably was another factor contributing to Betsy's ignoring the stated standards and procedures.

Ensure availability of training and information

Managers can eliminate many problems in controlling by ensuring that subordinates are sufficiently trained to carry out their duties and are informed about the standards of their jobs and the methods of carrying them out. Thus training (Chapter 13) and communication (Chapter 15) are intimately linked to the ability of a manager to control effectively and to mitigate against possible human-related side effects of a control system. Susie Waterman (Chapter 15) would have been much more effective in her job if Jake Deveneux had been a more effective trainer and communicator.

The same is true with regard to information. One cannot expect the job to be done if information about the job is not available. Often, for example, service technicians for appliances or automobiles are sent out on service calls with the barest of basic training and insufficient information about particular brands of machines. Some technicians may then take to reading the customer manual on a machine that they were supposed to be trained to repair. If there are many return calls, technicians obviously cannot be held responsible (although they often are); the information should have been available, and the technicians should have been certified as competent on the product before being sent out on the job.

Flexibility in control

Managers can reduce the negative feedback to efforts at controlling if they remain alert to instances when control and correction must vary from the expected. For example, many managers vary the correction process, depending on the longevity of the employee within the organization. New employees, who will be expected to know less or be able to perform less effectively for a period of time, often will be given a more understanding response to their failures to meet standards. As their longevity on the job increases, however, the expectation that they must meet the standards as well as everyone else increases also. You might have noted that Helen LeBlanc stated that Betsy Blinker would be expected to handle twenty-five to thirty clients an hour "after a week or two." At the start, however, her output could have been less.

A manager might also want to be flexible when illness, physical disability, time delays in delivery of components, or other such events occur. But here too the manager should let it be known that the flexibility in his or her control and corrective behavior is not the common approach to controlling within the organizational unit.

One of the quickest ways a manager's efforts at controlling will break down is if he or she does not exhibit firmness and fairness in control—evaluation and corrective action. This injunction against ease is not meant to necessarily contradict the call for flexibility cited in the previous paragraph, however. Rather, managers must be capable of discerning between situations calling for flexibility and those calling for firmness. Legitimate situations requiring flexibility should be recognized; others, in which the excuses are not good enough to rationalize the shortfall from expected standards, should be rejected firmly. If the manager does not react quickly, the control will break down, since the reaction of employees to controls that are not enforced will be to simply ignore them. For example, when Betsy "got away with" cashing her friend's $250 check—a violation of the bank's policy—she knew that she could do it more often, without fear of repercussions.

Firmness in control

Another injunction in discussing firmness is that firmness does not mean unfairness. Never should a control process be applied strictly because the manager wants to show who the boss is. The control process should be related to a standard (which is in turn related to overall organizational objectives), and the evaluation and corrective measures should take place at the appropriate times—not at the whims of a manager trying to flex muscles.

Managers can minimize the human problems associated with control if they simply establish a minimum number of control points in a process or system. This will mean fewer places or times when a subordinate reaction to control will grate against a superior's desire for control. Again, this is not meant to downgrade or minimize the need for control and control systems.

Minimize control points

Controls, however, should be related to achieving the objectives of the organization, and the manager should determine when the cost of control—including the costs of handling the inevitable human reactions to controls—exceeds the benefits of such controls. There is really no need for overcontrol that stifles initiative and dulls motivation and at the same time costs the organization more time and money than it is worth.

Many public agencies build in more control points than are necessary, simply because the public supposedly is given to expect honesty, and more controls are thought necessary to ensure that honesty. A more realistic reason, however, may be that public bureaucracies build up faster, and controllers build up with them. They are more difficult to get out of the system, since the departments and divisions of public institutions—including control units—become favorites of important legislators who cannot see fit to eliminate them for any reason.

Technology is also a factor behind building up the number of control points. With the advent of the electronic computer and the development of data-transmission systems, managers are now able to check out much more information and establish automatic flagging mechanisms at more points in the system. This is all done automatically, and the cost may be lower than a previous smaller number of manual control points or stations. The human reaction to the increased control may be less antagonistic simply because the control is not carried out according to the whims of some person, but by an impersonal, inanimate machine. On the other hand, the idea of machine-controlled humans is also a problem that organizations must cope with; the reactions of the workers at the Lordstown plant were as much against a mechanically controlled manufacturing process as against the pace of the line and the General Motors Assembly Division philosophy of manufacturing.

Recognize factors beyond subordinate's control

Managers must be careful to hold subordinates responsible only for events and processes that are completely under the control of those subordinates. The primary example of this is one that we cited earlier—the piece-rate worker who should not be held responsible if people who are not on piece rate, but whose work affects his or her ability to make the piece-rate quota, didn't perform. In any sequential process, the previous steps are always prerequisites for the steps being controlled, and the possible insufficient performance in those steps must always be considered reasons for leniency or a moderation of the control process for later steps in the process.

Similarly, if responsibilities are split between two or more units, the control process must account for the fact that each manager could not possibly be held accountable individually for the entire project. In many government situations, because of the unique way in which public projects are doled out to the various agencies, responsibility is often split among two or more groups. Thus, for example, in an intelligence operation the CIA, FBI, the various intelligence units of the separate armed forces, and other agencies may have parts of the responsibility. Apart from the political problems involved, evaluation and correction in such a situation are difficult at best because of the split responsibility.

Similar situations arise in industry, whether by design or simply by happenstance. For example, final hiring decisions often are taken over by the personnel department from the line supervisors. The responsibility still rests with the line supervisor (who can never relinquish that), but any evaluative or corrective process applied to the hiring system should recognize the role of the personnel department as well. That is, the line supervisor should not bear the total brunt of the control system.

Recognizing the need for individualism and growth

Theory X managers probably are inclined to introduce more control points and to utilize them more often—i.e., more concurrent control—than are Theory Y managers, who respect the need for human individuality and growth. It is often extraordinarily difficult for managers to understand their value structures which lead them to conclude a necessity for constant and ever-present overcontrol. Hence managers who overcontrol may not recognize that many individuals have an inherent need for autonomy and growth. Although values are difficult to alter, such managers are in need of organization development–type training and sensitivity sessions to understand and perhaps change their perceptions of people. These types of training often are very effective. Managers who manage other managers also should be on the alert for the symptoms—shown by their lower-level managers—of overcontrol and underlying mistrust of subordinates and employees.

Suffice it to say here that any aspiring manager should examine the underlying assumptions of his or her own management philosophy, because those assumptions do condition the approach to control, in terms of both the number of points in a process and the times. And as we have already noted, excessive control may be costly to the organization as well as debilitating to the human relationships between superior and subordinates.

Later on in this book, we shall stress the importance of the organizational audit—the complete and periodic reassessment of all of an organization's plans, procedures, personnel, allocations of resources, systems, etc.—to determine if each of those mechanisms is being utilized most efficiently and effectively in pursuit of the organization's objectives. Here, however, we want to emphasize only one part of that management audit, albeit a very important part: the periodic and systematic assessment of whether all of the controls and corrective systems employed by the organization are: (1) doing what they are supposed to be doing; (2) necessary even when and if they are doing what they are supposed to be doing; and (3) doing what they are supposed to be doing in the most efficient manner.

Auditing and the control package

Many organizations schedule management audits every five years (some, unfortunately, don't schedule them at all). Certain parts of the organization and its systems and processes should have their audits even more frequently. And the control systems imposed on the organization quite possibly are one of those areas, since it is extremely easy and always tempting to add controls. The audit is certainly a good tool to remedy overzealous managers who are imposing too much control over the organization. It is also useful for pointing out managers whose control is insufficient and whose units are not performing well because of it.

SUMMARY AND CONCLUSION

This chapter has been concerned with the human reactions to the control process. As such, it is an extension of the preceding chapter, which detailed the control process and its parts. In this chapter we studied some of the human reactions to control processes, including defensive behavior, ineffective achievement of goals, and lowered motivation and personal dissatisfaction. Then we discussed some of the organizational and managerial causes of the human reactions to control processes. These include inadequate feedback and information, measurement of the wrong things, inflexibility in the application of controls, inconsistency in the application of controls, overcontrol, the substitution of procedures for end results, and too little confidence in the abilities and individual growth of people.

Finally, we considered some possible managerial adjustments of control systems to the human factor. These include feedback of results, adequate training and information of the people being controlled, flexible control, firm control, the minimization of control points, the recognition of factors beyond the control of subordinates, and the recognition of the need for human individualism and growth. In addition, we recommended the periodic auditing of the organization's entire control package.

As we stated earlier, the control process assumes that the standards are correct and that it is generally the organizational components or resources that must be altered. But sometimes the standards are at fault; no planner is so omnipotent that his or her plans or standards must never be altered. When the standards rather than the organizational components are altered, we call such a process adaptation. It is to that managerial task that we turn in the next chapter.

DISCUSSION QUESTIONS

1 Human reactions to control may take the form of defensive behavior, ineffective performance, and lower motivation. Give examples of each of these categories of reaction.

2 Define: (a) frustration and (b) regression.

3 How does inadequate feedback affect a person's reaction to control?

4 Why is an inflexibly applied control a contributor to human dysfunctional reactions to control processes?

5 What do we mean when we say a process is overcontrolled? Illustrate.

6 Define "trained incapacity." As a management consultant, how would you recommend eliminating it?

7 Illustrate some of the managerial methods that executives can utilize to overcome dysfunctional human reactions to control.

8 Why is an audit of the control package considered necessary? How often should such an audit be done?

CASE: ANDY STENKOWSKI (B)

■ "For a company the size of Ajax, you would think that they would already have some standards," complained Andy Stenkowski to his wife, Edith, after a particularly trying day. Today was the frustrating culmination of about two months of managerial ups and downs for Andy.

He had been in his foreman's job for about a month when top management called a meeting of all the foremen. "Gentlemen, we're not getting the product out fast enough. Some of our smaller grocers are starting to complain that we're letting them down. Now each of you guys have some slower men in your sections; let's see if we can get them speeded up."

"About how much should each man be picking an hour?" asked Andy. "There's nothing in the union contract that specifies standards for each job."

"No, that means that the authority is left to management. We can set those standards if we want to," replied the vice-president of operations.

"Do we have any, then?" asked another foreman.

"Nothing, plantwide," replied the vice-president. "We've thought about it, and maybe we'll have something in the next year or so. Meanwhile, though, we've got some real loafers out there, and you guys had better shape them up."

Andy's section generally met their day's orders, but often just barely. There was very little slack, however, and when an unusually large order or a new account came in, the section would leave some orders for the next day or the next shift, depending on the next shift's workload. But Andy knew that the productivity of his people varied. Whereas his best person could pick over 180 pieces an hour, his poorest barely did 90. Andy suspected that the average was about 140.

Andy decided to chart the production of his men for about a month. Then he would establish an average "pick" rate, which he would use as a standard against which to push some of the less productive pickers. He also wanted to check any industry publications to see what other companies the size and type of Ajax were doing.

A month later, Andy called his crew together and announced that the average pick rate in the unit was 142 pieces an hour, compared with an industry average of 144. He said that he wanted those pickers at or above the average to stay with their production, but that he was going to work on those in the 90–125 range to get them up to average.

"Hey, Andy, when did you turn into a company slave driver?" called out one of the men.

"I hope you guys realize that the top guys are on my back to increase production," replied Andy. "Now, let's get back to work."

Only four people were picking fewer than 130 pieces an hour, but one was Charlie Vitrello, whose output rarely exceeded 100 pieces an hour. The three others gradually inched up to 130 and over, but Charlie stayed under 100. Andy spoke to Charlie and asked him why he wasn't cooperating.

"Hell, Andy, you've got no authority to set standards. Look, there's nothing in the contract, management has set no standards, so I can set my own pace. Now, just stay off my back, will you?"

"C'mon Charlie, we're old friends, and I know you can do a better job. I'll give you another month. Let's see if we can come near average."

"Or what, Andy?" asked Charlie.

"Let's not get to that, Charlie," replied Andy as he walked off.

Another month went by and Charlie's output stayed under 100. Andy finally went to Charlie and said, "Look, Charlie, I've tried to be good to you. Everyone but you is trying to meet the standard. I'm afraid I'm going to have to send you home for a week without pay."

"What? What for?" yelled an irate Charlie.

"Disregard of orders and unwillingness to meet a management standard," replied Andy.

Charlie marched off and an hour later, accompanied by Lou Votrovich, the shop steward, approached Andy. "Andy, what is this nonsense about standards?" asked Lou. "You know that there are no standards specified in the contract."

"Then it's up to management to set them," replied Andy.

"And management hasn't set any in this plant," said Lou.

"I'm the foreman, and I set them for this section," said Andy. "Charlie refuses to cut it here."

"C'mon Andy. Don't let the power go to your head. Who the hell gave you the authority to set standards?"

"Sorry, Lou, but Charlie stays out. I'm not budging on this one. Top management gets on my tail, and I've got to get output out of this group."

"Okay, Andy. We're going to grieve. I think we've got a winner here," announced Lou.

"Be my guest," replied Andy.

Andy reported the incident to the vice-president of operations and got very little response. "Okay, Andy, we'll see you at the first-level hearing. I'll be there and so will the personnel manager. Let me sleep on our case for a while."

At the hearing, the company and the union were working on four grievances, this one being the first. Andy recounted how he set the standards and that the rest of his crew was trying to meet them.

Charlie replied that Andy was overstepping his power. Lou Votrovich and the local president reasserted that there were no standards in the contract and that management had set a precedent by not enforcing company-wide standards. "Now, how can they justify one foreman's setting standards unilaterally? Besides," argued the president, "Charlie didn't even get a proper warning."

The vice-president for operations replied that for the record, he was not conceding management's right to set standards, but they would not press this case. Charlie would be reinstated with back pay.

Andy sat there stunned for a moment and then got up and left the hearing room. Charlie could barely conceal the grin on his face.

Later in the day, the vice-president of operations called Andy in and said, "Andy, I think you're on the right track, but this case wasn't as important for us to win as two of the others. We're going to set companywide standards, and I'm glad you started the ball rolling. At least the union knows we're moving in that direction. I want you to keep trying to get your production up. For the time being, you'll just have to find another way."

When Andy got home, the first words out of his mouth were, "Darn it, why did I ever take that foreman's job?" ∎

Case questions

1. Why did Charlie Vitrello react negatively to Andy's attempt to set standards?

2. What company managerial actions made it difficult for Andy to get Charlie (or any other reluctant employee) to respond to the new standards?

3. What now remains of Andy's capacity to lead, motivate, and, in particular, control?

SELECTED READINGS

Beaumont, R. A., and R. B. Helfgott, *Management, Automation, and People* (New York: Industrial Relation Counselors, 1964).

Benson, J. K., ed., *Organizational Analysis—Critique and Innovation* (Beverly Hills, Calif.: Sage, 1977).

Blau, B. A., "Understanding Midcareer Stress," *Management Review* **67**, 8 (August 1978): 57–62.

Cammann, C., and D. A. Nadler, "Fit Control Systems to your Managerial Style," *Harvard Business Review* **54** (January/February 1976): 65–72.

Dew, R. B., and K. P. Gee, *Management Control and Information: Studies in the Use of Control Information by Middle Management in Manufacturing Companies* (London: Macmillan, 1973).

Fournies, F. F., *Coaching for Improved Work Performance* (New York: Van Nostrand, Reinhold, 1978).

French, J. R. P., Jr., and B. Raven, "The Bases of Social Power," in D. Cartwright and A. Zander, eds., *Group Dynamics: Research and Theory* (New York: Harper & Row, 1960).

Graham, G. H., *Management: The Individual, the Organization, the Process* (Belmont, Calif.: Wadsworth, 1975).

Greene, R. M., *The Management Game: How to Win with People* (Homewood, Ill.: Dow Jones-Irwin, 1969).

Hackman, J. R., "The Design of Work in the 1980s," *Organizational Dynamics* **7**, 1 (Summer 1978): 2–17.

Hall, D. M., *The Management of Human Systems* (Cleveland: Association for Systems Management, 1971).

Hanson, C. A., and D. K. Hanson, "Motivation: Are the Old Theories Still True?" *Supervisory Management* **23**, 6 (June 1978): 9–15.

Lateiner, A. R., and H. W. Heinrich, *Management and Controlling Employee Performance* (West New York, N.J.: Lateiner Publishing, 1969).

Lippiti, G. L., "Quality of Work: Organization Review in Action," *Training and Development Journal* **32**, 7 (July 1978): 4–10.

McClelland, D. C., and D. H. Burnham, "Power Is the Great Motivator," *Harvard Business Review* **54** (March/April 1976): 100–110.

McMahon, J. T., and J. M. Ivancevich, "A Study of Control in a Manufacturing Organization: Managers and Non-Managers," *Administrative Science Quarterly* **21** (March 1976): 66–83.

Odiorne, G. S., *Management and the Activity Trap* (New York: Harper & Row, 1974).

Pugh, D. S., and R. L. Payne, *Organizational Behavior in Its Context* (New York: Saxon House, 1977).

Robey, D., "Individual Moderators of the Task Design, Job Attitude Relationship: A Note on Measurement," *Journal of Management Studies* **15**, 1 (February 1978): 68–76.

Scott, W. H., *The Management of Conflict: An Appeal Systems in Organizations* (Homewood, Ill.: Richard D. Irwin, 1965).

Swingle, P. G., *The Management of Power* (Hillsdale, N.J.: Halsted Press, 1976).

Szilagyi, A. D., Jr., *et al.*, "Role Dynamics, Locus of Control, and Employee Attitudes and Behavior," *Academy of Management Journal* **19** (June 1976): 259–276.

Tannenbaum, A. S., "Control in Organizations: Individual Adjustment and Organizational Performance," *Administration Science Quarterly* **8** (1962): 236–257.

Thompson, D. W., *The Manager: Understanding and Influencing Behavioral Change* (Chicago: Bradford Press, 1974).

Tricker, R. I., *Management Information and Control Systems* (New York: Wiley, 1976).

Whetten, D. A., "Coping with Incompatible Expectations: An Integrated View of Role Conflict," *Administrative Science Quarterly* **23**, 2 (June 1978): 254–271.

Chapter 19
ADAPTATION: OBJECTIVE AND STRATEGY CHANGE

CHAPTER HIGHLIGHTS

In this chapter we cover adaptation situations—when the standards and strategies are not assumed to be unchangeable. We study the adaptive process and then some reasons for altering organizational goals and strategy—changing environments, personnel, and other internal resources; inadequate initial planning; unreachable forecasts; and changing clientele needs. We then cover some of the various adaptive responses engaged in by organizations, including strategy redesign, product or service discontinuation, selective pruning, merger, or cessation of operations.

LEARNING OBJECTIVES

1 To be able to define the process of adaptation and to know its applications.

2 To understand how the adaptive process is an extension of the control process.

3 To learn the effects of changing environmental parameters: specifically, the effects of changes in the economic, political, social, technological, institutional, and international environments.

4 To understand the effects of changing personnel and internal resources on the organization.

5 To appreciate the effects on the organization of inadequate past planning and goal setting and poor forecasting.

6 To learn to expect the needs of clients to change often.

7 To understand how the various adaptation processes at various levels of the organization operate.

8 To learn to avoid the sunk-cost argument.

CASE: GRECO-ROMAN CHAIR COMPANY (B)

■ Something was happening to the Samson chair, and so far nobody could figure it out. The company had spent more than $200,000 researching the design and hiring top design consultants for that piece and another $250,000 market researching and test marketing the design. Those were the largest expenditures that Greco-Roman had ever made on a new product. Expectations were high, but the chair wasn't selling!

Achilles and Paris, the company's advertising agency, could not explain the low sales either. The agency had put its top people to work on the market research for that chair and had used established procedures which in the past had proved reliable for predicting success or failure, but something was wrong in this case. The chair wasn't selling, despite a complete recheck of the data and a rerun of the design through the market research testing process. Both of these indicated again that the design should have been successful and that the chair should be selling.

Chuck Martinelli, sales manager for Greco-Roman, carefully reviewed the progress of the Samson chair. The product had started out as Model 48 and was named Samson later, in accord with the company's policy of naming products after biblical and mythical characters. Achilles and Paris came up with a campaign that pictured Samson as a religious character and also emphasized his strength, but the advertising project was stopped while Greco-Roman and the Achilles and Paris people determined if the religious symbolism would have any negative repercussions. They finally decided to modify the appeal a bit, but to continue to put the emphasis on strength. The Achilles and Paris people were confident—at that time—that the design of the product and the theme of the advertising campaign responded perfectly to the assessment of the market need as indicated by the market research data.

Martinelli then reviewed the firm's own sales efforts. The discount schedule corresponded to that for G-R's other products and was identical to those of the other firms in the industry. The price of Samson was a little higher than that of the nearest competitive chair, but Greco-Roman products always carried a premium price. The salespeople's commission schedules actually were higher for Samson than for other pieces in the line; Greco-Roman always used a higher commission schedule for a new product until it was about two years into the line, when it was revised downward to the regular schedule. Salespeople never complained about that policy, and it gave them an incentive to push new products. Salespeople's call sheets were checked and their reports reviewed; only one report had anything derogatory to say about the product. It contained a complaint about the chair's massive-looking legs!!

Martinelli was stymied; he called Harry Cleaver, vice-president for marketing, and arranged a meeting for the next morning. When he was in Cleaver's office, Chuck pointed out that sales of Samson were well below projections, but that the advertising campaign, discount schedule, sales efforts, commission schedule—in fact, all aspects of the marketing efforts—were going according to plan, which was based on good, hard, sound data. Also, the quality of the product was excellent. Few complaints and returns were coming in.

"Chuck, let's sleep on this for a few days and see if we can come up with the reason Samson is bombing out. If we can't come up with anything, we'll bring it to the weekly executive meeting. Maybe they'll want to cut our losses and drop the whole project."

"Wow, Harry, we'd better be sure. There's a lot of hours and a lot of money sunk into this chair." ■

INTRODUCTION

In Chapter 17 we noted that adaptation differs from control in that in the latter, the standards are presumed to be fixed and the correctives are in the performance, whereas in the former, the goals and plans are assumed to be variable and can be changed. Figure 19.1 illustrates the adaptation process (dark lines) superimposed over the control process (lighter lines).

Adaptive thinking is not generally widespread among managements, and organizations continue to pursue goals long after many years of obvious failure and in spite of all manners of noneffective corrective action applied within the organization to the systems and personnel. Other managements continue to pursue goals and objectives long after independent and expert observers have indicated that the original goals were either unattainable or worthless.

Generally, the larger and more complex the organization, the more difficult it is for it to practice adaptation. However, it is precisely in the larger organizations and because of the complexity that their managers must be especially alert for adaptive possibilities. For example, government programs

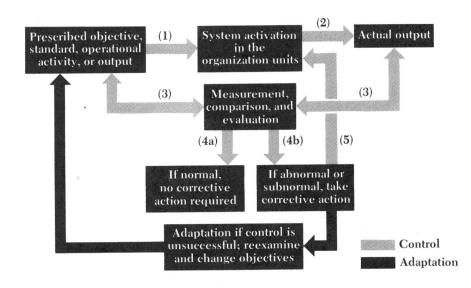

FIG. 19.1
The adaptation process, superimposed on the control process.

are often extremely stable and resistant to change, and legislative bodies continue to pour money into objectives long after it is evident that the programs have failed, the objectives are unreachable, or even after there are serious questions as to whether they are worthwhile. But because of the particular process of legislative enactment, public programs are extremely difficult to eliminate. Such programs, even those that do not accomplish their objectives, acquire a constituency of articulate and powerful supporters. Many legislatures, however, are now starting to enact "sunset" laws, establishing a time limit on the life of all programs. Those proving useful will be reenacted and refunded; those not achieving their promise will be allowed to expire.

Of course, the need to adapt is not confined to public programs. Private businesses may be equally blind to the process, and this is usually uncalled for. Ideally, the concepts of long-range and strategic planning call for a reevaluation of the very planning premises from time to time and a revamping of the plan when the parameters on which the plan was based are found to be changing. This is often called *dynamic planning*, and in some organizations dynamic planning is prescribed as the policy of organization relative to its design effort. Nevertheless, continual chasing of the proverbial nonexistent brass ring continues in many private organizations as well as public ones.

In this chapter we shall explore some of the specific reasons why organizations might be forced to practice adaptation. These concern primarily the *internal and external organizational parameters that are subject to rapid change*—and which should be continually evaluated and reevaluated—and the replanning necessary because of *past inadequate planning, poor forecasting,* and *changing client needs*. We shall then explore adaptive mechanisms: strategy change, organizational change, and adaptation at the various levels of the organization.

CAUSES FOR ADAPTATION

A number of the parameters on which the organization's plan is essentially based can change more rapidly or slowly than anticipated or indeed can change when such a change was not even anticipated. We shall cover several of these parameters, along with some of the design-process reasons for adaptive behavior (see Fig. 19.2).

Earlier in the book, we mentioned that some organizations engage in futurist thinking: brainstorming and trying to project well into the future in order to modify old plans and create new ones.* As more and more or-

---

* The Delphi method is often used in these projection exercises (see Chapter 6). One author who specializes in futurist projections is Herman Kahn. *See* Herman Kahn, William Brown, and Leon Martel, *The Next 200 Years* (New York: Morrow, 1976). It should be noted that Kahn's optimistic views of the future are not universally shared.

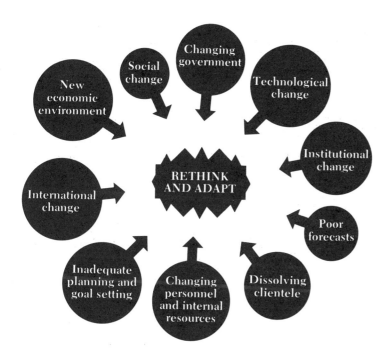

FIG. 19.2
Reasons for adaptation.

ganizations do this type of thinking, the practice of adaptation should become more widespread. Futurist thinking will not guarantee success, of course, but it will spur organizations to at least consider the possibility that what they are aiming for now may not be correct—too little, too much, or the wrong things.

The environment of organizations can, for our purposes here, be classified into six parts: economic, governmental, social, technological, institutional, and international. This breakdown, of course, is strictly for our own analytical approach; there is overlap among and between these areas, and they are not mutually exclusive in their effects on the organization and its planning.

    For many of the components in each of these areas, forecasting is done before the planning is undertaken and goals are set. But sometimes the forecasts are too imperfect. And often, as we pointed out above, goals become cast in concrete despite planners' best intentions. Adaptation, as we might expect, is a difficult thing to learn, because of loss of face on the part of the planner, a natural tendency to protect one's reputation and ideas, and a blinderlike attitude toward change. But environmental change in this day and age may be too powerful a force for adaptation to be avoided or neglected.

Changing environments

The economic environment   Here controllers and replanners must consider trends in basic business conditions: income, production, employment, prices and price levels, investment, consumer demand, government spending, and the like. (Chuck Martinelli considered some of these factors when doing his analysis of Greco-Roman's Midlands district.)

Precipitous changes in any one of the economic areas can be the cause of a serious shock to an organization. For example, sharp increases in prices can cause inventory revaluations which if missed, can be of extreme danger to the control of the organization. For example, prices of silver were rising spectacularly during the 1970s. One silver flatware company had its inventory valued by the last-in–first-out method, and it was courted by suitors for merger and corporate raiders who might have been interested in liquidating the company and selling off the silver for a handsome profit. Either no one in the company had thought to revalue the inventory, or the company was locked into a thought process that did not question long-held and cherished ways of doing business.

Similarly, defense contractors have often failed to discern abrupt changes in defense-procurement and spending policy (frequently related to changes in the governmental and international environments as well) and have had contracts cancelled, resulting in numerous layoffs and complete wreckage of profit projections and plans.

The governmental environment   Transfers of governmental power from one party to the other and changes in the approaches of the parties can have significant effects on many types of organizations and on the effectiveness of their plans. Goals and plans are often changed to reflect the possible opportunities and risks created by such changes.

Examples of political and governmental processes affecting business goals and procedures are numerous: employment (equal opportunity laws and affirmative action orders), environmental protection legislation (air, water, solid waste, noise), and urban renewal, to mention a few. On the local and plant level, zoning and planning restrictions have a tremendous impact on organizational planning. For example, one developer came to a New England college town with a 2600-unit housing development. However, he had failed to do his homework on the governmental system and the political climate of the town, with its complex network of zoning, planning, and citizens' review boards. Once he ran into resistance initially, however, he was astute enough to go back to the planning board and explore not only why he wasn't getting his original project through, but also whether the original project was right for this political environment. Eventually, the scope of the project was cut in half and was then accepted by the town. By that time, however, economic conditions had changed sufficiently so that the original project had to be scrapped and be replaced by something more in line with the revised economic projections.*

Social environment   Most organizations are affected by social changes and should keep their antennae attuned to changes in social indicators. For example, demography has an important effect on many business organizations and educational institutions; they continually readjust their goals to service different parts of the population as birth and death rates change. Baby food manufacturers, for example, noting the recent decrease in the birth rate, have looked around for new areas to enter. Some have tried to expand their original project lines into new international markets; others have looked for new product markets. Although many are still heavily involved in baby foods, they are also moving into other products such as insurance, juvenile toys, and recreation equipment.

Universities, reacting to the lower birth rates, are now searching about for new client groups to serve: renewal education, reaching out to off-campus clientele, executive development, etc. Some resistance is encountered as certain units within the universities believe that they can continue to function as they always have with the traditional student body. Some units may be able to continue traditional ways, due to the shifting preferences among the traditional students, but in general the total university cannot, and boards of trustees will be reevaluating the objectives and changing them.† On the other hand, many universities have one problem that is forcing them to find new ways to service the declining teenage population. Many institutions overbuilt dormitory buildings and other facilities during the days when the birth rate looked as though it would never abate, and they are now committed to bond payments over several decades. This, of course, makes any reevaluation of goals doubly difficult, as old decisions have committed the organization to a course of action that new decisions must take into account.

Technological environment   In the mid-1800s someone suggested closing the United States Patent Office because everything that had to be invented had already been invented! Of course, he was wrong. Organizations continue to be affected by technological changes, and even the smallest organization can have its controls and procedures automated and its goals changed by technological possibilities. A new discovery can make products and processes obsolete overnight. Technological breakthroughs in packaging, as much as any other social or economic reason, led to the rise of discount department stores and supermarkets, and the change in that industry is con-

---

* Since then, the environmental conditions—chiefly economic and political—have changed so much that the project is essentially dead, and the land is being sold off.
† For some interesting insights and opinions here, *see* Warren Bennis, *The Unconscious Conspiracy: Why Leaders Can't Lead* (New York: AMACOM, 1978).

stant. Optical scanning, generic foods, automatic funds transfer, and the mixed store are threatening further changes in the retail food business.

One interesting example of technology's affecting an industry is in banking, traditionally a conservative business. Banking has become so fully automated that in many parts of the country, the customer never has to see a teller anymore. Machine banking, which can take place at any hour of the day and in remote locations, expedites service. What happens to the bank, however, which tries to live up to its motto of personalized service under such circumstances? Some customers wanting speed would prefer the automatic service; others, desiring instead personalized services, would prefer to see a teller. A complete switch to either one of the methods is bound to lose customers, yet the automatic service is much more cost-efficient. One bank compromised very nicely; in addition to providing an automatic teller system, it put tellers at desks for those customers who wanted personalized service. The older, traditional cages and counters were eliminated, creating a feeling of warmth as well as resulting in some significant saving in floor space.

The airlines' customer services have been affected by the technology of jet- over piston-powered aircraft. With the piston plane, the cabin crews could serve a gourmet dinner without having to rush, and the passengers could enjoy a leisurely meal. With jet-powered aircraft reducing flying time by half, however, flight crews simply cannot get full meals served and the cabin cleared and secured before landing. So many airline companies have snack flights, with minimal meal service. Incidentally, many airline executives (albeit after deregulation moves by the Civil Aeronautics Board and Congress) are now rediscovering the notion that much of the public wants only low-cost, fast transportation anyway, particularly on short flights. But it was the technology of the jet engine that played the major role in changing the expectations of the flying public.

Institutional environment   "Institutional environment" refers to the changing societal and cultural perceptions of roles of the institutions of the society. For example, the changing perceptions of the roles of the corporation, labor union, government, charitable associations, voluntary organizations, etc., have resulted in a reassessment of goals and objectives within those organizations.

Although many of the functions of private agencies and institutions have been taken over by government in the past thirty to forty years, a possible change in the expected role of the corporation is now occurring. Today corporations, either voluntarily or reluctantly, are taking on social obligations or are being forced to consider social factors in what previously were strictly economic decisions.* Pollution, hiring practices, and ethical behavior are

* See Arthur Elkins and Dennis W. Callaghan, A Managerial Odyssey: Problems in Business and Its Environment, 2d ed. (Reading, Mass.: Addison-Wesley, 1978), especially Chapter 1, for a discussion of the pros and cons of social involvement.

only a few of these areas. These new expectations are forcing corporations to rearrange their objectives according to new social and institutional standards. For example, the plant-location decision discussed in Chapter 14 may now have to also consider environmental cleanliness, local employment, zoning, and other goals deemed socially responsible.

Most institutions in society and the associated organizations are subject to changing societal or client expectations, but none so much and so pervasively as the corporation and government during the past two decades. Some of the voluntary organizations and charitable organizations have seen their publics' expectations decreased, but the business corporation especially is expected by many to now do more. And often so is government. Congress or legislatures, reflecting the popular will or that of powerful and sometimes vociferous political groups frequently add functions to governmental organizations, redefining the goals and objectives of those units or organizations. For example, on the state levels prisons are more and more becoming places of rehabilitation rather than incarceration. This means a whole new role for the executives of the prison organization—perhaps new skills—and sometimes their inability to adjust old norms and attitudes to the new function and objectives is all too obvious.

The point here is that society creates new institutions or alters the expectations it seeks from older ones. When this happens, a reevaluation of objectives and plans, and sometimes a redefinition of the organization itself, must be made.

International environment   Actions on the international front affect not only the multinational firms and the internationally oriented organizations, but domestic organizations as well. Although most observers trace the energy crisis much further back than 1973, it was the Arab oil embargo of that year that brought the results of the crisis down to the level of most individuals. That embargo probably caused more adaptation on the part of managers than any single event, barring all-out world war. One survey of managers found that they raised prices, substituted raw materials, changed production processes or techniques, invested in energy-saving equipment, simplified product lines, rationed customers, and sometimes closed their facilities.* Other firms, particularly utilities, substituted fuels—in most cases changing to coal for gas or oil. Such changes are mainly adaptation, the changing of objectives or plans because the older ones were no longer attainable or viable.

The formal recognition by the United States of the People's Republic of China in January 1979, the 1977 coffee crop freeze in Brazil, the economic woes in Great Britain, the dollar's decreasing value overseas, and the government assistance rendered to firms in Japan—these are only a few of the

---

* *See* James K. Brown, "The Energy Crisis and the Manufacturer," *The Conference Board Record* (June 1974): 45–48.

events in the international arena that are and have been affecting the ability of organizations in the United States to reach objectives and hence necessitate a call for adaptation and reevaluation of objectives.

Changing personnel and internal resources

Sometimes, as we have noted, the internal strength of an organization results in its setting objectives in order to capitalize on that strength. When that strength dissipates through attrition, death, movement of executives, or any other reason, it may be necessary to change the objectives rather than hold a new team responsible for outputs that it can't possibly reach.

For example, suppose that sales objectives for a particular territory were based partly on the potential for the territory but mostly on the experience of a long-time salesperson who had developed personal contacts with buyers and was able to practically write the orders for certain customers. If that salesperson were pirated away by another firm, that change would be a loss for the one firm, but a new, positive factor for the competitive firm. The first firm would have to radically alter its sales objectives for that area; no new salesperson could be held responsible for meeting the old objectives in the face of such a handicap of competing against the superstar of that territory, who was now in the employ of another firm.

On the other hand, a change in personnel or internal resources can alter the objectives in a positive way. Consider a small firm that always made it by on its owner's personal reputation and entrepreneurial skill, but was lacking in capital and managerial expertise to grow in any substantial manner. If that owner sells out, the skill and reputation are now gone, and the objectives of the firm should be changed to reflect the owner's absence. But that absence may be more than compensated for by the new capital and resources that can be poured into the firm by the new owners. Thus the objectives will also change positively, according to the capabilities of those new resources.

Overcoming inadequate past planning and goal setting

Adaptation ought to take place if the goal-setting and planning processes of the organization were inadequate to begin with. Often goals are set with little or no research into their attainability; as a result, they are either nonattainable or very easy to reach. In the first case new goals must be set, taking into account the correct environment and an adequate assessment of the capabilities of the organization.

When goals are reached too easily, adaptation should take the form of raising expectations. In other words, control and adaptation do not apply only to the nonachievement or underachievement of goals. If goals are reached too easily, the revaluation process should recognize that the planning process was incomplete, did not correctly estimate either external or internal factors, and should revise the goals upward.

But planning and goal setting may also *overestimate* the potential of markets, resources, and personnel. In this case the subordinates who have to operate in the real environment cannot be held responsible for inadequate planning and goal setting.

Closely related to poor planning is the possibility of an unreachable forecast. Because forecasting is not an exact science, errors do occur. One need only scan the various governmental, university, and private economic forecasts to see that errors have occurred, and frequently. Most industrial or business forecasts are built on the basis of either commercial or public economic forecasts, market research data, or a combination of the two. Errors can be easily magnified as one forecast becomes the basic data source for another. Furthermore, as the forecast becomes longer-range in nature, the errors can become more plentiful, since even the best forecasters' crystal balls become more cloudy as the variable of time is added in.

Unreachable forecasts

Most organizational plans are based on fulfilling some need of a customer or a client, potential benefactee, or a citizen. If that need changes or disappears, the organization should be changing strategies. Ordinarily, such a need change can be foreseen and forecasted for. But often it changes abruptly. When the Salk antipolio vaccine was introduced (followed by the Sabin oral vaccine) and quickly administered almost universally, it eliminated the reason for existence of the March of Dimes. That organization quickly found another crippling disease to campaign against—birth defects—but some organizations do not and go out of existence. Adaptation in the face of total client need change may call for the utmost in imagination and creativity on the part of top-level managers.

Changes in clientele need

Sometimes projects are kept going "because we have spent so much already, it would all be wasted if we didn't go ahead with the project." (Chuck Martinelli said as much at the end of the case opening this chapter.)

Avoiding the sunk-cost argument

However, those costs are sunk, may never be recovered, and should not generally be a factor in a decision to drop or alter a project. Even if the current project has a positive return, it may never recover the invested amount, *or* resources could be committed to a project yielding a higher return.

In the governmental sphere, one group of consultants advised a town school board not to build a new school. The population of school-age children was projected to decrease, and the town was showing no potential for economic expansion; in fact, the place was just a nice, quiet, no-growth town. "You know," the town administrator answered, "the town just finished paying for the land for the school, and we'll never get that amount back. What about the money we put into that land?"

The consultants' advice was to sell the land for whatever the town could get, but not to put any more money into a school. In essence, "don't pour good money after bad. The land cost is gone, cannot be completely recovered, and the town's available resources should be used for another, more beneficial project, or perhaps no project should be planned at all, resulting in a possible decrease in taxes."

In essence, if the environment or any other factor calls for a change, the fact that money was spent on a project in the past—and has not yet been totally recovered—should not blind one to the possible necessity to change directions or projects.

ADAPTATION AT VARIOUS ORGANIZATIONAL LEVELS

Changes in standards, plans, or objectives can occur at any level of the organization; that is, adaptation can take place at any of the levels at which planning took place. For example, adaptation may concern nothing more than a minor change in standards or a change in production techniques. Many of the automobile-recall changes, for example, resulted from nothing more than lower-level production specifications that did not perform as expected in the market. A simple change in the specifications solved the problem for the future.

But adaptation is most important at the top levels of the organization, where long-range plans, organizational directions, and strategies are devised. It is there where the most time and effort are committed to the planning effort and the most risk is assumed in terms of the resources committed to the implementation of the organizationwide plan. We shall now review various types of adaptive responses to plans that did not go according to expectations. Generally, when a strategy or a plan is not working and the problem cannot be overcome by operational control methods, there are several types of options open to the adaptive decision makers.

Redesign the entire or part of the program

This adaptive technique is probably the most common. Parts of a process or a product are replanned and then phased into the remains of the total strategy; or, the entire process is replanned and abruptly entered onto the market (perhaps as the new, improved version) at a certain date, replacing the strategy previously used. Often, for example, a company may have a product that all its research confirmed and reconfirmed would be useful and desirable in the marketplace. But for some reason, the product does not sell. A redesign of the advertising campaign or a rethinking of the channels of distribution may be the solution. But maybe the original sales objective was too optimistic. One distributor of classical records found it very difficult to meet its projections on sales for the first two years of a ten-year expansion plan. On rechecking the data and reevaluating the environment, managers found

- Redesign part of or the entire program
- Drop the program or process
- Selectively prune
- Merge
- Go out of business

Adaptive responses

that they had aimed too high in the first place, given their own resources and the need to "build," rather than conquer easily, markets in such a stable field of music.

In a sense, then, the most prevalent adaptation process is one that prevents the baby from being thrown out with the bath water. That is, strategies, objectives, and plans are evaluated in parts, and those parts needing revamping are revamped; those that are salvagable are salvaged.

Sometimes the best revision of a strategy is to cut one's losses and get out of the situation. This could mean discontinuing a product, selling off a division, dropping a trademark, closing a plant or office, or any other such drastic action. Harry Cleaver is suggesting consideration of this approach for the Samson chair in the case at the beginning of this chapter.

Stop the entire process

Despite the popular conviction that large—particularly multinational—businesses can sell anything they put onto the marketplace, the graveyard of discarded products is too full of mistakes to substantiate that contention. The most famous project deletion was Ford Motor Company's Edsel. Ford spent millions of dollars on market research, product design, and product promotion in getting the Edsel ready for market. But within a year or two it was obvious that the car had flopped; the market just was not yet ready for a car of its type. There may have been the utmost of remorse at Ford headquarters, but the product was cut and the losses minimized. Similar decisions have been made by other large companies with products such as simulated leather (DuPont's Corfam), toothpaste (Vote), and breakfast cereals (Kellogg's cereals with dehydrated fruits). All of these products were dropped not during a testing stage or even a test market stage, but after a full-blown marketing effort had been launched and millions of dollars of promotion committed to them.

Often a company finds that it is no longer able to sustain itself in a particular line of business. Technology may be too advanced in that line; internal or external environmental factors may have changed significantly. But some other organization may have the resources and skills necessary to capitalize on the line. So the company that cannot meet its objectives may sell off the entire line or the entire division to the other company. Motorola, for example, was consistently losing money on its home television line; the entire line, complete with its manufacturing facilities, was sold off to Matsushita Electric, a Japanese manufacturer of electronic products.

Such loss cutting may mean closing a plant, dropping a trademark (Chrysler's dropping of the DeSoto line and American Motors' dropping the venerable old Nash and Hudson labels). Such adaptive reactions to changing environmental conditions or to inadequate planning processes may be painful to the organization, but they are less so than causing the demise of the entire organization.

Selective pruning   An organization may decide to prune only those parts of a line that are not used or that do not sell. For example, automobile companies may drop certain options if the market for them is not as great as expected. Clothing manufacturers drop styles that did not catch on and take off as expected. These actions are really not drastic adaptive responses (although they may be to the individuals who might be left unemployed when such an action is undertaken), but are another possible response to the inability to reach unreachable objectives or to carry out plans.

Merger   One adaptive reaction to not meeting objectives, particularly when those objectives are not met because of internal or organizational weaknesses, is to merge with another organization whose strengths complement those of the original organization. Merger, in this context, is not for reasons of tax loss carryover and other financial considerations; rather, even though the organization has weaknesses in meeting its objectives, it still has sufficient strength left to keep operating with the added resources and talents of the other organization.

On the other hand, many mergers are not voluntary, and often the very notion of merger conflicts with the unwillingness of shareholders or key executives to relinquish control of the organization. But to reiterate, for many situations, particularly when the organization lacks particular strengths to allow it to reach its objectives, merger may be the only solution to the problem.

Go out of business   The ultimate adaptive response is to liquidate the organization. If the market for a business is no longer there, the reason for an organization or unit's being established no longer exists, or the resources are so specialized that there is little or no flexibility to change the organization's directions, liquidation may be the only logical adaptive alternative.

Liquidation is usually painful, and for an observer or writer to recommend it might seem surprising. But not counting those businesses which fail because of poor management, there are always those that simply fold up and die because the constituency they served no longer exists or because the skills necessary to continue to survive are not present and cannot be acquired through hire or merger. Of course, one may always still indict the managers of those businesses for not keeping abreast of their environments, but in a fast-paced technological society, such a situation may be beyond the powers of managers, particularly in smaller organizations.

For example, prior to the 1950s, the manufacture of paint was a relatively simple process. Lead, linseed oil, a little zinc, and some color were generally the only ingredients; small manufacturers needed but a minimum of equipment (some vats for mixing and a pouring and canning machine) and a good eye for color, and they were in business. Rarely did these small firms engage in research and development or even maintain a laboratory for testing. With the advent of vinyls, alkyds, latex, and other bases and the outlawing of lead-based paints in most areas, however, the paint business went well beyond the capability of many of the early small companies. Since they had few assets to offer anyone and trademarks were for the most part known only locally, they were not even very good merger partners. Many of them just vanished, leaving the business to the larger, more research-oriented firms.

Greco-Roman faces a possible problem of adaptation with the Samson chair. All of the controllable behaviors and processes seem to be holding up well; even replanning on the operational level looks unnecessary, as the planners seem to have covered all of the bases. The salespeople are working hard, the price of the chair is not out of line, the advertising campaign seems sound, and the product quality seems good. Only two things could be wrong: (1) customers don't need, want, or like the chair; and relatedly, (2) the forecast on which the planning was based was too optimistic. The Achilles and Paris agency could have been wrong in both its determination of product need and in its estimate of the number of units that could be sold.

Back to the Greco-Roman Chair Company

This leaves Greco-Roman with some options. One might be to drop the product, much like DuPont dropped Corfam. Despite Martinelli's protests about sunk costs, if few people want the Samson chair, there is no use spending more money telling them they should want something they don't want.

Another option might be to decrease sales expectations. If the forecast was wrong—despite the claim by Achilles and Paris that the agency used tried-and-true methods—perhaps the sales expectations were overly optimistic. Of course, a decision of this nature—to reduce sales expectations—would depend on a recalculation of profits from a lower sales objective. Perhaps an alternative project would then become more attractive.

In any event, what Martinelli and Cleaver must do is rethink the very concept of the Samson chair, not the variables or behaviors that are going into the selling of it.

SUMMARY AND CONCLUSION

In this chapter we covered the concept of adaptation as a category of control. Adaptation occurs when the objectives or plans are not assumed to be fixed and unchallengeable; in operational control, by contrast, the standards are assumed to be fixed, and the operations, personnel, and/or equipment are assumed to be at fault.

We reviewed the reasons for organizational adaptation. In most cases adaptation results from the altering of the parameters on which the original plan was based. The key factors relate to the organization's environment, which for the sake of analysis can be divided into six categories: economic, political, social, technological, institutional, and international. Additional reasons for adaptation are the changing personnel and internal strengths or special resources of the organization, unreachable forecasts, inadequate planning and goal setting in the first place, and changes in client need.

We then discussed adaptation and the various levels of the organization, noting briefly adaptation at the operational level and then the adaptive techniques of the top level, e.g., a redesign of all or part of the original strategy; a cessation of the entire process; selective pruning, particularly of products; merger; and as a last resort liquidation of the organization.

DISCUSSION QUESTIONS

1 Define adaptation and differentiate it from organizational control.

2 Illustrate the process of adaptation.

3 Define dynamic planning. How does that concept relate to adaptation?

4 Illustrate how environmental change—for example, social change— would force adaptive response.

5 Why is it important for a company to be aware of economic indicators such as income, production, price levels, government spending, etc.?

6 Explain the impact on changing internal resources on adaptive processes within the organization.

7 What are some of the top-level adaptive responses? Differentiate among some of them.

8 Why would merger be considered an adaptive response?

9 Going out of business is the ultimate adaptive response. Why is this sometimes the most logical choice?

CASE: STANTON PRODUCTS DIVISION

■ The news hit Langdon City like a bolt of lightning. Skyway Aeronautics had not received the expected engine contract for the new, record-breaking order of planes from Intercoastal Airways. Since this was the first major order for the new Transtar model H6M wide-body jet, the outlook for future engine business looked very dim. This contract loss, coupled with the inability of Skyway to land the engine contract for the new F23 fighter made the potential for Skyway look gloomy indeed. The Company had only one contract left—for helicopter engines—and that had only two years to run. The future also looked gloomy for the area around Langdon City and the Stanton Products Division of Continental Industries in particular.

Continental Industries had purchased Stanton Products in 1966. Stanton, which specialized in precision grinding and forming, had been founded by Ed Stanton in 1956 specifically to work alongside Skyway. A former Air Force officer, Stanton knew that Skyway needed subcontractors to grind and finish turbine blades and other parts for jet engines. Continental came in when Stanton let it be known that he was looking for a comfortable retirement. The steady infusion of military contracts plus the almost certain purchase of new-generation aircraft by the civilian airlines made Stanton Products an attractive purchase for Continental.

Skyway announced that approximately 7000 of its 10,000 employees would be laid off as the helicopter contracts were fulfilled. Stanton's employment would probably drop from 480 to a plant labor force of about 100. Without Skyway, Stanton would have a few orders from small, specialty manufacturers and some transfer work from other Continental divisions, but nothing major.

"It seems to me that we have two options open to us," announced Continental's president. "We can find a totally new strategy for Stanton and get it off its dependence on Skyway, or we can pick up our marbles and go home. Does anyone have any other suggestions?" ■

Case questions

1. What past efforts did Continental Industries make with respect to Stanton Products Division?

2. Is going out of business a viable option for Stanton? Why?

3. What alternative adaptive responses would you recommend for Stanton? Be specific.

SELECTED READINGS

Anshen, Melvin, ed. *Managing the Social Responsible Corporation: The 1972–1973 Paul Garrett Lectures* (New York: Macmillan, 1974).

Basil, D. C., and C. W. Cook, *The Management of Change* (New York: McGraw-Hill, 1974).

Cole, S., J. Gershung, and I. Miles, "Scenarios of World

Development," *Futures* **10,** 1 (February 1978): 3–20.

Eppink, D. I., "Planning for Strategic Flexibility," *Long-Range Planning* **11** (August 1978): 9–15.

Farmer, R. N., *Management in the Future* (Belmont, Calif.: Wadsworth, 1967).

Gluck, F. W., R. N. Foster, and J. L. Forbis, "Cure for Strategic Malnutrition," *Harvard Business Review* **54** (November/December 1976): 154–165.

Haimann, T., and W. G. Scott, *Management in the Modern Organization,* 2d ed. (Boston: Houghton Mifflin, 1974).

Holroyd, P., "Change and Discontinuity: Forecasting for the 1980s," *Futures* **10,** 1 (February 1978): 31–52.

Hutchinson, J. C., *Management Strategy and Tactics* (New York: Holt, Rinehart and Winston, 1971).

Kane, E. J., "EFT and Monetary Policy," *Journal of Contemporary Business* **7,** 2 (Spring 1978): 29–50.

Kilmann, R. H., L. R. Pondy, and D. P. Slevin, eds., *The Management of Organization Design* (New York: North Holland, 1976).

Lorange, P., and R. F. Vancil, "How to Design a Strategic Planning System," *Harvard Business Review* **54** (September/October 1976): 75–81.

Louden, J. K., *Managing at the Top: Roles and Responsibilities of the Chief Executive* (New York: AMACOM, 1977).

McCosh, A. M., "Inflationary Adjustments of Some Elements of the Planning and Control Cycle in Investment Centers," *Management International Review* **16,** 4 (1976): 35–49.

McFarland, E., *Management Principles and Practices,* 3rd ed. (New York: Macmillan, 1970).

McGrath, P. S., *Managing Corporate External Relations: Changing Perspectives and Responses. A Research Report from the Conference Board Division of Management Research* (New York: The Conference Board, 1976).

Miller, D., and P. H. Friesen, "Archetypes of Strategy Formulation," *Management Science* **24** (May 1978): 921–933.

Miner, J. B., *The Management Process, Theory, Research, and Practice* (New York: Macmillan, 1973).

Moch, H., "Transition Management in a Changing Environment," *Personnel Journal* **57,** 9 (September 1978): 492–495.

Mockler, R. J., *Business Planning and Policy Formulation* (New York: Appleton-Century-Crofts, 1972).

Murray, W., *Management Controls in Action* (Dublin: Irish National Productivity Committee, Development Division, 1970).

Rogers, D., *Can Business Management Save the Cities? The Case of New York* (New York: Free Press, 1978).

Torgersen, P. E., and I. T. Weinstock, *Management: An Integrated Approach* (Englewood Cliffs, N.J.: Prentice-Hall, 1972).

Chapter 20
THE ORGANIZATIONAL AUDIT

CHAPTER HIGHLIGHTS

In this chapter we explore the concept of the organizational audit, an instrument or process by which management and the organization periodically examine their purposes, processes, plans, structure, managerial behavior and goal pursuit, and legal compliance. In addition, we relate the organizational audit to the more traditional financial audit and to the newer concerns considered in a social audit.

LEARNING OBJECTIVES

1 To be able to define and apply the term "organizational audit."

2 To know and to be able to develop the areas to be covered in an organizational audit: strategies and goals, planning processes, organization structure, standing plans, managerial performance, adherence to corporate or organizational objectives, and legal compliance.

3 To understand the function of a financial audit and to relate it to the organizational audit.

4 To be able to define a social audit and to relate that instrument to the organizational audit.

INTRODUCTION

In Chapter 18 we discussed briefly the audit of controls and control systems as one way of eliminating unnecessary hindrances to effective organizational operations. That audit was, as we mentioned then, only a small portion of a more comprehensive concept that may be called an organizational audit.

In Chapter 19 we explored the need for a reevaluation and possible change in strategy or objectives when operational control is ineffective or inapplicable. But adaptation usually occurs when something goes wrong and a corrective must be found. And adaptation may relate to one program or one set of programs, not necessarily to the systematic investigation of the entire organization. This latter is called an organizational audit—a much broader term than "adaptation."

In this chapter we explore the concept of an organizational audit. Although much of the management literature refers to a management audit, here we will broaden the coverage to include the concept of the total organization, reflecting total management and organizational activities and processes.* Also, social and political trends are manifesting themselves in increased restrictive legislation, regulation, and external pressures on the organization and management. And there are increasingly severe penalties for strategic failure in terms of resources lost. Thus in order for the organization to adapt and respond to the demands of its increasing number of publics—sometimes in ways not measured by financial statements, ratios, or bottom-line numbers—new trends in management evaluation will have to be developed.

The organizational audit, then, is defined as a periodic examination of the entire organization—its objectives, strategies, functions, and processes. As such, the organizational audit is a definitely prescribed event in the life of the organization, scheduled once every so many years—often five or ten years, in some cases more frequently.

Business firms are not the only institutions that should undergo organizational audits. Every once in a while, government agencies are studied and recommendations made for their streamlining; whether anything results from those recommendations is another story, but at least the attempt is made to consider change in the organization and its processes. Another example of the audit process is accreditation for universities and colleges. Typically, reaccreditation takes place every ten years. In reality, that accreditation process is an audit very similar to that for business and government.

In a true organizational audit, nothing should be held back from investigation or evaluation; nor is any part of the organization immune from investigation. Organizations that do audits—such as universities when evaluating particular schools and departments—often hire outside consultants or teams of selected professionals and experts to do the auditing job in order to preclude any part or process of the organization from being withheld from the investigation. Before the outsiders do come in, an internal self-study report is generally done by the organization's own staff units.

COVERAGE IN AN ORGANIZATIONAL AUDIT

As a comprehensive overlook of the entire organization and its processes, an organizational audit is designed to answer several types of questions. After briefly considering the scope of an organizational audit, we shall deal with some specific parts of an organization and its processes and try to determine some of the specific questions a complete audit will be investigating.

* One example is Jackson Martindell, *The Scientific Appraisal of Management* (New York: Harper and Brothers, 1950).

Basically, an audit asks "Why?" of just about every process and every instrument of the organization. Why is this particular procedure engaged in? Why does this particular organizational unit exist? Why can't we do better another way?

Thus generally, an audit team asks: "Is what we are doing the right thing to do? If it is the right thing to do, are we doing it in the best way possible? Are there alternative, more efficient, and more effective ways of doing what we are doing now? What would happen if we eliminated the process or the unit that we are investigating?" Each of these questions probes the very nature and existence of the unit, and this process should occur if the organization is really committed to clearing the deadwood in objectives, procedures, and personnel that inevitably builds up over a period of years.

Given that general backdrop, we can now explore some of the *specific* topics that an organizational audit would encompass, along with some of the specific types of questions that should be asked and some of the reasons that these areas are important.

Corporate objectives

A true complete audit begins with the top-level strategic questions, such as "Should we be in this business or in these businesses?" or "Is the business we think we're in really the business we are in?" Even though any contemplated change is difficult, an audit should question whether the organization can do better in another line or lines or whether it should place its resources into a better-paying operation.

Economists have long assumed the mobility of resources—at least in the long run. But a switch in businesses is not an easy thing to accomplish. Additional questions must be asked before an affirmative answer to a change in businesses or even mode of operation is made. For example, "Do we owe anything to our steady customers?" "With consumerism so strong today, do we dare abandon users and owners of our product?" "What new resources would be required if we decided to move into new lines?" "Do we have familiarity with any new contemplated services or businesses?" "Can we turn around the present trends of our business?" "What about the state of competition in a projected endeavor?"

Libraries form an interesting subject for an audit of corporate purpose. The very word "library" is derived from the Latin word "*Libra*," meaning book, and for many the institution of a library is associated with books only. But libraries can be more than just books. If one contemplates the changes in population mix, technology, costs, communication processes, and the like, one may easily envision a library of the future without books. Consider, for example, a patron with a television set tied into the library (among other services) by a cablevision system. Consider the entire library computerized and tied to a microfiche system or some similar information-storage system. The patron could, by manipulating a series of buttons attached to the television set, check the catalog, access that material, and read right from the screen. A patron having his or her own duplicating process could also copy the material for reading at leisure. Similarly, a patron could access and watch a concert, ballet, lecture, or any other type of stored program.

In essence, the library of the future may be an institution with few books, but a great deal of information and entertainment. In fact, I once suggested to a group of librarians that the name of the public library be changed to "Information Storage and Retrieval Center," a name that would more adequately reflect its function.

In truth, however, very few organizations audit the nature of their existences. Because of the value commitments of top management and perhaps the owners of the business, the very nature of the business is rarely questioned. If, however, the business were to change hands or if the environment were to alter very rapidly, such an evaluation of corporate purpose might be made.

The planning and objective-setting process

Here the audit team is concerned not so much with the objective, plan, or strategy per se, but with the processes by which those substantive plans are developed. An audit team investigating an organization would recapitulate and reconstruct the managers' processes in planning and establishing objectives. The audit team would explore for and point out external factors that were ignored, alternatives that were missed, information sources and information that were passed up, linkages among plans that were not accounted for, resources deleted or not used, and other failures in the planning techniques. The auditors would also determine whether managers had accurately scanned their environments—threats, challenges, and potential changes—and accurately determined the strengths and weaknesses of the organization available to them for implementing plans.

Organizational auditors would be especially concerned about determining whether the organization's long- and short-range plans had been integrated and whether short-range operational planning had been undertaken within the context of the general long-range planning. The auditors would also investigate the relationship of planning to policy; how did planning effect the changes in policy? How did policy constrict the planning effort? Did the constriction by policy have any negative effect on the firm in terms of opportunities missed or resources committed for less than maximum return?

Organizational structure

An audit team investigating an organization might find the structure of the organization to be one of the more complex areas being surveyed. In general, the team would be concerned that the total structure was conducive to the accomplishment of the organization's plans and objectives, but a number of specific issues would be confronted also.

First, an auditor should determine whether all of the units currently in existence are really necessary. Inevitably, over a period of years institutions build up a number of units that may be superfluous to the organization if the environment in which the firm or organization operates or the firm's objectives were to change. Such units should be either eliminated or consolidated with others if a definite rationale for their existence cannot be established.

Similarly, the audit team should discover whether units are contributing to organizational purposes in accordance with their cost. Because of the power, prestige, or influence of certain managers or the result of previous allocations of resources within the organization, some units may have more than enough resources to accomplish their present objectives. This excess of resources may create an imbalance in the organization, as other units may be short of resources that they may need to accomplish their missions. In universities, for example, resources move extremely slowly between departments and schools, even though the student demand moves more swiftly. Because of tenure among faculty, who may have been hired when demand in some subjects was high, and the need to offer innumerable specialties, some departments with low student demand now are overloaded with faculty, whereas other departments with high student demand have a shortage of faculty. An organizational audit should discover and address this imbalance.

Another question that an audit would seek to answer is if the arrangement among units is as efficient as possible. For example, if the business firm is arranged in a functional breakdown, e.g., production, marketing, finance, the question might be asked whether the organization is ready to move to a divisionalized, product-type, or even a matrix organization structure. Conversely, if the company is in a divisionalized state, the audit should ask about the staff or service units. Is the arrangement of those units sufficient to ensure adequate attention, or is there too much support? Are duplicate units throughout the company efficient, or should services be consolidated into single companywide units serving all divisions and departments?

Audits should reveal whether any units within the organization are understrength or overstrength, as well as whether any executives are supervising too many subordinates. If the audit is on the lookout for an excess of organizational units, it should also be aware of the fact that some units may have to be added to the organization. For example, many organizations are now strengthening both their personnel departments and their training centers in response to both the new government regulations in the areas of equal opportunity and affirmative action and the need to upgrade and train previously untrained personnel. Safety departments, in the face of OSHA, are also assuming greater importance.

While reviewing the structure, the audit team would also consider the age distribution of the top executives and managers throughout the organization. It should also investigate the plans made to groom new managers to replace retirees. Any organization should have a well-planned schedule of succession for new managers and executives; too often no plans are made, and chaos reigns when a management team departs or a key executive must be replaced quickly.

Policies, procedures, and methods—standing plans

Most organizations develop detailed manuals of policies, procedures, and methods. But some organizations never stop to determine whether all of those standing or permanent plans are necessary or whether they have become obsolete. An audit of the organization should include a periodic revaluation of all policies, procedures, and methods to determine their timeliness, necessity, and usefulness.

This policy review is one of the most important reasons for conducting a managerial or organizational audit in the first place. Often an organization will accumulate a mountain of policies that can develop into a stranglehold on organizational progress or a blockage to the realistic assessment of changing conditions. Some commentators have even recommended doing away with a detailed policy manual in the first place, calling it a defense for the incompetent on the one hand and a weapon for the manipulators within the organization on the other.*

Thus the well-oiled organization will review its policies, procedures, and methods as a vital part of the organizational audit. This section of the audit takes place more frequently than other parts of the audit if the organization is inclined to keep its rules streamlined.

Often the organization structure is described as the frame of the company or the institution, with the policies and procedures being described as the flesh and the vital organs. It is important that the guts of the organization be kept as lean and as capable of moving to exploit available opportunities as possible. Organizations burdened with rules and procedures for every possible incident cannot make the quick necessary adjustments to exploit available strategic opportunities.

None of this, of course, is to suggest that policy is not necessary within the organization. As we have pointed out, it is much more efficient for an organization to maintain one rule or set of rules for a recurring situation than to have a manager or even an employee make a new and perhaps inconsistent rule or decision for each occurrence of the situation. What we are cautioning about here is the overburdening of the organization with rules and regulations, the nonpruning of a policy or procedure when its usefulness has expired, and the overconstraining of the creativity and initiative of subordinate managers and employees alike. For example, it was reported that during the dying days of W. T. Grant and Company, an old and honorable retailer which went bankrupt in 1976, store managers, including many who

* Robert Townsend, *Up the Organization* (New York: Knopf, 1970).

had many years of experience of on-line operation, were being bombarded with numerous conflicting policies and procedures from the New York office. No creativity or imagination at the local level was allowed, leading to intense frustration on the part of the experienced local managers. Even more important, however, the policy was being made by executives who were really unaware of the problems that local managers were facing.* Such a process should have been stopped by a management or organizational audit long before it contributed to a decrease in the vitality of the organization and its personnel.

As we noted in Chapter 1, managers generally function as part of a team. Although lone-wolf managers still exist in modern organizations, most of today's management is the process of joint decision making and consultative arrangement. Decisions are generally group decisions; or, if they are made by individuals, there typically is consultation, information gathering, confirmation, advising, or ratification offered by or required of other managers within the organization.

Managerial performance as a team

    A management or organizational audit would thus be concerned with how these linkages among managers function. Is consultation effective and are the right people consulted? Where in the organization are the information centers located, and can the necessary information be gathered easily? What units are responsible for keeping abreast of information about the organization's environment? Who advises, and is the advice accurate and necessary? Who scans for changes and threats, and are alerts sounded swiftly within the organization?

    In one organization, for example, a central data bank was responsible for storing production capacity, output, and loading information, and this information was received and should have been inputted into the system on a near real-time basis as soon as it occurred. Yet the center was so inefficient that the data were often not available to staff planning units, which consequently had to go to the line units over and over for the same types of information already laboriously submitted to central data storage. Needless to say, these requests for the same information from several staff units were not well received by the line units and caused resentment.

    The audit would also focus closely on the communication system of the organization. Is communication effective? Do communications travel directly? Are there unnecessary blockages in communication? For example, in one organization the purchasing agent conveniently dropped purchase requisitions from the various departments into his desk drawer and then forget them for long periods of time. Operating managers, frustrated at not receiving their orders for material (or not receiving information on the fate of

---

* See R. Loving, Jr., "W. T. Grant's Last Days—As Seen from Store 1192," *Fortune* **93** (April 1976): 108–112. Also reprinted in the Appendix of this book.

their requisitions), would double or triple their next orders, but then the purchasing agent would suddenly find the old requisitions and process both the old and the new ones! Materials piled up in the line units because of this blockage in the communications system of the organization.

Even more important is the linkage of information flow to strategic decision making within the organization. Is it effective and direct? Does it offer the decision maker the necessary information, forecasts, environmental scanning, and predictions so that effective strategic and long-range planning can take place?

Finally, the audit team would attempt to spot clashing personalities and personal differences among members of the management team *if* those clashes affected the performance of the team. No one should ever expect that every member of a large organization will get along with every other member. In most instances these inevitable personality clashes will have no effect on the operation of the organization. But occasionally an argument or a long-term feud will have that effect, and although this cause-and-effect relationship may remain hidden within the organization's normal operation, it should be looked for as part of the audit.

Managerial adherence to corporate or organizational objectives

An organizational audit should determine whether management's commitment throughout the organization is complete and relevant to the organizational objectives. A number of theorists have proposed, and studies have verified, that the real objectives of an organization are those framed and practiced by management and executives, not those written in corporate charters or corporate philosophies.* This transformation of objectives may be done purposefully, but more likely it is the natural effect of executives' having power, operating a large organization with great amounts of resources, and turning that organization and its resources—either consciously or subconsciously—toward their favored ends. Sometimes this transformation is done very slowly, with the real objectives of the organization gradually shifting from product or residual (profit) maximization to maximization of managerial benefits. At other times, particularly as a result of a merger or a corporate raid, the transformation of objectives may be much more dramatic and open. If the attempted raid on the silver plate company (described earlier), had been successful, organizational objectives would have shifted very rapidly to reflect the personal objectives of the new owners, who were interested not in producing flatware, but in cashing in on the increased value of the silver inventory.

The objective of good and effective management is to effect the completion of organizational plans and objectives. Although the completion of corporate plans should simultaneously reward the manager's personal goals,

* R. J. Monsen, B. O. Saxberg, and R. A. Sutermeister, "The Modern Manager: What Makes Him RUN? *Business Horizons* (Fall 1966): 23–34.

those personal aspirations are not primary. The organizational audit ought to point out directions for redirecting errant managerial effort should that be necessary. Indeed, this is another reason why an audit team should be independent of the management of the organization; if the audit were undertaken by the firm's executives, there would be a tendency to either forego investigation of the personal-organizational conflict in goals or refuse to recognize its existence.

Increasingly, organizations are interfacing with government and coming under a growing volume of regulation. In the United States, this means that organizations must comply with a greater volume of complex federal, state, and local regulations. It is not our intent here to catalog all of the legal areas in which the firm interfaces with government, but merely to illustrate some of the potential problem areas that an organizational audit can be effective in uncovering—either blatant violations of the law or ignorance of the law—and pointing out where corrective action is possible or necessary.*

Legal compliance

Increasing amounts of legislation and regulation may change the entire job requirements of an individual unit or manager, but the ineffectiveness of a particular manager who does not keep up to date may not be known until the organization becomes involved in a substantial legal entanglement. For example, equal opportunity legislation, affirmative action, and occupational safety and health regulations have made the personnel manager an increasingly important and prominent figure within the organization. In the past, the personnel manager was primarily a record keeper, whose knowledge of the law was limited to wage and hour regulation. Personnel management was a mechanical process, operating with a great deal of mythology—particularly relating to women and work situations—involved in it. Now the field is extraordinarily technical, requiring constant attention to changing regulations and legal interpretations not only in equal opportunity, but in pensions, benefits, insurance, and other areas as well. So the organizational audit is important in this area to point out this type of change and perhaps pinpoint the inadequacies of existing units relative to new environmental factors.

Another important area for the organizational audit to be concerned with is antitrust compliance. Executives may not know whether a particular activity in which they are engaged is in violation of the law. The organizational audit ought to point out where executive education in this area is necessary.

At other times executives know the law, but ignore it. In one major antitrust case cited earlier, executives knew not only about the law, but also that the company had a policy supporting the law. Yet they violated both

* A standard text in business government relations is Clair Wilcox and W. G. Shepherd, *Public Policies Toward Business,* 5th ed. (Homewood, Ill.: Richard D. Irwin, 1975).

the law and the policy. Executives were signaling to subordinates that the law could be violated or that company policy in that matter really didn't have to be followed. Such encouragement to violate the law could have serious costs to the company in terms of actual cost, future litigation, and reputation (in this case, the monetary cost was substantial, and the loss in reputation was temporary). Organizational audits should seek to uncover this defiance of law and policy.

ORGANIZATIONAL AUDITS RELATED TO FINANCIAL AND SOCIAL AUDITS

Financial audits   We have already mentioned the necessity of a financial audit as a control device, and it is beyond the scope of this book to cover the concept in much detail. Most managers and observers realize the necessity of the financial audit as a control device. The financial audit is a yearly occurrence and generally is concerned with accurately portraying the financial results of the organization's activity and its financial condition at a particular time. During the investigation, certain standards are employed to ensure that the organization followed proper financial procedures and behavior and that safeguards against chicanery and embezzlement were in effect and enforced.

The financial audit can uncover instances calling for a broader organizational audit. For example, if certain financial transactions were questioned and found to be illegal or improper, the result should be an investigation into the organization relationships that allowed such negligence and illegal behavior to occur. As such, the financial audit acts as a trigger for the broader organizational audit.

On the other hand, top management should not wait for the financial audit to uncover possible improper behavior before considering the use of an organizational audit. The organizational audit is a necessary, broader concept that should be planned for periodic and consistent application to the organization.

Social audits   With the increasing emphasis on social responsibility, or the role of the corporation in solving social problems, it should not be surprising that some forms of measurement or accounting for corporate social activity would be attempted.* Although there is not much to show yet in the area (the techniques are nonstandard, undeveloped, and not universally accepted), the area of social audit or social accounting is becoming popular fare at corpo-

---

* The social-audit literature is very diverse. For example, *see* Raymond A. Bauer and Dan H. Fenn, Jr., *The Corporate Social Audit* (New York: Russell Sage Foundation, 1972); David F. Linowes, "Let's Get on with the Social Audit: A Specific Proposal," *Business and Society Review* (Winter 1972–1973): 41–47; and David H. Blake, William C. Frederick, and Mildred S. Myers, *Social Auditing: Evaluating the Impact of Corporate Programs* (New York: Praeger, 1976).

rate and business meetings and has found growing interest among scholars and practitioners alike.

Managers and organizations have all sorts of reasons to undertake or advocate social audits. Some simply seek to forestall any activist protests that might be brewing. If these managers can present some form of data, they hope they can at least fend off accusations and condemnations by activist groups. Other executives want to know how much they are really spending on social activities. After all, corporations for years have been lending executive time, operative time, facilities, and equipment to all sorts of civic and charitable causes; few ever bothered to calculate the real costs of those contributions. Still other managers firmly believe in the social-responsibility doctrine and want to develop social audits for planning, control, and reward purposes. In some companies official policy, publicly announced at least, is that the rewards given to lower-level managers will be partially based on social performance. Finally, some managements are looking to find a net social-benefit figure.

The problem with the concept of social audit is that there is little agreement on what to measure and how to do it. As the concept has evolved, there seem to be at least three schools of thought on the approach an audit should take: one advocates starting right now to find a measure of corporate net social benefit; a second centers on a more traditional determination of the direct costs involved; and a third approach is for programs in which adequate performance measures are difficult to determine, and that includes most of the corporate social programs. For those, some writers have recommended that the firm adopt a "process audit," or a description and subjective evaluation of origins, goals, rationale, and actual operations of the programs.

We would suggest here something very similar to, yet broader than, the process audit. That is, rather than have a separate social audit concerned with some perhaps unattainable quantitative evaluation of social good or social harm—most of which cannot be measured—the organization should include the social issues and their effects within the total organization audit described above.

Planners, managers, and decision makers and the organization need to be audited even more now because social issues are forcing increasing excellence in managing and there are more publics to which managers must respond. However, any social audit that a company contemplates ought to be a fully integral part of the organizational audit, since the issues are generally integral parts of the traditional issues with which managers deal. For example, OSHA decisions are not unique; what OSHA does is to expand the parameters that decision makers deal with on decisions such as plant location, plant design, and equipment design. The same is true for issues such as pollution control and equal opportunity. *In short, most social issues have only widened the required planning spectrum for managers.* Hence the organiza-

- Should we be in this business?
- Are our objectives the right ones?
- Do we really know where we are headed?
- Is the business we think we're in really the one we are in?
- Do we have a good planning process?
    Were there any external factors ignored?
    Did we cover all alternatives in planning?
    Did we get all of the available information?
    Were our plans linked together?
        Short range to long range?
        Unit to department to division, etc.?
    Was planning overly constricted by policy?
- Is our organization functioning well?
    Do we need all of the units we have?
    Are all units worth their cost?
    Is the arrangement of units as efficient as possible?
    Are any units understrength? Overstrength?
    Do we need any new types of units?
    Do we have a plan for managerial succession?
- What is the state of our policy manual?
    Are policies up to date?
    Do we need any new policies? In what area?
    Are policies restricting initiative and creativity?
- What is the state of our management group?
    Do managers operate effectively as a team?
    Do they consult one another?
    Where are information centers located, and are they effective?
    Do strategic decision makers have access to the information needed?
    Do personality clashes inhibit the functioning of the management team?
- Do managers pursue official objectives?
    Do personal objectives clash with organizational objectives?
- Is the organization complying with the law?
- Do all managers comply with the law?
    Equal employment opportunity?
    Antitrust?
    Payoffs and bribes?
    Other laws and regulations?
- Are we in tune with social issues?
- Do we operate in accord with prevailing ethics?
- Do we accommodate interest groups?

Some key questions in an organizational audit— a checklist

tional audit, under which such issues are integrated with the total picture in the evaluation, is probably a more appropriate vehicle for review than a more limited and indeed nebulous social audit.

SUMMARY AND CONCLUSION

In this chapter we focused on the concept of the organizational audit—a scheduled periodic examination of the entire organization's endeavors and processes. As such, it is definitely prescribed and should be undertaken every so many years.

We concluded that there is nothing that an organization should hold back from inclusion in a management audit. Top-management activities—strategies—as well as the lowest-level procedures are included in the audit. Some of the topics covered in the audit are a review of corporate objectives, planning and decision-making processes, organizational structure, policies and procedures, managerial performance, managerial commitment, and legal compliance. Then we related financial audits, the more traditional types of audits, to the evolving concepts of organizational audits. Finally, we noted the emerging concept of the social audit and stated a preference for the material to be integrated into the broader organizational audit concept, since in general social values are being integrated into traditional business decision making.

Periodic auditing is important to the organization whose philosophy is to clear deadwood and keep the processes vibrant and successful. Only an alert management can keep its objectives clear and current and its processes directed toward those objectives. The prescribed management audit—using questions such as those posed in the box on p. 452—is one tool to facilitate that effective and efficient operation of the management role.

DISCUSSION QUESTIONS

1 Define organizational audit.

2 Why should organizational audits be carried out by outside agencies or consultants?

3 In an audit of corporate objectives, what would be some considerations to a change in the basic corporate purpose?

4 How would you audit the planning process of an organization?

5 Why is a policy review one of the most important reasons for conducting an organizational audit?

6 Why should communication linkages among managers be reviewed?

7 Why should we expect that managers will always respect and adhere to stated corporate objectives? Explain.

8 The popular view of a business organization is one thought to be trying to avoid legal compliance. Do you agree? What is the role of the organizational audit in determining legal compliance?

9 How do financial audits relate to organizational audits?

10 Define social audit and critique the concept.

SELECTED READINGS

Albanese, R., *Management: Toward Accountability for Performance* (Homewood, Ill.: Richard D. Irwin, 1975).

Anthony, R. N., *Management Accounting Principles*, rev. ed. (Homewood, Ill.: Richard D. Irwin, 1970).

———, *Management Accounting: Text and Cases*, 3rd ed. (Homewood, Ill.: Richard D. Irwin, 1964).

Anthony, R. N., and R. E. Herlinger, *Management Control in Nonprofit Organizations* (Homewood, Ill.: Richard D. Irwin, 1975).

Bauer, R. A., and D. H. Fenn, Jr., "What Is a Corporate Social Audit?" *Harvard Business Review* 51 (January/February 1973): 37–48.

Beresford, D. F., and S. A. Feldman, "Companies Increase Social Responsibility Disclosure," *Management Accounting*, 58 (March 1976): 51–57.

Blake, D. H., W. C. Frederick, and M. S. Myers, *Social Auditing: Evaluating the Impact of Corporate Programs* (New York: Praeger, 1976).

Broad, H. W., and K. S. Carmichael, *A Guide to Management Accounting*, 4th ed. (London: H.F.L. Publishers, 1965).

Campbell, J. P., *et al.*, *Managerial Behavior, Performance, and Effectiveness* (New York: McGraw-Hill, 1970).

Churchill, N. C., and A. B. Toan, "Reporting on Corporate Social Responsibility: A Progress Report," *Journal of Contemporary Business* 7 (Winter 1978): 5–17.

DeCoster, D. T., and E. L. Schafer, *Management Accounting: A Decision Emphasis* (New York: Wiley, 1976).

Estes, R., *Corporate Social Accounting* (New York: Wiley, 1976).

Gale, J., "Social Decision-Oriented Measurement: Some

Considerations," *Journal of Contemporary Business* 7 (Winter 1978): 55–74.

Hermoso, J. R., "Enter: The ECO Accountant," *Accountants' Journal* 27, 1 (1977): 27–30.

Herzberg, F., *The Managerial Choice: To Be Efficient and to Be Human* (Homewood, Ill.: Dow Jones/Irwin, 1976).

Kapnick, H., "Changing Role of Public Accounting," *Accounting Forum* 48 (May 1978): 31–39.

Keller, I. W., and W. L. Ferrara, *Management Accounting for Profit Control*, 2d ed. (New York: McGraw-Hill, 1966).

Koontz, H., and C. J. O'Donnell, *Management: A Systems and Contingency Analysis of Managerial Functions*, 6th ed. (New York: McGraw-Hill, 1976). *See* Part 4, Staffing, especially Chapter 21, "Appraisal of Managers."

Kuong, J. F., *Audit and Control of Computerized Systems* (Wellesley Hills, Mass.: Management Advisory Publications, 1977).

Levinson, H., "Appraisal of What Performance?" *Harvard Business Review* 54 (July/August 1976): 30–49.

McComb, D., "Some Guidelines on Social Accounting in the U.S.," *Accounting* 89 (April 1978): 50–52.

Martindell, J., *The Appraisal of Management: For Executives and Investors*, rev. ed. (New York: Harper & Row, 1965).

Seidler, L. J., and L. L. Seidler, *Social Accounting* (Los Angeles: Melville Publishing, 1975).

Stiner, F. M., "Accountants' Attitudes Toward Social Accounting," *Journal of Business* 16 (May 1978): 3–12.

Teel, K., "Self-Appraisal Revisited," *Personnel Journal* 57, 7 (July 1978): 364–367.

Illustrative
Comprehensive Cases

The following articles were selected to illustrate how some real-world organizations faced problems and challenges requiring the application of many of the concepts, corrective practices, and managerial skills discussed in this book. Organizations illustrated include a government contractor, a public utility, two major retailers, and the largest automobile manufacturer. Also, the managerial problems and challenges in the cases occur at all managerial levels —from the chief executive officer to first-line supervisor.

We have included the entire articles to illustrate the attempted cures as well as the problems. As you will note, in many of the cases the managerial challenges are far from being completely overcome. Indeed, in one case the organization met its demise.

ELECTRIC BOAT

General Dynamics has just swept away a dark cloud of financial uncertainty, creating great expectations on Wall Street. The settlement of long-disputed claims on eighteen attack submarines has lifted the corporation's stock to the highest level in more than a decade. Though its $359-million write-offs on those subs will plunge General Dynamics far into the red this year, Chairman David Lewis describes the future as "very bright"—and in general that is true. The company stands to make money on most of its other business, which includes such promising new weapons systems as the F-16 fighter plane for NATO and the Tomahawk cruise missile. There is, however, an expensive skeleton that looms as large in the future of General Dynamics as it does on the dockside at Groton, Connecticut . . . : the Trident submarine.

Potentially worth some $20 billion in business, the missile-firing monster is endangered by huge cost overruns and serious delays. Washington blames the continuing snarls in the project largely on lapses in management by its sole producer, the Electric Boat Division of General Dynamics. The company has orders for seven of the submarines, and the Pentagon had envisioned a fleet of more than twenty—until the effort to build them turned into what one of its senior officials describes as "a disaster."

On the drawing boards, at least, the Trident looked to be a whale of a weapons system. The submarine is as long as a destroyer and as heavy as a cruiser, displacing 18,700 tons. Its mission is to deter nuclear war by patrolling beneath the seas, carrying twenty-four long-range missiles, eight more than the Polaris and Poseidon subs it was designed to replace. So far, however, all that can be said for certain about Trident is that it has become the most expensive weapons program the U.S. has ever launched. The cost estimate for the first submarine alone, not including its missiles, has shot up to $1.2 billion, 50 percent over the original figure. With costs still rising and the program way behind schedule, both Congress and the Defense Department are beginning to doubt the wisdom of the venture and look about for cheaper alternatives.

A lot of the troubles with Trident can be traced to a hasty start and a stubborn admiral named Hyman Rickover, the father of the Navy's nuclear program and still its iron boss. The Pentagon decided that it had to move fast in 1972, when the first strategic-arms deal gave the Soviet Union a numerical edge in missile-firing submarines: sixty-two to the U.S.'s forty-four.

Louis Kraar, "Electric Boat's Whale of a Mess: The Trident Sub." Reprinted from the July 31, 1978, issue of *Fortune Magazine* by special permission; © 1978 Time Inc.

To compensate, the Navy wanted to assure that the maximum number of its subs would survive a Soviet first strike. The means to this end was a longer-range missile, the Trident, which would let the subs hide anywhere within 4,000 miles of the target.

Admiral Elmo Zumwalt Jr., then chief of naval operations, wanted to put the missiles on a new sub not much bigger than Poseidon, but he ran out of time to argue further with Rickover, who insisted on a very large reactor. Rickover contended that it was needed for higher speeds—a dubious advantage in a sub that must move quietly and lie low to escape detection. In any case, Rickover's reactor required a huge hull, which, Zumwalt says, had to be fitted "with an unprecedentedly large number of missiles to justify its size and costs." The Trident does not give the U.S. the option of deploying more sub-launched missiles while staying within the SALT limit on subs, because there is a separate limit on launching tubes, 710 for the U.S. and 950 for the U.S.S.R.

From that point, the procurement of Trident becomes an incredible tale of overoptimism and misjudgments by both General Dynamics and its customer. In July, 1974, the Navy signed its first production contract for four subs without having completed the detailed design plans. An unpublished audit by the General Accounting Office says that there was no "valid basis for establishing realistic cost estimates." The congressional watchdog agency discovered that the Navy had calculated a price based on the company's costs of labor and materials for vastly smaller submarines, then adjusted it mostly on the basis of guesswork. Its figures were not even supported by price quotations from suppliers. General Dynamics blithely accepted the Navy's terms, despite its own earlier warnings of "uncertainties in costs."

The contract includes some unusual provisions for profits amid hefty cost overruns. General Dynamics would earn 12.8 percent if it built the first sub at the Navy's estimated cost, termed the "target price." But if construction expenses rise, the profit margin gradually drops. The Trident becomes only a break-even proposition if costs climb to about two and a half times the target price. Any additional overrun comes out of the company's pocket. This exceptional spread, Navy officials contend, gave the company an incentive for undertaking the risky job, while still putting a ceiling on the government's liability.

General Dynamics is fully protected against inflation, however, which is computed from agreed-upon indexes for labor and material. The more its timetable slips, of course, the longer the Trident program is exposed to inflation—at the taxpayers' expense. While the first sub was supposed to be delivered no later than April, 1979, the contract does not penalize the builder for failing to meet the deadline. General Dynamics now says the first Trident won't be ready before November, 1980, about a year after the oldest of the Polaris subs is due to be retired.

The Defense Department, the Navy, and congressional investigators are in rare agreement about what went wrong at the Groton shipyard. General Dynamics got too greedy when it took on contracts for both the Trident and the attack submarines. As the work force was doubled to a peak of 30,000 in mid-1977, the yard suffered the corporate equivalent of a nervous break-down. Vice Admiral C. R. Bryan, head of Naval Sea Systems Command, which is Trident's customer, reports: "Electric Boat expanded its work force too rapidly, which lowered productivity. It lost control of its materials for Trident, and everything cascaded at once onto the heads of its managers." During the worst of the chaos at Groton, poorly supervised workers often waited around for hours because the parts they needed were not available. Electric Boat had simply failed to order them, but had no reliable system for knowing that.

As Admiral Bryan notes, the skills and crafts for building submarines "do not automatically exist in hiring halls, the streets, or at the corner service station." To meet its needs, Electric Boat hastily promoted many of its journeymen to supervisors and replaced them with unskilled workers. The shipyard wound up with managers and production workers who lacked sufficient experience in their jobs. Stanley Eno Jr., a former supervisor of labor relations, says, "The growing pains were unbelievable." The normal quota of three or four learners working under one skilled mechanic jumped to as high as a dozen learners, "with no one learning anything and produc-tivity dropping tremendously."

Sudden, disruptive social change in the traditionally male, white shipyard compounded the troubles. The hordes of new workers included many women and members of minority groups—a lot of them from the hardcore unemployed. To be sure, Electric Boat was responding to the usual govern-ment pressures and incentives for "affirmative action" on behalf of women and minorities. But in its eagerness to expand the work force, the company hired indiscriminately and then failed to train and control its new employees adequately.

At the least harmful level, there was a lot of distraction. As Eno says, "When women walked by bra-less with their T-shirts bouncing—and I'm not trying to be funny—production slowed down because everybody stopped what they were doing to take a look." Men and women began sneaking off to secluded parts of the shipyard for what he calls "hanky-panky." Even more serious, adds Eno, "we had every problem of a major city right within our shipyard. Drugs, alcoholism, sex, and fights over incidents of racial discrim-ination became a way of life." Company training programs for new foremen were "half-baked," Eno charges. And because workers were not given enough to do, "they had time to stand around and smoke pot, pop a few pills, or pull a bottle out of their pockets to take a drink."

While confirming the thrust of Eno's appraisal, Admiral Bryan doubts that vice and racial problems at the Groton yard "would be more than a sensible person might expect in this society." He is more concerned about another measure of Electric Boat's decline: its percentage of skilled workers in the essential trades fell from 80 to 53 percent, remaining alarmingly low until this year.

The company had planned to build the Trident in sections on a sort of production line, and it sank $150 million of its own money into the facilities it needed, but the scheme has not yet worked well. Electric Boat added to the confusion by revamping the yard's organization several times. Summing up, Admiral Bryan says: "The dominant cause of delays and cost increases that were avoidable boils down to shipyard management."

General Dynamics is trying to clean up the mess with a tough new manager at Electric Boat, its third in four years. P. Takis Veliotis has brought a very hard-nosed approach to Groton. He has dismissed thousands of workers in order to get payroll costs under control. Those who are left have complained bitterly to local newspapers about all the stern discipline—they must now get permission to go to the rest room, for example. Judging from their accounts, Veliotis says, "you would think we were running a Marine boot camp. It's not quite that bad."

But Veliotis, who is a six-footer with a pencil-line mustache, does look—and act—like a drill sergeant. He learned his trade at his father's shipyard in Greece, his native land, and aides say that the new boss "has no time for arguments or discussions." As manager of General Dynamics' civilian shipbuilding division at Quincy, Massachusetts, he helped avert a financial disaster by getting costs under control on some contracts for LNG tankers. Though work on the sensitive Trident project is normally limited to American citizens, the Navy granted Veliotis (now a Canadian national) the necessary clearances because of what it calls "the special circumstances."

Veliotis took over at Electric Boat in October, and began firing people his first day on the job. The initial batch of 2,000 salaried employees, including engineers and designers, were given a half hour to clean out their desks and leave. Some who had been with the company for years were stunned and tearful. Soon the layoffs spread through the ranks of blue-collar employees, reaching a total of 5,000.

Gradually, Electric Boat is rehiring some of the journeymen who were made instant supervisors—this time as production workers. While the purge has embittered union leaders, Veliotis argues: "This was not a pleasant thing to do, but we did it quickly and got it behind us." The situation is still tense, however, and Veliotis has evidently taken precautions for his own safety. He had a new wall built in front of Electric Boat's executive suite and travels to work with bodyguards in a chauffeured limousine.

To find the weaknesses at higher levels of the organization, Veliotis brought with him from Quincy a group of executives who serve as his eyes and ears. These super-managers, inserted into every key department, became known at Electric Boat as "the Quincy eight." They discovered—as government auditors had been telling the company for months—that the shipyard had no comprehensive list of the parts and materials needed to build the Trident and no clear idea of what was on hand. Some parts had been double- or triple-ordered and others never ordered at all. In January, Veliotis curtailed production for nine days to take the yard's first wall-to-wall inventory in a quarter century, cataloguing 60 million items.

Now that the housecleaning job is behind him, Veliotis says he is confident he can turn over the first Trident late in 1980, with the next three following within twenty-eight months. But no one in the Pentagon is willing to stake his reputation on the new dates, for they depend on continuing improvements in productivity at the shipyard. Admiral Bryan sees "a number of positive signs," including the company's tighter reign on its materials and its labor, but he warns that there is still "some risk" that Electric Boat will fail to keep its promises.

Rather than risking a possible gap in the U.S. nuclear deterrent, the Navy plans to refurbish some of the Poseidon subs to keep them in service beyond their normal twenty-year life. Ten of them will be equipped with the longer-range Trident missile. But all the Polaris subs and most of the Poseidons will still have to be retired during the next decade, and it is still not clear just what will replace them.

In retrospect, the Navy clearly put too much faith in both its own rough estimates and General Dynamics' proved ability to build large, complex weapons systems quickly. Admiral Bryan says he is told quite often these days that the Navy should have known better. "Everyone was working on the basis of Electric Boat's past performance," he explains in his defense. "Each new class of subs had been bigger than the last, and we had not encountered these problems."

General Dynamics still has a chance to make a profit on its seven Trident subs, but it may not get the opportunity to build a lot more of them. Congress is upset about the delays and cost overruns, and the armed-services committees have refused to authorize money for another Trident next fiscal year. Influential committee members fear that Trident may be pricing itself out of existence. Indeed, a Pentagon panel of technical experts drawn from industry and government is considering alternatives, including a smaller and cheaper substitute. William Perry, the under secretary of Defense for research and engineering, says that halting Trident in favor of another submarine "is more than a remote possibility," and Veliotis concedes that "there is no built-in guarantee Trident won't go down the drain." The final decision depends upon the outcome of studies that will be completed during the next twelve months.

If the Pentagon does launch a new program—perhaps for an updated version of Poseidon or for a missile-bearing version of the largest attack sub —the business won't necessarily go to General Dynamics. Its rival in nuclear subs, Newport News Shipbuilding Co., a division of Tenneco, has impressed the Pentagon by bringing in attack subs for as much as 30 percent less per vessel than the cost of the same subs from General Dynamics. Newport News refused to bid on Trident, arguing that the Navy should order a prototype first to find out where the problems lay and what the job might cost. In retrospect, that unusual act of self-control looks exceptionally wise.

Case questions

1. Discuss the problems with the government's planning process for the Trident submarine program.
2. Evaluate Electric Boat's original hiring and upgrading program (when the contract was first awarded). How might it have been handled differently?
3. What controls over the work force were lacking? Outline a set of controls that should have been put in place originally.
4. Evaluate Electric Boat's managerial design function.
5. What do you think of the actions of Veliotis? Evaluate him and his actions in terms of the leadership models discussed in the book.
6. How would you have handled the planning for the Trident project?

A&P

When Jonathan Scott took over as chairman and chief executive of A&P almost four years ago, the company was in desperate straits. It still is. On the record so far, Scott's performance at A&P has been one of the most disappointing management failures of recent years.

It's not that Scott hasn't *done* anything—he's done a lot. Among other things, he closed down almost half of the company's 3,468 stores, replaced almost all of top management, and spent hundreds of millions of dollars on new facilities. But all this has not translated into decent operating results. There have been serious errors of judgment or perception. The five-year recovery plan Scott announced in 1975 is a shambles and the company is back in the red. It lost $9.9 million in the first quarter of this year and $6.9 million in the second, and will almost certainly end up with a loss for the year. Most of the company's twenty-three operating divisions are unprofitable. Even a good many of the newer stores opened since 1970 are losing money. Operating expenses are out of line with those of competitors. Labor costs, which represent over 60 percent of total operating costs, run to 12.4 percent of sales, 2.3 percentage points above the industry average. An A&P executive says the company's administrative costs amount to approximately 2 percent, compared with an industry average of 1.25 percent. Stymied and overwhelmed by these problems, A&P has called in high-priced management consultants for the second time in five years. Concedes one A&P executive: "The company is in the same position today that it was in in 1971."

A couple of points should be made in Scott's defense. For one thing, this is an unfavorable time to be trying to improve the sales and earnings of a supermarket chain. Partly because the huge growth of the fast-food industry has been taking away a lot of business, supermarket sales have been growing only a little faster than inflation in recent years. This slow growth in the real volume of sales has crimped profits. Supermarket executives are beginning to look back with some nostalgia on the days when the standard profit margin was 1 percent of sales. Last year the industry's overall margin came to a thin 0.72 percent.

The big chains, moreover, are feeling tough competition from savvy and aggressive independents (operators of ten or fewer stores). There are many cases where an independent bought a former red-ink store unloaded by one of the chains and made it profitable by virtue of his merchandising flexibility and lower operating costs. (See box, page 464.) Supermarket chains, in short,

Peter W. Bernstein, "Jonathan Scott's Surprising Failure at A&P." Reprinted from the November 6, 1978, issue of *Fortune Magazine* by special permission; © 1978 Time Inc.

have been having a rough time lately. Some are losing money, and one large chain, Philadelphia-based Food Fair, recently filed for protection under Chapter 11 of the Bankruptcy Act.

GEORGE SHELTON'S INSTRUCTIVE SUCCESS IN A FORMER A&P STORE

When A&P closed its store at 500 Twelfth Street, S.E., in Washington, D.C., just twelve blocks from the Capitol, it was a loser. Today, almost three years later, another supermarket occupies the same premises, and it's thriving. Called Shelton's Marketbasket, the store does about twice the volume it did as an A&P. The man responsible for this transformation is George Shelton, forty, a wily and aggressive businessman who took over the store nine months after A&P closed it.

Shelton is one of a sizable number of independents who have snapped up A&P stores that the company closed and turned them into profitable enterprises. A&P estimates that 85 percent of the approximately 1,800 stores it has closed down since February, 1975, are still operating as food stores. (Some were acquired by chains.)

The one Shelton bought was small as supermarkets go (11,500 square feet). Shelving and freezers had not been replaced in at least fifteen years. "My negotiations with A&P were short and sweet," Shelton says. "They agreed to sell me all the equipment for $1." In its last year as an A&P, he estimates, the store had weekly sales of about $30,000. "It was a classic A&P inner-city store with the A&P coffee-grind smell," he remembers. Most of the customers were people of low or moderate income. Unruly youngsters from the neighborhood often gathered outside the store, which made shopping there unpleasant at times.

Treating caviar like orange juice

When he took over, with the help of a $160,000 bank loan guaranteed by the Small Business Administration, Shelton had a good bit of supermarket experience behind him. In various capacities, he had spent about a dozen years at Kroger, the nation's third-largest supermarket chain. He opened up Shelton's Marketbasket on December 8, 1976, and was disappointed but not dismayed that it did only $8,000 worth of business the first

week. The level has been rising ever since, and weekly sales now average around $55,000.

The key to Shelton's success has been his merchandising. Operating in a neighborhood with a variety of income levels and ethnic groups, he has attracted many different segments of the community to his store. He stocks Spanish, Italian, Jewish, and Chinese foods, among others. Observes one customer, Betty Ann Kane, a member of Washington's Board of Education: "He has Häagen-Dazs ice cream as well as ribs and chitlins." Shelton points out that his prices are good, especially on gourmet products. "Capitol Hill is notorious for the gourmet-shop rip-off," he says, "but I use the same basic markup on caviar as orange juice." Although there are two elementary schools across the street, he does not sell small candies, because he does not want children clogging the aisles. Nor does he sell beer by the can. "I want to attract the stable shopper," he says.

Shelton's must be about the friendliest grocery store in town. The boss himself is often in the store weighing vegetables or working the checkout, sometimes wearing a "Love Thy Grocer" button. When asked where something is, employees are supposed to lead the customer to it rather than just give directions. In the winter, Shelton runs a bus to and from the local senior citizens housing. Because the store lacks a parking lot, he hires youngsters to carry groceries to customers' cars. Last Christmas, he sent out greeting cards to his customers, thanking them for their patronage. Such gestures are winning him loyal customers. Says Congressman James R. Jones: "Shelton's is just like the neighborhood grocery store in Muskogee, Oklahoma, where I grew up."

Only two members of management

The store is also safe, an important consideration in a city with high crime rates. Shelton employs eight off-duty policemen. Police regulations prohibit them from working as security guards, so Shelton puts them to work as cashiers and stockmen; but in accord with another police regulation, they still carry their guns.

Shelton employs non-union help and keeps his labor cost to about 10 percent of sales, the industry average. Administrative expenses are very low. There are just two members of management: Shelton, who pays himself $38,000, and a $20,000 store manager. Shelton's office is an unadorned room in the store's basement, without air conditioning. The net profit of about 1.5 percent of sales ($50,000 last year) is a bit above average for an independent—and about double the average margin of supermarket chains these days.

Far from satisfied with his store, Shelton plans to remodel, replacing the old refrigeration equipment, adding a deli, and expanding the frozen-food and dairy departments. All that will cost $250,000. He hopes to complete his modernization by the end of the year, before the Safeway a few blocks away finishes an announced expansion project. He has also begun thinking about possible sites for another store.

Also, it should be acknowledged that A&P was a very backward company when Scott took over. It lacked the financial controls of a modern corporation. The management had been late in following its customers to the suburbs, and there were too many small, inefficient stores tucked away in deteriorating urban neighborhoods. Stores were overstocked with A&P's private-label merchandise (notably Jane Parker and Ann Page brands), one consequence of the company's excessive emphasis on its manufacturing plants. With all this, A&P's sales were nearly flat for the Sixties, gaining an average of only 0.9 percent a year. A&P's share of the grocery business in the U.S. declined from nearly 10 percent in the early Sixties to 6 percent ten years later. In 1973, the company lost its position as America's No. 1 grocery chain—in total sales—to Safeway Stores.

Past managements had failed to take care for the company's future. During the Sixties, Scott points out, there were no borrowings of any kind for investment in growth and little reinvestment of capital in retail facilities. At the same time, Scott notes, the company was paying cash dividends that, in proportion to earnings, ran to nearly double those of other large food retailers. One of the principal beneficiaries of that dividend policy was the John A. Hartford Foundation, set up by a son of A&P founder George Huntington Hartford (it supports medical research). The foundation, which was then dominated by retired A&P executives, owned one-third of the company's stock (but has since reduced its holdings to about 25 percent). As one observer recently put it, "A&P was being milked."

Jonathan Scott, now forty-eight, seemed to possess both the business ability and the personal qualities that would be needed to turn A&P around. He was recruited by Booz, Allen & Hamilton, the management-consulting firm that the A&P board turned to in 1974 when it decided to go outside for help. At the time he was the chief executive of Idaho-based Albertson's, the country's tenth-largest supermarket chain, where he had started as a management trainee in 1953. Some men reach the top because they marry the boss's daughter; Scott performed the unusual feat of reaching the top in spite of divorcing the boss's daughter. In 1965, after the divorce (he has since re-married), his former father-in-law, J. A. Albertson, named him president of the chain. He became chief executive in 1972.

Albertson's faith in Scott was well placed. Revenues more than tripled in the decade after Scott became president, reaching $852 million in fiscal 1974, and earnings more than doubled, to $9 million. In the process, Scott won a reputation as a hardheaded and innovative retailer who pioneered Albertson's geographic expansion as well as its development of large com-bination food-and-drug stores. Along with his business acumen, Scott has other commendable attributes. His quiet informality—almost everybody calls him Scotty—and an open, forthright manner make it hard not to like him. In fact, there are those who think that Scott's biggest problem in managing A&P has been that he is too nice. Says one man who has come to know him pretty well: "He is not heartless enough to do it."

For whatever reason, the approach Scott took to the store-closing program, which he embarked upon immediately after he took over in February, 1975, was fundamentally flawed. With the company's condition deteriorating rap-idly, there was no question that Scott had to act quickly. The immediate problem was deciding which stores to close and which to save, a matter of considerable complexity. The shutting of a single store can have significant ramifications on a marketing area's distribution costs, its warehousing opera-tions, its advertising expenses, and its labor situation, as well as on the A&P manufacturing facilities that are deprived of an outlet for their products.

Scott confronted a choice between two strategies. One was to close down the company's worst operating units, store by store, warehouse by ware-house, plant by plant. A more radical course of action was to shut down en-tire operating divisions. Scott opted for the first alternative. "We made a conscious decision to close down on a store-by-store basis," he recalls. "We decided to weed out the very worst and try to turn around the rest. We wanted to save as much as we could."

The plan Scott adopted was the keystone of the five-year recovery pro-gram that Booz, Allen had formulated for A&P after a year-long study that cost $1 million. It called for the immediate closing of 1,250 unprofitable or marginal stores as well as certain warehouses and manufacturing plants. To cover the estimated cost of the program, A&P set up a $200-million reserve taken as a charge against earnings in the fourth quarter of 1974. The result was an after-tax loss of $157 million for the year. "This is hard medicine to take," Scott told the stockholders in June, 1975. "Major surgery is always costly and painful."

In retrospect, it is clear that Scott's basic decision was a mistake. Be-sides closing individual stores that were too small or badly located, the company should have shut down several operating divisions, retreating completely from geographical areas where it was having especially bad toubles. The store-by-store approach, leaving A&P spread thin in some areas, sacrificed potential economies that could have been gained from geographical concentration. What's more, A&P continued to hang on in places where it had only a weak position in the marketplace. Capital invested in remodeling stores in such areas could have been better spent where A&P's position was stronger (or competition relatively weak). As one astute competitor put it: "The challenge of turning the business around turned out to be greater than A&P ever imagined. Closing small stores was not the kind of amputation they needed."

Scott's strategic error was not immediately apparent, however. Once the company decided to operate, the actual "surgery" proceeded smoothly enough. In fact, it did not take as long or cost as much as A&P at first suspected it would. A year after Scott unveiled the program, he announced that it "was completed ahead of schedule and well below estimated cost." Altogether, the company closed 1,433 stores, more than 40 percent of the number it had when Scott took over, as well as thirty-six food-processing plants and warehouses. Only two operating divisions—Dallas and Buffalo—were entirely eliminated. (A third, St. Louis, was closed down later on.) Even though the plan had been altered to include some additional facilities, the company decided that not all of the $200-million reserve would be needed, and it was reduced by $35 million during fiscal 1975. For one thing, A&P realized more money from the sale of property and the disposition of leases than it had originally estimated.

Initially the company seemed to respond well to the drastic cutback in operations. Despite the loss of stores that had accounted for $1.5 billion in annual sales, A&P nearly maintained its volume during the first year of the recovery program. The following year, fiscal 1976, total sales climbed to a record of $7.2 billion, almost 11 percent more than the $6.5 billion the year before. The company was profitable in 1975 and 1976, and after another successful quarter management declared its first dividend in thirty-three months. Store by store, things looked even better. With the closing of many of the company's small stores, the average size of an A&P had increased from about 16,000 square feet to almost 20,000, a jump that quickly gave the company better operating results. Average weekly sales per store climbed from $37,308 in 1974 to $69,871 in 1976, a remarkable improvement. A&P still lagged behind the industry average of $72,425, but a year later, with further improvement, A&P's average weekly sales per store virtually matched the industry figure of $75,000.

The company was able to maintain its sales volume partly because the employees felt good about the new management. Spurred on by Price & Pride, the new corporate-advertising campaign that was directed as much at the employees as it was at the customers, and excited by the plans to make

A&P healthy again, the employees rallied around Scott, cleaning up the stores and working harder.

The company also benefited from good will among consumers. Some loyal customers who found their old A&P closed down looked for another nearby. When other consumers heard the commercials saying there was a "new" A&P, one that put price and pride together again, they were willing to give the store another chance. After all, the A&P (which employees used to call "Grandma") was something of an American institution. The customers, however, were disappointed by what they found. "The ads featured better-looking stores with very wide aisles and attractive-looking merchandise," laments one A&P vice president, "but the customer who left us two or three years ago would come in and find the same bad situation that she left. A&P simply got ahead of itself in its advertising."

The encouraging results, then, were misleading. As several A&P executives now admit, the volume increases that came in the wake of the store-closing program were "false," the result of a short-term change in circumstances rather than any fundamental improvement in the company's operating habits. Scott agrees. "When the enthusiasm wore off," he said recently, "we could not sustain the volume increases because we did not have the real tools and the systems to work with."

Whether or not the lack of "real tools" and "systems" had anything to do with it, volume did fall off. In fiscal 1977, sales in dollars increased by less than 1 percent, which meant, of course, that real volume declined considerably. The decline continued in the current fiscal year, with first-half sales up only 2 percent from a year earlier, quite a bit less than the rate of inflation. Profits sank dismally: from $23.8 million in fiscal 1976 to $4.8 million in 1977, to heavy losses in the current fiscal year.

Now that the company is back in the red and the initial buoyancy in sales has fizzled, it is all too evident that the store-closing program failed as a remedy for A&P's difficulties. One reason it failed was that it was not accompanied by an adequate effort to overcome the managerial problems of the stores A&P retained. A&P had traditionally been a "manage by memo" company, run from the top down. Corporate management had given the store managers little decision-making power. The managers were not really running the stores and they were ill-equipped to do so. In many cases, managers had no idea of the prices they were paying for goods delivered to the stores, and thus were unable to make proper pricing decisions.

Upper management, moreover, failed to establish sound merchandising programs in the stores. Store managers operated without proper shelf-allocation programs. Inventory controls were spotty. What came in from the warehouse was often decided by higher-ups, and there was little concern for demands of customers in particular neighborhoods. Says Willis Lonn, executive vice president for merchandising and procurement: "A&P people had been conditioned over the years to not making money. They were conditioned to being unsuccessful."

It took the new management under Scott a while to perceive the severity of the problems. As a result, the reconditioning process—the retraining of personnel, the installation of management-information systems, and the setting up of basic merchandising programs, among other things—took much longer than Scott had hoped. Some of the new management's remedial measures, moreover, were pretty ineffective. Millions of dollars, Scott admits, were wasted on store-personnel training programs that did not have any impact—partly, it appears, because there was too little follow-up.

In addition, management's lack of adequate information about store operations made the closing program a somewhat hit-or-miss affair. Because of the absence of detailed profit-and-loss statements, and a cost-allocation system that did not reflect true costs, A&P's strategists could not be sure whether an individual store was really unprofitable. For example, distribution costs were shared equally among all the stores in a marketing area without regard to such factors as a store's distance from the warehouse. Says one close observer of the company: "When they wanted to close a store, they had to wing it. They could not make rational decisions, because they did not have a fact basis."

The store-closing program had the perverse effect of increasing the company's labor costs in some markets. A&P's average hourly wage is $6.74 without fringe benefits—at least $1.64 higher than the average of the competitors in the same operating areas. Because of union contracts that guarantee employees jobs on a seniority basis as long as A&P operates some stores in an area, young and less highly paid workers were "bumped" off the payroll when the company shut stores. Older and more highly paid employees kept their jobs, though many were transferred to other locations. In the Long Island and Pittsburgh divisions, two areas where A&P is burdened with especially stiff contracts, the average age is fifty-six. While paying more, the company was getting less. As a rule, A&P's older store employees are less productive than their younger counterparts.

A&P's new management also did not fare very well in calculating what effects the store closings would have on the company's manufacturing plants, which have absorbed a lot of capital resources over the years. As of early 1975, the company operated forty-six plants. Twenty-one were bakeries. The others turned out everything from "frozen potato morsels" to mouthwash.

Private-label products from these plants were flooding A&P stores. The customer who wanted a wider choice was forced to shop elsewhere. Sales suffered. Booz, Allen concluded that A&P was often making retail-merchandising decisions based on the needs of its manufacturing units. As Allan Feder, A&P's executive vice president for manufacturing, put it, "The tail was wagging the dog."

For a while, A&P's new management had hopes that increased volume in its remaining stores would lift its manufacturing sales. In fact, the company was so confident of getting increased sales that the five-year plan called for *adding* some manufacturing plants. Instead, when volume did not increase, twenty-seven of the plants were closed. Some of the remaining nineteen are operating at uneconomic rates. By one recent unofficial estimate, the huge grocery-products plant at Horseheads, New York, is now running at just over 50 percent of capacity. Under Scott, A&P has been moderately successful in finding markets outside the U.S. for its manufactured products, but this business, Compass Foods, has not yet built up enough volume to make much of a difference at the plants.

Even more embarrassing than the disappointing results of the facilities-closing program is the poor showing of the program to build new and larger stores. Altogether, the new management planned to spend $500 million in five years. In the first two years alone, A&P announced, it would lay out $230 million to open 200 newly built or acquired stores, remodel and enlarge 600, and give an additional 1,400 a face-lift. Some of the financing came from $200 million worth of credit agreements that A&P negotiated with eleven banks. As a result, A&P's long-term debt jumped from $39 million in 1974 to $134 million three years later. (The company had no long-term debt at all as recently as 1971.) The redevelopment program was, as Scott told the stockholders in June, 1975, "a tremendous undertaking."

Although A&P had the financial means, it lacked the ability to carry out the program. After two years, the company had spent $161 million, $69 million less than planned; it opened 191 new or acquired stores but fell far behind in the remodeling program. For fiscal 1977, seventy new stores were planned but only forty-six were opened. Increasingly concerned about the company's disappointing earnings, management decided to scale capital expenditures down to $85 million in fiscal 1978.

Much of the money invested in facilities was badly spent. With all of the company's divisions competing for funds, the money was dispersed somewhat haphazardly, based on area sales volume and what one vice president calls "a certain amount of emotionalism." Proposals for new stores were brought in by the operating people who wanted to run them, and they would hazard a guess as to what the new store's sales would be. The results were poor. Laments Scott: "Hundreds of millions of dollars have been invested in the wrong place."

Scott feels that most of the blame belongs with the old management, which had made most of the bad decisions about where to invest in building or remodeling stores before he took over. He halted work on about forty stores that were being worked on when he arrived. Since then, moreover, real-estate development at A&P has become more scientific. The company now uses an elaborate formula to estimate each project's potential return on investment, instead of relying on the arguments of store operators. Of the approximately 200 new stores—constructed or purchased—that Scott's management is solely responsible for, "a good majority," says an A&P executive, can be counted as successful. That's fine, but the new management can be faulted for throwing good money after bad in carrying out some of the old management's investment plans.

What's more, Scott has made blunders of his own in the deployment of capital. Perhaps the biggest and most expensive was the decision to sink sizable resources into the Chicago area. In the face of heavy losses from operations there—$10 million in 1976—A&P decided to make a big bid for more business. In late 1976, the company purchased sixty-two stores from National Tea, which had decided to withdraw from the Chicago market. The price was $22 million. So far, the move has turned out badly. "We miscalculated our breakeven point," concedes Lowell Peters, the executive vice president who oversees the division. He explains that A&P's labor and advertising costs as a percent of sales did not decrease as hoped. A more fundamental problem, according to a local competitor, was that even though A&P was able to choose the stores it wanted, it did not pick very good ones. At any rate, the company is still losing money in the Chicago market.

The carrying-out of the store-closing and modernization programs was made more difficult by the cumbersome way Scott organized the company's chain of command. At the urging of Booz, Allen, he tried to decentralize decision-making downward, reorganizing the company along the lines of the regional chains that had been achieving the greatest growth in the supermarket industry. Scott hoped that A&P would, in effect, become a group of regional chains, united at the top. So the company set up eight regional offices, each of which had a president (annual salary: $75,000) and its own accounting, merchandising, real-estate, and sales staffs. Each region, in turn, supervised the operations of three or four divisions. Says Scott: "We had to be ready for increased volume and growth."

When A&P's volume failed to increase, the regional offices quickly became a layer of burdensome and expensive bureaucracy. The result, in the words of one divisional vice president, was "total chaos." Adds another: "We just didn't get anything done." In September, 1977, after a three-day huddle of top management in Bermuda, a decision was made to abolish the regions, eliminating approximately 400 jobs and saving A&P $20 million a year. Subsequently, the company named three group executive vice presidents to supervise the twenty-three operating divisions. A few months ago, each group head was also given a small staff.

Aside from the store closings, the stiffest medicine Scott has administered to A&P has been a massive injection of new people into the corporate management. Of the seventy people in top management (vice president and above), only twenty have been with the company longer than Scott, according to an organization chart prepared for the board of directors. A mere six have been in their present positions for longer than three years. All of the top ten officers under Scott have come to A&P since he arrived. Three of them, including David Morrow, the president and chief operating officer, came from Scott's old company, Albertson's. Most of the old A&P hands still with the company are now divisional vice presidents, although some once held higher posts. Twelve of the twenty-three divisional chiefs have been with the company more than a quarter of a century.

The shake-up at the lower levels has been less turbulent, but still considerable. By one estimate, about 25 percent of A&P's store managers have left within the last three and a half years, more than double what would be considered normal turnover. Managers were changed so often in the Long Island division that when a new vice president was installed in June, he put a moratorium on further changes, to relieve the anxiety of the people under him.

The hovering presence of management consultants along with the constant personnel changes created not only a lot of stress but also a lot of hard feelings. What's more, there are indications that some of the new people in management represent no improvement over the people they displaced. A former employee says the company has hired "a lot of floaters and drifters." A competitor notes that most of the people A&P hired from his organization were employees he did not mind losing. Another longtime A&P hand says that while initially he was convinced that Scott intended "to blend the best of the old with the new," it later became clear that "all the career people at A&P were being eliminated one by one"—either fired or asked to move back in the organization. Certainly, all the changes made it more difficult for Scott to carry out the recovery plan. But, Scott says lamely, "we have to expect change while we are finding the right solutions."

Scott has been urgently looking for ways to get A&P moving again. Last December A&P instituted "action prices," a merchandising program that passes manufacturers' specials directly on to the consumer. Then in January, A&P decided to drop the stale Price & Pride campaign. A new one was launched in September, promising that "You'll Do Better at A&P." Following the lead of other chains, the company also began promoting plainly labeled generic products in special "economy corners." Finally, the search for larger sales led A&P to trading stamps, which are now being dispersed in the ten operating divisions where gains are most badly needed. In earlier days, Scott had been strongly opposed to trading stamps.

Still searching for a long-term solution to its many ills, the company has once again turned to management consultants. McKinsey & Co. was hired a year ago to do essentially the same thing Booz, Allen did—work out a new strategy for A&P. The fee: $100,000 a month. To be sure, McKinsey is looking at a very different company from the one Booz, Allen studied four years ago. A&P is smaller and the physical plant is more modern. Scott has spent a considerable amount of energy overhauling the organization—bringing in new people, building a sound real-estate department, putting in tighter financial controls, improving the company's cash management, and installing information systems. But it remains to be seen whether these management-manual improvements at the corporate level will translate into better performance where it counts—in the operation of A&P stores. A&P's future depends on increased sales and lower operating costs in the stores, and in these nitty-gritty matters, Scott's record so far has been grimly disappointing.

The results of the McKinsey study are not expected to be announced until early next year, but there has already been quite a bit of speculation inside and outside the company about what will happen next. Management is currently reviewing the information generated by McKinsey and, in Scott's words, "determining our strategy by area." Scott gave the stockholders a clue about what they might expect at the annual meeting in June. "It does seem clear," he said, "that we will have to take further consolidation steps in some areas." Since then Scott has been reluctant to add much, except to say that the changes in the company will be "material."

Other members of top management have been less guarded about A&P's future direction. There is unanimous agreement that A&P will get smaller before it gets bigger. One distinct possibility, according to one executive, is that "whole divisions will be closed down." Long Island, Pittsburgh, Milwaukee, Florida, and parts of New England are most frequently mentioned as the marketing areas where that could happen. Chicago is another sore spot, but the company seems less inclined to do anything drastic about it. Earlier this year, in what might be regarded as a prelude to future actions, A&P left the Columbus, Ohio, market, selling off seventeen stores in the area. Another more familiar course of action would be for A&P to continue to close down its weakest stores. One executive points out that McKinsey has already identified 100 stores that the company should abandon. Says a competitor: "If there is radical enough surgery, A&P can still survive."

At the same time, A&P executives talk of the company's rejuvenation. Some divisions, such as Baltimore, Richmond, the Carolinas, Atlanta, and Philadelphia, will probably be identified as growth areas where the company should channel most of its future investment. Money will also go to fortify

A&P's position in some parts of the New York metropolitan region, the company's biggest market. One certain target for growth will be the Family Center subsidiary, which Scott set up in 1976 to operate large (56,000-square-foot) combination food-and-drug stores. So far, there are twelve Family Marts, as they are called, all in the Southeast. Two more are scheduled to be opened this year.

Whatever the strategy, A&P's management is convinced that the old Great Atlantic & Pacific Tea Co. will continue to exist. Talk of A&P's demise is certainly premature. The company currently seems able to generate enough cash that bankruptcy is not a near-term possibility. At the corporate headquarters in Montvale, New Jersey, the mood, in the words of one executive, is one of "superconfidence." Talk of failure is dismissed as an absurdity. Says one executive vice president: "We would have to be totally incompetent for A&P to fail." Scott himself says, "I have not the slightest doubt that A&P is going to make it." He insists that it is just a matter of time until management is able to turn the company around. But in order for that to happen, Jonathan Scott will have to, in the words of the new advertising slogan, do better at A&P.

Case questions

1. Evaluate A&P's planning process. Did the company account correctly for environmental conditions and corporate strengths and weaknesses? Did it overcome "trained incapacity"?

2. Was A&P centralized or decentralized? What effects did the placement of decision centers have on the company's ability to implement the new plan?

3. Were A&P's objectives market-oriented? Or, were objectives determined by internal conditions? Discuss.

4. Evaluate A&P's forecasting in this case.

5. Discuss and evaluate Scott's reorganization plans involving regional and then group managers. What were the basic reasons for such a structure?

6. Discuss in terms of objectives, planning, and organization why George Shilton was able to make the Washington, D.C., store succeed, although it had failed under A&P. If A&P had done some things differently, might such stores have been made as successful as they eventually became under other ownership?

7. Evaluate Scott's leadership role.

8. Discuss the latest A&P moves. Are they well planned?

9. As a management consultant (or a staff planning person) to A&P and doing an organizational audit, what strategy or long-term plan would you recommend?

G.M.

The perpetuation of leadership is sometimes more difficult than the attainment of that leadership in the first place. This is the greatest challenge to be met by the leader of an industry. It is a challenge to be met by the General Motors of the future.

—former Chairman Alfred P. Sloan Jr.
My Years with General Motors (1963)

With giant corporations as with giant oil tankers, bigness confers advantages, but the ability to turn around easily is not one of them. Though General Motors does some things very well, one just doesn't expect it to be nimble. In so huge an organization, decision-making processes are inherently complex, and sheer mass generates a great deal of inertia. Four years ago, however, G.M. came up against the sort of challenge foreseen by Alfred Sloan. Though the company seemed ill prepared for change, it not only met the challenge but did so with a resounding success that surprised many observers of the U.S. auto industry.

The clearest evidence of G.M.'s effective response to that challenge is the transformation of its product line to meet the demands of the marketplace—and the federal government—for better gas mileage. When the Arab oil embargo hit at the end of 1973, G.M. had the worst average gas mileage among U.S. automakers—a dismal twelve miles per gallon. As buyers turned away from gas-guzzlers in panic during the following year, G.M.'s share of the U.S. new-car market slid to 42 percent, the lowest point since 1952 (not counting the strike year of 1970). Just three years later, in the 1977-model year, the average mileage of G.M. cars, 17.8 mpg, was the *best* among the Big Three automakers. G.M.'s big cars alone averaged 15 mpg, or 3 mpg better than the entire 1974 fleet. Largely as a result, the company's market share has rebounded to about 46 percent.

At the center of this product revolution was G.M.'s downsizing strategy, which began last year with the big cars. G.M. gambled that it could redefine the meaning of "big" in the American marketplace, from its traditional connotation of exterior bulk to a more functional, European-style definition based on interior space and driving quality. The gamble succeeded. In what proved to be a good year for big cars in general, G.M.'s more than held their own against the conventional offerings of Ford and Chrysler.

Charles G. Burck, "How G.M. Turned Itself Around." Reprinted from the January 16, 1978, issue of *Fortune Magazine* by special permission; © 1978 Time Inc.

The downsizing strategy is also the key to G.M.'s hopes for the future. Despite the many difficulties and uncertainties of the auto market, General Motors is notably more confident than the other U.S. automakers of its ability to meet the government's tightening schedule of mileage laws for the years to come with cars that will still satisfy the American consumer. Says President Elliott M. Estes: "We're working on three or four scenarios for getting to 27.5 miles per gallon by 1985. It's a problem now of economics—how can we do it for the least cost?"

G.M.'s headquarters are awash in self-assurance these days. There is more than a hint of that spirit in Chairman Thomas Aquinas Murphy's outspoken optimism about the economy, the automobile industry, and General motors itself. Most remarkable is Murphy's unabashed determination to increase market share as much as possible—indeed, he has said on more than one occasion that he will not be satisfied "until we sell every car that's sold." That's an astonishing departure from the posture of earlier G.M. chief executives, who avoided *any* talk about expanding market share for fear of unleashing the hounds of antitrust.

Murphy explains his outspokenness by asking and then answering a rhetorical question. "Should there be a limit to our return or our market penetration? I say no. The risks of the business today are as high as or higher than they've ever been, and the returns ought to be high. And if we're obeying the law, doing the best job of serving the customer, and discharging all the other responsibilities we have as a good employer and responsible citizen, then we've earned whatever we get."

Such spirit was nowhere to be found at G.M. four years ago. Nineteen seventy-four, in fact, seemed to confirm what many observers had been suspecting for some time—that G.M. was losing its capacity to lead the industry. Sloan, the man who established that leadership in the first place during the 1920's, had observed that "success may bring self-satisfaction . . . the spirit of venture is lost in the inertia of the mind against change," and it appeared in the early 1970's that his own company was fulfilling the prophecy.

Between 1962 and 1972, G.M.'s market share drifted down from its all-time high of 51.9 percent to 44.2 percent. Most of the lost sales went to imports and did not greatly trouble G.M. Following a strictly financial logic, the company concluded that it was sensible to stick with its traditional policies, which had earned it dominance of the highly profitable big-car market, rather than compete head-on in the less profitable small-car field.

For a while, events seemed to justify this reasoning. Measured in dollars, sales continued to rise. G.M. indisputably knew who the prime automobile customers were and how to make what they wanted.

But G.M. was slow to realize what besides efficiency made the imports so attractive: agility and a certain sporty functionalism were increasingly appealing to a broader public than what G.M. understood as the economy market. There were executives at G.M. in 1970 who actually thought that —as one explained to a reporter—"there's something wrong with people who like small cars." G.M.'s domestic and foreign competitors, knowing better, captured a lot of the growth while G.M.'s chosen territory was contracting. Ford's market share during those years slipped only two percentage points, to 24.3, while Chrysler's actually rose.

G.M. also seemed fundamentally out of touch with the outside world. Its size made it a natural target for antibusiness critics—especially the militant autophobes who held the auto industry responsible for everything from urban pollution to suburban sprawl. The company's reaction to its critics, as well as to the pollution and safety legislation pushed forth by the government, was defensive and even uncomprehending. Its labor relations presented a similarly sorry sight. The problems of the highly automated plant at Lordstown, Ohio, for example, which began building Vegas in 1971, became celebrated as a classic management failure to understand or communicate with employees.

Yet despite G.M.'s insularity and self-preoccupation, managerial machinery was grinding along, resolutely if ponderously, in search of new directions. Sloan had, after all, set up a management system predicated upon change. But even important management decisions rarely show up visibly or dramatically on the outside. As Thomas Murphy says, "Drama in business lies mostly in doing well the job right before you."

New policies, moreover, like new cars, require lead times. Indeed, G.M.'s top officers are not inclined to react with high emotion to the events of any given year, for the practical reason that in so massive an institution there is little they can do to affect the short run in any case. Experience has taught patience. They know, for example, that even a new division head cannot do much that will influence his division's results for a good twenty to thirty months. Asked about the process of change at G.M., they invariably reply that it is "evolutionary, not revolutionary."

It is a characteristic of evolutionary processes, of course, that they are hard to perceive until after they have been going on for a while. G.M.'s first response to those social-minded critics was aloof and almost brusque. But after handily turning aside their most flamboyant challenge—"Campaign G.M.," at the 1970 annual meeting—the company set up extensive machinery to bring new and critical thinking into its corporate planning process. It created a new public-policy committee, staffed entirely with outsiders, and the fresh viewpoints the committee brought to G.M. were listened to. The company also hired a number of important managers from outside—a radical departure from the tradition of near-exclusive reliance on internal management development. These people were assigned to key posts. For example,

Stephen H. Fuller, who had been professor of business administration at Harvard Business School, was put in charge of the personnel administration and development staff. Ernest S. Starkman, from the school of engineering at the University of California, Berkeley, was made head of environmental activities.

The rapid turnaround of G.M.'s product line over the past three years could not have been accomplished without a good deal of earlier thinking and planning. As far back as 1972, the board of directors created an ad hoc group called the energy task force, headed by David C. Collier, then G.M.'s treasurer and now head of the Buick division. Collier's group included people from manufacturing, research, design, finance, and the economics staff, and it spent half a year on its research. "We came to three conclusions," said Collier. "First, that there was an energy problem. Second, the government had no particular plan to deal with it. Third, the energy problem would have a profound effect upon our business. We went to the board with those conclusions in March of 1973."

Collier's report made for a good deal of discussion throughout the company in the months following. "We were trying to get other people to think about it," says Richard C. Gerstenberg, who was then chairman of G.M. Meantime, Collier's group was assigned to examine G.M.'s product program, and when Collier reported back to the board again in October, the talk turned to what Gerstenberg refers to as "getting some downsizing in our cars."

The embargo, of course, intruded dramatically upon this rather studied planning process. But while no specific decisions had yet been made on the basis of Collier's report, the work of the task force had done much to create the right frame of mind at all levels of management. G.M.'s board was able within two months to approve several specific proposals. Two were "crash" decisions for the 1976-model year. The Chevette would be built, using component designs from Opel and other overseas divisions, mainly Brazil; and so would the car that would become the Seville, under consideration for more than a year. And then, as Gerstenberg says, "the possible long-term program was to find a way to redesign all of our regular lines so we could get them all in a much more fuel-efficient area."

G.M.'s product-policy committee had already decided, in April, to scale down the 1977 standard cars, but the reductions were to be modest, totaling about 400 pounds, and they were calculated to improve economy by only about one mile per gallon. By the end of 1973, however, mileage had suddenly become the overriding concern, and it was clear that practically the entire product line would eventually have to be redesigned. The biggest question, recalls Pete Estes, then executive vice president in charge of operations staffs, was where to begin. The committee's deliberations were intense, but not lengthy. The consensus that emerged, says Estes, was that "our business was family cars, so we had to start there. If we had started at the bottom, there would have been a gap for a year or so where the competition could have moved in."

The policy committee's new proposals went to the executive committee, which makes all of G.M.'s major operational decisions (its members include the seven top officers). In December the executive committee instructed the company's engineers to come up with a plan for substantial reductions in the 1977 big cars, and to start on the reductions for other body sizes in the years after.

Even as the product plans were being redrawn, G.M. was taking a broader look at itself—investigating how it had failed to deal with its problems, and working up recommendations for change. Every summer, the executive committee undertakes what Gerstenberg calls "an inventory of people"—a review of the company's 6,000 or so top managers for possible promotion and replacement. In 1974, moreover, it was charged with picking successors to Gerstenberg and President Edward N. Cole, both of whom were retiring. In addition, the board asked the committee to take an inventory of G.M.'s problems. Both inventories, in turn, were presented to the newly created organization review committee, consisting mainly of the outside directors who serve on G.M.'s bonus and salary committee. The job of this review committee was to analyze the problems and propose organizational solutions.

Many of those problems were in the process of being dealt with, of course—particularly in the transformation of the product line. But some of the most important were not so easily defined or specifically addressed. The process of running G.M. had grown considerably more complex since the 1950's. The business environment was still uncertain, and outside constraints had to be taken increasingly into account. The review committee wrestled with the implications of such matters during that summer; toward the end of its assignment, it was augmented by Murphy, who had been nominated to replace Gerstenberg as chairman.

What the committee recommended, in September, 1974, was a major reorganization at the top. That reorganization, says Murphy, "expanded importantly the top management group. Looking beyond where we were at the time, we designed it to bring new executives into a higher echelon." Complicated in its details, the reorganization upgraded the responsibilities of the executive vice presidents, and added a fourth to the three already existing. The upgrading brought forward four relatively young men, all future prospects for the top, to serve on the board and the executive committee. Since the divisions now answer to top management through those executive vice presidents, the reorganization strengthened lines of authority and communication.

The reorganization also redefined and strengthened the jobs of the president and of the new vice chairman, Richard L. Terrell. Supervision of G.M.'s eight operating staffs had previously been split between the president and the vice chairman; all were brought together under Terrell. That move freed the new president, Estes, to concentrate more fully on operations—and especially upon overseas operations, which were transferred to him from the vice chairman. Along with Ford and Chrysler, G.M. is planning a growing number of "world cars"—essentially similar models that can be built in the U.S., Europe, or anywhere else. Though the first of those, the Chevette, was barely on the drawing boards for the U.S. that year, G.M. reasoned that overseas and domestic work could be more directly and effectively integrated if both divisions reported to Estes.

If the reorganization was a landmark event, it was in some ways less important than another change wrought in 1974—the adoption of the project center, a new concept in engineering management, devised to coordinate the efforts of the five automobile divisions. A G.M. project center, made up of engineers lent by the divisions, has no exact counterpart elsewhere in the auto industry—and perhaps in all of U.S. industry. NASA used the concept for the space program, and Terrell spotted it there when he was head of the nonautomotive divisions, one of which—Delco Electronics—was a NASA contractor. Sloan himself would have appreciated the concept, for it is right in line with the coordinated-decentralization approach to management.

G.M. adopted the project-center idea in order to meet the special demands created by the downsizing decision. Coordinating the development of a new body line among the various divisions is a complex undertaking even in normal times. To do what it wanted, the company would have to engineer its cars in a new way, using new design techniques and technologies, during a time when the margins for error and correction would be tighter than usual. Particularly under these circumstances, G.M. could no longer afford the old problem (by no means unique to G.M.) of what Estes calls "N-I-H, not invented here, a kind of disease engineers have." An engineer suffering from N-I-H resists new ideas that originate outside his bailiwick.

The project center is not a permanent group. Every time a major new effort is planned—a body changeover, say—a project center is formed, and it operates for the duration of the undertaking. Thus the A-body center, which shepherded this year's intermediates through development, ran from late 1975 until this past fall. The X-body center is now at work on next year's front-wheel-drive compacts. All project centers report to a board composed of the chief engineers of the automotive divisions.

Project centers work on parts and engineering problems common to all divisions, such as frames, electrical systems, steering gear, and brakes. Many of these are identical in every division; many others are what G.M. calls "common family parts"—e.g., shock absorbers—that are basically the same but are calibrated or adjusted to divisional specifications. The project center augments, but does not replace, G.M.'s traditional "lead division" concept, in which one division is assigned primary responsibility for bringing some technical innovation into production.

The project center was probably G.M.'s single most important managerial tool in carrying out that bold decision to downsize. It has eliminated a great deal of redundant effort, and has speeded numerous new technologies into production. Its success, however, rests on the same delicate balance between the powers of persuasion and coercion that underlies G.M.'s basic system of coordinated decentralization. "We become masters of diplomacy," says Edward Mertz, assistant chief engineer at Pontiac, who was manager of the now-disbanded A-body project center. "It's impossible to work closely on a design without influencing it somewhat. But the center can't force a common part on a division." Indeed, many of G.M.'s engineers feel the project-center innovation has actually helped enhance the divisions' individuality, by freeing some of them to work on divisional projects.

The turnaround of the past few years has worked powerfully to lift G.M.'s self-esteem and spirit. Spirit, of course, is a nebulous part of management, difficult to quantify. G.M.'s state of mind has always been particularly hard to assess. Its elaborate management systems seem designed to function almost regardless of the people who work in them, and G.M. officers rarely waste much time telling outsiders how they feel about themselves or their company. They are practical men who choose to be judged by results.

Indeed, the great defect of Sloan's landmark book as a management treatise was that it dealt exclusively with the practical aspects of professional management. As Peter Drucker pointed out in a critique of *My Years with General Motors*, "Something essential is lacking: people, ideas, and, above all, passion and compassion and a commitment to something more, and larger, than just the business." Sloan himself, Drucker was quick to observe, excelled at leading men and inspiring them, and was a man of ideas and large commitment. But he did not talk about such matters, and it may well be that his paper legacy outlasted his personal legacy, contributing to the rather impersonal quality that has seemed to characterize G.M.'s management during much of its recent history.

Nevertheless, there is an inescapable difference between the spirit at G.M. headquarters these days and what was observable a few years back. John DeLorean, who was one of G.M.'s rising management stars, quit the company in 1973 complaining that it had "gotten to be totally insulated from the world." And Edward N. Cole retired from the presidency in 1974 with the gloomy remark that "the fun is gone . . . I wouldn't go into the automobile business again."

Today it is hard to find a top executive at G.M. who does not evidence enthusiasm for what he or the company is doing. The enthusiasm is most often expressed as excitement over the current "challenge" of the automobile business, and it is especially common among engineers. They agree that some of the fun may indeed have gone out of the business—as Mertz says, "You haven't got the same freedom; more of the targets are set in Washington." But meeting those targets has required a great deal of ingenuity and hard work, and the job has been enormously satisfying.

Indeed, the bottom line of change at G.M. is the company's state of mind—which today reflects a revivified sense of purpose and a much sharper understanding of the external world. As a practical example, it was difficult for engineers to muster much enthusiasm for their work on safety and emissions controls when the company was publicly condemning the requirements as onerous and ill conceived. G.M. has long since stopped complaining and has adopted a deliberately cooperative stance, in good part to restore its credibility and its battered public image. In doing so, it has transformed a major problem—the need for compliance with illogical and unfair policies—into a managerial and technical challenge.

More fundamentally, G.M.'s entire approach to its business has changed. The company's downsizing plan was its first comprehensive new strategic attack upon the marketplace in many years. And it was shaped by a far better understanding of the market's changing nature than the strategies of the immediate past. The new top-management team that took over in 1974, moreover, was especially capable of making the new strategies work. To a degree rare among G.M. top managers over the years, Murphy, Estes, and Terrell are all confident, relaxed, and straightforward men, good at speaking and at listening, and broad in their vision and experience.

Indeed, a case can be made that G.M. has passed through one of the major turning points of its history. One authority who holds this view is Eugene E. Jennings, professor of management at Michigan State University, a consultant to top executives of numerous American corporations and a close observer of G.M. for more than twenty years. "In the late 1960's and early 1970's, G.M. was one of the most insular and inner-directed companies around," he says. "Now, more than any other company in the auto business, and more than most companies anywhere, it has moved up to a higher level of organizational effectiveness. It has learned how to be outer-directed and strategic—to use its head, rather than trying to use its clout." Jennings thinks those practical managers at G.M. don't fully realize as yet what they have accomplished—but he predicts that they will within a few years as they see the results accumulate.

There are tough years ahead for General Motors, unquestionably, as well as for the rest of the industry. The tug-of-war between emissions controls and fuel economy, for example, will intensify sharply under the proposed emissions standards for 1981. Publicly, G.M. is committed to good citizenship on the subject—the company has learned to its sorrow that credibility suffers badly when it complains about unreachable standards and then subsequently manages to meet them. But by any realistic measure, the 1981 standards are irrationally severe, and, in terms of their costs, will levy enormous social disbenefits. People at G.M. do not talk much about the problem at present, but they may have to make the issue public at some point in the future.

The coming year, moreover, may challenge G.M.'s downsizing strategy. The new G.M. intermediates are not the spectacular improvements over their predecessors that the standard cars were, and they face much stiffer competition. Ford's compact Fairmont and Zephyr, for example, are elegant designs, cleverly engineered, and are functionally comparable to the G.M. intermediates.

The costs of redoing the entire product line are enormous, of course. G.M.'s R. and D. expenditures are running at an annual rate of well over $1 billion, which is equivalent to more than a third of 1976 net income ($2.9 billion, on revenues of $47 billion). By 1980, G.M. estimates, capital expenditure for the decade will have amounted to more than $25 billion, most of which will go to meet the demands of emissions, safety, and downsizing. And some tactical requirements are costly too. The company is selling Chevettes at a loss right now, for example—G.M. feels it must pay that price to establish itself more securely in the small end of the market.

Along with the problems, however, come opportunities. By downsizing the top of its line first, while competitors started from the bottom, G.M. has ended up with the standard-car market almost to itself for the next year or so. And that market is hardly the dinosaur preserve it may seem to be. Although all American cars are growing smaller, some will always be bigger than others. G.M. estimates that around 25 percent of the public will continue to want six-passenger cars into the foreseeable future.

Small cars, moreover, are turning out to be a great deal more profitable than the industry once believed them to be. Consumers at all but the rock-bottom level are evidently opting for as much automotive luxury as they can afford. As domestic automakers emerge from the struggle of meeting a concentration of expensive government demands, they can almost surely look to climbing rates of return. Those enormous capital outlays will be making a positive contribution too—they are hastening plant overhaul, providing opportunities for productivity gains and new operating efficiencies. Murphy sees no reason why G.M.'s return on shareholders' equity should not climb back to the level of the mid-1960's—consistently above 20 percent.

Indeed, to G.M.'s officers these days, the problems of the future look pretty pallid in comparison with those of the past few years. The system that Sloan built, with its capacity for change and evolution, has weathered a major crisis of adaptation and emerged stronger than ever. It is hard to imagine what might come along in the foreseeable future that could test General Motors more severely.

Case questions

1. Evaluate G.M.'s forecasting process and the establishment of planning parameters.

2. Why should a large organization intrinsically be "evolutionary, not revolutionary"?

3. Discuss the "downsizing strategy." Why was G.M. able to do that job so much more quickly than its competitors?

4. Why was the project center such a significant event for G.M.'s organization?

5. G.M. has always been known as a decentralized organization, with the divisions making all significant decisions on their products. Do you detect a trend toward centralization in G.M.'s reorganization? Why?

6. Why was the redesign of the organization an integral part of the planning and strategic changes that the company undertook?

7. Discuss G.M.'s managerial-design function as it responded to environmental change. What elements of the company's environment did it respond to? Did the company essentially perform an organizational audit in making its changes? Discuss.

AT&T

By the time John D. deButts retires from American Telephone & Telegraph Co. next February, he may have established himself as a corporate strategist with few peers. He ruled AT&T during its most turbulent era, one in which technological innovation made its standard products and services increasingly obsolete. And it was a time when Bell, sheltered for nearly seven decades under the umbrella of a government-regulated monopoly, was suddenly and unwillingly thrust into a new era of competition with companies that had a better command over the new technology. Though at heart deButts believed monopoly was good for Bell and its customers, and though he fought bitterly to maintain it, he ultimately realized that Bell's choice boiled down to changing—or not surviving.

As he steps down, it is becoming apparent that in his six years at the top of the world's largest corporation he has carefully crafted a total change in strategy that few other men would have dared to undertake. Recognizing competition as a new fact of life for Bell, deButts' plan is to meet the challenge by totally revamping the company's structure, broadening its concept of the products and services that are within its realm, and changing its goal from that of mastering the regulatory process to meeting the needs of the marketplace.

BEHIND AT&T'S CHANGE AT THE TOP

In short, he has set in motion a plan designed to change Bell from a regulated telephone company into a fiercely competitive supplier of all forms of communications systems, including computerized services that bear little resemblance to what AT&T has traditionally represented. The new direction will take AT&T into certain battle with the country's most technologically sophisticated and marketing-wise company—International Business Machines Corp. (page 486). And if it all works, the word "telephone"—at least as we know the telephone today—will have about as much place in the company's name as the word "telegraph."

Setting the stage

The Oct. 18 announcement that deButts is retiring one year early and that Charles L. Brown is succeeding him surprised even top officers at AT&T and, on the surface, seemed ill-timed. But the changing of the guard, too, fits

AT&T vs. IBM

As communications and computers merge, it is increasingly evident that in the 1980s American Telephone & Telegraph Co. and International Business Machines Corp. will each be the other's major competitor. Other companies will play large roles in both markets, but only AT&T and IBM seem powerful enough to slug it out toe-to-toe.

The two will make unique competitors, just as they already make a classic study of contrasts. Although both dominate their respective fields, with 82% of the nation's phone service in AT&T's hands and 50% of data processing controlled by IBM, one is regulated by government while the other is not, resulting in two companies of totally different character. Under a shelter of government regulation, AT&T has maintained its significant edge in size, but competition has made IBM sharper, leaner, and richer.

Size

IBM's growth is the most storied in industry. AT&T, however, has grown as fast in the last decade, and the computer maker has not been able to reduce the 2-to-1 revenue lead of the telephone giant. Ma Bell is nearly five times as big in terms of assets, and each year it pours about three times as much into capital investment as IBM. For 1977 the two giants showed these financial results:

	AT&T	IBM
	Billions of dollars	
Sales	$36.5	$18.1
Operating income	9.7	4.6
Net income	4.5	2.7
Cash flow	9.7	4.7
Capital spending	11.3	3.4
Assets	93.9	18.9
Number of employees	767,254	310,155

But a closer comparison shows that the size is not all that counts and that the contest between the two corporations is not at all as lopsided on the telephone company's side as the bottom line of financial statements might suggest. In fact, on most other points of comparison, IBM has the competitive edge, which may explain why, despite Bell's size, the stock market currently puts a total value of $41 billion on IBM shares, some $3 billion more than it values all of AT&T's.

Products and services

While both companies have an almost equal reputation for product quality and dependable maintenance services, their product mixes and product innovation rates are not at all alike. Recent competition has forced Bell to step up its development and marketing of sophisticated communications hardware, but the great bulk of its offerings is still limited to fairly standardized residential and business telephones. Voice telephone service accounts for about 90% of Bell's revenues, with about 55% of that coming from business customers. Product lifetimes tend to be very long; the standard black telephone has not changed significantly since candlestick phones were retired in the early 1930s.

Most of IBM's products, in contrast, are technologically more sophisticated, and almost all of its products are marketed to business—a concentrated market with high revenues per customer. Data processing equipment still accounts for 80% of its revenues, but the company is also the leader in typewriters and a strong contender in office copiers. The next step will almost surely be to blend its office products into business systems to encompass all forms of communications, including satellites that will carry communication in digital form.

IBM's product life cycle is much shorter than Bell's. Historically, its main computer systems have gone through total change every six years. In order to compete effectively, AT&T will have to dramatically accelerate its product development.

Productivity

IBM consistently works its money, its people, and its plants much harder and more efficiently than its regulated competitor. It generated $58,465 per employee last year, 23% more than Bell. Similarly, for each dollar it has invested in net plant, IBM last year generated revenues of $4.62, compared with only 44¢ for Bell.

Much of that difference comes about because regulators base Bell's rates and its regulated return on capitalized assets, which encourages the company to follow a much more liberal capitalization policy than IBM. For example, AT&T pays full market value, including profit, for the equipment it buys from Western Electric Co., and it capitalizes all of that, plus installation costs. IBM capitalizes only the bare cost of producing its rental machines, excluding profits and installation costs. Its practice is to write off those costs in five years, using accelerated depreciation schedules.

And because of regulatory pressure to keep telephone rates down, AT&T must depreciate its equipment over a much longer life span than IBM. Last year, IBM wrote off 23% of its entire net plant, compared with a mere 6% for Bell. As a result, only 19% of Bell's total investment of $101.8 billion has been depreciated, compared with 53% of IBM's total plant investment of $17.7 billion. Thus, while AT&T is carrying aging and overvalued plant that has not been expensed as it became obsolete, IBM's plant falls into two neat categories—completely written off or spanking new.

Financial strength

Such differences in depreciation, of course, suggest that there is more quality in the earnings and asset figures that IBM reports than in those of Bell's. But IBM's superior financial strength shows up in other ways. Its pretax return on capital last year was 39%, three times greater than AT&T's. And if AT&T had depreciated its plant at the same rate, the company would have lost money. IBM's cash position is almost ludicrous: With $5.4 billion in cash at yearend, four times as much as AT&T, the interest earned on it could have paid off its $256 million in long-term debt twice over.

And it is in the area of long-term debt that the two companies show their greatest disparity. AT&T's debt of $32.5 billion (compared with equity of $37.4 billion) is 127 times that of IBM's, and the company's interest payment last year was almost 10 times greater than IBM's entire debt. As a regulated monopoly, AT&T has seldom had trouble borrowing money, but as it exposes itself to the risks of competition, there is little question that IBM's debt-free status will become more critical in determining which one gets the capital it needs.

Marketing

Given its vast sales and service operation already in place around the country, AT&T's presence in the marketplace is second to none. But compared with IBM, it is a neophyte in marketing. AT&T is accustomed to delivering service when ordered, not to actively soliciting orders. If it can learn to sell, its contact with the market can make it a marketing threat to IBM, but it has a long way to go on that score. Last year, AT&T's sales, general, and administrative costs amounted to $5.5 billion, compared with $7.2 billion for IBM.

From its beginning, IBM has had to fight for and hold all its customers against some of the toughest and strongest competitors in U.S. industry, including General Electric, RCA, and Xerox. Though it suffered a late start in computers against Sperry Rand Corp.'s Univacs, its marketing savvy soon regained it leadership in that part of the office equipment industry. IBM's current competition (which is AT&T's, too) is lean and mean, and many are giants in their own right, with NCR, Burroughs, Sperry Univac, and Digital Equipment all in the $2 billion revenue class.

Research and development

Though industrial research and Bell Labs sometimes seem almost synonymous, IBM actually outspent the phone company on research last year, $1.1 billion to $717 million. Such developments as the transistor have produced a record at Bell Labs that any company would envy, but partly because regulation forces a slower depreciation schedule, AT&T has not been the innovator in a number of important areas, such as electronic switchboards. And more than a few industry critics wonder why Bell is still developing new analog systems when the rest of the world has accepted digital technology as the wave of the future. Though technology is a hard race to evaluate, IBM may now be running neck and neck with AT&T.

nicely into deButts' grand scheme. Now that the strategy is worked out, deButts may well have reasoned, what better way is there to tell Bell's massive organization—three-quarters-of-a-million people strong—that the stage is set to unleash its new assault on the market. "DeButts is the Moses who took the people to the edge of the promised land, and Brown is the Joshua who must fight the Canaanites," observes Asher Ende, a 27-year veteran (now retired) of the Federal Communications Commission who was instrumental in the commission's landmark Carterfone decision in 1968. That ruling was the first of a series of FCC moves that have allowed scores of competitors, many of them from the data processing industry, into what had previously been Bell's regulated communications domain.

By all accounts, Brown is most of all an operations expert (page 489) who is well-suited to take deButts' new strategy and run with it. But it is deButts who gets credit for making the first major change in AT&T's business approach since Theodore Vail (AT&T's first president) nearly 70 years ago established himself as a legend in telecommunications by accepting government regulation in order to keep antitrusters from breaking up the phone company and then by fashioning an approach that capitalized on the regulatory process and made Bell the most successful of regulated utilities. With 1977 revenues of $36.5 billion, Bell ranks fourth among corporations, and it is easily the largest in assets with $94 billion, more than double those of second-ranked Exxon Corp. As Vail saw the inevitability of regulation, deButts has seen the inevitability of its ending. "When I took this job, the Carterfone decision had just been made," recalls deButts. "With competition coming, it was pretty obvious that we had to become more market-oriented." Adds Robert E. La Blanc, a general partner at Salomon Bros. and longtime analyst of AT&T: "DeButts will leave his mark [on Bell] second only to Vail."

DeButts' strategy calls for:

1 *Total revamping of* AT&T's *operation:* In what is clearly the largest corporate reorganization in history, Bell will change either the titles, assignments, or responsibilities of a third of its work force. And the change in the company's structure will touch every level, from the $600,000-a-year chairman's position to the $18,000-a-year telephone installer.

2 *Overhauling of the company's marketing program:* In an effort to strike back at its new competitors from the data processing business, Bell is making its move into the computer business. Though it will not go up against IBM in mainframes, AT&T has already begun introducing a steady stream of new products—from computer-like switchboards and terminals to computerized communications networks—all designed to allow the phone company to catch up with a data processing revolution that was passing it by.

AT&T'S BROWN: TAILORED TO THE TASK AT HAND

Charles L. "Charlie" Brown is probably just the type of chairman American Telephone & Telegraph Co. needs right now—a flexible, pragmatic, and broadly experienced operations man. A far less outspoken and publicly visible man than his predecessor, John D. deButts, Brown is much more likely to work quietly behind the curtain of Bell's massive organization. But in retiring from his post one year early, even deButts may be conceding that while he was the man best suited to draft a strategy to guide his company into a new competitive era, Brown is better suited to implement it.

Virtually all of his fellow executives at AT&T prefer to describe the 57-year-old Brown as a disciplined operator, not a creative strategist. "He's the kind of person you come to with both the analysis and a recommendation," says Charles Marshall, president of Illinois Bell Telephone Co., a post Brown held before being promoted to executive vice-president at AT&T in 1974. "He's a man who brings out the best because people know they have to be prepared."

Up from under

Brown is also the quintessential Bell manager. His father spent 37 years with AT&T, and Brown, like many other top Bell managers, began working for the company in a blue-collar job, collecting $13 a week for summer work as a ditchdigger installing cables. Few executives in Bell have operating experience more varied: His resume lists 23 different positions with the phone company in 10 cities.

But Brown's jobs at AT&T also seem to provide just the preparation he needs to move forward the company's new strategy of computers and competition. An electrical engineer by training (University of Virginia), Brown in 1961 was named the first dean of AT&T's Data Communications School in Cooperstown, N.Y. It was Bell's first effort to train its people to provide communications equipment to a data processing market. "The fact that Charlie ran that school shows the way-back-when of his dedication to the marriage of data and communications," says Marshall.

In the late 1960's, just after the Federal Communications Commission's Carterfone decision had broadened

competition in telephone instruments and switchboards, Brown, then president of Illinois Bell, showed he could quickly adapt to a competitive marketplace. He responded to the FCC's decision by creating Illinois Bell's first separate marketing department as part of a broader plan to respond faster to needs of business customers. Brown even began meeting with customers personally, making a previously unnecessary pitch on why they should order Bell equipment. "He felt comfortable with it [Carterfone], because he's a competitor by nature," observes William H. Springer, controller at Illinois Bell.

Funds juggler

Brown's tenure as AT&T's chief financial officer for three years prior to becoming president in 1977 will also be a key factor in helping him implement Bell's new strategy, which will require balancing the need for funds to speed up new product development with the need to generate more funds internally. Reducing the company's debt burden is a prerequisite of moving away from regulation and into a riskier competitive environment. As chief financial officer, Brown leveled off AT&T's long-term debt and reduced the company's percentage of debt to total capital from a record high of 46.4% in 1974 to 38.3% last year.

As an operations expert, Brown is also seen as less rigid in his thinking than deButts, whose fierce attachment to principles made him an outspoken advocate of preserving Bell's vertical structure when some in government called for breaking it up. That dedication explains deButts' desire to reorganize Bell for competition, but it nevertheless also made him—and Bell—many enemies in Washington.

Brown may make compromises to get Bell out of its regulatory jam. "He won't be a slave to some prior position [of his own] or that deButts may have stood for," says Springer. Adds Harry Edelson, a vice-president of Drexel, Burnham Lambert Inc.: "He can change some of the entrenched positions that deButts may have found himself in, and so maybe Brown is capable of gaining more for AT&T by playing ball, compromising to get a better deal instead of fighting."

3 *Dealing with the most confusing and potentially threatening regulatory environment that the company has ever seen:* Much of Bell's strategy hinges on FCC approval of AT&T's proposed computer offerings as regulated services and on Bell's cooling down the fever in Washington to deregulate interstate communications completely, a move the company is not yet prepared to accept. But in the long term, Bell seems to be readying itself for a major compromise with the regulators: It would accept competition if the government would drop its efforts to break AT&T into separate parts. The fact that deButts has chosen this moment to step down underscores just how important compromise now is to Bell. His rigid stand in favor of the old regulated monopoly so embittered progressive regulators and even some in his own industry that deButts may now realize that his successor is in a better position than he is to settle with the government.

4 *Reorienting personnel to competition:* Though this is a subtle test of the new strategy, it may ultimately be the most difficult. To tackle the job, AT&T is mounting its most ambitious training program ever in an effort to make its employees think in terms of selling and not of taking orders, of dealing with competitors and not regulators, and of making profits as well as providing services.

Realigning responsibilities

Though he speaks about his new assignment in terms far more controlled and less passionate than those used by deButts, Brown knows full well the extent of the undertaking. "This is a complete change, the largest change at any one time in [the company's] history," he says.

At least at first, the most obvious aspect of that change is the company's massive reorganization. Though deButts had begun gradually changing AT&T's corporate structure soon after he became chairman in 1972, the big move was revealed last year, when the company announced the creation of three new executive vice-presidential posts—one in charge of business services, one supervising residential services, and one with responsibility over network services. Amazingly, it was the company's first substantial effort to structure itself along the lines of its major market segments. Though most other companies had long ago abandoned functional organization, Bell clung to it into the 1970s, dividing responsibilities on the basis of the task performed, such as traffic management, plant supervision, and maintenance, installation, and engineering. All sales efforts were lumped together with billing and customer service into a department called "commercial," and it dealt with residential and business customers alike. Observes Kenneth J. Whalen, executive vice-president in charge of residential services: "There was not a traditional marketing structures as at Procter & Gamble, IBM, or General Electric."

Before competition, telephone service did not have to be tailored around the customer's needs. Now, with competition taking customers away from Bell, the company is at last turning to a structure designed to respond better to customer needs. With the new structure almost completely in place at the parent company's headquarters at 195 Broadway in New York City, Bell is pushing the new structure down to its 19 operating telephone companies. By the middle of this month, all of the subsidiaries had filed plans to duplicate the switch at the corporate level from a functional to a market-oriented organizational structure. But already many observers are skeptical about the company's prospects for implementing those plans smoothly. "You will see absolute chaos for about two years at Bell," predicts Howard Anderson, president of Yankee Group, a telecommunications market research firm based in Cambridge, Mass.

In an attempt to avoid that, Bell has carefully scheduled a gradual phasing in of the reorganization, working one management layer at a time from the top down. Coordinating the reorganization of the operating companies will be the task of William M. Ellinghaus, who replaces Brown as president. For the next 18 months, the expected duration of the reorganization, that job will take most of his time. "The biggest challenge now is to put [the new structure] in place and make sure it delivers," he says.

Essentially, the reorganization will touch some 250,000 Bell employees who have some form of contact with the customer. Even telephone installers will now work on either residential or business jobs, but not both. And each department will be totally responsible for serving all of the needs of its market segment, from developing new business and designing new systems all the way to installation and repair of equipment. Obviously, Bell is hoping the new structure will bring all of its managers closer to their particular market so that they can respond faster to customer needs and to the competition. "This will bring marketing into the bowels of the organization," says Thomas E. Bolger, executive vice-president of business services.

Until now marketing has always received short shrift at AT&T. "The merchandising and marketing that we did was very heavily regulated and tariff-oriented," admits Whalen.

Bell was so devoid of marketing expertise that when it began setting the foundation of the new organization it had to go outside to get it. Only a year after he took office, deButts created the company's first marketing department, with Whalen as its head. DeButts gave Whalen carte blanche to do whatever was needed to instill a market orientation at AT&T, and Whalen did what previously had been sacrilegious at Bell: He recruited an outsider, Archibald J. McGill, a former marketing vice-president at IBM, to take a newly created post of marketing manager and preach the marketing gospel to top managers.

It marked the first time that Bell had filled a high-level post without promoting from within, but since then recruitment from corporations known for their marketing skill has soared. Now, fully half of the 300 market managers in the business services operation are recent recruits from such marketing-oriented companies as Procter & Gamble, IBM, and Colgate-Palmolive.

A systems-selling strategy

Bell's new marketing whiz kids are now trying to make the telephone company's marketing program resemble that of IBM by adopting the computer maker's key marketing tactic: solution selling. Instead of focusing on equipment, such as a switchboard, AT&T will now attempt to analyze a customer's total communications needs and offer the system best designed to meet them. The new marketing approach even prompted Bell last year to drop a do-gooder, public relations motto ("We hear you") for a sharper, marketing one ("The system is the solution"), which also serves as a not-so-subtle defense of Bell's vertical integration. Systems selling is now the "key, heart, and soul to our marketing strategy," declares the business segment's Bolger. Adds J. Roger Moody, executive vice-president of Teletype Corp., AT&T's communications terminal subsidiary: "In going from a monopoly to a competitive company, AT&T must convert from a telephone company to a communications systems company."

To give its new and more aggressive marketing organization something to sell, Bell has lately been spewing forth a continuous stream of new products to meet the requirements of systems selling, products based on the concept that advanced technologies in data processing and communications have merged into one. The new products are Bell's answer to the dozens of new competitors it has had to face since the FCC a decade ago began handing down decisions that permitted effective competition in telephone instruments and communications terminals, in switchboards, and in private business satellite and microwave networks sold to business customers (page 499). As a result of those decisions, Bell has had to fend off some 50 innovative competitors in terminals and switchboards and some 15 competitors, including RCA and ITT, in private networks (BW—Feb. 13).

Bell is also fending off competitors in the long-distance telephone market, where independent companies such as MCI Communications Corp. set up competitive long-distance lines and then hook into the local Bell network. By doing this, they can undercut such Bell services as Message Telephone Service/Wide Area Telephone Service (MTS/WATS). Services such as WATS are sold mainly to the 500 largest corporations, from which Bell gets half its revenues, so competitive services such as these are especially frightening to AT&T.

New software packages

Just as the reorganization touches every level of the company, the new product push attempts to inject advanced computer technology into every aspect of the company's communications offerings. But none of the proposed new computerized services is as ambitious—or potentially as threatening to competitors—as Advanced Communications Service.... Announced last July, ACS is a nationwide computerized network service that will store data, automatically switch it to different areas of the country, and code and decode messages in order to break down the incompatibility between computer mainframes and terminals of different manufacturers. Now, only Telenet Corp. and Tymnet Inc. offer such a business network service. "In the 1980s, I believe [ACS] will be at the core of solving our business and government customers' needs," says McGill.

Even with FCC approval, the new service would not be ready for the market until 1980, but the potential competitive consequences are staggering. With its built-in data processing capabilities, a manufacturer could use the network to break up an order automatically into a series of messages to tell production plants how many products to make, its shipping department where to send the order, its accounting department where to send the bill, and its purchasing department how much raw material to order to replace that used in filling the order. Since it now takes hundreds of computer time-sharing companies to provide these and other basic data processing services, ACS could immediately threaten their survival. Jack Biddle, president of the Computer & Communications Industry Assn., refers to ACS as "the world's largest time-sharing network."

But with the addition of software packages that would perform more complicated duties, ACS could ultimately make a large dent in the market for computer equipment, because such tasks are now performed by sophisticated computer hardware and software, sold by IBM and others, costing $30,000 and up.

With its new switchboards, AT&T is following the same trend toward computerization. In 1975, Bell introduced its first electronic switchboard, called Dimension. That was years behind more innovative PBX competitors, which are now grabbing one out of every five sales in a market where Bell had a monopoly a decade ago. Now Bell is trying to close the gap. Earlier this year the company unveiled the first of several dozen software packages designed for different industries that will allow customers to use the Dimension PBX for a number of data-processing functions. With its first such package, for the hotel-motel industry, Dimension can be used to make wake-up calls automatically and keep track of room availability.

So far, some of the company's most advanced product computerization has taken place at its obscure Teletype subsidiary (page 503). Because Teletype did not even roll out computer-like terminals until 1975, several years after competitors, the subsidiary's share of the communications and data-processing terminal market plunged from more than 90% in the mid-1960s to less than 5% in the mid-1970s. But by last July, Teletype was already introducing its second-generation computer terminals, and that aggressiveness explains why the subsidiary last year reported a 50% increase in sales.

The basic telephone instrument is not escaping the new product push either, but again Bell is responding to innovations of others instead of making the innovations itself. Nevertheless, AT&T two years ago began opening stores around the country where customers select from a new, broader line of designer phones. For a few dollars a month, the company also offers call forwarding and holding services. And now Bell is speeding up development of new communications systems that could connect the home to distant computerized data bases to deliver a wide variety of educational, entertainment, and financial services through both video and voice communications.

Such new products pit Bell in a bitter confrontation against the data processing industry and its dominant factor, IBM. But since data processing equipment manufacturers have been using a new freedom given them by the FCC to poach on AT&T's communications market, it was only natural to expect Bell to return the favor. "The merger of data processing technology and communications technology is such that unless they [AT&T] do this, whole segments of the market are going to be excluded to them in the future," says La Blanc of Salomon. Adds John C. LeGates, president of the Center for Information Policy Research: "What's really going on is a war between two different kinds of industries for control of a brand new market."

By far, the two major opponents in that war will be IBM and AT&T. IBM, declares Teletype's Moody, is now "the biggest competition for the entire Bell System. We're on a collision course."

That collision could well put many smaller competitors in both industries out of business. Fearful that Bell might use profits from areas where it is still protected by government-regulated monopoly to underwrite predatory pricing in areas where it has competition, many of Bell's new competitors are complaining bitterly that the company should not be allowed to enter the data processing field. But current regulation tends to encourage this type of cross subsidy. For example, Bell's highly profitable long lines service contributes $3 billion a year to local telephone service to keep those rates down. "It's easy to argue that that's not right and it isn't except for social reasons," admits Richard R. Hough, executive vice president for network services. He concedes that Bell often does not really know how to pinpoint which services should bear a greater burden for maintaining the network.

Government regulators are losing patience with AT&T's inability to locate the origin of costs. "When [AT&T] tells me it will take three years to find out how much things cost, it tells me they don't want to know," says Ernest F. Hollings (D-S. C.), whose Senate subcommittee is currently studying the proposed new Communications Act.

AT&T is trying to eliminate such objections by working with the FCC to develop a new "functional" accounting system that would allocate costs more accurately to each service. The FCC—which would approve any changes—has been studying the problem for a few years now, "but satisfactory changes are still a long way down the road," says Frederick C. Heubner, administrator of the accounts and finance division of the Wisconsin Public Service Commission.

Bell complains that regulatory requirements further handicap it as a competitor by slowing down the introduction of new products. "When I wanted to introduce our new Snoopy phone," complains Bell's Whalen, "I had to go to 54 different regulatory bodies, and they are approving it at different times."

Clearly, Bell's entire new strategy hinges on how government changes its regulatory process. Ironically, the same government regulators that forced competition on Bell could now prevent it from responding to that competition by limiting its product offerings. Under a consent decree Bell signed with the Justice Dept. in 1956, Bell's operating companies are only permitted to market regulated communications services. On that basis, its new data processing-oriented products and services may be considered as falling outside the telephone company's realm. AT&T's monopoly "only allows them to move information—to own and operate the pipeline that moves messages. But over time they have taken on the oil wells, the refineries and the gas stations at both ends of the pipeline," complains Biddle of the CCIA.

Inquiries are now under way at the FCC to determine whether to allow AT&T to market the new terminals from Teletype, some of the Dimension PBX software packages, and ACS. Thus far, the commission has generally favored Bell's new direction. "We in government are saddled with AT&T because it operated under federal policy, and we are partly responsible for this situation," explains a staff member at the newly created National Telecommunications & Information Agency (NTIA) in the Commerce Dept. Much the same feeling exists among state regulators, who are beginning to take a more active role in overseeing Bell's new marketing efforts. "If you're going to get into competition, you can't have [AT&T] competing with one hand tied behind its back," says the Wisconsin Public Service Commission's Heubner.

The 1956 consent decree is hardly the only reason for Bell's desire that the FCC classify its new computerized services under regulated communications. While the company is now hurriedly changing to be more competitive, it is also desperately hoping Washington will slow down its deregulation of telecommunications.

That seemingly incongruous position is partly explained by the fact that Bell is stuck with so much undepreciated and yet obsolete equipment. Only 19% of the company's gross plant of $101.8 billion has been depreciated, primarily because regulators, attempting to keep telephone rates from rising, have forced Bell to follow a depreciation schedule that is slower than the company would like. Yet, if those regulators now allow competition in other presently monopolized services, Bell could effectively compete only by tak-

Undepreciated, obsolete equipment

ing large write-offs of aging equipment that would be made obsolete by newer equipment introduced by competitors.

"Depreciation policy is a real dilemma," says Larry F. Darby, chief of the FCC's Common Carrier Bureau. "Bell would like to write it off faster than we are willing to and a lot faster than the states, which are far more conservative." Thus, regulators are not altogether unsympathetic with Bell's need to slow the introduction of competition in order to preserve the company's financial viability. Says an NTIA official: "A certain period of transition is clearly in order."

At best, however, Bell's attempt to hold back competition can only be a delaying action. Bell's last-ditch attempt to solidify its monopoly position under regulatory supervision came in 1976 when it sponsored the Consumer Communications Reform Act. Dubbed the "Bell Bill" by opponents who saw it as "self-serving," it was soon derailed despite an unprecedented lobbying effort by a Ma Bell team. The demand for competition in telecommunications is actually gaining broader support in government. The FCC is studying a proposal to introduce competition in long-distance networks that can switch calls between different points, and that strikes at the heart of Bell's hold on the business market. In an effort to overhaul the Communications Act of 1934, Representative Lionel Van Deerlin (D-Calif.) has introduced the Communications Act of 1978, which would free Bell from the constraints of the consent decree in return for Bell's running its $8 billion-a-year Western Electric operation as an arm's length subsidiary.

More than any other government threat, it is divestiture that really panics Bell, since it believes that its vertical operation is critical to its new marketing strategy. Yet the possibility of divestiture is probably greater now than at any other time in the company's history. The most serious threat, of course, comes from a four-year-old Justice Dept. anti-trust suit—slated for trial in 18 months—that seeks Bell's divestiture of not only Western Electric but also of its highly profitable Long Lines Dept. forcing a division of Bell Labs. It is anathema to Bell. "It will never happen voluntarily under any conditions," vows deButts. Adds marketing expert McGill: "It would be a prescription for disaster. In a high-technology industry, you have no choice but to be vertically integrated."

Naturally, a nonintegrated AT&T would find it all but impossible to compete effectively with a vertically integrated IBM, but Bell argues that the Justice suit would also affect phone service to the consumer. If it had to buy its equipment from outside suppliers, AT&T says, it would have to pay 20% more, and that alone, say industry experts, could increase the average telephone bill by 17%.

Even some of Bell's competitors worry that an independent Western Electric might be an even greater menace. With $8 billion in revenues last year, the manufacturing subsidiary is several times larger than its nearest

U.S. competitor, International Telephone & Telegraph Corp. And already Western has begun looking beyond Bell for supply contracts in the international markets, such as the $500 million contract—$107 million of which goes to Western—it recently landed to provide a communications network for the government of Saudi Arabia. "If you take Western Electric out of the Bell System," predicts Salomon's La Blanc, "you're going to turn a whale into a shark that would eat competition alive."

Yet the government's own pressure to end the Bell monopoly by introducing competition into more telecommunications markets may be Bell's best defense against divestiture. In short, it puts Bell in a position of making a grand compromise with government that would be the very opposite of the one Theodore Vail made nearly seven decades ago: accepting more competition in order to hang on to its vertical structure.

Compromise with government

Since deButts has been so vociferously opposed to competition in any form, he is clearly not the best man Bell could send to the bargaining table, and his realization of that fact more than anything else may explain his early retirement. Brown, who is not wedded to deButts' earlier positions, is in a better position to negotiate, and already he is sounding what appears to be a call for compromise: "Our major corporate goal is to try to reach a national consensus from a regulatory, legislative, and legal standpoint which defines the ground rules under which this company can and should operate."

Even if Brown is able to pull off that compromise, Bell still will face a major internal constraint to implementing its new market-oriented strategy: its people. Bell managers have been brought up to prosper in a politically oriented, regulatory environment, where it is more important to get favorable rate increases from state regulators than to provide a service that is tailored to individual customer needs. To gain approval from regulators, Bell managers think of providing good service to an entire community, and it is no coincidence that they are encouraged to join every community organization that will make them visible and appreciated.

Now Bell managers will be forced to recognize that they must service the needs of varying market segments, but changing attitudes that have been ingrained in Bell management since the turn of the century is no easy task. "I was brought on board to help the company understand the marketplace and how to establish management systems," recalls McGill. "It's missionary work I'm doing."

With the advent of competition, of course, comes the risk of loss, and that may involve the biggest attitude change for Bell employees. It means that the Bell System will have to generate a new profit motivation, since profits will no longer be guaranteed by regulators. As a regulated utility, AT&T's revenues and profits are based on the size of its assets, not on the productivity of those assets. On productivity, AT&T compares poorly with its big, new competitor, IBM. Thus, in a free market, AT&T would likely have to trim a lot of its fat to stay in the game. "This is a mentality AT&T has never developed, but it has to in this new business [environment]," observes Robert Harcharik, president of Tymnet. Adds William S. Cashel Jr., Bell's vice-chairman and chief financial officer: "The concern for profitability [will] go deeper in the organization than it had before. Now we have the dual objective of profitability along with service."

To make those attitude changes, AT&T has embarked on a major retraining drive. Its top 1,800 managers have already gone through a corporate policy seminar on how to manage and market in Bell's changing environment. And some 15,000 lower-level managers and supervisors are now going through some form of marketing training.

The Picturephone failure   While the company may still have a long way to go to instill a profit orientation into its employees, it is already imposing a more stringent financial test to its new product development program. "We had always measured things that we felt were important," admits marketer Whalen. "Now we have to be sure to measure what the customer wants."

Nowhere was the previous attitude more evident than in Bell's multi-million-dollar program to develop the picture telephone in the 1960s. So enthusiastic were Bell executives about their technical achievement that when the new product was introduced with great fanfare in 1969, they predicted that annual sales of the picture phone would reach $1 billion by 1980. As it turned out, they were far more enthusiastic about their new gadgetry than were potential customers, who did not want the new service badly enough to pay the more than $100 per month that Bell was asking for it. With virtually no demand for its Picturephone, Bell was forced to pull the product out of test-market a couple of years after its introduction. "Before a new product comes on stream now," pledges Cashel, "we will know how it will do over time."

To many of its customers, Bell's change to a market-oriented approach may not yet be all that apparent. An executive with one corporate customer, which purchases about $1 million in communications services each month—mostly from Bell, insists that while AT&T's new competitors are consistently developing products to meet his company's needs, Bell is still trying "to make us change the way we do business in order to fit the systems they have to offer." He adds: "You can't move an elephant as fast as a mouse."

AT&T's Brown concedes that getting the new market message down through the corporate ranks is "not complete in any sense." To get the message across, Brown must convince Bell's employees that despite a proud history as a regulated monopoly, AT&T has no other choice than to be a competitor, because when Bell fails to deliver what customers want, they now will have another place to go.

"We are restructuring our organization so that we will be able to take care of ourselves, our customers, and our shareholders under whatever circumstances arise," says Brown. "But whatever happens, we will be competitive."

COMPROMISING THE REGULATORY RESTRAINTS

As much as anyone else, federal regulators can take a lot of the credit for the bold new competitive strategy of American Telephone & Telegraph Co. When the Federal Communications Commission a decade ago began allowing data processing companies and other competitors into what had previously been Bell's regulated telecommunications monopoly, it not only began reversing nearly 100 years of telephone regulation, it also forced AT&T to drop a strategy well-suited for regulation and adopt one better suited for deregulation. Now, as a marketing-oriented telephone company attempts to strike back at its new competitors by entering their computer business, government is in the curious position of having to decide just how tough a competitor Bell itself should be.

In Washington, the regulatory debate on that question has built to a fever pitch and has spread even to Congress, which a few years ago showed almost no interest in telephone regulation, but which now is considering rewriting its landmark Communications Act of 1934. Never in its history has Bell's future rested on so many decisions being made by so many key regulatory, judicial, and legislative bodies. Juxtaposed as it is with telephone regulations that have evolved over decades, the new effort is producing the most bewildering regulatory environment Bell has ever seen. But from all the confusion, one fact emerges clearly: Federal regulators are now intent on promoting as much free enterprise as they can in an industry that not too long ago was universally considered a "natural monopoly."

For AT&T, which built its monopoly by grudgingly accepting regulation and then learning how to master it, the conversion to competition must involve a strategy for dealing with government. Since much of its regulatory framework is still on the books, it must somehow justify its move into computers under old rules and policies that never envisioned such a thrust. On the other hand, it must fend off those who are pushing the notion of competition to its extreme by calling for the dismemberment of Bell itself.

If history provides any clues, Bell is up to the task, since no other regulated company has had quite as much success in defusing attacks from government and in getting what it wants from regulators. When the states, beginning with Indiana in 1885, started regulating rates on local telephone service, AT&T opposed the action as unfair discrimination. But by the time J. P. Morgan interests took control of the board and elected Theodore N. Vail as president in 1907, Bell's monopoly was nearly complete. Vail, the architect of the strategy AT&T was to follow for the next seven decades, concluded that regulation of telephones not only was inevitable but even afforded the Bell System protection from having to fight upstart telephone companies. By 1910, when the Interstate Commerce Commission was granted regulatory authority over interstate phone service, most states were regulating intrastate service. In 1934 federal telephone regulation shifted to the newly created FCC, but telephone regulation itself remained largely a matter of Bell's managers successfully persuading their regulators to grant them the rates they wanted to charge and to approve the services they wanted to provide.

Bell has been able to live with the antitrusters, too. When the Justice Dept. in 1913 first notified Bell that it was considered in violation of antitrust laws, it was responding to growing fears that AT&T would eventually wind up with total control over all communications. Vail assuaged the trustbusters by agreeing to allow independent phone companies to plug into Bell's network. He also agreed to acquire independents only with government approval and to relinquish control over Western Union Corp. Although the agreement appeared to be an antitrust coup, it did not prevent Bell from tightening its grip on communications: From 50% control over local phone service at the time of its first antitrust battle, Bell's control over telephones has grown to 82% today.

Western Electric compromise

In 1949 the Justice Dept. struck at AT&T again, charging that the company's ownership of Western Electric Co. made rate regulation meaningless, since Bell bought its equipment from its own subsidiary and included that in an asset base on which its rates are set. Without a competitive market for that equipment, government lawyers argued, the prices Bell set on it were arbitrary and probably too high. The antitrust suit, therefore, sought to split Western Electric into three entities separate from Bell.

Seven years later, under an Eisenhower Administration that was less interested in prosecuting the case, the antitrust litigation was dropped when Bell signed a favorable compromise, the so-called 1956 consent decree, which allowed it to retain Western Electric. In return, Bell agreed for the first time that its phone companies could provide only regulated communications services, although Western Electric would be left free to make and sell any products intended for use in communications, conceivably anything from computers to green vans.

The consent decree is the pivot around which revolves today's massive and confusing web of litigation and regulation. Because the decree failed to eliminate any of the problems antitrusters saw with Bell's supply monopoly, the Justice Dept. four years ago took its third shot at Bell by filing an even more ambitious antitrust suit that calls for divestiture by AT&T of its Western Electric subsidiary, its Long Lines Dept., and some of its 23 operating phone companies.

The case, which will take years to litigate, is scheduled for trial in early 1980, and there is no compromise in the wind. "We're not about to settle for fuzzy compromises this time," vows a Justice Dept. attorney. "We want divestiture—separate arms, legs, and torso laid out on the table." AT&T's stand is just as intransigent, particularly since creeping deregulation of communications is forcing Bell to be more competitive. "If you are going to be a more competitive organization," says Charles L. Brown, AT&T's next chairman, "you don't trade off your manufacturer and developer."

Dissatisfaction with the consent decree and a desire to foster more competition are also encouraging Congress to make a total review of Bell's vertical structure as well as its regulated monopoly. Initially, it was a move by Bell to thwart the FCC's pro-competitive decision that stimulated Congress to act fast on telecommunications. Unfortunately for Bell, its initiative backfired. In 1976, the telephone industry, led by Bell, lobbied desperately for a bill that would have granted AT&T a congressionally mandated monopoly over long-distance telephone service. The bill was stopped dead in subcommittees of both the House and the Senate, and last year those committees began working on their own bills.

In the first serious attempt to rewrite the Communications Act of 1934, Representative Lionel Van Deerlin (D-Calif.), chairman of the House subcommittee on communications, last June introduced the Communications Act of 1978, which would permit wide open competition in interstate telecommunications and require total separation of Western Electric from Bell's phone companies.

But Bell's plan to use its vertical integration to compete aggressively against the computer companies is getting much more sympathy from the FCC, mainly because the commission is responsible for forcing competition on Bell in communications. Beginning in 1968, when its Carterfone Communications Corp. decision effectively introduced competition in telephone instruments and other communications terminals, the FCC has steadily riddled Bell's regulatory umbrella with some large holes. In a series of decisions after Carterfone, the commission allowed specialized carriers to provide private or point-to-point satellite and microwave networks to compete with Bell's long-distance private lines.

Now the commission is studying the possibility of allowing competitive interstate networks that provide switching services to many points. Bell's response to such decisions is to strike back at its new competitors by marketing computerized communications services, and so far the FCC has reacted favorably to that. Explains former Commissioner Kennéth A. Cox: "The commission feels that since IBM wants into communications, they have to let AT&T into the computer business."

Under the 1956 consent decree, however, the only way to do that is for the commission to classify AT&T's new services as part of the "common carrier communication services" that must be regulated. Without that, Western Electric can make and sell the new computer hardware, but not in conjunction with communications services sold by the operating phone companies. Although data processing companies argue that Bell's new drive into their business violates the consent decree's requirement for Bell to stick to communications, Bell's president-designate, William M. Ellinghaus, retorts: "With the blurring lines of data processing and communications processing, it is becoming increasingly difficult to determine what it [the consent decree] means." Asking whether a service properly belongs to communications or data processing, adds John LeGates, president of the Center for Information Policy Research, "is like asking whether Palestine belongs to the Arabs or the Israelis. It clearly belongs to both, depending on who you ask."

Confusion over definitions   The most dramatic evidence of the FCC's intent to allow Bell to capitalize on that confusion came early last year, when it let Bell market its new Dataspeed computerlike terminals (page 503). With that decision, it all but abandoned a 1971 policy, which grew out of the commission's vaunted "Computer Inquiry I." It concluded then that any transmission that changes the nature of the data being transmitted should fall under unregulated data processing and thus outside Bell's reach. Now the FCC staff is working on "Computer Inquiry II" to define further what does and does not fall under regulated communications services, and presumably the outcome of that study will determine whether Bell's requests for tariffs on even more sophisticated computerized communications services will be granted.

Such confusion over definitions is further evidence that the quickening pace of technological change makes it increasingly difficult to enforce not only the consent decree but any other regulation of telecommunications. And as Bell accepts more competition, it is better positioned to claim a right to the same vertical integration its new competitors possess. If it cites deregulation to fend off the antitrusters successfully for a third time, the remaining question will be whether government, by protecting Bell for decades as a regulated monopoly, has created a behemoth that by virtue of its sheer size, scope of operations, and inbred traditions will remain anticompetitive even when regulation ends. Addressing an International Communications Assn. meeting last May, Walter R. Hinchman, former chief of the FCC's Common Carrier Bureau, sounds a gloomy note on that prospect: "I am virtually convinced that the [Bell] System is largely beyond the reach of both federal and state regulation, and may therefore be impervious to competition as well."

TELETYPE TESTS THE NEW MARKETING STRATEGY

Although it is easily the most obscure operation in American Telephone & Telegraph Co., Teletype Corp. has quickly become the most dramatic example of what Bell can accomplish with its new market-oriented strategy. Only 1½ years ago, Teletype was a small and virtually forgotten factor in the $2.5 billion communications and data processing terminal business. Since then, it has begun marketing its first computer-like terminal as part of a bold plan to capture a major piece of the fastest-growing segment of the data processing business, the furiously competitive terminal market dominated by International Business Machines Corp. and 50 or so innovative competitors.

Led by a former IBM executive who makes no bones about trying to grab as much of the market as he can by underpricing his big competitor, Teletype has stunned the terminal industry with its performance in recent months. Last year, its first full year under the new marketing strategy, Teletype's sales grew 50% to $300 million.

For Teletype, it is a desperate comeback bid. The company once so dominated the terminal business that its name is still often used to refer to any message transmitted from one machine to another. Unfortunately for Teletype, which was purchased by AT&T in 1930 and merged into its Western Electric Co. subsidiary, its name is now often misused, since many "teletypes" are no longer sent on terminals Teletype makes.

In fact, nowhere has AT&T been more devastated by competition from the computer industry than at its Teletype subsidiary. Until the 1960s, Teletype controlled more than 90% of the market for "record" communications terminals, but when IBM and other data processing equipment producers began manufacturing terminals about that time, Teletype all but ignored the fact that its new competitors were revolutionizing its business. It clung to its old electromechanical machines, while others were marketing faster electronic machines equipped with TV-screen displays and featuring computer-like systems that allowed for editing, formatting, and storing messages. Teletype did not even introduce an electronic model until 1973, and even that had few electronic capabilities. By then, Teletype seemed terminally ill; its share of the burgeoning terminal market had shriveled to less than 5%. "When the technology changed to electronic and electronic took the form of a computer, we said that wasn't our business," says J. Roger Moody, the former IBM executive who was tapped by AT&T last year to become Teletype's executive vice-president and given the task of instilling in the subsidiary a zest for marketing.

Thanks partly to Moody, Bell's new-found determination to take on its rivals from the computer industry is most apparent at Skokie (Ill.)-based Teletype. Last year, after it overcame regulatory obstacles at the Federal

Communications Commission, Teletype began full-scale marketing of the Dataspeed 40/4 model, its first terminal designed for use in data processing systems. The response was immediate: Though sales of Teletype's mechanical units continued to fall, demand for the Dataspeed more than made up for that and produced last year's sales surge.

Last June, Teletype stepped up its marketing drive by announcing a new line of computer-like terminals called the 4500 series. The first model in that line performs much the same editing, formatting, and storing functions as the Dataspeed 40/4, but thanks to improved electronics it transmits 33% faster and costs half as much. Indeed, the new Teletypes are strikingly similar to IBM's most popular models, but a six-terminal system costs $17,000, compared to the $23,000 price tag on a similar IBM setup.

Though Teletype is now playing a catch-up game, it is conceivable that with Bell's sheer size and its expertise in communications, it could again be defining the standards in terminals. In the past two years, the AT&T subsidiary expanded its research staff by 50%, to more than 400, and Moody says that later models in the 4500 series will be programmable and have vastly expanded computer capabilities. Such improvements are already encouraging some industry analysts to predict that Teletype will again become a major factor in the terminal market. "If Teletype terminals are bundled with all the other Bell plans for getting into the computer business, they could acquire 30% of the market by 1985," speculates Jack Biddle, president of the Computer & Communications Industry Assn., which represents independent terminal manufacturers.

In addition to putting more stress on new product development, Teletype is also trying to cover the market more effectively with sales and service personnel. By 1981 it will roughly double its service operation to 600 specialists in 90 centers around the country. This year the company appointed a vice-president to head a new sales group that will specialize in selling directly to customers outside the Bell system. Up to now, most sales of Teletype equipment have been made to AT&T's 23 operating phone companies, which install the units as part of the regulated communications services they provide and use them internally, as well. But as customers increasingly turn to private network services offered by Bell's new competitors, they are more disposed than ever to get their terminals elsewhere. Thus Teletype is recognizing that it can no longer cling so tightly to Bell's coattails, and its expanded sales force is already giving it increased independence. Though 60% of Teletype's sales this year are being made to AT&T phone companies, that percentage is down from 70% last year.

Tangling with legal issues Despite Teletype's growing independence, its existing link to the Bell system —and the marketing clout that goes with that—is what worries competitors in the terminal business. As long as Teletype operates under Bell's regulatory umbrella, they fear that AT&T's regulated telephone rates will be used to subsidize Teletype's expansion. And while IBM is obviously strong enough to withstand that pressure, many smaller terminal manufacturers fear that a duel between the giants will drive some of them out of business. "AT&T is just plain going into the data processing business via Teletype," argues Ralph H. O'Brien, president of Mohawk Data Sciences Corp., a terminal manufacturer. "As far as we're concerned, they will be in total competition with people who will be fighting with one hand tied behind their back."

Teletype is a crucial part of the broader plan to deal with Bell's new competitors in the communications industry by moving into the information systems business with the latest computer technology. "The idea is for AT&T to enter the computer field by providing all the equipment sold outside the host computer," says Gerald Lapidus, a consultant with Quantum Science Corp., a computer consulting firm. "And without Teletype's capability to manufacture terminals and market them, that plan is greatly impaired."

More than anything else, that explains why Teletype's strategy is touching off a fierce legal dispute that goes to the heart of the controversy over whether Bell should be allowed to go into the computer business. Competing manufacturers are charging that Teletype's new push into computer-like terminals violates the antitrust decree Bell signed with the Justice Dept. in 1956. Under that decree Bell's 23 operating companies can provide only regulated communications services.

The case of the competitors rests on their contention that Teletype's newest machines are not just communications terminals, but data processing terminals as well. As such, they claim, Teletype's products violate a landmark FCC ruling in 1971 that keeps data processing an unregulated business and requires that common carriers enter it only through unregulated subsidiaries. If Teletype's new terminals were considered data processing machines, distributing them through AT&T phone companies would violate both the 1971 rule and the consent decree.

When Teletype introduced its first computer-like terminal in 1975, IBM and independent terminal makers made just such a claim before the FCC. The commission's Common Carrier Bureau sided with them, ruling that Teletype's new Dataspeed 40/4 could not be included in Bell's interstate communication services. That greatly restricted sales of the new unit, but only a year later, after lengthy and heated hearings, the FCC reversed the bureau and granted an interstate tariff on services involving the Dataspeed 40/4. Almost immediately, sales of the new terminal took off.

Meanwhile, Teletype's aggressive marketing plans faced still another regulatory threat. Even as the FCC approved the Dataspeed 40/4, it was reshaping its policy on the distinctions between communications and data processing, in the light of technological changes since 1971. Last July the FCC's Common Carrier Bureau recommended that the commission deregulate all but the simplest kind of communications terminals. But fearing that approval of that recommendation might be tantamount to kicking Bell totally out of the terminal business because of the consent decree, the FCC tabled the matter until late November for further study.

If the computer industry fails to convince the FCC and the commissioners decide that computer terminals are legitimate regulated services, that action could defang the consent decree almost entirely, allowing telephone companies to market computer terminals freely. But even if the FCC decides to deregulate and not permit complex terminals under tariff rates, Teletype still has an out. The consent decree is much broader in its treatment of Teletype's parent, Western Electric, than of telephone operating companies. It allows Western Electric to make and sell any products used or intended to be used in providing communications services. Because telephone companies use many Teletype terminals in their internal operations, Teletype feels free to market them outside the Bell System directly to end customers, under the terms of the decree.

Stepping over the line

"It's what we call the creeping computerization of AT&T, and it's exactly how we built our business," says Edward Gistaro, who heads the data processing division of Datapoint Corp. "We give a customer a little intelligence in the terminal, and he's going to get hooked. For me, it's legal. But for them [Teletype] it isn't." Adds Biddle of the Computer & Communications Industry Assn.: "If the 40/4 was borderline [between communications and computers], the 4500 is a big step over that line."

Teletype's Moody argues that Bell is merely exercising a right other companies take for granted—using computer technology to improve its services. Whether an intelligent terminal is a data or a communications processor, he says, depends on customer perception. "It would be intolerable to tell a user, 'there's a piece of gear that's got a computer capability, but you can use it only for communications processing,'" observes Moody. "That's like selling a person a car and telling him he can only drive north, not south."

It is this confusion in terminology that may allow Teletype to pursue its expansionist strategy despite the protests of its competitors. The FCC, thus far, has refused to deregulate all electronic terminals, which would have delivered a near-fatal blow to Teletype. "The problem the commissioners confronted head-on was that use of the smart terminal is determined not by the carrier, but by customers," explains an FCC lawyer. "Today it's a communications device under any definition, and tomorrow it's a data processing terminal."

Case questions

1. What kinds of leadership styles can you expect from Brown as opposed to deButts?

2. In undergoing a reorganization, what kinds of changes is AT&T making, and how do they relate to corporate strategies and long-range plans?

3. How do environmental factors figure in the long-range planning or strategy building of AT&T? Would you recommend that any other factors be considered?

4. Evaluate deButts's four-point strategy in terms of the types of items that should be considered in an organizational audit. Why didn't AT&T engage in periodic auditing of its organization's purposes, goals, and programs earlier?

5. Discuss the changes in contexts of the long-run objectives and plans as AT&T enters more competitive businesses, e.g., computers. What kinds of special forecasting problems does the company now face?

6. What special environmental factors temper AT&T's organizational design and planning processes? How would they affect them?

7. What are some of AT&T's internal strengths and weaknesses? Compared with IBM's? How do these affect the company's planning or designing?

W. T. GRANT

At 9:30 in the morning last February 10, lawyers for the creditors' committee of W. T. Grant Co. walked into a federal courtroom in New York with a surprising proposal. For months, Grant's had been trying to reorganize under the protection of a bankruptcy court, and the once vast retail chain had shrunk from 1,100 stores to 359, and from 75,000 employees to 30,000. With no warning, the creditors' lawyers declared that the seventy-year-old business should be liquidated at once.

Two days later Federal Bankruptcy Judge John J. Galgay granted the committee's request, and the company's stores were padlocked to await a closeout sale. It was the final chapter in the largest bankruptcy proceeding in the history of retailing—the company's debt totaled more than $800 million.

FIGHTING FOR THEIR LIVELIHOOD

The liquidation of a multimillion-dollar enterprise is a poignant business drama even as it is played out where the public most often views it—at the level of the lawyers, the accountants, and the creditors' committees. But Grant's decline and fall takes on a different, more human perspective when it is perceived at store-level, so to speak, where men and women were fighting for their livelihood as well as the survival of the organization. The view from Store 1192, Grant's branch in Westerly, Rhode Island, also tells a good deal about what went wrong with the company and why it couldn't keep itself off the rocks.

The manager of Store 1192 was Albert J. Duclos (pronounced "du-close"), forty-one, a man whose hazel eyes sparkled with an enthusiasm that seemed almost unquenchable. He is methodical and, surprisingly for one so immersed in detail, articulate as well. His thoughts roll out decisively in a voice edged with the clipped, harsh accents of southeastern Massachusetts. His decisiveness helped to dispense confidence, and some small measure of comfort, among the eighty employees of Store 1192 during Grant's last uncertain hours.

Rush Loving, Jr., "W. T. Grant's Last Days—as Seen from Store 1192." Reprinted from the April 1976 issue of *Fortune Magazine* by special permission; © 1976 Time Inc.

A DISTRICT LEADER

Duclos spent nineteen years with Grant's, his entire working career, and over the past ten years he managed six Grant's stores in various New England towns. In that decade his annual income multiplied from $8,000 to $37,000, largely because of bonuses. He was so successful a manager that he led his district in sales and profits for six years.

Duclos took over the Westerly store in 1971. A seacoast town on the Connecticut border, Westerly is a marketing center for 140,000 families. Many shoppers come from across the state line, where the sales tax is a penny higher, and during the summer extra thousands from New York and central New England fill the shingled cottages that line the nearby beaches. Most of these people shop at the Franklin Plaza Shopping Center, a strip of sixteen stores just outside town. The largest of the stores was Grant's.

The year-round residents, many of whom work at the submarine yards of General Dynamics in Groton, Connecticut, shopped in Store 1192 for such staples as work clothes, cosmetics, and housewares. The vacationers, who knew the Grant's name from back home, came for fishing tackle, toothpaste, and similar traveling needs. And both groups patronized the Bradford Room, the store's restaurant. One of the most popular eating establishments in Westerly, the Bradford Room earned 30 cents on the dollar, making it the most profitable department in the store.

During his years in Westerly, Duclos played to this market well. Within two years after his arrival he had increased his store's sales by 19 percent, to more than $2.5 million, while doubling profits to $245,000. This 10 percent return on sales was about twice the average for all America's retailers. Under Duclos, 1192 became Grant's twenty-third most profitable store, and continued to make a little money even after the company had fallen into the red.

Every morning Duclos made the hour-long drive to Westerly from his home in Attleboro, Massachusetts. The commute was inconvenient, but not unusually long for that part of New England, and Duclos and his wife, Val, preferred Attleboro to Westerly as a place to bring up their two daughters. The store was open from 10:00 A.M. until 9:00 P.M., and Duclos was always there an hour or more before opening time. He rarely left before 6:30 or 7:00 P.M.

CUTTING HIS TEETH ON KOOL-AID

At the store Duclos was used to feeling like the captain of a ship—in charge of just about everything that went on. With the aid of his merchandise manager and two assistant managers, he oversaw all orders for new stock and plotted the mix of goods that Grant's offered Westerly's shoppers. He could raise or lower prices at will to beat the competition, and he had the power to concoct special promotions, even drawing up his own newspaper and radio ads. Once his bosses in New York City tried to keep him from stocking swimming pools, on the ground that pools wouldn't sell in a seaside community. Duclos went ahead anyway and ordered $5,000 worth, selling out in a week. Duclos had been in love with merchandising since the age of eleven, when he set up a Kool-Aid stand outside the neighborhood grocery in Fall River.

Duclos felt his first qualms about Grant's policies in the early 1970's. New York headquarters had ordered the stores to begin selling furniture and large appliances. To bolster those sales, the company had entered the hazardous credit-card business full steam ahead. Clerks were offered $1 bounties for each customer they signed up for a card, and Duclos was ordered to push the credit-card campaign above everything else. The pressure grew so intense that at one point his district credit manager called hourly asking how many accounts he had opened. "We hated the goddam things," says Duclos.

On New York's insistence, only cursory credit checks were conducted. When one manager insisted on making thorough inquiries, New York threatened to fire him. Meanwhile the new card holders were using their new credit to haul away hundreds of dollars worth of washing machines and beds. Duclos and virtually every other manager warned that the cards were brewing trouble, but New York didn't listen. By last year Grant's credit-card receivables totaled $500 million, and half of that was deemed uncollectible.

UNDOING DISASTER

The day of reckoning finally came early last year when the company plunged into the red—$177 million for fiscal 1975. Despite the immensity of the loss, Duclos's hope still ran high; he'd heard rumors that the directors were already searching for a new president who could turn the company around. And, sure enough, one morning last April, Duclos's district manager called to say that the directors had found their man. His name was Robert H. Anderson; he was a merchandising vice president from Sears.

Through the summer Duclos thought Anderson really might be able to do the job. The new boss sent order after order from New York undoing disastrous policies of the old regime. The best news Duclos got was a bulletin from headquarters telling him to stop issuing credit cards; Anderson had ordered the entire operation to be phased out. At a meeting of managers came more good news: Duclos was ordered to close out appliances and furniture. These higher-priced stocks turned over too slowly and did not generate enough sales per square foot of floor space. His district manager told Duclos to rearrange the store so that the first thing customers saw when they entered was women's fashions. Someone in New York had finally discovered that 80 percent of Grant's customers were women.

Despite these favorable signs, Duclos kept hearing rumors that Grant's might go bankrupt. After his district manager informed him that there would be no semiannual bonus coming up in September, Duclos canceled plans for his family's annual vacation trip. He spent the three-week holiday in July on a ladder painting the house, because now he also could not afford to hire anyone for the job.

One morning several months later, a customer walked into the Westerly store and told a clerk that she had just heard on the radio that Grant's had gone bankrupt. The report spread rapidly across the sales floor. In the office Duclos and his immediate subordinates clustered around a portable radio on a secretary's desk as the 10:30 news came on. The news about Grant's was all they had feared—the company had indeed plunged into bankruptcy.

There had been no warning from New York, no word at all. Everyone stood there in stunned silence. Finally Duclos spoke up, trying to reassure his people. "This could be the best thing for this company that could happen to us," he said. He tried to explain that bankruptcy would permit them to get out of some bad contracts. "This may be the best way to save the company."

THE NEST EGG GETS FRIED

But for all his reassurances, the bankruptcy hit Duclos with a jolt. In Grant's better days he had invested more than $20,000 in company stock, drawing on most of his savings and borrowing from a bank to finance his purchases. Now his holdings were virtually worthless, and he still owed the bank $5,000.

Several days after the bankruptcy five clerks came to his office and announced that each of them would raise $10,000 and buy the store if he would run it for them. Duclos was moved, but he told them the idea would not work—they would need more backing than they could get. But Duclos was impressed by their morale.

Meanwhile, his own morale was being severely shaken. Hundreds of his fellow managers, many of them respected friends, were laid off as New York headquarters closed down their stores. Val Duclos, an outgoing and equally outspoken woman in her late thirties, kept telling him to quit, that the company was doomed. But Duclos was determined to stick it out.

Into the winter word kept coming down that Anderson was changing the chain's merchandise mix, orienting it more to a narrow line of items that sold the fastest. In November, just as Grant's biggest selling season got under way, Duclos was told to begin a series of clearance sales. He fretted about the timing. November and December are the months that can determine a chain's year-end profit, and when managers are ordered to slash prices at such times, profits can only suffer. The creditors' committee was watching the turnaround from the sidelines. Duclos feared that if Anderson misjudged the committee's mood, climbing losses might impel the creditors to push for liquidation.

A DAY IN "GRANT'S TOMB"

In mid-January Duclos and his fellow managers were summoned to New York for a special briefing. It was the only time he had ever been inside "Grant's Tomb," which is what employees called the fifty-three-story headquarters building on Times Square that had been completed only five years before. They assembled in a third-floor auditorium, one wall of which sported a banner proclaiming: "Best of the Stores . . . Best of the Items!" Remembering the many old friends who were not there because their stores had been closed, Duclos resented the insensitivity of the slogan.

In a marathon of speeches and slide shows, Anderson and his key executives outlined a bold new plan for creating a "New Grant's." First off, they said, all stores would be "fashionized," a term Anderson had coined; it meant emphasizing women's fashions. And, since they were discontinuing slow-selling items, the managers would have to put their stores through "compaction," another Anderson coinage meaning to squeeze the sales area into a smaller space. They must also "colorize" their stores, i.e., paint counters and walls a selection of bright colors, in shades and types of paint decreed by New York.

Anderson warned his managers that every store must be spotless. "If the windows are washed at nine o'clock, and it rains at ten, they'll be washed again at eleven," he snapped. "That's the way we're going to run our stores." Anderson said the New Grant's would be launched on February 1, the beginning of their new fiscal year. They would open with a "supersale," featuring drastic markdowns of such items as boots, toasters, and electric saws.

On the evening train back to Providence, Duclos pondered the day's events. He was elated by a promise that, come spring, he and the other managers would get those canceled bonuses after all. Of far more importance to company and career, he felt a sense of excitement about the New Grant's.

Here at last was something definite and creative, a plan a real merchant could get enthusiastic about.

Yet, there were things that troubled Duclos. More than once during that day at Grant's Tomb, they had been told to charge all the costs of the transformation to the current fiscal year. Duclos worried that this would push the company's year-end losses higher than the creditors might stand for. On a more personal level, he and the other managers were rankled by the New York office's increasingly patronizing attitude, signalized by the excruciating detail of its edicts for paint hues and merchandise mixes. "We did something wrong, but we're not all stupid," Duclos had grumbled during a coffee break. As he and the other managers had reminded one another, it had not been they who had bankrupted Grant's, but the executives who sat in New York.

SELLING THE WRONG GOODS

Within days, Duclos was well on his way toward creating a new store. His clerks and stockboys were painting the counters, and Duclos had "compacted" the sales floor from 60,000 square feet to 41,000. Over on one side, two dozen shoppers picked over the clearance sale, where everything not on New York's checklist of approved merchandise had been stacked and marked down 75 percent. The checklist had not included such popular items as paper towels and barbecue grills, meaning that Duclos had to put them in the sale. Then, it turned out that New York, incredibly, had sent out an incomplete list. So Duclos had to reorder paper towels to replace those that he had sold at a loss.

The carpenters arrived to rebuild some of the walls. A floor man showed up and began replacing cracked tiles. Duclos juggled his maintenance budget and hired a cleaning contractor to strip old wax and polish the floor. "I can feel it all coming together," he said happily.

But then the district manager, Paul Carlson, a jovial but nervous little man, called with the news that Anderson had decided to make an inspection tour of the area on February 4, just after the scheduled opening of the New Grant's. And the Westerly store would be his first stop. Duclos was unshaken. But Carlson was jittery; he began pushing Duclos hard to create a perfect store.

Carlson had good reason to worry, because on a previous visit to New England Anderson had been displeased with the stores he had seen and had abruptly dismissed Carlson's predecessor. "Come on now, Paul, calm down," Duclos joked. "If they fire me, they fire you first. It'll take them so long to get to me it'll be like having two weeks' notice."

THE MANNEQUIN CRISIS

Word of the president's visit spread through the store, and everyone seemed to work more feverishly. While they toiled, a clerk talked about Anderson's previous trip to Rhode Island. "Mr. Duclos and the others stood at the door waiting," she recalled. "Someone was on the telephone calling that he was forty minutes away, then thirty minutes away, but he never came."

By early afternoon five regional and district merchandising and display men had arrived; they had been dispatched urgently from Massachusetts. The regional office near Boston seemed to have been swallowed up by panic, but Duclos was philosophical: presidential inspections create panic in every corporation.

Duclos showed his visitors how low he was on stock and displays. His own people had called New York and the warehouses, pushing for shipments, only to be rebuffed. One display man looked around the fashions department and turned to Duclos in surprise: "You don't have any mannequins at all?" "Just toss-ups," said Duclos—meaning simple cardboard figures. The display man hurried off to call New York and round up some mannequins. All afternoon the store's two phone lines were tied up, as the five men made call after call, using their authority—and the imminence of Anderson's visit —to get quick deliveries of displays and goods.

While Duclos wandered about the sales floor checking on the progress of the stockboys and clerks, one of the regional men informed him that the bright yellow paint on the infant's-wear counters was the wrong shade. Together they called the display manager in New York, who confirmed that he had just changed the specifications. "A bulletin is in the mail to you," he said cheerily. Duclos hung up, disgusted. Now they had to paint the department all over again.

Soon the two regional men were back; one of them announced that his colleague did not like the layout of the candy counters. "It's not according to the plan from New York," he explained. The Westerly store had never received the candy-department plan.

It became obvious that what really troubled the regional men was the layout of the entire store. They thought it should have the broad aisles and affluent look of a department store. Duclos was happy to hear this, because he and his merchandise manager had proposed just that sort of layout when they had gone through their "compaction." The regional office had turned them down.

"GET GOD TO MAKE IT SNOW!"

Duclos and his visitors tried out new counter arrangements, shifting one department and then another, but after each move a neighboring area would cry out for a change of its own. Into the evening a half dozen stockboys and the older men sweated and puffed and pushed and pulled counter after counter. Five of the stockboys were teenagers who had been off from school that day because of snow. Duclos had hired them part-time, and at nine o'clock they put on their jackets to leave.

"Al! You're letting the boys go?" called a display man.

"They have school tomorrow."

"Get God to make it snow! Hasn't He ever heard of Bob Anderson?"

Wherever possible, during the coming days, Duclos used Anderson's visit to help get his store remade. When the tape of background music began to drag, he called the Boston company that leased the equipment and asked for a new player. The man in Boston said it would take ten days. "My president is visiting next week," replied Duclos, "and if he hears that thing dragging he'll probably order your machines pulled out of all Grant's stores." The new machine arrived in two days.

JOTTING NOTES AT 55 MPH

Duclos worked ceaselessly, arriving at 8:00 A.M., leaving at 10:00 P.M. for the hour-long drive home. Sometimes he jotted down reminders for the next day on folded pieces of note paper while steering his Vega down Interstate 95 with his knees. After he got home he would sit for an hour or more making more notes and sipping a Seven and Seven (Seagram's 7 with 7-Up).

The thing that plagued him increasingly was the lack of merchandise. He even rented a truck and dispatched an assistant to a Grant's warehouse in Windsor Locks, Connecticut, to bring back a special load of auto accessories. Despite this effort at self-help, Duclos found himself trying to serve his customers from a stockroom and shelves that remained too bare. The warehouses seemed unable to distribute fast enough; the flow of goods to all stores was so slow that Carlson called to say that New York had ordered the supersale delayed. Now the New Grant's would open on the very day of Anderson's visit.

As the big day loomed, the truckloads of merchandise began arriving at last, and the shelves and racks were filling with goods. But then Carlson called again: Anderson was not coming. He could not leave New York— something about a meeting with the creditors.

The New Grant's blossomed forth on schedule. Shoppers poured in. Some women asked if this were a new store; others commented on the fresh colors. Sales for the day reflected the customers' positive attitude: volume was up 60 percent from a normal Wednesday.

Sales were still running high the next week. Monday two vice presidents visited and offered nothing but praise. But soon after he arrived at the store on Tuesday morning, Duclos received a severe jolt. The manager of another

New England store telephoned to say that he had just called a New York buyer about some needed goods, and the buyer had told him that the creditors were going to court to ask that Grant's be liquidated. Duclos called his wife, who had planned a shopping trip that day. "Don't spend any money," he warned.

$1 MILLION FOR THE BOSS

He was on the phone the rest of the day seeking information. A manager in Warren, Rhode Island, told him that the creditors had pulled the plug after discovering that the year's losses were running higher than they had been led to expect. Duclos had feared just that reaction. Another manager passed the word that the bonus was now dead.

Like the other managers, Duclos was growing increasingly bitter with each call, especially when he remembered that the same bankers who were now closing the company had guaranteed Anderson's salary for five years, to the tune altogether of $1,050,000. Through the entire day there was never any word from New York. "I figure we'll get notified when the guy is putting the lock on the door," Duclos grumbled.

Duclos kept hoping that the report of liquidation was merely another rumor. But late that afternoon a friend called to report that New York had put out a press release confirming everything. "What can I say?" Duclos said, his voice hollow. "It was a great company." He was close to tears.

But only as Duclos drove home that night did he finally realize what this all really meant: he had to find another job. "This is it, boy," he said to himself. "You'd better get moving." What kind of work should he seek? Did he want to stay in retailing and put up with the long hours? Duclos thought of the past two weeks: "I loved it," he thought. "That's the kind of thing I want to do."

That night the emotions and the shock kept thundering over him. He drank five Seven and Sevens, sitting in the family room. When he went to bed he could not sleep; he just lay there watching a Frankenstein movie on TV.

Wednesday morning Duclos performed the most heartrending task of his entire career. Although he still had heard nothing from New York, he broke the news to his clerks, calling them into a conference room that the carpenters had just finished paneling. "It's nothing official," he said. "I have nothing official, but it looks like the Grant Co. will go out of business." Several women wept.

Thursday afternoon the judge signed the order to liquidate. All stores were to be locked that night. Duclos received his instructions about 6:30. It was the first direct word he'd had from New York in all those three days.

FRIDAY THE THIRTEENTH

The next morning Duclos was sitting with his merchandise manager in the restaurant silently sipping coffee and staring out the window at the jammed parking lot. The other stores at Franklin Plaza were beginning their Washington's birthday sales. It was Friday the thirteenth. While they sat there one of the district display men came in.

"Sit down, and have a cup of coffee," Duclos said dejectedly. "It may be your last cup of coffee at Grant's."

"We were really up after Monday," said the merchandise manager.

"Yeah, we were 400 ahead in sales," said Duclos.

"Then someone zapped us."

Duclos looked out the window again. "Look at all those cars out there," he said wistfully.

After awhile they got up and went back to the sales floor. Most of the lights were out, and they wandered among the counters, thinking about how beautiful it looked and how the customers at the liquidation sale would ravage it. The floor seemed to gleam brighter than ever. All the merchandise sat in neat rows. The store was immaculate. "Now the animals will come," Duclos blurted out angrily.

"They'll tear the place up," said the display man, Bob DeBroisse. "You'll never recognize it by the first night."

The tape of background music was still running, and as they passed a counter of coffee makers and toasters that were about to be marked down for the liquidation, it blared gaily into "The Best Things in Life Are Free."

They walked on, and the display man began worrying aloud about being out of work. Duclos suddenly regained some of his old bounce and tried to cheer him up.

"You've known hard times before, Bob."

"Yeah, but I never had a big house to unload fast."

"They're not going to take your house," Duclos said, putting his hand on the man's shoulder. "The banks don't want your house."

But no sooner had the display man left than Duclos was somber again. Head down, thinking, he walked once more through the empty store with a friend who had come to commiserate with him. He walked very slowly in silence. Through the fashions, down the back row past the draperies, back up along the housewares and the toys, past the records and the jewelry. He stopped and leaned against a checkout stand and looked into the gloom of the unlighted store. He stayed there for some time thinking, remembering. Two customers came to the door, read the "Closed" sign and walked off to Fishers Big Wheel, the discount store down the way.

A VERY TIGHT COMPANY

"I really think it would have worked," he spoke up at last. "But Anderson went about it the wrong way. He went too fast. You don't give away a quarter of a billion in merchandise in the last quarter of the year. If we'd come up with a better profit picture for last year I think the creditors would have gone along.

"This has always been a very tight company," Duclos went on, his voice rising, the words now tumbling out. "His idea of cleanliness has always been in my book, but . . . goddamit! . . . you don't do it in a year when you're not making money. I don't mean leaving crud on the floor, but . . . goddam! . . . you don't paint the whole goddam store in a bad year! He said: 'Get it all done; get all the expenses in this year and get it clear before 1976,'" Duclos paused. His tired, black-rimmed eyes looked over the store once more, and he said bitterly: "There wasn't any 1976."

Case questions

1. Evaluate the planning process going on while W. T. Grant was going through its "last days." As a management consultant, what courses of action might you have recommended?

2. Evaluate Grant's adaptive responses to environmental changes.

3. Discuss the distribution of vertical managerial authority or the decentralization of decision making in W. T. Grant. What effect did this have on the fortunes of the company? Would you have alternative recommendations?

4. Evaluate Duclos in terms of the leadership models discussed in Chapter 16.

5. What kinds of motivational systems were used on store managers? On store personnel? What alternative ways can you design?

6. Discuss staff/line relationships within the W. T. Grant organization. As a consultant, would you have had any recommendations in this area?

7. It is often said that the credit card mania "caused" the downfall of W. T. Grant. Do you agree? Or was it something more fundamental?

8. Were there any communications problems in the organization? What kinds of changes might have improved the communications flow?

9. How would you have acted in Duclos's place? In Anderson's place? As a staff person in New York headquarters? As a creditor?

10. What do you think of "going out of business" as an adaptive response in this case?

GLOSSARY

Acid test ratio The balance sheet ratio of cash and accounts receivable to current liabilities.

Activity In PERT diagrams, an activity is the action that must occur in order to achieve an objective. Activities link events to form a network.

Activity trap Odiorne's term for managerial behavior that emphasizes activity rather than output. Wheel spinning, looking busy, making work—the expenditure of energy that is not meaningfully related to the achievement of organizational goals.

Adaptation A managerial process of change, revision, and control in which goals, plans, and standards are assumed to be variable.

Administration That body of activities concerned with the planning, forecasting, scheduling, output control, work allocation, and performance evaluation of an organization.

Advocating The presentation of the needs, wants, or complaints of the work group of a manager to higher levels of management.

Affirmative action Executive Orders 11246 and 11375, requiring a federal contractor with fifty or more employees or federal contracts in excess of $50,000 to set goals for the employment and utilization of minorities and women and to develop policies and procedures for affirmatively reaching those goals.

Age Discrimination in Employment Act of 1967 An act protecting individuals between the ages of forty and seventy from being discriminated against because of age in employment and job conditions.

Arbitrating A managerial skill concerned with resolving conflicts among organizational members or departments.

Authority A relationship (that includes elements of power or influence) between two parties under which one party (subordinate) accepts the dominant and decision-making role of the other (superior).

Bakke case (See **Regents of the University of California v. Allan Bakke.**)

Behavior modification A school of psychology that suggests that desired behavior may be elicited by conditioning individuals through the use of positive rewards as reinforcement for correct responses.

BFOQ *Bona fide occupational qualification*—the only reason why an employer may discriminate on the basis of religion or sex.

Bogies Production norms set by an informal group, often in conflict with organizationally desired goals or norms.

Book value The accounting value of an asset. Generally, original cost less depreciation.

Break-even analysis A decision tool used under conditions of certainty to determine at what level of output volume a firm will start to turn a profit.

Bureaucracy A formal organization. Often the term is used to denote an organization whose administration is so tied to adherence to rules that effective action is impeded.

Business An organization whose objectives are met through dealings in the marketplace. Profit-oriented.

Capital budgeting Planning expenditures on assets whose returns will extend beyond one year.

Capitalized expenditure An expenditure that is depreciated over the life of the equipment.

Carrying costs Those costs related to holding an inventory on hand, e.g., interest, insurance.

Centralization An organizational mode that concentrates decision-making and design functions in higher levels of the organization.

Certainty Under conditions of certainty, the various possible values of all of the variables and outcomes, or of the variables interacting, are known, and each is attainable or controllable; the decision maker simply has to arrange operations in their most efficient configuration according to the objectives sought.

Chain organization A chain form of communication allows for some intercommunication among network members, but is more limited in information accessibility than the free form. In a chain a person generally communicates only with the persons on either side of him or her.

Civil Rights Act of 1964 (Title VII) A congressional act specifically outlawing discrimination in companies of fifteen or more employees on the basis of race, religion, national origin, or sex in any personnel-related matter such as hiring, wages, job assignment, promotion, or personnel facilities.

Classical school of management Those theories and that research according to which organizations should be designed around tasks, not people. It was assumed that tasks could always be efficiently related one to another, that people were motivated by simple things, and that thus they could be easily manipulated into the *one* efficiently designed productive system.

Closure Completion of a task. In job enlargement closure refers to structuring tasks so that workers can perceive the product of their efforts.

Coercive power Person A's ability to apply sanctions to person B, as person B perceives the situation.

Command units Line units.

Communication A process whereby one person transmits signals to another; the process is effective when the second person or group comprehends exactly what the first one has transmitted and is able to act as the first person intended.

Communication distortions Those elements that either interrupt the communication process or effectively stifle the objective of commonality on the part of sender and receiver.

Compounding The method of determining the value of a compound interest–bearing payment or flow of payments at some point in the future.

Conciliating A managerial skill focused on restoring harmony among conflicting members or units of an organization.

Concurrent controls Control applied to an ongoing functioning process, with the goal of *preventing* deviation from a standard.

Conglomerate An organization of diverse, and often unrelated, elements, usually built through mergers and acquisitions.

Consideration An underlying dimension of leadership, identified in the Ohio State leadership studies, that is focused on such people-related concerns as fair treatment of subordinates, subordinates' welfare, and a friendly work environment.

Contingency theories of leadership Theories of leadership that focus on the interrelationships among a number of variables, such as leader power, the task, and the relationship between followers and leaders.

Control process A managerial process composed of setting standards, measuring and comparing the actual versus the standard, evaluating the results, and correcting for discrepancies between actual and intended results.

Controls The process of organizational change or correction whereby the goals, plans, or standards against which output is being compared are assumed to be basically correct, infallible, or unalterable. The general managerial process by which the output of an activity is compared and contrasted with a preestablished standard or plan.

Corner-point solution In linear programming one of the corner points of the feasibility space will provide the maximum attainable profit solution to the problem.

Corporation A group of individuals who, through the granting of a charter, are recognized as a separate entity having powers and rights distinct from those of its members.

Correction In the control process, the adjustment made to bring actual performance into congruency with a preestablished, standard level of performance.

Counseling A managerial skill directed toward the seeking of solutions for the personal, work-, or career-related problems of organizational members.

Critical path In PERT the critical path to total project completion is the longest path in terms of time.

Current expenses An expenditure that is totally charged off in the accounting period in which it is incurred.

Current ratio The balance sheet ratio of current assets to current liabilities.

Debt ratio The balance sheet ratio of total debt to total assets.

Decentralization The structuring of an organization such that some decision-making and administrative functions are performed at lower levels, in more dispersed fashion.

Decision center An area of an organization in which decision making for a particular purpose is concentrated.

Decision making The mental activity that takes place in moving an organization from an existing state of affairs to an anticipated, desired state. The process involves passing judgment or coming to a conclusion on a problem with several alternative solutions.

Decision process A seven-part process consisting of: (1) problem search and formulation; (2) information gathering and evaluation ; (3) formulation of alternative courses of action; (4) application of decision rules and tools; (5) choice of desired alternative; (6) choice of implementation scheme; (7) provision of check and audit procedures.

Decision rule A predetermined direction for conduct or a formula that facilitates passing judgment on an issue under consideration.

Delphi technique Developed by the RAND corporation, this technique for group decision making avoids the problems of face-to-face meetings by using a series of questionnaires and iterative opinion composites in an attempt to achieve a group consensus.

Depreciation In accounting, the allocation of the cost of equipment and buildings over the length of their useful lives.

Descriptive goal model Goal systems and models abstracted from observations of functioning organizations.

Design A manager's activity of mentally interrelating problems, resources, needs, and outputs into goals, plans, organizations, and systems.

Development The provision of resources and opportunities which encourage the overall, long-term, organizational maturation of an individual.

Discounting The method of determining the present value of a future stream of cash flows.

Dynamic planning A concept of long-range or strategic planning that calls for a periodic reevaluation of the planning premises (e.g., environments, internal strengths) and a revamping or updating of the plan when the parameters on which the plan is based are found to be changing. Generally such review processes are mandated by policy.

Earnings The profits of a business firm.

Economic goal model A model of organizational goal setting that assumes that: (1) decision makers are rational, i.e., that they are aware of all of the information necessary to make the best possible decision; and (2) the maximization of profit (minimization of loss) is the primary goal.

EEOC Equal Employment Opportunity Commission—created by the 1964 Civil Rights Act and empowered to enforce compliance with the requirements of Title VII of the Civil Rights Act.

Effectiveness The achievement of objectives.

Efficiency The achieving of goals when resources are limited. Standards of efficiency are usually measured by profits, but other standards, such as economical use of personnel, time, or space, may also be used for evaluation.

Entrepreneur An individual who organizes, energizes, directs, and assumes the responsibility for a business. Generally refers to the person who conceives of and starts the business.

Equal Pay Act of 1963 A law that forbids pay and fringe-benefit differentials based on sex.

ERG model Developed by Clayton Alderfer, ERG is a theory of motivation, similar to Maslow's hierarchy of needs, which postulates that individuals have three basic need sets—existence, relatedness, and growth.

Espinosa v. Farah Manufacturing Co. A case in which the Supreme Court ruled that the 1964 Civil Right Act's prohibition of discrimination based on nationality does not protect noncitizens of the United States against an employment policy of hiring only natives.

Evaluating Measuring mechanical or human output against a standard or set of standards.

Evaluative listening The type of listening that occurs when the receiver tries to combat the sender or argue against the sender's message.

Evaluator A person or machine that compares the actual output with the objective or standard.

Event Within a PERT diagram, an event in an objective. A series of events linked by activities constitutes a PERT network.

Expectancy of outcomes In expectancy theory the probability of gaining personal goals that an individual assigns to achieving a particular organizationally demanded goal.

Expectancy theory A group of theories predicated on the assumption that individuals make rational choices, e.g., if an individual regards a reward as important and if a certain performance will provide that reward, he or she will perform the reward-eliciting behavior.

Expected value The product of the conditional payoff within the cell of a payoff matrix times the probability of the occurrence of the particular state of nature associated with that cell.

Expert power The power that person A has because person B perceives A's knowledge in a certain area to be greater than B's own. Facilitates influence and acceptance of authority.

Expertise Specialized knowledge of a particular subject, e.g., data-processing expertise.

Feasibility space In linear programming the area bounded by the horizontal and vertical product axes and the inner perimeter of the various input constraints. This area defines all of the feasible solutions to the problem, given the input constraints.

Financial audit An annual assessment of the organization's financial activity and its financial condition at a particular time.

Fixed costs Those costs that a firm incurs regardless of the level of output.

Follower theories of leadership Leadership theories that focus on the psychology and behavior of followers as the most important variable in leadership.

"Forces in the manager" One of three factors in Tannenbaum and Schmidt's continuum of leadership. Those forces are the manager's value system, confidence in subordinates, leadership inclinations, and feelings of security in an uncertain situation.

"Forces in the situation" One of the three factors in Tannenbaum and Schmidt's continuum of leadership. The relevant forces in the situation include the type of organization, group effectiveness, the complexity of the problem itself, and the pressure of time on the situation.

"Forces in the subordinate" One of three factors in Tannenbaum and Schmidt's continuum of leadership. The forces in the subordinate include the need for independence, the readiness to assume responsibility for decision making, tolerance for ambiguity, interest in the problem at hand, understanding and identification with the goals of the organization, knowledge and experience to deal with the problem, and learned expectations of sharing in the decision-making process.

Formal organization Individuals or groups having stated duties and delineated relationships and united toward achieving specific, stated objectives.

Free-form organization A communication organization in which all members are in easy communication with one another. Ready accessibility to information allows for maximum input into the solving of complex problems.

Functional breakaway The increasing vertical or horizontal specialization of an organization or the growth of secondary functions into specialized or general staff units.

Functional staff unit A staff unit that has been granted the authority to issue policies and disseminate decisions throughout an organization only in its area of expertise.

Gantt chart A scheduling chart most often used in scheduling an order through certain production functions.

General Electric v. Gilbert A case in which the Supreme Court ruled that a company is not obligated to include pregnancy within the coverage of health insurance plans; however, subsequent legislation has required that pregnancy insurance be included.

Generic products Nondifferentiated products that are sold without the use of brand names or trademarks.

GIGO A computer science acronym: garbage in–garbage out. The quality of output can be only as good as the quality of input.

Goal The stated end toward which organizational or unit activity is directed.

Goal displacement A process in which the means used to attain organizational goals become goals in themselves.

Grapevine The informal communication network in organizations that allows for passage of nonofficial information through and to the members of the organization.

Griggs v. Duke Power The case in which the Supreme Court ruled that test and educational requirements in hiring must have explicit job-relatedness.

Halo effect A predetermination of an opinion or decision on one matter due to the subjective perception of the results from a previous, similar situation.

Hawthorne effect Changes in responses caused by the very act of being involved in an experiment.

Hierarchy of needs The five levels of needs postulated by Abraham Maslow—physiological, safety, social, self-esteem, and self-actualization.

Hierarchy of objectives The form of the goal structure of organizations, with higher-level goals expressed in broad, general terms and lower-level goals expressed more specifically. Each subunit has goals that are consistent with, and subordinate to, the goals of the next higher administrative unit.

Horizontal specialization A phenomenon of complex organizations in which workers on the same organizational level perform differentiated tasks. Location, product, process, time, and function are often bases for the differentiation.

Human resource planning That area of management concerned with the recruitment, placement, and promotion of individuals within the organization.

Implementation The instituting or putting into effect of a plan or procedure to ensure the achievement of an objective.

Informal leaders Leaders who hold their position through acceptance by the group rather than through appointment by management.

Information processing The translating and transferring of information into and out of an organizational unit Communicating.

Initiating structure An underlying dimension of leadership, identified in the Ohio State leadership studies, that has to do with task-oriented, goal-directed behavior.

Insufficient reason, principle of A decision criterion in which, having no reason to assume that one state of nature will occur over any other, each state of nature is assigned an equal probability of occurring.

International corporation (multinational corporation) A corporation that engages in trade in more than one country.

Intervention The second stage of team building; the process of dissecting the existing values of an organization.

Inventory control A decision tool used to determine the minimum combination of costs to be incurred to keep an adequate inventory flowing. It determines the optimum number of orders per time period and the optimum size of the orders.

Inventory turnover The ratio of net sales to inventory.

Investments Capital expenditures for items that: (1) are not directly a part of the product being manufactured or service rendered; (2) do not wear out within one year; but (3) whose cost is recoverable over a part of the period of time it is being used.

Isoprofit line   In linear programming an isoprofit line shows the combination of outputs that will provide the same amount of profit.

Job enlargement   The addition of operative tasks to a worker's responsibility; expanding a job horizontally in order to increase satisfaction and motivation through an increased sense of worker responsibility.

Job enrichment   The addition of managerial and decision-making tasks to a worker's job in order to respond to the higher-level, creative needs of that individual.

Lead time   The time that elapses between placement of an order and its arrival at the company's door.

Leadership   The process that brings about the transformation and integration of the human resources of the organization into willing, compliant, and cooperative, if not enthusiastic, participants in the achievement of organizational purposes.

Learning theory   A body of knowledge directed toward explaining and improving manners of teaching and ways of learning.

Legitimate power   The power person A has, as seen by person B, that has its basis in the cultural values or norms of person B.

Line organization   That part of the organization which works primarily on the functions that contribute directly to the organization's primary objectives.

Line/staff conflict   Conflict arising from the differing goals, interests, beliefs, ages, locations, or educations of line and staff members.

Linear programming   A decision tool used under conditions of certainty to determine the optimal allocation of limited resources among multiple uses—that allocation that will maximize output and profit. The underlying assumption of this tool is the condition of linearity among variables.

Liquidity ratios   Financial-control tools, such as the current ratio or the acid test ratio, used to evaluate an organization's ability to carry current liabilities with either current assets or current assets less inventories.

Long-term planning   The formulating of organizational strategy through the linking of several short-term plans. Starts with specification of long-range or strategic objectives.

LPC   A questionnaire developed by Fred Fiedler to measure the propensity of a leader to use a particular leadership style by rating his or her least preferred co-worker (LPC) on a series of semantic-differential scales.

Management   A professional vocation concerned with the directing of organizational activity and the achievement of organizational goals.

Management by Objectives   A management technique using predetermined and formal cycles to map out and review the progress toward a set of objectives that a subordinate is to attain in a given time period. The objectives are determined by consensus between subordinate and superior.

Manager   One who designs interrelationships between systems and resources, implements plans and procedures, and controls, audits, and adapts the outcomes of activities in order to achieve specified organizational goals and objectives.

Managerial functions   The three general functions a manager performs are design, implementation, and control/audit/adaptation activities.

Managerial skills   The three major categories of managerial skills are: (1) knowledge of subordinate functions—technical and administrative; (2) interactive skills; and (3) administrative skills.

Manning tables   Charts used in determining organizational human resource needs that contain individuals' names, ages, retirement dates, and specific job descriptions.

Marginal cost   The costs a firm incurs from producing one additional unit of product.

Marginal listening   The type of listening that occurs when the listener is thinking of some other subject or occasion while the sender is attempting to communicate.

Marginal revenue   The increment in total income received by a firm from the last unit sold.

Market value   The value of an asset if it were to be sold today.

Matrix organization   A type of organization whose structure entails coordination of the relationship of many and varied products or programs overlaid on a group of multipurpose functional resources.

Maximax   An optimistic decision criterion that assumes that the best possible state of nature will always occur.

Maximin   A decision criterion that assumes that the worst possible state of nature will always occur. Maximize the minimum expected value.

Mentoring   In a training program using mentoring, an inexperienced employee is guided through the rules, regulations, and policies of the organization by a more experienced employee.

Minimax regret   A decision criterion that attempts to minimize the amount of regret to be suffered in a decision situation. Minimize the maximum regret.

Modern school of management   Modern management theories stress that there may be several or many modes of efficient production and that human beings are more complex in needs, wants, and feelings than the classical theorists believed. Managerial styles are seen as being dependent on task/people combinations, rather than just task alone.

Motivation   In managerial theory the desire to perform in an organizationally useful manner.

Motivation hygiene theory   (See **Two-factor theory**.)

Movement to change   The third stage of team building. The process of improving organizational effectiveness through the building of new cooperative values.

Multinational corporation   A business organization that operates, has investments, or owns subsidiaries in more than one country.

Multipath planning   Planning in which several different chains of events must take place simultaneously in order for an event to occur.

Multiunit organization   An organization in which more than one unit performs the same activity, e.g., a chain of fast-food restaurants.

Network   A communication system that has multiple sending and receiving units in which the same message is communicated to more than one unit.

Nonverbal communication   Communication expressed physically through hand gestures, facial expressions, and eye movements.

Normative goal model   A goal model prescribed on the basis of some underlying value system.

Not-for-profit organizations   Organizations that, though operating in the nonbusiness sector of the economy and not seeking profit, employ some or all of the standards of business, e.g., hospitals, universities, and churches.

OFCC   Office of Federal Contract Compliance—a watchdog agency of the Department of Labor, directed toward guiding compliance in affirmative action.

On-the-job training (OJT)   A training program in which the trainee works under the direct supervision of his or her future supervisor while getting hands-on experience in the actual workplace.

Opportunity costs   The rate of return on the best foregone alternative investment.

Ordering costs   Those clerical, freight, and other costs related to placing and receiving an order.

Ordering point   That level of inventory or stock which, when reached, indicates the need to reorder in order to maintain an adequate, flowing inventory.

Organization   In its ideal form, an organization is an integrated set of units pursuing interrelated and coordinated goals and subgoals such that the achievement of lower-order goals furthers the achievement of higher-level goals.

Organization development   A body of knowledge and processes that attempts to improve the effectiveness and efficiency of organizations through the use of various psychological and social-psychological techniques, e.g., team building and sensitivity training.

"Organization man"   A popularized stereotype of the organization member as an ulcer-ridden, hypertensive, frustrated automaton.

Organizational audit   The complete and periodic reassessment of all of an organization's plans, procedures, personnel, allocation of resources, systems, etc., to determine if each of those mechanisms is being utilized most efficiently and effectively in pursuit of the organization's objectives.

Overcontrol   A degree of control that results in diminished effectiveness and efficiency.

Overrun   The amount by which actual costs exceed estimated costs for work covered by a contract.

Pay-back period   The length of time needed for the cost of an investment to be recurred by the stream of net revenues.

Payoff matrix   An arrangement in matrix form of conditional payoffs resulting from various combinations of management strategies and states of nature.

Perpetual goal   The long-range, stable, general objectives of a firm. A continuing goal.

"Person-in-the-middle"   The role conflict that may result from the expectations of a manager's supervisor and opposing expectations from a manager's subordinates.

PERT (Program Evaluation Review Technique)   A planning tool developed to aid managers when large numbers of interrelated processes must be brought together into an integrated plan. Utilizes notions of activities, events, critical path, and slack time.

Piece-rate systems   Remunerative schemes that pay workers according to the amount of product they produce.

Planning   A mental managerial activity involving the arrangement of multiple linked decisions on ends and on means to accomplish a long-range, or major, objective.

Planning backwards   A process of working backward from the final objective to the initial starting point. This process entails determining what must be achieved before that final objective is attained and is done by detailing in reverse the preceding subobjectives that must be met.

Planning matrix   A planning tool that brings order to the planning process by providing benchmarks in terms of times, responsibilities, interrelationships, and control while the plan is being implemented.

Policy   General guides to actions that are standard within and throughout an entire organization or particular administrative unit.

Policy audit   A regularly scheduled review of policy and procedures to determine if they are still efficient, effective, and applicable to the organization and its functions.

Postcontrols   Control that is applied after a process is complete to determine the effectiveness and efficiency of the performance.

Power The ability to control behavior through the control of rewards and punishments. Power in an organization results from the unequal distribution of resources and skills, and a power relationship can shift as resources, skills, and knowledge are differently distributed. Power is a basis for acceptance of authority.

Precontrols Controls applied to a process before it starts to prevent deviations from the standard.

Present-value analysis A method of capital investment analysis that determines the present value of a future stream of payments, discounted by the appropriate discount rate.

Primary functions Those organizational functions which contribute directly to the achievement of organizational objectives.

Probability The likelihood of an event's occurring where there is a risk that the event will not occur.

Problem A less than optimal existing state of affairs in an organization. A problem may also be a challenge or opportunity that has been overlooked.

Procedure The standard sequential process for carrying out policy.

Process audit A particular type of social audit. A descriptive and subjective evaluation of the origins, goals, rationale, and actual operations of an organization's social programs.

Procurement The acquisition of products or services necessary for the organization. Often called purchasing.

Product manager Within a matrix organization, a manager who is responsible for a single product's production, sales, and marketing through interaction with functional-area managers, such as finance or production.

Profit The difference between total revenue and total costs.

Profit maximization When marginal cost is equal to marginal revenue or when the slope of the total-cost function is parallel to the slope of the total-revenue function, profits are at their maximum point.

Projective listening Listening in which the receiver attempts to project himself or herself into the situation and state of mind of the sender, seeking to learn all of the message, understand its content, and understand the context in which the message was sent.

Rate of return The discount rate that equates the cost of an investment to the present value of a future stream of cash flows.

Rational-goal model A theoretical organizational model in which each integrated subunit pursues subgoals in such a manner that in a cooperative and coordinated fashion, the achievement of the specific lower-order subgoals leads to the achievement of more general higher-level goals.

Referent power The power person A enjoys due to the fact that person B identifies with, or wants to be associated with, person A.

Refreezing The final stage of team building. The process of inculcating new cooperative organizational values into the managerial style of the various groups.

Regents of the University of California v. Allan Bakke In this test of reverse discrimination, the Supreme Court ruled that although race could be used as a factor in school admissions, specific affirmative action quotas could not be used as a remedy except where there was a legal finding of past discrimination.

Reinforcement A reward or punishment, significant to the recipient, which, by its application or withdrawal, can be used to shape or elicit a particular behavioral response.

Resource supplying An administrative skill directed toward providing a manager's work unit with the resources necessary to achieve the unit's objectives, given budgetary and temporal constraints.

Revenues The income a firm receives from the sale of product.

Reverse discrimination Alleged abuse of the civil rights of white males or others from attempting to comply with equal rights or affirmative action guidelines.

Reward power Person A's ability to give rewards to person B, as person B perceives the situation.

Risk Under conditions of risk the decision maker may be aware of the values of all the variables and/or the possible outcomes; however, the likelihood of an event's occurring may be neither under the control of the decision maker nor certain to occur. The decision maker has available the objective probabilities of each value or outcome's occurring and can make decisions based on probable occurrence.

Role playing A management-training tool whereby an individual acts out a role or pretends to be another or himself or herself responding to a specific problem situation or predicament.

Rumor clinic An instrument used by organizations to show the effects of perception and biases on a message as it passes through the various stations of a communication network.

Sales-maximization goal model A model suggesting that the primary goal of managers is to serve themselves before the organization and that this goal is achieved through sales maximization as opposed to profit maximization.

Salvage value The value of a capital asset at the end of some specified period of time.

Satisfaction   The fulfillment of a need or want.

Satisfice   The *realistic counterpart* of the assumption of rationality in theoretical, rational goal models. A condition in which enough information is sought or enough effort applied to make adequate or "good enough" decisions.

Savings   The decrease in fixed and variable expenses.

Scheduling   A type of planning that entails assigning a certain project through various functions or processes within certain time constraints.

Scientific management   The school of management developed by Frederick Taylor that assumed that financial rewards were the prime motivation to work. The research from this school delved into the interactions between money and production through piece-rate systems, work analysis, time-and-motivation studies, and production-based reward plans.

Secondary functions   Those organizational functions which facilitate the achievement of the primary functions and contribute indirectly to the objectives of the organization.

Sensitivity training   An organizational technique that focuses on helping organizational members expose their inner feelings in order to create a free, open environment in which to work. T-group.

Separate-facility training programs   A type of program often used for operative trainees when the training effort would have serious disruptive effects on job processes or when the training is so technical that it requires specialized equipment and personnel.

Service units   Units specializing in the performance of physical secondary functions, e.g., mailroom, filing office.

Service-objective goal model   A normative goal model predicated on the belief that the primary objective of the organization is to provide and distribute utility in an optimal fashion.

Short-term planning   Short-range planning that is an integrated part of a long-term strategy.

Situational theories of leadership   Theories that focus on the situation as the central factor inducing leadership.

Skills transfer   Certain general managerial skills may be used in a variety of situations; however, other skills, particularly technical ones, are much more job-specific.

Slack time   In PERT slack time for an event is found by subtracting the accumulated expected time (t_e summed from the beginning of a project) from the latest time (t_l subtracted from the proposed end of the project—T_i).

Social audit   A review and assessment of an organization's social responsibilities and activities.

Social-responsibility goal model   A model based on the belief that the goals of an organization should be directed toward enhancing the welfare of multiple interest groups surrounding the organization rather than maximizing the return to the group controlling the organization.

Span of control   The number of units or subordinates that a manager supervises.

Staff organization   The component of an organization that specializes in the performance of secondary functions.

Staff units   Specialized planning units assisting line officers in studies, development of policy, etc.

Standards   The basis on which performance is evaluated. For management, standards of efficiency and effectiveness, measured by profitability and goal achievement, are often used. Also, a preestablished objective deadline or desired behavior.

Standing plans   Policies and procedures—instruments designed to cover repetitive situations.

Structure   The arrangement by which tasks, responsibilities, authority, and chains of command within an organization are delegated, implemented, and maintained.

Subgoal   The objective of a short-term plan as part of a longer-range plan.

Subjective probability   The assignment of a personal best guess to the possible occurrence of an event. The input into the guess may be intuition, a reservoir of information concerning previous similar events, or expert advice.

Suboptimization   A process of goal conflict, occurring when personal or subunit needs, values, or objectives are incongruent with organizational goals, which forces a reassessment and lowering of organizational goals.

Subsidiary   A firm that is financially controlled by a parent firm, but often maintains some separate market identity.

Sunk cost   An unrecoverable cost that has already occurred due to a past decision.

Team building   A technique that attempts to develop cooperation, rather than competition, among various organizational groups in order to facilitate goal achievement.

Technology   The application of science, its materials, and its methods to industrial or commercial objectives.

Theory X   Douglas McGregor's Theory X manager assumes that: (1) work is inherently distasteful to employees and therefore they try to avoid it; (2) since people don't want to work, they must be directed, coerced, and controlled in work situations; (3) individuals work only to make money to be secure.

Theory Y   Douglas McGregor's Theory Y manager assumes that: (1) work is a natural activity for individuals; (2) individuals will commit themselves to work objectives; (3) the degree of commitment is a function of the rewards; (4) the average person seeks responsibility and does not shun it; (5) the capacity for psychological growth is widely, rather than narrowly, distributed within the population.

Three-need theory   David McClelland has hypothesized several relationships among the need for achievement, the need for affiliation, and the need for power.

Title IX, Educational Amendments Act (1972)   Legislation that directed schools and colleges receiving federal funds to develop plans to ensure that equal opportunity was offered to both sexes in all activities.

Total costs   The summation of the fixed costs and variable costs of a firm.

Trade-off   A situation of limited resources in which one or more goals or standards can be achieved only at the partial expense of some other.

Trained incapacity   An organizational dysfunction in which adherence to, and satisfaction of, the procedure becomes more important than the contribution of those procedures toward the objectives of the organization. Adherence to policy becomes an end rather than a means to an end.

Training   Training is a short-term concept relating to the teaching of a particular skill, job, or task performance to an individual.

Trait theories of leadership   Theories of leadership based on the assumption that effective leaders share a set of personal characteristics that are different in either kind or degree from the characteristics of nonleaders.

Transportation method   A variant of linear programming that maximizes service and delivery with a minimum of costs from the various combination of plants.

Transsending station   A component of a communication network that transfers the same message from a sender unit to another receiver unit.

Tunnel vision   In organizations the misperception of a variable as an immutable, unchangeable fixed factor.

Turnover rate   The percentage of resignations, terminations, and retirements relative to the particular work force over a specified period of time.

TWA v. Hardeson   In this case the Supreme Court ruled that an employer's duty to accommodate an employee's religious beliefs does not require violation of seniority rights of other employees or require the employer to incur additional costs.

Two-factor theory   Frederick Herzberg's theory of motivation is based on two individual needs—the need to grow psychologically (the motivating factor) and the need to avoid pain (the hygiene factor).

Uncertainty   Under uncertainty the decision maker knows the possible outcomes, but can assign neither definite certainty nor objective probabilities to their occurrence.

Unfreezing   The first stage of team building, directed toward diagnosing the problems of an organization resulting from internecine competition.

Unipath planning   A simple plan that entails moving beyond a single decision to a string of decisions, each a part of a single sequence of events to be implemented.

United Steelworkers of America and Kaiser Aluminum & Chemical Corporation v. Weber   A 1979 case in which the Supreme Court ruled that a voluntary affirmative action plan favoring minorities and women is legal under the Civil Rights Act of 1964.

Valence   In expectancy theory valence is a measure of the importance of a reward to an individual.

Variable costs   Those costs that are directly related to the production level of a firm, e.g., labor, raw materials.

Vehicle noise   The distortions in communication that result from mechanical breakdowns, static, misprints, erasures, and various kinds of interruptions.

Vertical specialization   The hierarchical structure of an organization such that those positions at the top have broad, more encompassing functions, with increasingly specialized functions occurring at the lower levels of the organization.

Vested interest   In organizational theory a vested interest occurs when personal needs are included in making decisions concerning the organization.

Vestibule training   A type of separate training in which the trainee is placed in an environment that is a duplicate of the forthcoming workplace.

Weber case   (See **United Steelworkers of America and Kaiser Aluminum and Chemical Corporation v. Weber.**)

Weighted optimism   A decision criterion that uses the decision maker's subjective probabilities of his or her optimism or pessimism in determining the expected values of different strategies. Also called the Hurwicz criterion.

Wheel organization   The archetype of the bureaucratic organization. The communication network is such that communication is received, issued, and controlled at a central hub. Members on the spokes have little opportunity to communicate among themselves.

Work ethic   The belief that working is good in, and of, itself.

Yield   The rate of return of an investment.

Zone of acceptance   A frame of reference that determines under what circumstances an individual is willing to accept authority. Varies with the mix of power and possessed resources and among individuals.

INDEX